Welcome

Welcome to **Photoshop For Beginners**, your essential guide to using all versions of Photoshop. Whether you have Photoshop CS2 or CS5, or even Photoshop Elements, this book will take you through all the key tools and commands step by step. The title is split into ten easy-to-navigate sections, so you can jump right in to the bits you want, be that retouching, adjusting, transforming or outputting. We go through the program's interface in detail and look at how to make your first-ever edit in Photoshop. As you get more comfortable with the tools on offer, then we have a bunch of creative ideas to take your artwork one step further. This book also comes with a free disc, which has some great stock images and brushes, bonus video tuition and project files for the book's tutorials. We hope that you enjoy this title and your newfound Photoshop skills.

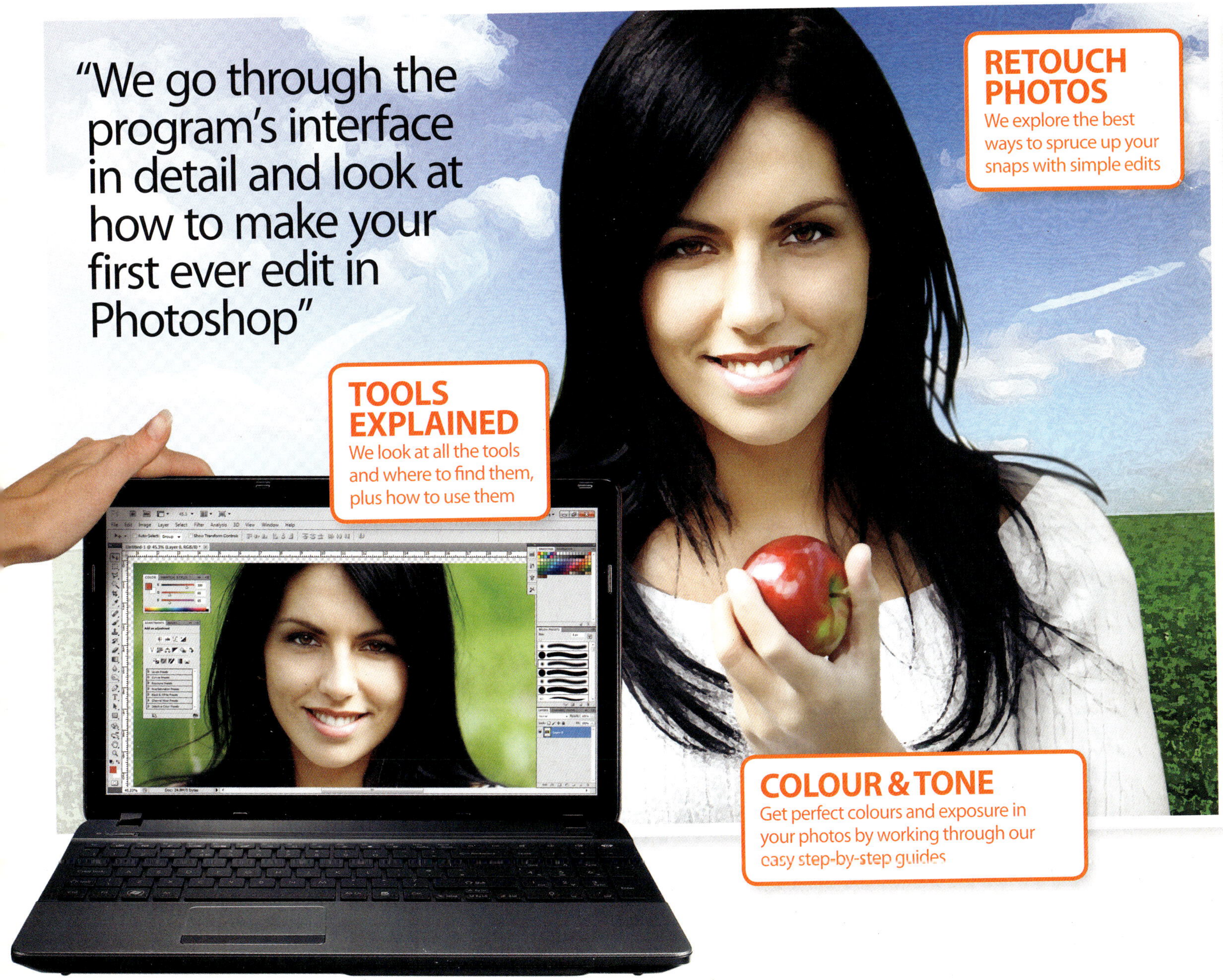

"We go through the program's interface in detail and look at how to make your first ever edit in Photoshop"

RETOUCH PHOTOS
We explore the best ways to spruce up your snaps with simple edits

TOOLS EXPLAINED
We look at all the tools and where to find them, plus how to use them

COLOUR & TONE
Get perfect colours and exposure in your photos by working through our easy step-by-step guides

Photoshop® for Beginners™

Imagine Publishing Ltd
Richmond House
33 Richmond Hill
Bournemouth
Dorset BH2 6EZ
☎ +44 (0) 1202 586200
Website: www.imagine-publishing.co.uk

Editor in Chief
Jo Cole

Production Editor
Julie Bassett

Design
Charles Goddard

Printed by
William Gibbons, 26 Planetary Road, Willenhall, West Midlands, WV13 3XT

Distributed in the UK & Eire by
Imagine Publishing Ltd, www.imagineshop.co.uk. Tel 01202 586200

Distributed in Australia by
Gordon & Gotch, Equinox Centre, 18 Rodborough Road, Frenchs Forest, NSW 2086. Tel + 61 2 9972 8800

Distributed in the Rest of the World by
Marketforce, Blue Fin Building, 110 Southwark Street, London, SE1 0SU.

ISBN 978-1-908222-2-51

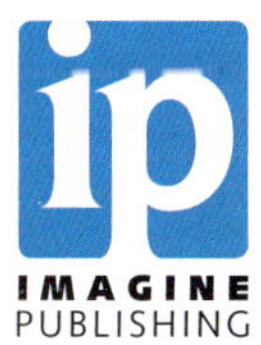

Contents

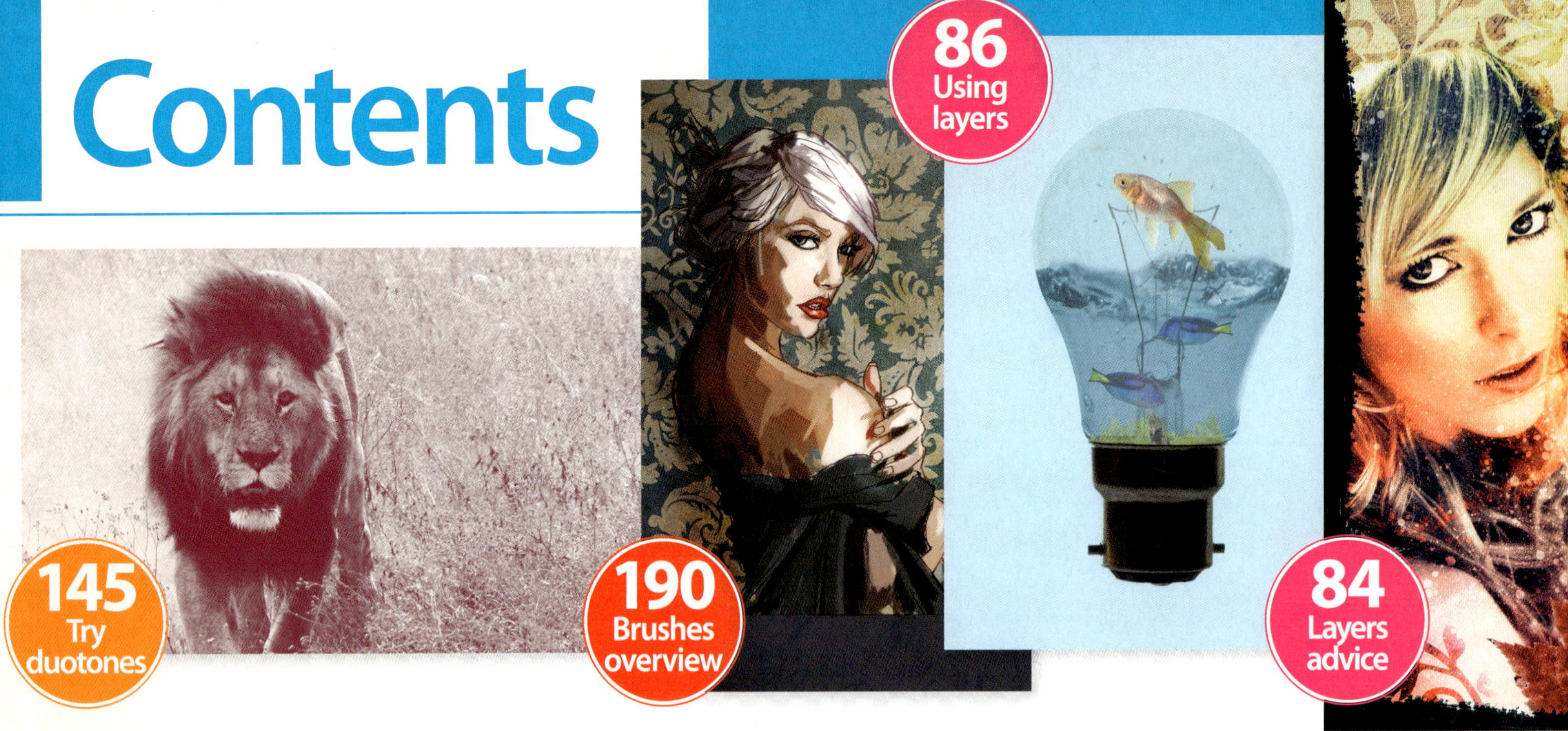

"Find your way around Photoshop and Photoshop Elements in a flash"

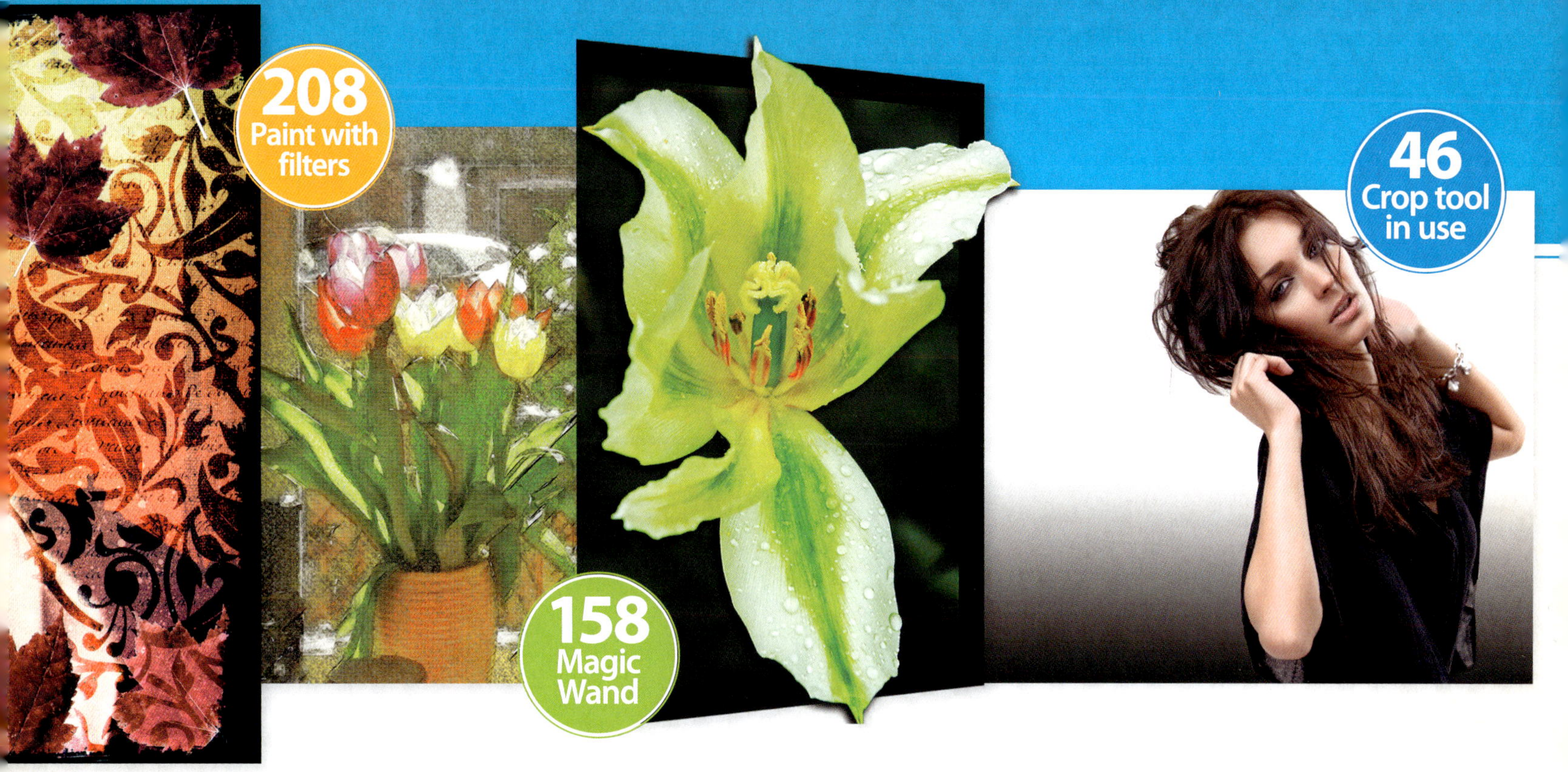

208 Paint with filters

46 Crop tool in use

158 Magic Wand

Selections

Brushes

Filters

Output

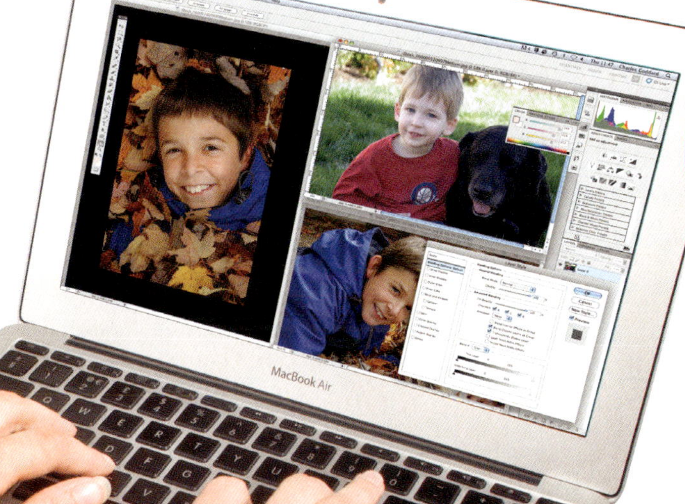

238 Save for the web

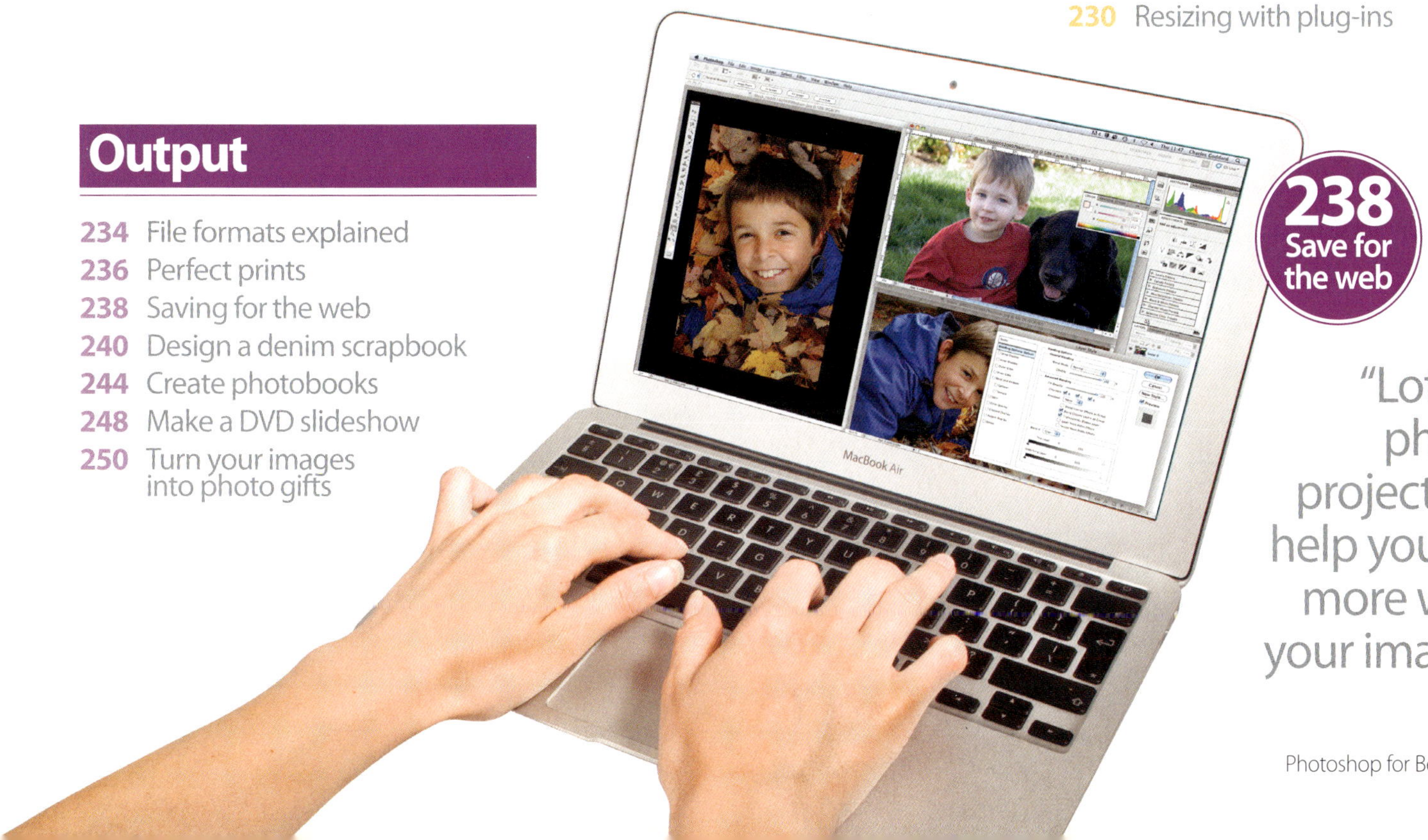

"Lots of photo projects to help you do more with your images"

Getting started

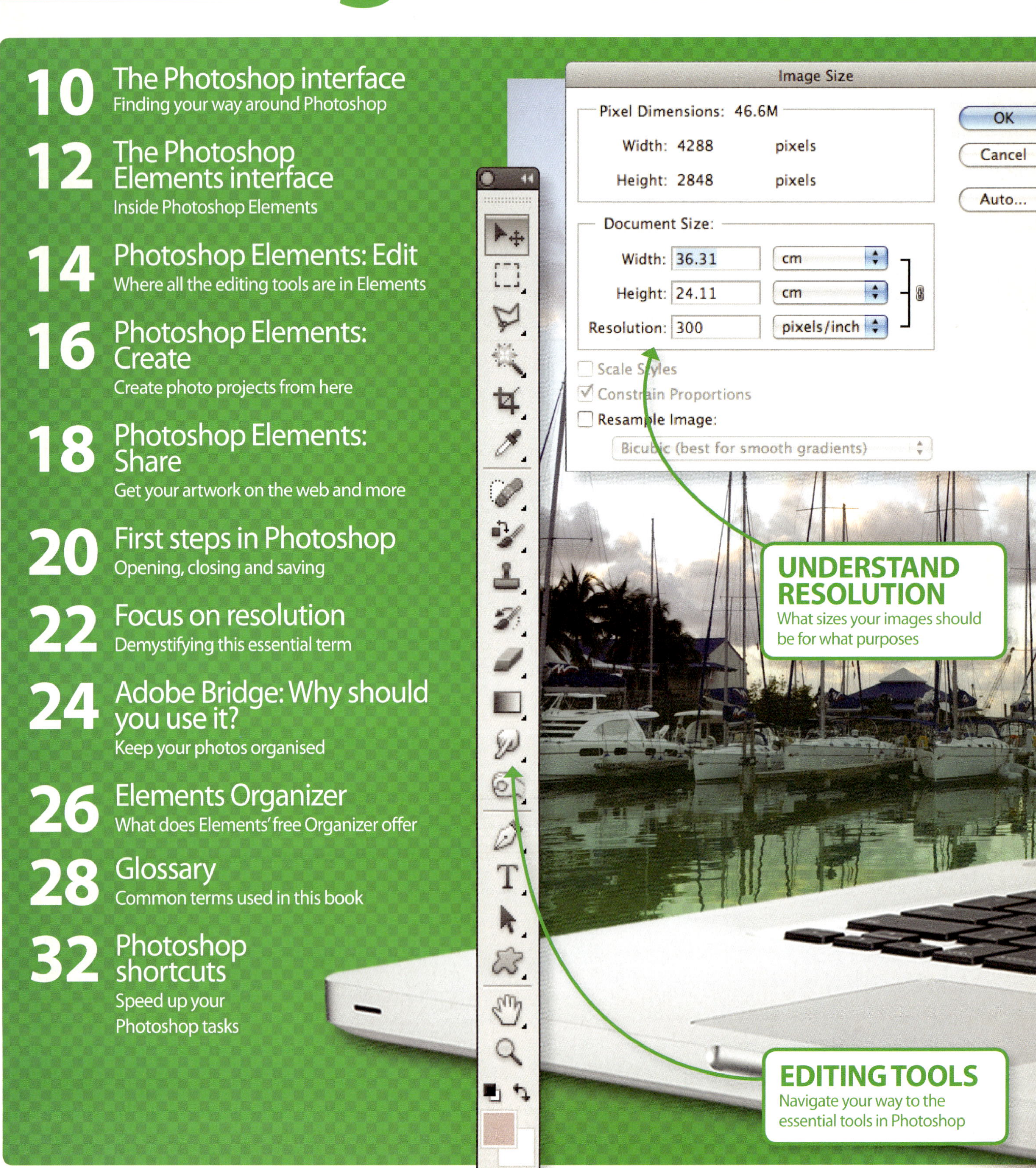

UNDERSTAND RESOLUTION
What sizes your images should be for what purposes

EDITING TOOLS
Navigate your way to the essential tools in Photoshop

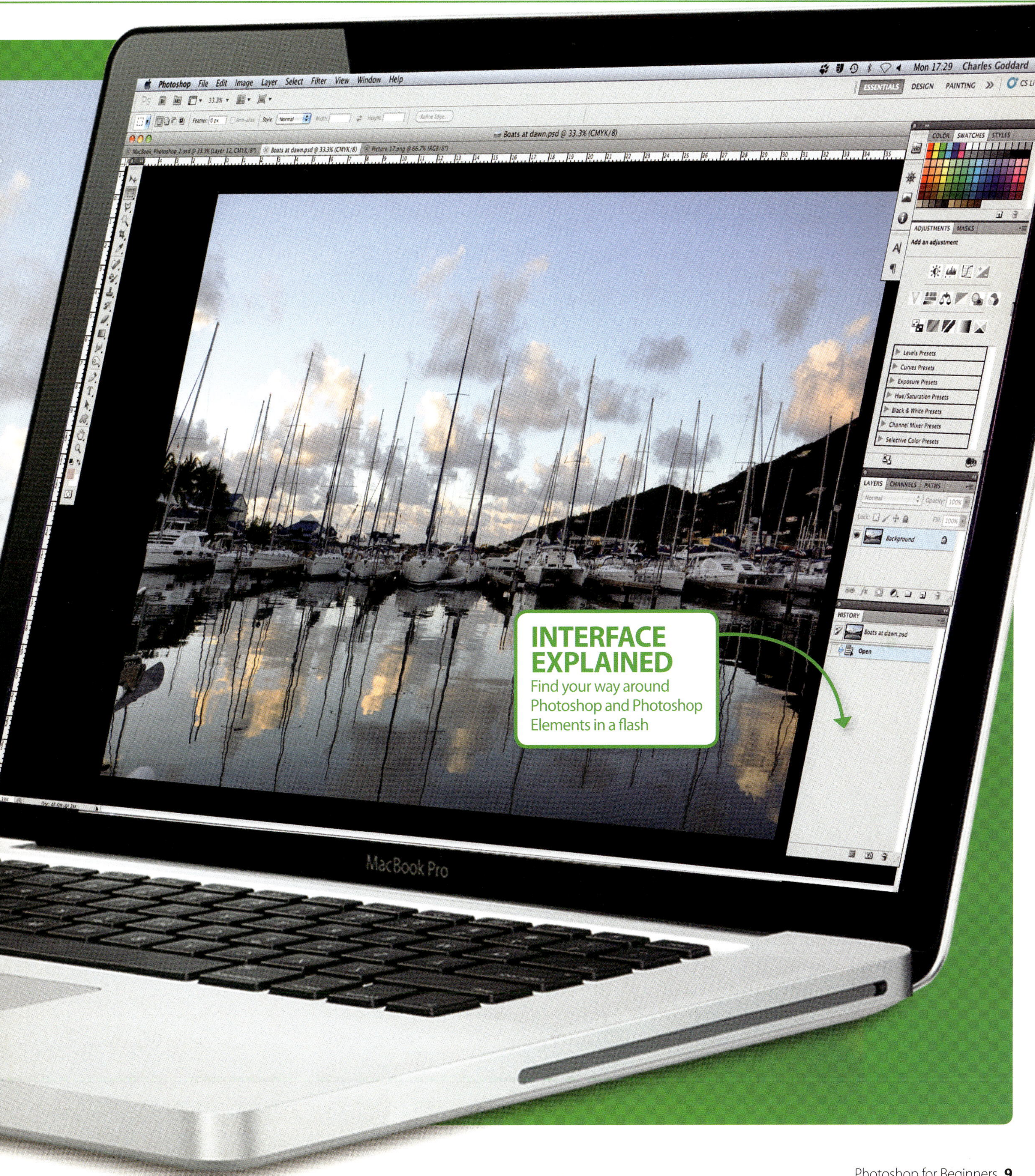

INTERFACE EXPLAINED

Find your way around Photoshop and Photoshop Elements in a flash

The Photoshop interface

Photoshop has more tools and options than Elements, as you'd expect, but this extra power doesn't mean that you have to jump through hoops to get to something

Photoshop hasn't got a reputation as being the best photo editor around for no reason. It isn't a cheap program, by any standard, but it is also incredibly powerful and once you start to learn how to use it, you will realise that anything is possible.

The main interface consists of a large window, which is where your current project is seen. You can open more than one image at a time. In older versions of Photoshop, these will be shown in different, individual windows that you can switch between. In more recent versions of the program, multiple images are shown in tabs, exactly as you might have seen on an internet browser when you have more than one page open. Down the right of the screen are all your open palettes, and down the left is the toolbar, for accessing all the tools in Photoshop.

In the top right of the screen, you will see the word Essentials, and this refers to the 'workspace' that you have open. We will look at this in more detail on later in the book, but workspaces are preset layouts for the Photoshop interface that opens just the palettes that you need for a specific task. You can even create your own custom layout.

Unlike Photoshop Elements (see the next page), there aren't set workspaces for sharing or creating different projects, but there are a few sharing options in there if you know where to look… and we will later in the book!

"Once you start to learn how to use Photoshop, you will realise that anything is possible"

GETTING AROUND

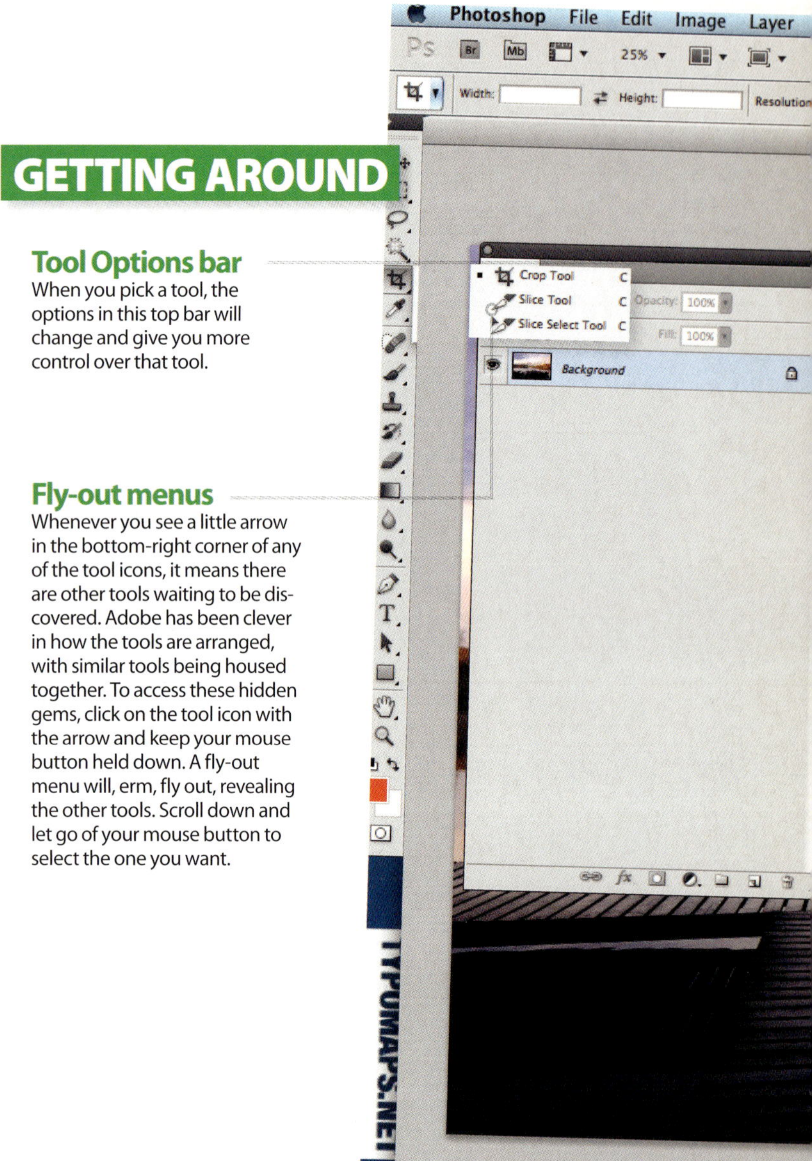

Tool Options bar

When you pick a tool, the options in this top bar will change and give you more control over that tool.

Fly-out menus

Whenever you see a little arrow in the bottom-right corner of any of the tool icons, it means there are other tools waiting to be discovered. Adobe has been clever in how the tools are arranged, with similar tools being housed together. To access these hidden gems, click on the tool icon with the arrow and keep your mouse button held down. A fly-out menu will, erm, fly out, revealing the other tools. Scroll down and let go of your mouse button to select the one you want.

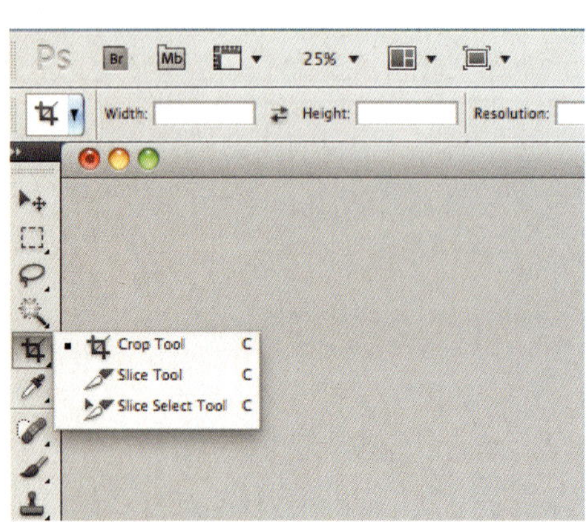

01 Toolbar

Many of your 'go to' tools will be found in the toolbar. Accessing one of the tools is just a case of clicking on the tool icon for it to be activated.

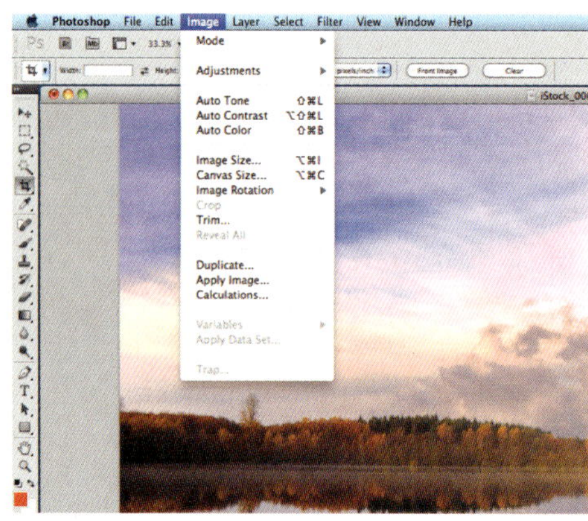

02 Menu bar

These menus are drop-down menus, so you get to see the contents by clicking one of the headers to make them drop down.

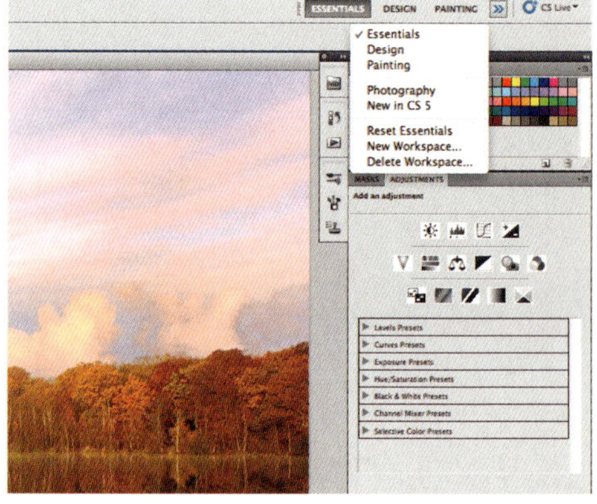

03 Workspaces

Photoshop has prepared some workspaces that you can use for specific tasks. The default is the Essentials, but we'll look at them in detail later.

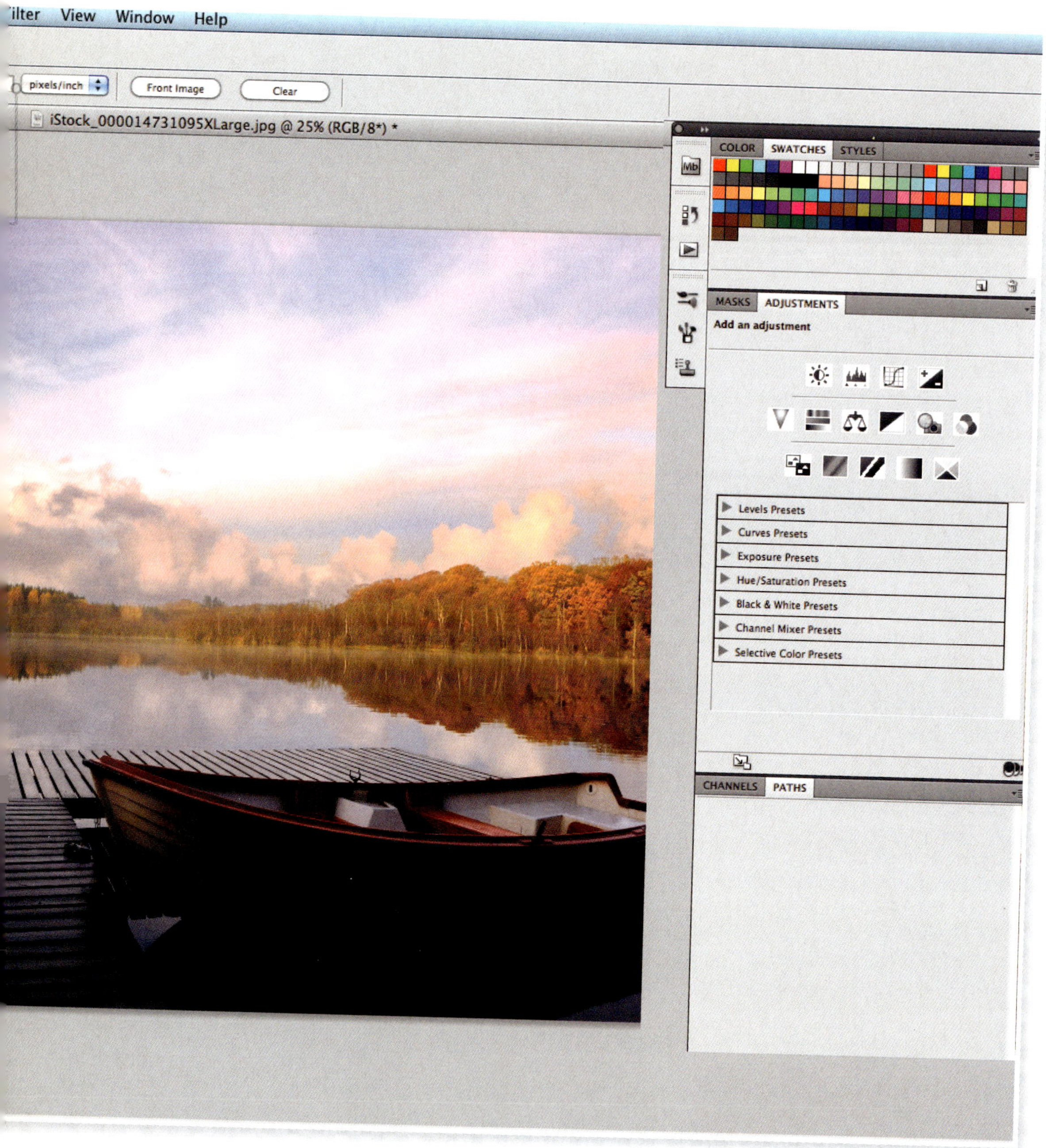

Mini Bridge

Bridge is Photoshop's way of managing images and lets you navigate through folders on your hard drive. It is a powerful tool and has more than enough options to warrant a book of its own. CS5 also boasts the Mini Bridge feature, which works within the Photoshop interface.

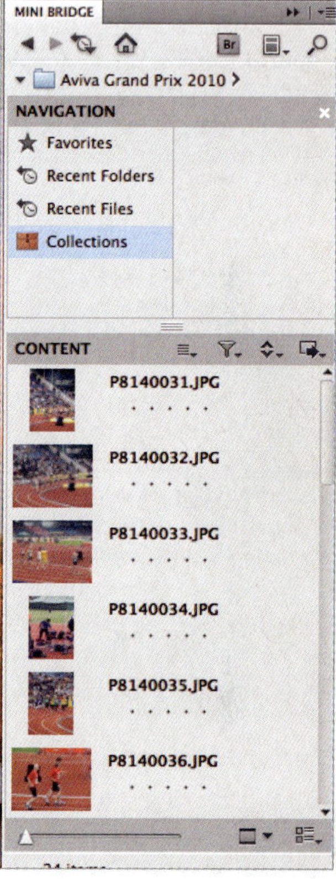

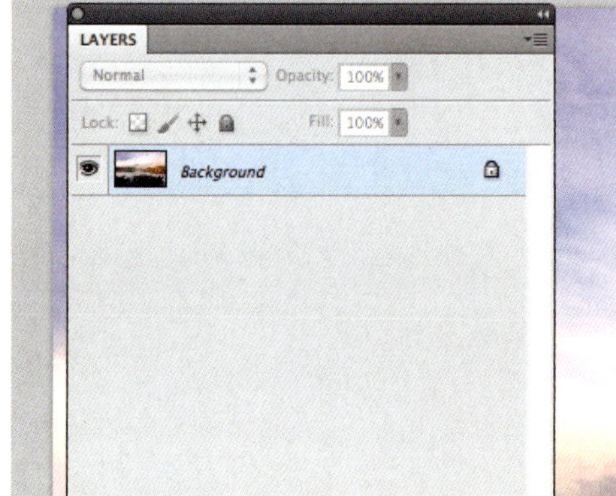

04 Palettes

These are the backbone to all the other tools and commands, giving you extra functionality and control. One of the most useful is Layers.

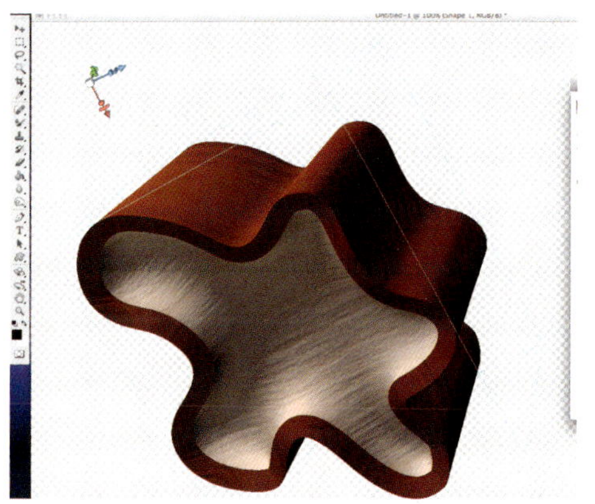

05 3D in CS5

Photoshop has been flirting with 3D for a little while now. Don't dismiss this as too complicated – you can create amazing titles and shapes easily.

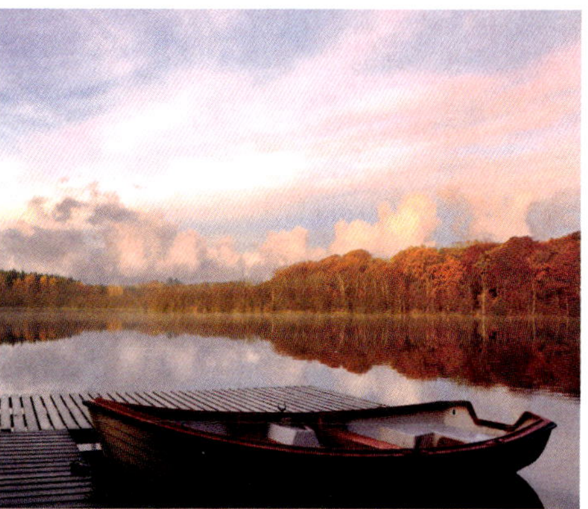

06 Main window

Any image you open or file you create will appear in this area. You can zoom in and out and use the Navigator (top-right corner) to see where you are.

The Photoshop Elements interface

The Photoshop Elements interface holds a treasure trove of tools and commands for users at all skill levels. Here's a primer in what the most important ones are

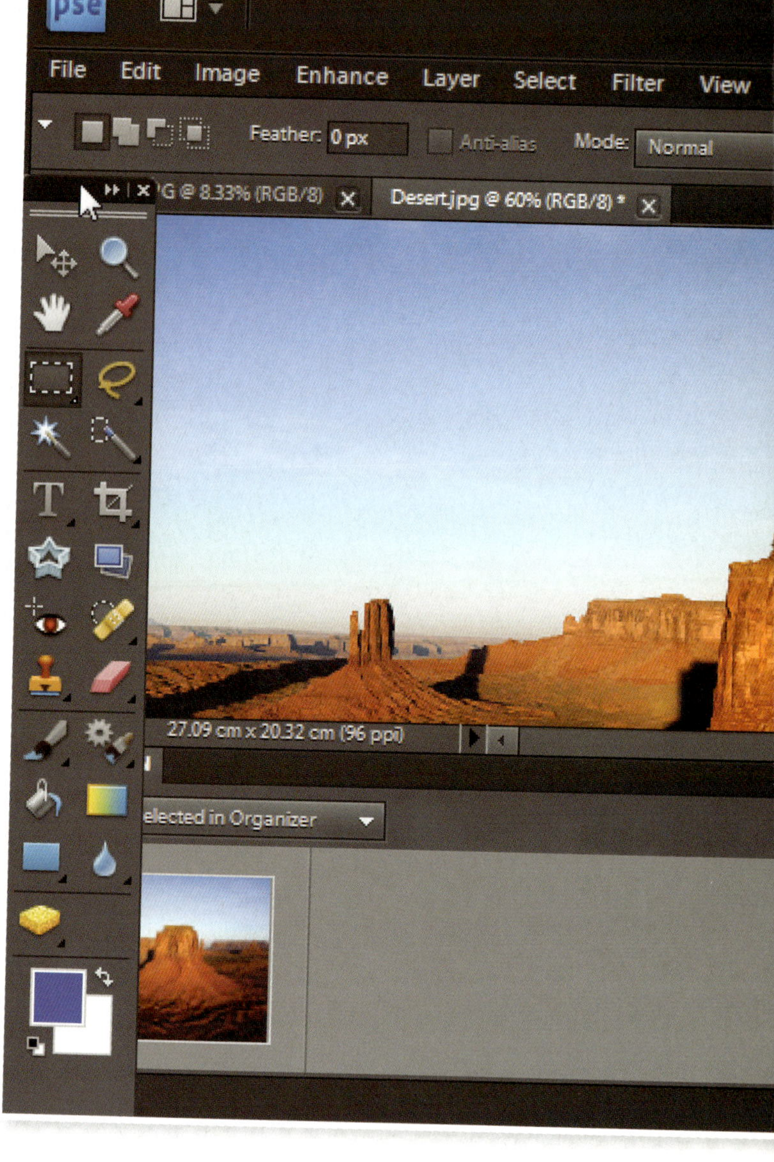

Photoshop Elements is a great little program if you're just starting out with image editing. This is because it has all the tools that you need to make any edits to your image right in front of you in easy to find locations. It also has a loads of automated options , which let the program do the hard work for you.

On these pages we mainly look at the Edit options, as these are the ones that you will be using time and time again. This is where the magic happens, as it were, with all the tools that you will ever need in one handy toolbar down the left-hand side. Along the top are all the menu options, which are where you go to open and save photos, as well as customise your interface layout. You'll see on the right-hand side all the editing options that you are working with, organised into palettes.

However, there are two other interfaces that you can enter. In the top-right, next to Edit, you will see another tab called Create. This is where you can make creative projects using your images, such as photo books, collages, slideshows, and so on. The Share option which sits next to this does what it says on the tin; it enables you to share your edited photos with the wider world, by enabling you to upload to Facebook or Flickr, for example. You can also print and email images from directly within the Elements interface as well. We'll be looking at these options in more detail throughout this book, so for now, let's just take a closer look at the main interface.

"This is where the magic happens with all the tools that you will ever need in one handy toolbar"

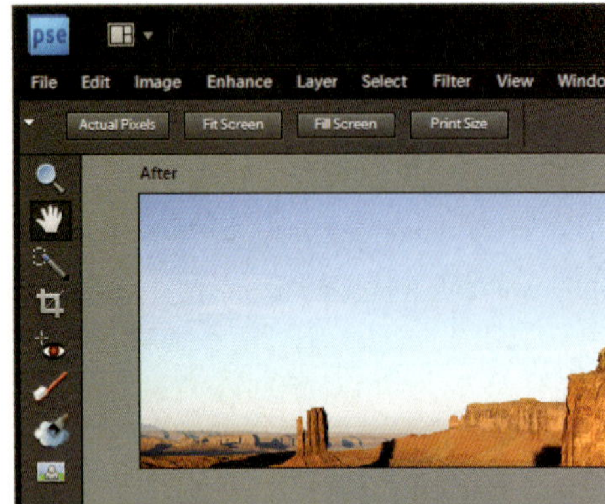

01 Toolbar

This is where a lot of the major tools in Elements live. To select a tool, simply move the cursor over to the tool you want and then click.

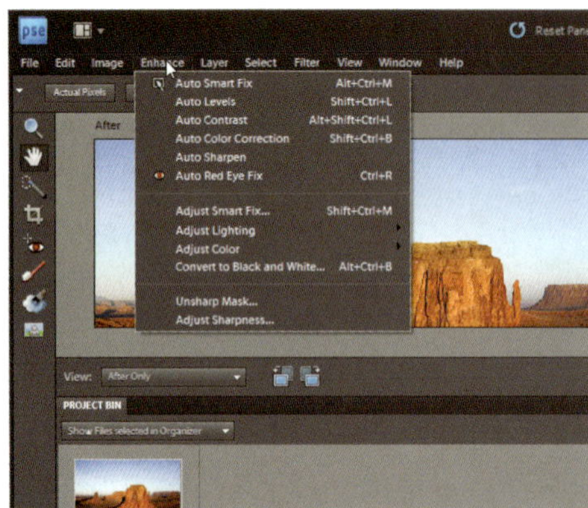

02 Menu bar

Click on one of the menu headers to see the list of commands held in there. Scroll down and click the mouse again to select the command you want.

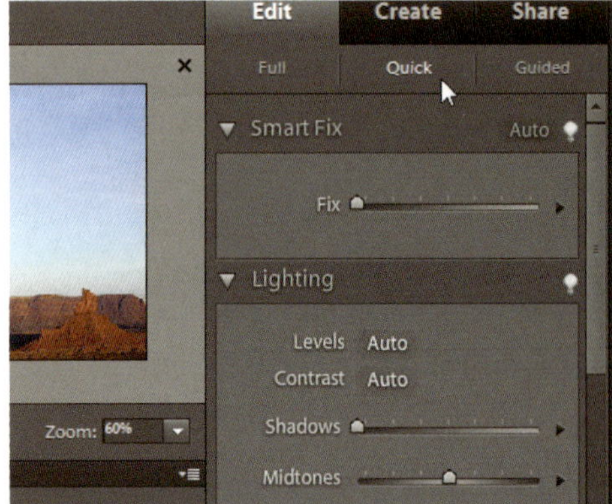

03 Editing window

Elements offers users a choice of areas to edit in, which are accessible from here. Simply click the tab to enter that space.

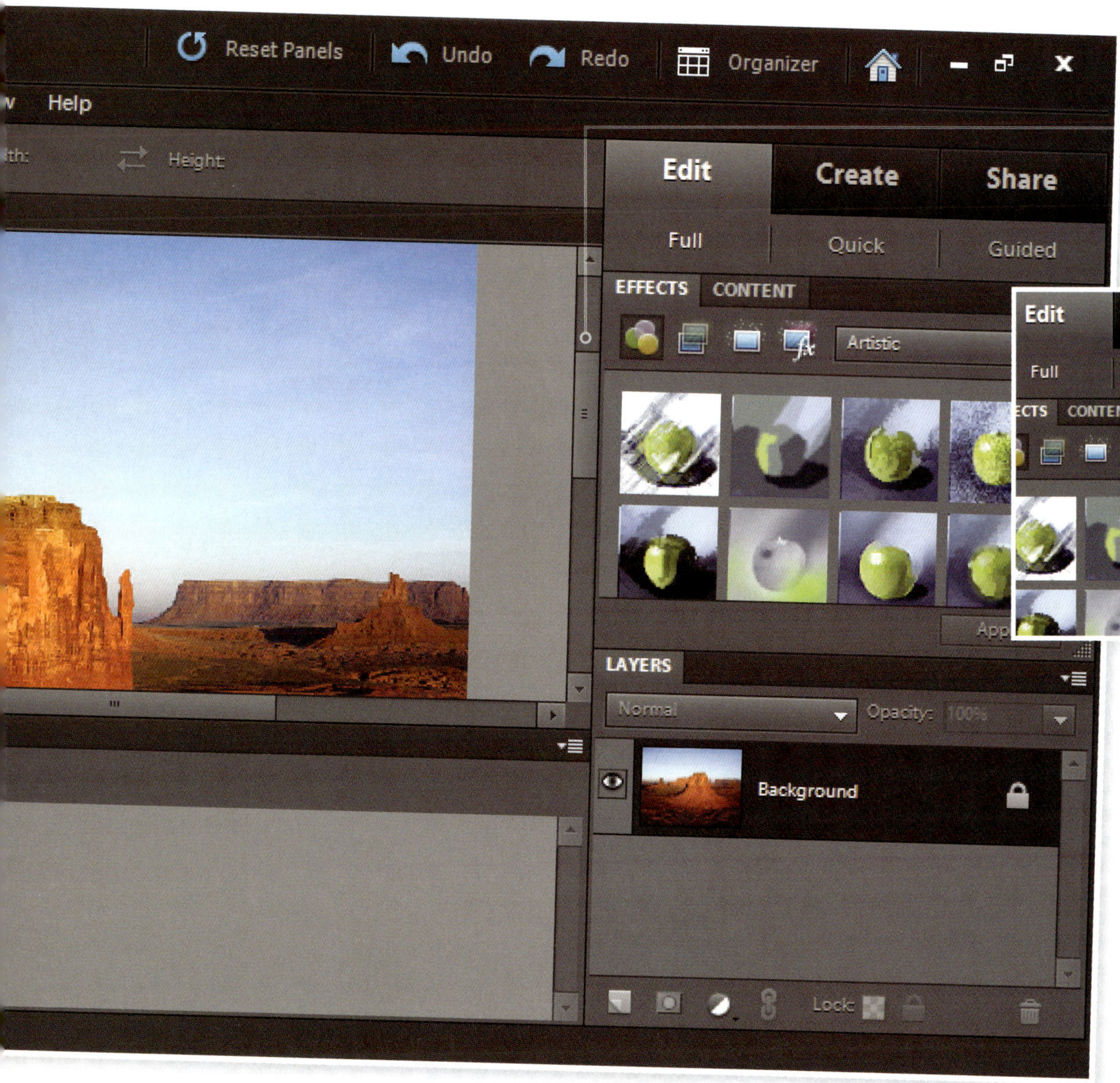

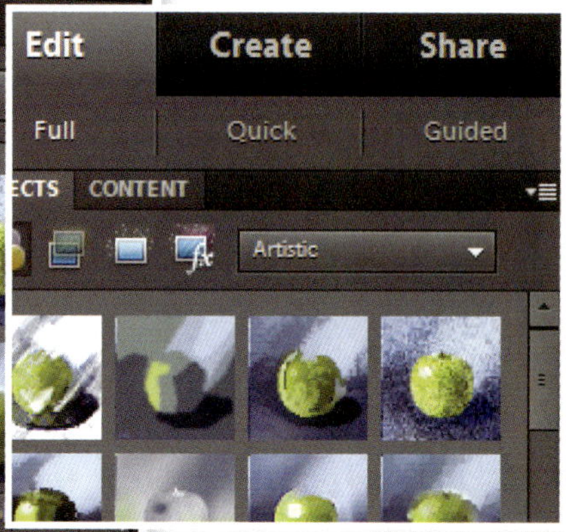

Scrollbar

Use this to navigate around the workspace. You can scroll vertically as well as horizontally. Click and drag a bar to move it, or click on the arrows.

Editing windows

Edit offers the full range of tools, Quick is perfect for complete newbies as it condenses all of the major edits into a series of sliders. Guided walks you through key edits to help you learn the tools better.

Toolbar

If you see a small arrow in the bottom-right of the tool icon, it means that there are other tools hidden behind the main one. To access these, simply click and hold your mouse button to make a fly-out menu appear. Keep your mouse button held down, and move to the tool you want. Let go of the mouse to select.

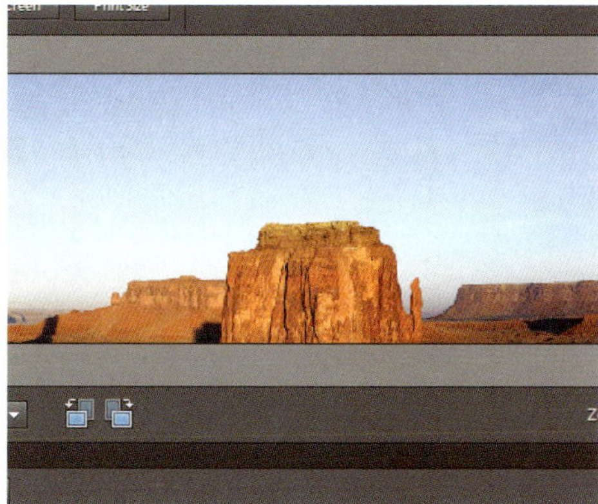

04 Workspace

This is where all of your editing takes place. When you load or create a new file, it will appear in here. You can open more than one image.

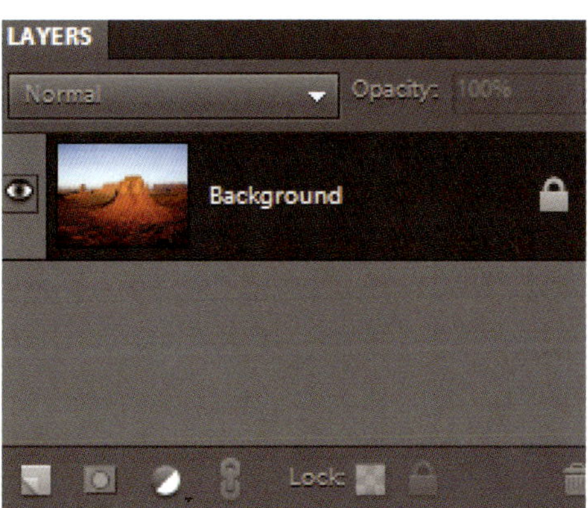

05 Palettes

Palettes are docking areas for various commands and tasks. To access a palette, click on it. To see more, click Window and scroll to the one you want.

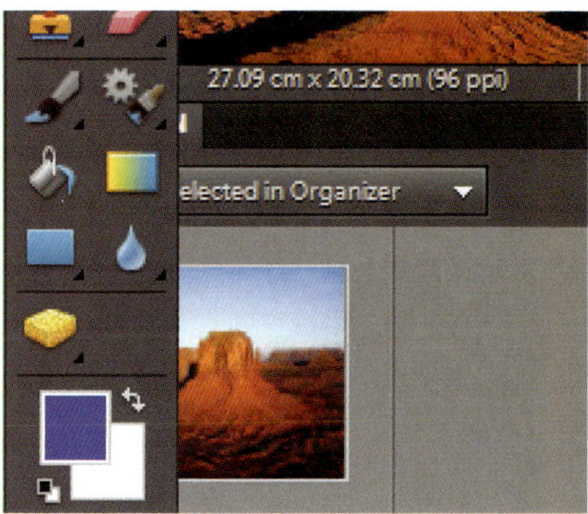

06 Project Bin

This allows you to see all of the images that you have open at once. Click on one of the thumbnails to open it up in the main workspace.

What's new in Elements 9?

Photoshop Elements has always boasted an impressive feature set – discover how the latest incarnation packs in even more

The past few versions of Photoshop Elements have introduced some innovative new features and version 9 carries on this tradition. With this latest incarnation, users can wield even greater control over their images than ever before, and be able to do it without emptying the coffers. It works seamlessly with its sister product, Premiere Elements, so if you have video to work with as well as photos, then consider the bundled offers.

In addition to the existing range of tools and commands, Elements 9 has some enticing new tricks up its sleeve. Layer masks make their debut appearance as does the ability to quickly apply photo styles and effects. You can produce creative projects within the program and also send your latest works straight to Facebook.

The Content-Aware ability of the Spot Healing brush first seen in Photoshop CS5 is now available in Elements, making photo editing even easier. And as with previous versions, you can set the interface to work with your ability.

Want a simple approach? Pick the Quick flavour. Go for Full if you want complete control or pick Guided to be shown exactly what to do. In short you have all you need to do whatever you need to your photos. This article will take a look at the new and enhanced features, giving you a taste of what version 9 has to offer, as well as summarising the key features of other versions of the Elements package.

"Go for Full if you want complete control or pick Guided to be shown exactly what to do"

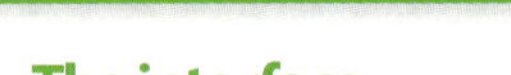

The interface

The Elements 9 interface carries on the smart grey appearance of recent versions, with easy to read icons and various workspaces to make editing as straightforward as possible.

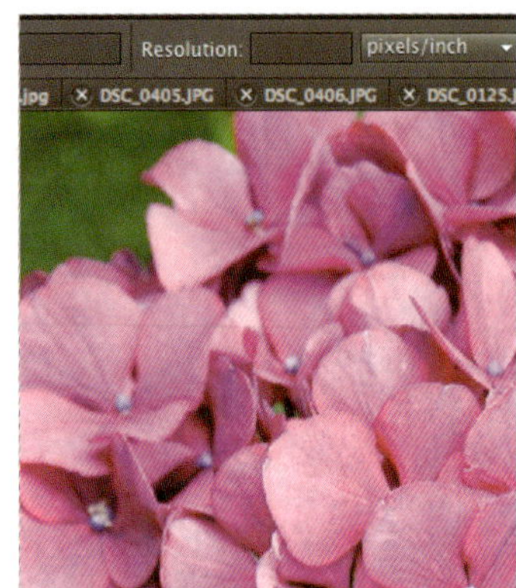

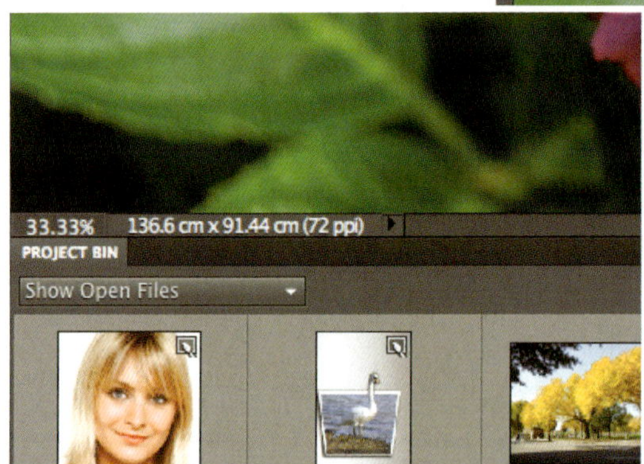

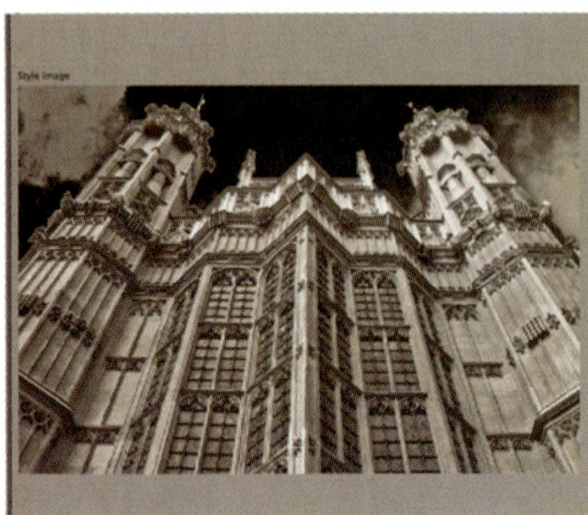

01 Photomerge

The Photomerge Style Match feature is a new way to quickly edit your images. The basic idea is that you apply the style of one image to another.

02 Style Match

Go to File>New>Photomerge Style Match, drag the image whose style you want to copy next to the image you want to edit. Use the sliders to perfect.

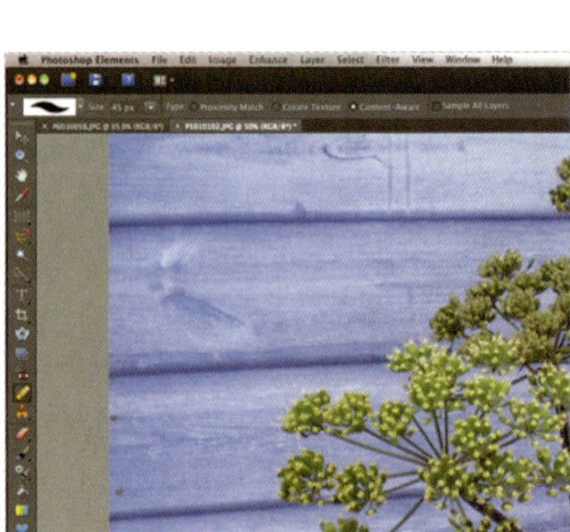

03 Better cloning

Elements users can now enjoy Content-Aware capability with the Spot Healing brush. Pick the tool and click Content-Aware in the top bar.

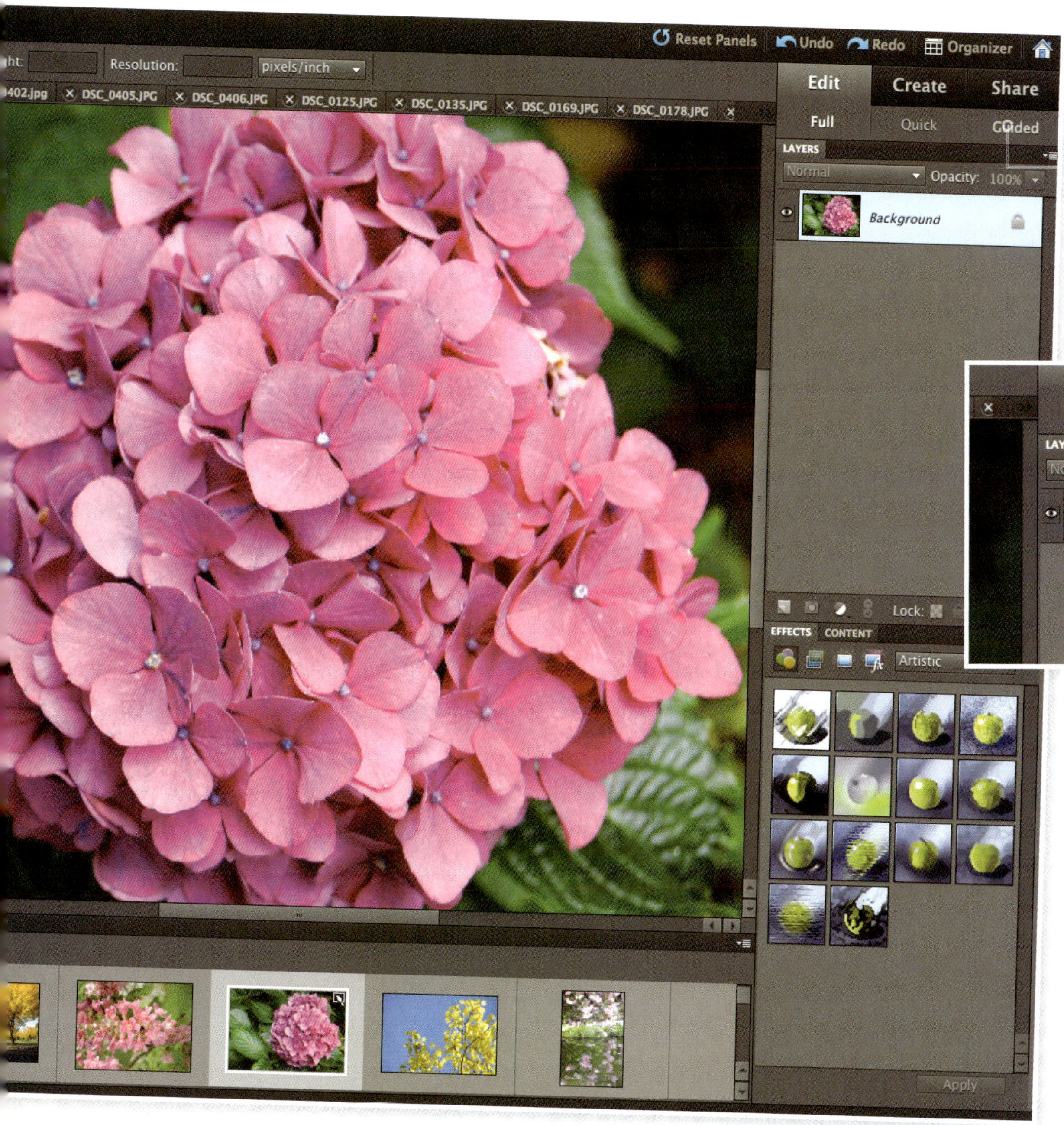

Guiding light

The Guided work area walks you through a series of creative processes. Elements 9 introduces new effects, which are detailed on page 52. It's just a case of following the steps and really couldn't be easier.

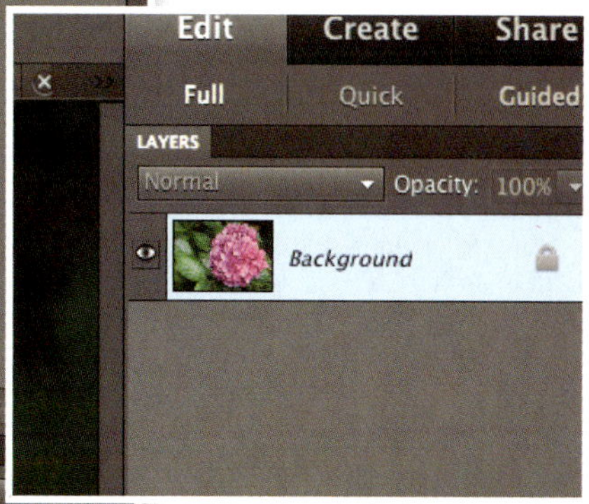

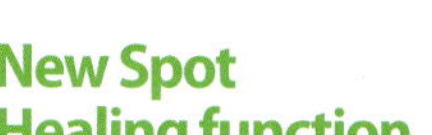

New Spot Healing function

One of the most exciting new features of Elements is the Content-Aware option in the Spot Healing brush. This allows you to remove unwanted objects with just a few strokes of the brush.

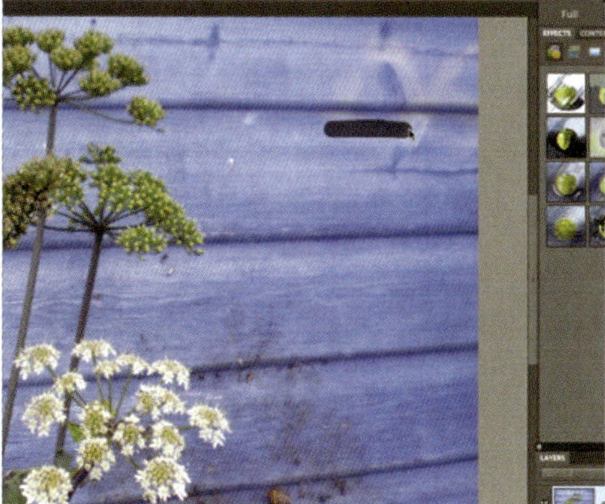

04 Clone away

Zoom into your image so you can see what's going on, adjust the brush size and then simply paint over the area you want to remove.

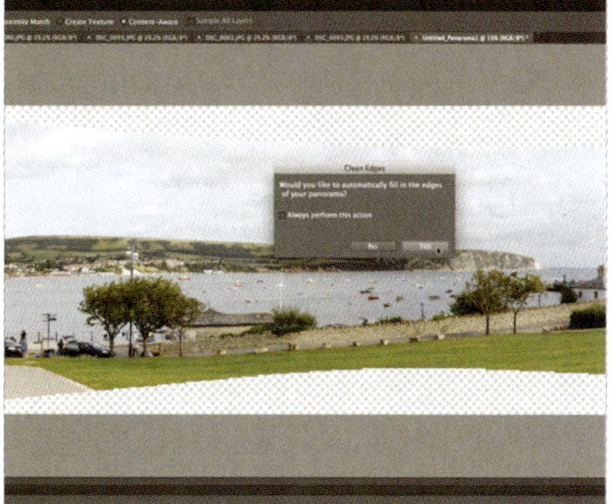

05 Panoramas

Panoramas are a fantastic way of capturing an entire scene but they don't seem to have achieved the popularity they should have done.

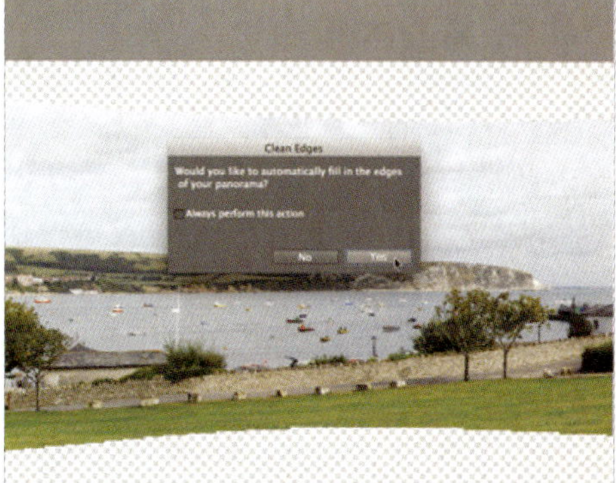

06 Stitch in time

You get to stitch together images as normal and once Elements has done its thing, you will be given an option for those outside spaces to be filled.

Elements: Create options

Photoshop Elements has a dedicated interface for all kinds of photo projects, so you can do more with your pics

It's so easy to build up a massive collection of photos that sit on your desktop and do nothing, gathering digital dust and forgotten about. As we have mentioned, there are a number of different interfaces within Photoshop Elements, which each deal with different tasks. Here we are taking a look at the Create interface, which promises to give a new lease of life to these photographs.

This enables you to create exciting photo projects from within Photoshop Elements, including books, calendars and more. Each project guides you through step by step, and you can pick templates, add text, upload images and more, without any prior knowledge. Your can select images to add to your projects from the Elements Organizer, or from your computer, and then it's time for the fun part – experimenting!

You can keep trying out new ideas again and again, as nothing is set in stone. When you are done, you can use the dedicated Adobe Photoshop Services to get your project printed professionally. There are also online suppliers for some of the categories that you can choose from, including Kodak Gallery and Shutterfly. You can even use the Create interface to order prints from your photo library.

This is a really plus point of the Elements software, and it is not something that you will find in the standard Photoshop version. There is a real emphasis on creating and sharing, doing more with your photos.

"Create exciting photo projects from within Elements, including books, calendars and more"

QUICK PHOTOSHOP TIPS

Printing

You will see a selection of printing options here too, which enable you to do more than the standard Print menu as you can send pictures to be directly printed by an online supplier.

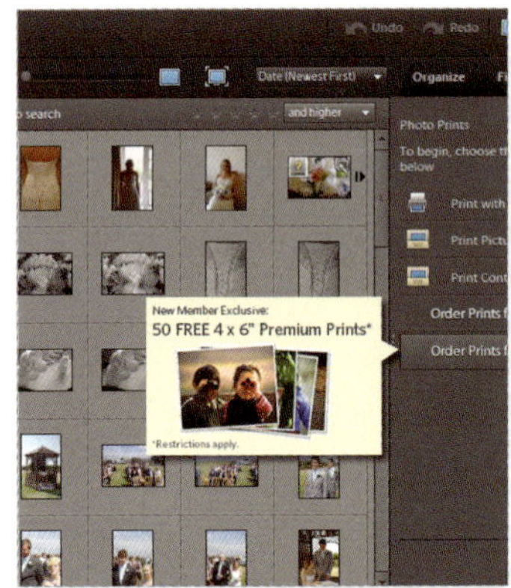

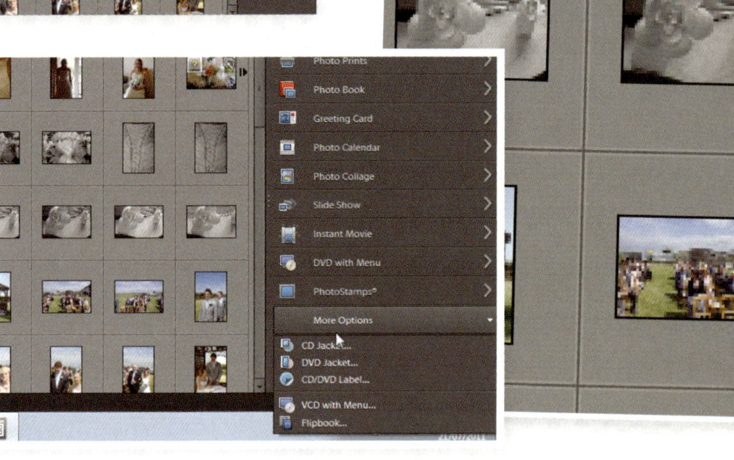

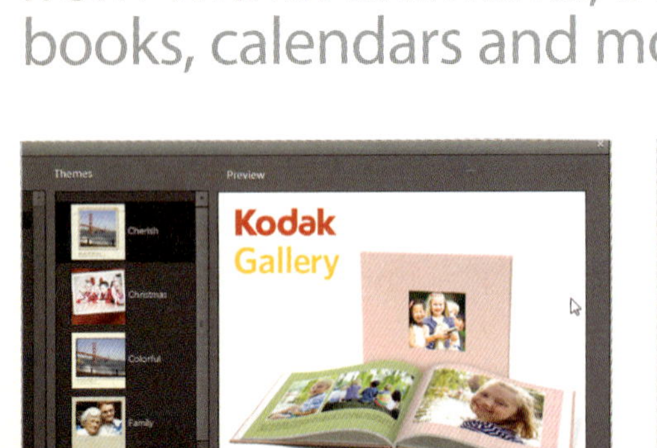

01 Photo Book

The classic presentation method, the Photo Book is as popular as ever. Design the book through Elements, then order it online.

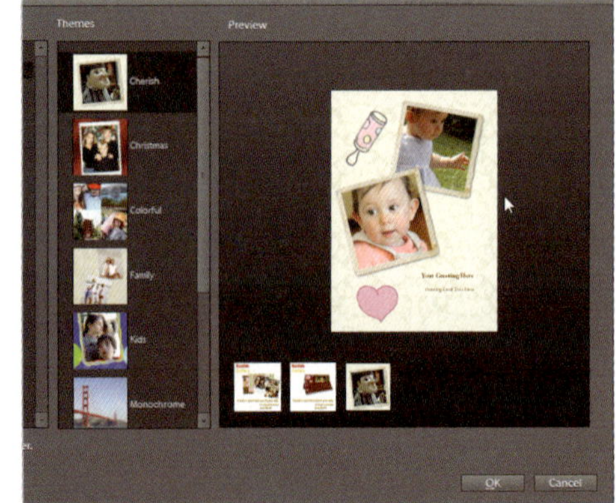

02 Greeting Card

A really fun way to personalise greetings cards for birthdays, Christmas and any other occasion. It's really easy to create as well.

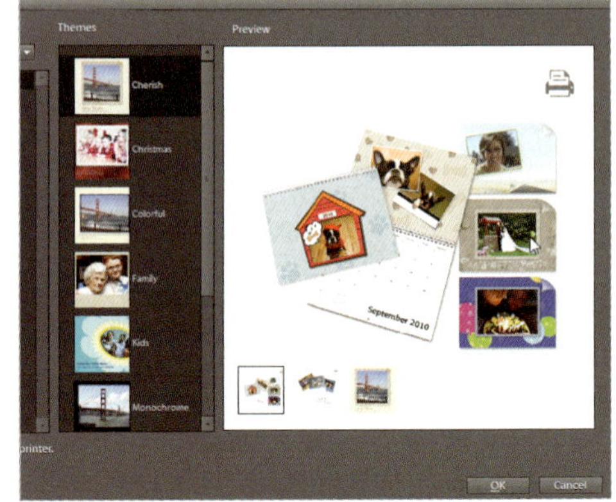

03 Photo Calendar

This is purchased through Adobe Photoshop Services, which enables you to get your calendar design printed and bound.

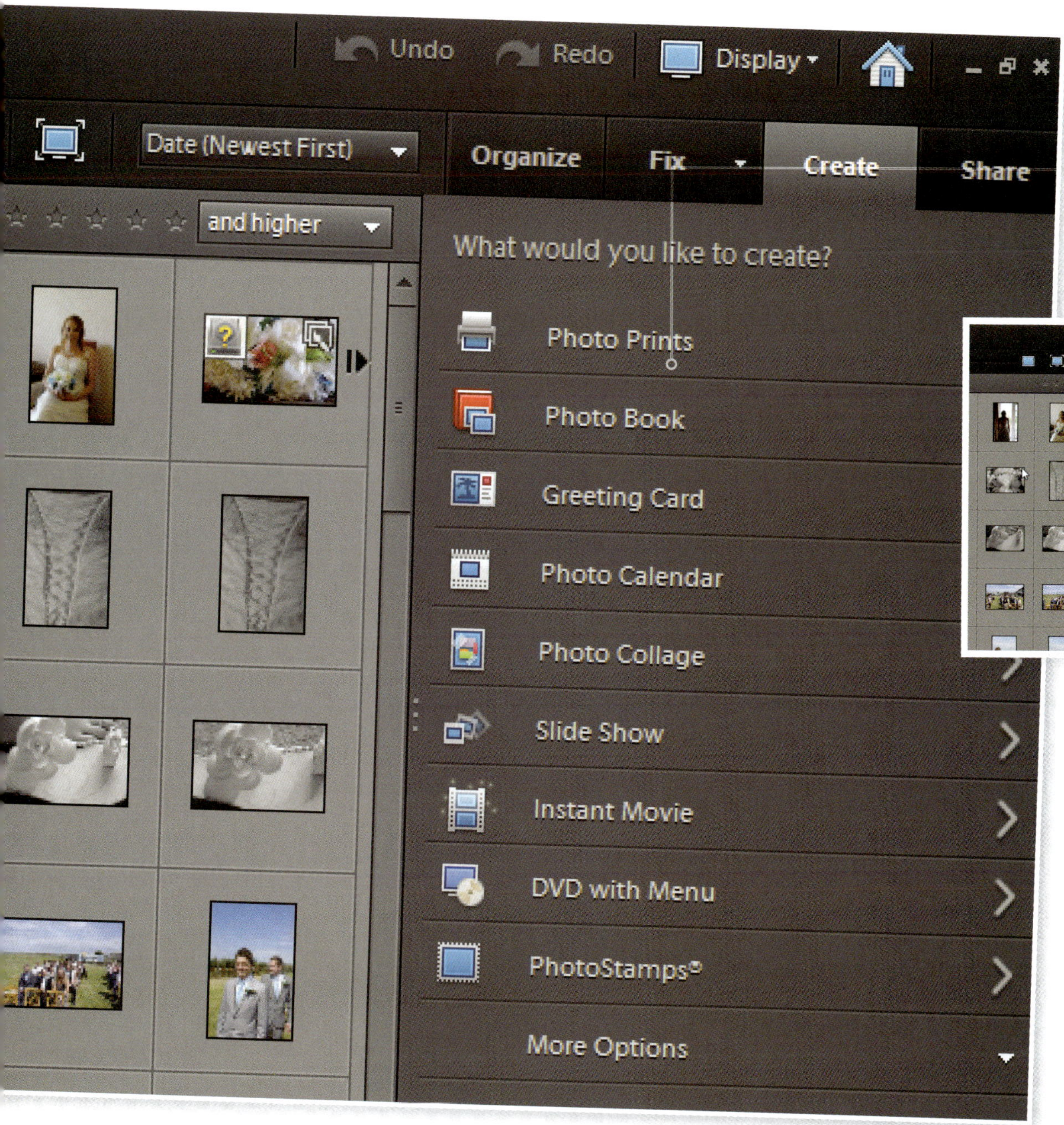

Creative options
Down the right-hand side are all of the options for what you can create using Photoshop Elements, which are all easy-to-follow guides.

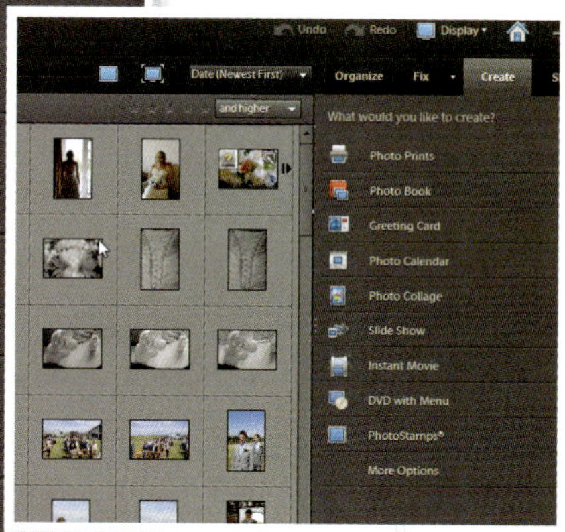

Open images
Your open images are here in the Project Bin, but when you choose to start a new photo project, you will be able to go back in and select more images to use.

Templates
Each project gives you a choice of templates that you can use as you create your product, and you can customise these with text and images.

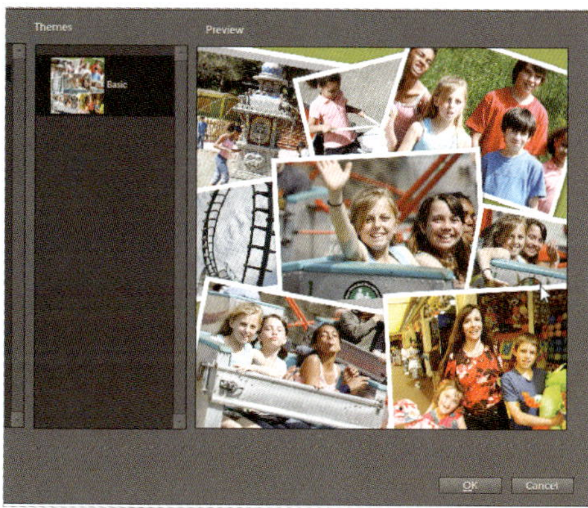

04 Photo Collage
A lovely way to show off lots of your images in one go, you can have a lot of fun with your collage projects and get creative with text too.

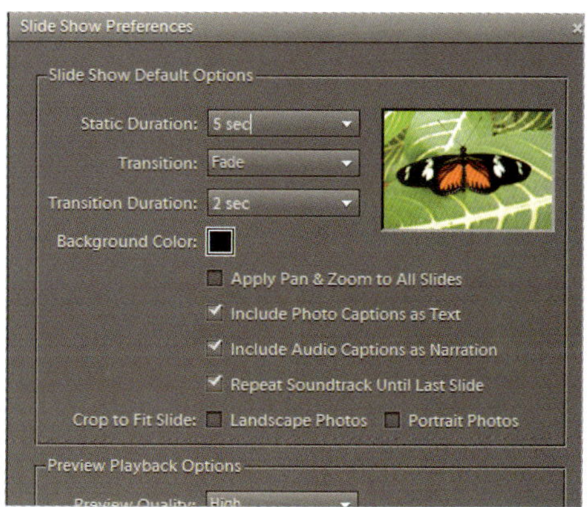

05 Slideshow
A simple way of displaying your photos, you can add pictures and music, then burn them DVD to give as gifts.

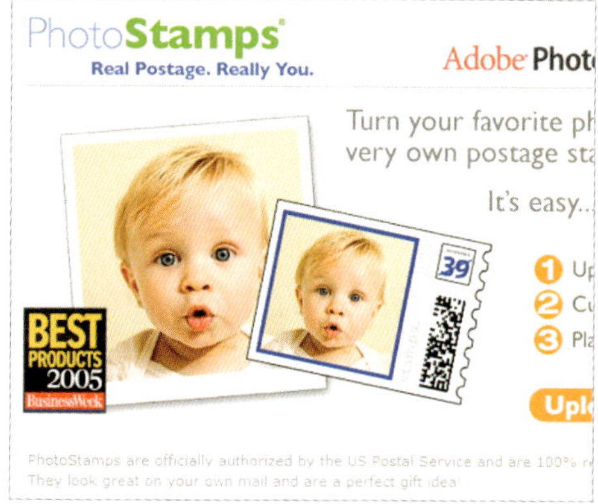

06 PhotoStamps
An unusual use for your photos, you can create postage stamps from any photo, but you need to sign up to be bale to order your stamps for use.

Photoshop Elements: Share

Don't keep your images to yourself; let everyone see and enjoy them with Elements' built-in Share options

We are living in a digital world, where sharing ideas, images, text and, well, anything, is easily done via the web. Photoshop Elements has obviously been following this trend and has incorporated the sharing options into the main interface.

There are the classic options here, such as sending images via email to friends and relatives. However, there are some more modern integrations, such as direct upload to Facebook and Flickr. Photoshop Elements will prepare your images for upload and then post them to your account. The engine that Elements uses is faster than the one on Facebook, for example, as it does the compression using your computer's power so that when it uploads to Facebook it does so in a flash. There are other options here too, but we have focused on the ones that are the most popular.

Sharing images is great if you have family and friends spread around the country, or the world, as it lets them instantly see what you have been up to. Even better, if you have organised your images with the Organizer and tagged people in your pictures (see page 26 for more on this), these tags are automatically added to Facebook – a real timesaver.

We'll have a closer look at some of the built-in Share options over these two pages, but check out our full Output section, starting from page 232, where we have loads of creative ideas for what you can do with your photos and Photoshop artworks.

"There are some more modern integrations, such as direct upload to Facebook and Flickr"

LEARN TO SHARE

Facebook tagging

Tag your photos using the Elements Organizer, which even does a lot of the hard work for you by tagging familiar subjects for you, and these will be translated straight into Facebook – clever stuff!

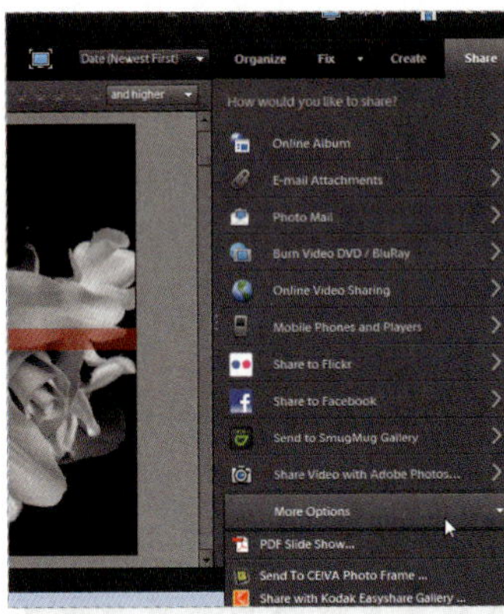

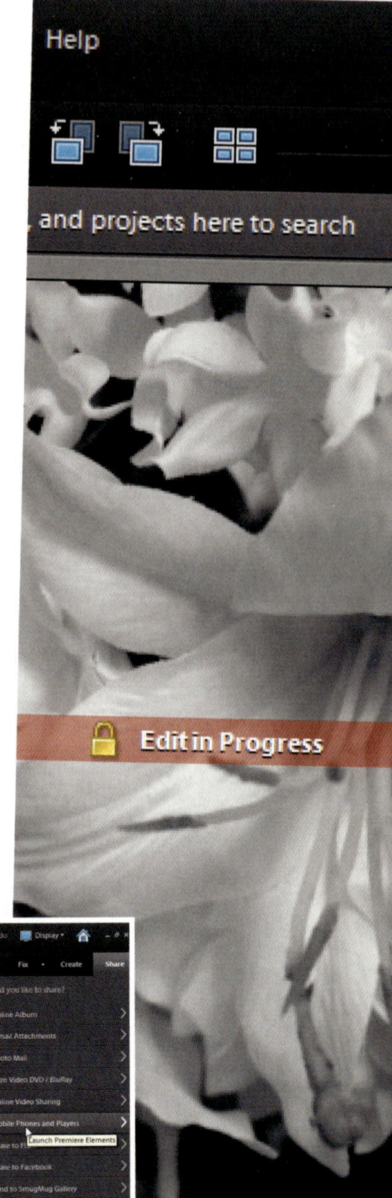

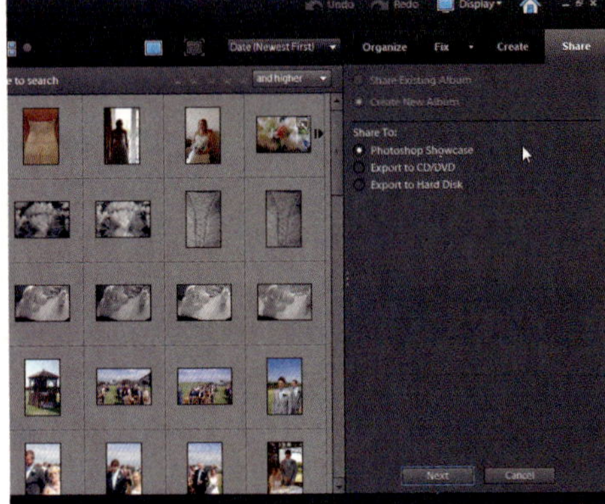

01 Online Album

Use this option if you want to upload a set of pictures to your own web page, so that you can share your images with your friends.

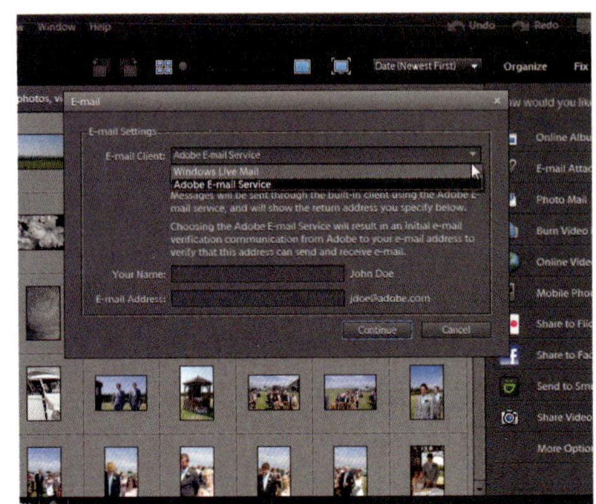

02 Email

You can instantly attach a picture to an email via your desktop account by using this option. It's super-simple and it's quicker too.

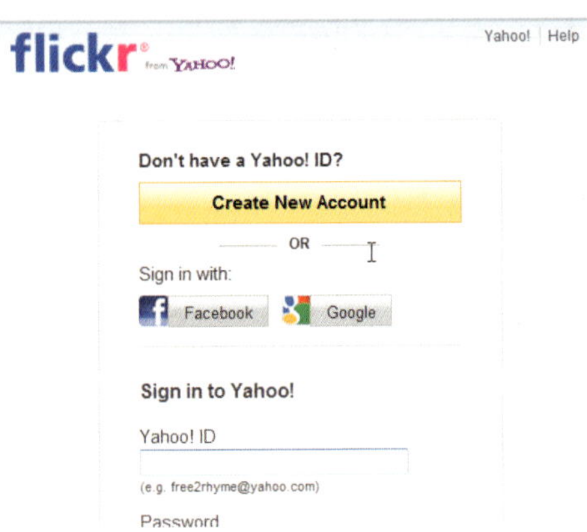

03 Flickr

The world's best-known photo-sharing site is at your fingerprints. Once you have an account, then you can quickly add images to your albums.

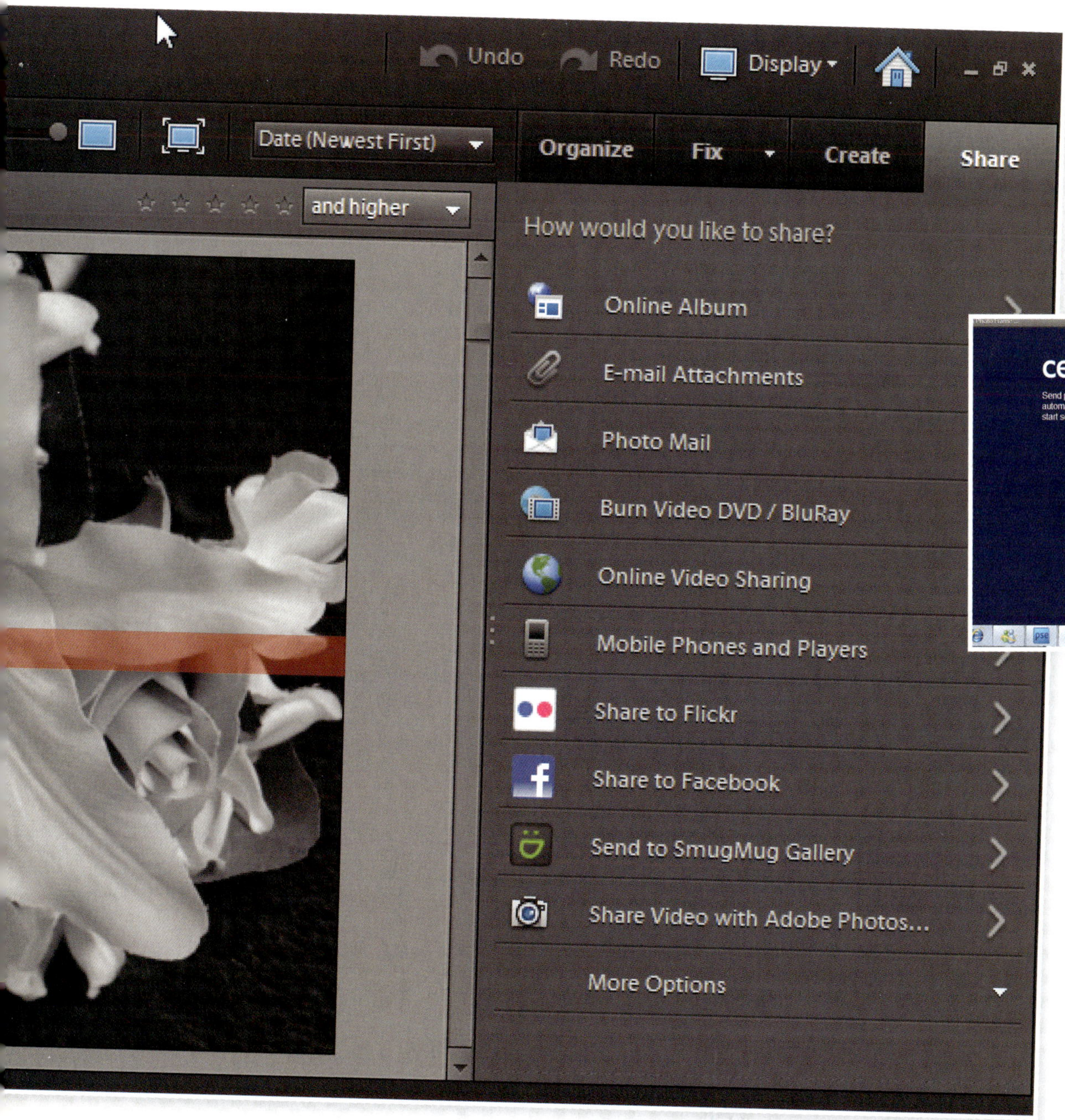

Online galleries

Supported galleries here include Flickr and SmugMug. As long as you have an online account, then you can directly upload your photos to these sites from Elements .

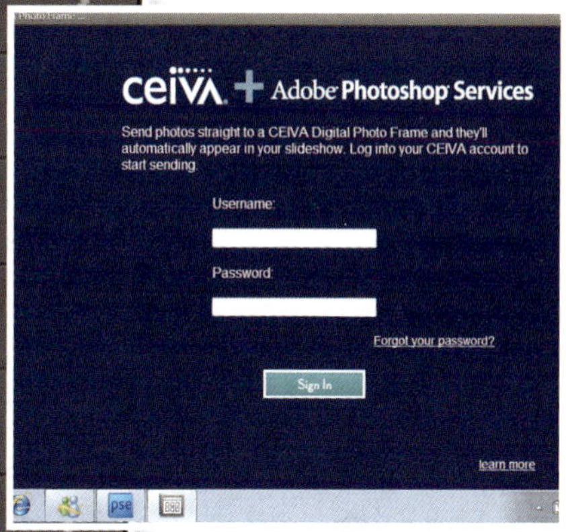

CEIVA

This is a clever piece of technology. These are connected photo frames, to which images can be sent from anywhere. So, if you have frame or someone you know does, you can send images to it from Elements.

Photo Mail

This is really a fancy email. You can embed your photos within a decorated template, with loads of customisable options to play with, that can then be sent out to your email contacts

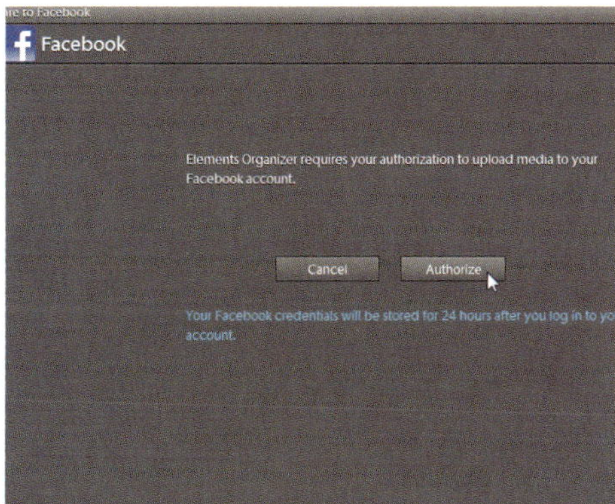

04 Facebook

If Facebook is your choice of sharing platform, you can easily. Images are compressed and sent directly from within the Adobe interface.

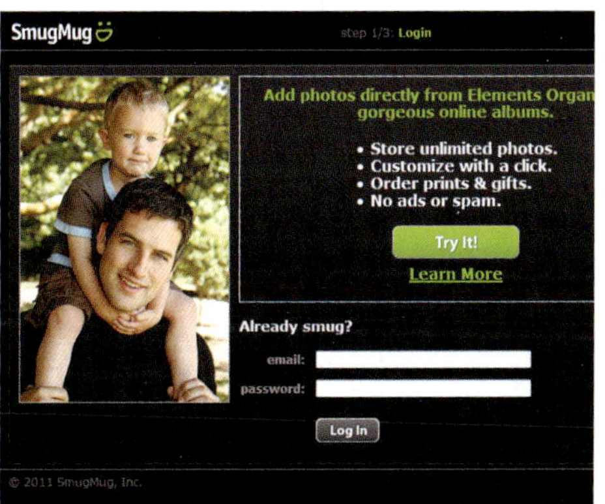

05 SmugMug

Another popular photo-sharing site that you can directly upload to. Find out more about this service at www.smugmug.com.

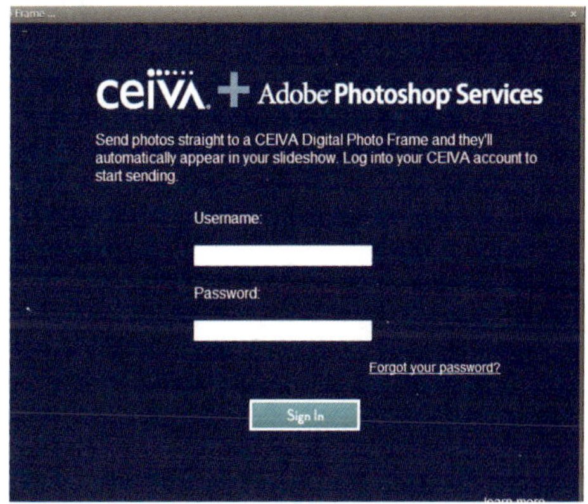

06 CEIVA Photo Frame

This innovative product is a digital photo frame to which images can be sent directly. You can even send them to other CEIVA frames.

First steps in Photoshop

First time in Photoshop? Use this primer to get up to speed with the basics in our essential guide

The first time you open Photoshop, it can seem a bewildering mess of icons, menus and palettes. You no doubt realise that there are two flavours of Photoshop – Photoshop CS and Photoshop Elements. It is generally thought that Photoshop is for professionals and that Elements is purely for beginners. The interface of Elements is a bit more intuitive than Photoshop, and features such as the Quick Edit mode mean that it's incredibly easy to make your first edit. But Elements still has a lot of the same tools as Photoshop so don't dismiss it is 'Photoshop Lite'. It might be that the tool is called something slightly different or that it's in a different place, but there's generally a workaround to give Elements users the same wealth of editing options as Photoshop users. In places where there is a difference between Photoshop and Elements, we've included the Elements way of carrying out a technique. If you don't see an alternative way, then it's the same.

There are three core skills that you need when you first start using Photoshop. You need to be able to load a file, open a new file and also save a file. These three tasks all require extra knowledge, such as understanding resolution and file formats.

The other essential ability that you need is to get access to all of the tools. If you think the Photoshop interface is confusing as it is, it would cause your brain to explode if all of the tools were on display at once! To avoid this, a lot of tools are grouped together and hidden behind a major tool.

One other thing that is worth mentioning is shortcuts. We always give the menu commands for performing tasks as it's a good way to get used to where things are and how things are organised. But once you get more comfortable with moving around the interface, you can start to use your keyboard to carry out the most common commands.

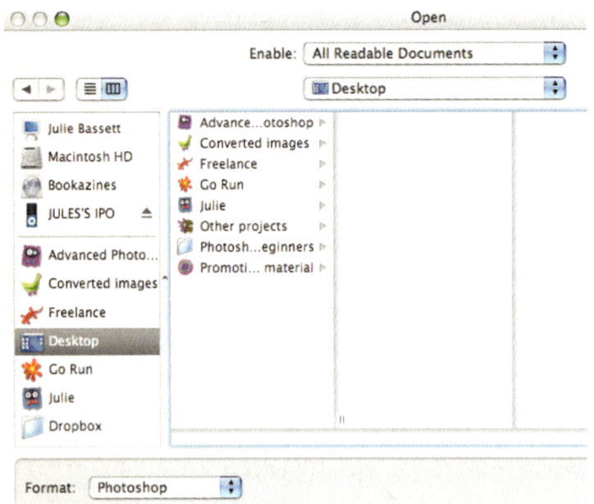

01 Open a file

To load an image, go to File>Open and then use the window browser to navigate to the file you want. Once found, simply click Open.

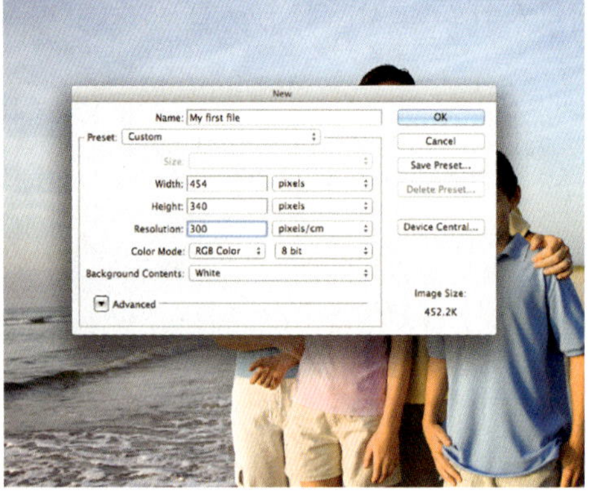

02 Create a file

To open a new file, go to File>New and enter a name, a size and a resolution. Click OK to create it. In Elements, go to File>New>Blank File.

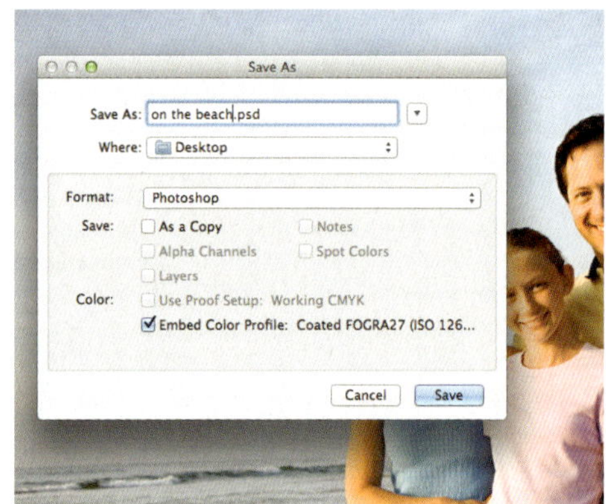

03 Save a file

Saving is also a straightforward affair. Go to File>Save As. You can rename the file if you want and, more importantly, set the file format.

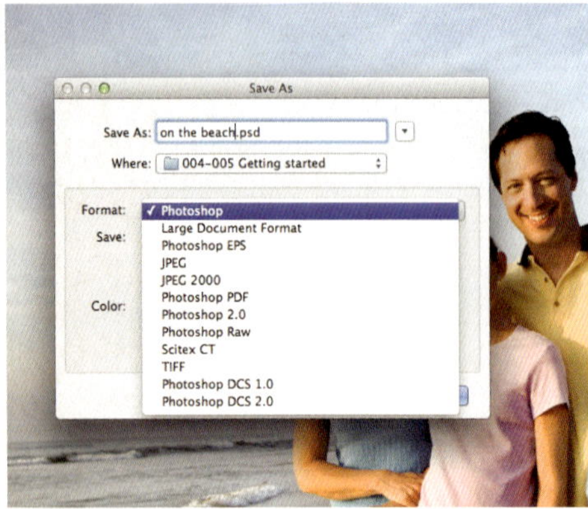

04 File formats

Adobe has supplied a lot of different file formats for you to save your image in and we'll be looking at this in more detail throughout this book.

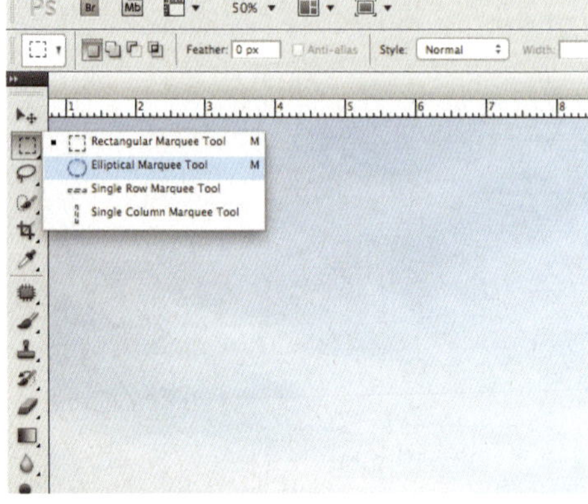

05 Selecting tools

Adobe has bundled similar tools together. If you see a small arrow in the bottom-right corner of a tool, then there are other tools hidden behind.

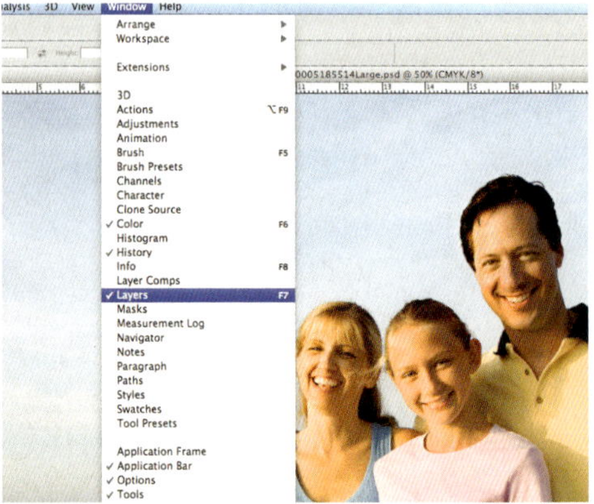

06 Options

Tools and commands are found in a series of palettes. You can set which palettes are seen using the Window menu.

QUICK PHOTOSHOP TIPS

Quick save

The first time that you save a new file, use the Save As command as we have described, so that you can set the file name and format. Then, if you continue working on the image, you can just use File>Save instead, which saves your progress to the same file. It can be easier to get used to the keyboard shortcut, which is the Apple/Cmd key if you're using a Mac, or the Ctrl key if you're using a PC, plus the 'S' key at the same time.

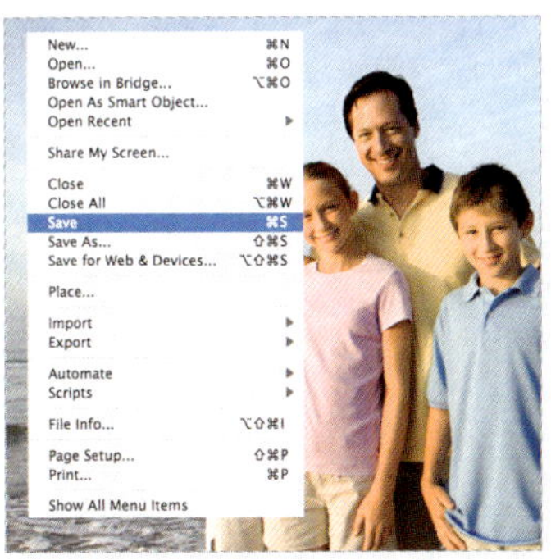

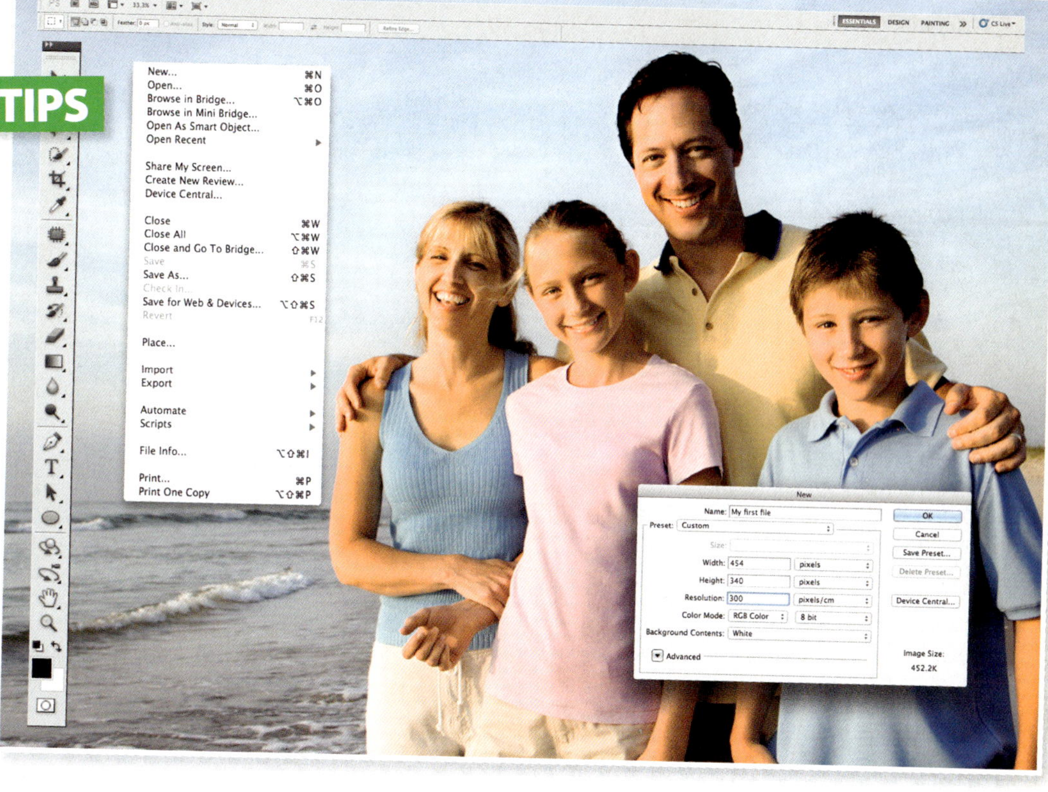

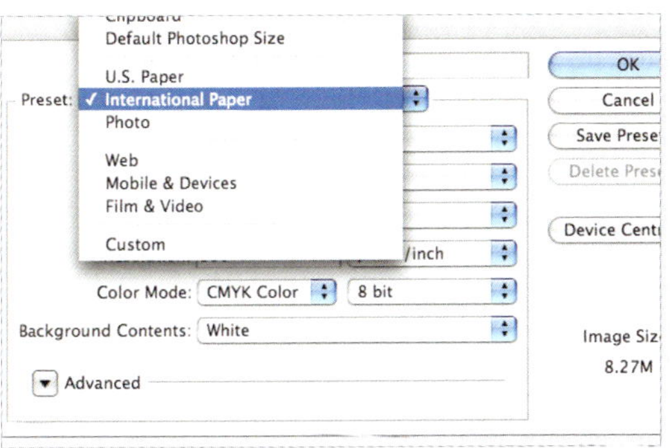

File sizes

When you are creating a new file from scratch, you can use the Preset menu to see different pre-defined sizes. International Paper offers you A4 and A5, for example, for quick setup of new documents to the right dimensions.

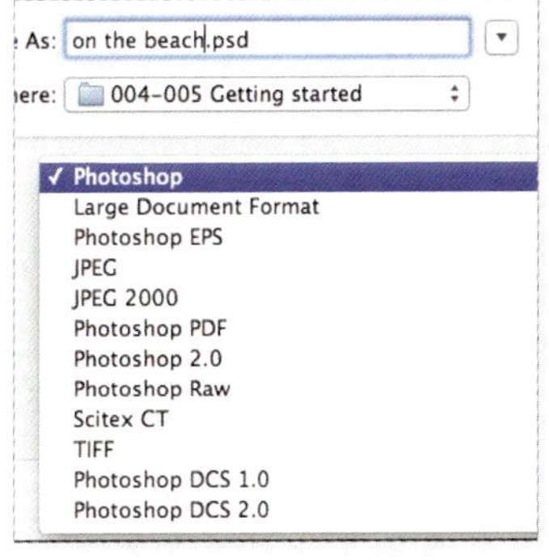

Common file types

JPEG is the most common file format. It is used because it offers smaller file sizes but that can lead to loss of quality. When you choose to save in JPEG, you are given a slider to set the quality. PSD is a Photoshop document and is needed if you are saving a multi-layered document. TIFF results in larger but in good quality files. Use this when you need the optimum quality.

Resolution Get it right the first time

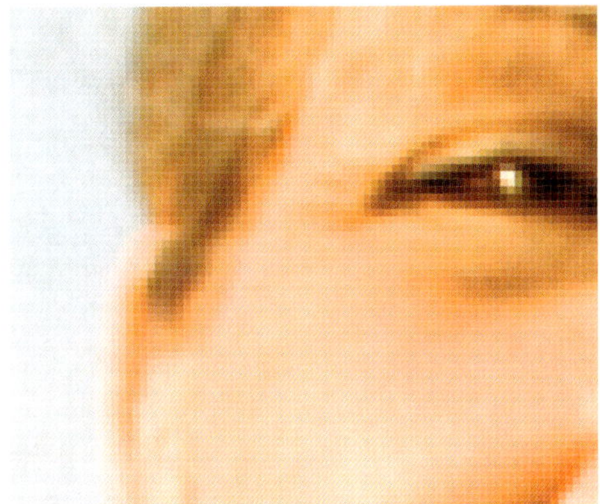

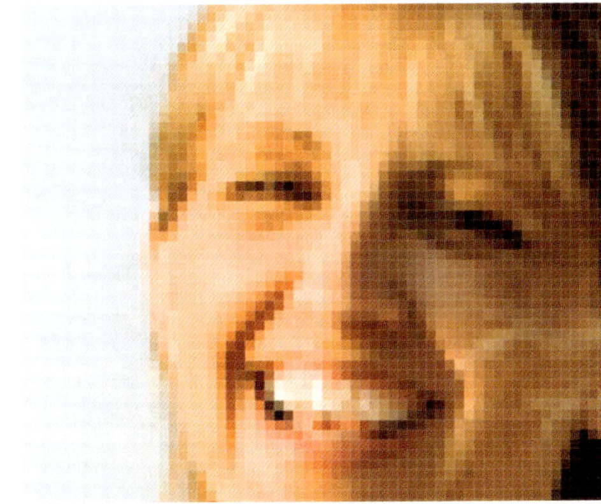

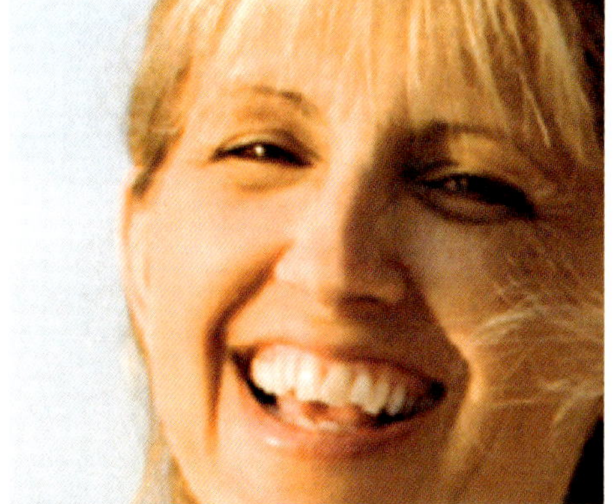

01 What is resolution?

All images are made up of square pixels. These pixels control how detailed an image is – put simply the more pixels the better the image.

02 Start with 72ppi

Photoshop measures pixels in inches (or ppi). Our screens work in 72ppi, so if you are doing something that will never be printed, 72ppi is fine.

03 Go 300ppi for quality

If you need quality or you want to print an image, work in 300ppi. The extra pixels mean that an image has more information.

Focus on resolution

Understand the nature of every pixel in your image and learn the right way to resize your photos without damaging them

The foundation of everything we do digitally is dictated by pixels – tiny bits of colour that we can barely see. When we talk about quality, pixels are more often than not part of the equation, and this is where resolution comes into play.

Resolution is the number of pixels per inch in your image, and for short this is known as ppi. There are two resolution values which are commonly used in digital artwork and photography: 72 and 300ppi. The larger the ppi, the bigger an image can be printed – and for on-screen purposes 72ppi is used, and 300ppi is best suited for printing.

But the factor that decides the final quality of an image is its pixel dimensions. The lower the pixel dimensions, the smaller the image size. When you increase the resolution (ppi) of an image that already has small pixel dimensions, you effectively make its print size even smaller.

Resolution is the difference between an image with lots of definition and an image with a blocky, pixelated appearance. Always look out for high-resolution stock images to use in your artwork. This enables you to print bigger, zoom in closer and still have good definition.

In this guide you'll learn how to control resolution, whether for print or for on-screen purposes. Discover what happens to your image when you resample pixels – and we also uncover what the tick boxes in the Image Size menu really mean.

"In this guide you'll learn how to control resolution, whether for print or for on-screen purposes"

CHANGING IMAGE RESOLUTION

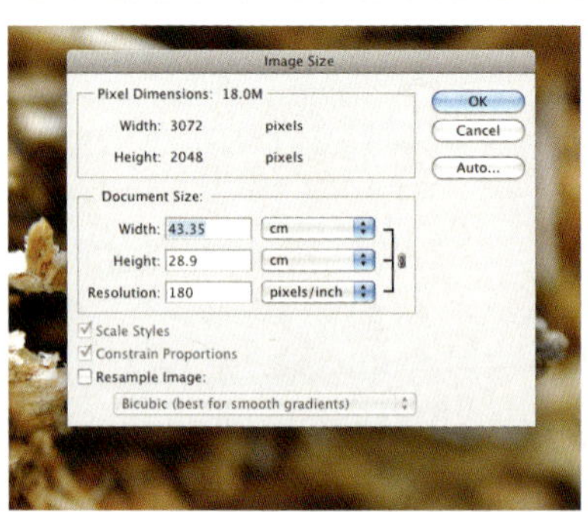

Constrain sizes

Open the dialog box and make sure the Constrain Proportions box is ticked. Keep the Scale Styles box ticked and uncheck the Resample Image box. The pixel dimensions section should grey out.

Adjust resolution

Using the Resolution field, enter a value suited to your purpose. For printing enter 300, and for on-screen use enter 72. You'll notice the Width and Height values change to show the document's size.

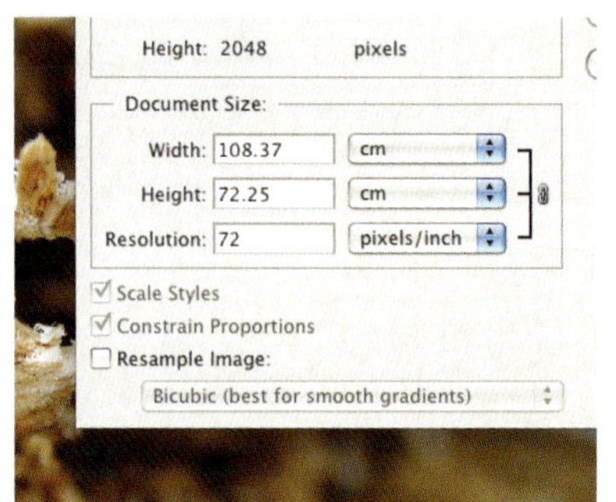

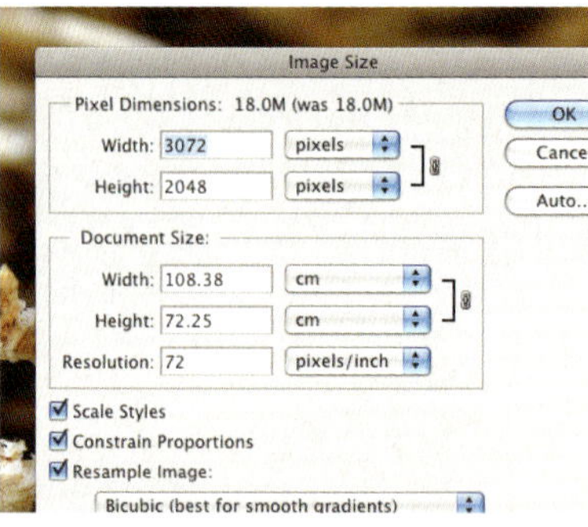

Adjusting pixels

Tick Resample Image to change the pixel dimensions of your image. PS adds/removes pixels to cater for the change in size. Pick the Resample method for best results, depending on your image.

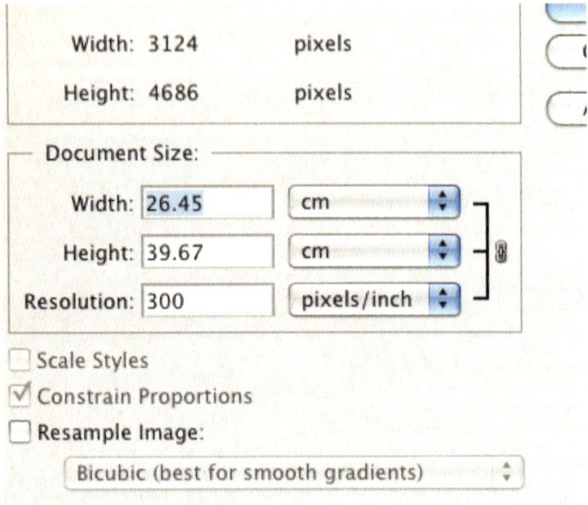

01 Printing advice

When you print an image, the best resolution is 300ppi. When printing with inkjet printers with photo paper, 200-300ppi would suffice.

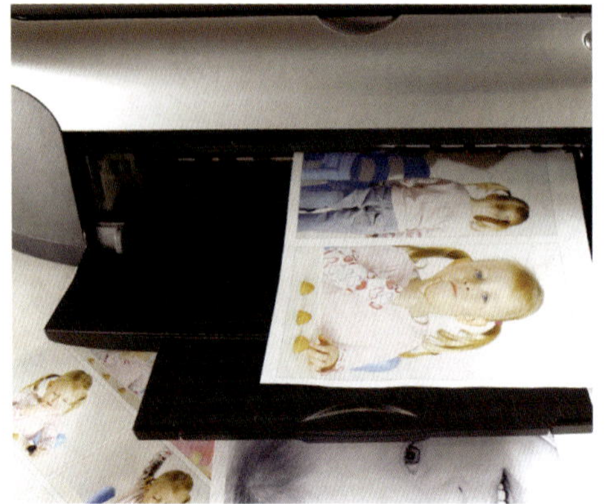

02 Inkjet printing

The difference is in the definition and clarity of the result. More definition can be seen in an image printed at 300ppi than at 200ppi.

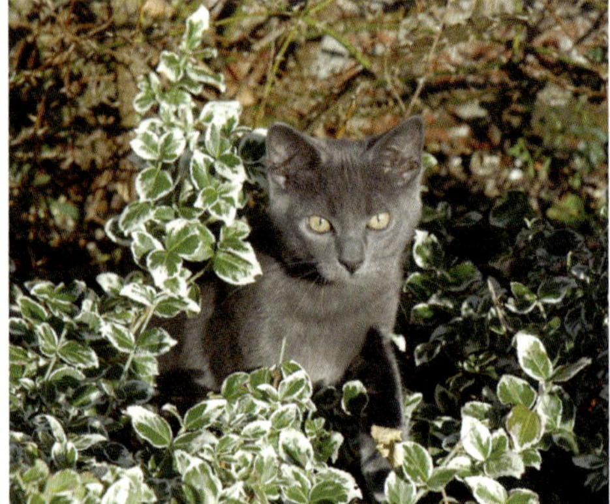

03 On-screen resolution

If your artwork is for the web, image resolution should be 72ppi. The extra pixels in 300ppi become redundant for displaying on-screen.

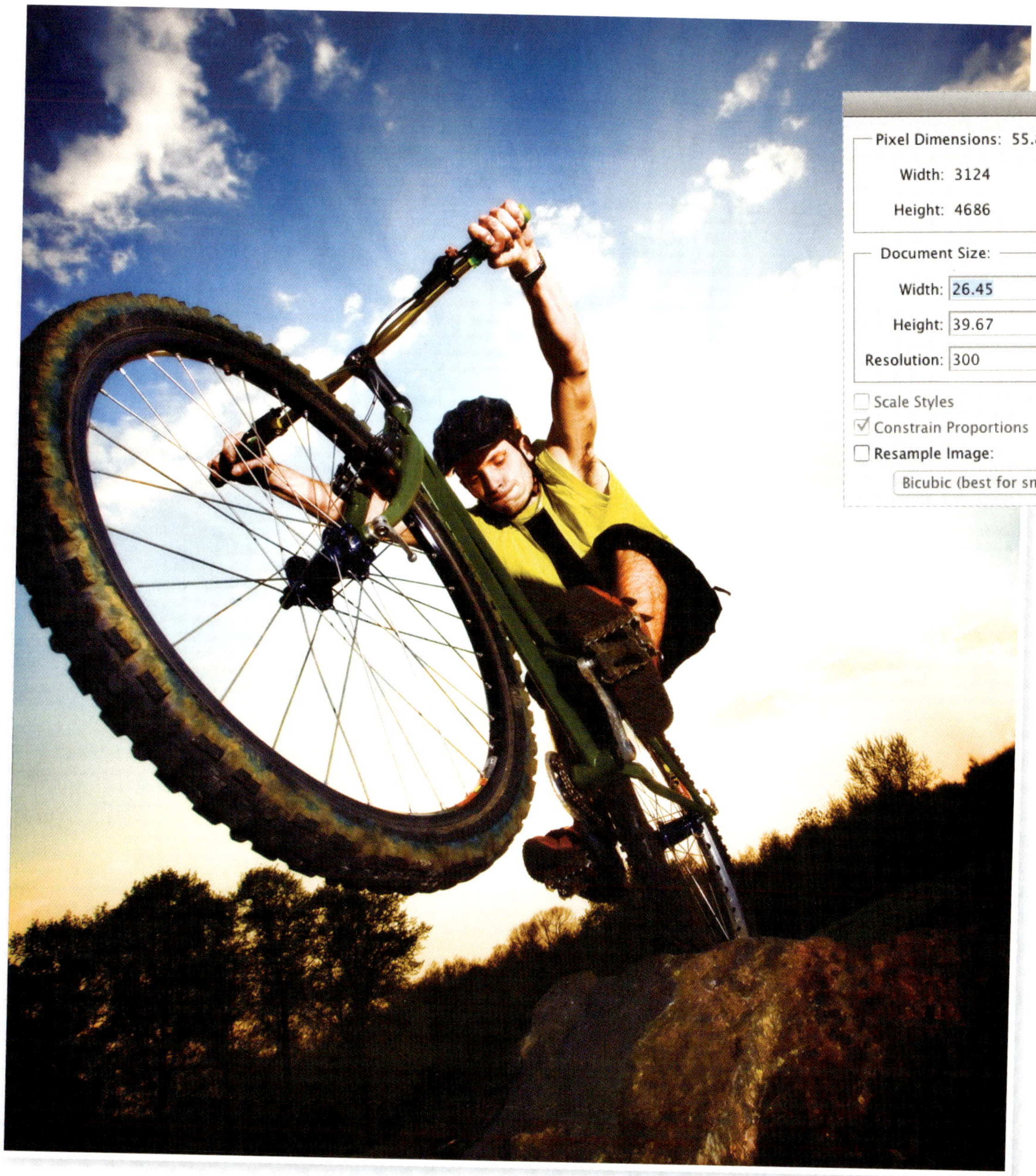

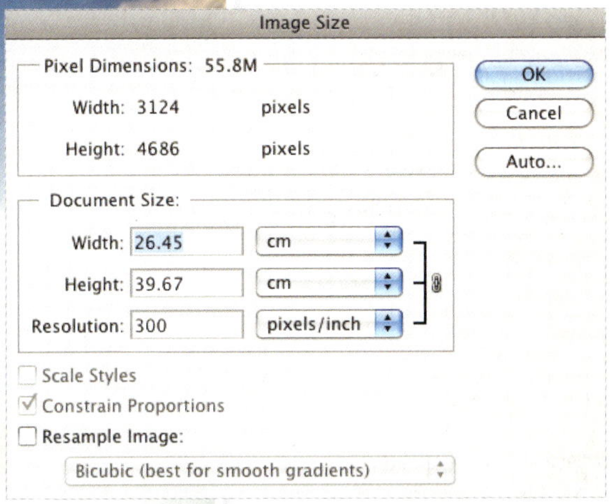

Image Size menu

Under Image>Image Size, the image's pixel dimensions are given, as well as document size and resolution. The resolution is in pixels per inch (ppi for short). The resolution of 300ppi is used for print.

Image definition

This image has a large pixel dimension, so at 300ppi its print size is close to A3. Image clarity is good too, and we can see closer to the details when we zoom into the image at 100%.

Crop tool

Using the Crop tool removes important pixels from your image, and as a result lowers an image's resolution (ppi) and ultimately reduces print size.

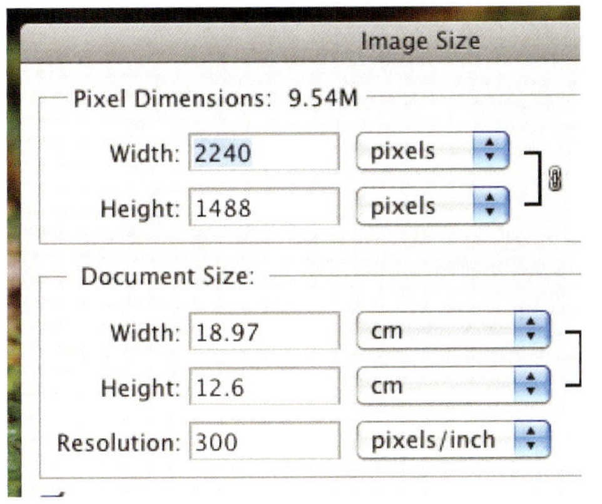

04 Resample dimensions

The Resample option enables you to adjust the number of pixels in your image, resulting in pixels being either added in or taken out by Photoshop.

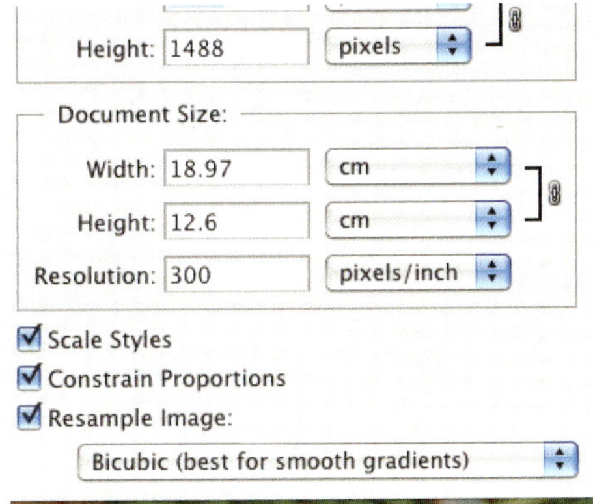

05 Interpolation

A list of options becomes available for methods of interpolation – the way PS blends each pixel. Resampling affects quality and definition.

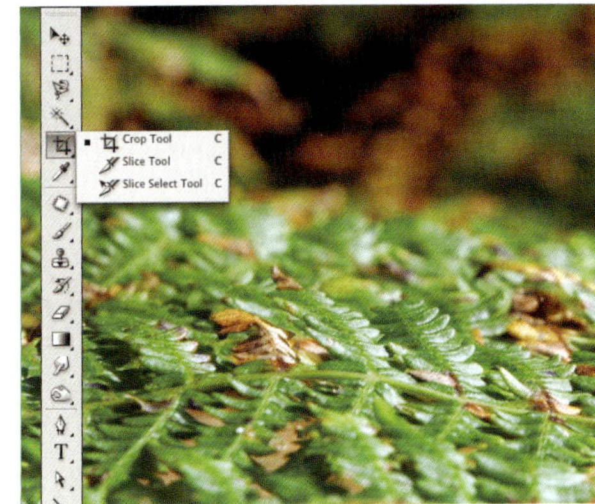

06 Cropping

The Crop tool lowers an image's pixel dimensions, and affects its print size. The Crop tool can be set to a certain resolution for the cropped image.

Adobe Bridge: Why should you use it?

Keep on top of your workflow with Photoshop's closest friend and image-editing partner, Bridge

Adobe Bridge has been on the scene for many versions of Photoshop and actually sits unassumingly hidden as soon as you've purchased the software (it's also in the latest version of Elements too). With Bridge supplied from the offset, it's surprising just how many artists avoid it or have never even heard of it. Though it's fair to say that Bridge takes time to get used to, it's only when you dig deep into what it can do that it will persuade you to stick with it for the ride ahead.

Bridge has many uses for improving and organising your workflow. Whether you're importing batches of freshly shot images or making sense of an overflowing library of images on your hard drive, use Bridge to organise things and to keep your workflow finely tuned, streamlined and practical from start to finish. Bridge uses collections, filters and keywords to tag images and search for the ones you need all within one interface. It can save you time searching through hard drive folders for that specific image of a person's birthday or wedding event, for example.

Keywords speed up the time it takes to find certain images. You can create your own keywords, such as a place or family name, and tag images relating to the word. Keywords are listed in a palette in the Bridge interface next to the main preview window and by right-clicking on a keyword and selecting Find, you can hunt down the assigned images. Images can also be found by searching exposure settings, colour profiles or by width and height. Utilising this palette will speed up the searching process of your workflow if you find yourself with a huge library of images hidden in the corners of your computer's hard drive.

There's a handy shortcut in Bridge that allows you to upload images directly from a camera or any attached storage device. Photo Downloader lets you make a new folder and save images to it. They can be renamed and saved according to their date or file name. You can delete originals and save copies, and a copyright tag can be given to images with the creator's name so other artists know where the files originated.

> "Bridge uses collections, filters and keywords to tag images and search for the ones you need all within one interface to save you time searching"

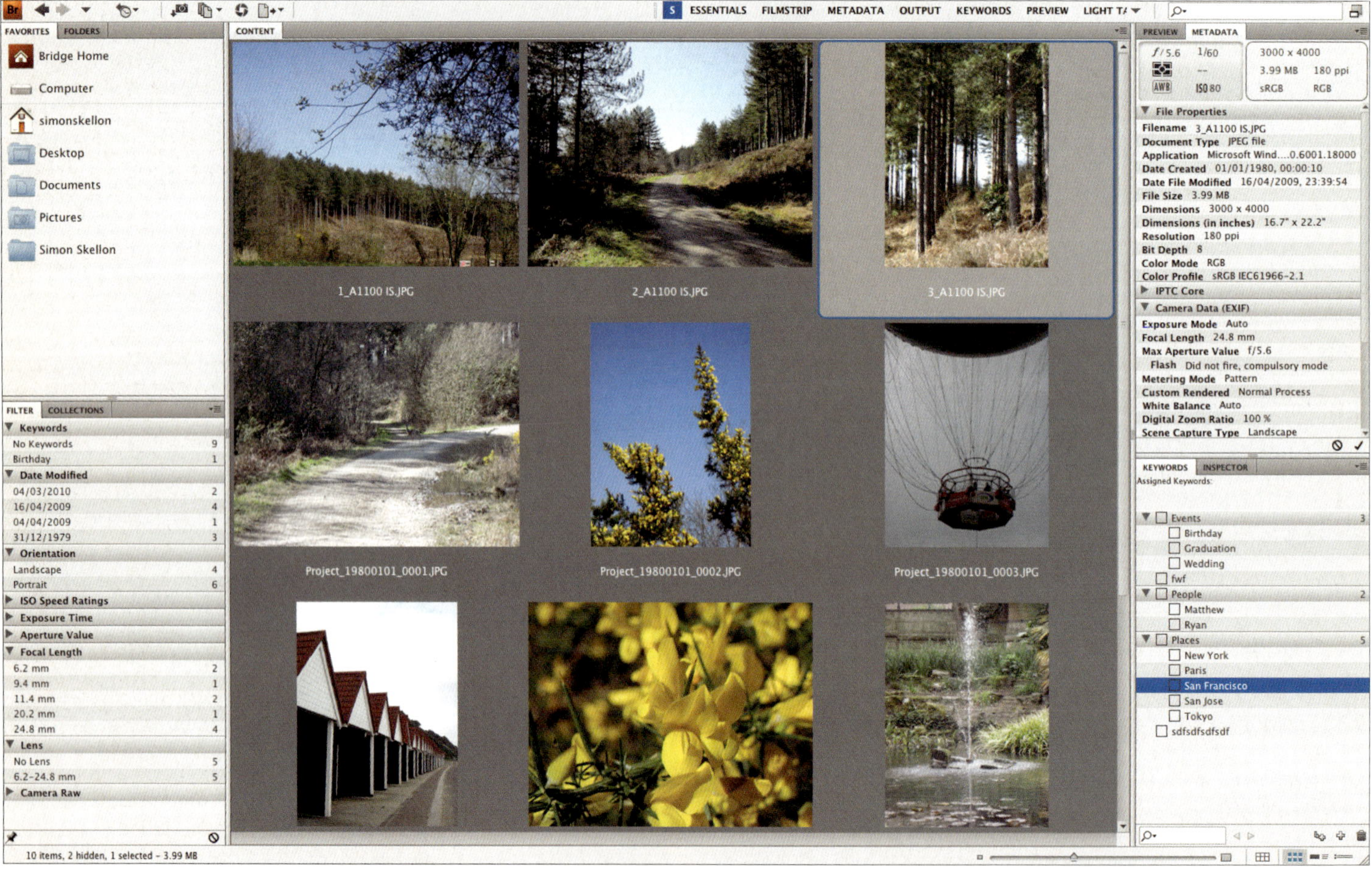

Navigating through Bridge How to find your photos

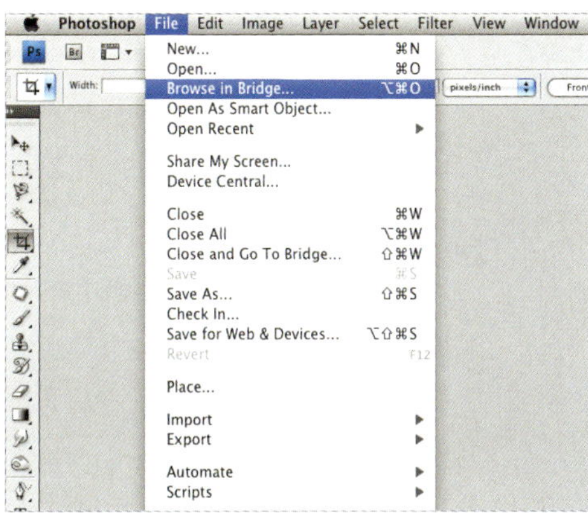

01 Found in Photoshop

Bridge can be opened from inside Photoshop. Go to File>Browse in Bridge to open up the Bridge interface.

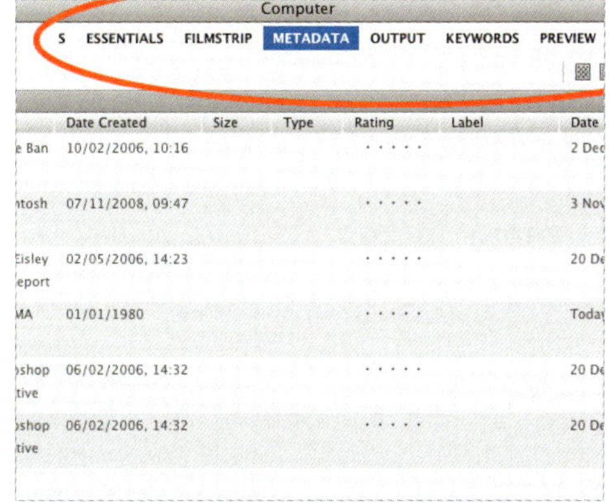

02 Set up the interface

Along the top of Bridge are options for arranging the interface such as Essentials and Preview. Cycle through them to see which works best for you.

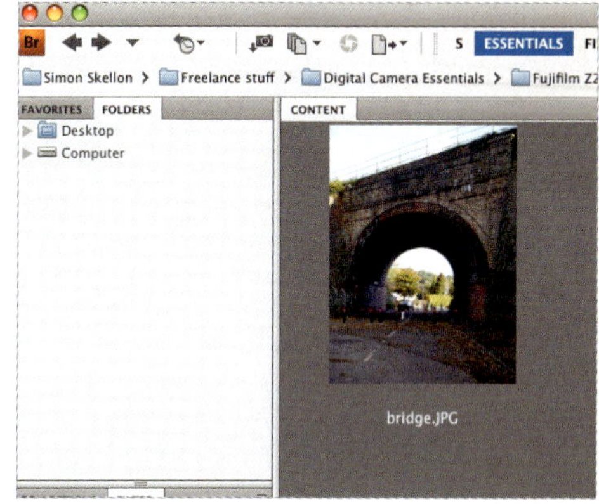

03 Load images

In the top left are the Favorites and Folders palettes. Hunt down the images you need to organise and the images will load in the centre.

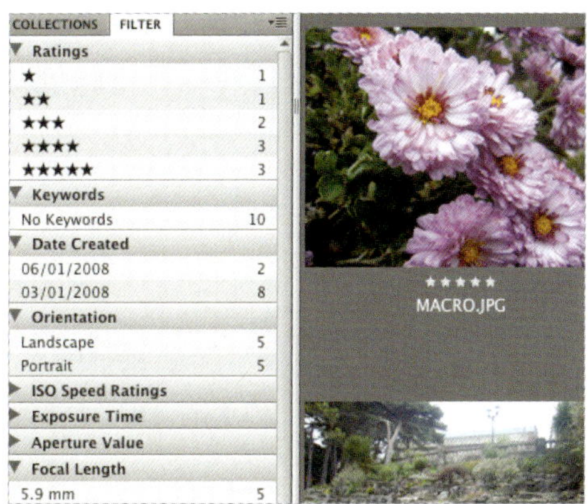

04 A star rating

Under each image are five dots that represent stars. Click on the rating for each image. In the Filter, images can be chosen by stars.

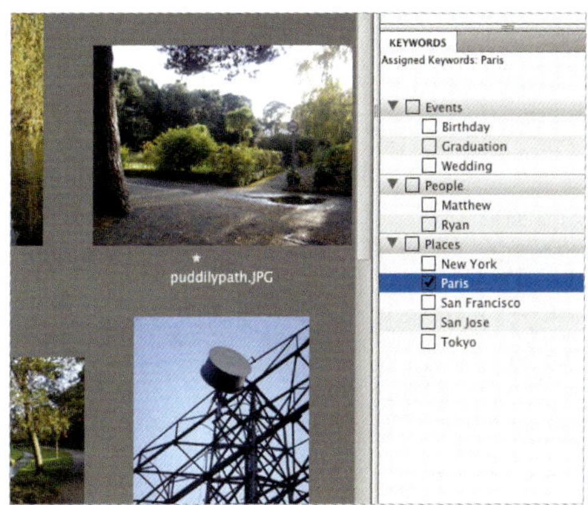

05 Apply keywords

To add keywords, highlight a single or group of images and in the Keywords palette tick an option that applies, such as a place name.

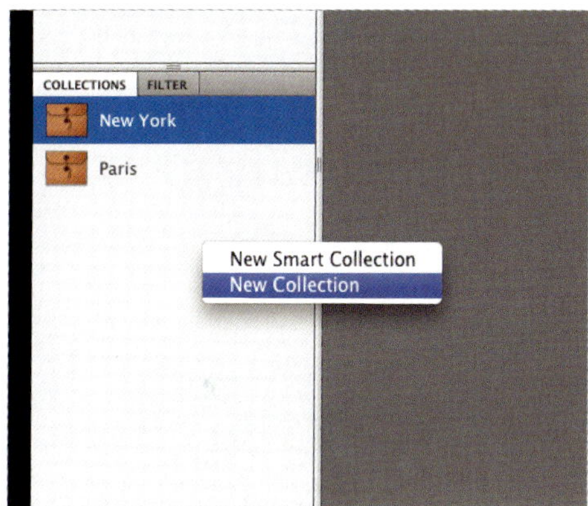

06 Create collections

Create new collections and you can give the grouped images keywords. Add your files into their own Collection folders to help stay organised.

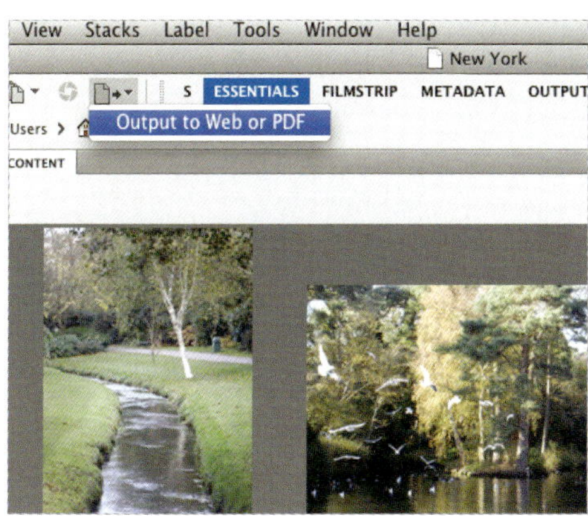

07 Enter output mode

At the top of Bridge is the option to Output to Web or PDF. Selecting this option takes you into the output screen where you can lay out your images.

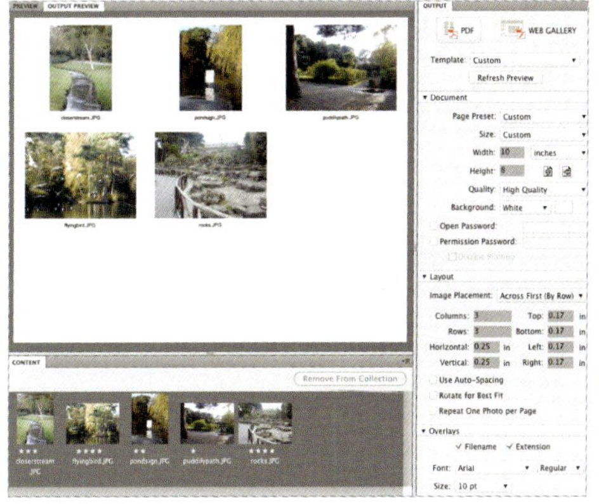

08 Choose output settings

In Output you can create a layout of your images to print as a thumbnail reference. You can watermark images with text or create a web slideshow.

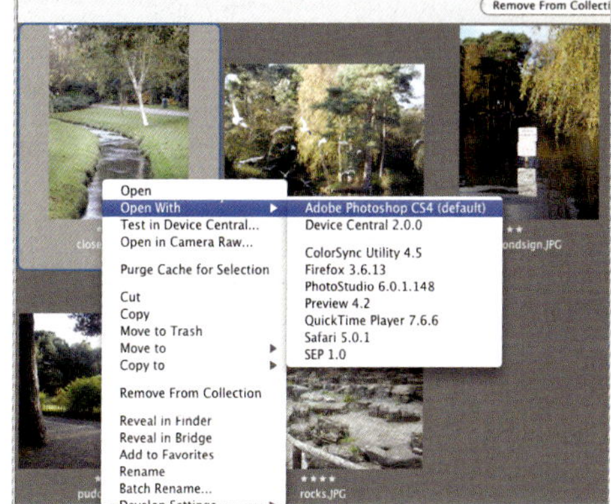

09 Open in Photoshop

To open images in Photoshop, Ctrl/right click an image and select Open With. Alternatively, double-click an image and it'll open straight into PS.

Using the Elements Organizer

Keep your photo collection in order with this essential extra that comes with Photoshop Elements

The latest version of Photoshop Elements not only includes new features for image editors to enjoy, it boasts enhanced tools too. In Photoshop Elements 9 there is a new welcome screen from which you can choose between Organize and Edit tabs to either begin image manipulations straight away or sort through your library of images first.

The Organize function in Elements is handy for arranging all of your photos and videos in one place. Due to the thumbnail displays, which can be customised to suit how you prefer to view images, it is easy and quick to locate just the photos you want to work with and arrange them accordingly. The latest version even includes automatic People Recognition that cleverly detects the faces of people in your photos.

This technology analyses your people shots and brings up a window with all of the faces highlighted. You can then tag these people, and in the future, you can just type in someone's name to find all the pictures of them. You can also add a simple star rating to images. There are five stars underneath each image and you can click on them to light them up. You can then choose to filter your images based on their star rating – a good way to find all your best shots, or even the bad ones that need to be edited further.

Your images can be keyworded, which means that you can add personal tags that identify your images. There are a preset selection of tags, such as people, location and so on, and each of these can be used as search criteria.

The Organizer used to just be available for PCs, but the latest version, Version 9, now offers the Organizer to Mac users. If you have Premiere Elements for video-editing too, then you can use the same Organizer for both still and moving images, helping to keep your entire media collection in one place and happily sorted.

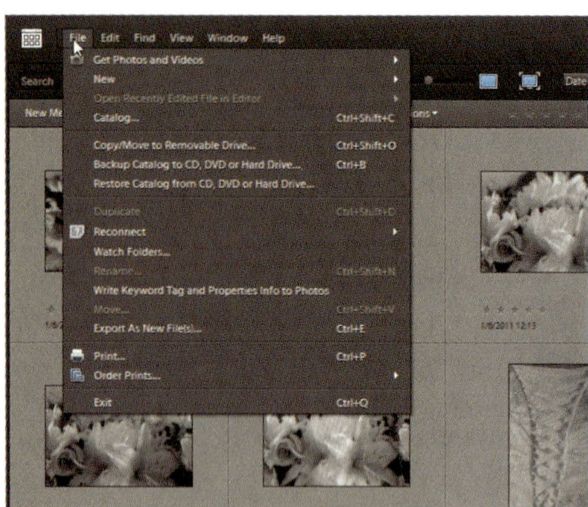

01 Add images

The first thing that you need to do is add images to the Organizer, which you can easily do from the File menu.

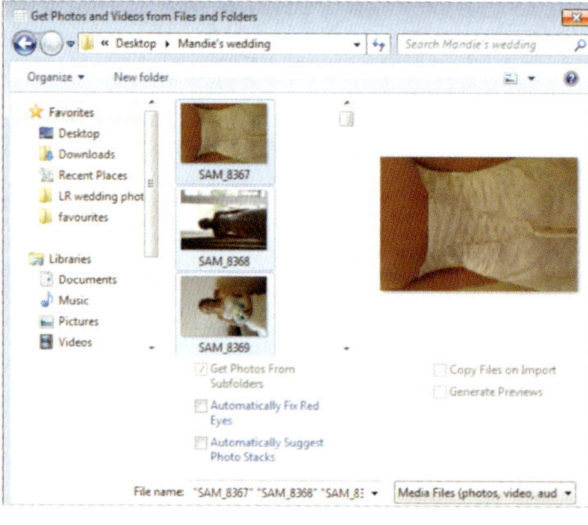

02 Import options

When you are importing pictures you can ask Elements to correct red eye as it goes, or to suggest photo stacks of similar images.

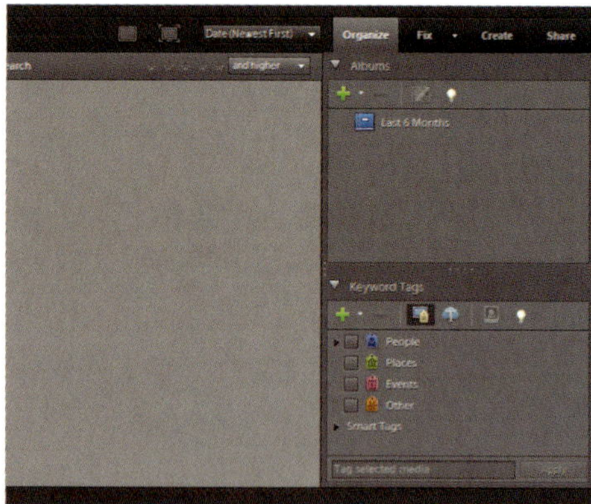

03 Sort the view

By default, you will see the last images imported, however if you want to change this, you can pick a different album to view.

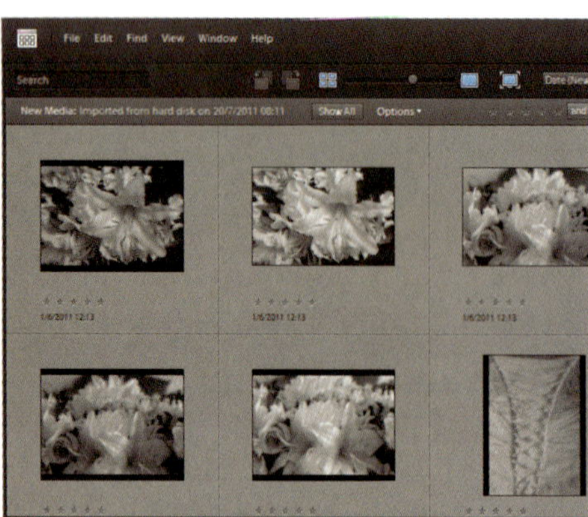

04 Show all

Hit the Show All button to see all of your images in one go. Using the stars underneath you can set individual ratings for your images too.

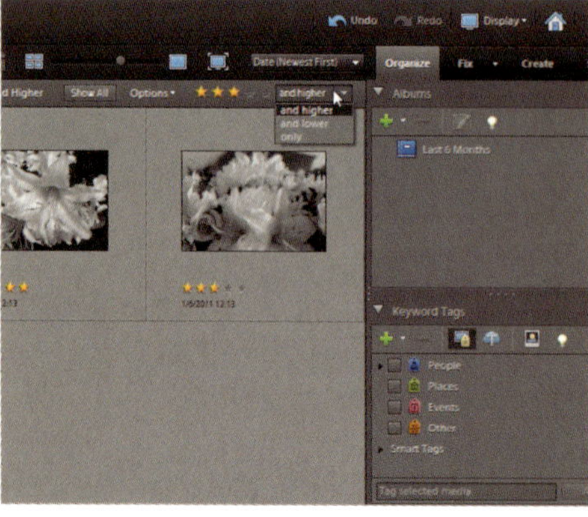

05 Filter by rating

When you have rated all your images, you can then use the rating filter to isolate just the images that you want to use.

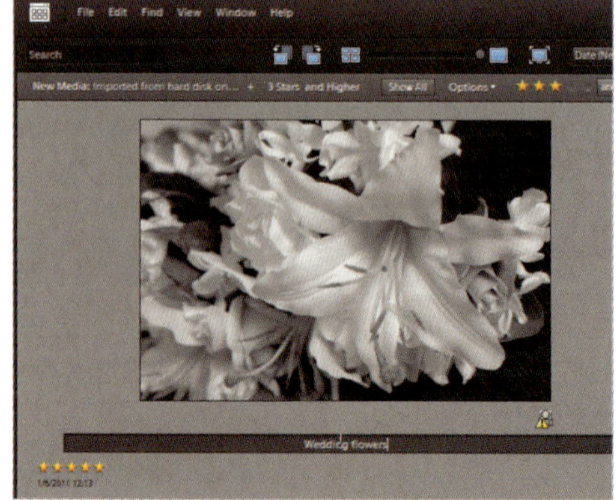

06 Large view

Click on any image in the Organizer and you can see it bigger in the central screen, where you can add a caption, for example.

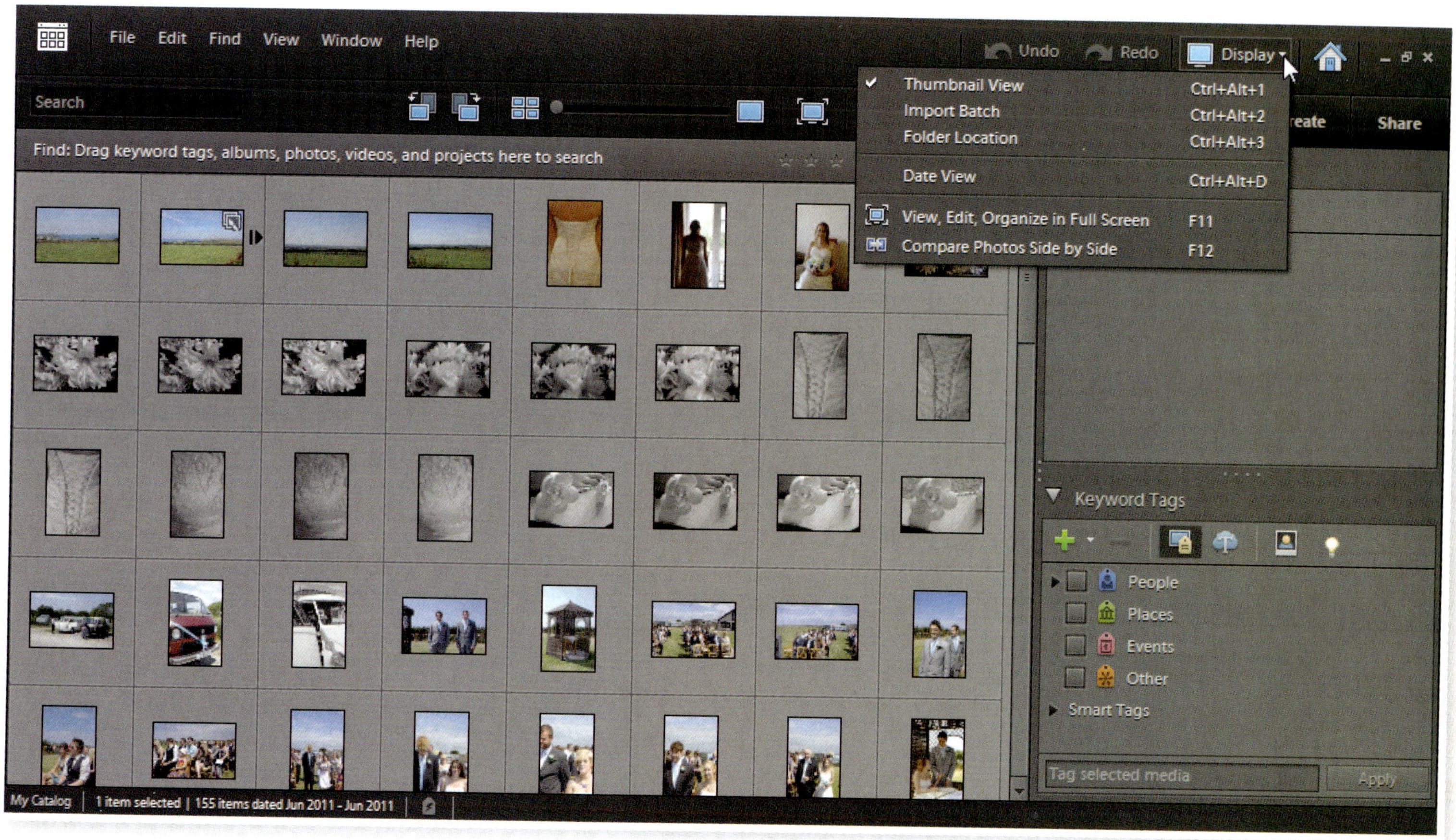

Quick save

The first time that you save a new file, use the Save As command as we have described, so that you can set the file name and format. Then, if you continue working on the image, you can just use File>Save instead, which saves your progress to the same file. It can be easier to get used to the keyboard shortcut, which is the Apple/Cmd key if you're using a Mac, or the Ctrl key if you're using a PC, plus the 'S' key at the same time.

Thumbnail views

There are a number of ways that you can choose to view your images which are selected here. You can have thumbnails of various sizes and you can filter by star rating to give a more accurate choice of photos.

Common file types

JPEG is the most common file format. It is used because it offers smaller file sizes but that can lead to loss of quality. When you choose to save in JPEG, you are given a slider to set the quality. PSD is a Photoshop document and is needed if you are saving a multi-layered document. TIFF results in larger but in good quality files. Use this when you need the optimum quality.

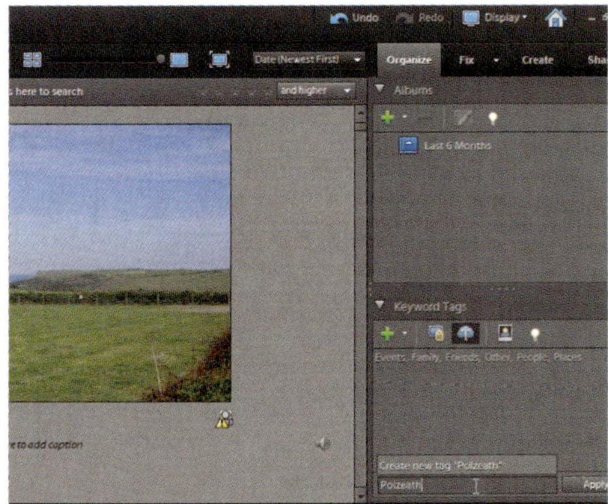

07 Tagging

Using the Keyword Tags panel, you can enter things like location, which you can use to sort your images at a later date.

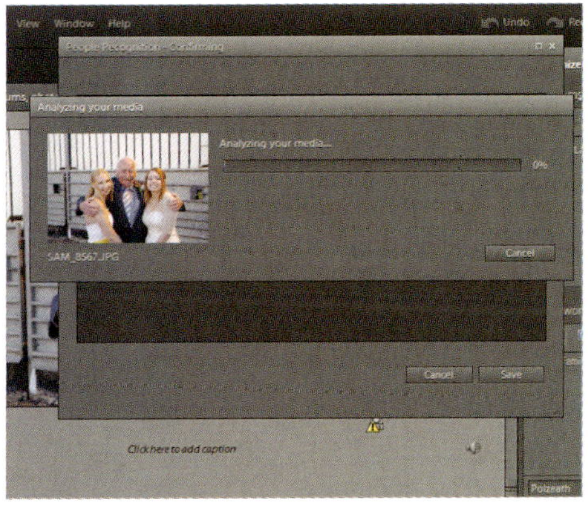

08 Get tagging

If there are people in your shot, you can ask Photoshop Elements to use People Recognition, which searches a photo for faces.

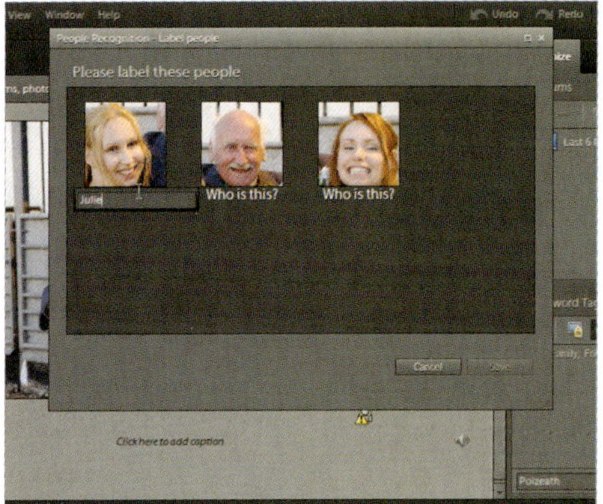

09 Name game

When all of the faces have been found, you can see them individually and then add names for these people underneath their pics.

Glossary of key terms

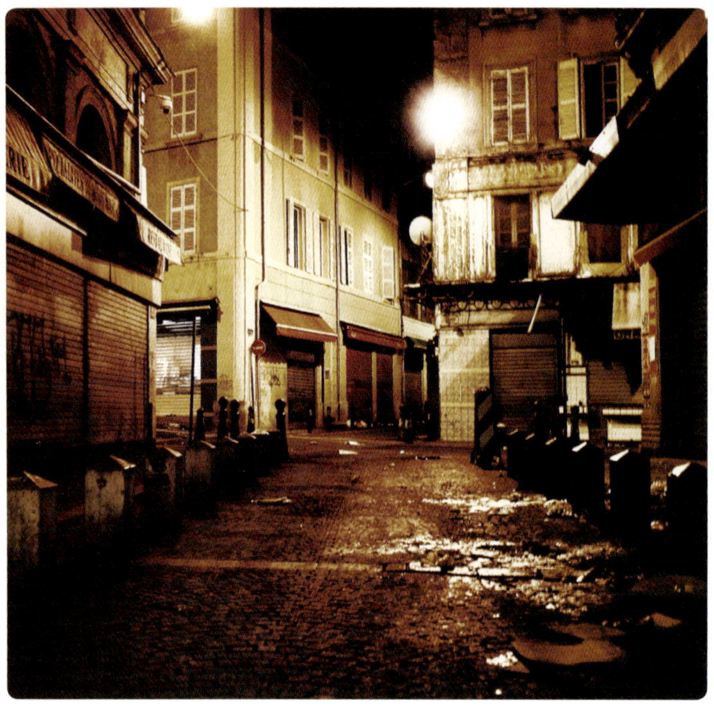

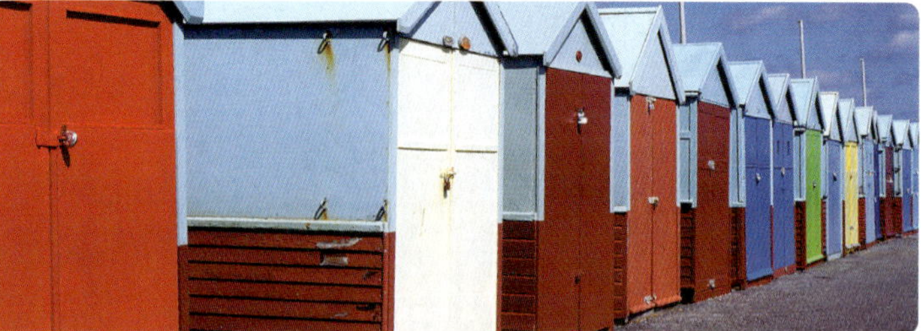

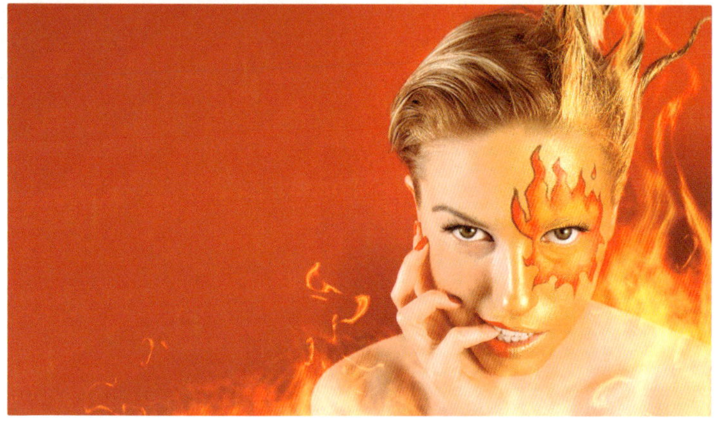

Adjustment layers

These are non-destructive layers that enable you to make changes to your image, such as correcting exposure, turning the image black and white and more, without affecting your original image. You can also go back to adjustment layers in the future and change the settings.

Artifact

We usually use this term when images are saved as JPEGs or shot in low light and have a lot of noise. Artifacts are unwanted elements that creep into photos when they undergo heavy compression or editing.

Background layer

This is the original layer that you open in Photoshop. By default this layer is locked to protect it from changes, but you can double-click on the layer to turn it into a regular, editable layer.

Blending mode

The blending mode options in the Layers palette determine how the pixels in the layer interact with the pixels in the layers below it, giving different effects (see page 100 for more information).

Brush Preset

Photoshop comes with lots of Presets for its different tools and with brushes this means that different combinations of size and thickness, etc, have been stored for you to use. You can also create your own if you find a brush setup that works for you.

Camera Raw

This is Photoshop's built-in RAW-processing plug-in, which enables you to open photographs that have been shot in the RAW format, rather than JPEG, and you can edit these before taking the image into Photoshop.

Clipboard

This is where file elements are stored if you cut or copy from one image to another. If the Clipboard gets too full, then you might find that it starts to slow down Photoshop processing.

Clone

This is the processing of taking a clean area from a photograph and applying it over a flawed area of the image. This is done with the Clone Stamp tool. Click on the clean area while pressing Opt/Alt to 'source' the sample, then paint over the flaw and the source will be applied here.

CMYK

This stands for Cyan, Magenta, Yellow and Black, which is a common Image Mode for printing. Photoshop Elements does not support CMYK images. Most printers will convert RGB images into CMYK for printing, but if you have Photoshop you may want to work in CMYK so you can see how the final image will look more accurately. Some filters and adjustments only work in RGB, in which case you will need to flatten or merge your layers before converting to CMYK, as this may have adverse effects on your image's colours.

Colour cast

This is when an unwanted colour is 'cast' over your photograph. The Color Balance command can fix this in a flash though.

Contrast

This is the difference between the light and dark areas in an image, and can be altered using Levels and Curves, as well as the Brightness/Contrast command.

Crop

This is the act of trimming an image, discarding unwanted pixels from the final composition.

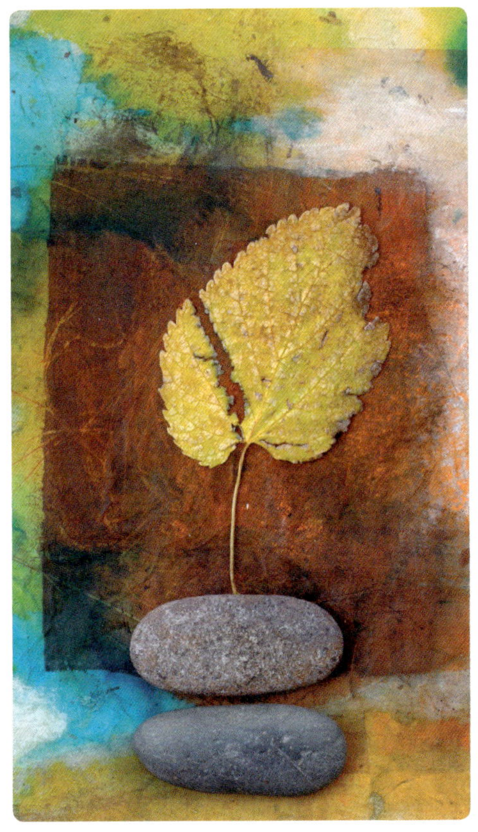

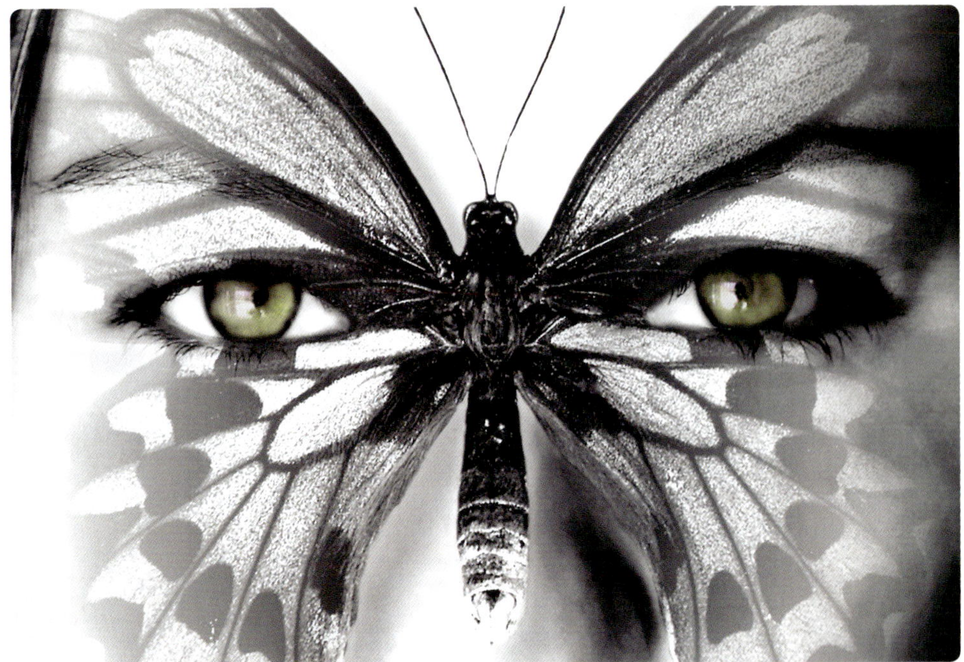

"Exposure is the amount of light in which a photograph is taken"

DPI

This stands for Dots Per Inch and it is a measure of printer resolution. Use higher DPI settings for better prints. We recommend working at 300dpi where possible if your image is intended for print.

Duotone

This is a greyscale image that uses two colour inks of your choosing to tint the photos. This is not available in Photoshop Elements.

Exposure

This is the amount of light in which a photograph is taken. You can fix underexposure (too dark) or overexposure (too light) in Photoshop to some extent.

Feathering

When you make selections, the Feather command softens the edge of the selection so that it blends more naturally into the background.

Filters

These are preset controls that give special effects to your photos. There are loads built into Photoshop and Photoshop Elements (see page 206 for more), and you can also purchase or download more filters.

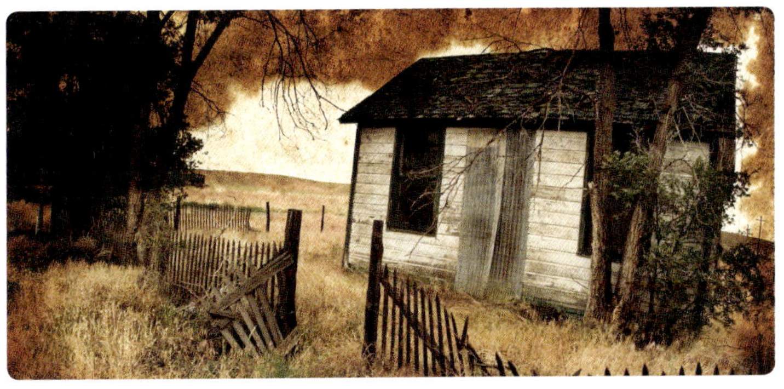

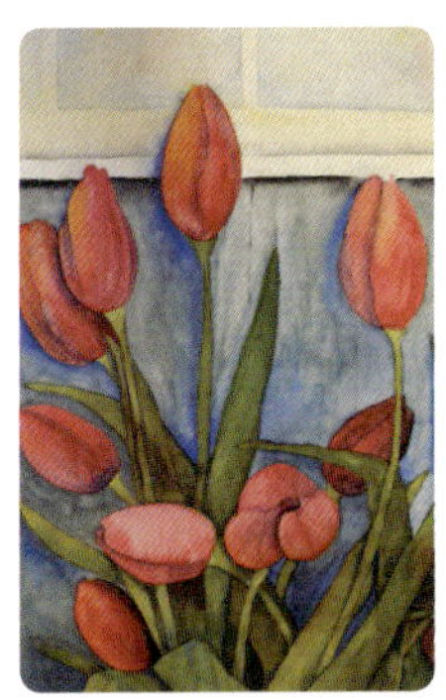

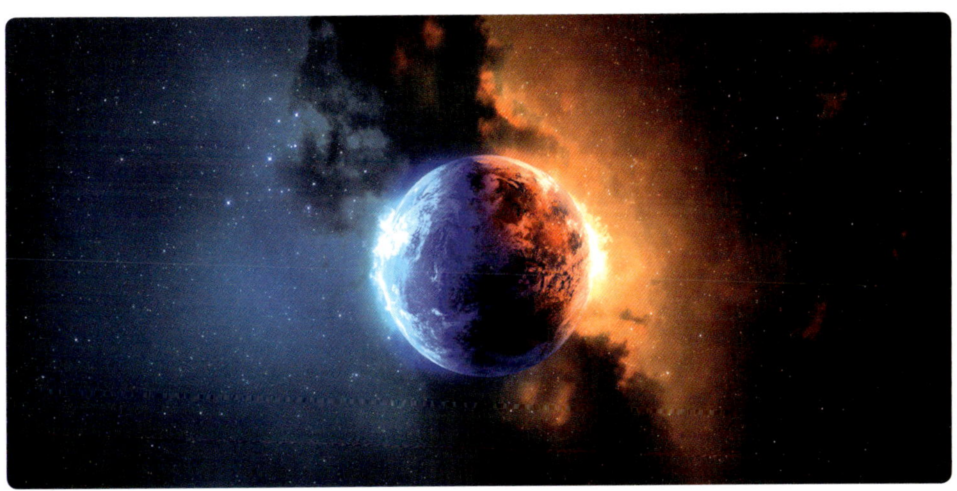

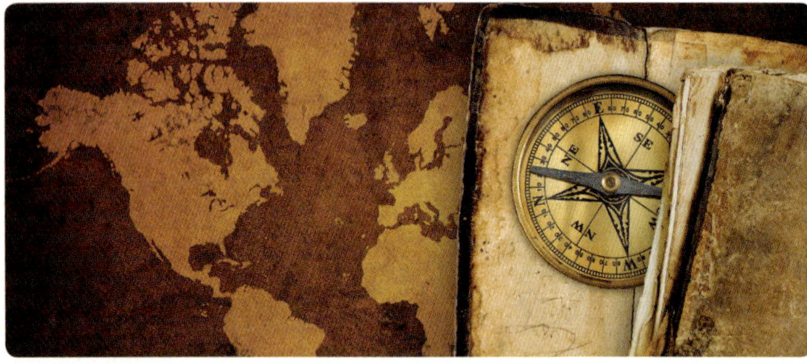

"You can use the History palette to backtrack if something goes wrong"

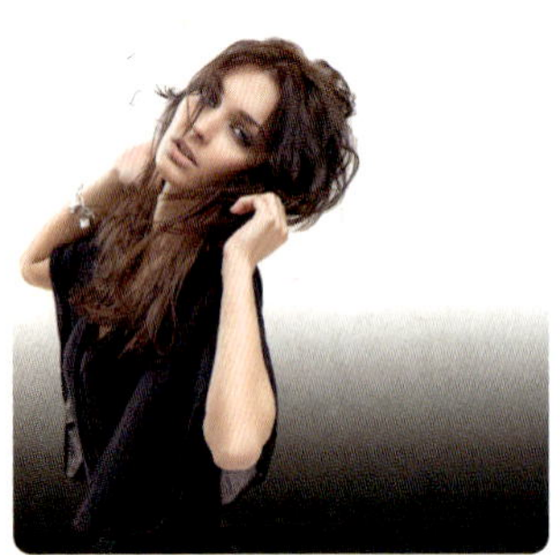

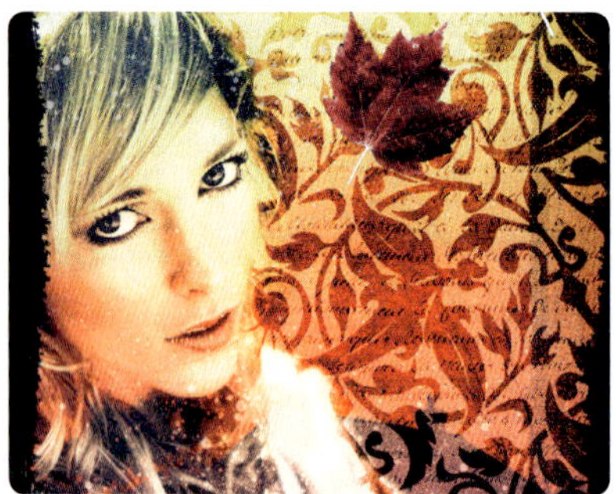

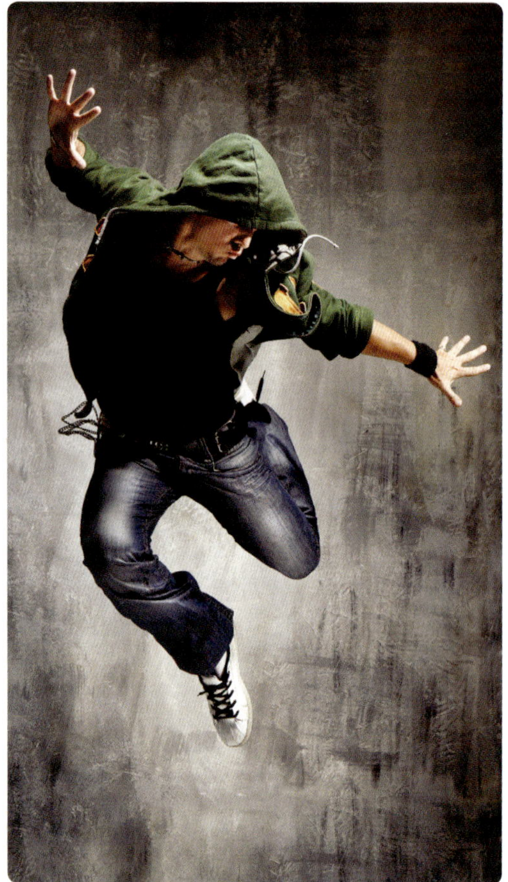

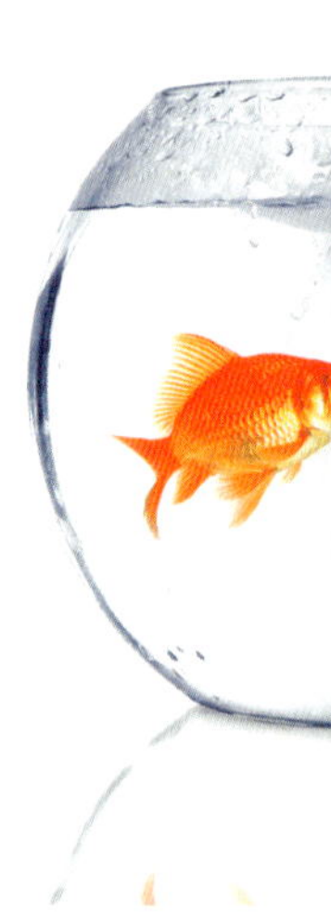

Flatten

You can flatten all your layers into one layer to keep file sizes down. However, bear in mind that you will lose all your layers so you won't be able to go back and change things in your image.

Gaussian Blur

One of the Blur filter options in Photoshop. This is one of the most common blurs used and it softens through a 'bell-shaped' distribution of colour and tone.

Gradient

A transition effect from one colour to another. You can set your own colours for custom effects.

Grayscale

This removes all colour from an image, using just black, white and grey on one channel. If you want to turn your image black and white, however, there are more accurate methods.

Highlights

This is the brightest elements in an image.

Histogram

Many cameras have a built-in histogram, as does the Levels palette. This is a graph that shows how the pixels are distributed in an image. The horizontal axis shows the 'levels' from the darkest to the brightest pixels (0-255), whereas the vertical axis shows how many pixels there are at each level. You are looking for an even distribution of tones.

History

Your commands are saved as History States, so that you can use the History palette to backtrack if something goes wrong.

Image Mode

This is the name given to image modes, such as RGB, CMYK, etc. This can be changed by going to Image>Mode.

JPEG

This is the most common file format used by digital cameras and it does compress image information to keep file sizes down.

Layer

This is how you can overlay different images or image elements over one another. We go into layers in much more detail from page 82.

Layer group

To help you stay organised when you are working on lots of layers, you can collect layers into groups so that all the layers that relate to the same thing are together.

Layer masks

Layer masks let you control how much of one layer shows through to the one below it. You paint directly on the mask in white or black to reveal or hide.

Levels

This is a control that helps you control the colour and tone in your images.

Midtone

This is the term for the area of tones that fall between the brightest and darkest pixels.

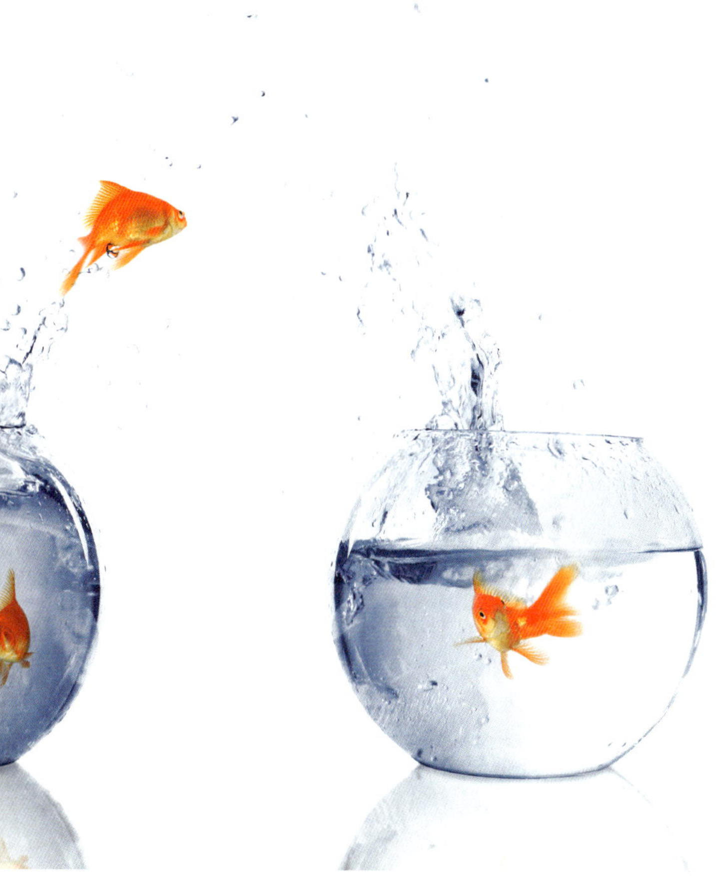

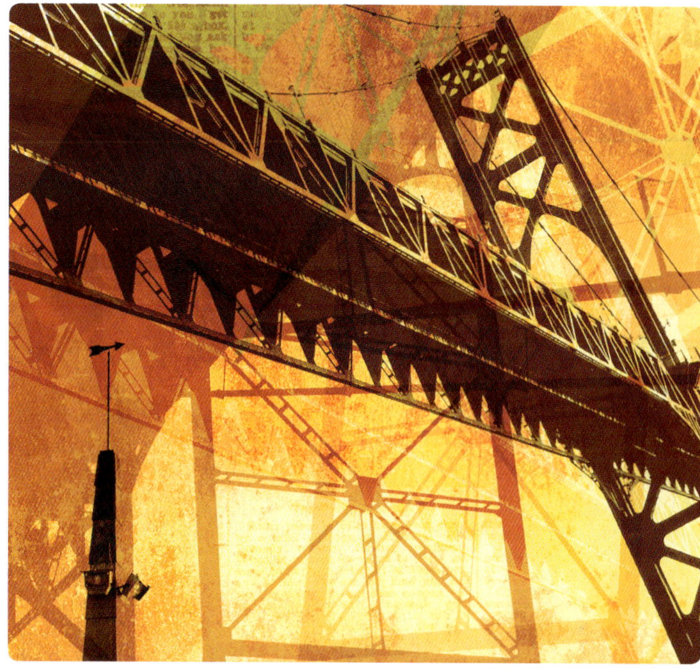

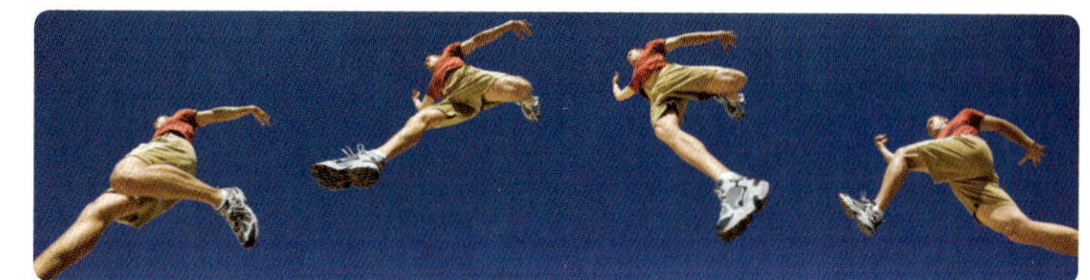

Noise

This is an artifact that shows up as grain on your photos. This is common when images have been compressed, or shot in low light. There is an option to remove noise in photos.

Opacity

This is the control used in the Layers palette or in the Brush controls, which determines how 'visible' or 'transparent' an effect is. In Levels, it controls how much of the underlying layer cam be seen on the one(s) above it. With brushes, this determines the strength of the paint being used.

Pixel

These are the tiny, rectangular points of colour that a digital image is composed of.

PPI

Pixels Per Inch is a measure of image resolution used by cameras and computers.

PSD

This is Photoshop's own file format and it can be used to save multiple layers.

Quick Mask

Available in Photoshop only, this is a quick way of masking areas in an image to form a selection.

Red eye

This is a common flaw in digital portrait photographs, caused by the use of camera flash.

Resolution

This is a measure of clarity and sharpness in an image. The higher the resolution, the better-quality the image, but also the bigger you can print it.

RGB

This is the Red, Green, Blue image makeup that is used by computer screens.

Saturation

This is the strength of a given colour and it can be altered in the Hue/ Saturation options.

Selection

This is the name given when you isolate a certain part of any image.

Shadows

These are the darkest elements in an image.

Sharpening

This is the process of enhancing details in an image. Be careful when sharpening though, as too much can lead to unwanted artefacts.

Swatches

This is a selection of preset colours that you can pick from in Photoshop. You can create or download more of these.

TIFF

This is a file format that is often used for printing. It is compressed in such a manner that it does not affect the image quality, however it can lead to bigger file sizes.

Transform

This is the set of controls that enables you to distort, skew, scale, etc, an image.

Unsharp Mask

This is a popular filter used for sharpening, as it increases detail.

Photoshop shortcuts

Dramatically speed up your workflow with these handy shortcuts

Once you've got to grips with the basic Photoshop tools and features, it's a great idea to start practising some of the shortcuts. Whether you are editing, retouching, creating and more, you can save loads of time by learning shortcuts. Over these two pages we've compiled an essential shortcut guide, which we've split into sections based on the type of tasks you perform. Make sure you have this cut-out-and-keep guide close to your computer and use it whenever you have a Photoshop project on the go. We're certain you will know these shortcuts off by heart in no time! We have given both Mac and PC commands, so Cmd/Ctrl means the Apple or Command key on a Mac, and Control on a PC.

Handy shortcuts for everyday tools

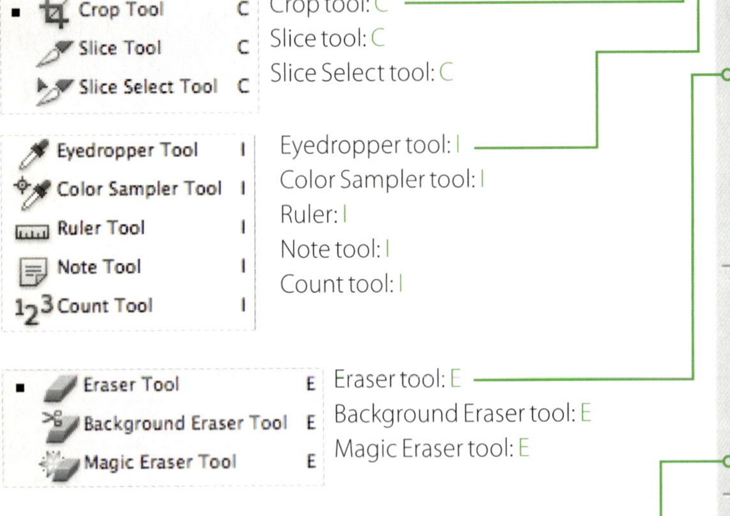

Crop tool: C
Slice tool: C
Slice Select tool: C

Eyedropper tool: I
Color Sampler tool: I
Ruler: I
Note tool: I
Count tool: I

Eraser tool: E
Background Eraser tool: E
Magic Eraser tool: E

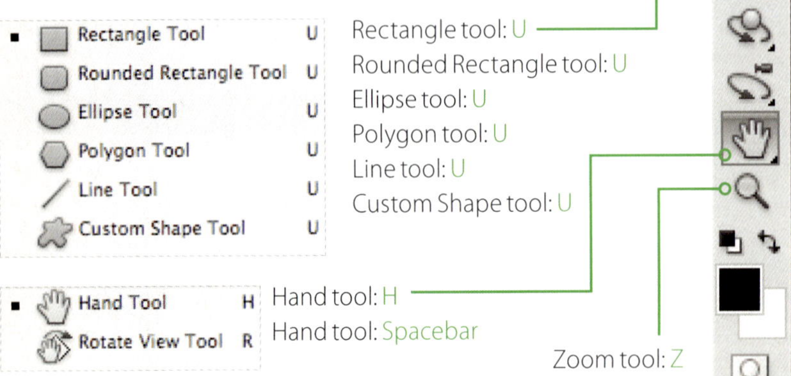

Rectangle tool: U
Rounded Rectangle tool: U
Ellipse tool: U
Polygon tool: U
Line tool: U
Custom Shape tool: U

Hand tool: H
Hand tool: Spacebar

Zoom tool: Z

Select and Selection tools

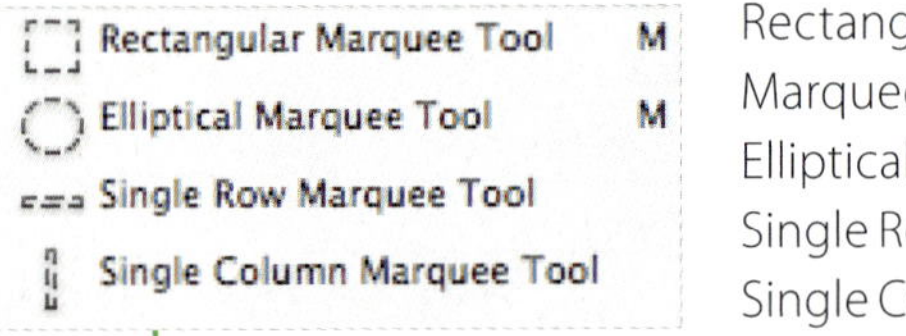

Rectangular Marquee tool: M
Elliptical Marquee tool: M
Single Row Marquee tool: M
Single Column Marquee tool: M

Lasso Tool L
Polygonal Lasso Tool L
Magnetic Lasso Tool L

Lasso tool: L
Polygonal Lasso tool: L
Magnetic Lasso tool: L

Quick Selection Tool W
Magic Wand Tool W

Magic Wand tool: W
Quick Selection Tool: W

Toggle Standard/Quick Mask modes: Q
Cycle Path/Direct Selection tools: Shift+A
Toggle Slice/Slice Select tools: Shift+K
Cycle Lasso tools: Shift+L
Toggle Rectangular/Elliptical Marquee: Shift+M
Toggle Pen/Freeform Pen tools: Shift+P
Select All: Cmd/Ctrl+A
Select All Layers: Cmd+Opt+A/Ctrl+Alt+A
Deselect: Cmd/Ctrl+D
Feather: Cmd+Opt+D/Ctrl+Alt+D
Inverse: Cmd/Ctrl+Shift+I
Reselect: Cmd/Ctrl+Shift+D

Painting tools

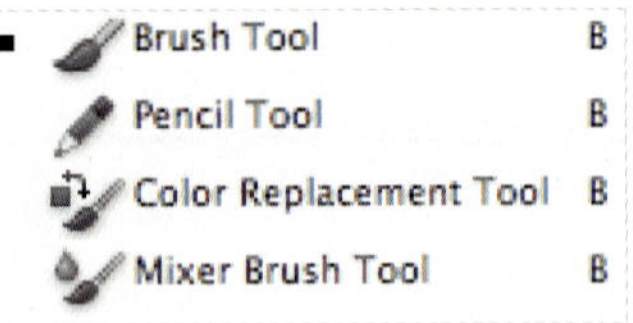

Brush tool: B
Pencil tool: B
Color Replacement tool: B
Mixer Brush tool: B

Decrease/Increase Brush Size: [/]
Decrease/Increase Brush Hardness: {/}
Previous Brush: ,
Next Brush: .
First Brush: <
Last Brush: >
Brush tool: B
Pencil tool: B
Gradient tool: G
Paint Bucket tool: G
Sponge tool: O

History Brush Tool Y
Art History Brush Tool Y

History Brush tool: Y
Art History Brush Tool: B
Tool Opacity 10%-100%: 1-0
Flow/Airbrush Opacity 10%-100%: Shift+ 1-0

Image-editing tools

Spot Healing Brush tool: J
Healing Brush tool: J
Patch tool: J
Red Eye tool: J

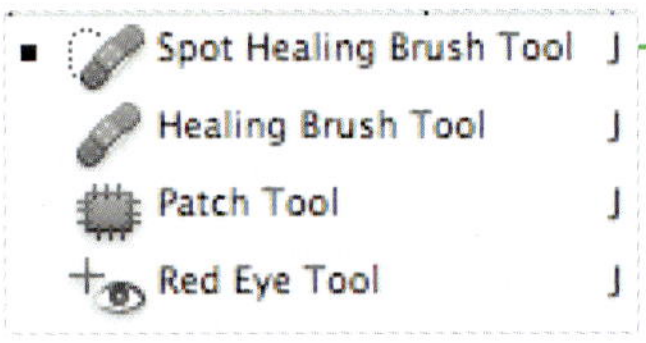

Clone Stamp tool: S
Pattern Stamp tool: S

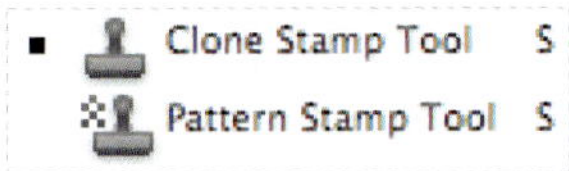

Dodge tool: O
Burn tool: O

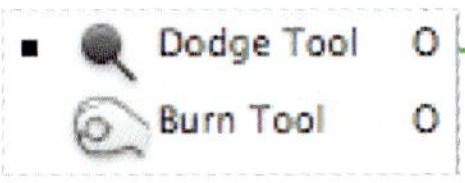

Toggle Clone/Pattern Stamp: Shift+S
Auto Color: Cmd/Ctrl+Shift+B
Auto Contrast: Cmd+Opt+Shift+L/Ctrl+Alt+Shift+L
Auto Levels: Cmd/Ctrl+Shift+L
Canvas Size: Cmd+Opt+C/Ctrl+Alt+C
Color Balance: Cmd/Ctrl+B
Color Balance (last settings): Cmd+Opt+M/Ctrl+Alt+M
Curves (last settings): Cmd+Opt+M/Ctrl+Alt+M
Curves: Cmd/Ctrl+M
Desaturate: Cmd/Ctrl+Shift+U
Hue/Saturation: Cmd/Ctrl+U
Hue/Saturation (last settings): Cmd+Opt+U/Ctrl+Alt+U
Image size: Cmd+Opt+I/Ctrl+Alt+I
Invert: Cmd/Ctrl+I
Levels: Cmd/Ctrl+L
Levels (last settings): Cmd+Opt+L/Ctrl+Alt+L

Foreground/Background colours
Default colours: D
Switch colours: X
Edit in Quick Mask Mode: Q

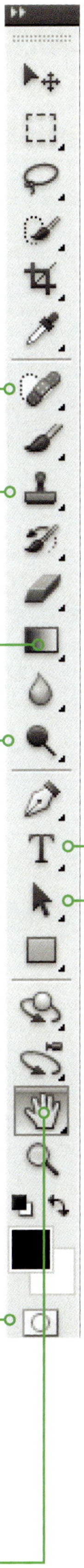

More tools to play with in CS5

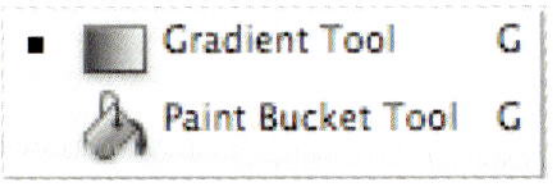

Gradient tool: G
Paint Bucket tool: G

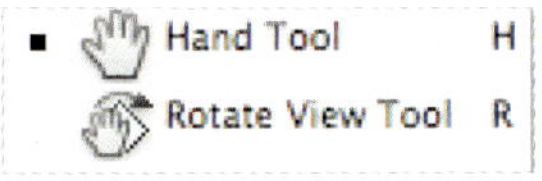

Hand tool: H
Rotate View tool: R

Type tools

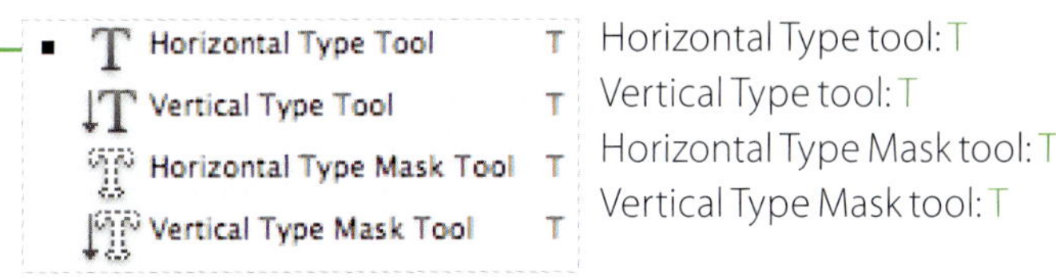

Horizontal Type tool: T
Vertical Type tool: T
Horizontal Type Mask tool: T
Vertical Type Mask tool: T

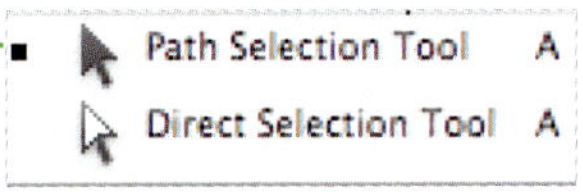

Path Selection tool: A
Direct Selection tool: A

Align Left: Cmd/Ctrl+Shift+L
Align Right: Cmd/Ctrl+Shift+R
Bold (toggle): Cmd/Ctrl+Shift+B
Centre text: Cmd/Ctrl+Shift+C
Decrease/Increase Type Size by 10pt: Cmd+Opt+ Shift+<, /Ctrl+Alt+Shift+<, >
Hyphenation (toggle): Cmd+Opt+Shift+H/Ctrl+Alt+Shift+H
Italics (toggle): Cmd/Ctrl+Shift+I
Justify Paragraph (Force last line): Cmd/Ctrl+Shift+F
Justify Paragraph (Left align last line): Cmd/Ctrl+Shift+J
Underlining (toggle): Cmd/Ctrl+Shift+U
Uppercase (toggle): Cmd/Ctrl+Shift+K

Layers

Bring Forward: Cmd/Ctrl+]
Bring to Front: Cmd/Ctrl+Shift+]
Create/Release Clipping Mask (toggle): Cmd+Opt+G/Ctrl+Alt+G
Group Layers: Cmd/Ctrl+G
Layer Opacity 10%-100%: 1-0
Layer Via Copy: Cmd+ Opt+J/Ctrl+Alt+J
Layer Via Copy (with dialog): Cmd/Ctrl+Shift+I
Merge Layers: Cmd/Ctrl+E Merge Visible: Cmd/Ctrl+Shift+E
New Layer: Cmd/Ctrl+Shift+N
New Layer (no dialog): Cmd+Opt+Shift+N/Ctrl+Alt+Shift+N
Next Layer: Opt/Alt+]
Previous Layer: Opt/Alt+[
Select Previous Layer: Opt/Alt+Shift+[
Select Next Layer: Opt/Alt+Shift+]
Send Backward: Cmd/Ctrl+[
Send to Back: Cmd/Ctrl+Shift+[
Stamp Down: Cmd+Opt+E/Ctrl+Alt+E
Stamp Visible: Cmd+Opt+Shift+E/Ctrl+Alt+Shift+E
Select Bottom Layer: Opt/Alt+, Select Top Layer: Opt/Alt+.

Basic corrections

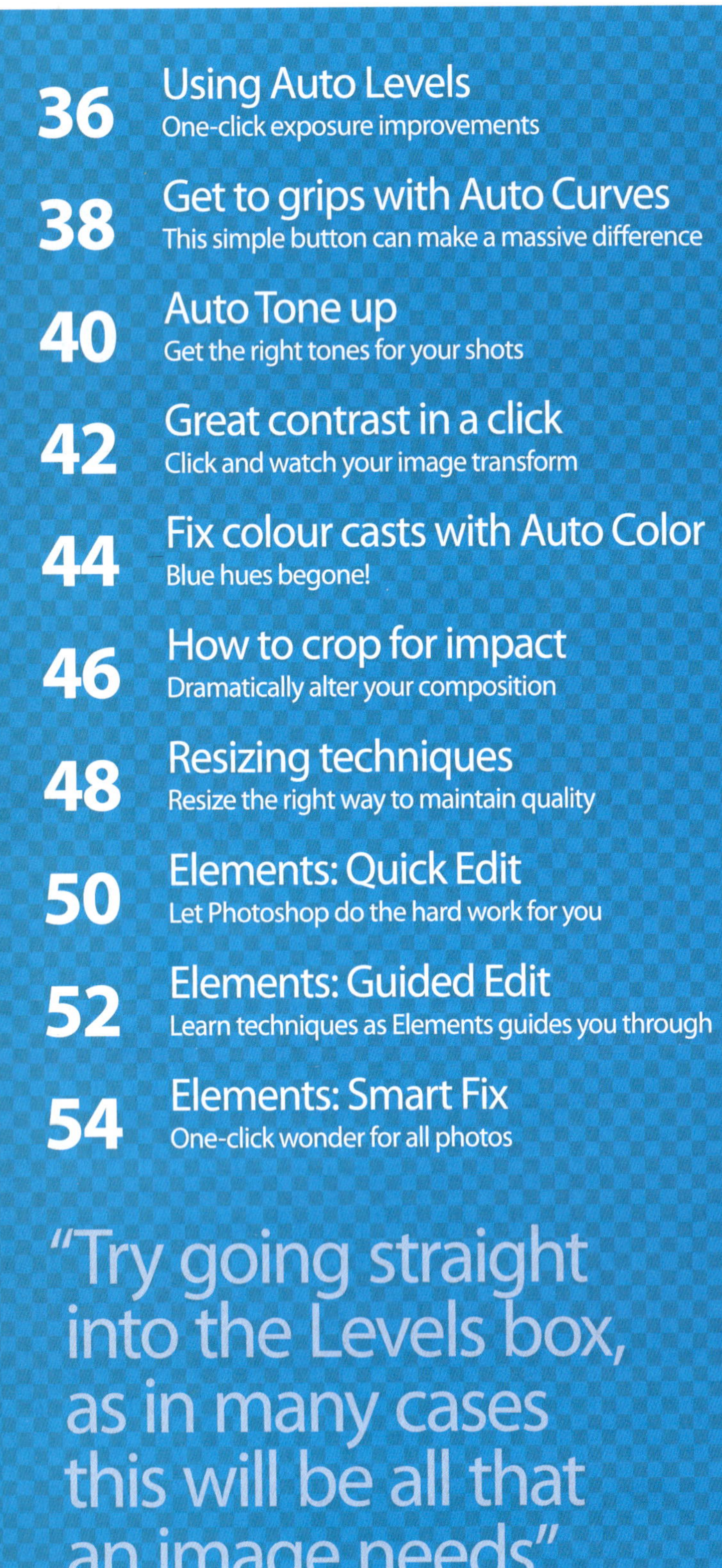

"Try going straight into the Levels box, as in many cases this will be all that an image needs"

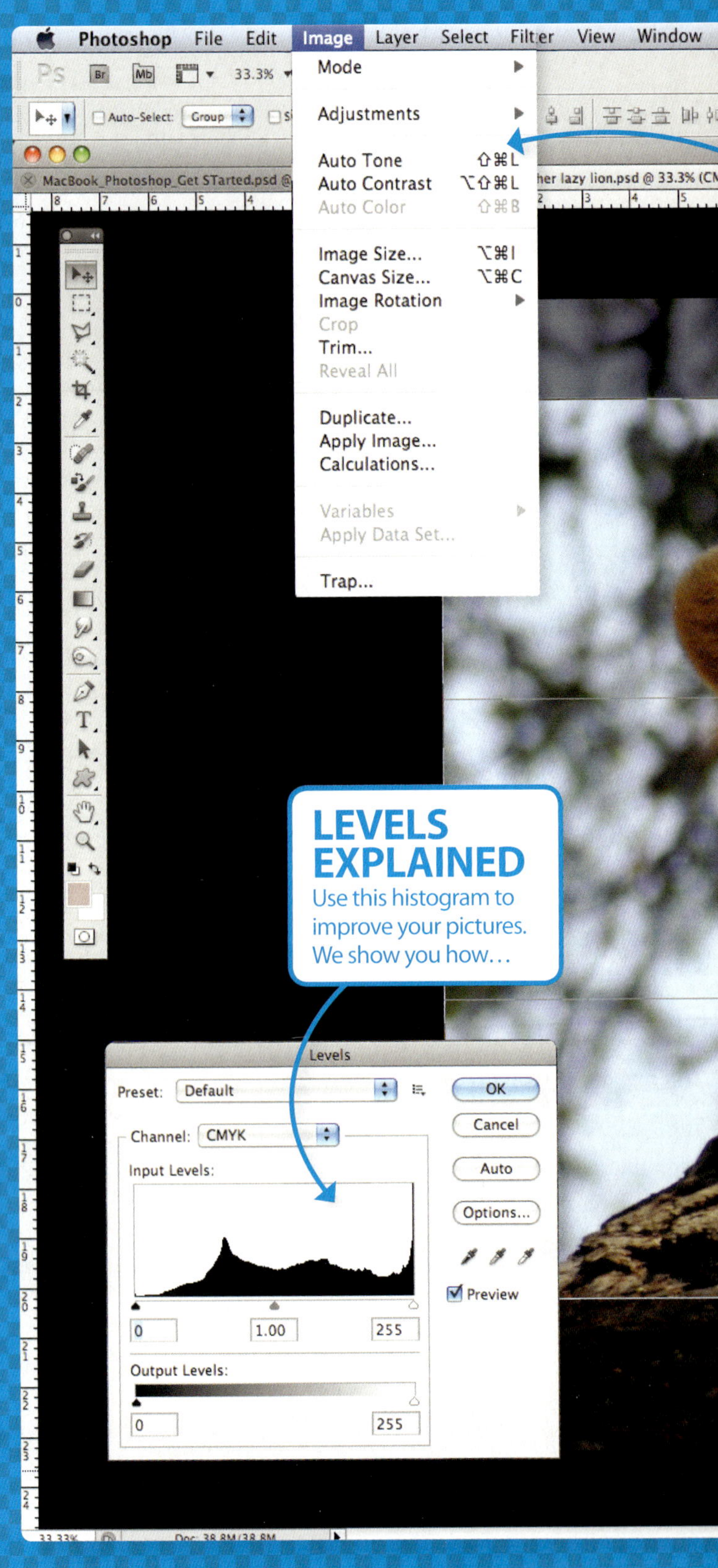

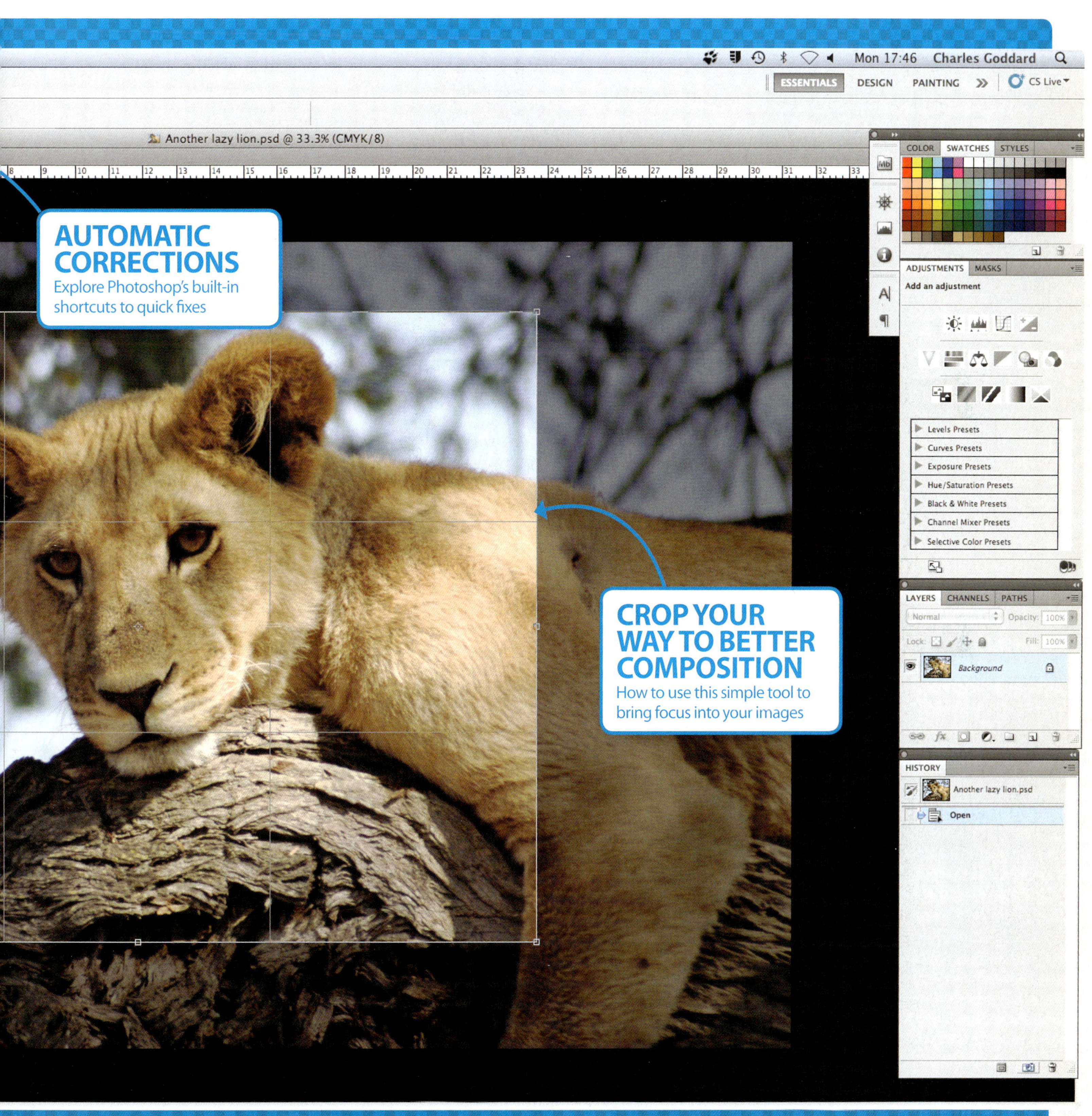
Mon 17:46 Charles Goddard
ESSENTIALS
DESIGN
PAINTING
CS Live
Another lazy lion.psd @ 33.3% (CMYK/8)
COLOR
SWATCHES
STYLES
ADJUSTMENTS
MASKS
Add an adjustment
Levels Presets
Curves Presets
Exposure Presets
Hue/Saturation Presets
Black & White Presets
Channel Mixer Presets
Selective Color Presets
LAYERS
CHANNELS
PATHS
Normal
Opacity: 100%
Lock:
Fill: 100%
Background
HISTORY
Another lazy lion.psd
Open
AUTOMATIC CORRECTIONS
Explore Photoshop's built-in shortcuts to quick fixes
CROP YOUR WAY TO BETTER COMPOSITION
How to use this simple tool to bring focus into your images

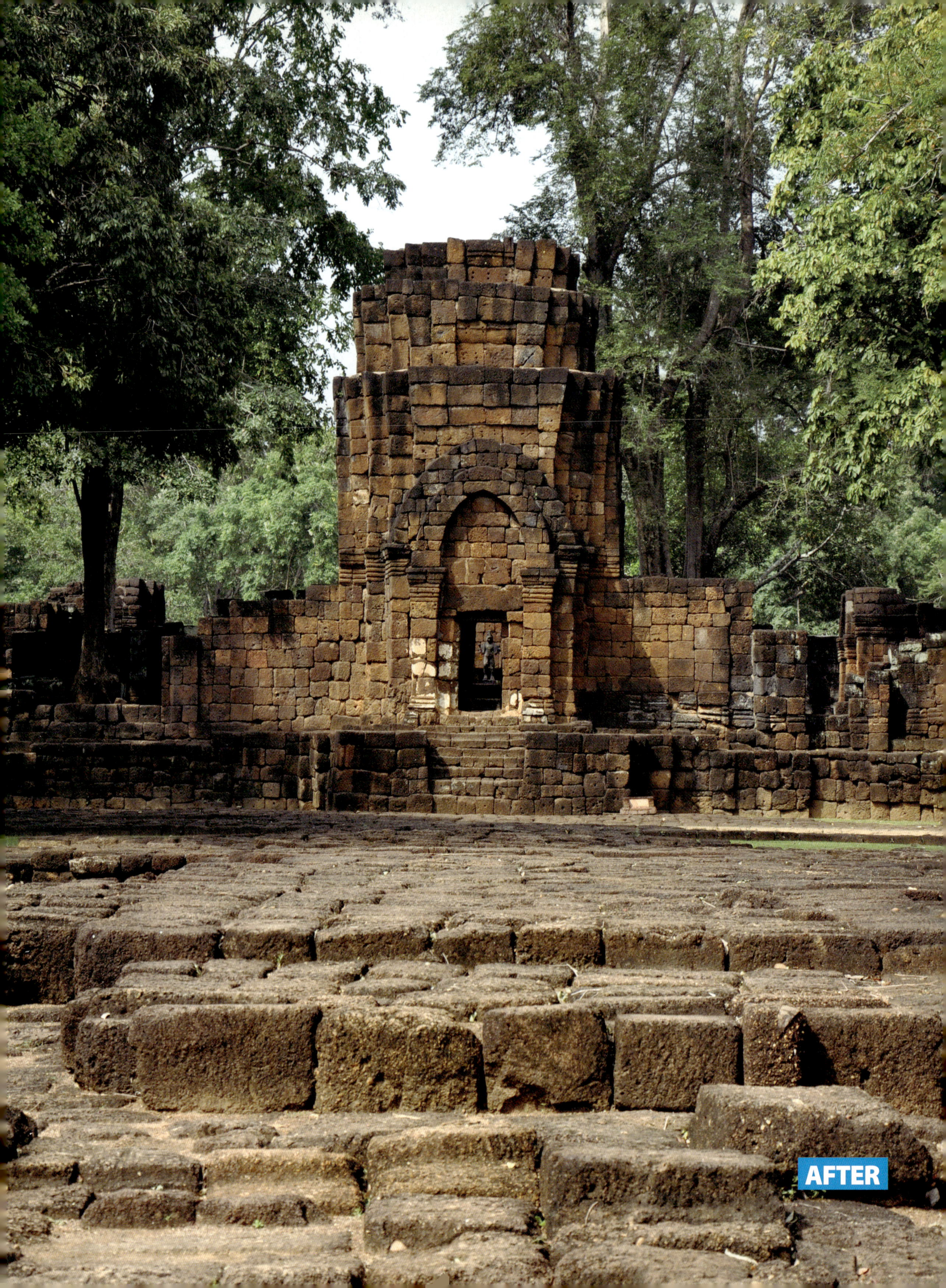
AFTER

Using Auto Levels

Make sure that you have perfect exposure across your photographs

The Levels dialog is probably the first one that you need to learn when it comes to correcting basic flaws in your images. Luckily, it is not as complex as it looks and it will fix and control the overall tonal and colour ranges in your images. There are various ways of applying Levels, from using the dialog box that comes up when you go to Image>Adjustments>Levels, or as an adjustment layer. For now, though, we are just looking at what happens when you use the Auto option.

As soon as you open an image in Photoshop, it is worth going straight into the Levels box and using the Auto option, as in many cases this will be all that an image needs, and it will certainly act as a good starting point for any further adjustments that you need to make. The Levels dialog analyses your image and creates a histogram with values for shadows and highlights in your photo. The Auto command levels out these values, so that the contrast is well balanced between both extremes of the tonal range.

"It will fix and control the overall tonal and colour ranges in your images"

SIMPLE LEVEL CONTROL

Auto button

When you hit the Auto button Photoshop will analyse your photo and apply the corrections it deems necessary to get a good tonal range across your shot.

Preview

When Preview is ticked, you will see the change on your main image. Uncheck it to see the original image for comparison, then click OK to commit.

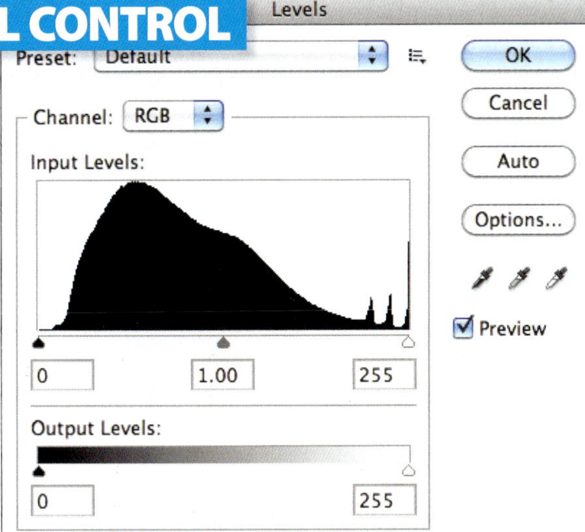

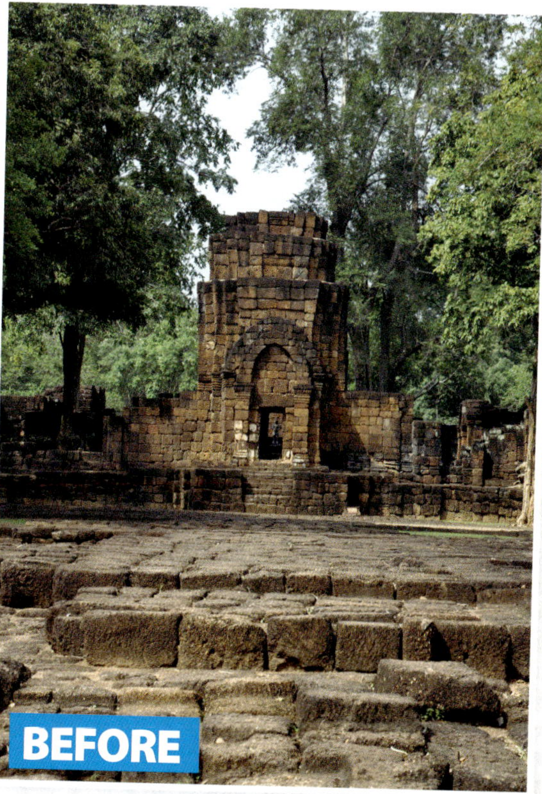

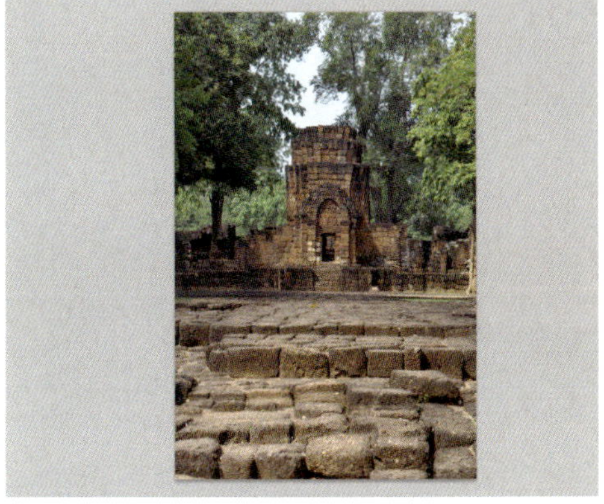

01 Start image

Our start image is a good composition with some nice colours, by the tonal range is a little on the dull side.

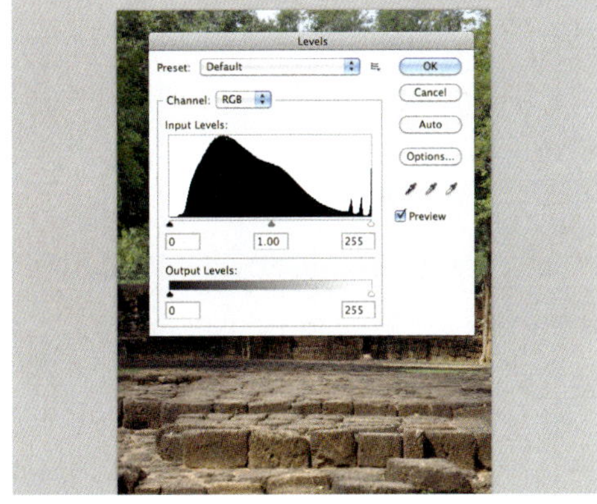

02 Opening the Levels dialog

Go to Image>Adjustments>Levels and you will bring up this Levels dialog, with a histogram in the middle showing your tonal range.

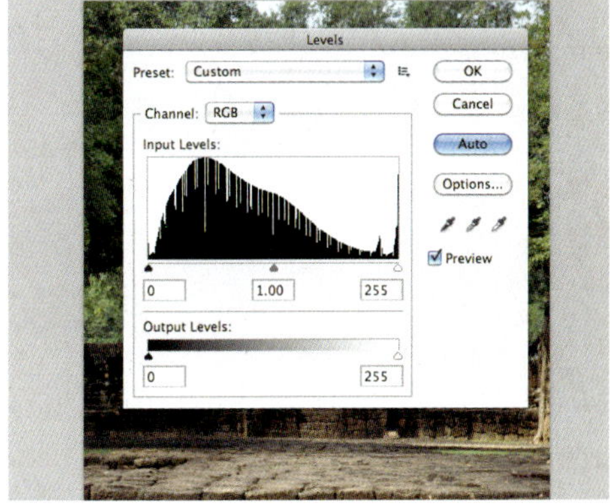

03 Auto it up

We will be looking in more detail about the other options in this box in the Colour & tone section (page 56), but for now, just hit Auto for a quick fix.

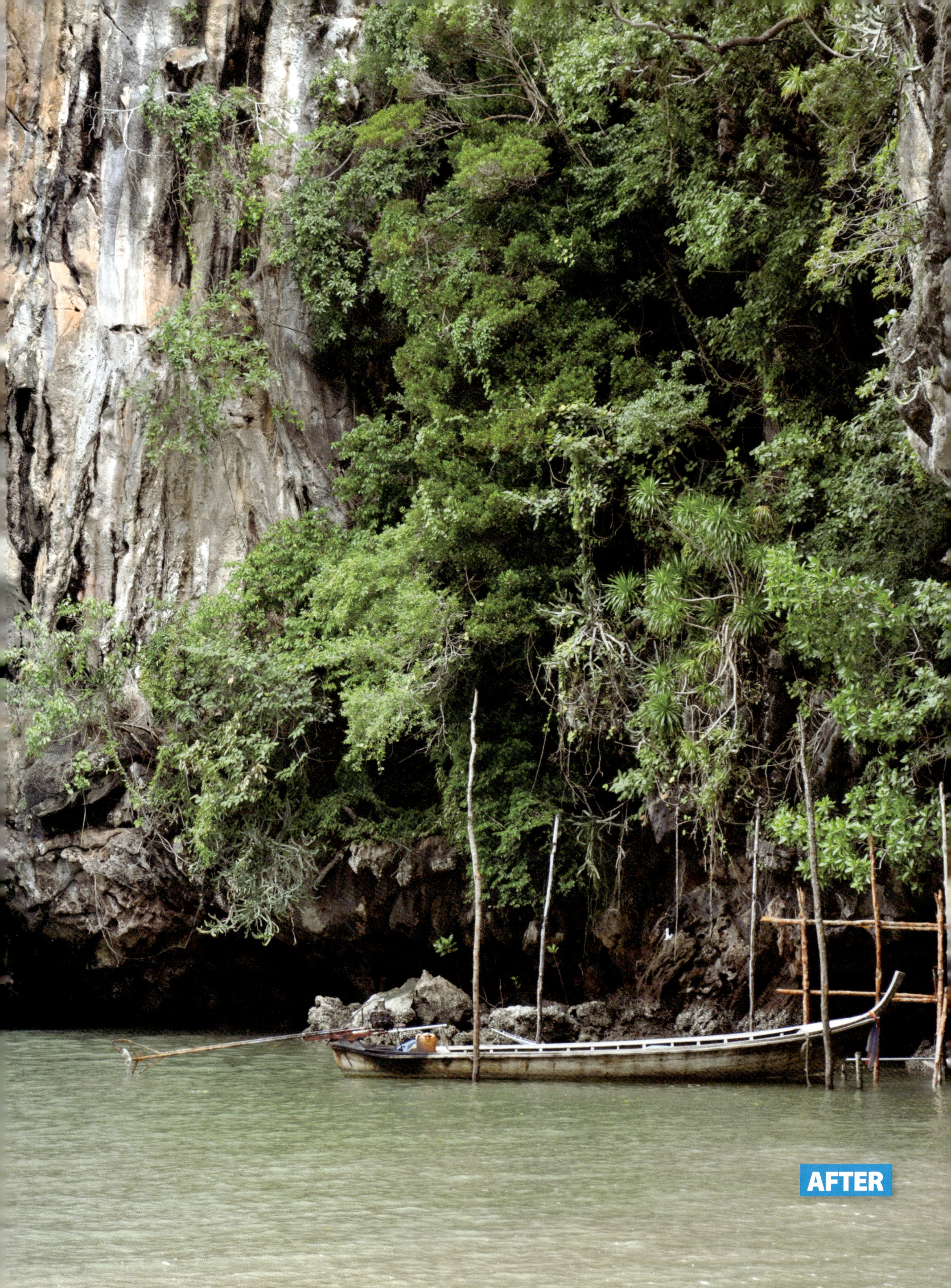
AFTER

Get to grips with Auto Curves

A simple one-click control that hides a very powerful editing tool

Curves and Levels are often talked about in the same sentence as they both affect the tonal range of your photos. However, though they do the same sort of thing, they do so in different ways.

With Levels, you can control the tonal range of the Highlights, Midpoints and Shadows, which is good for making global changes to your image as a whole. However, with Curves, you can pick literally any value in your whole image and tweak the tonal range at that point. This makes it an incredibly precise tool for getting perfect exposure and contrast. It can be a bit more intimidating though, as Curves is not something we see that often, whereas the histogram, that is present in the Levels dialog is similar to the histogram that is often used by digital cameras to help you ensure even exposure when shooting.

Still, even a push of the Auto button in the Curves dialog can make a big difference to your image and you can worry about understanding the ins and outs of it at a later date.

"Pick any value in your image and tweak the tonal range at that point"

GET SOME CURVES

Presets

There are various presets that can be used to tweak your image, but when working fast make sure that this is on the Default setting.

Why Curves?

Curves are very precise, which means that they also take more getting used to than Levels. You can grab any point on the line to affect the tonal range in that specific area.

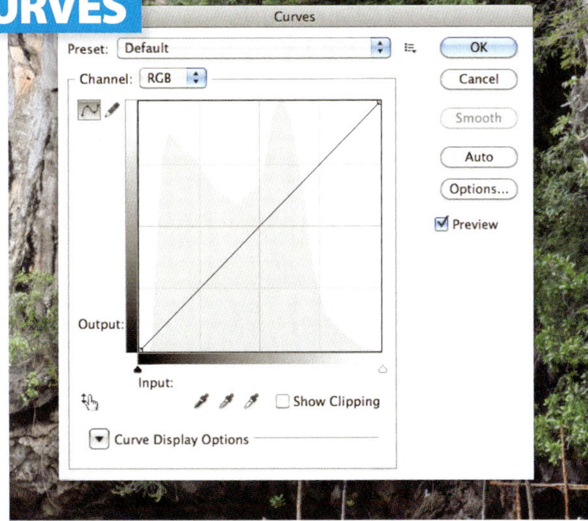

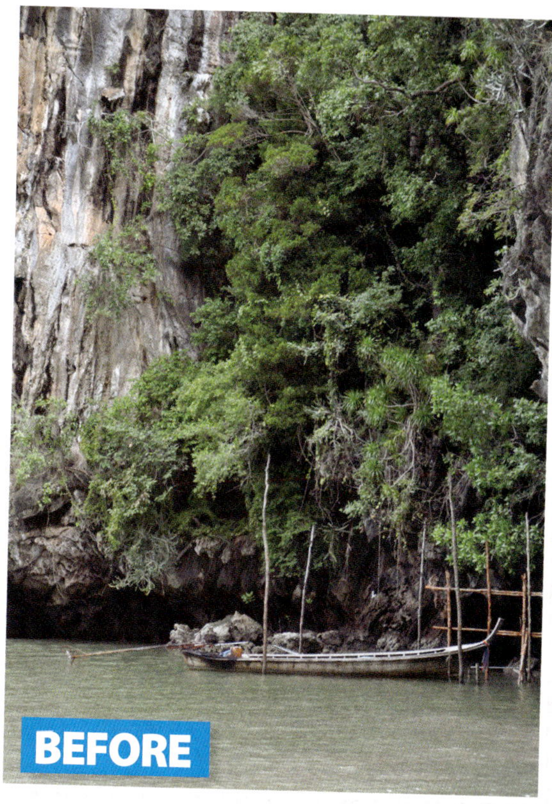

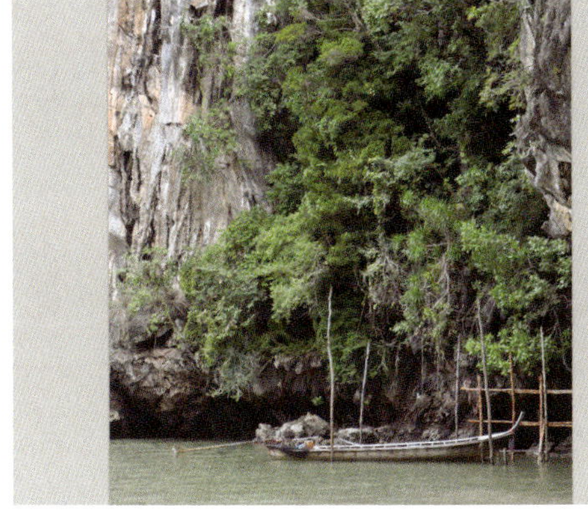

01 Open your image

Our image that we are going to work on is a little on the washed-out side. The greens aren't very vibrant and everything is blending together.

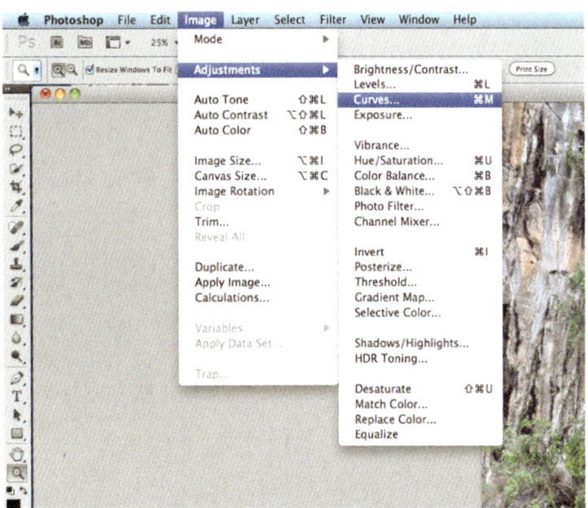

02 Access the Curves

Go to Image>Adjustments>Curves and you will bring up the Curves window. This can also be opening by using the shortcut Cmd/Ctrl+M.

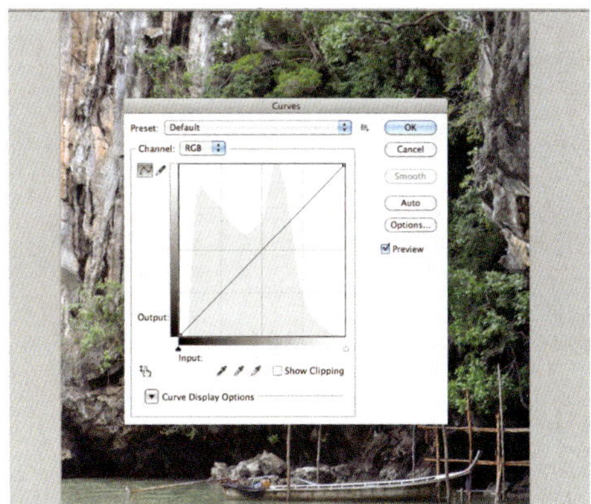

03 Automatic control

The Curves dialog maps the tones in your image using a curved line. For now, just hit Auto and you'll see the curve change and the tonal range fixed.

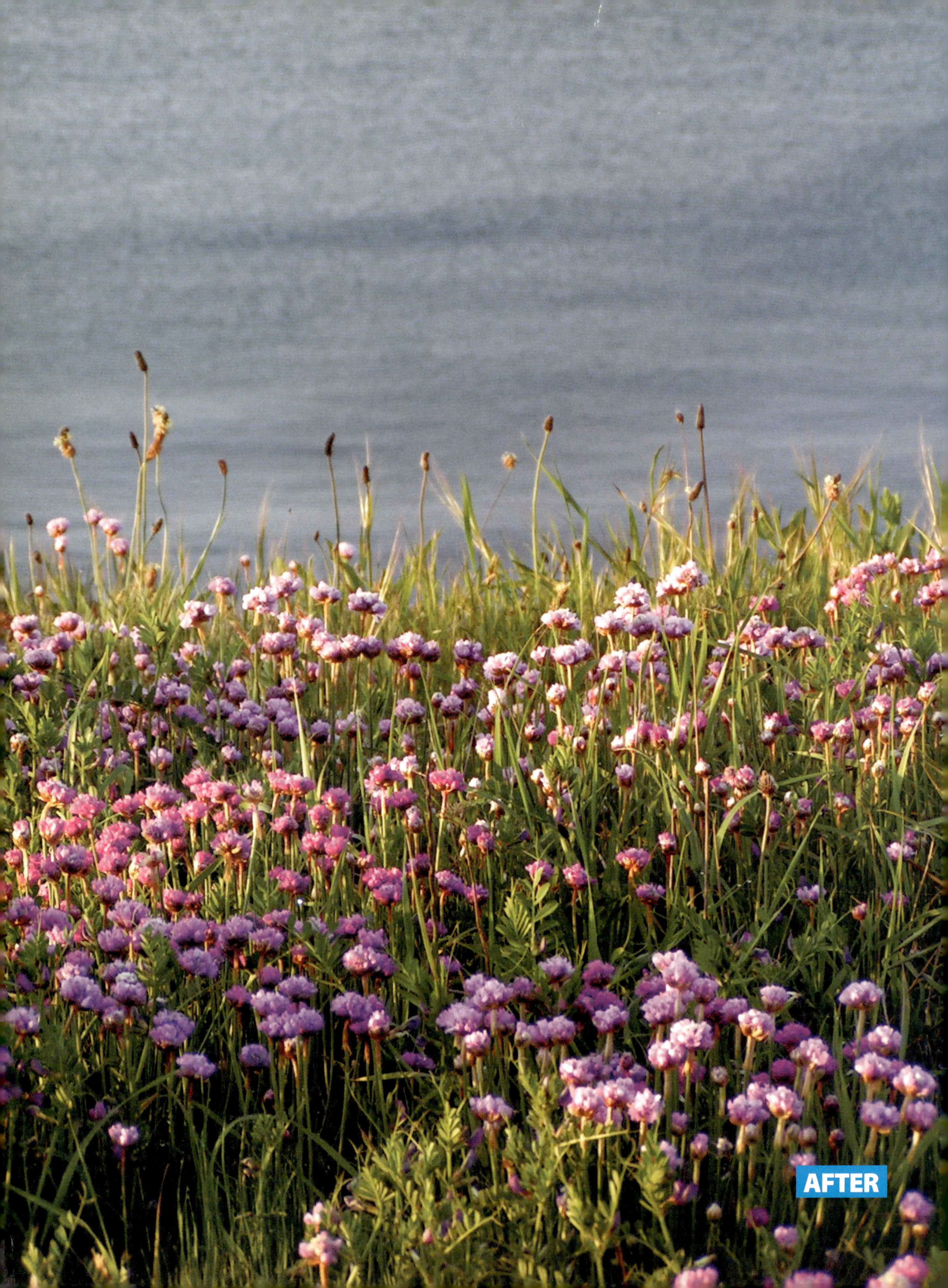
AFTER

Auto Tone up

A real one-click miracle control courtesy of Photoshop's Image menu

We've looked at Levels and Curves, and we'll come back to them later. But it you are looking for the ultimate quick fix for your photos, then we have a little trick for you.

While Photoshop Elements users have a whole host of automated controls to fix your images in a flash (we'll be looking at these further in the book), smart fix options aren't on display in Photoshop in your main interface.. However, take a visit to the Image menu from the top toolbar in Photoshop and you will find three completely automatic options. These use the power of Photoshop's more advanced colour and tone controls, like Levels and Curves, and improve the exposure and tonal range of your photos in literally seconds. If you're unhappy with the result after applying you can also use the Undo command, which is easily found in the File menu, or by using the handy shortcut Cmd/Ctrl+Z. But even if you don't get the results you want, it's a good way to ensure you are editing on a well tonally balanced image.

"Improve the exposure and tonal range of your photos in literally seconds"

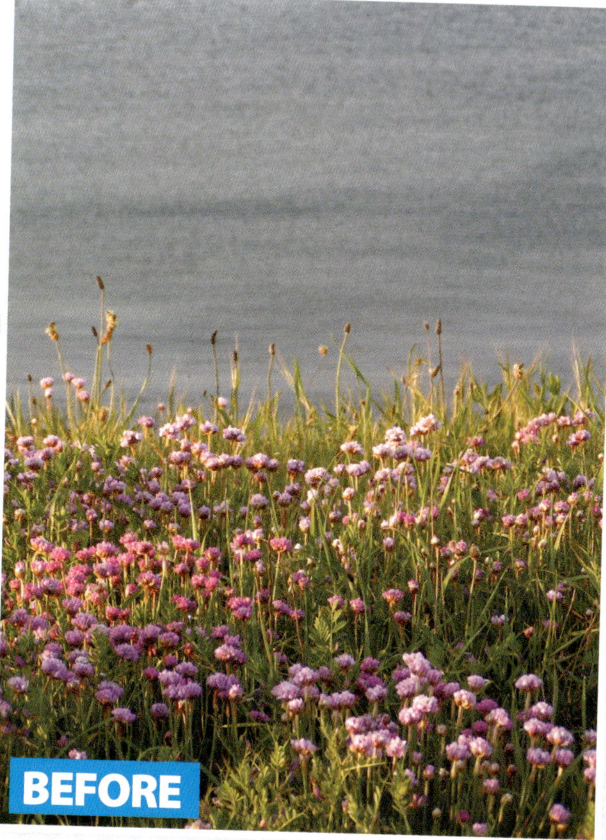

GET TONED

Auto Tone

Auto Tone is a one-click command that is accessed from the Image menu and can be great for a quick fix.

Shortcut

Save even more time by using the handy keyboard shortcut assigned to Auto Tone. It's Cmd/Ctrl+Shift+L.

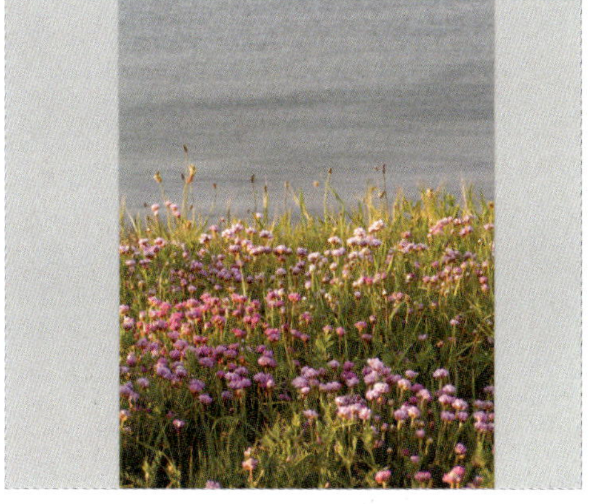

01 Image analysis

When you open an image, have a look at the tone and contrast. Your eye can usually spot when something isn't quite right.

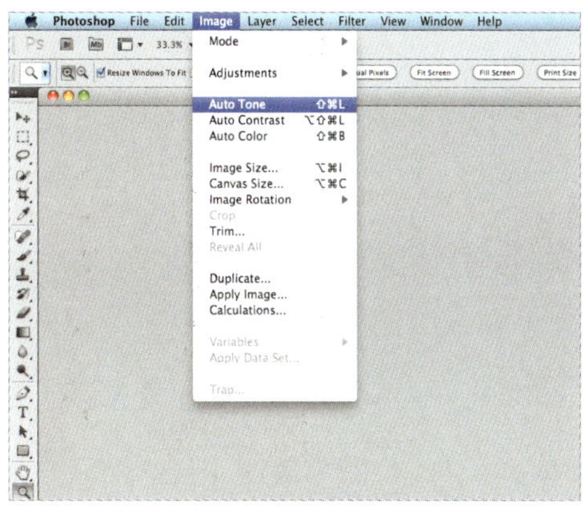

02 Try a tone up

Auto Tone is one of three automatic commands that reside within the Image menu. Click it once to affect your photo.

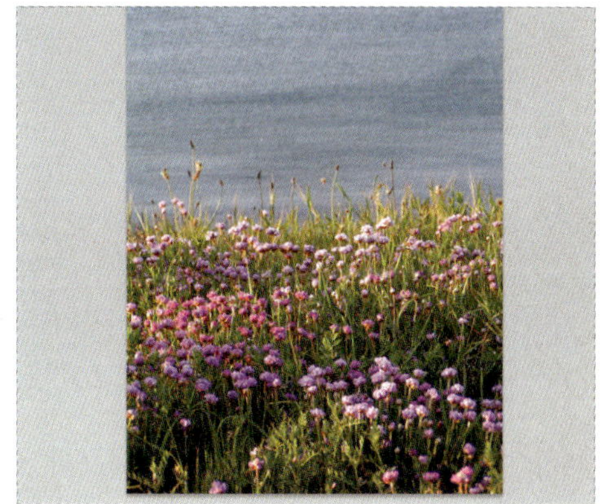

03 And you're done!

Within once entering the Levels or Curves dialogs, we have brought out the purples in our flowers and the blue in our sea.

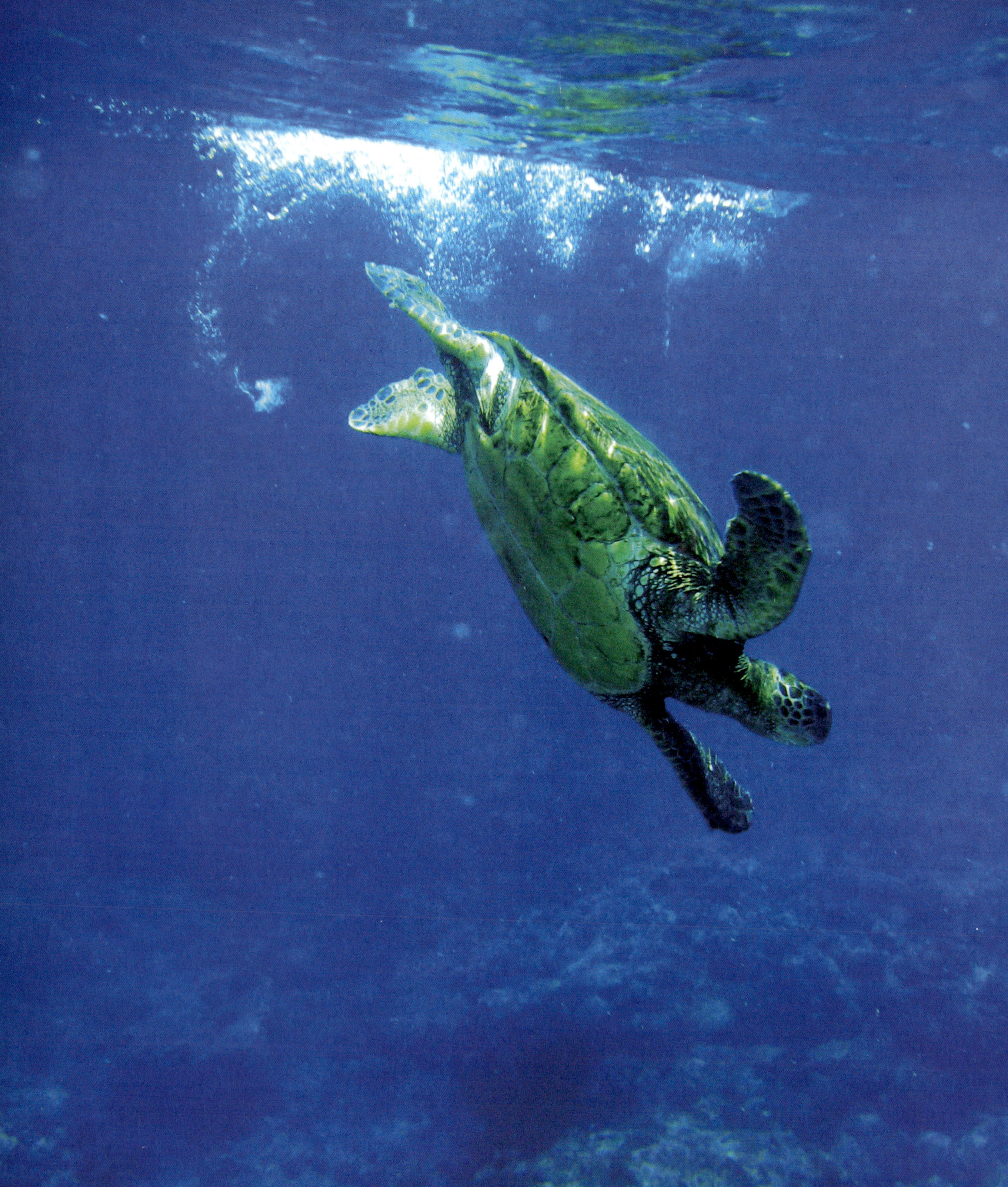

AFTER

Great contrast in a click

Take a so-so image into a keeper by using this handy automated command

Just as we have seen with Auto Tone in the last couple of pages, there is also a simple solution to alter the contrast in your image, ie the difference between the high and low tones in a photograph. If you have an image that is low contrast, tones will start to blend into one another and this can lead to a washed out effect.

Luckily we don't have to put up with these images as there is a really easy way to fix them. The Auto Contrast control will take your image and improve the contrast using powerful behind-the-scenes technology, which results in much better tone and colour across a scene.

The image that we are using here is a typical example of a low contrast image. The blue of the water against the turtle's shell makes everything looks very, well, blue. By upping the contrast, more tones come through, such as the green on the shell, clearly defining the subject against its environment and transforming the image.

"It will fix and control the overall tonal and colour ranges in your images"

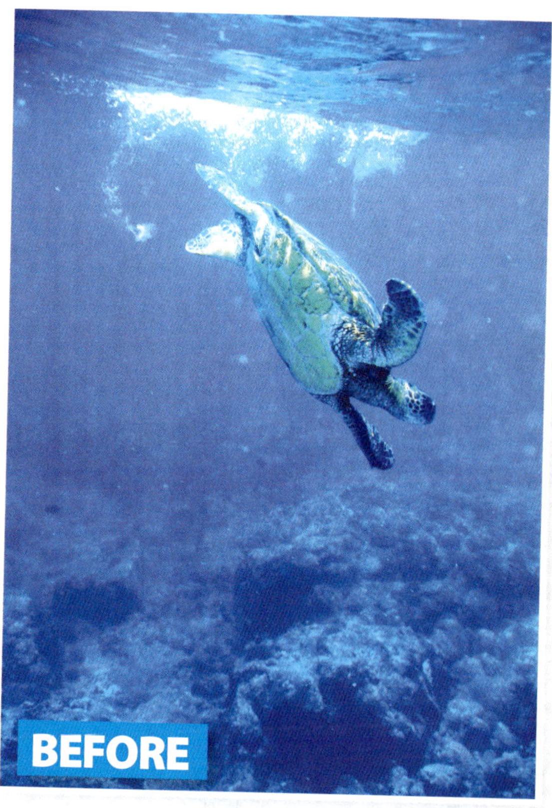

SEE THE CONTRAST

Contrast

The contrast in your image can have a massive effect on the final image. Our start image suffers from being low contrast, in that colours are not very defined from one another. One quick visit to the Image menu and suddenly we have a much stronger overall image.

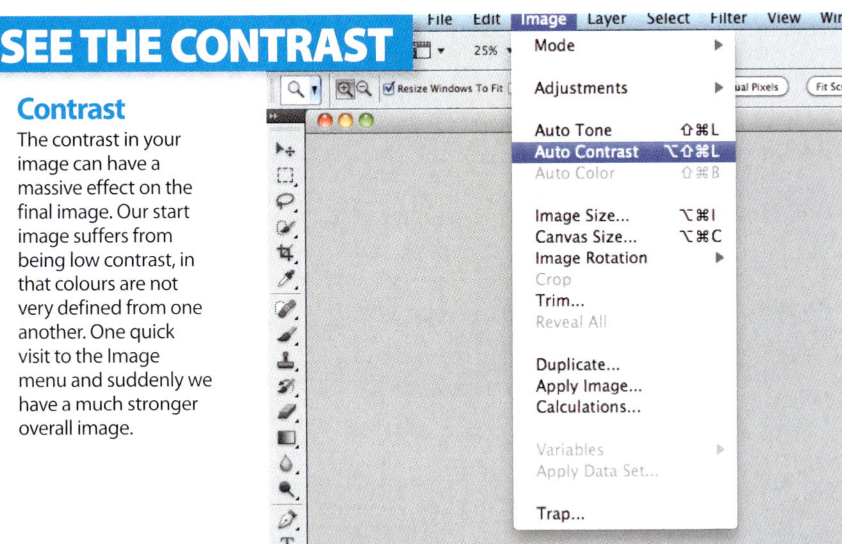

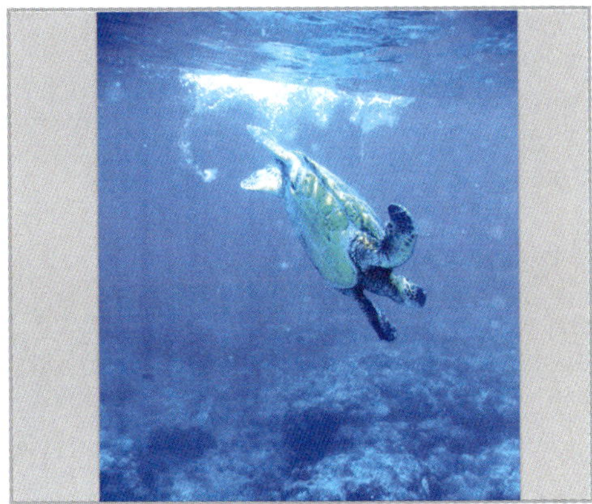

01 Wishy washy
This image is rather stunning, but it is let down by the faded colours that appear washed out, stopping the turtle from being prominent.

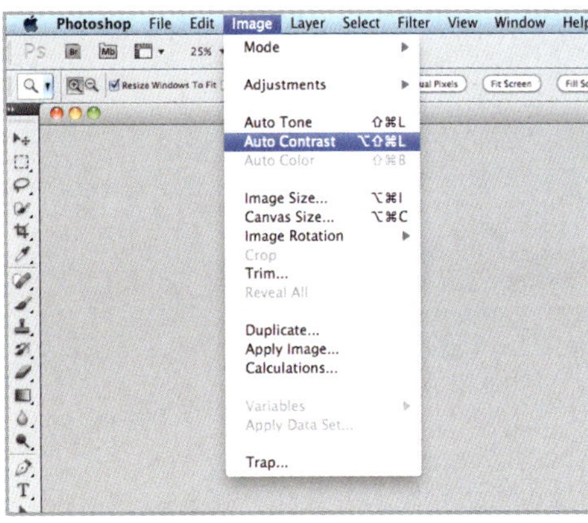

02 Auto Contrast
The Auto Contrast one-click solution is found under the Image menu in Photoshop and it will sort your image out super fast.

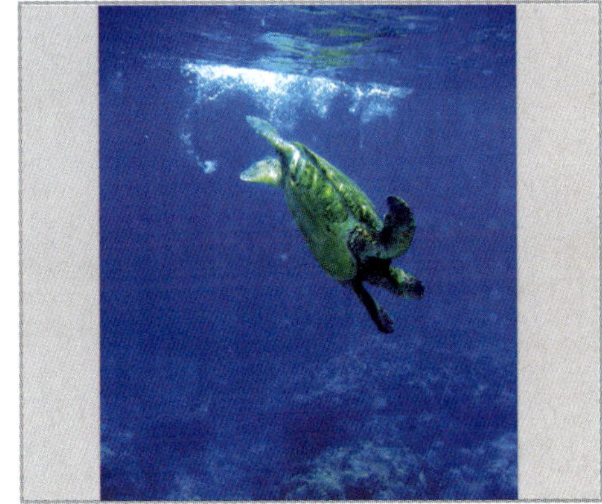

03 Final image
Our final image has a much deeper blue and the details and colour of the turtle are a lot brighter, making the creature stand out.

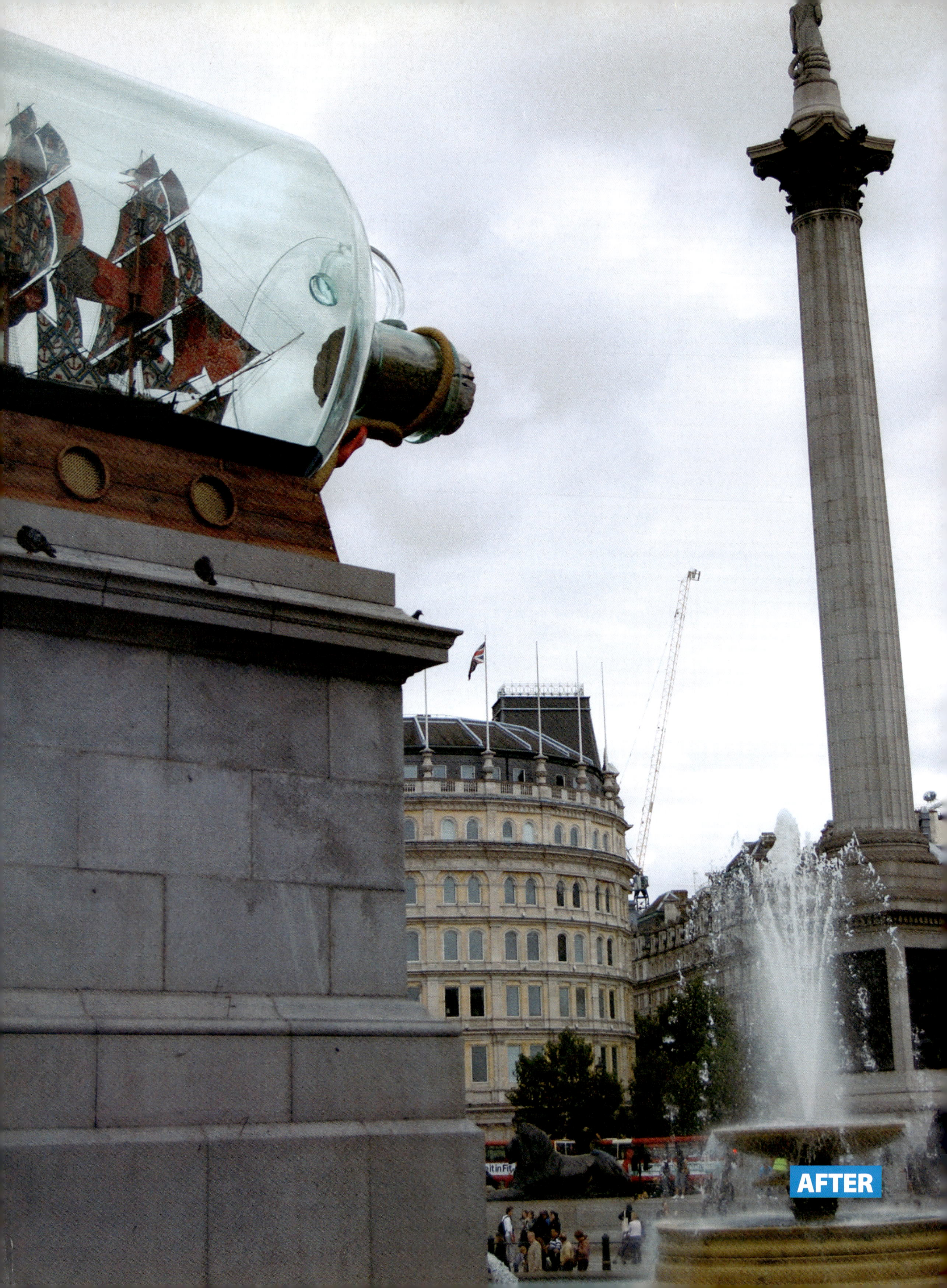
AFTER

Fix colour casts with Auto Color

Get rid of comment white balance problems with this auto option

The final automatic command of the three in the Image menu is Auto Color. This does not work on CMYK images, so if it is greyed out, then you cannot access it without changing the Image Mode to RGB.

This simple command comes into its own if you have a colour cast over your image. This can be caused by a number of things when taking the photo, for example the lighting in which you are taking a shot. Different lights, like fluorescent or tungsten bulbs, will leave a cast over your photo, such as yellow or blue. Also, setting the wrong white balance setting can lead to an unwanted colour cast as well.

In our image we have a very noticeable blue colour cast across our image, the result of taking a photo by setting the wrong white balance option on our camera. However, one click on the Auto Color command gets rid of this, and restores the colours to a more natural state, giving us a great base to do further work on.

> "One click on the Auto Color command gets rid of our colour cast"

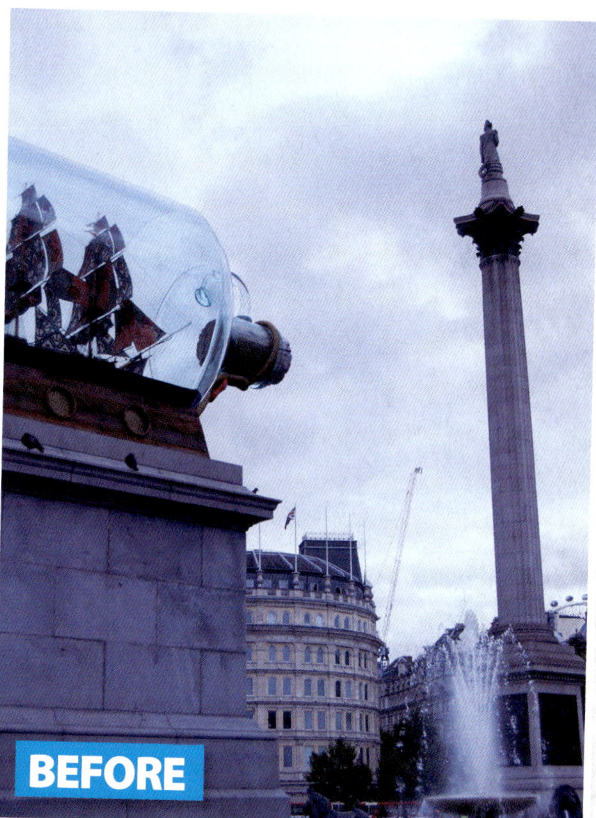

CAST YOUR SPELL

Mix your commands

Now that we have looked at all three automatic commands in the Image menu, don't be afraid to apply more than one to your photos. They each deal with a slightly different problem, so by using all three, you can perfect your image massively in just seconds.

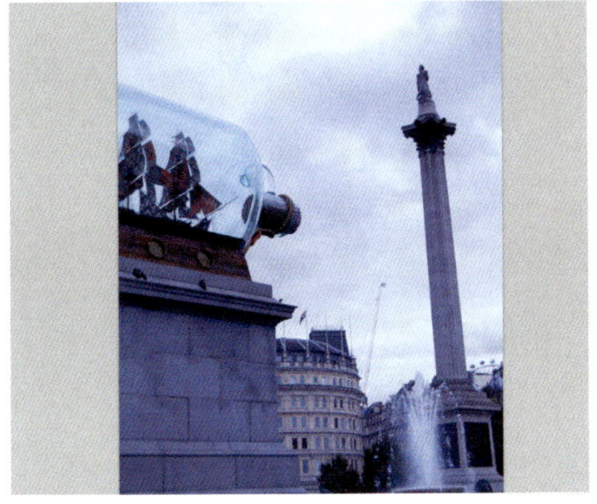

01 Got the blues

We're pretty sure that this scene wasn't blue when we took it! But there is definitely a noticeable cast on our photograph.

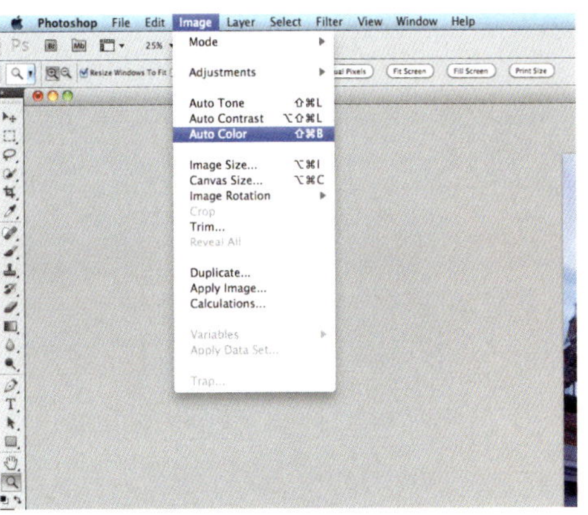

02 Locate your auto control

Go to Image>Auto Color in the Photoshop interface. This option will only be available is you are working in RGB.

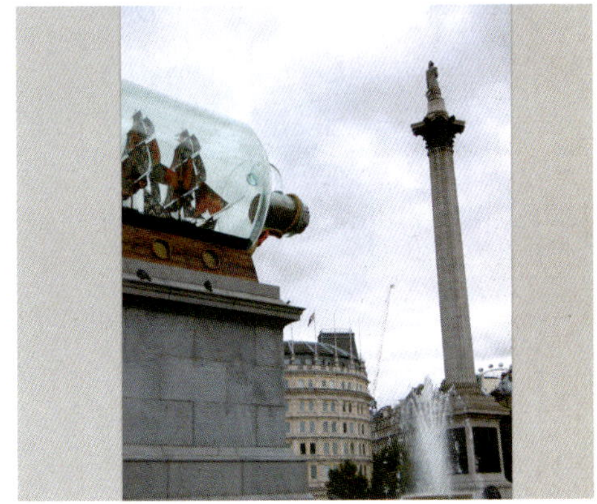

03 That's better!

Our blue cast is magically gone. However, the tones are still flat. Using the other auto options will give us a great final image.

How to crop for impact

Don't worry if your image lacks punch. You can trim away excess with the Crop tool

It's easy to forget about composition when taking photos – it's more important to capture the main area of focus than spend hours worrying about the position of it. However, one of the many joys of Photoshop is that you don't have to keep images as you captured them. You can change the composition and the focus using a wealth of tools in the program, which can make a huge impact on the final photograph.

In many cases, the simplest of tools in Photoshop can have the greatest effect. In this mini tutorial, we will be looking at the Crop tool. This is found in the left-hand toolbar and it looks like a little square, but with the corner lines extended so that they cross. It's the same in both Photoshop and Photoshop Elements. Once selected, it's as simple as clicking and dragging over your image to create a crop area – the bits that you want to keep stay bright, and the bits to delete go dark.

It's worth bearing in mind that when you crop, you are deleting the unwanted image information, so make sure that you have a copy of the original if you don't want to lose it. Should you realise you have made a mistake straight away, Cmd/Ctrl+Z is your ultimate shortcut – that will undo the last thing that you did. And while we are talking about shortcuts, another handy one to learn is Cmd/Ctrl+C, which will let you access the Crop tool at any time.

By simply cropping an image you are changing the focus of your photo. In our example, the poor couple are being overlooked in favour of that amazing scene behind them. We move them off-centre and suddenly it is the couple that draws you in. We have supplied the start image for this tutorial so you can give it a go, but you can try this out on any of your own images using the exact same method. You'll be surprised at what a difference a change of composition can make.

WHAT YOU'LL LEARN

What's the focus?
We want to make the couple the main subject in this image, but at the moment they are being swallowed up by this stunning backdrop.

Crop tool
Whether you are using Photoshop or Photoshop Elements, you will find the Crop tool in the main toolbar down the left-hand side of the screen.

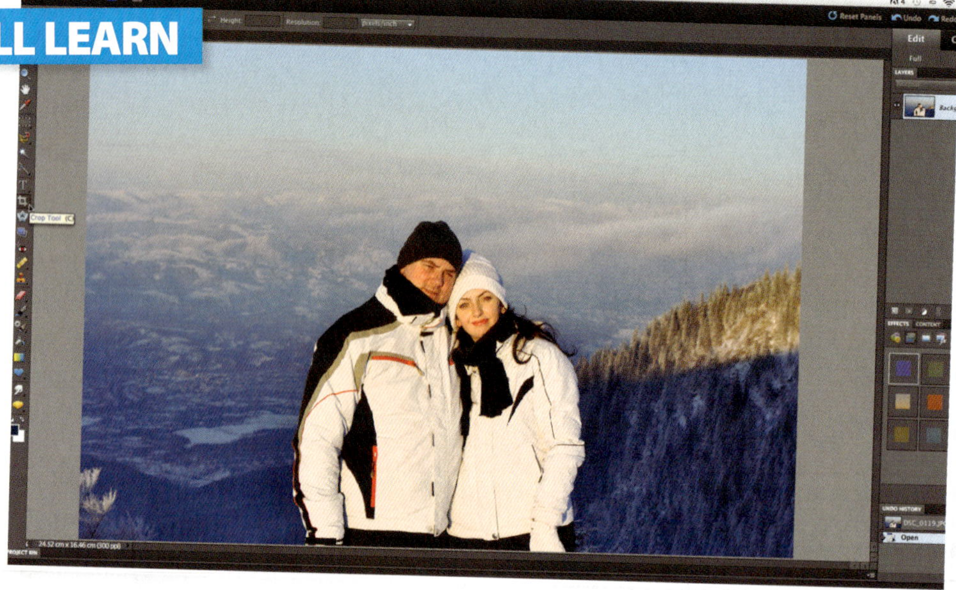

See the Crop area
When you are cropping, the parts of the image that will be deleted are darkened so you can preview the crop before committing.

Commit to the crop
To finish cropping, you can simply click with the mouse over the crop area, or use the little tick icon in the top Options toolbar.

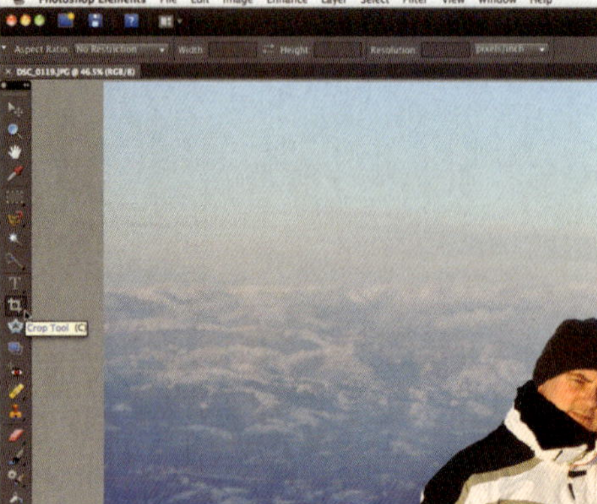

01 Select the tool
Open up the supplied image. Let's get to work with the Crop tool and see if we can come up with a better composition.

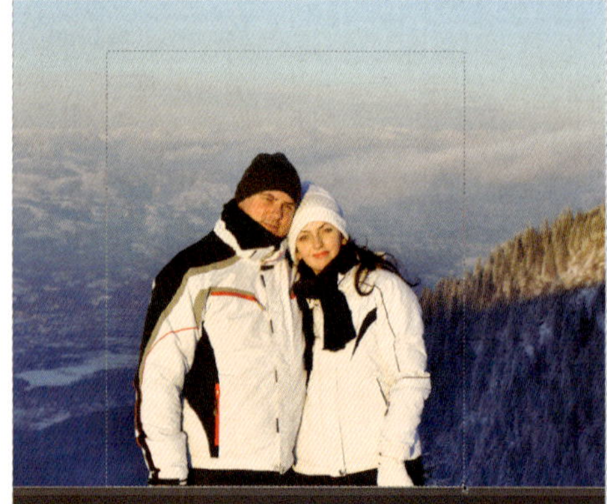

02 Draw the area
With the tool selected, go over to your image and then click and drag over the area you want to keep. Make sure you keep the mouse button held down.

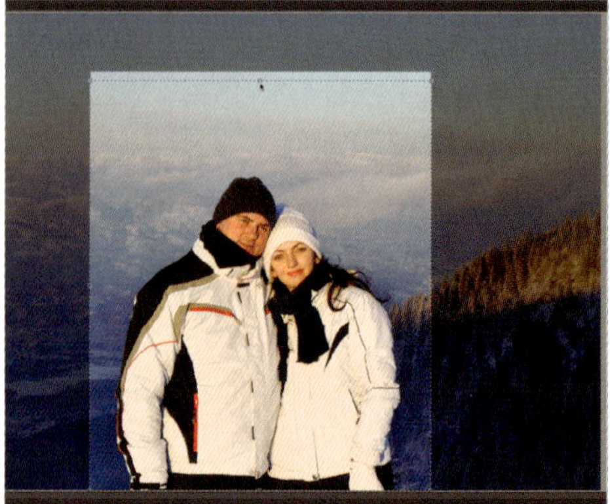

03 Refine and crop
If you want to adjust the crop area, simply click on one of the little square corner points and then drag it to the position you want.

"One of the many joys of Photoshop is that you don't have to keep images as you captured them"

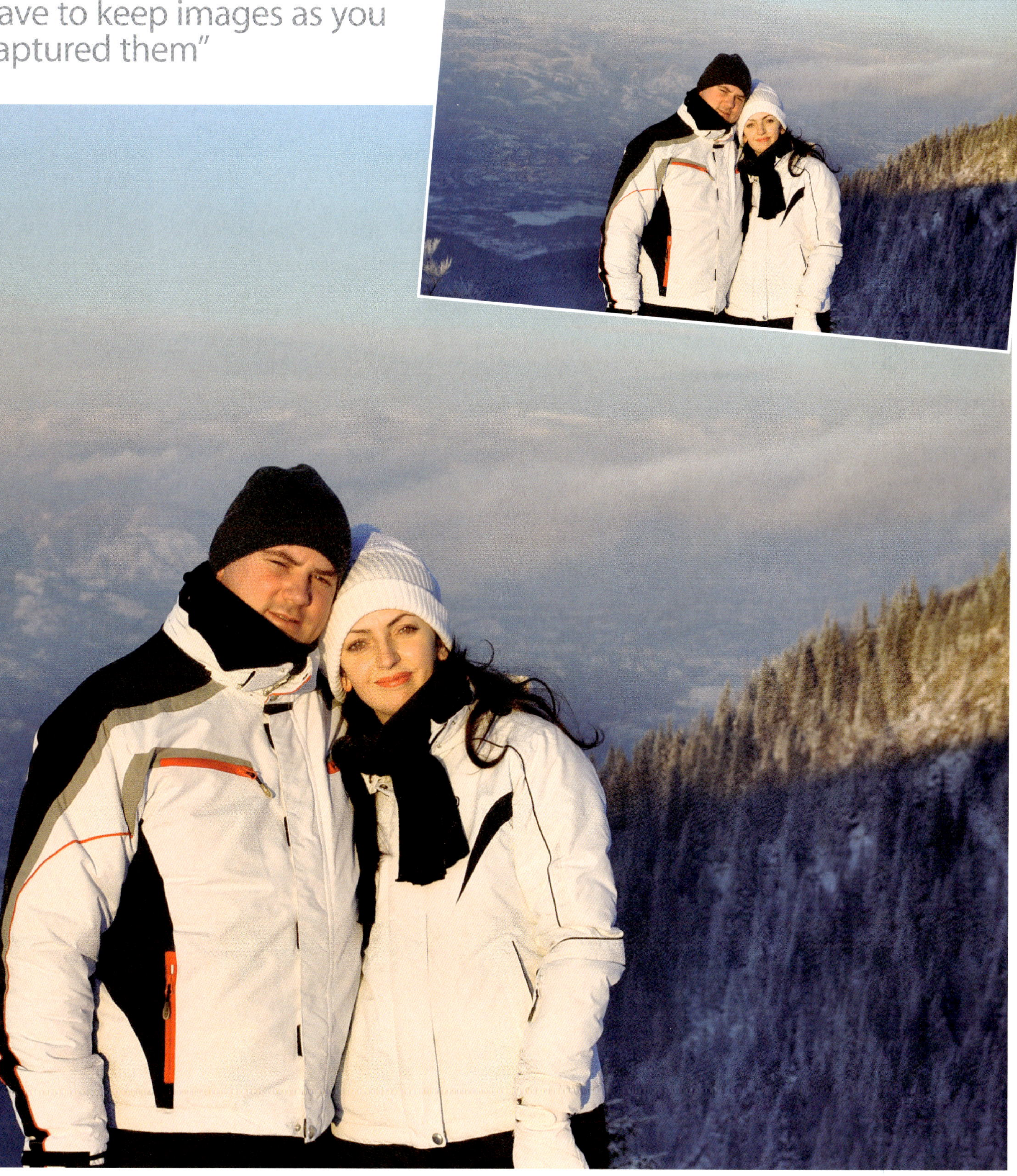

Resizing techniques

Resizing images is easy in Photoshop – deciding on the best composition is the hard part

A crucial factor in composing an image is how it has been framed, cropped or resized. Photoshop has a variety of methods for either shrinking or blowing up to bigger dimensions.

It's amazing how the slightest change of framing changes an image's message and how that message is perceived by the viewer. When you come to print your artwork, its size and shape are both important visual clues to its message. The decision of framing an image mostly comes down to the lines of composition, or direction, within it.

Photoshop, and Elements, has a lot on offer for such a simple job as resizing. The Crop tool, found in the toolbar, offers a quick way to trim an image to size, whether it's changing orientation or cropping out distracting subjects from the edge of a frame. The Content-Aware Scale feature in Photoshop CS4/CS5 and Recompose in Elements 8/9 rescales your image, leaving important subjects intact. Subjects such as people are recognised as one object, and only the areas around are stretched or squashed.

Use these two pages as a guide to picking the best resizing method for your image. It'll work equally well whether you want to add more punch with a tightly cropped composition, or enlarge an image and add a Resample method for smooth results.

"Add more punch with a tightly cropped composition, or enlarge an image and add a Resample method for smooth results"

QUICK PHOTOSHOP TIPS

Editable layers

Before you can use any of the Transform tools, you first have to make sure the layer is an editable one. If the layer is locked then double-click on it and hit OK in the New Layer dialog box.

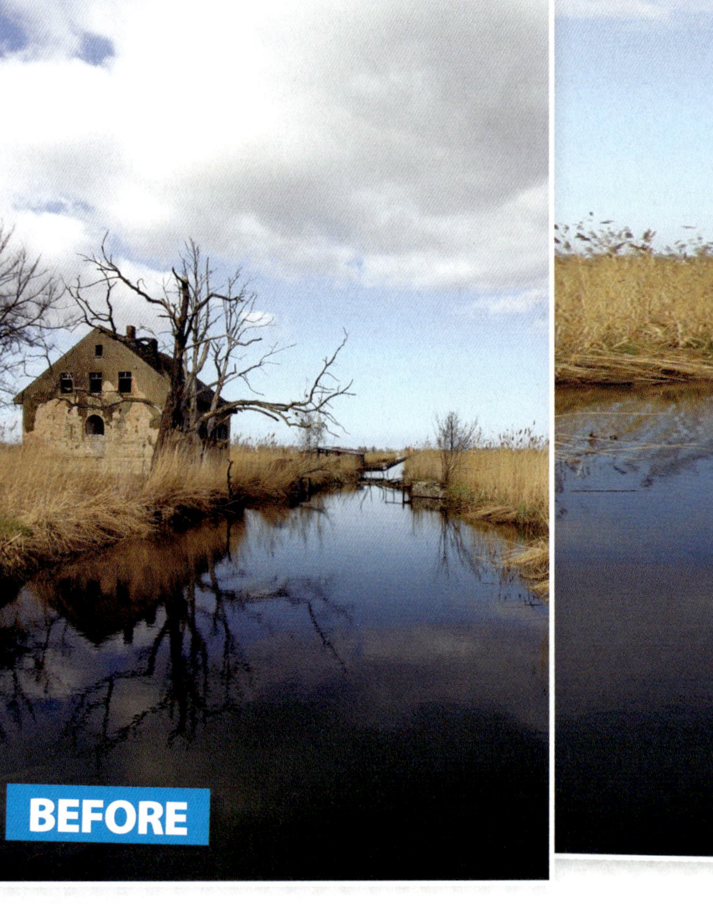

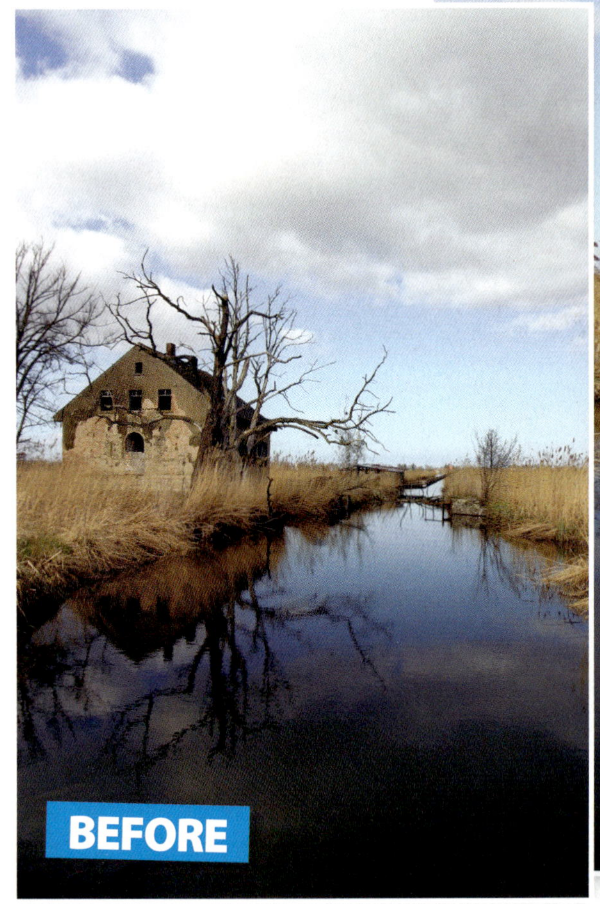

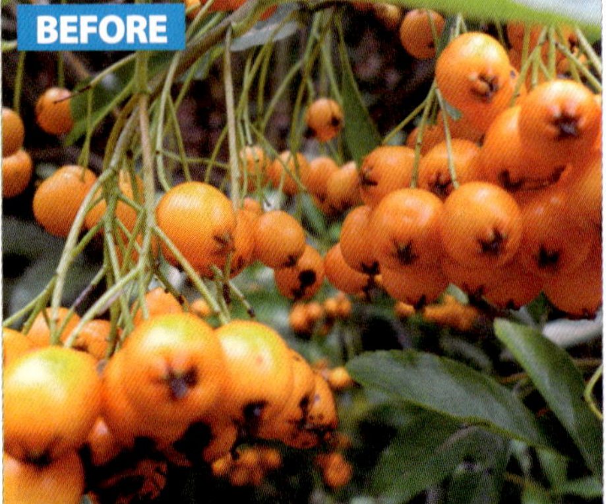

01 Crop tool

The Crop tool can be set to specific dimensions and resolution by entering values in the Options bar. Leave blank to play with the resolution freely.

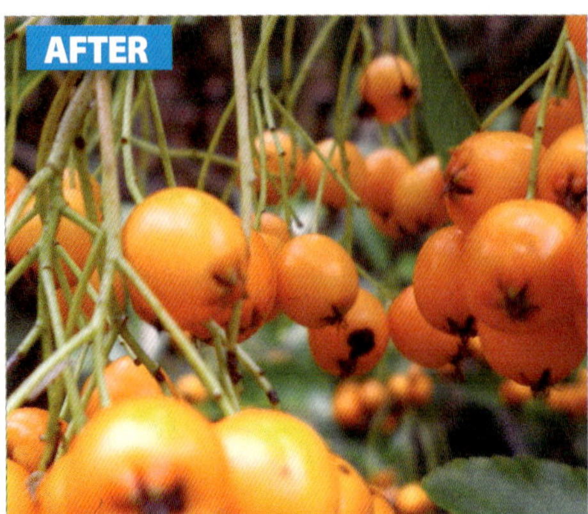

02 Crop tool 2

Once the cropping frame is added to your image, you can black out the outer areas with the Shield command in the Options bar.

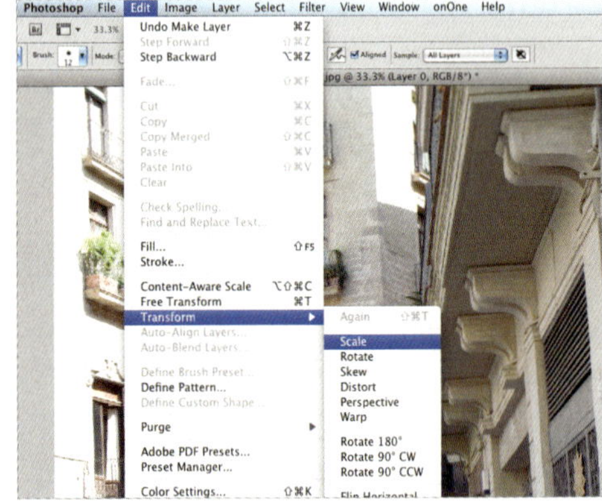

03 Transform menu

The Free Transform option is a quick way to shrink an image, whether to throw it out of proportion or keep the resize constrained by holding Shift.

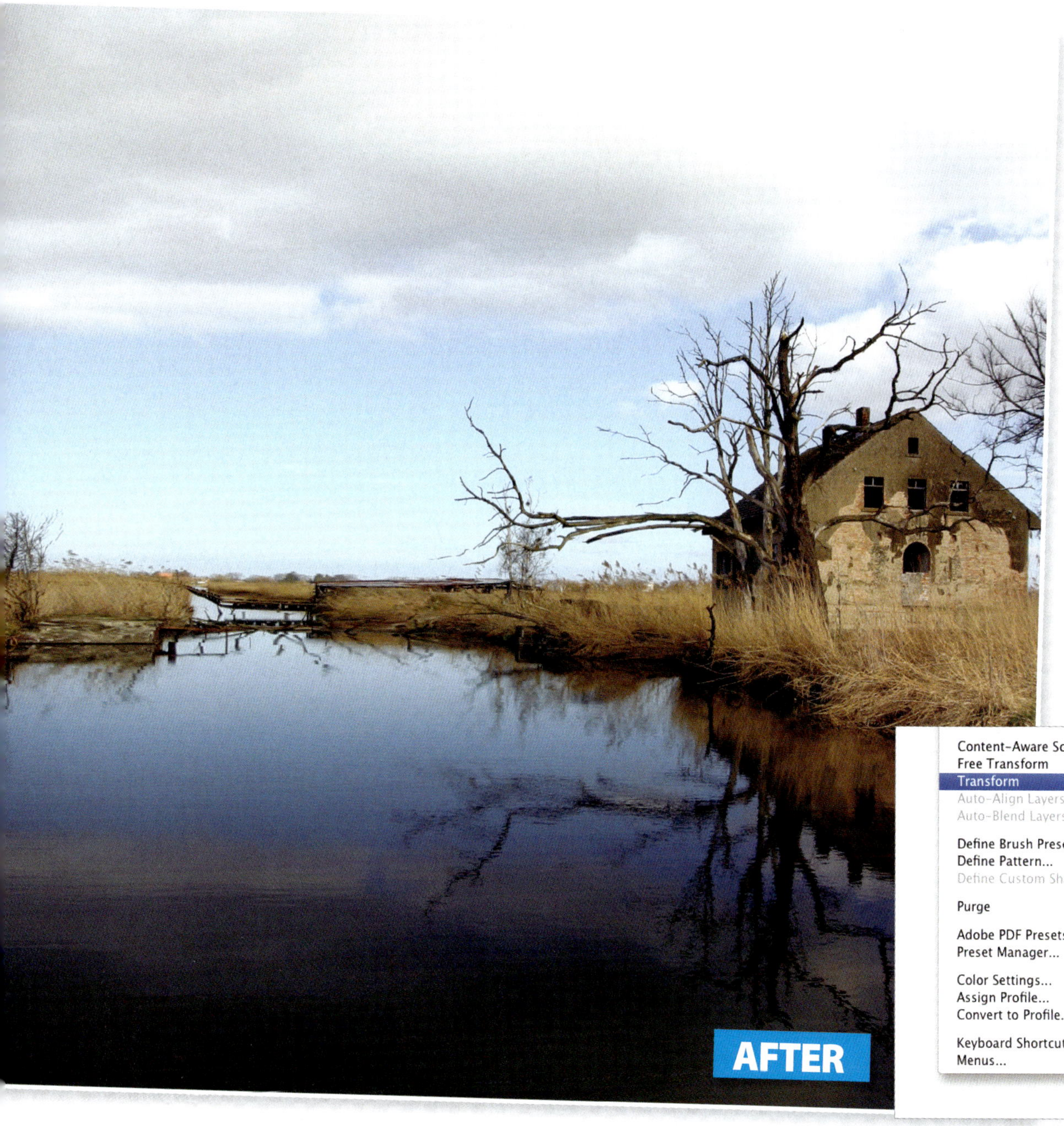

Content-Aware Scaling

Under Edit>Content-Aware Scale, an image can be resized while keeping each subject the same shape. We've kept the building in this image in one piece but stretched the sky and river.

Edit menu

In the Edit menu the group of Transform commands are grouped along with the Free Transform and Content-Aware Scale options.

Options bar

In the Options bar the dimensions of the cropping can be set depending on print size, frame size or orientation to suit your composition. You can set these with the Crop tool or Free Transform and Content-Aware Scale features.

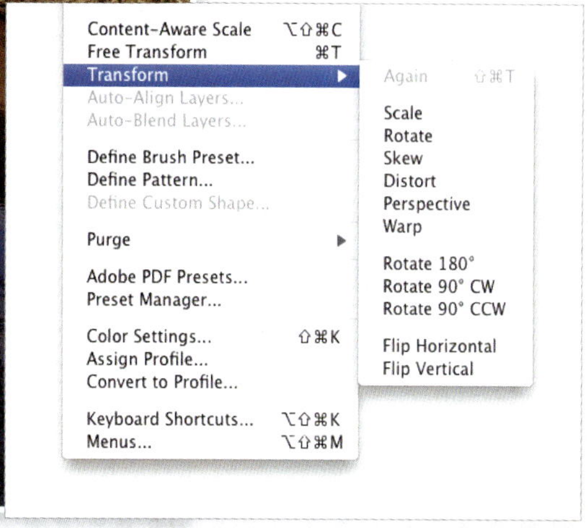

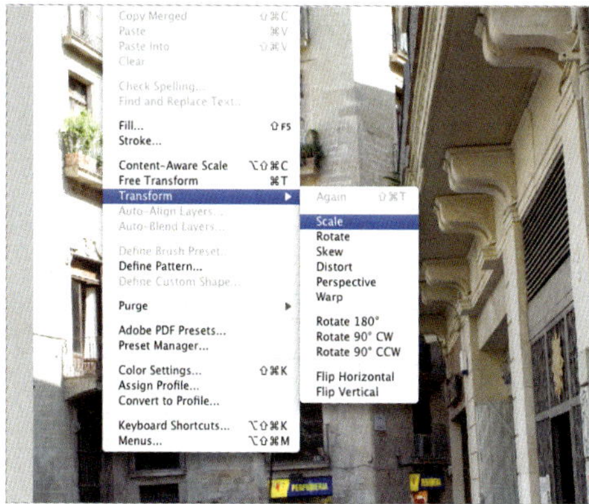

04 More options

Other Transform options include Skew, Warp and Distort. You can be specific with the angle, height and skew of the Transform using the Options bar.

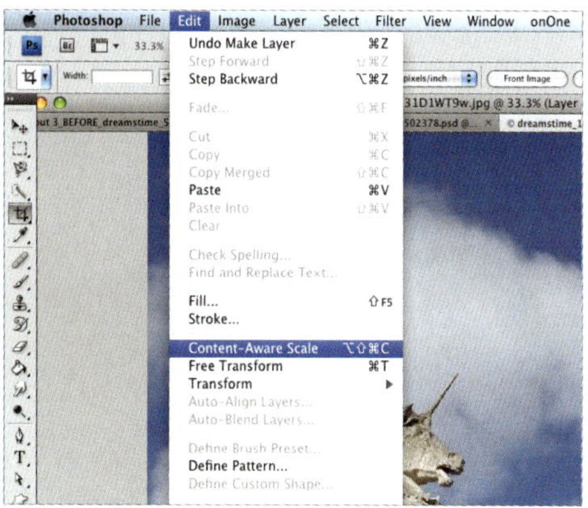

05 Content-Aware Scaling

Content-Aware Scale (CS4) considers the subjects in your image when resizing, and only areas of repetitiveness (for example a blue sky) are affected.

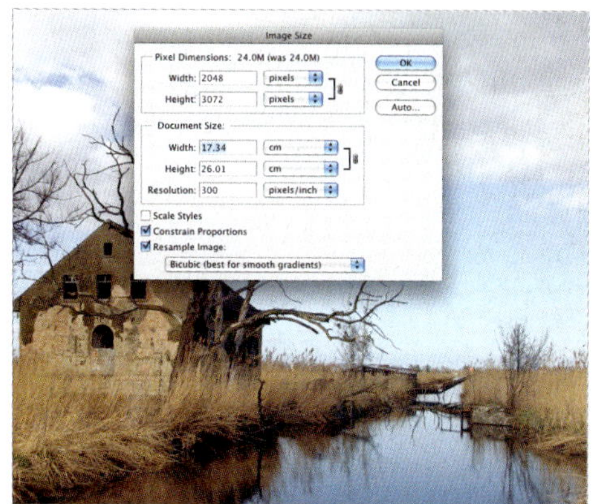

06 Image Size

For precision, use Image>Image Size. Here you can set the exact sizes of the pixel dimensions and the document size too.

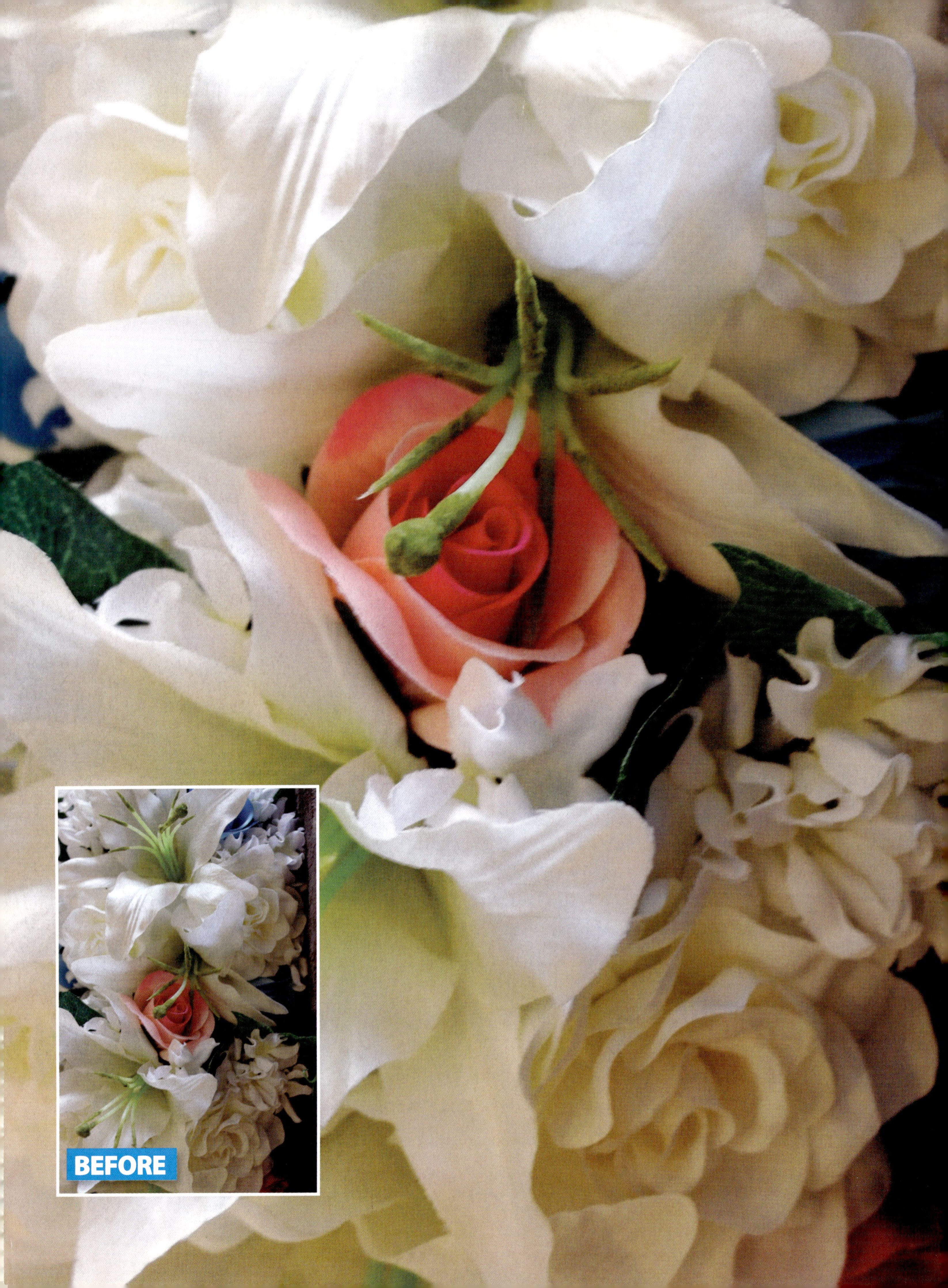
BEFORE

Use the Quick Edit option

Who says that image editing has to take time – Elements has a speedy solution

Of the three editing modes in Elements, Quick Edit really does live up to its promise. In Quick Edit mode the panel to the right has a whole bunch of sliders that you can use to give fast and effective results.

These cover everything from Lighting and Color to Balance and Sharpness. There are a number of these controls that have an Auto button, which enables Elements to do the hard work. You can always tweak the sliders further to help get the exact results that you need.

You can just jump right in, however, and play around with the sliders. If you don't like the results then there is a Reset button at the moment that can be hit at any time to put the sliders back to the default. The smallest tweak of the slider can make a really big difference here, so make sure that you keep your images looking realistic.

The Quick Edit options can be accessed from the Elements Organizer as well as the Edit interface, so if you see a shot that needs a quick fix, you can click and retouch in just seconds.

If you see a little lightbulb next to the slider headers, this means that you can access the Help menu and read more about the control that you are trying to use. Give it a go and you can transform your photos easily.

"Of the three editing modes in Elements, Quick Edit really does live up to its promise"

QUICK EDIT OPTIONS

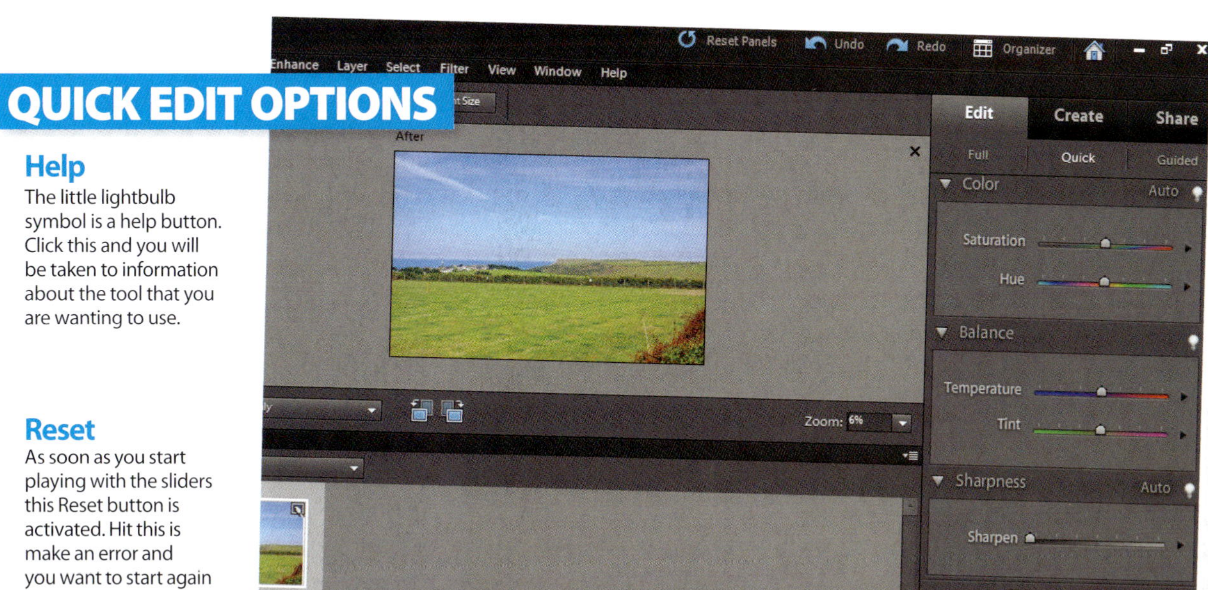

Help
The little lightbulb symbol is a help button. Click this and you will be taken to information about the tool that you are wanting to use.

Reset
As soon as you start playing with the sliders this Reset button is activated. Hit this is make an error and you want to start again from scratch.

Sliders
These sliders are pretty self-explanatory and you can make a very big difference to your shots just using these. Take it slow though; you can always add more if you think the image needs it.

Quick mode
If you are in the Edit interface, then you can click on the Quick option in the top-right. If you're in the Organizer, then go to the Edit tab, and from the drop-down menu choose Quick Edit.

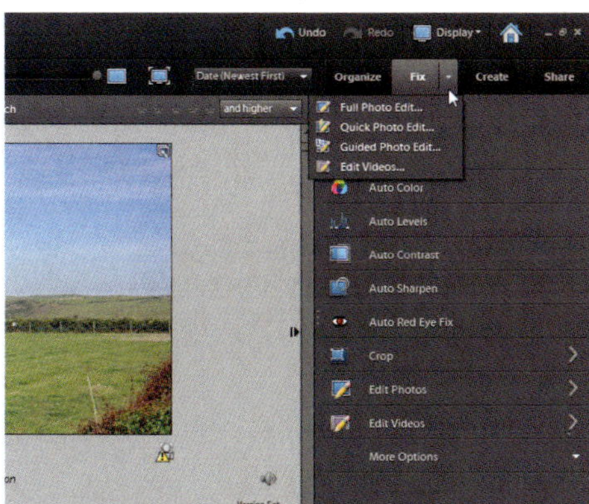

01 Choose your mode
Click on the Edit tab from the Organizer, the drop down gives you the choice of which Edit mode you want to use. We're going to choose Quick Edit.

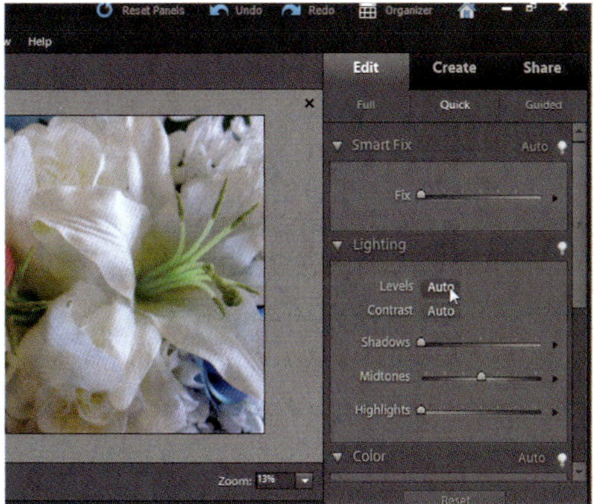

02 Auto options
We're going to use the Auto Levels option, which will help to balance the tones, followed by the Auto Contrast. This gives a good starting point.

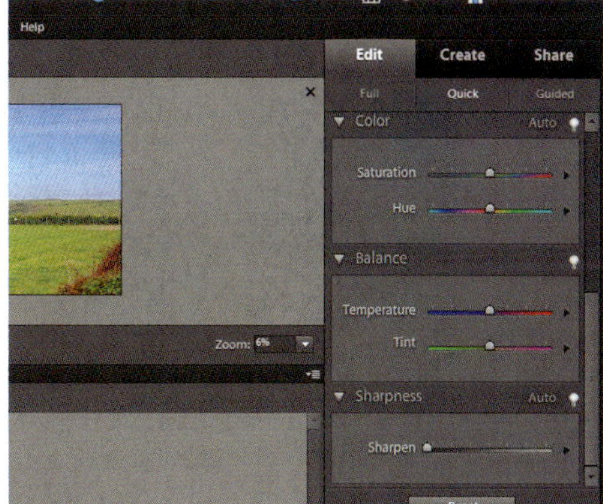

03 Tweak the sliders
Now we work down the rest of the sliders making subtle tweaks until we're happy with the way that the image looks. Don't forget to press Save.

Make Guided edits in PS Elements

From essential retouch options to more creative edits, the Guided walkthroughs help make the most of your pictures

Photoshop Elements has a load of different ways that you can edit your images. The Guided edits are a great way of learning more about the program and what it can do, as they walk you through different tasks step by step, explaining which tools you are using and why.

There are both practical and creative edits that come under this category, and some are relatively complex to do, but when broken down into steps, it's suddenly much simpler.

The first lot of Guided edits are all very simple and straightforward, helping you to crop, transform, lighten, colour correct and retouch your photos. There are also some more creative options, such as different ways to tint your images, merge them together and so on. Right at the bottom of the extensive list are some great effects such as the Out Of Bounds and Pop Art.

The best bit is that you can always start again if something goes wrong – though with Guided edits it's hard to stray far from the path. Here we will look at one of the Guided edits in more detail and you can see more of the creative options in the boxes to the right. Go on, give it a try and see what you can come up with!

"The best bit is that you can always start again if something goes wrong"

CREATIVE GUIDED EDITS

Lomo Camera Effect

This re-creates the traditional look of a Lomo camera.

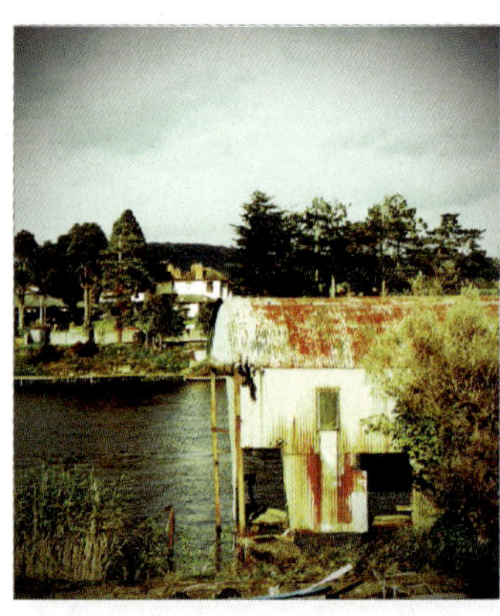

Out Of Bounds

This is a fun effect that lets you make an object spring out of a frame.

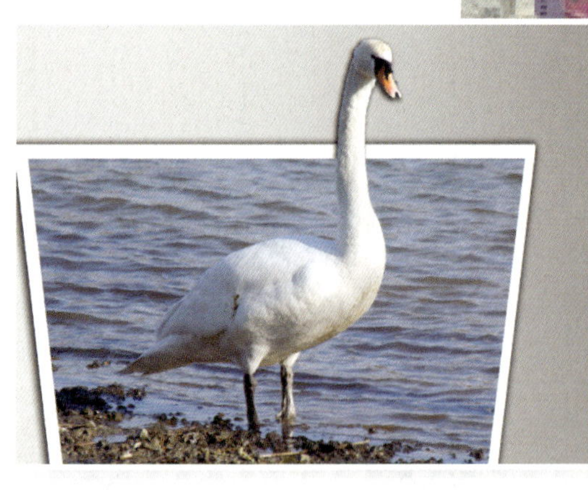

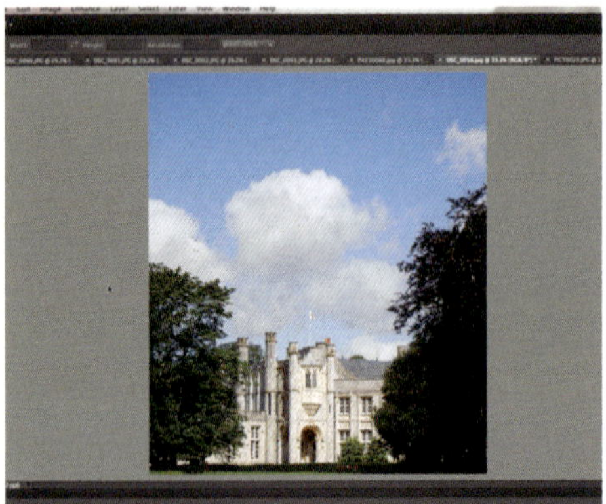

01 Creative effects made easy

One area where Elements' ease of use is apparent is in its new guided photo edits. These babies walk you through a variety of great effects.

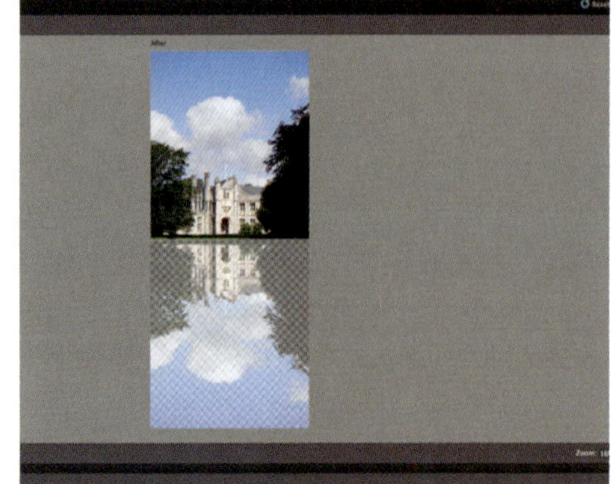

02 Get to the guides

Open up your image and then click the Guided tab. Scroll down to Fun Edits and click the one you want (we have picked Create Reflections).

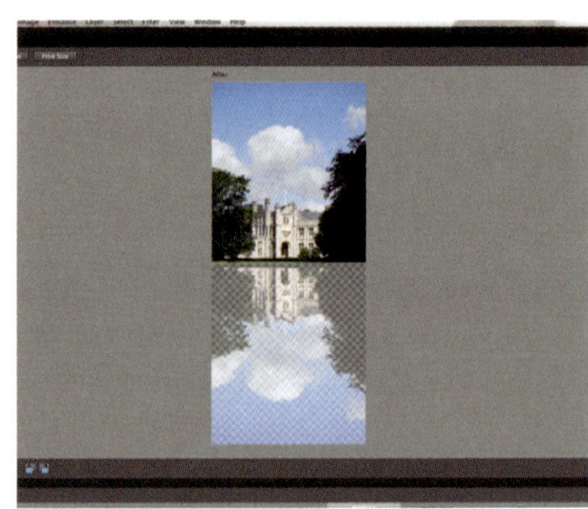

03 Watch and learn

Elements has created a flipped version of the start image. The next step is to pick the Eyedropper tool and set a background colour.

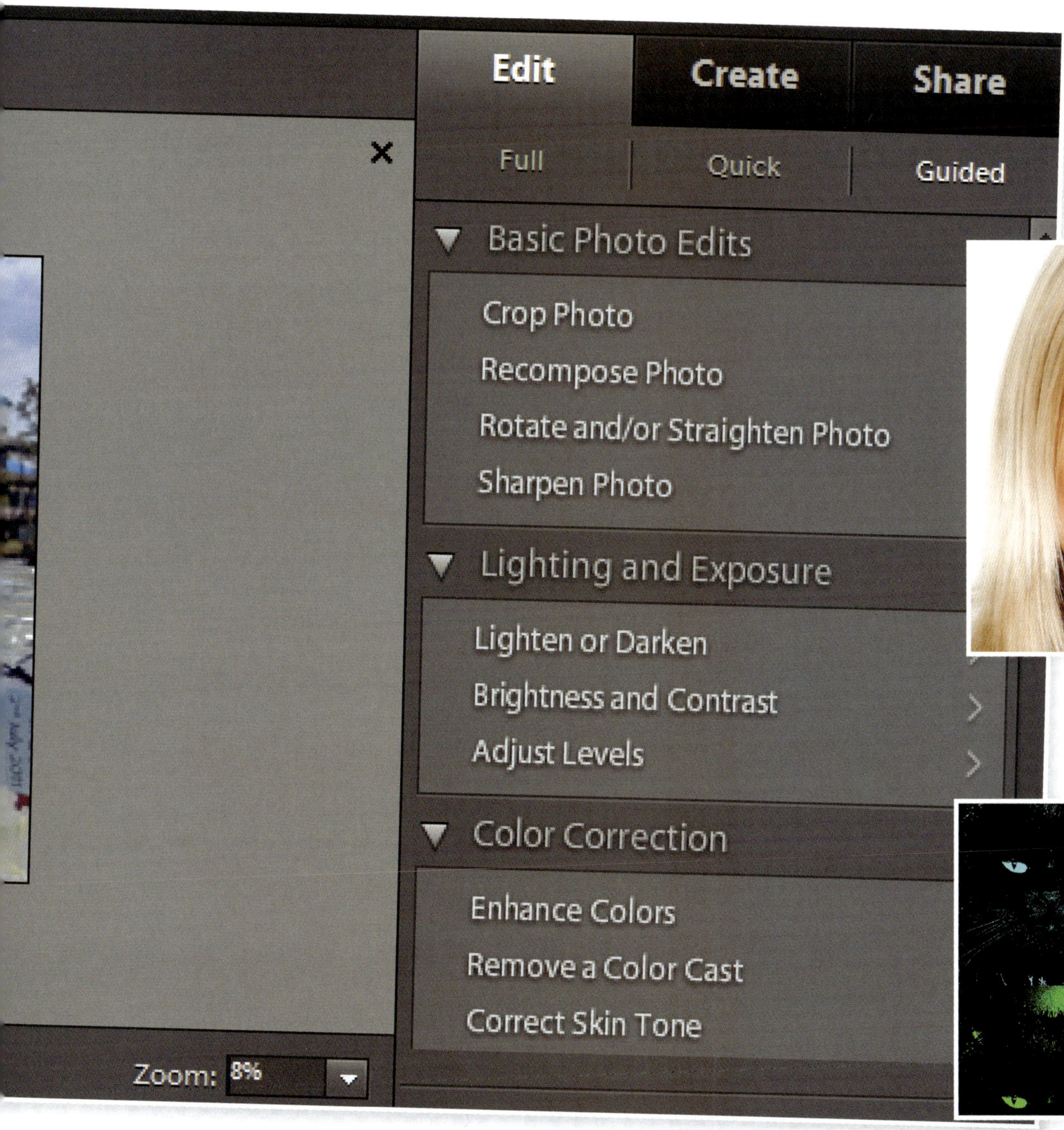

Perfect portraits
Retouching portraits can be a tricky job, but this edit makes things simple.

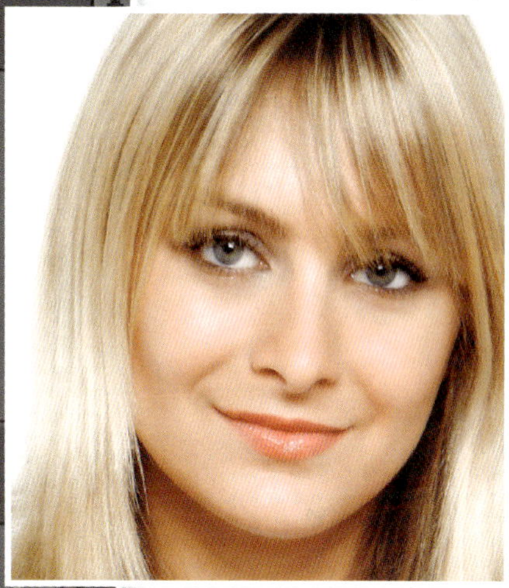

Pop Art
A classic look that is made as easy as pie in Photoshop Elements 9.

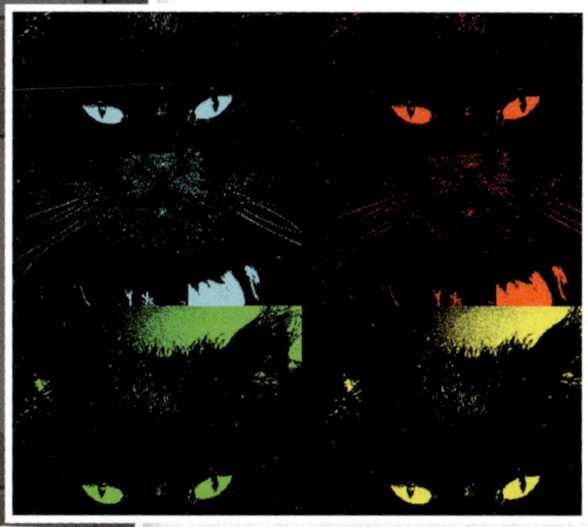

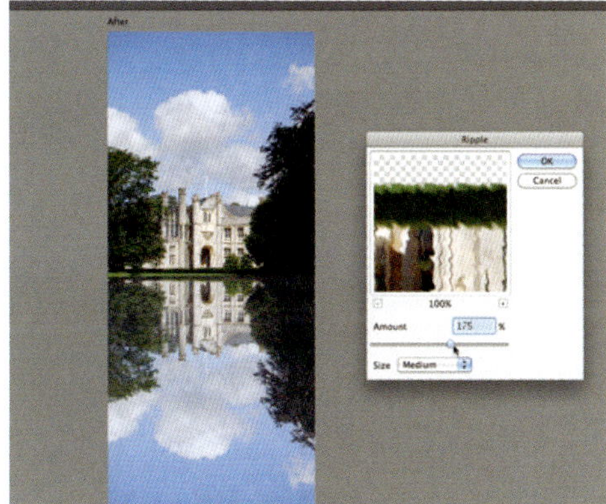

04 A bit of control

For our reflection, there is a choice of the sort of reflection to have. There's even a slider to help you tinker with the intensity of the effect.

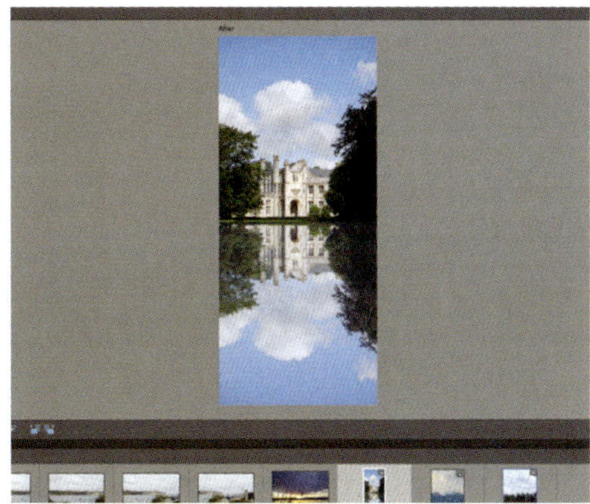

05 If it all goes wrong

As you work through the steps, you may find that you get a bit clicking-happy and need to go back. The Undo command will take you back.

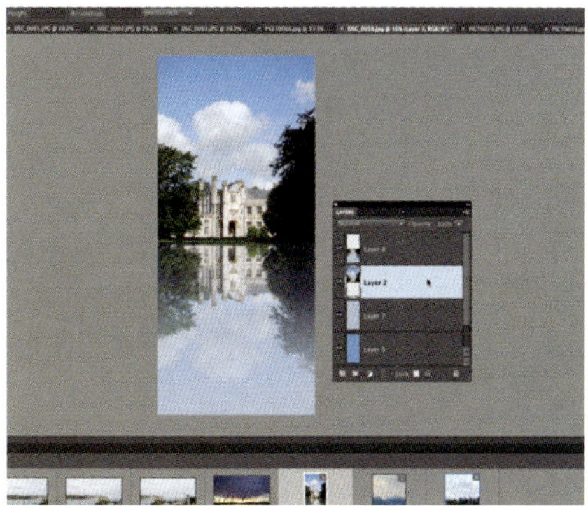

06 Get to the heart of things

Click Done. If you click on the Full tab, you will see that all of the steps are split into separate layers so you can use the layers to make adjustments.

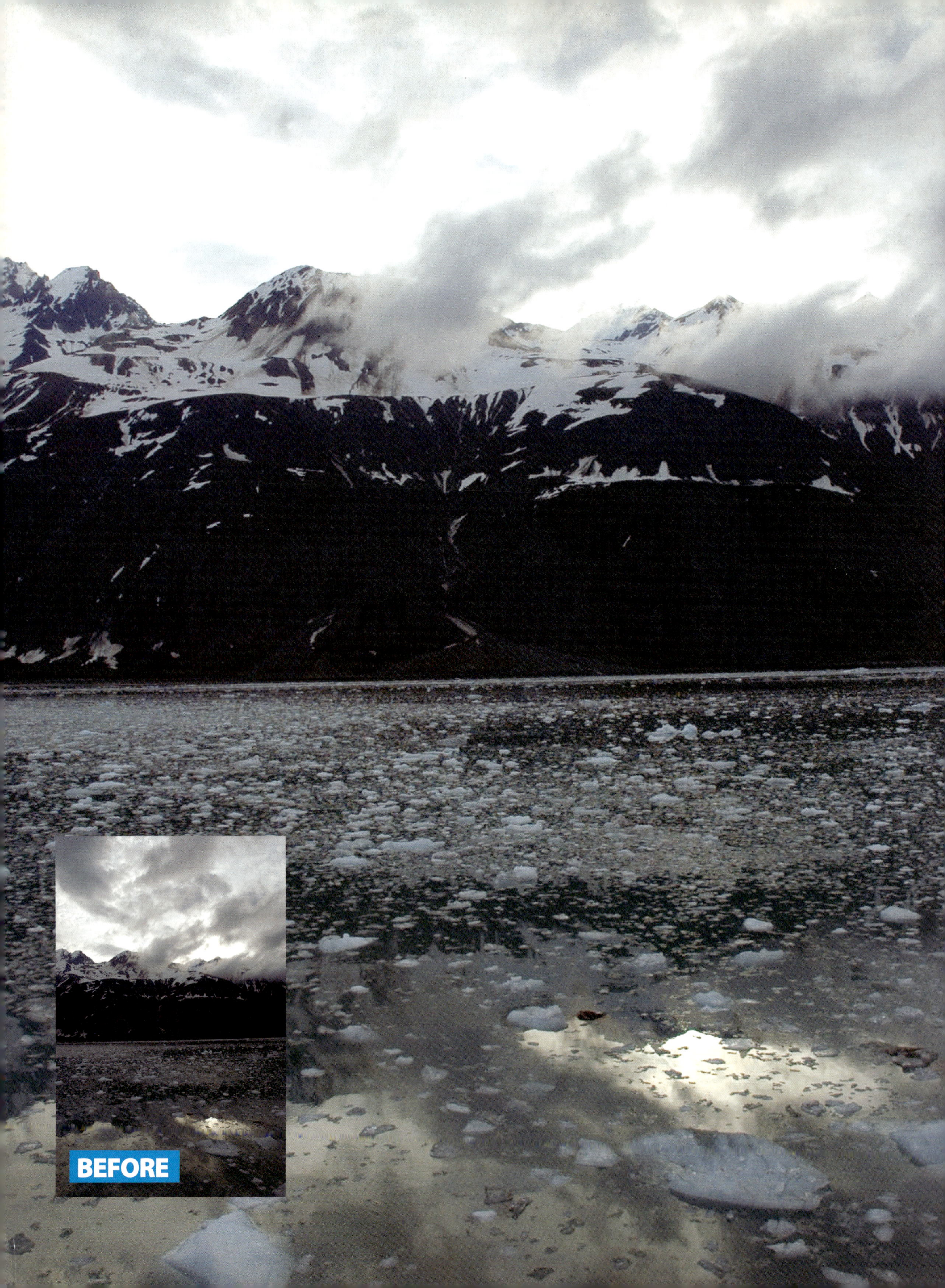
BEFORE

Fix images the Smart way

We take a look inside Photoshop Element's Smart Fix option for perfect pics

Photoshop Elements prides itself on making good images great with the minimum of effort. The Smart Fix control is definitely a tool that we promise you will be using time and again.

It is a simple command that can be found in both the Edit and Organizer interfaces. If you are already in the Edit window, then you can go to the Quick Edit interface, which we have already covered in more detail on page 50.

Right at the top is the Smart Fix slider, which can be moved to the right to set the level of 'fixing' needed. Try taking it one notch at a time until you are happy with the result as a little can make a huge difference to the tonal range of your photos. Of course you could just hit the Auto key and the program will analyse your image and decide what tonal and colour edits are needed. You can also find the Auto Smart Fix option by going to the Enhance menu in the top toolbar. And if you want to get your fingers in a twist, then you can use the Auto Smart Fix shortcut, which is Opt/Alt+Shift+M.

If you are in the Photoshop Elements Organizer section of the program, then you can use the Auto Smart Fix button in the right-hand panel when you select the Fix tab, so you don't have to even go into Elements to make quick changes.

> "The Smart Fix control is definitely a tool that we promise you will be using time and again"

SMART FIX OPTIONS

What it does

Smart Fix looks to help the tones, exposure and colours in your image in one step. It basically combines all the common automatic tools into one step.

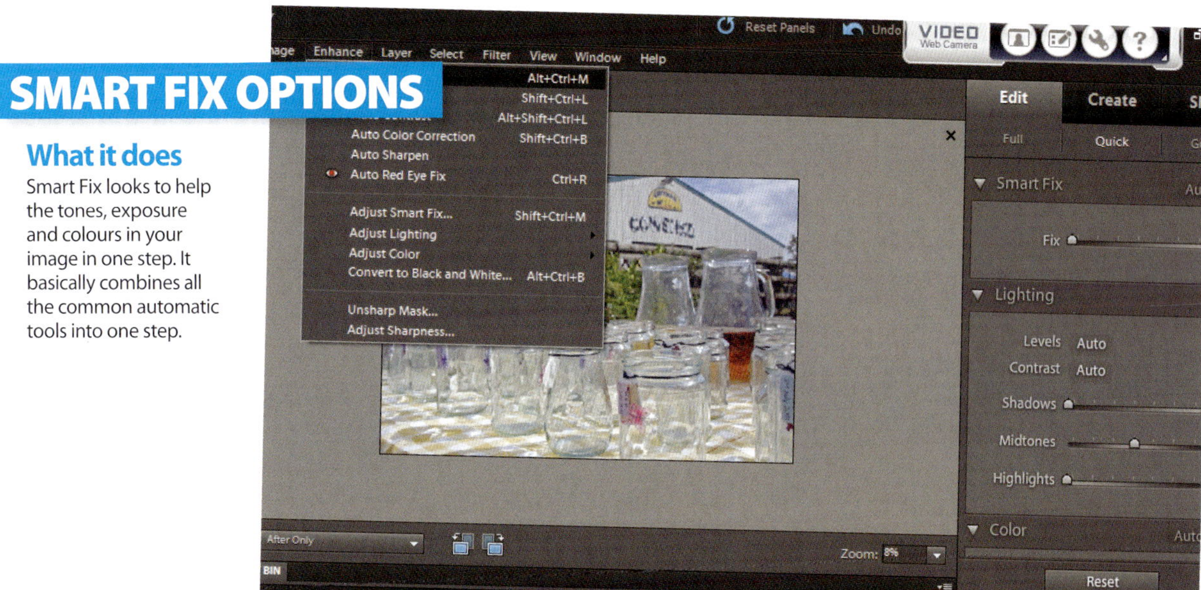

Smart Fix slider

This is the slider that controls your Smart Fix strength. You can do this one notch at a time to get the right result.

Menu options

Use this menu to access the Auto Smart Fix controls, or use the three-key shortcut that is denoted here.

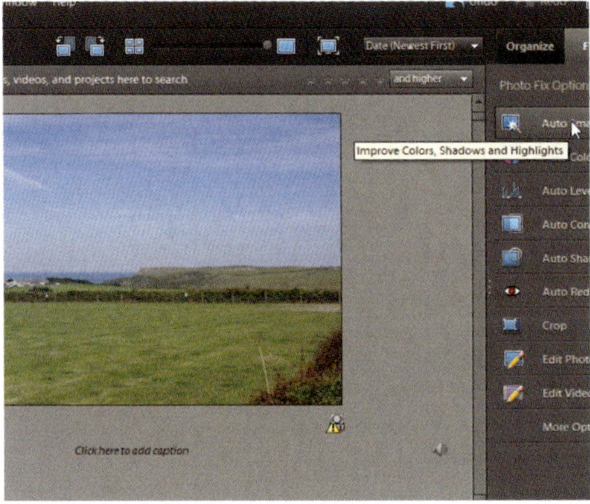

01 Auto Smart Fix

Directly from the interface within the Elements Organizer you can hit the Fix tab and then select the Auto Smart Fix from the menu here.

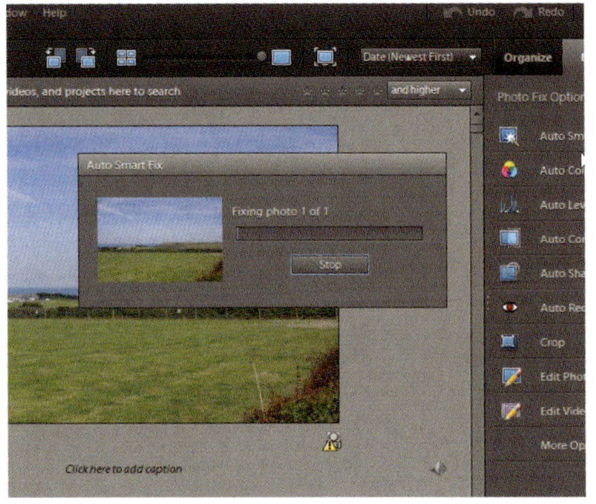

02 Photoshop does its bit

A dialog box will pop up to show you that Photoshop is thinking and analysing, which usually only takes a number of seconds.

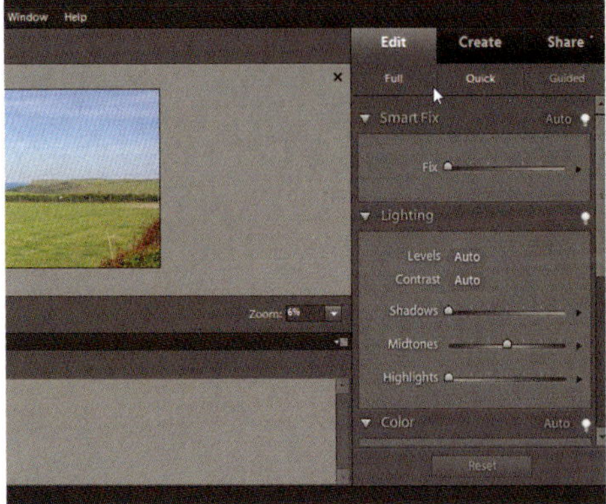

03 Control it

If you prefer to have a bit more control over the way that the image is fixed, then use the slider under Smart Fix in the Quick option.

Colour & tone

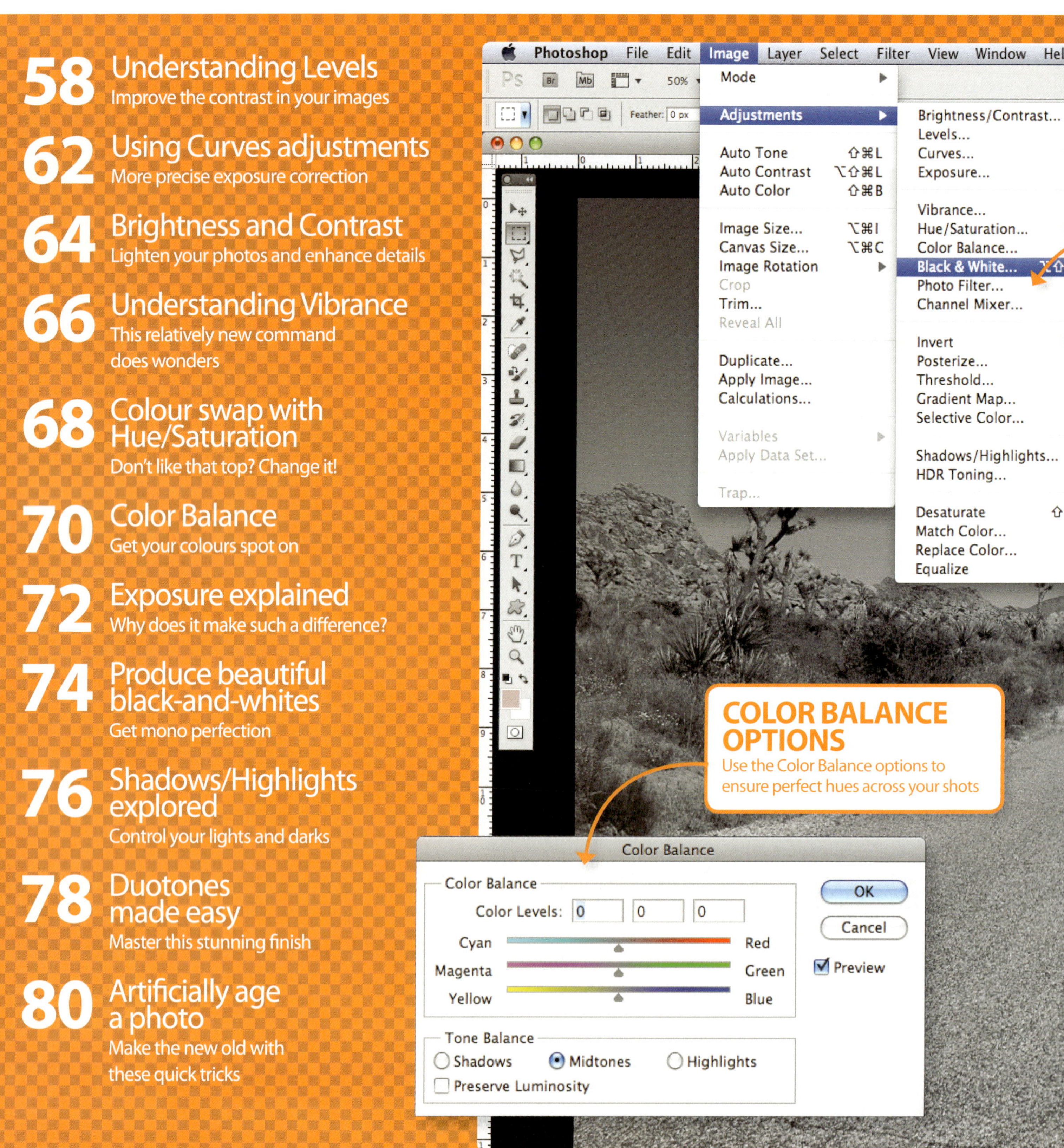

COLOR BALANCE OPTIONS
Use the Color Balance options to ensure perfect hues across your shots

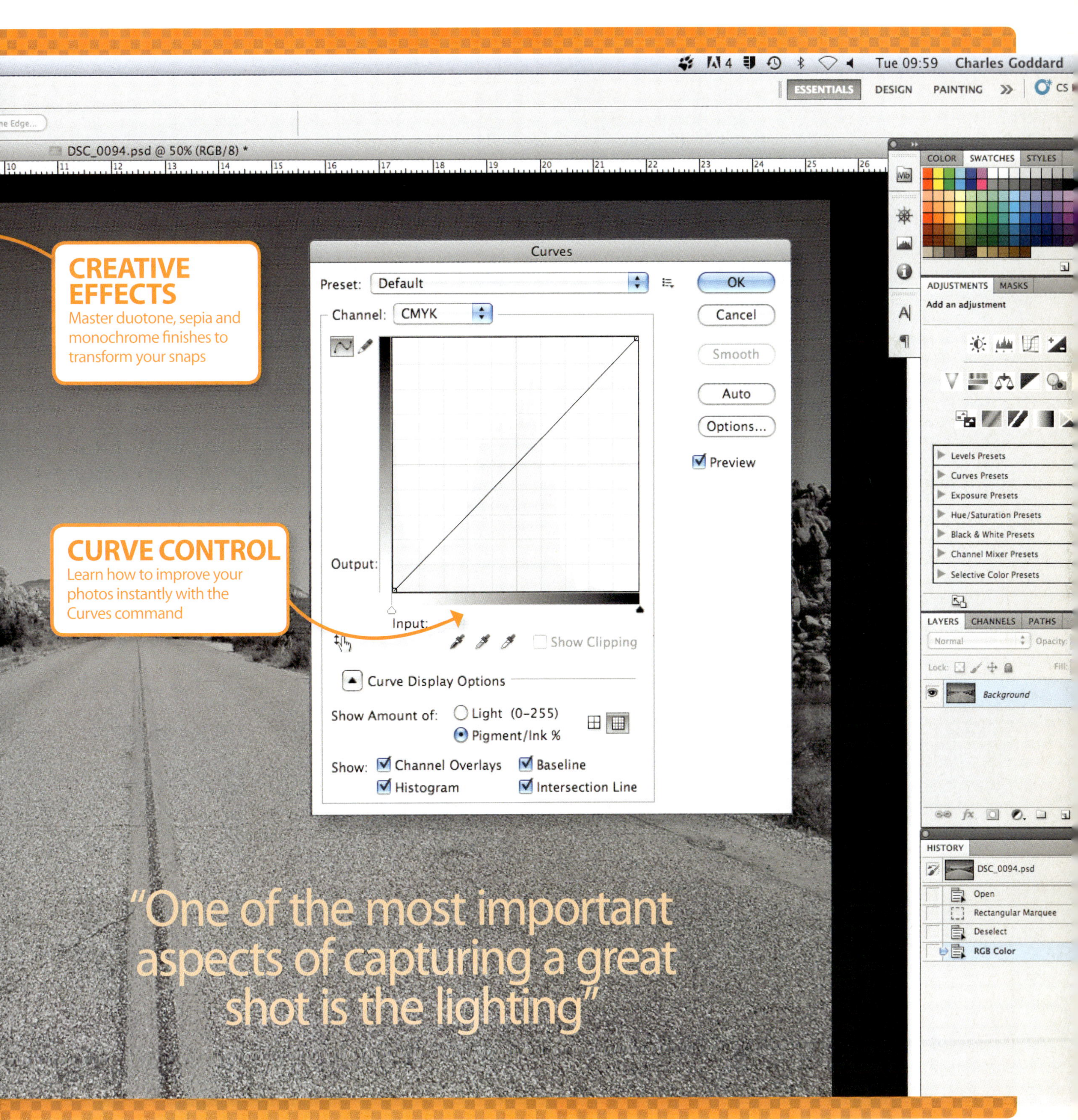
CREATIVE EFFECTS
Master duotone, sepia and monochrome finishes to transform your snaps
CURVE CONTROL
Learn how to improve your photos instantly with the Curves command
"One of the most important aspects of capturing a great shot is the lighting"
Curves
Preset: Default
Channel: CMYK
OK
Cancel
Smooth
Auto
Options...
Preview
Output:
Input:
Show Clipping
Curve Display Options
Show Amount of: Light (0-255)
Pigment/Ink %
Show: Channel Overlays
Baseline
Histogram
Intersection Line
Tue 09:59 Charles Goddard
ESSENTIALS
DESIGN
PAINTING
DSC_0094.psd @ 50% (RGB/8) *
COLOR SWATCHES STYLES
ADJUSTMENTS MASKS
Add an adjustment
Levels Presets
Curves Presets
Exposure Presets
Hue/Saturation Presets
Black & White Presets
Channel Mixer Presets
Selective Color Presets
LAYERS CHANNELS PATHS
Background
HISTORY
DSC_0094.psd
Open
Rectangular Marquee
Deselect
RGB Color

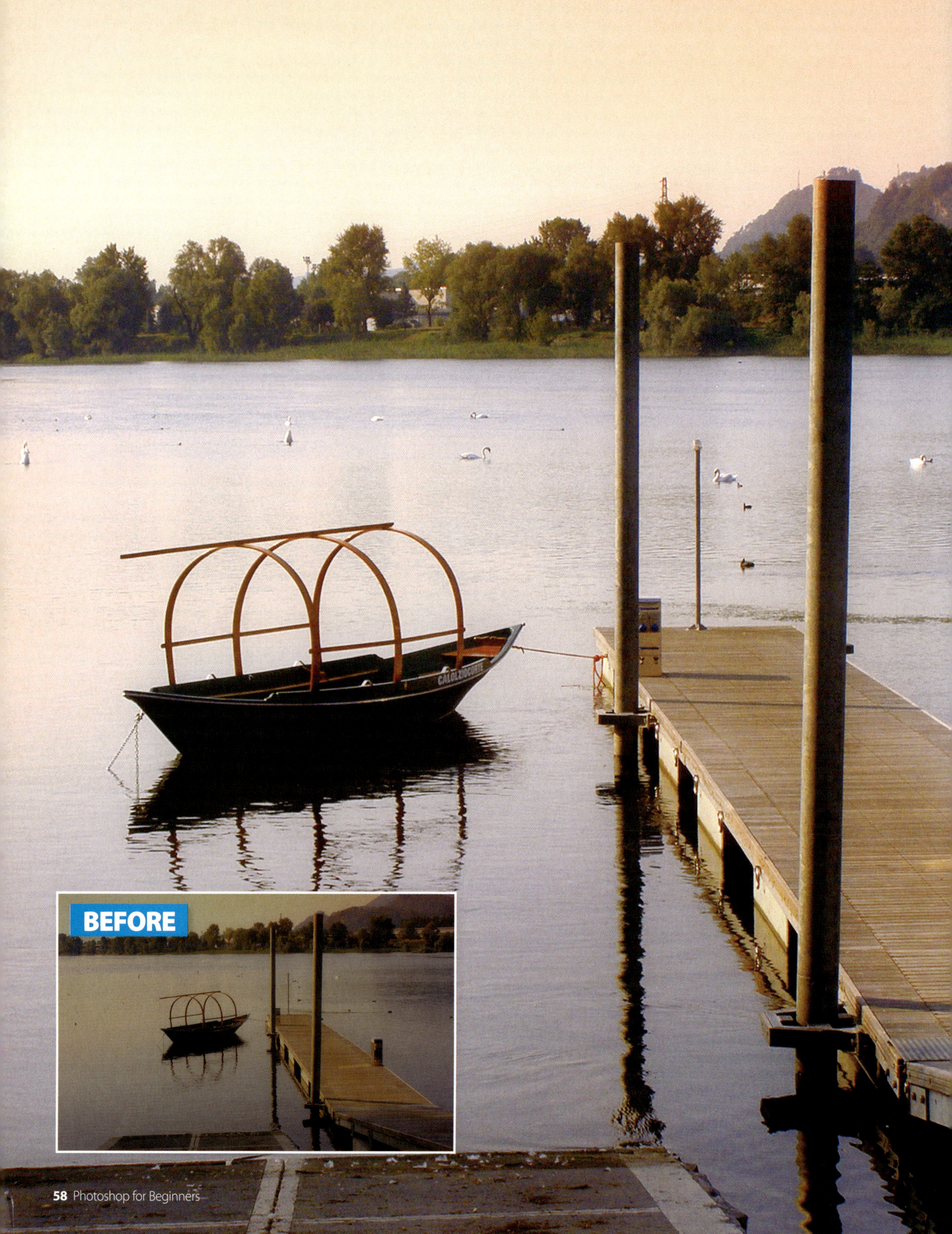
BEFORE

Understanding Levels

Learn to use Photoshop's most popular tool for working with light in a photograph

Any photographer will tell you that one of the most important aspects of capturing a great shot is the lighting. If the shot is accidentally under or overexposed, or if the white balance is off, even a well-composed shot can lose its appeal. Such shots generally are discarded – it's not as if you can go back and change the amount of light in a scene, is it?

Well, actually, in Photoshop, we can go a long way towards doing just that. There are several tools available to fix lighting issues, and Levels is a favourite. While Curves may be more powerful and Brightness/Contrast may be more user friendly, Levels offers the best mix of effectiveness and ease of use.

Let's begin by defining its name. Photoshop interprets images by breaking them down into colour channels and measuring how many pixels of each degree of brightness there are in that channel. When the colour channels are combined together, the measurement is referred to as 'luminous levels'. In a regular 8-bit image (that's the default for most images) there are 256 degrees of brightness, or levels of luminosity. That range goes from solid black, which means no brightness in each colour channel, to solid white, which is full brightness in every colour channel. Essentially, Photoshop looks at an image and immediately tracks how many pixels belong in each brightness slot. So the Levels command primarily enables you to adjust the end and midpoints of the luminous scale, and Photoshop remaps the remaining pixels accordingly.

> "Levels offers the best mix of effectiveness and ease of use"

THE LEVELS DIALOG

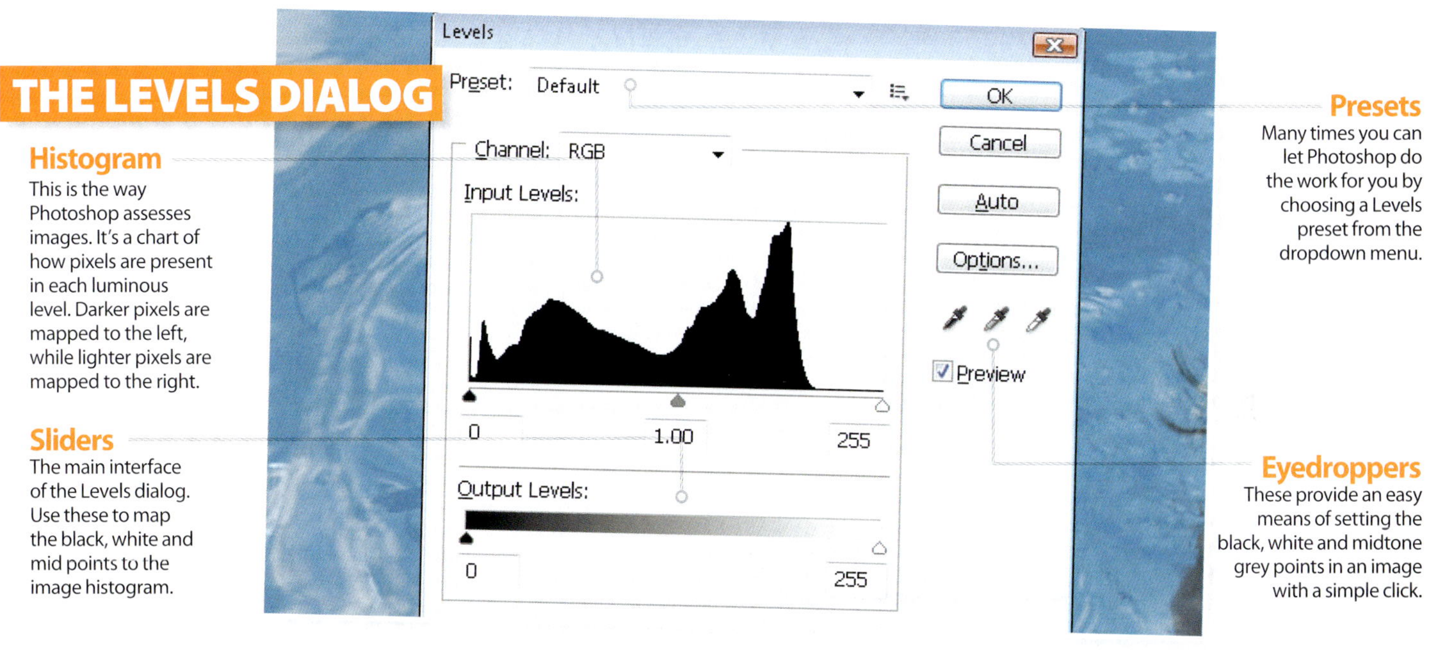

Histogram
This is the way Photoshop assesses images. It's a chart of how pixels are present in each luminous level. Darker pixels are mapped to the left, while lighter pixels are mapped to the right.

Sliders
The main interface of the Levels dialog. Use these to map the black, white and mid points to the image histogram.

Presets
Many times you can let Photoshop do the work for you by choosing a Levels preset from the dropdown menu.

Eyedroppers
These provide an easy means of setting the black, white and midtone grey points in an image with a simple click.

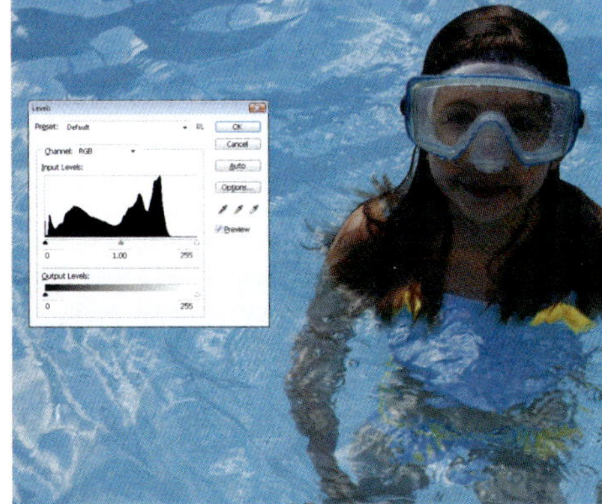

01 Histogram help
This image is clearly too dark. The histogram in the Levels window indicates this as there are almost no pixels to the far right, the light area of the graph.

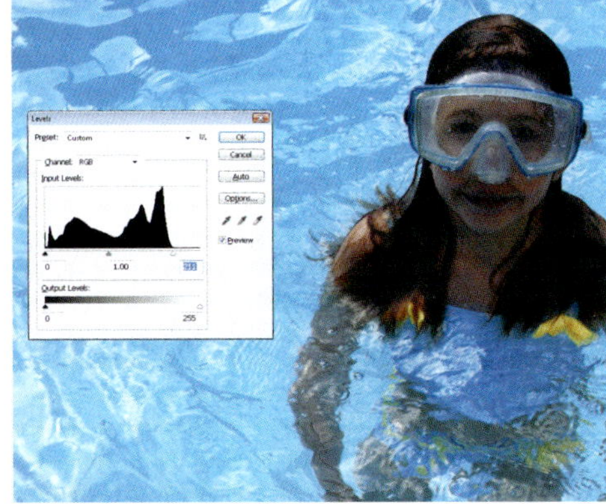

02 Easy lightening
By sliding the white handle left, the image instantly lightens to correct the poor exposure. Line up the handle with the right edge of the graph's curve.

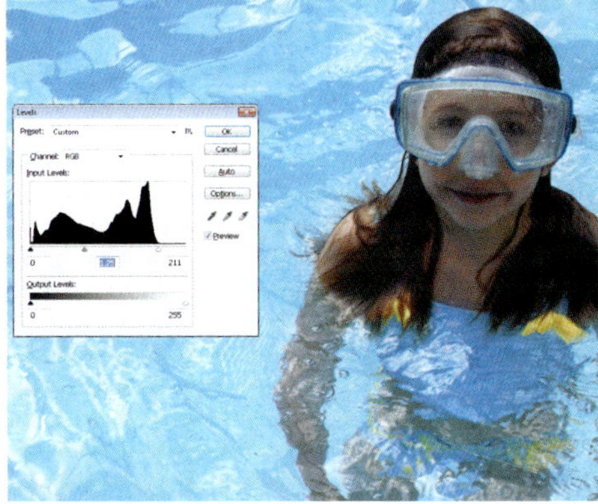

03 Midtone magic
The midtones are still too dark. Fix this by sliding the central grey handle to the left slightly. These handles are the easiest way to tweak exposure.

Level up Use Levels to correct several issues in a single image

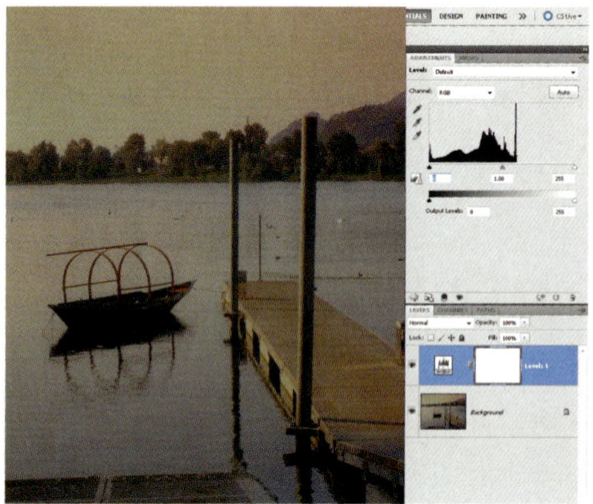

01 A different approach
Open the image 'LakeatDusk.jpg'. Usually Levels will be accessed via Cmd/Ctrl+L, but this time we'll go to Layer>New Adjustment Layer>Levels.

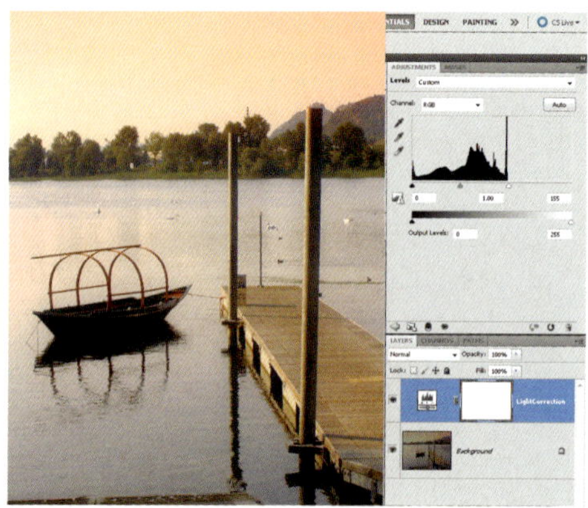

02 Lighting control
Double-click the layer to rename it 'Light Correction.' Then, in the Adjustment panel, grab the white slider handle and drag to meet the left edge of the graph.

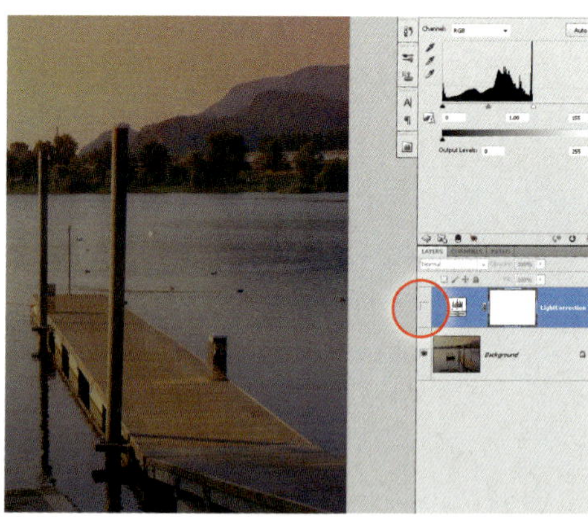

03 Before and after
To the left of the adjustment layer's thumbnail there is a small icon of an eye. Click this to hide the adjustment layer, then click again to reveal it.

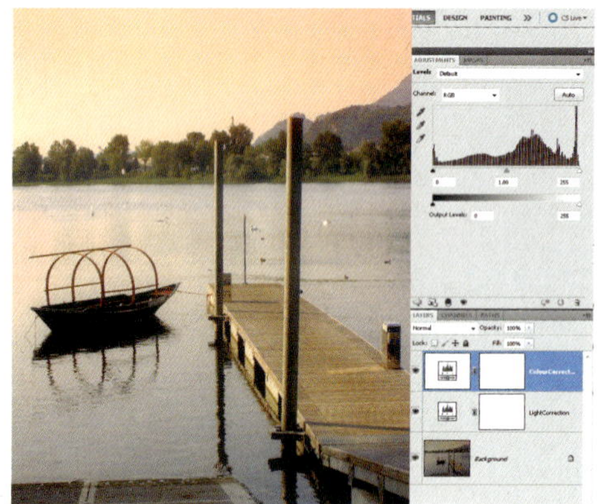

04 Stackable layers
Another advantage of this technique is the ability to stack effects. Add another Levels layer, as we did before. Rename this one 'Colour Correction'.

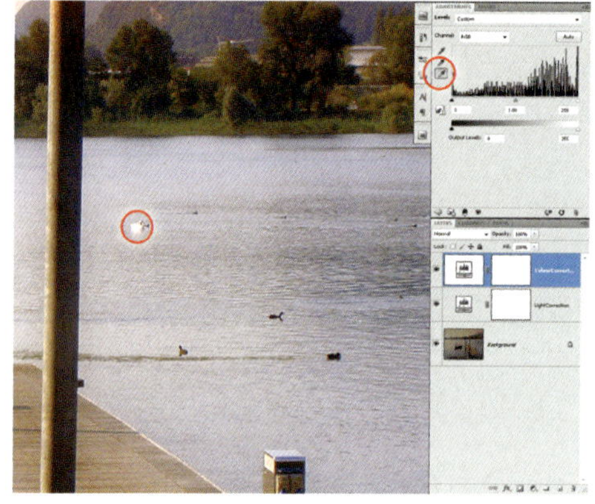

05 White balance
Click on the white eyedropper in the Adjustment panel, then set the white point by clicking on the swan in the scene. The orange tint should vanish!

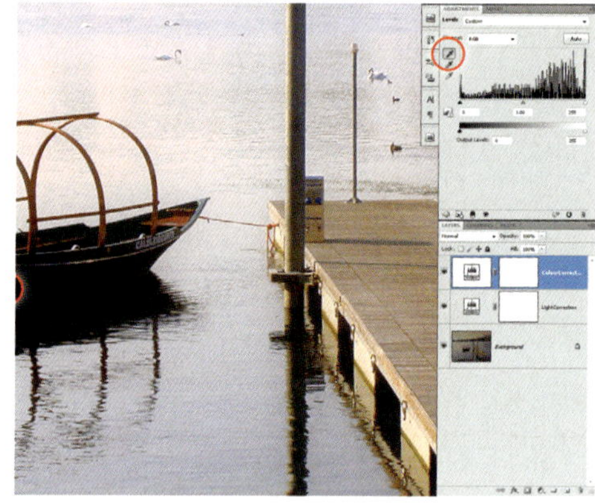

06 Black balance
Now click on the black eyedropper icon and set the black point by sampling the shady area under the boat. The colour shift will be slight at this stage.

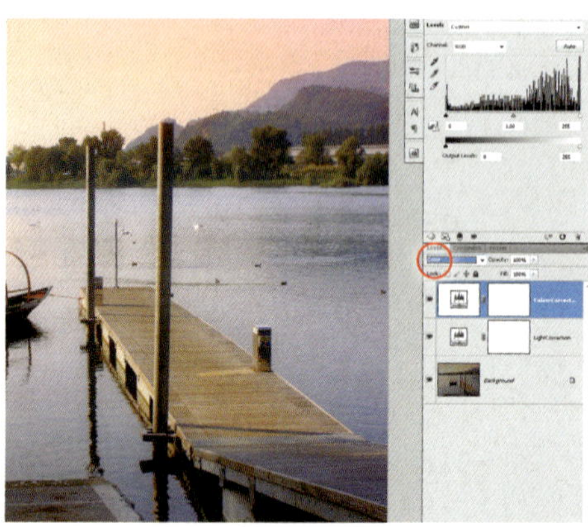

07 The perfect blend
A big bonus of adjustment layers is blending modes, available in the Layers palette. Change the Colour Correction layer's blend mode to Color.

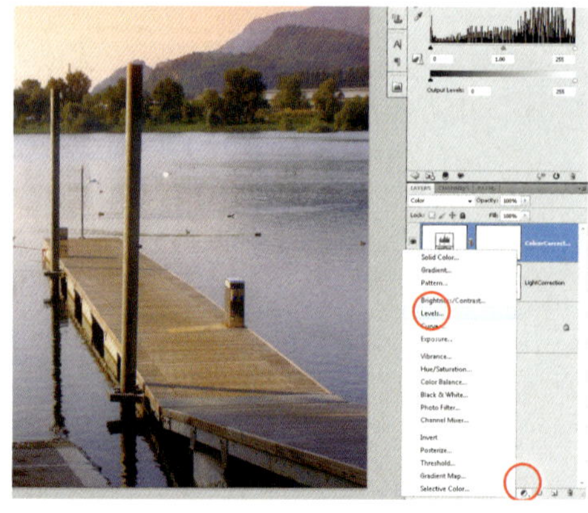

08 Shadow work
At the base of the Layers panel, click on the half-filled circle icon to add a third Levels adjustment layer. Rename this one 'Shadow Lighten'.

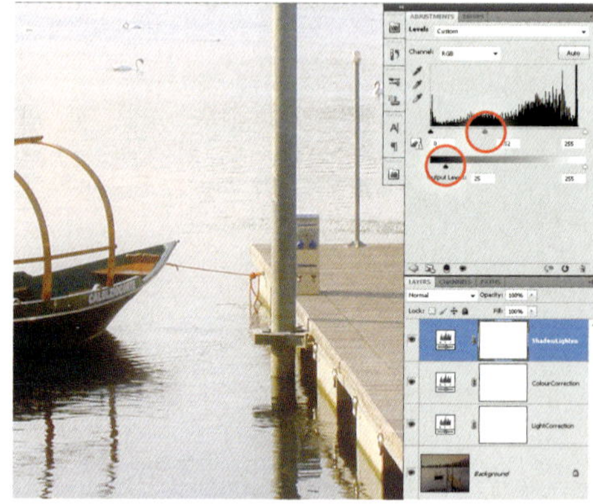

09 Brighten up
Nudge the central handle under the histogram left to brighten the midtones. Now move the dark handle on the Output Level bar to the right slightly.

QUICK PHOTOSHOP TIPS

Colour histograms

If histograms are your thing, you will love the option to see them broken down by colour. Go to Window>Histogram and use the flyout menu to the upper right to select the All Channels View.

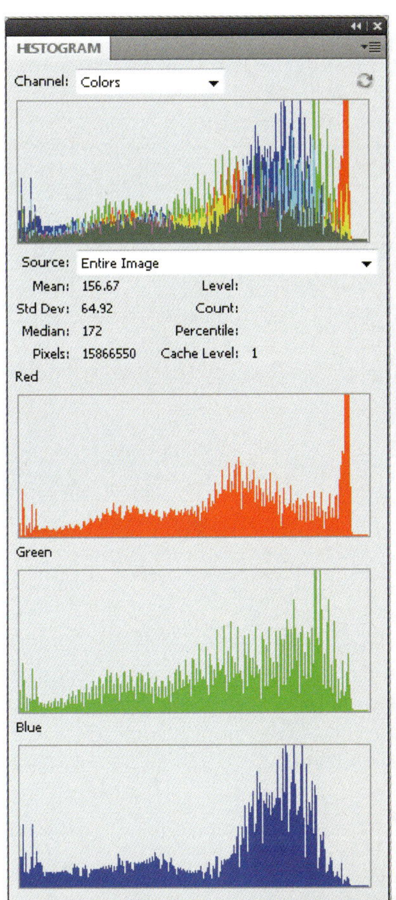

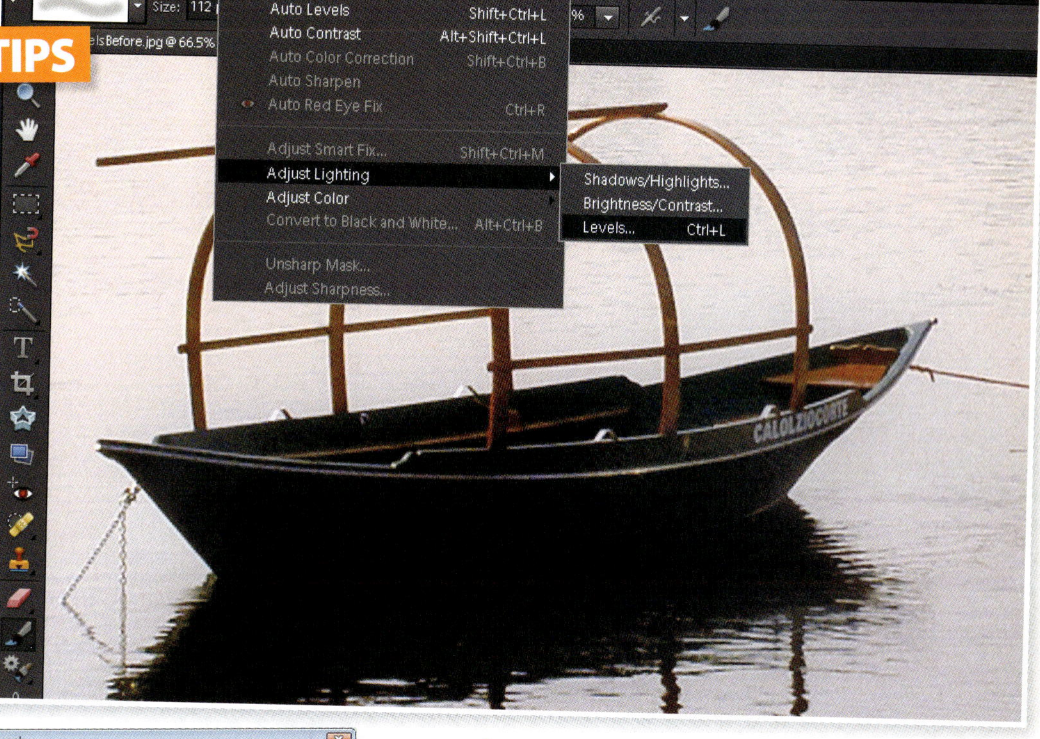

Getting there

In Photoshop proper, the Levels command is found under Image>Adjustments. In Photoshop Elements it is found under Enhance>Adjust Lighting. For both programs, the shortcut is Cmd/Ctrl+L.

Fine colour control

In the Levels dialog the Default operation is for the composite channel, but you can have the same control over levels in the individual colour channels by choosing them from the dropdown menu.

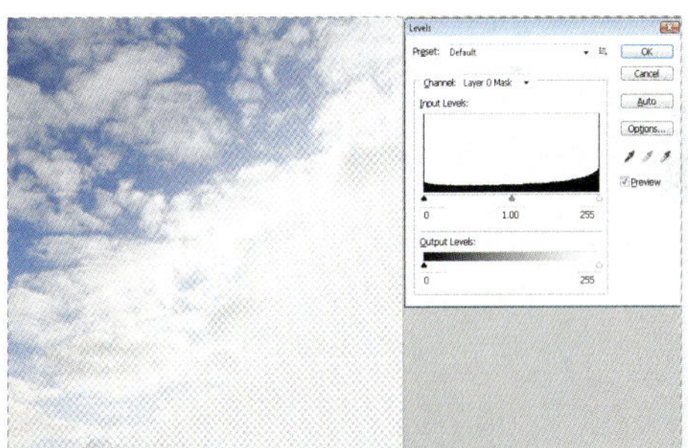

Level mask

Targeting a layer mask and running the Levels operation on it can give you even finer control over transitions in the mask. This is particularly helpful for masks which have gradients.

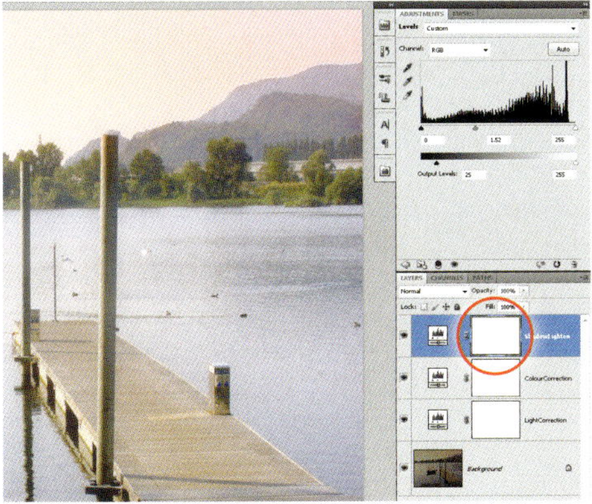

10 Use the mask

Click on the white icon next to the layer thumbnail; this is the mask thumbnail. Whatever you do next will be done to the layer mask, not the layer itself.

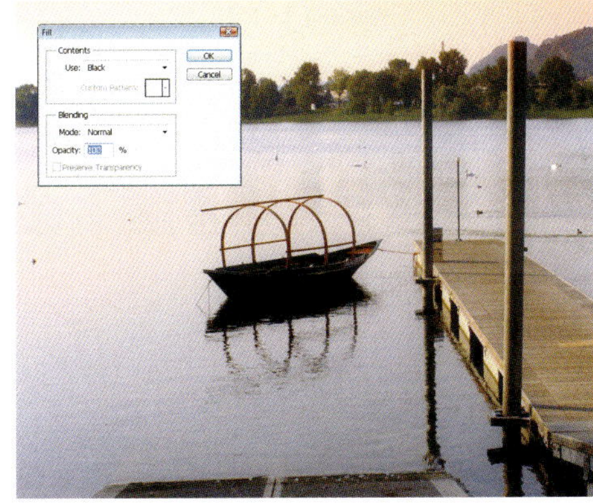

11 Black out

Go to Edit>Fill and, in the dialog, select Black from the Contents menu and click OK. This fills the mask with black and hides the Levels effect on this layer.

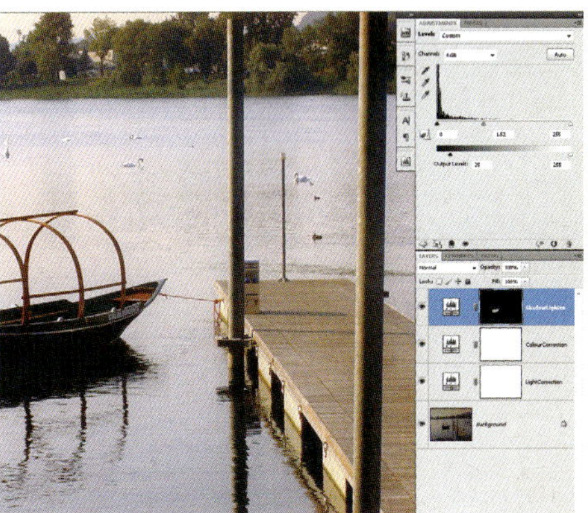

12 Paint with light

Grab the Brush tool, set the colour to white, and reduce Opacity in the tool Options bar to 20%. Gently paint in subtle accents to the boat's shadow.

Using Curves adjustments

Learn to use the most powerful luminosity control feature that Photoshop has to offer

Chances are you may have taken one look at the intimidating Curves interface with the mysterious graphs and charts and quickly closed it before running back to the comfortable sliders of Brightness/ Contrast. But when it comes to power and control of the luminous, or brightness, levels of an image in Photoshop, Curves is king! Curves can not only accomplish the same things as other features, but it also offers many additional capabilities. The tradeoff is the interface takes a little more effort to understand.

The first thing to notice is the familiar histogram behind the curves window. This is a chart of the luminous values of the image's pixels. The dark, or shadow, pixels are on the left while the light, or highlight, pixels are on the right.

Curves draws a line, or curve (hence the name), over this chart and, by setting points along the curve, you remap that luminous level to the new point on the curve. If that sounds really confusing and technical, that's because it is. To try to put it simply, you can lighten the shadows by moving points on the left upwards. Darken the highlights by pushing points on the right downwards. Adjust midtones by moving the middle of the graph up or down.

Curves in Photoshop Elements works slightly differently. In Elements the feature is found in Enhance>Adjust Color>Adjust Color Curves. The dialog presents you with four sliders: Highlights, Midtone Brightness, Midtone Contrast and Shadows; these control corresponding points on the curve.

"When it comes to controlling brightness levels, Curves is king!"

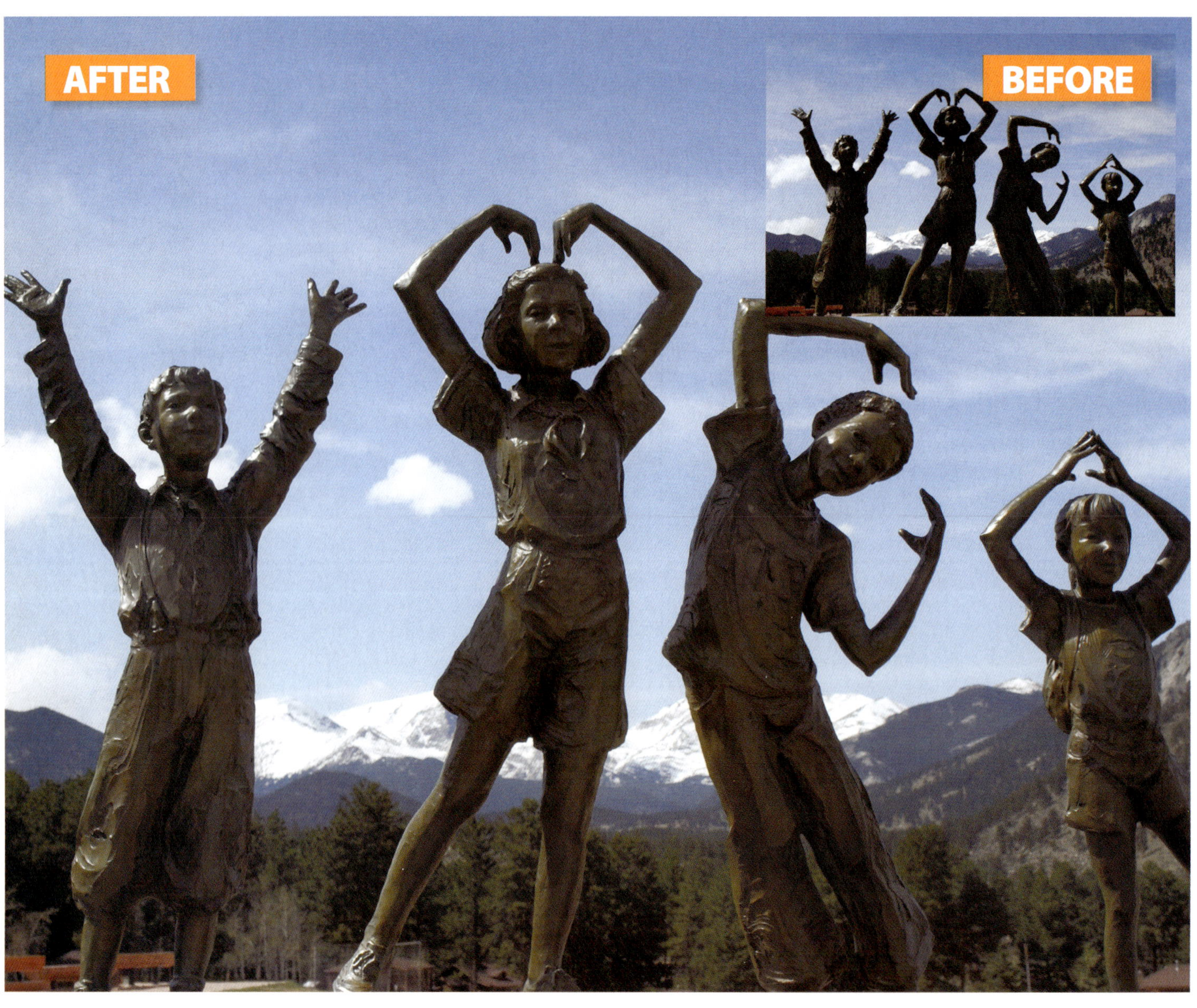

Complete curve control Harness the power of this remarkable tool

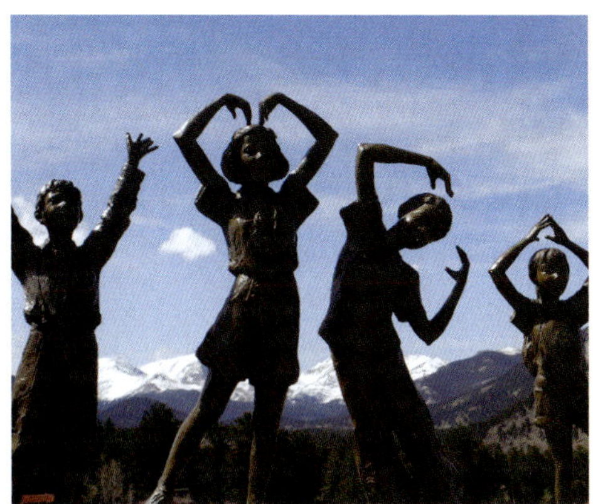

01 Open the image

Let's begin with an image where the subject is too dark. Open 'ymca.jpg' provided to follow along as we correct the lighting issues using Curves.

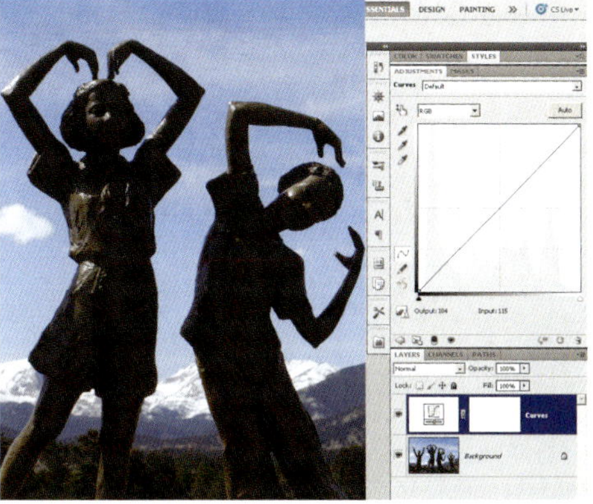

02 Accessing Curves

Go to Layer>New Adjustment Layer>Curves. Once named, it will pop up in the Layers panel and the Curves dialog will appear in the Adjustment panel.

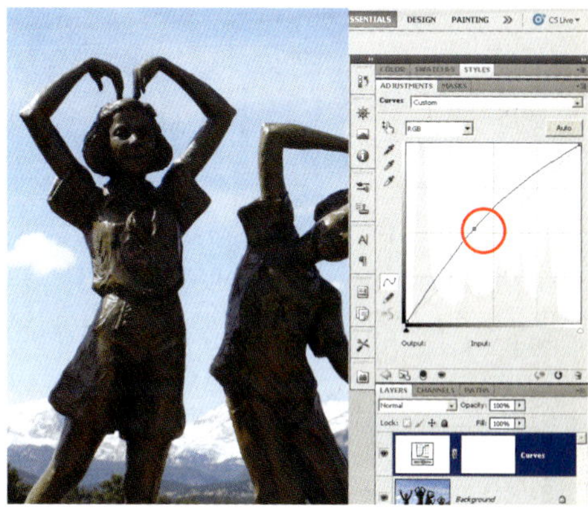

03 Make your point

In the dialog, click in the centre of the graph to add a point to the curve. Then drag that point up and to the left to see the image begin to lighten.

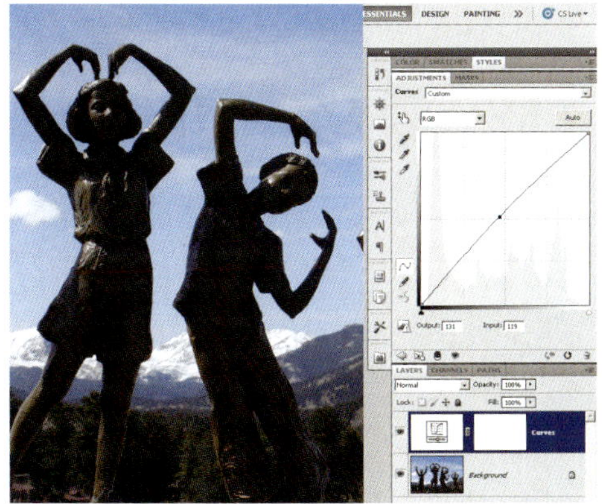

04 Fine adjustment

With the new point still active, use the arrow keys on your keyboard to nudge the point. This method provides finer control than using the mouse.

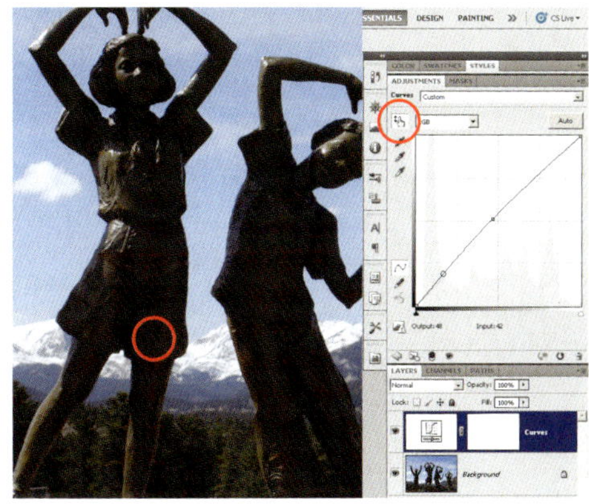

05 Targeted Adjustment tool

At the top of the Curves panel is a pointing finger icon; this is the Targeted Adjustment tool. Click it and roll over the image and watch the window.

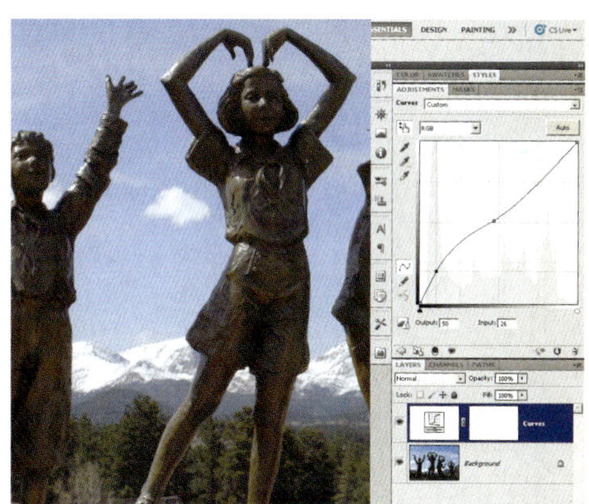

06 Bang on target

In a dark area of the statue, click and drag upwards slightly. The area you clicked on should get lighter, without impacting the other luminous areas.

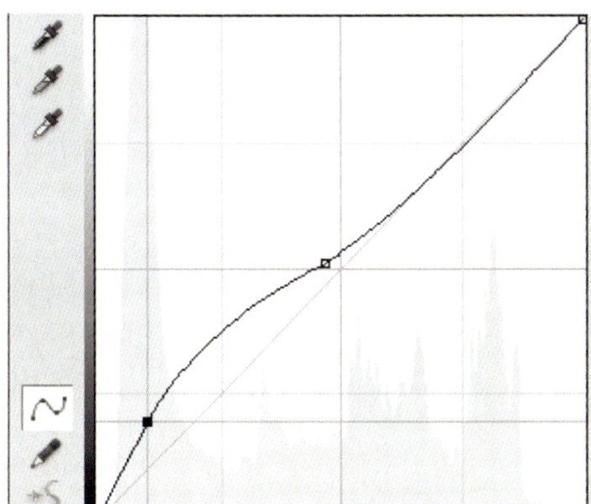

07 Watch the curves

When you used Targeted Adjustment, Photoshop added a point and modified it accordingly. This is a much easier option than doing it by eye.

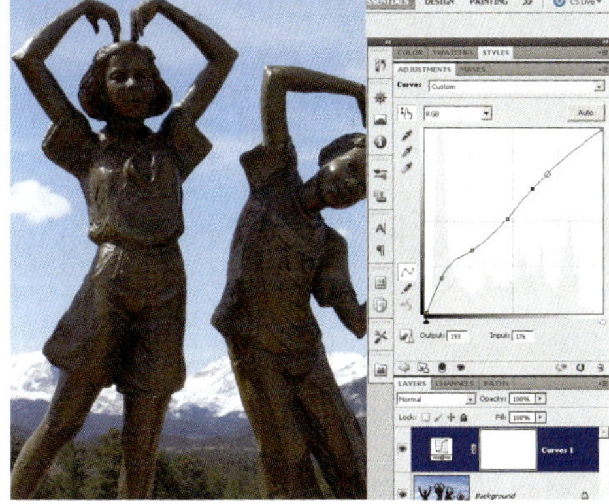

08 Keep going!

Use the same process to add more points to the curve to enhance the midtone shading. If you need to remove a point, grab it and drag it off the curve.

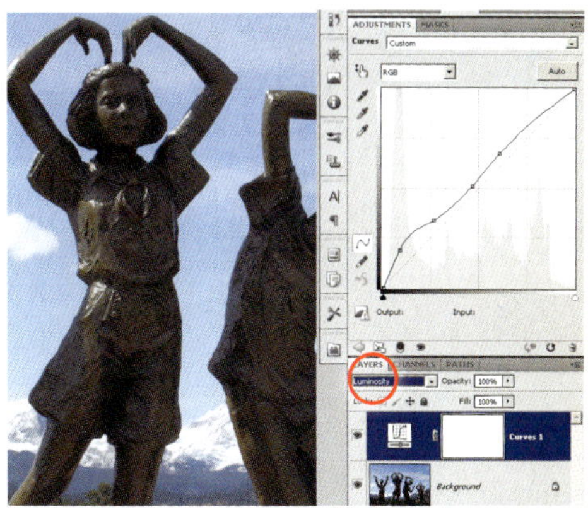

09 Happy bl-ending

Sometimes the Curves adjustment can introduce unwanted colour shifts. To prevent this, set the adjustment layer's blending mode to Luminosity.

Brightness and Contrast

This quick 'no-fuss' option is a surprisingly capable feature for exposure corrections and very easy to get to grips with

This adjustment feature is one of the oldest and most intuitive available for altering the lighting of a photograph in Photoshop. While Curves and Levels have an interface that includes a graph to explore and learn, Brightness/Contrast has just two sliders: rather predictably, the Brightness slider and the Contrast slider. And they do exactly what you would expect them to do.

Brightness lightens or darkens an image and Contrast enhances or removes conflicting tones. The Brightness slider is much the same as the middle slider handle in the Levels control (see pages 58-61) that adjusts the gamma of the midtones. In the same vein, the Contrast slider is similar to tweaking the two outer handles in Levels at the same time.

One of the dangers of this tool is the unwanted side effect of clipping the shadows and highlights. This means that dark pixels are turned completely black and pixels that are close to the white limit are turned completely white. This destroys details and is generally considered bad form.

Previous versions of Photoshop (ie pre-CS3) included a Brightness/Contrast adjustment that would easily clip the highlights and shadows. Now the feature is reworked to avoid this, but it can still happen if you're not careful. This is one of the rare tools that operates exactly the same in Photoshop as it does in its sibling Photoshop Elements. The Use Legacy option is missing in Elements, but other than that the tools are identical.

> "While Curves and Levels have… a graph to explore, Brightness/Contrast has just two sliders"

QUICK PHOTOSHOP TIPS

Simple sliders

Complete control with just two straightforward sliders. One for brightness, one for contrast. It really doesn't get much easier than that.

Brightness: 32

Contrast: -37

Use Legacy, or not

Prior to Photoshop CS3 the Brightness/Contrast controls would harshly clip highlights and shadows without care. To revert to this behaviour for effect, simply check the Use Legacy box.

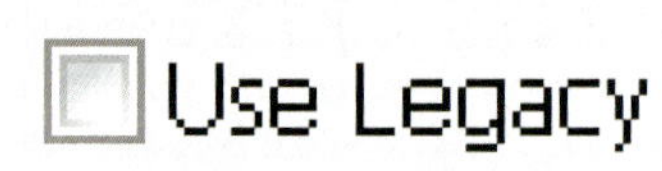

Shadow details

Look closely! The Brightness/Contrast adjustment has revealed details in shadow areas that were nearly imperceptible before it was applied.

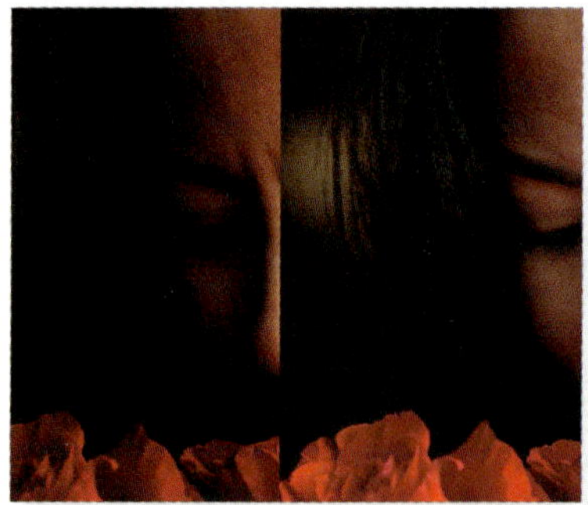

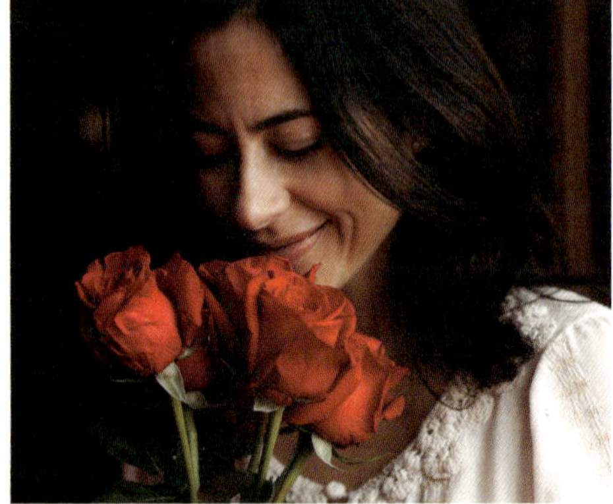

01 Photoshop proper

Launch Photoshop and open the 'Roses.jpg' file provided. The shot feels a bit dark and can use some work to pull details out of the shadows.

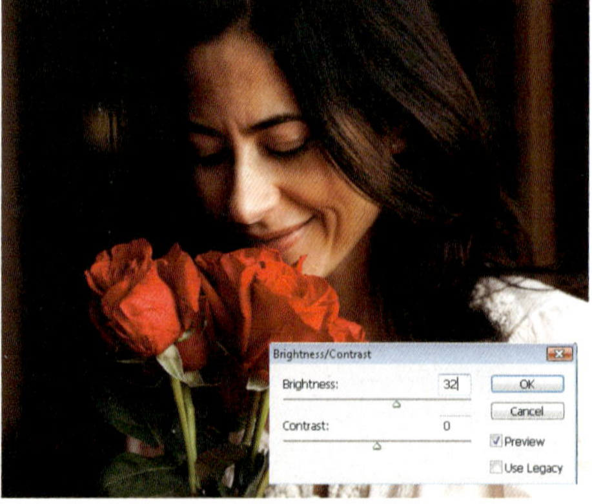

02 Adjust Brightness

In Image>Adjustments>Brightness/Contrast, uncheck the Use Legacy box. Up the Brightness to just before the highlights start to clip; we used 32.

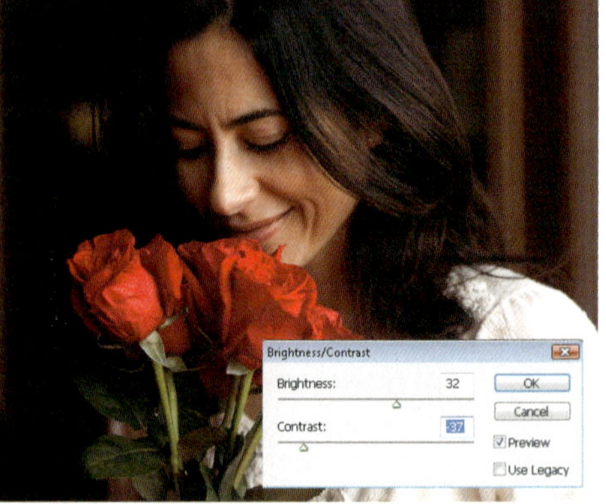

03 Adjust Contrast

Next reduce the Contrast to even out the midtones; we used -37. Toggle the Preview box to see how much the image changed. Then hit OK.

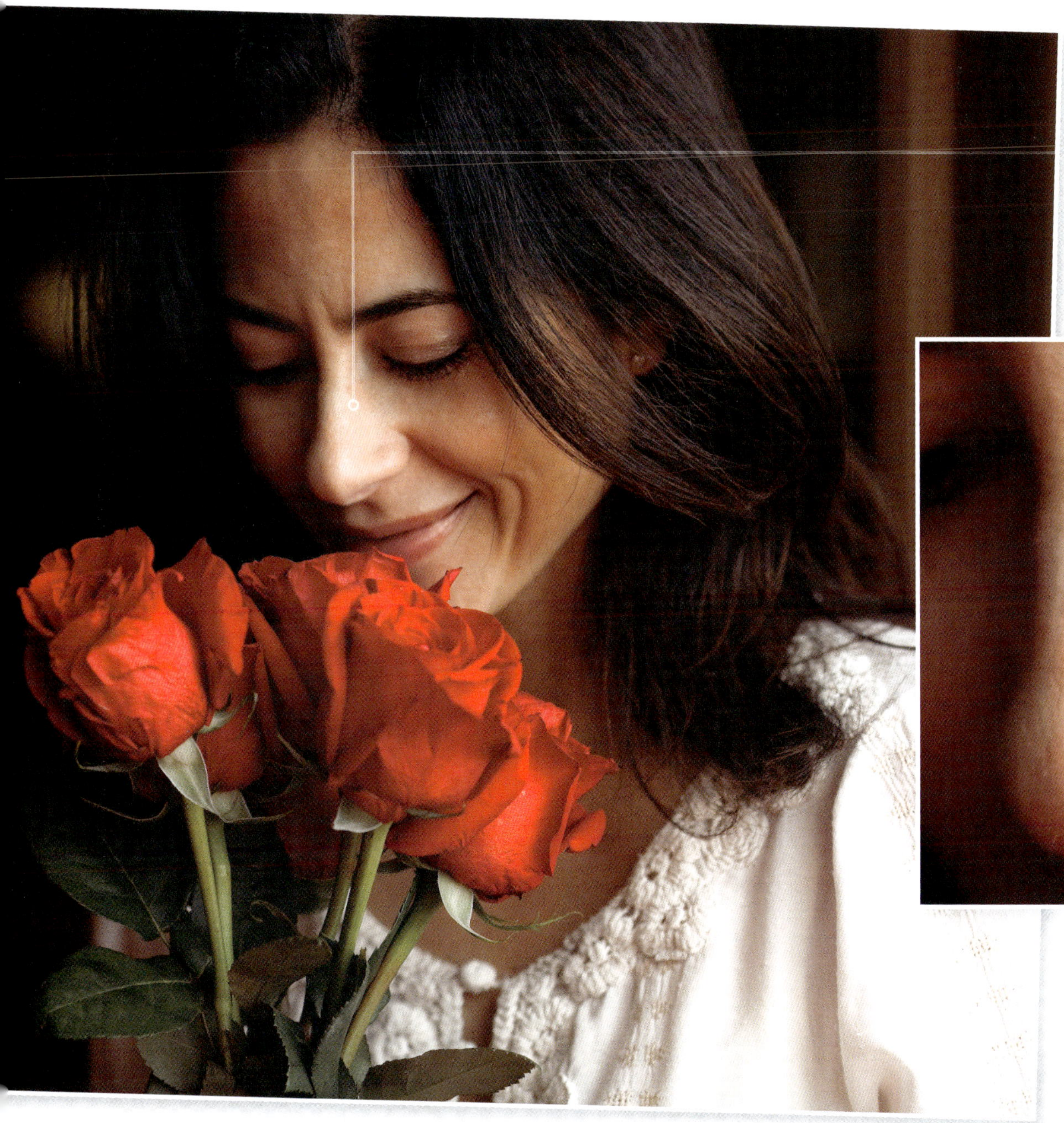

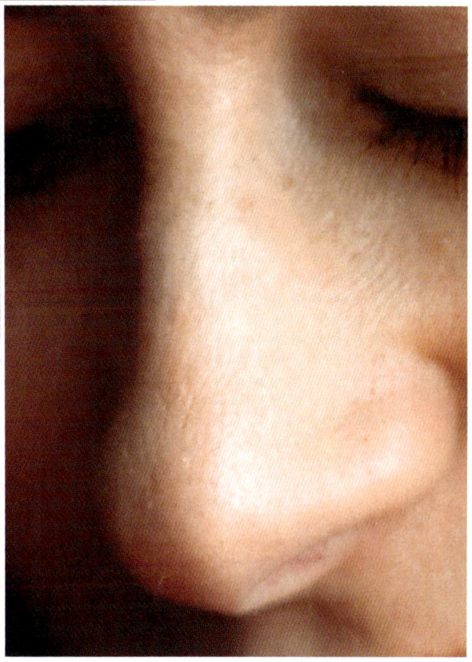

Beware of clipping

Watch the highlights carefully as you brighten the image. You want to avoid any clipping of the light areas, especially near a focal point.

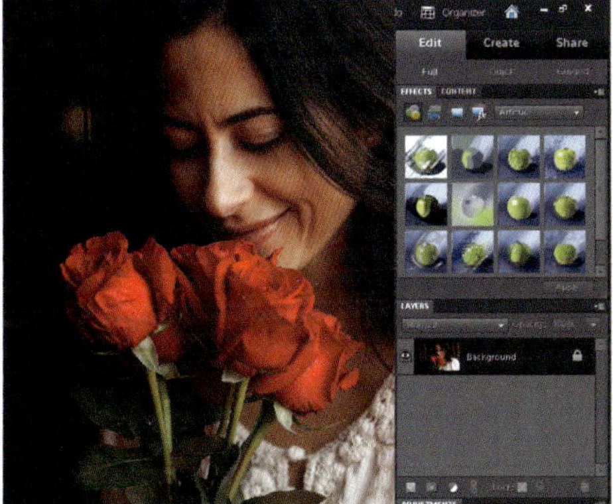

04 Photoshop Elements

Now let's try it in Photoshop Elements. Launch the app and open 'Roses.jpg' as before. The Elements interface makes the photo look even darker!

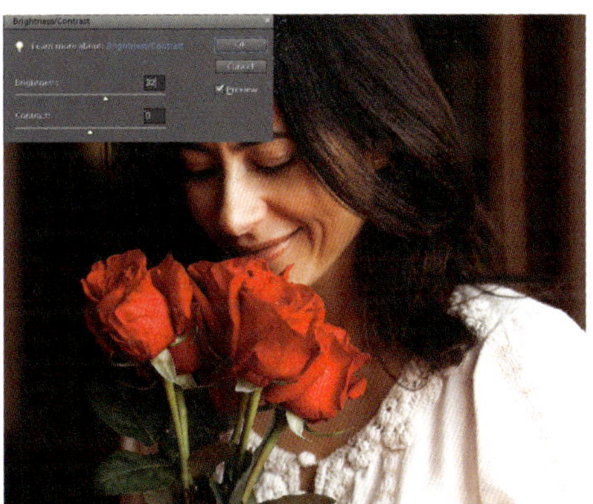

05 New program, same sliders

Go to Enhance>Adjust Lighting>Brightness/Contrast. A very familiar palette appears. Set the Brightness to 32, keeping an eye on highlights.

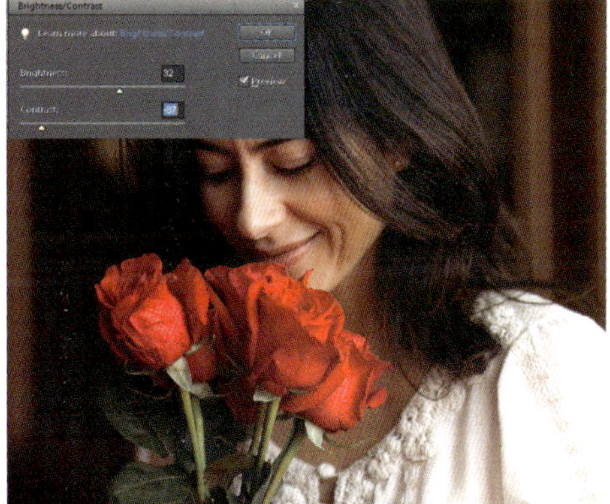

06 Compare and contrast

Pull the Contrast slider to around -37. Check the before and after via the Preview box. If you are satisfied with the adjustment, press OK.

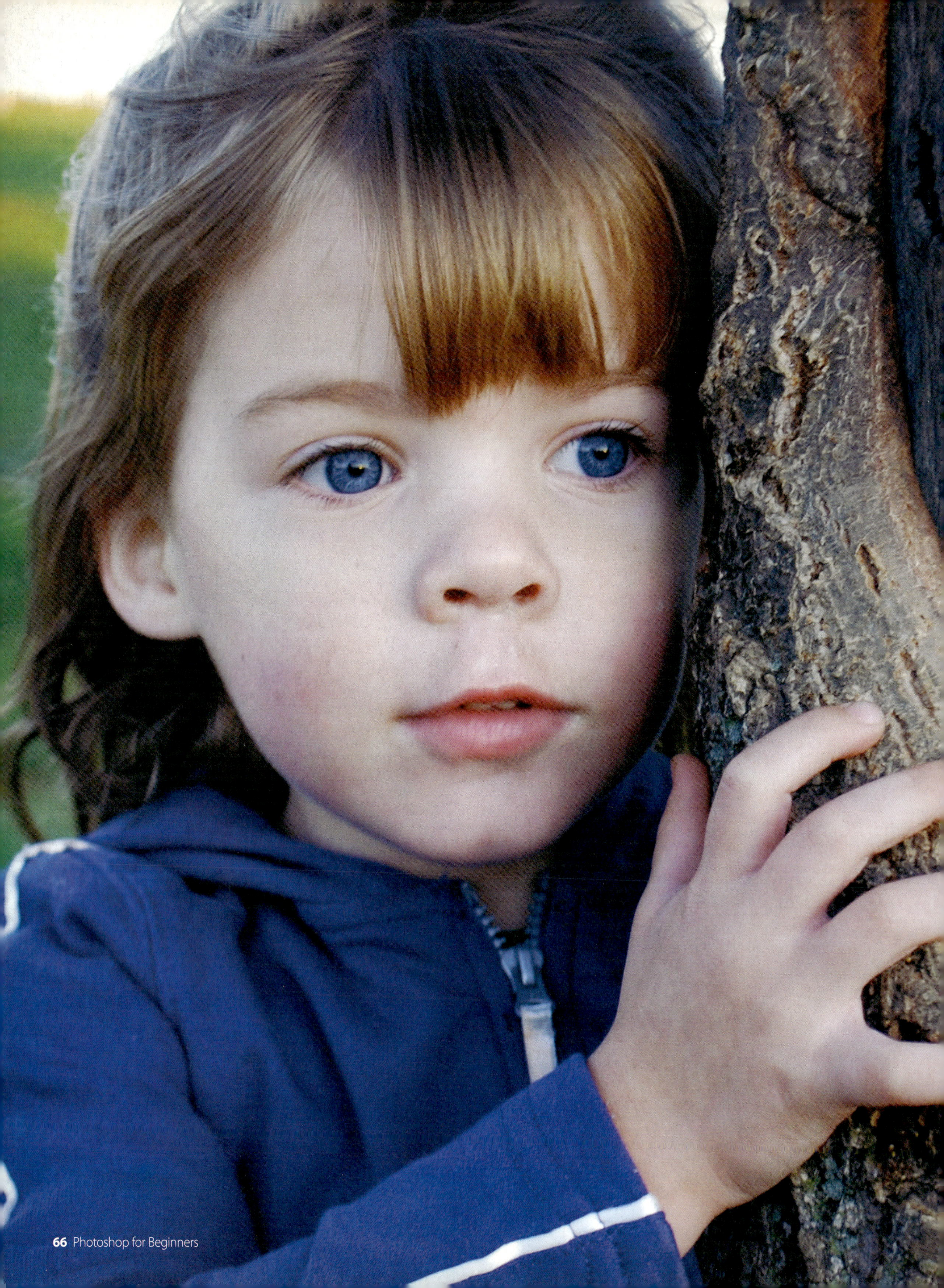

Understanding Vibrance

Give your images life with Vibrance. It's like Saturation but with a safety net

A common problem in many photos is the lack of bright, brilliant colours. Even a well-composed and carefully lit photo can be improved by a touch of colour treatment. For years, the method of choice to accomplish this in Photoshop was to adjust the saturation. While effective, this approach is frequently heavy handed. It has a tendency to oversaturate colours that were already well saturated and not boost the poorly saturated tones far enough. This can lead to frustration as you attempt to add richness to a low-saturated area and watch as the more saturated areas get blown out instead. Skin tones can be particularly troublesome using this technique.

The Vibrance adjustment was created to change the way colours are treated. It includes the familiar Saturation slider, which will still do the grunt work of infusing saturation into an image. But the Vibrance slider now is used to add saturation to those hard-to-reach areas without oversaturating the others. It also has a built-in safeguard to protect skin tones from turning overly yellow or red. The general process for using Vibrance is to start with the Saturation slider. Slide it slowly and carefully until you see some of the colour areas begin to clip, then draw it back away from that point. From there, use the Vibrance slider to make finer adjustments. Because of the restrictions to the Vibrance operation,

"Vibrance was created to change the way colours are treated"

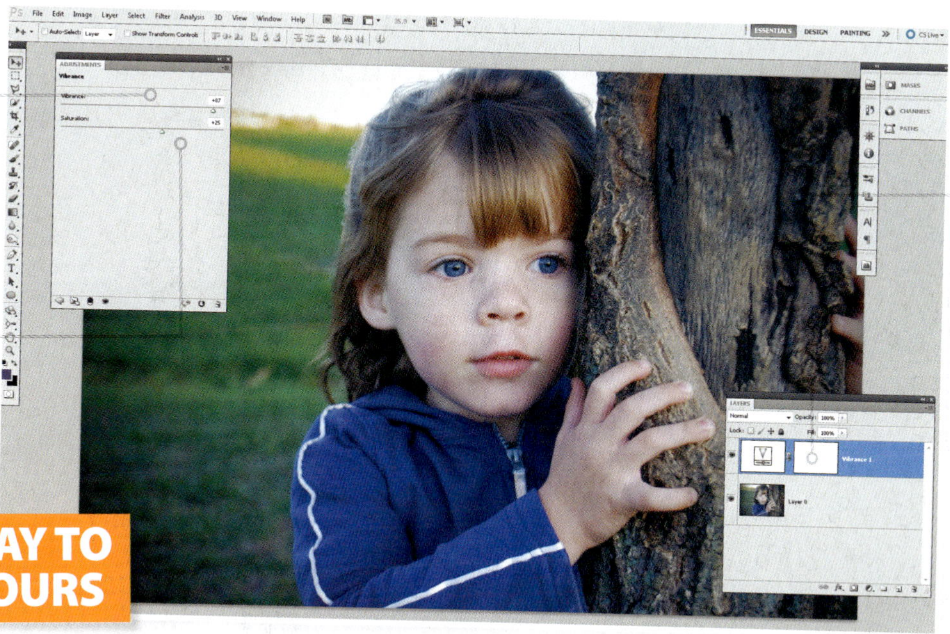

Vibrance slider
The safest way to adjust saturation. This slider has built-in restraints that protect against colour clipping, which particularly helps to preserve skin tones.

Saturation slider
Similar to using the Hue/Saturation control, but with less chance of banding in the result. Small tweaks do the trick.

Adjustment layer advantage
By implementing Vibrance as an adjustment layer you gain the benefits of retaining the original image and a layer mask being readily available.

Skin protection
The eye and lip colours are enhanced, but by using the Vibrance slider, the skin tones are well protected against any unnatural colour shifts.

THE SAFE WAY TO BOOST COLOURS

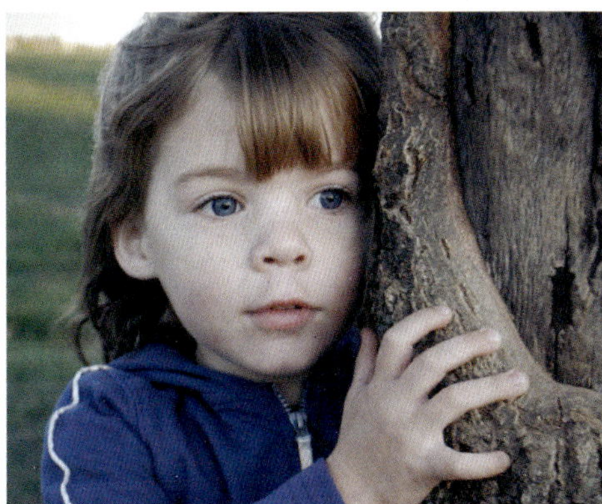

01 Take a drab image…

Find the 'HIdeNseek.jpg' image provided. Open it in Photoshop and notice how the dull and dingy colours can ruin even a well-composed shot.

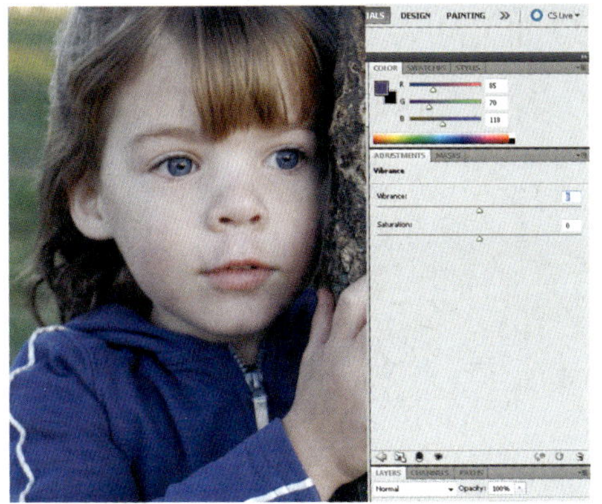

02 Enter the Vibrance

In the Adjustments panel, click on the 'V'-like icon to add a Vibrance adjustment layer. Notice how the layer automatically includes a layer mask.

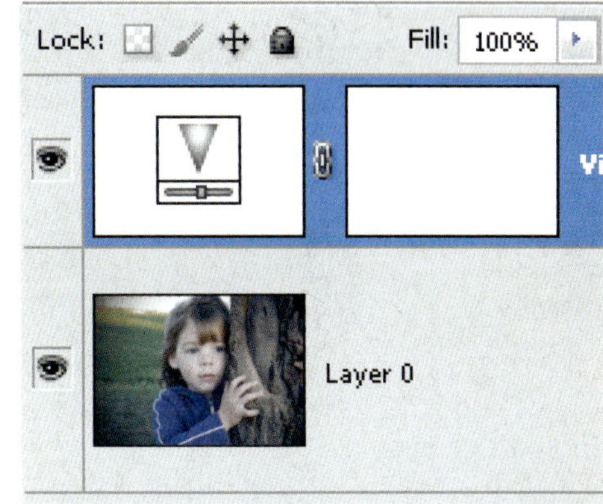

03 Super sliders

Adjust the Saturation slider first, just a tad; we used a setting of 25. Then push the Vibrance value until the colours pop. We found 87 to be a good point.

Colour swap with Hue/Saturation

Truly the 'big gun' when it comes to complete colour control in Photoshop, this is an essential tool to master

Making drastic colour changes in an image is one of the tasks Photoshop was built for. And when it comes to large colour adjustments, no tool is more capable than Hue/Saturation. No other tool can so convincingly shift red to blue without even blinking. If Vibrance is the scalpel of colour adjustments, then Hue/Saturation is the broadsword!

The Hue/Saturation controls are fairly straightforward and intuitive. The top slider bar is Hue, or the actual colour tint; this will make the most noticeable changes to an image. The colours within the bar can be a little misleading, however, so it's best to watch the image for visual feedback while using this. The next slider is Saturation, or colour intensity. This slider can turn an image into a black-and-white photo or a psychedelic nightmare; plus if all you need is to add a little colour boost, this is the one you want. The Lightness slider does exactly what you would expect it to do – adjusts the lightness. The popular Colorize box provides a quick way to add a specific colour cast to the entire image. Think sepia toning, but with the ability to select any colour.

But the feature that really makes Hue/Saturation different is the ability to target specific colour ranges without masking. For example, if you select the first eyedropper and sample a red area of the image, the top dropdown setting changes from Master to Reds and the changes will only impact the red pixels of an image. The bottom colour bars will even provide adjustable brackets so you can dial in the exact range of reds you wish to alter.

"If Vibrance is the scalpel of colour adjustments, then Hue/Saturation is the broadsword!"

HUE/SATURATION IN ACTION

Specify the colour

Only Hue/Saturation allows you to select which colour you wish to alter. You can even create different settings for each colour group in an image.

Master	Alt+2
Reds	Alt+3
Yellows	Alt+4
Greens	Alt+5
Cyans	Alt+6
Blues	Alt+7
Magentas	Alt+8

Target Adjustment

The Target Adjustment tool automatically selects the colour group you sample by clicking in the image. Then dragging left and right alters the saturation, while Cmd/Ctrl-dragging modifies the hue.

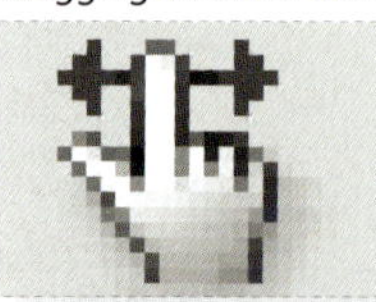

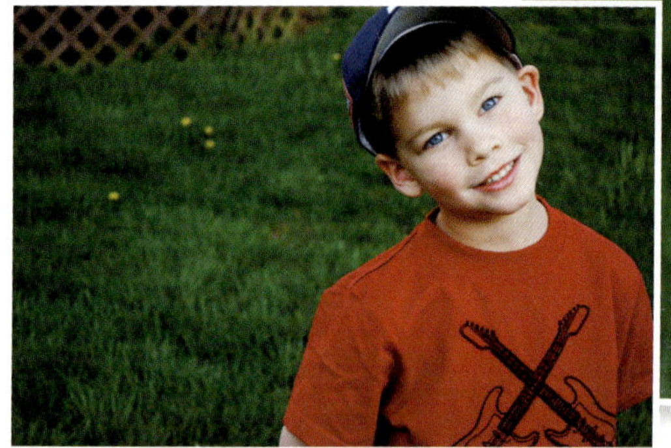

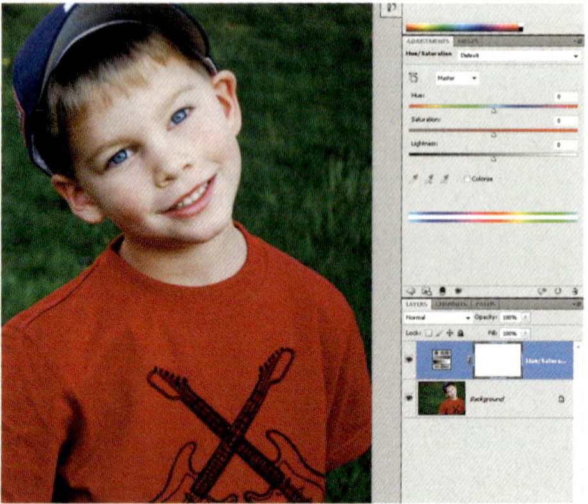

01 Let's begin
Open the 'BallPlayer.jpg' file provided. Go to Layer>New Adjustment Layer>Hue/Saturation. The controls are displayed in the Adjustments panel.

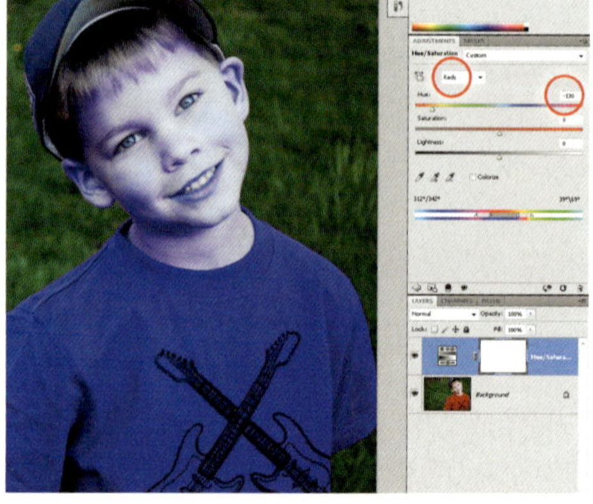

02 Target the Reds
In the Adjustments panel, change the dropdown from Master to Reds. Then slide the Hue control to change the colour of the shirt. We settled on -130.

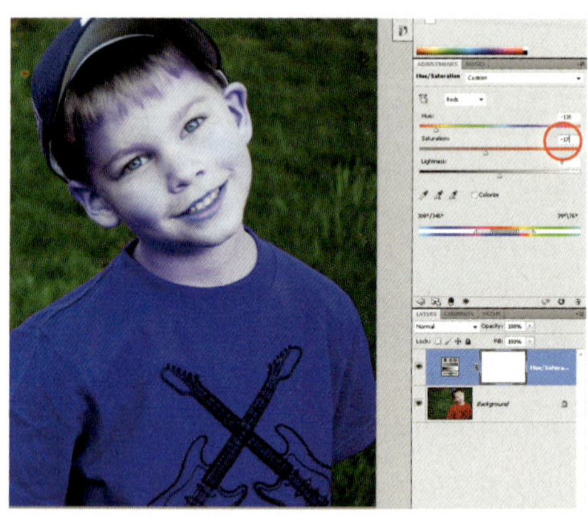

03 Spot of saturation
In the T-shirt, there are areas where the colours are clipping, so pull back on the Saturation slider to tone it down slightly. We set ours to -17.

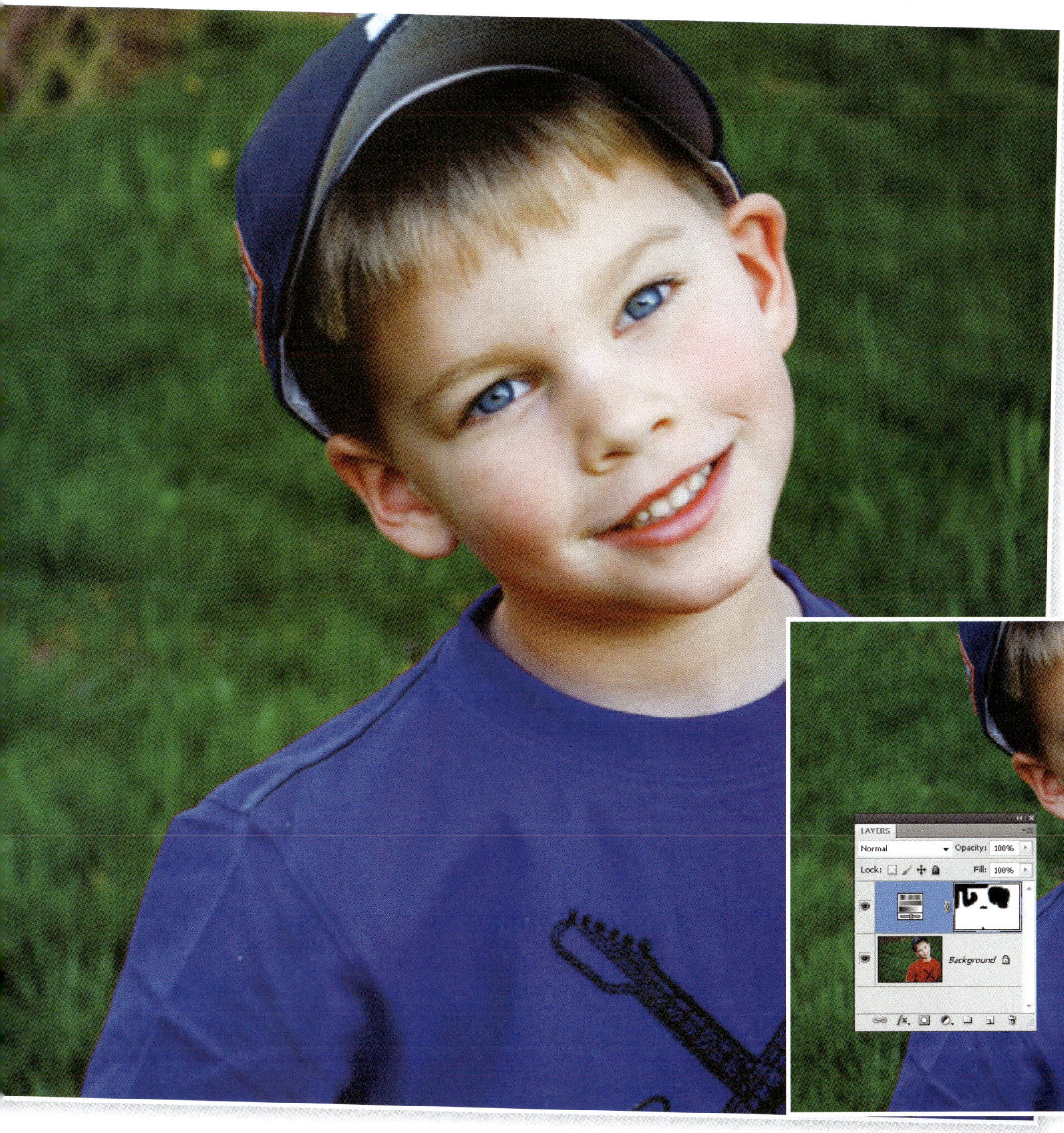

Helpful eyedroppers

These wonderful little gadgets in Hue/Saturation enable you to include or exclude sampled areas in the range of influence with just a single click!

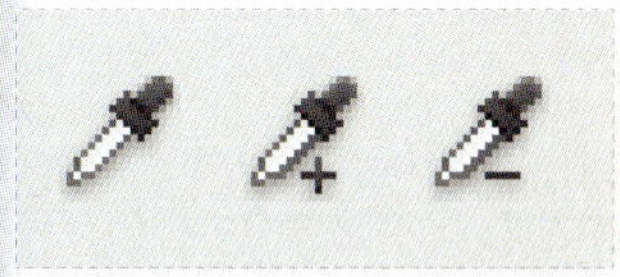

Making life easier

While a little masking was necessary to remove the adjustment from the face, Hue/Saturation did an excellent job of keeping the effect on the red shirt and not spilling over to the green grass behind.

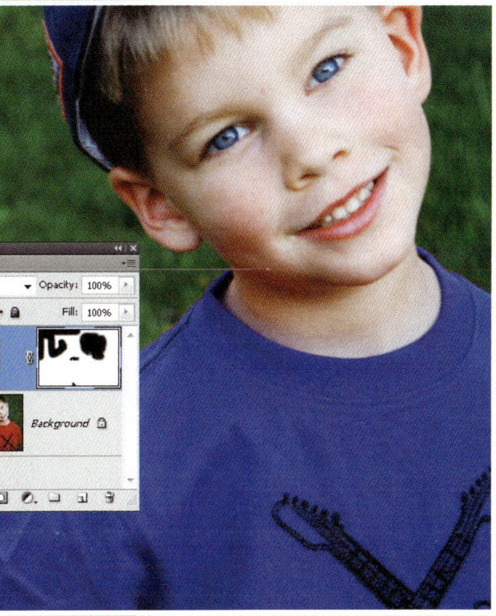

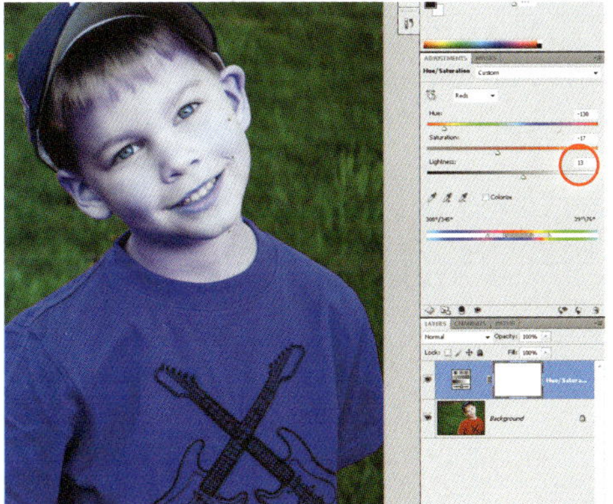

04 Lighten up

Next lighten the shirt by increasing the Lightness slider. We found a setting of 13 to be just enough to achieve the temperature we were looking for.

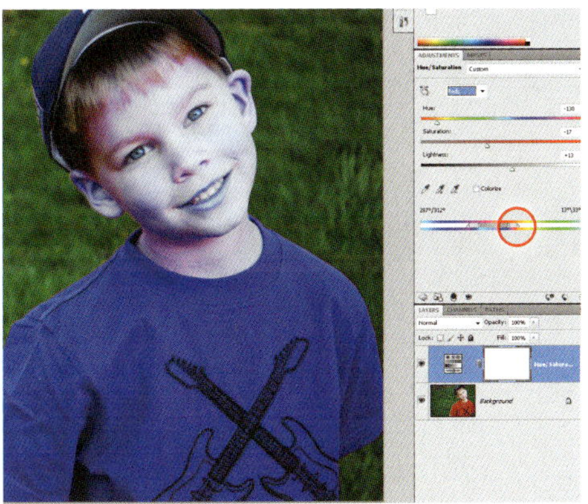

05 Adjust the range

The colour bar near the bottom represents the layer's range of influence. Drag the right handles towards the left to exclude the yellow areas.

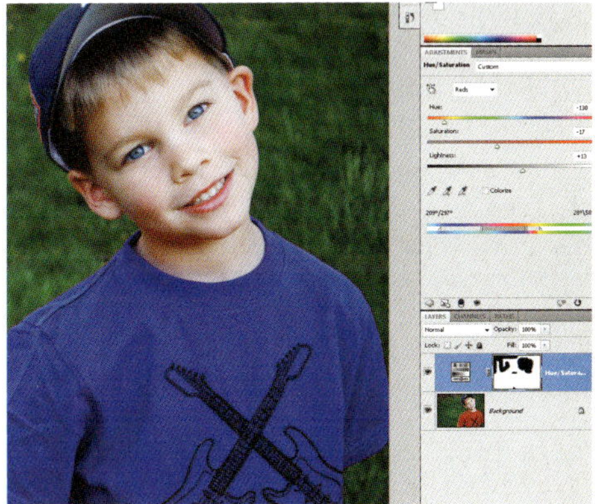

06 Use the mask

Select the mask thumbnail next to the layer thumbnail. Apply a soft brush with black to the face and any other areas you don't want affected.

The balance of colour

Learn how to treat common colour problems using the Color Balance adjustment

Eyes are marvellous things. One of the most amazing aspects about them is their ability to translate light that is slightly coloured into white. For example, if you are reading this in your living room, you see this page as white. But the light bulb you are using to read by is likely casting a yellow light. Your eye adjusts to this colour shift reflexively. Our cameras are not quite so adept at it. Unless the camera compensates for this change, the picture results in a colour cast created by the lighting. The real way to correct this problem is to use the white balance setting on your camera *before* you take the picture. But what if it's too late for that? Can an image be saved?

The Color Balance adjustment makes 'light' work of this type of conundrum. By providing a triplet of colour sliders each for the Shadows, Midtones and Highlights, this feature can rid an image of all but the most stubborn of colour casts. There's only a few general guidelines with Color Balance: start with the Midtones, make small adjustments and toggle the visibility so you can compare your work. The slider bars are very clear in the way they depict what colour is added by what slider, however practice makes perfect with this tool.

It does take an experienced eye to recognise which hue will best correct the photo, so the safe bet is to implement this control as an adjustment layer (Layers>New Adjustment Layer>Color Balance); that way you can tweak the

> "This tool can rid images of all but the most stubborn colour casts"

THE BALANCING ACT OF HUES

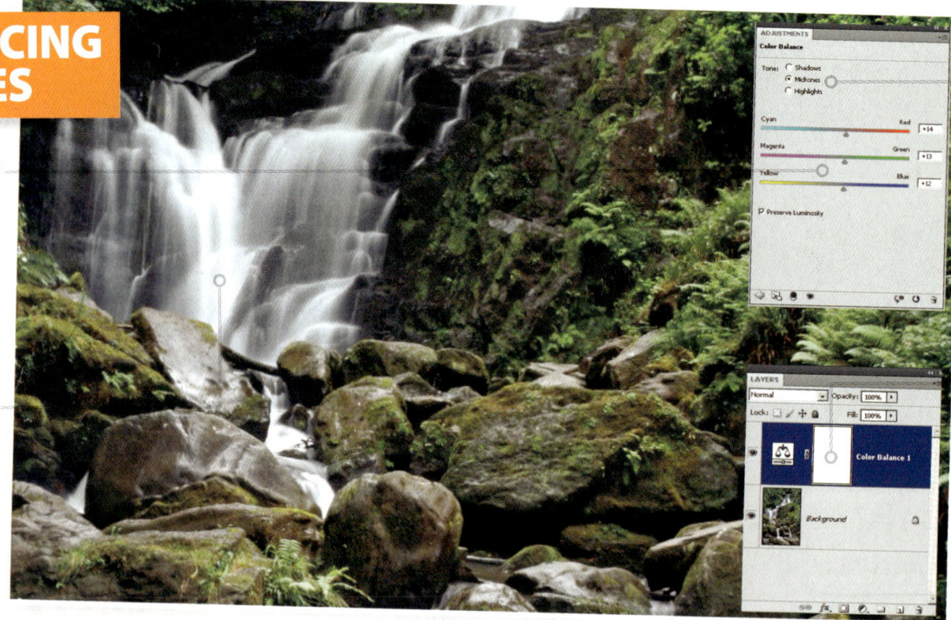

Slider serendipity
A slider for each colour channel allows for great control over specific hues within the image. The available sliders are dependent on the image colour mode.

Richer colours, whiter whites
Just like any good laundry detergent! Remove any off-white colour casts and create deeper, more vibrant colours in an image.

Select a target
Use the radio buttons to indicate where the adjustments should focus. This way you can create different balance settings for each of the main luminosity areas: shadows, midtones, and highlights.

Adjustment layer goodness
By implementing Color Balance as an adjustment layer, you can easily hide, edit, mask or completely remove the effect whenever you wish. The ultimate convenience!

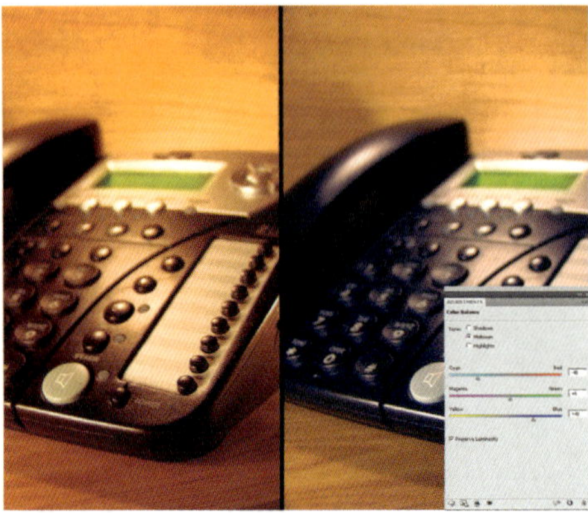

01 Tungsten trouble
Regular light bulbs cast a yellow-orange tint. Pull Color Balance sliders towards the Cyan and Blue to compensate. Focus on Midtones, then Shadows.

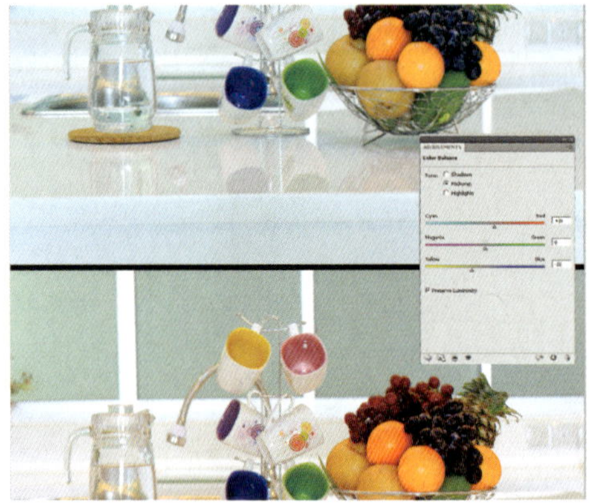

02 Fluorescent flaws
Fluorescent bulbs are known for casting a green-blue hue. Upping Red and Yellow in the Midtones will go a long way to repairing the image.

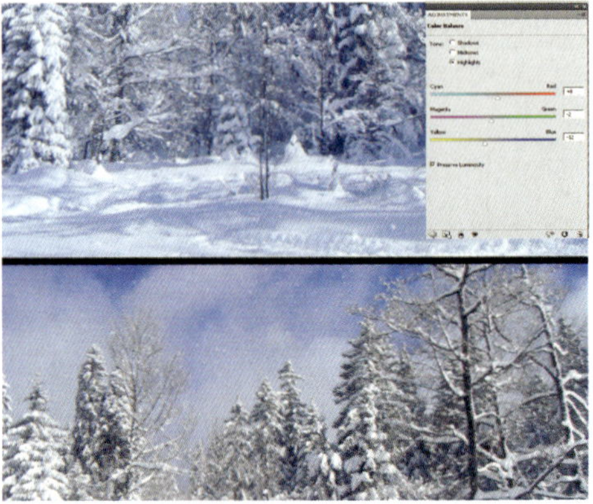

03 Snowy snare
Outdoor shots can often get a blue cast, especially in snow. To correct this, start with the Highlights, removing blue by pushing towards Yellow.

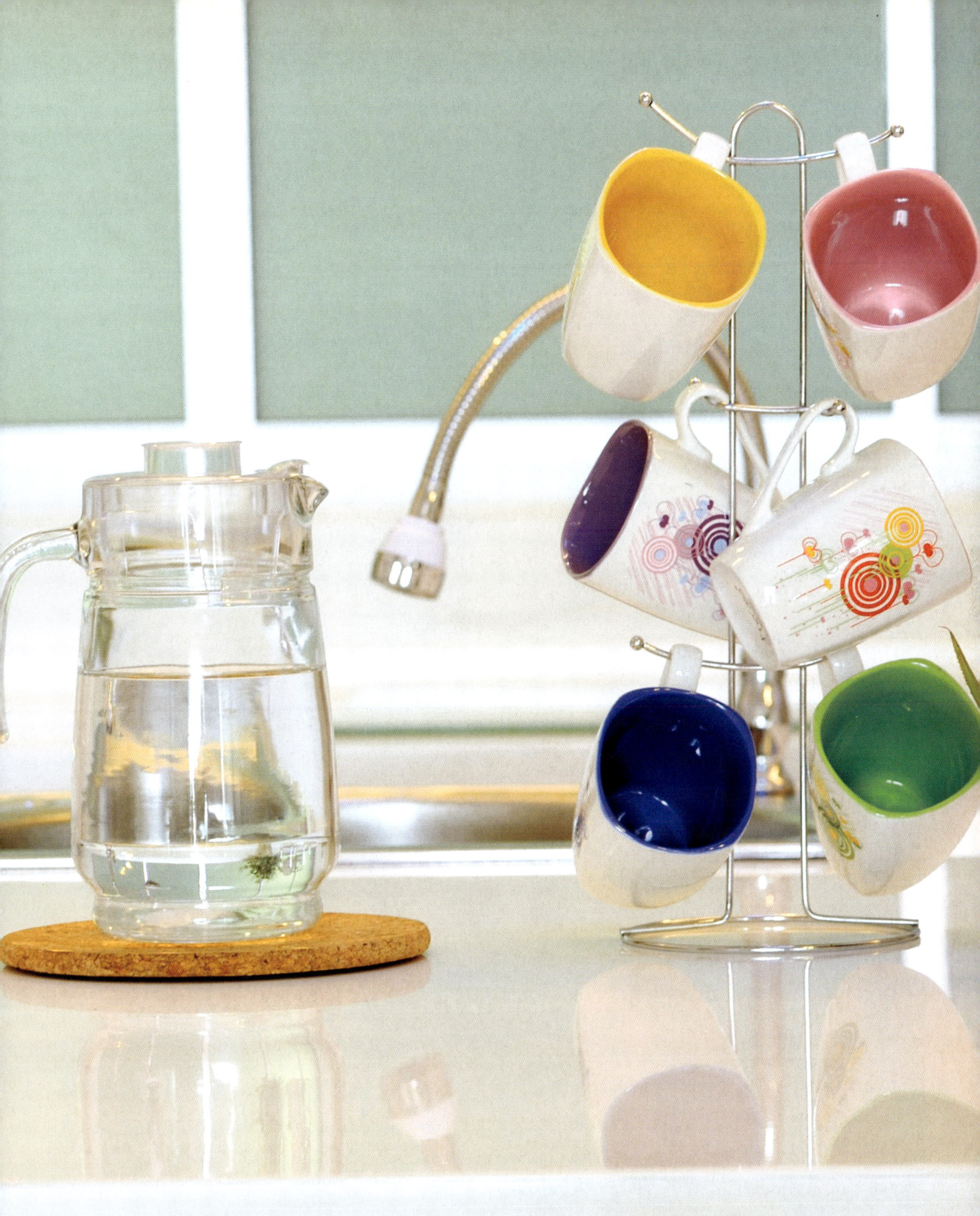

Exposure explained

Discover how to correct your poorly exposed photographs with just a few straightforward slider bars

Exposure touches on several aspects of the photographic process, which can be confusing. Generally the term is used to describe how much light is allowed to reach the camera's sensor, but it's sometimes used in reference to a shutter's cycle. Despite a bit of confusion over the use of the term, Photoshop regards exposure as the overall light and dark of a shot. An image that is overexposed has highlights that are blown out and seems altogether too bright. Alternatively, an underexposed shot will be too dark. The PS Exposure controls are geared primarily towards high dynamic range (HDR) imagery, but work fine for standard 8-bit shots too.

Adjusting Exposure is one of the areas where Photoshop Elements drastically differs from Photoshop. The latter implements Exposure either via an adjustment layer or through the Image>Adjustments menu. Either way generates a control panel with three sliders: Exposure, Offset and Gamma Correction. The Exposure slider targets the bright highlight portions of the image without affecting the darkest shadow areas. The Offset slider adjusts the darks and midtones without impacting the highlights. While the Gamma Correction slider deals with the brightness of the entire image.

Elements includes Exposure in the Guided Editing process. It's tucked away in the Lighting and Exposure area, and has an Auto button that actually works pretty well. But, if you prefer a manual approach, the sliders are easy to understand and clearly labelled. Let's see how Exposure works in both apps.

"The Exposure controls are geared primarily towards HDR imagery, but work fine for 8-bit shots too"

QUICK PHOTOSHOP TIPS

Auto exposure

The Auto button proves to be very helpful in easily correcting exposure problems. Just a single click provides instant and striking results.

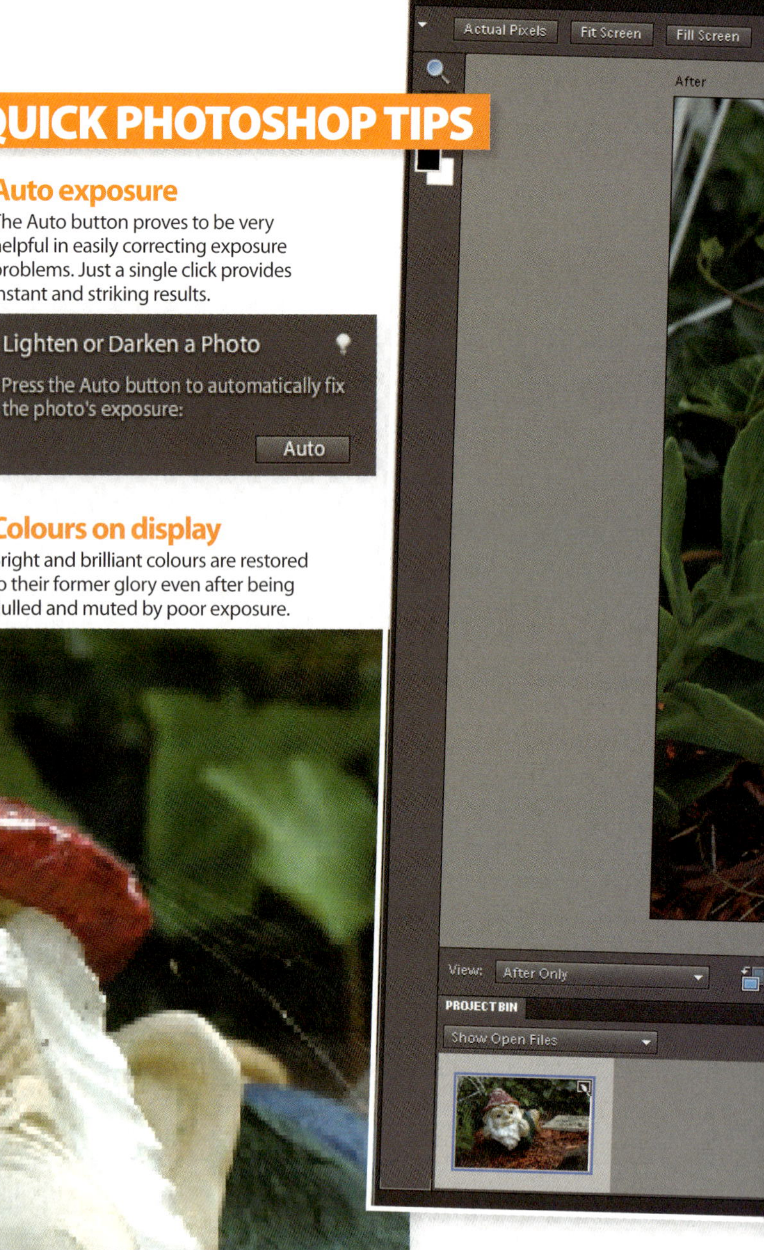

Colours on display

Bright and brilliant colours are restored to their former glory even after being dulled and muted by poor exposure.

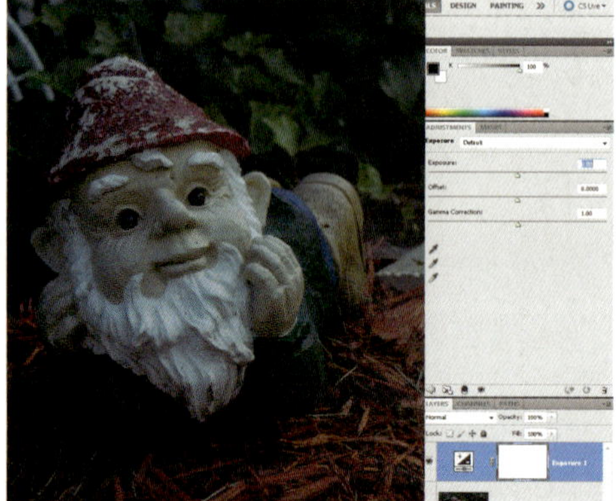

01 Exposure in Photoshop

In Photoshop, open 'GardenGnome.jpg'. In the Adjustments Panel, hit the icon with the plus and minus signs to add an Exposure adjustment layer.

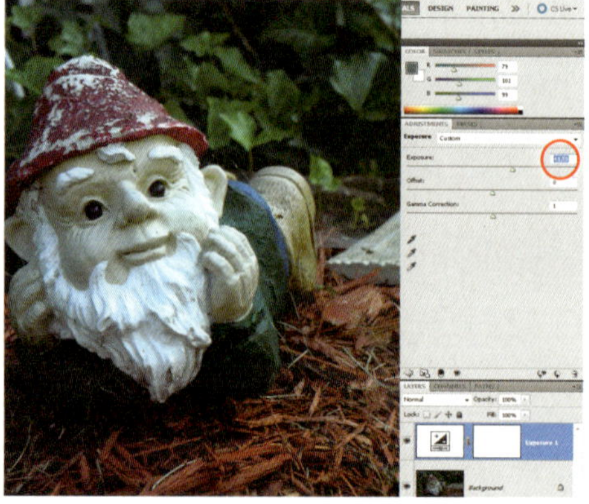

02 Brighten up!

Begin with the Exposure slider. Pull it to the right until the bright areas of the image lighten up considerably. A value of 1.59 works well in this case.

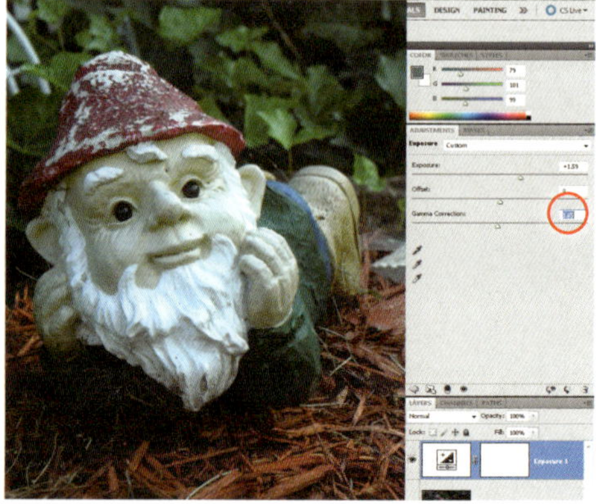

03 Other settings

If you feel the shadows need direct adjustments, up the Offset slider slightly. The last slider can be used for overall brightness; we set it just over 1.0.

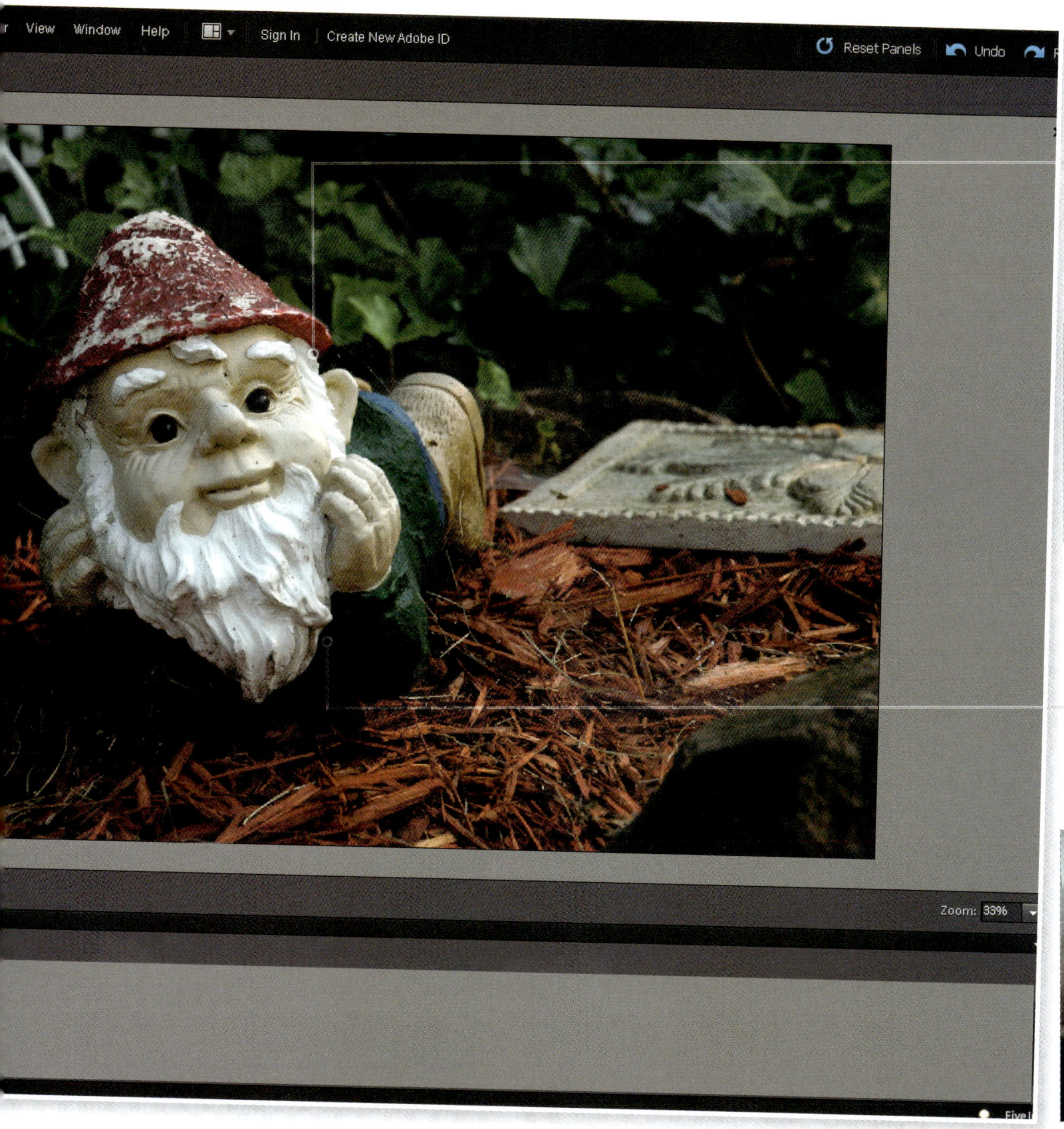

The whites have it

Highlights that once were murky and grey become bright whites. Be careful with the adjustments, as the feature can be over powered and blow out highlight areas if not used with caution.

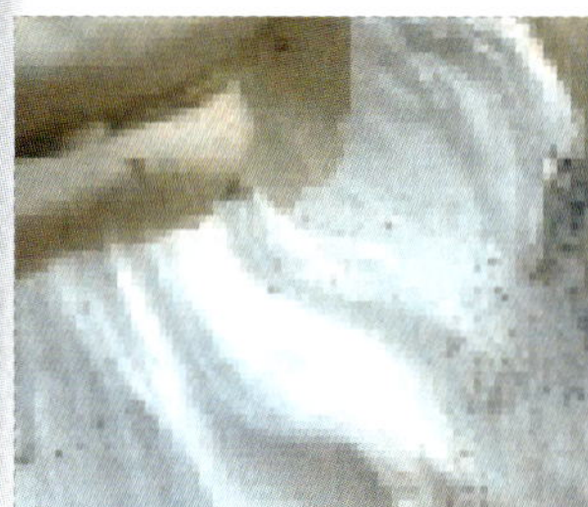

Sharp shadows

The dark areas are still deep shadows and those bring good contrast and balance to the image. If the shadows are too bright, the image begins to appear greyed out.

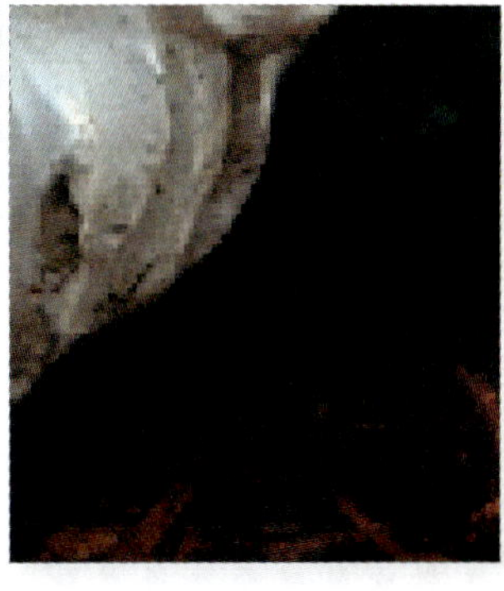

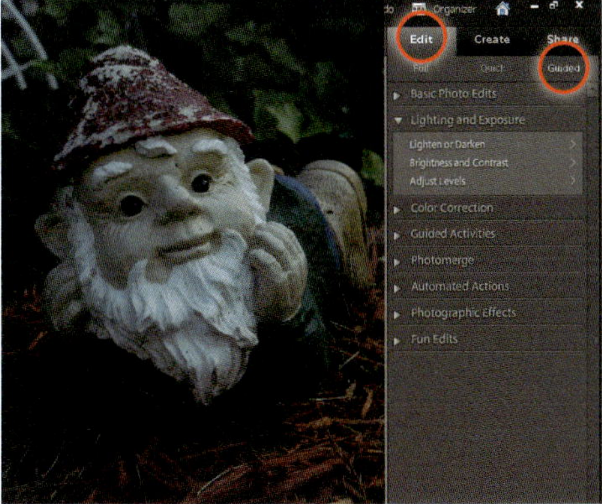

04 Exposure in Elements

Launch Elements and open 'GardenGnome.jpg' from the disc. Look to the right of the interface for the Edit panel then click on the Guided tab.

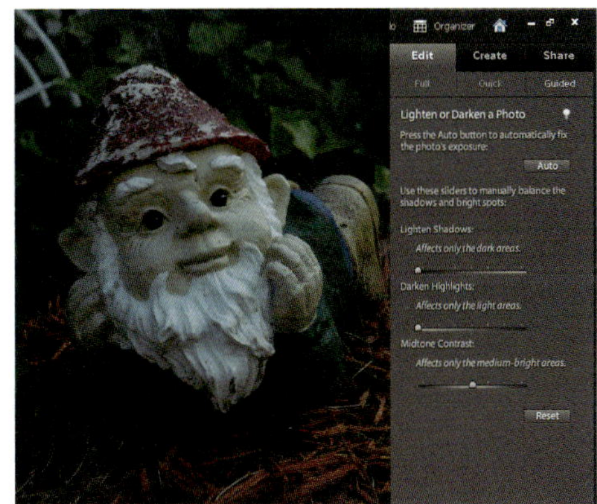

05 Find the Exposure section

Open up the Lighting and Exposure group then click on Lighten or Darken. The panel will change to present the options for adjusting exposure.

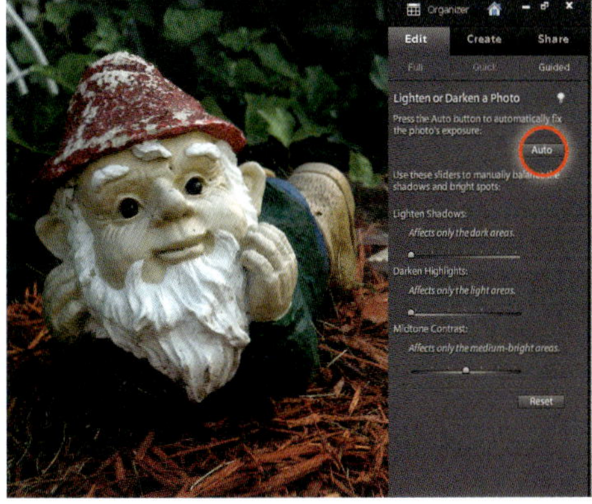

06 Quick and easy

Hit the Auto button and see the image's exposure instantly corrected. This won't always work, but the relevant sliders can be used for manual tweaks.

Produce beautiful black-and-whites

Photoshop gives you maximum creative control to transform colour snaps into stunning black-and-white imagery

Black-and-white photography is a study unto itself. By limiting colour range, the strength of a shot must be carried on tonal value and composition – a restriction which forces the photographer to focus on shapes, line and contrast. This can result in some wonderfully striking images that often seem to be even richer than their fully hued counterparts.

Black and white means more than just a lack of colour though. Photoshop provides several means of eliminating colour from an image, but simply desaturating a shot does not allow for the creative process required to produce a truly exceptional black-and-white image. The preferred method is to use the Black & White adjustment. This allows for fine control over the grey values of each colour family in the image. This can be remarkably useful if you are attempting to lighten a sky but darken skin tones, etc. By using Black & White, this requires no masking or selections of any kind. It truly strikes a wondrous balance between ease of use, high level of control and effectiveness.

Not every image is appropriate for black-and-white conversion. When evaluating a photo, consider the tonal range and contrast. Also, monochrome can give a sense of formality, so if the topic is serious, it will probably work well. Rich details like rusted metals or rugged portraits are always favourites too.

In this series of steps we'll show you how to take a pleasant enough full-colour image and transform it into a truly striking black-and-white one.

"Black & White allows for fine control over the grey values"

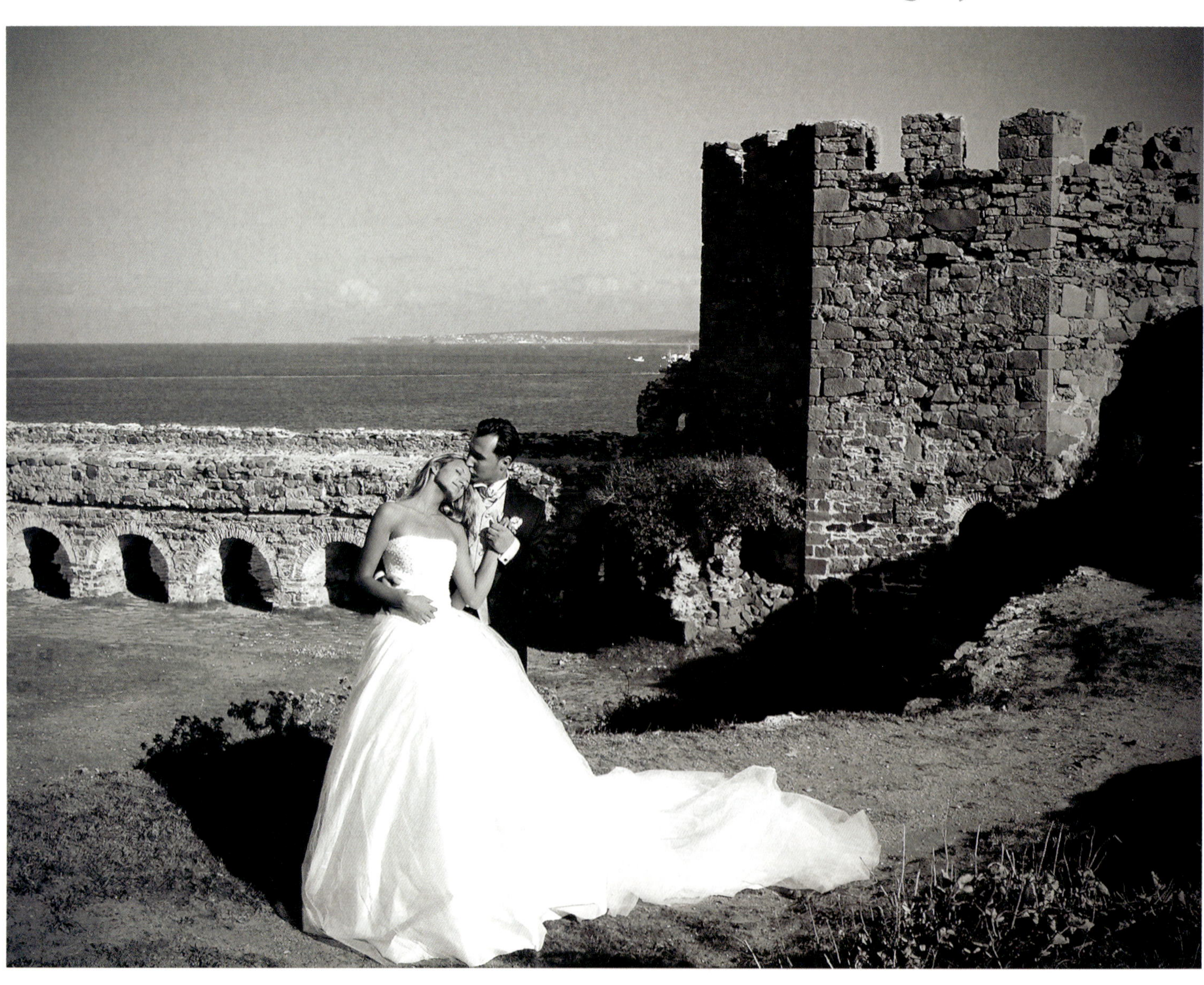

Best of Black & White Learn the ins and outs of this remarkable little adjustment tool

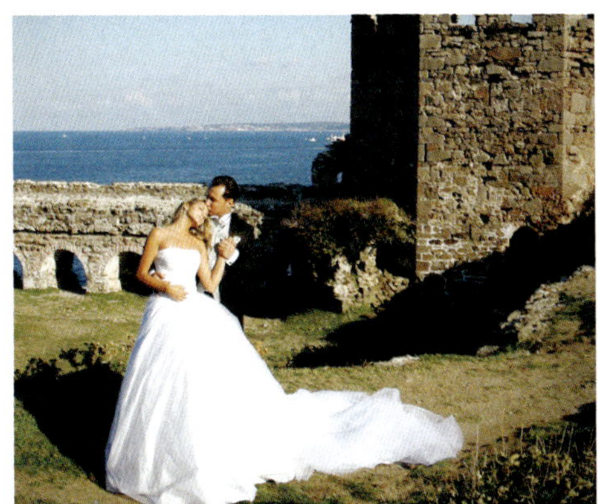

01 Select a photo

Black & White works best on shots with strong lines and contrast that don't rely on colour information. We invite you to use 'WeddingBW.jpg' provided.

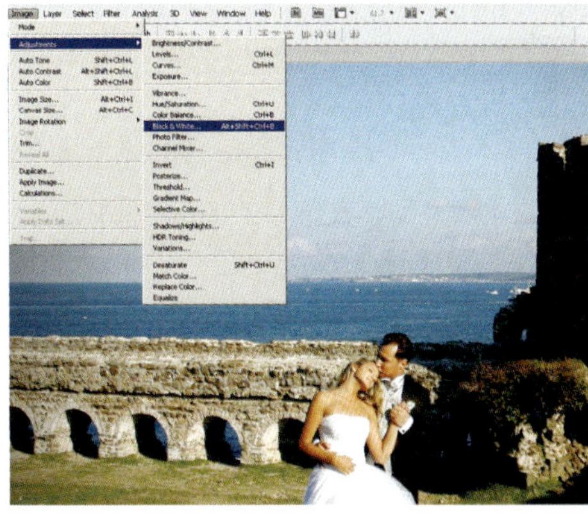

02 Black & White adjustment

This particular conversion feature is found under Image>Adjustments>Black & White. Or use the keyboard shortcut: Cmd/Ctrl+Opt/Alt+Shift+B.

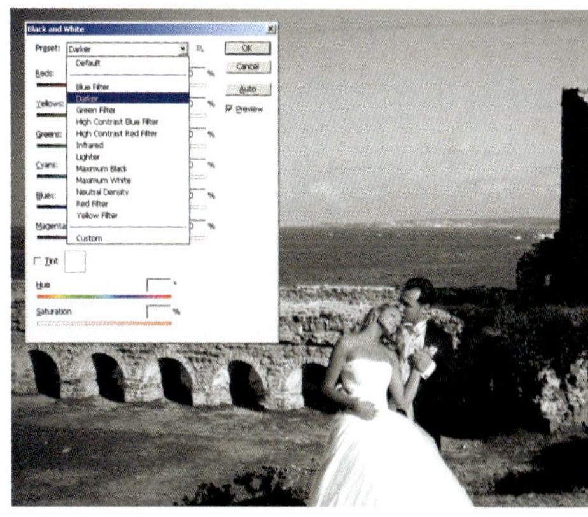

03 Browse the presets

Photoshop provides a host of preset conversions, worth browsing through to get a sense of what approach may or may not work for your image.

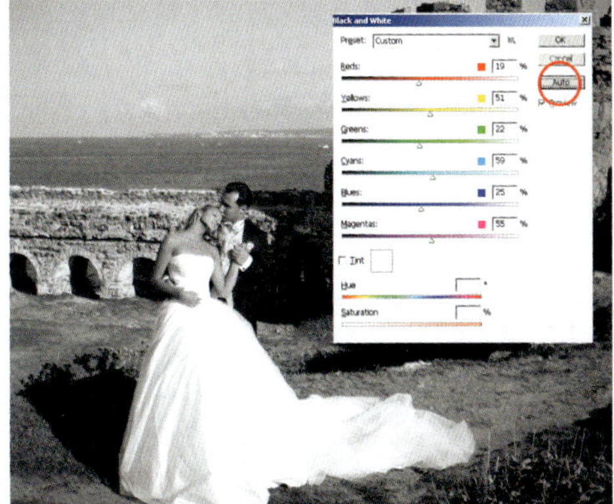

04 Auto button

Automatic PS functions are seldom reliable, but in this case, the Auto feature offers a solid starting point. The Auto button is on the right of the dialog.

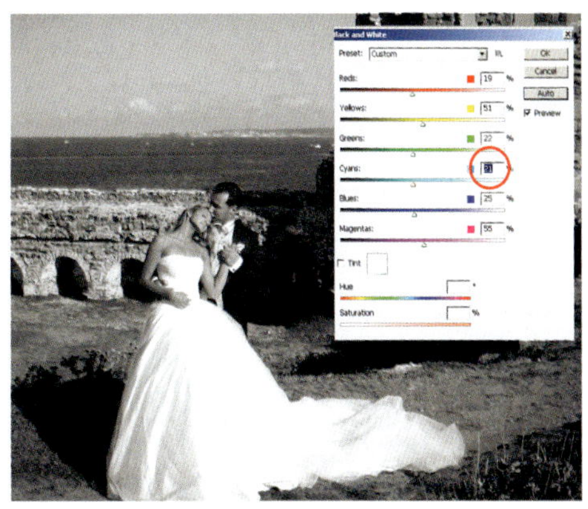

05 Adjustable skies

Bring down the brightness of the sky by adjusting the Cyan levels. The goal is to darken the sky just enough so it doesn't distract from the dress.

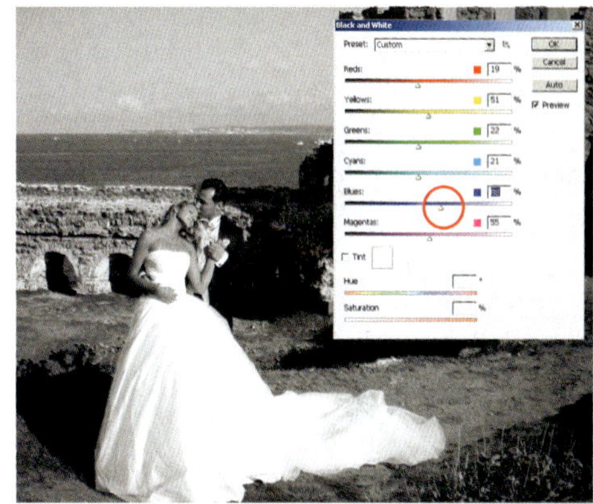

06 Ocean control

Next we'll brighten the sea by tweaking the slider bar for the Blues. Pull the slider handle towards the right a fair amount so the sea isn't quite so dark.

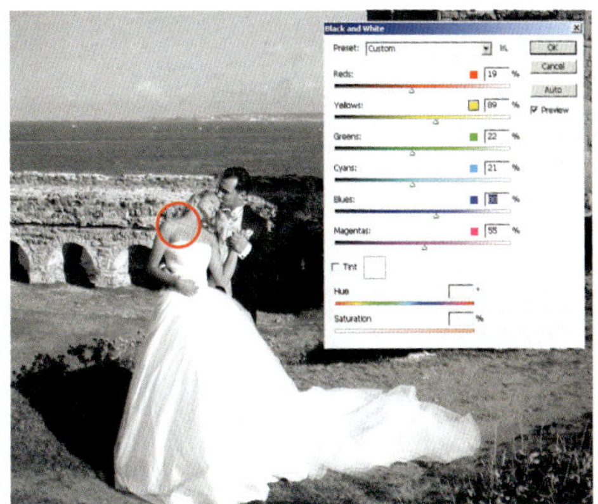

07 Beautiful skin tones

Mouse over the image and the cursor becomes an eyedropper. Click and drag on the bride's shoulder to adjust skin tones (watch the Yellows slider).

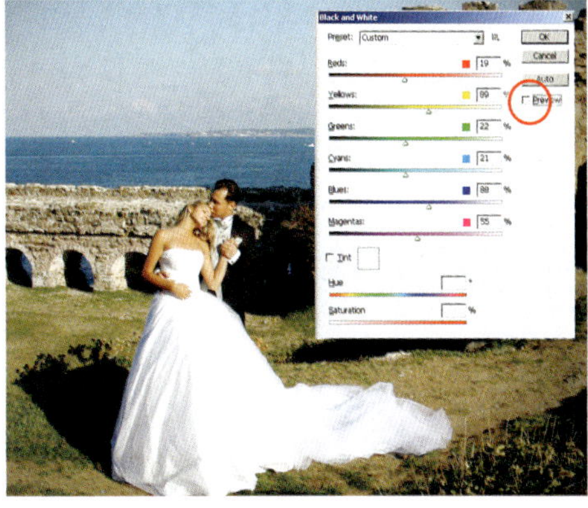

08 Check your work

Use the Preview checkbox to toggle the effect on and off. This provides great before and after visual feedback. Use it frequently to check your work.

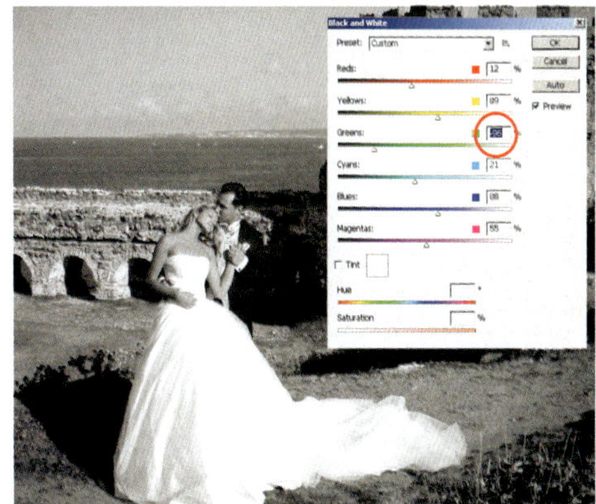

09 The grass is always greener...

To add more details to the grass, knock down the Greens slider substantially. Bringing out texture here helps visually balance details in the rock wall.

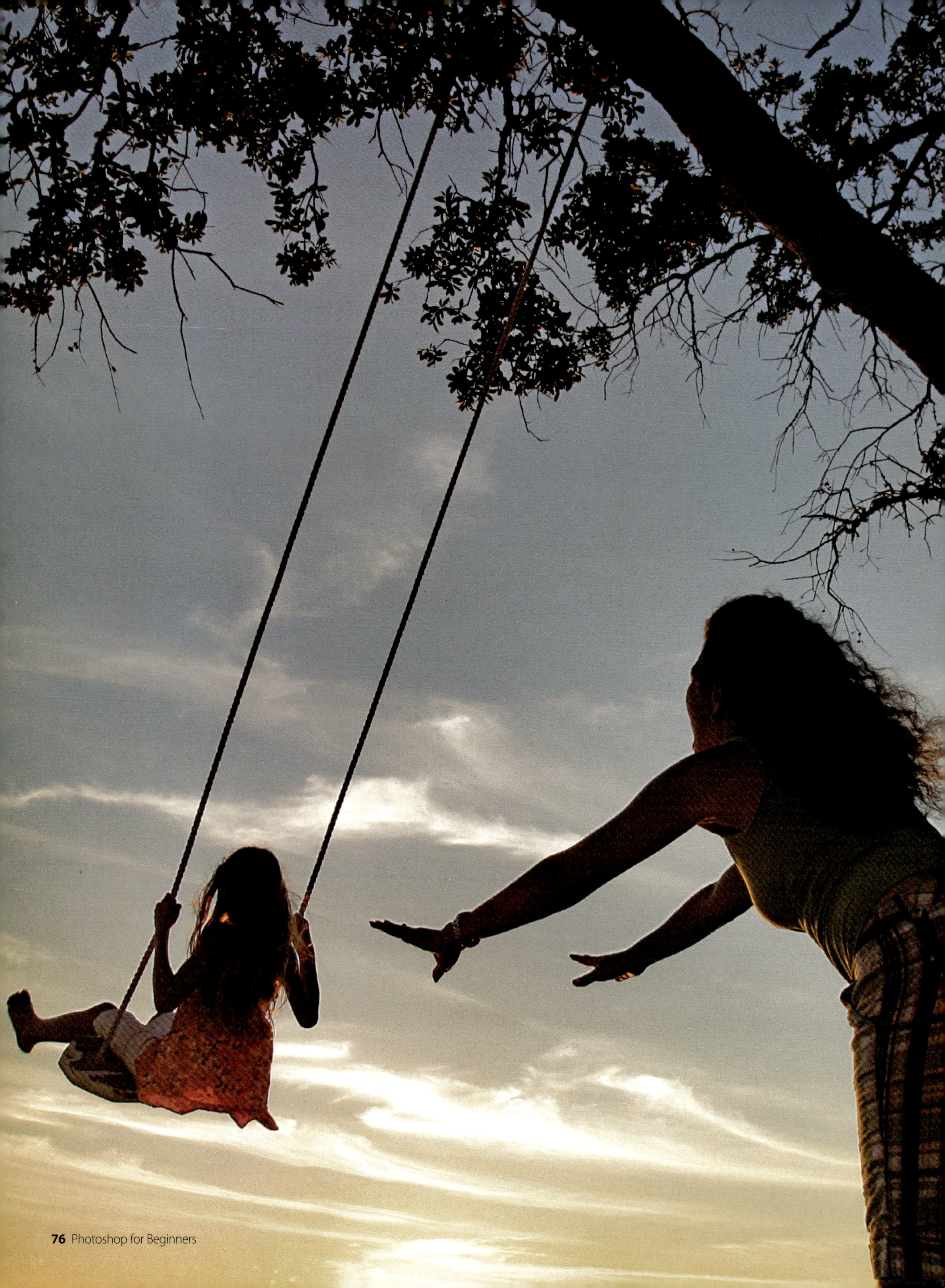

Shadows/Highlights explored

Use this sophisticated adjustment to pull more details out of a dark silhouette than you might have ever imagined

Backlit images can frequently pose quite a dilemma. How do you lighten the dark subject pixels while darkening the overblown background area? And how do you do this without spending endless hours creating a selection or mask? With Shadows/Highlights, that's how!

Even though it lives in the Adjustments menu, the Shadows/Highlights command is technically a filter. It cannot be applied through an adjustment layer. Therefore it's good practice to duplicate the Background layer before running this adjustment. That way, mistakes aren't permanent.

While this feature allows you to pull a remarkable amount of detail out of dark silhouettes, it will not create details out of total darkness. If the shadows are clipped, ie completely black, Photoshop can't create what is not there. So be aware that the subject must have some degree of detail left that hasn't been obliterated by the dark. In fact, while working to restore the details to the darkened areas, be on watch for introducing noise into the image.

Photoshop offers a plethora of controls in this feature, most of which you will probably never use, while PS Elements pares it down to just three sliders. Find them under Enhance>Adjust Lighting>Shadows/Highlights. Elements enables you to brighten Shadows, darken Highlights and make more subtle adjustments with the Midtone Contrast control. In this example we strive to illustrate just how much detail can be recovered from an image using this tool.

> "Duplicate the Background layer before running this adjustment"

WHAT YOU'LL LEARN

More options

The default operation of Shadows/Highlights has only two simple sliders. Check Show More Options to reveal many more useful controls.

Watch out for haloes

One thing you need to watch for with this adjustment is haloes around subject edges. The Radius settings will help spread them out but won't eliminate them completely.

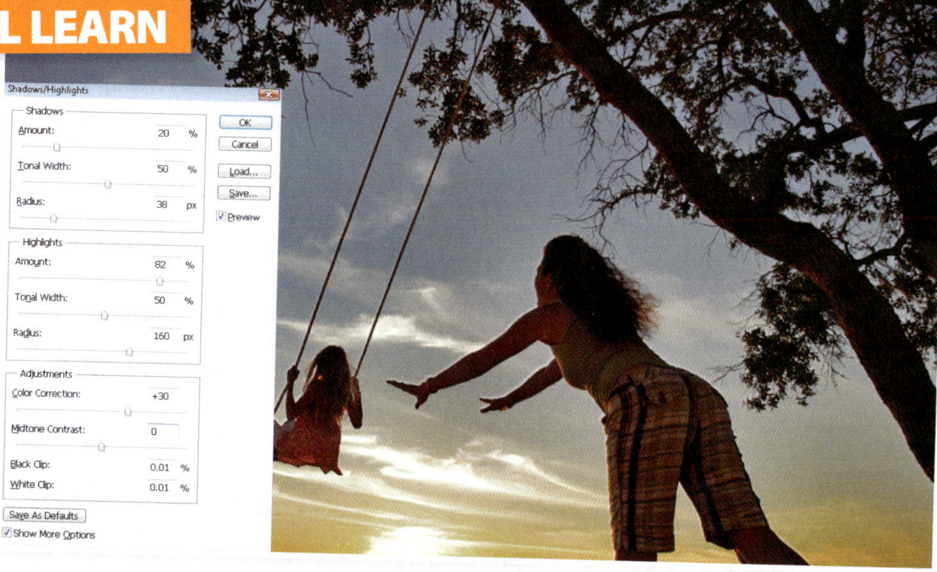

Tonal Width

It's recommended that these settings be left at their default 50%. However, if you change one, the other should be adjusted so that they equal 100% when combined.

Colour with caution

While this setting provides an easy way to boost colour values in the image, it's not always the best solution in that it can introduce undesired saturation values.

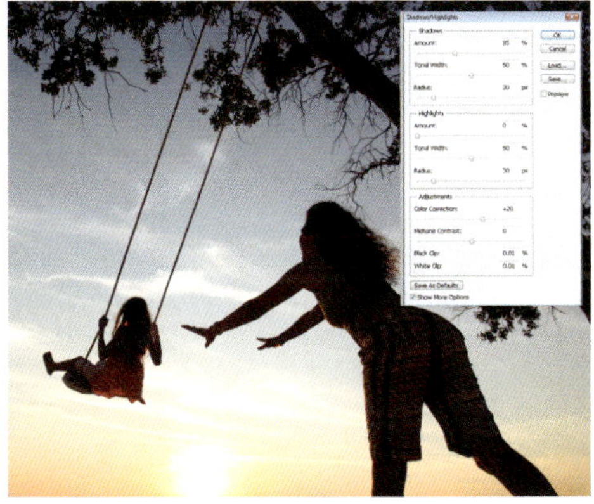

01 Into the swing of things…

Open 'SunsetSwing.jpg' provided. While backlight is clear, the subject details are also still there. Now go to Image>Adjustments>Shadows/Highlights.

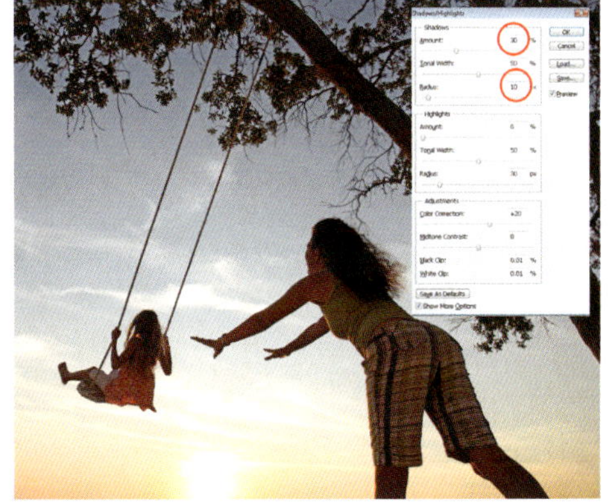

02 Open the shadows

Use the Shadows Amount slider to brighten the details in shade. We used a setting of 30%. Then, for the Radius, we applied a value of 10px.

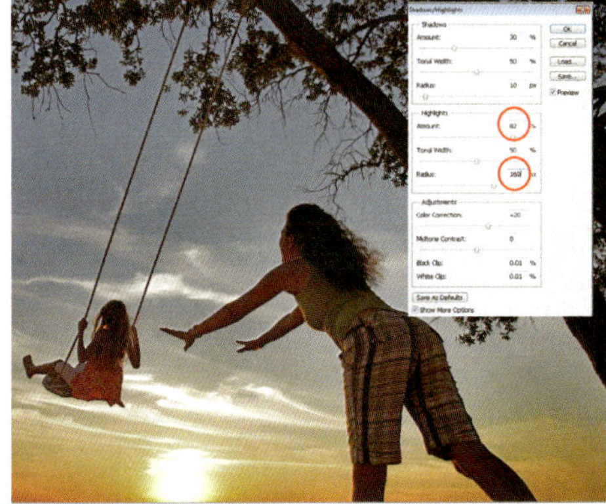

03 Pull in the highlights

To reveal details in the highlight areas, adjust the Amount slider to around 80%. If you get haloes, counter these with a high Radius setting of 160px.

Duotones made easy

What started out as a technical means of saving ink has turned into a creative outlet for photographers

Anybody who has ever had something printed will know all too well that ink isn't cheap. In fact the more types of ink you use in a single print, the more expensive the job is. To counter this, layout artists in the past have used a duotone process to help reduce costs. That means that every pixel in an image would be some combination of only two inks. Since most full-colour printing is done with at least four inks (cyan, magenta, yellow and black) plus any spot colours, working with only two inks can almost halve costs.

It didn't take photographers long to realise that this cost-saving measure could actually be used to create some very striking and creative imagery. Just adding that tint of colour can give life and interest to your images. Some photographers are so enamoured with the flavour of duotone imagery that they even use other techniques to mimic the appearance.

Here we explore the technical process for creating a true split-tone image. Photoshop's approach appears intimidatingly technical, but really is pretty easy. First, an image is converted to black and white (see page 74) and then split toning is applied. Photoshop provides fine control by allowing you to specify how much of each ink is given to each level of brightness. So you can easily assign one ink to the shadows and midtones and another to the highlights.

Traditionally, black is the first ink colour assigned. But we encourage you to experiment with different combinations to obtain more unusual results.

> "This cost-saving measure can create some very striking imagery"

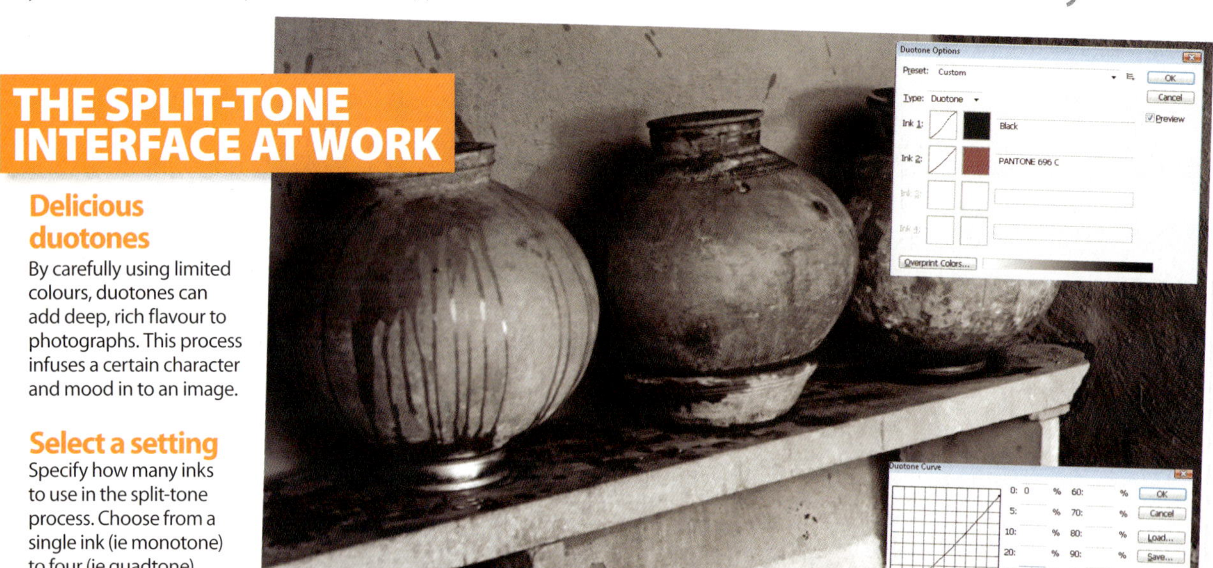

THE SPLIT-TONE INTERFACE AT WORK

Delicious duotones
By carefully using limited colours, duotones can add deep, rich flavour to photographs. This process infuses a certain character and mood in to an image.

Select a setting
Specify how many inks to use in the split-tone process. Choose from a single ink (ie monotone) to four (ie quadtone) and then assign the inks to be used.

Colour assignment
The control box allows you to assign specific colours to each ink. You may choose from a preset colour library or use the traditional picker.

Dangerous curves
Adjust points on the curve for each ink colour. This controls how much of the ink is given to each luminous value.

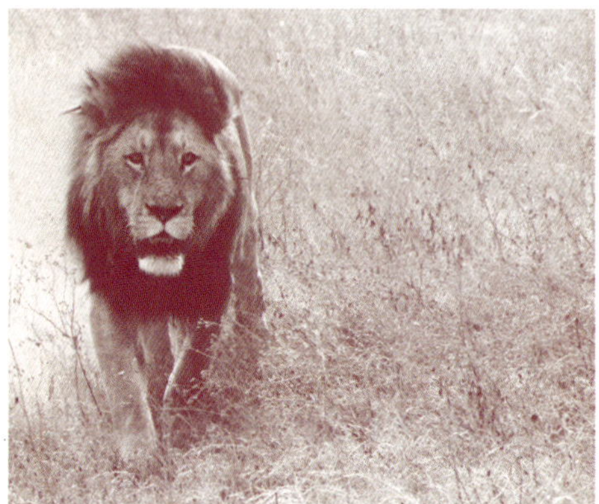

01 Majestic monotones
Usually monotone printing is straight black and white, which can look great. But the same process can be used for any ink colour, so experiment!

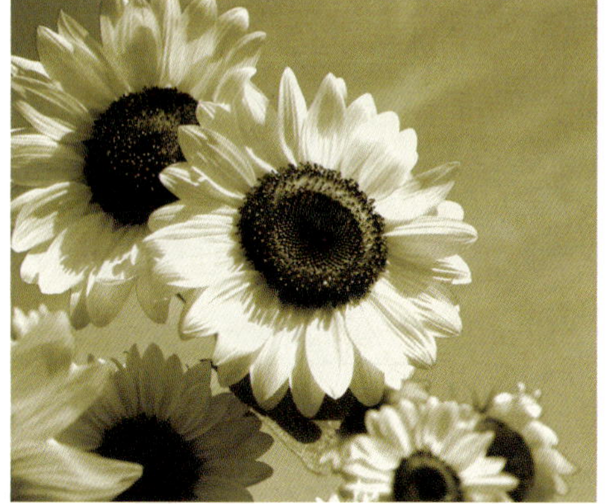

02 Dynamic duotones
Dual colouring is the main use for this tool. Two tones can add a subtle mood to a black-and-white photo. A common pairing is black and yellow.

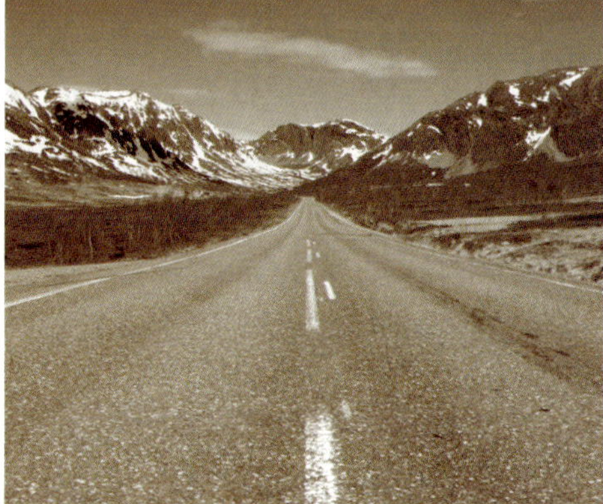

03 Terrific tritones
Simply adding one more ink to the mix can open up many new possibilities. This combo of black, magenta and yellow creates a sepia-toned image.

Duotone in Photoshop

Save on ink and add creativity to a photo with just one technique

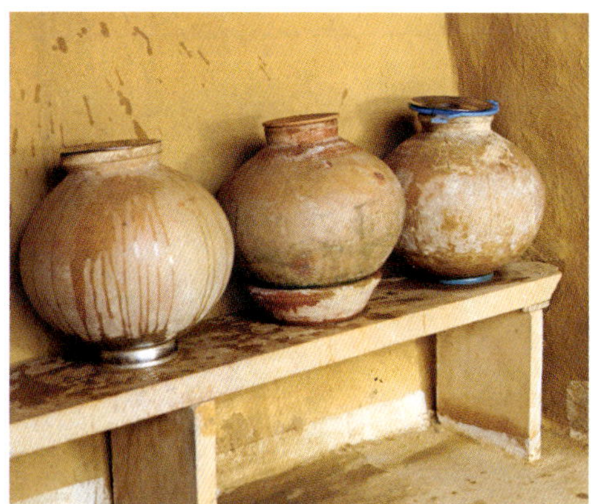

01 Find a file

Let's begin with a full-colour image to work with. If you wish to follow along with our steps, open the 'ClayPots.jpg' file which we have provided.

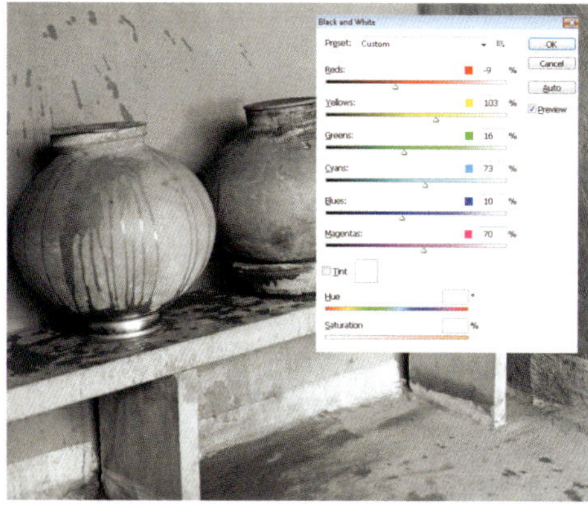

02 Lose the colour

Select Image>Adjustments>Black & White. For our image, we set Reds to -9, Yellows to 103, Greens to 16, Cyans to 73, Blues to 10 and Magentas to 70.

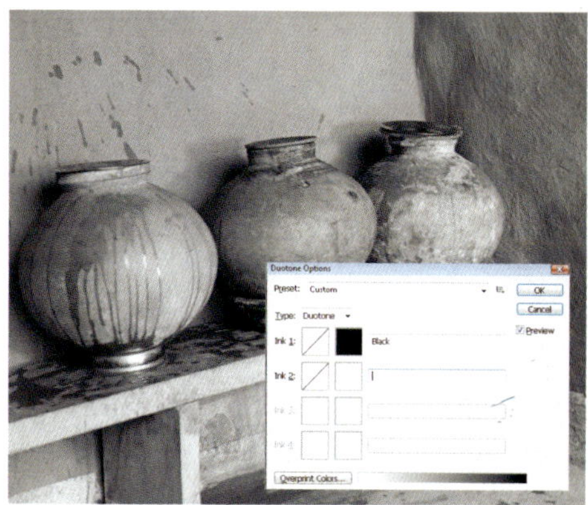

03 True colour loss

Next go to Image>Mode>Grayscale to discard all colour information. Now go to Image>Mode>Duotone. In the control box, set Type to Duotone.

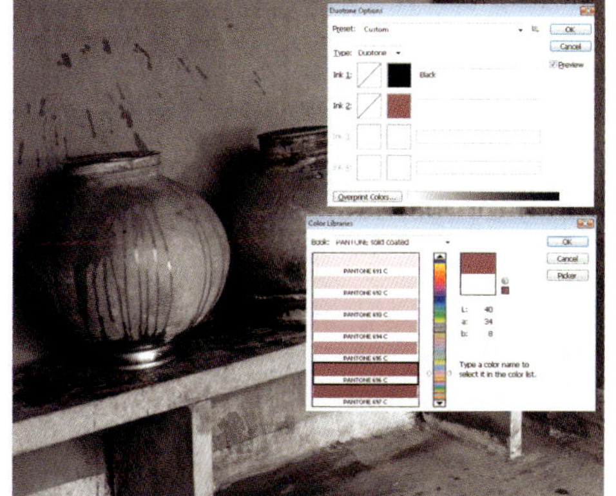

04 Ink 2 (PANTONE 696 c)

Click on the colour chip for Ink 2 to invoke another dialog. The default library is the PANTONE Solid Coated. Select the 'PANTONE 696 c' colour.

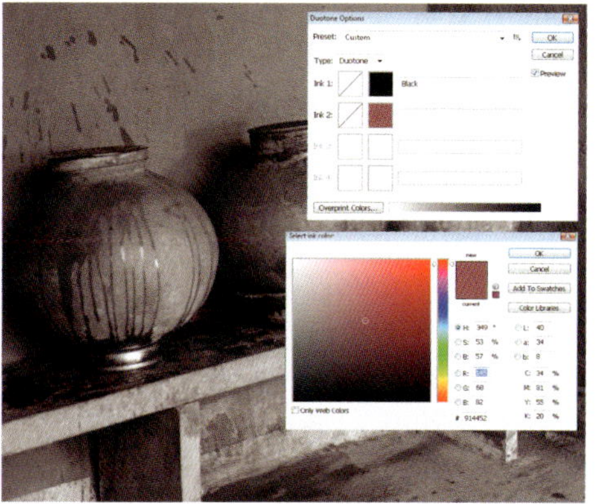

05 Color Picker

If you prefer the more traditional Color Picker over the library, click the Picker icon in the dialog. This method requires you to name the colour.

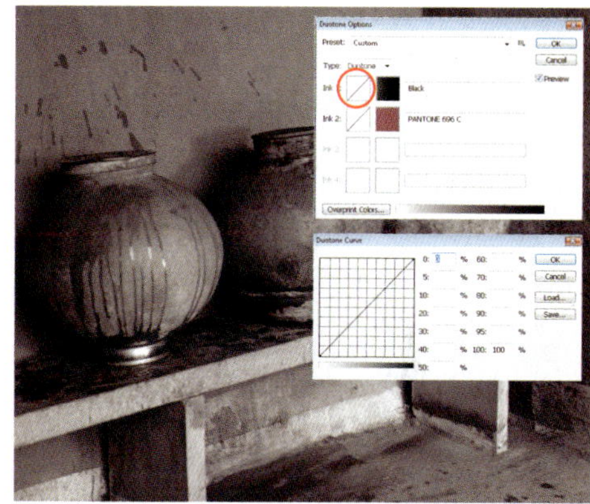

06 Curves ahead

With a colour picked, select the diagonal line icon for Ink 1. The new control box presents a graph that adjusts ink levels for each brightness level.

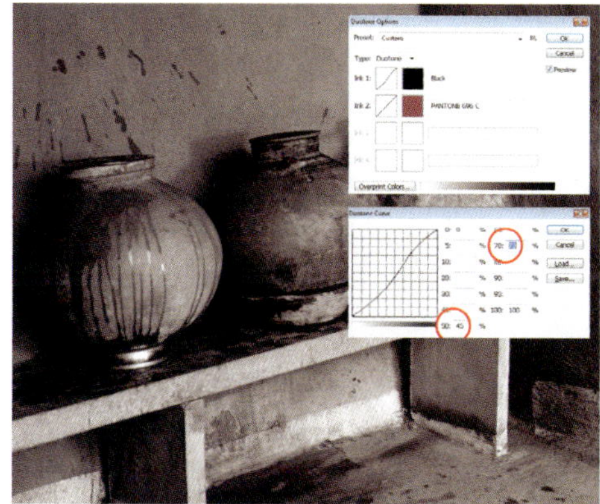

07 Small adjustments

Either by adding points to the curve or using the numerical boxes, set the 50 level to 45% and the 70 level to 73%. This will lighten midtones for starters.

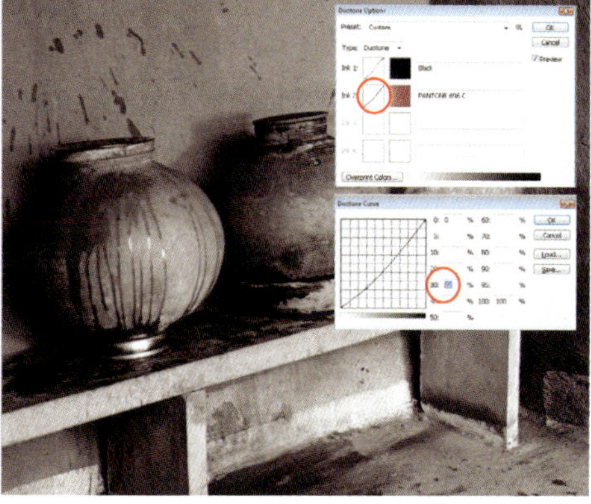

08 Further refinement

Now click on the curve icon for Ink 2. For this curve set the 30 level to 22%. This will help brighten the quarter tones and add more depth to the scene.

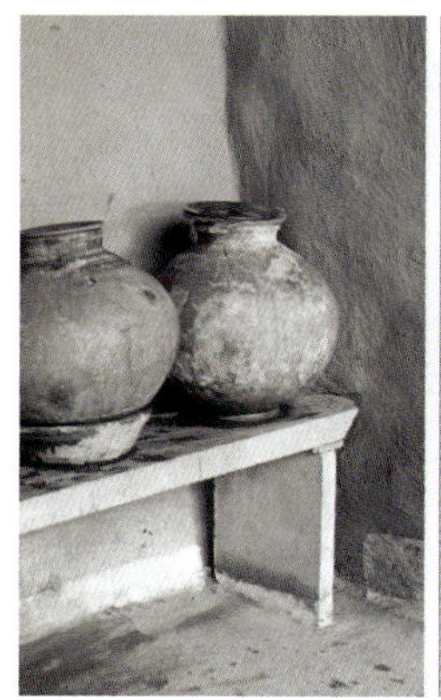

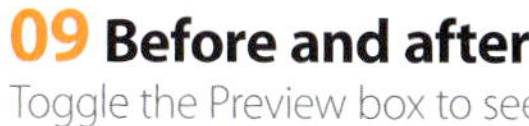

09 Before and after

Toggle the Preview box to see the results of your work contrasted with the greyscale version. You'll see the duotone has a much richer ambience.

Artificially age a photograph

In this quick creative project learn how to make a photo look decades old with an easy sepia-toning effect

By now, you've probably had your fill of instruction on different methods of working with tone and colour in Photoshop. We're guessing you are ready to see some creative outflow of the techniques we've been discussing. In this quick tutorial, we'll show you the 'how-to' for just one of the popular creative effects Photoshop is so well known for: we're going to artificially age a photograph!

There are several things that happen to photographs as they age. The inks begin to break apart and colour gets lost. The physical material the photo is on begins to break down, aiding in the deterioration process. One of the most tell-tale signs of age is the colours of the photo all turning to a yellowish-red colour known as sepia. Creating a sepia-toned image in Photoshop is very much like making your own sandwich. There are several different ways to do it, and the only 'right' way is the way you like the best. We will show you the easiest and most flexible method available.

Other age indicators are faded areas of the photo and visible film grain. In this guide we explain how to create all these effects in Photoshop to transform a modern snap into one that could have been taken decades ago.

So select an image you would like to experiment with, or load up ours. Keep in mind that the settings we recommend are merely that – recommendations. We encourage you to start with our suggestions and work from there to find the settings that are just right for your image.

"Creating a sepia-toned image in Photoshop is very much like making your own sandwich…"

OLD BEFORE ITS TIME

Tone of sepia

There are many ways to create a sepia-toned effect in Photoshop, but using the Colorize option in a Hue/Saturation layer is the easiest and most straightforward.

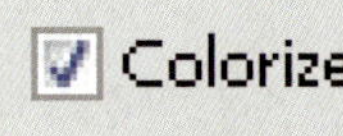

Signs of ageing

The faded corners and added film grain are applied with filters. When paired with the sepia tone, they help the aged effect appear much more realistic.

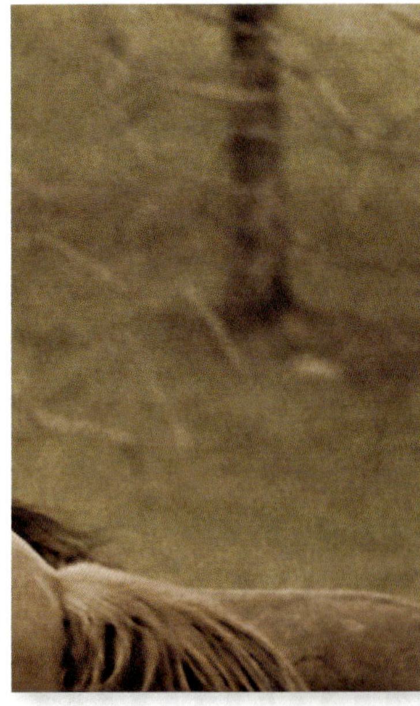

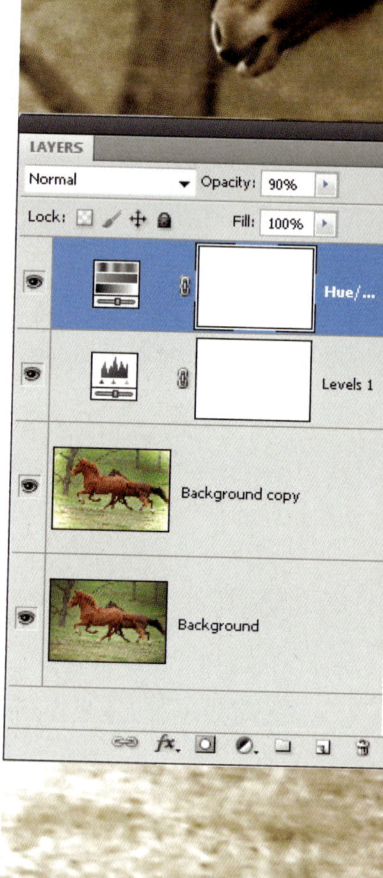

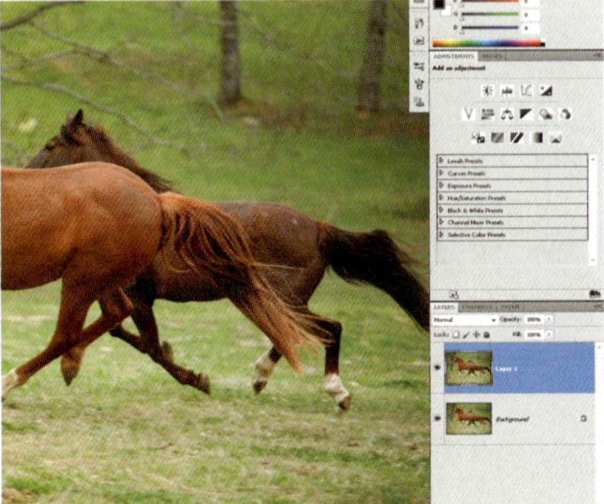

01 Common first step

In most projects you are going to want to retain the original image and work with a copy. Hit Cmd/Ctrl+J to duplicate the background to a new layer.

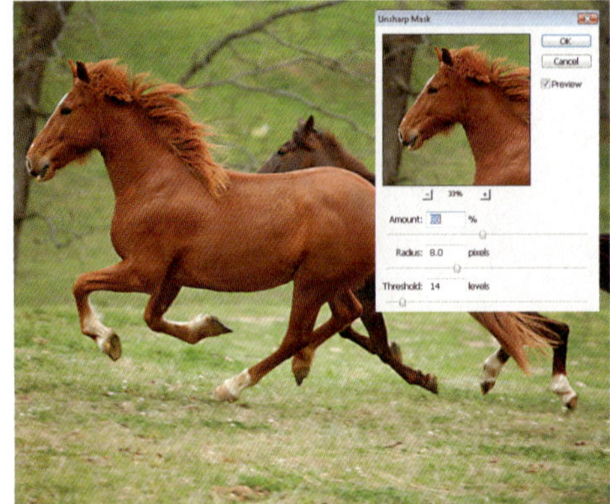

02 Sharpen up

Let's harden some of the edges by going to Filter>Sharpen>Unsharp Mask. Enter an Amount of 88%, Radius of 8px and Threshold of 14 levels.

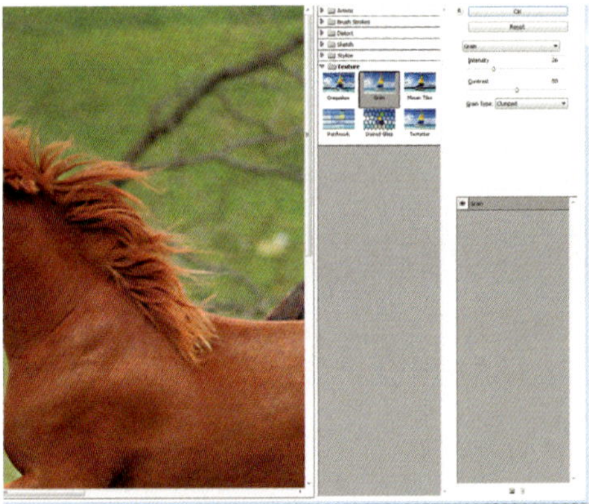

03 Old-fashioned grain

To add some aged film grain, go to Filter>Texture>Grain. Change the Grain Type to Clumped, Intensity to 26 and Contrast to 50. Hit OK to apply the effect.

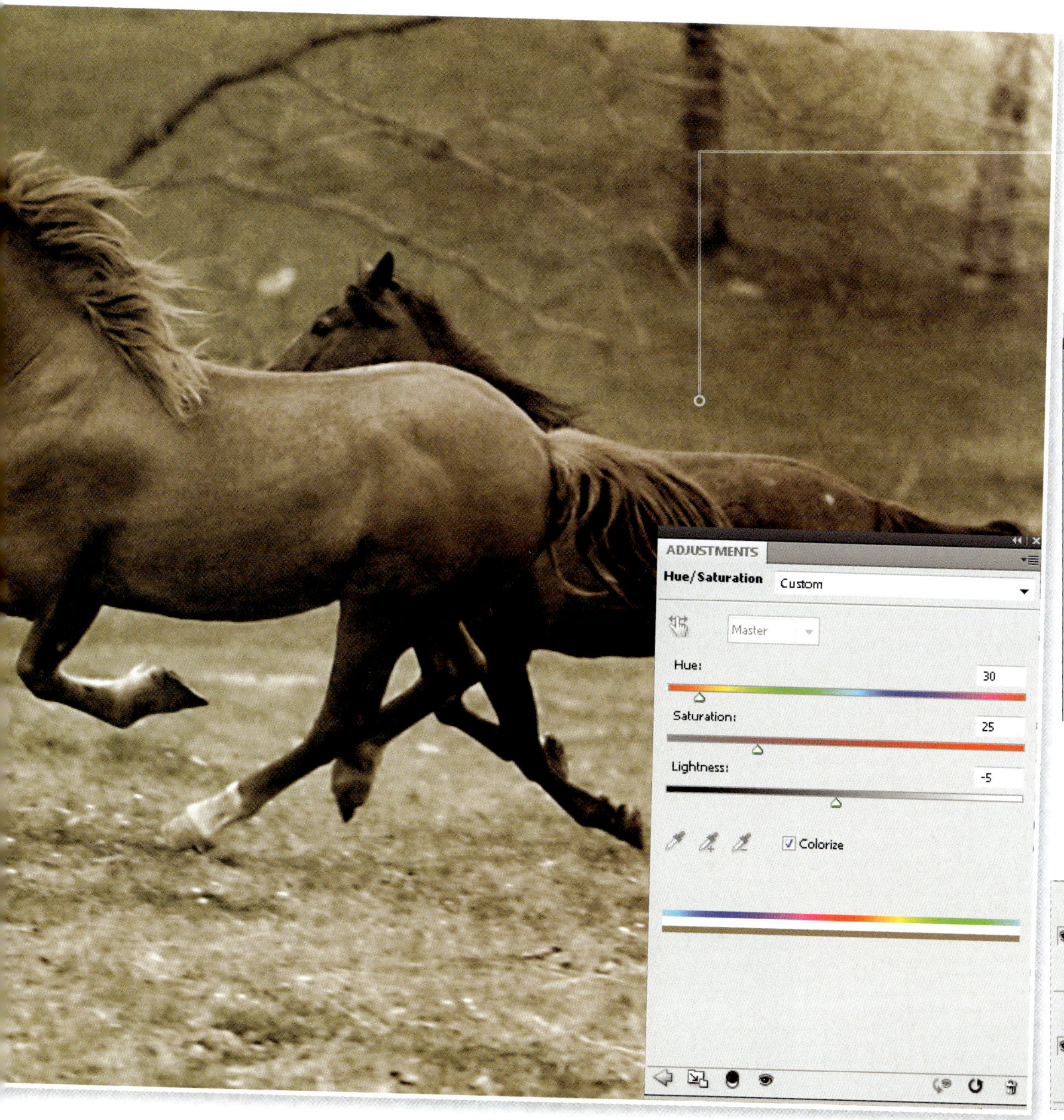

Adjustment layer benefits

By adding the Hue/Saturation as an adjustment layer, you can reduce the layer opacity, which allows just a hint of the original colour to peek through.

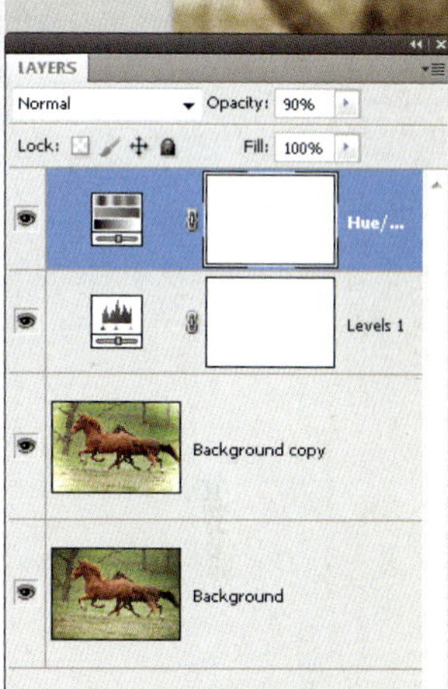

Work with a safety net

By working on a duplicate, the original background is preserved. That way you can always get back to the start if you make a mistake.

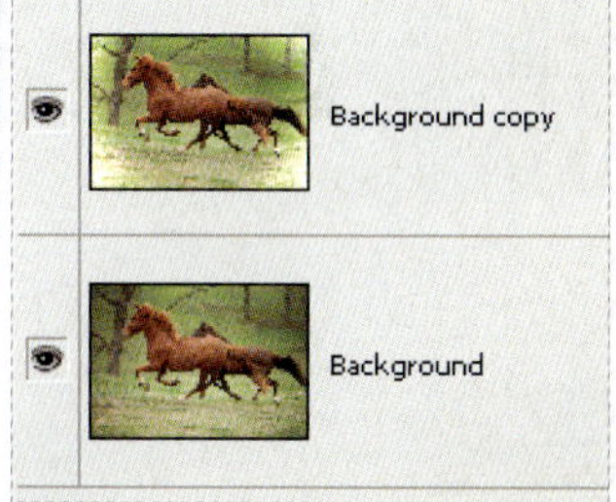

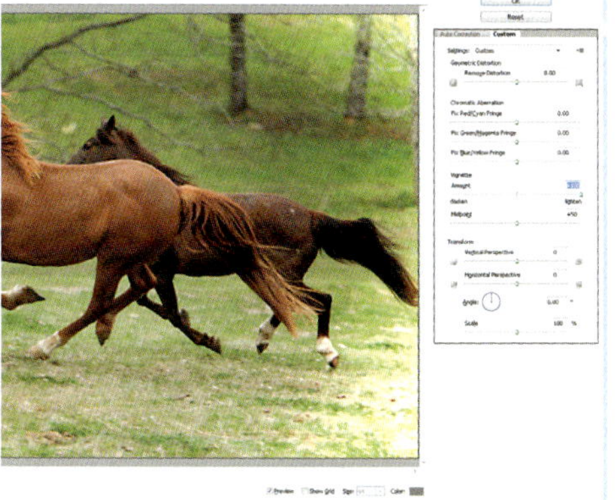

04 Faded edges

A quick way to fade the edges is to use Lens Correction found in the Filter menu. Look in the Custom tab and set the Vignette Amount to +100.

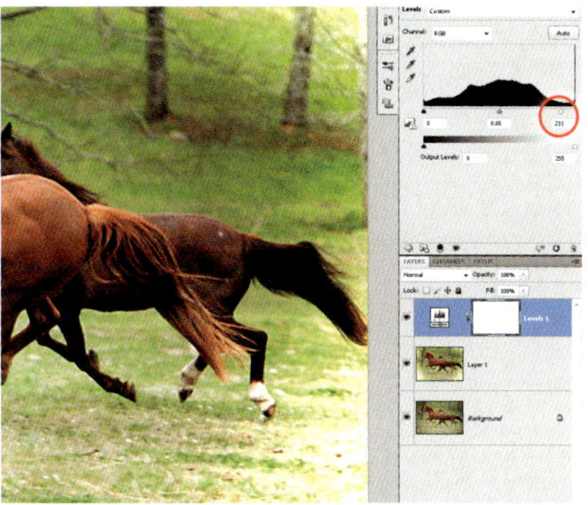

05 Increase contrast

Go to Layer>New Adjustment Layer>Levels. In the Adjustments panel pull the right-most slider slightly to the left. This will bump up the contrast.

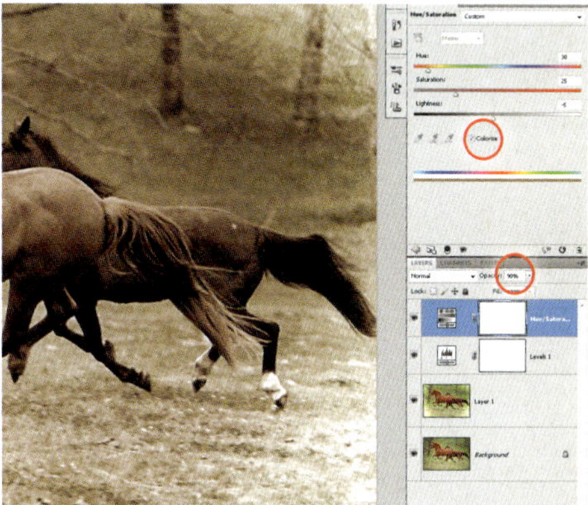

06 Colorize to finish

Add a Hue/Saturation layer and enable the Colorize option. Set Hue to 30, Saturation to 25 and Lightness to -5. Then reduce layer Opacity to 90%.

Layers

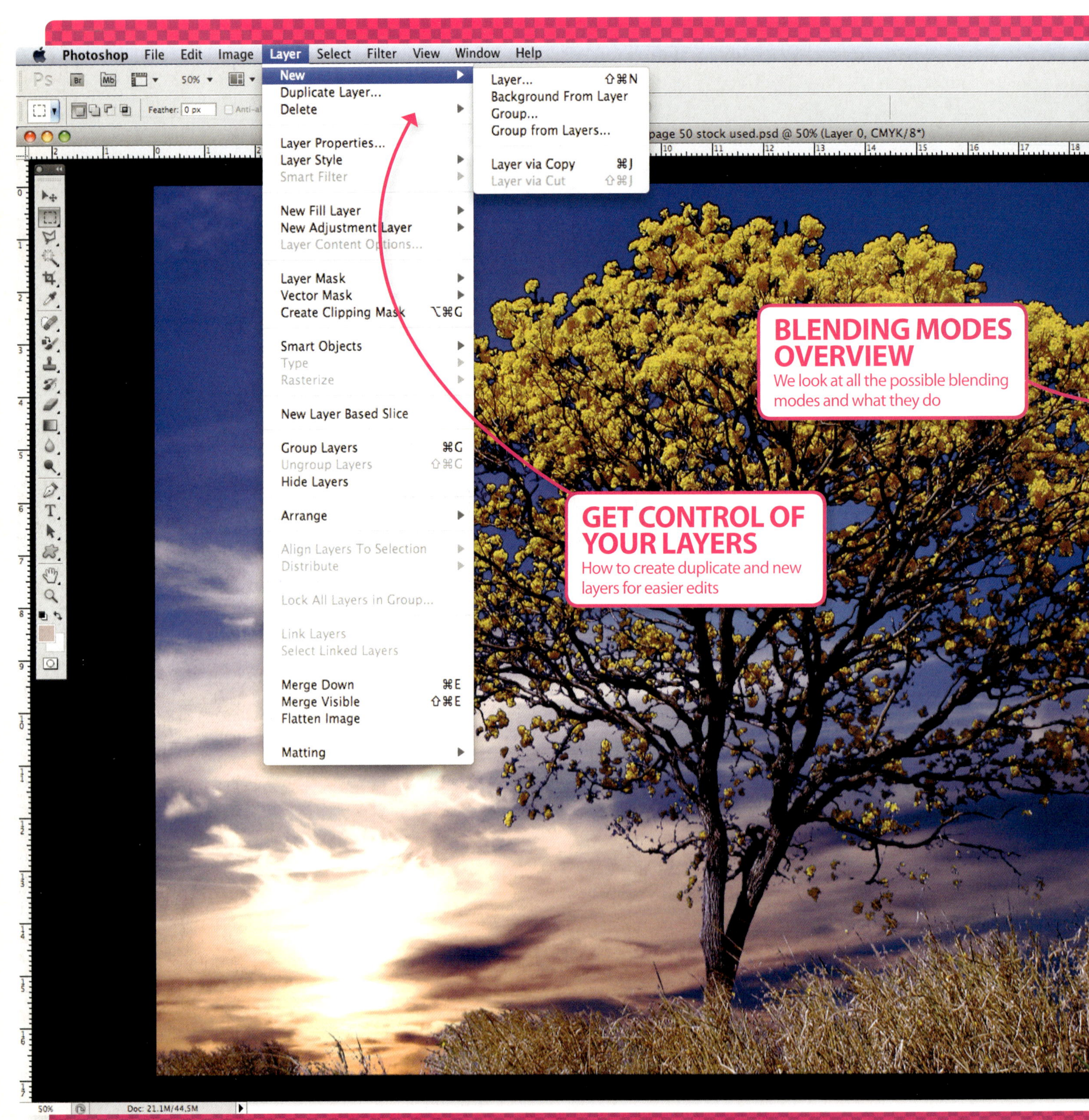

BLENDING MODES OVERVIEW
We look at all the possible blending modes and what they do

GET CONTROL OF YOUR LAYERS
How to create duplicate and new layers for easier edits

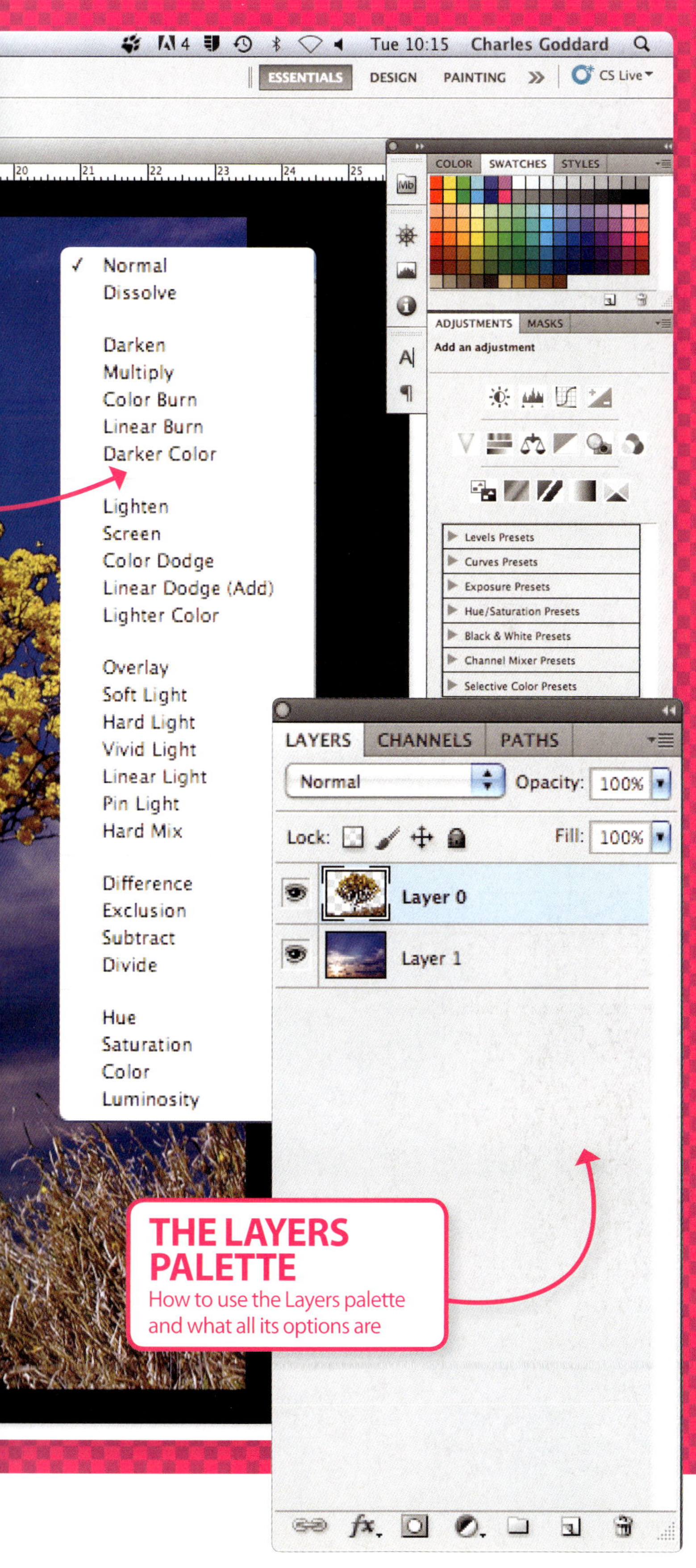

THE LAYERS PALETTE
How to use the Layers palette and what all its options are

"Layers are a vital part of your Photoshop experience and will save you much time and bother"

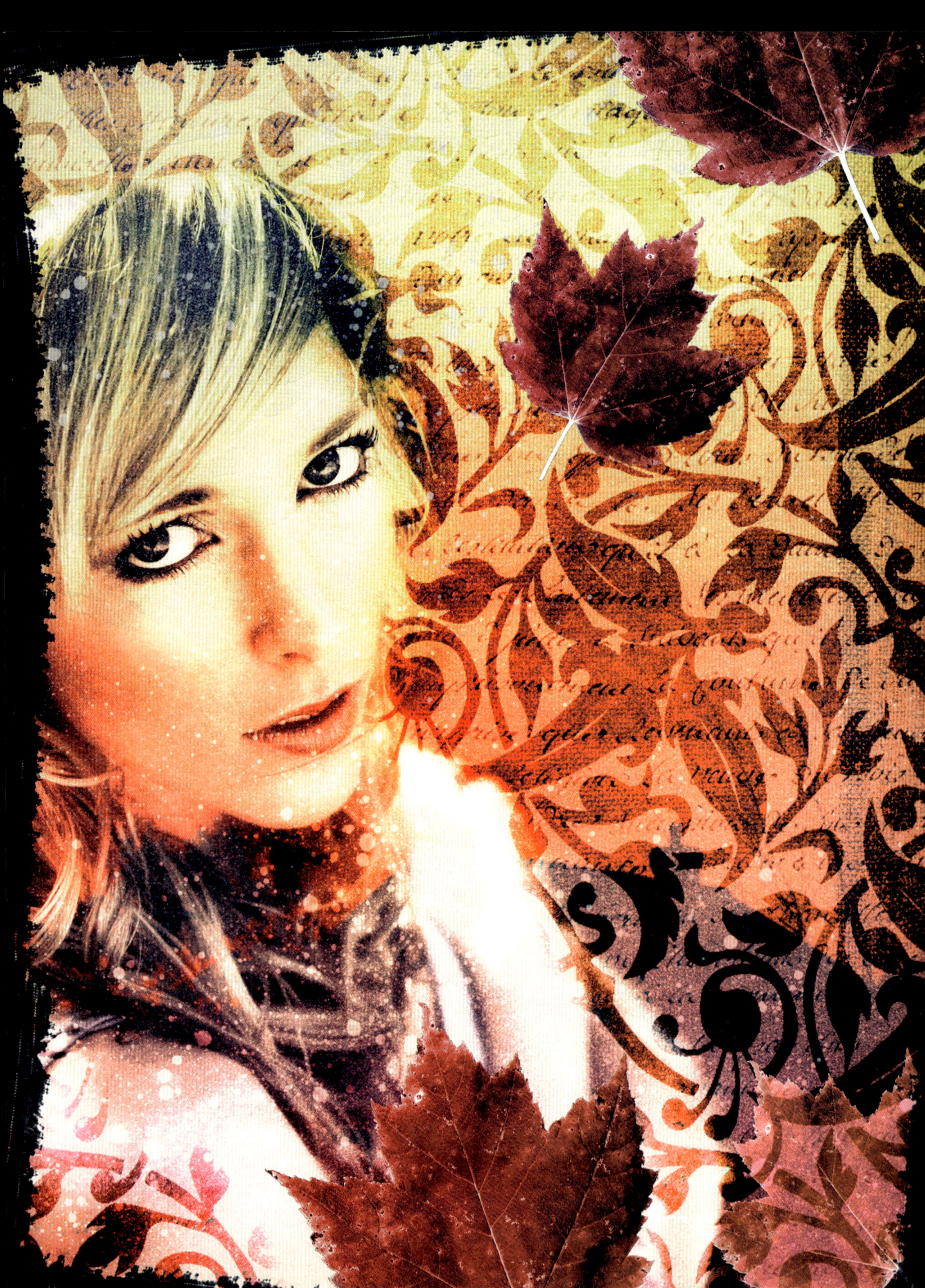

The Layers palette

Layers are a vital part of your Photoshop experience and will save you much time and bother. Here is a quick guide to the palette and its controls

As you work your way through any Photoshop tutorial you'll notice one thing – all of them use layers somewhere along the line. Layers allow you to break down your image into separate components, and work on each part without disturbing the others. In areas of an image that are transparent, you can see through to the layer below. As well as allowing you to work on parts of the image in isolation, layers let you alter the composition of an image by rearranging their order. You can create adjustment layers to make edits without making permanent changes to the image, and apply special effects to layers from the Styles menu. To make sure your layers don't get in a wild and unruly state, you have various management choices to help organise matters.

When you open an image or make a new file, it will appear on a layer. When you create a new layer, you can either make a clean layer or one that duplicates existing content. New layers appear above all the existing layers, although you can change the order. To create a new layer, click the New Layer button in the Layers palette. If you Option-click (Mac) or Alt-click (PC) on the New Layer button, you can give the layer a name and specify other options such as blending mode and colour. If you want to create a new layer that has the same content and effects as an existing layer, drag the layer to copy onto the New Layer button.

Because each layer helps build up an image bit by bit, it can get confusing to see what you're working on. To simplify matters you can turn the visibility of a layer on or off. This is done by clicking the little eye icon. If it's there, you can see the layer, if it's not the layer has been turned off. There is a lot that can be written about layers, so we've just concentrated on the basics here.

"Layers allow you to isolate parts of your image into separate components"

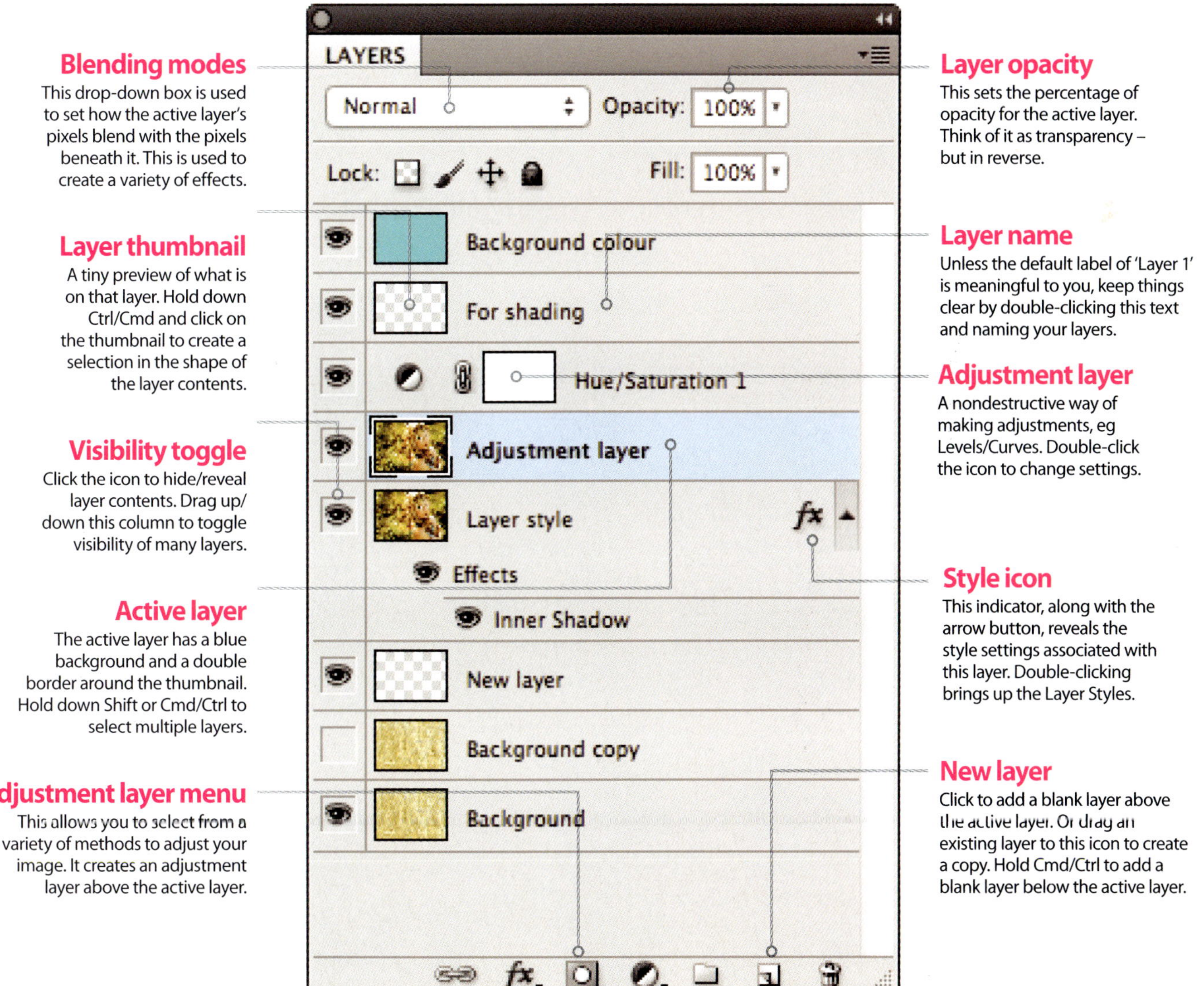

Blending modes
This drop-down box is used to set how the active layer's pixels blend with the pixels beneath it. This is used to create a variety of effects.

Layer thumbnail
A tiny preview of what is on that layer. Hold down Ctrl/Cmd and click on the thumbnail to create a selection in the shape of the layer contents.

Visibility toggle
Click the icon to hide/reveal layer contents. Drag up/down this column to toggle visibility of many layers.

Active layer
The active layer has a blue background and a double border around the thumbnail. Hold down Shift or Cmd/Ctrl to select multiple layers.

Adjustment layer menu
This allows you to select from a variety of methods to adjust your image. It creates an adjustment layer above the active layer.

Layer opacity
This sets the percentage of opacity for the active layer. Think of it as transparency – but in reverse.

Layer name
Unless the default label of 'Layer 1' is meaningful to you, keep things clear by double-clicking this text and naming your layers.

Adjustment layer
A nondestructive way of making adjustments, eg Levels/Curves. Double-click the icon to change settings.

Style icon
This indicator, along with the arrow button, reveals the style settings associated with this layer. Double-clicking brings up the Layer Styles.

New layer
Click to add a blank layer above the active layer. Or drag an existing layer to this icon to create a copy. Hold Cmd/Ctrl to add a blank layer below the active layer.

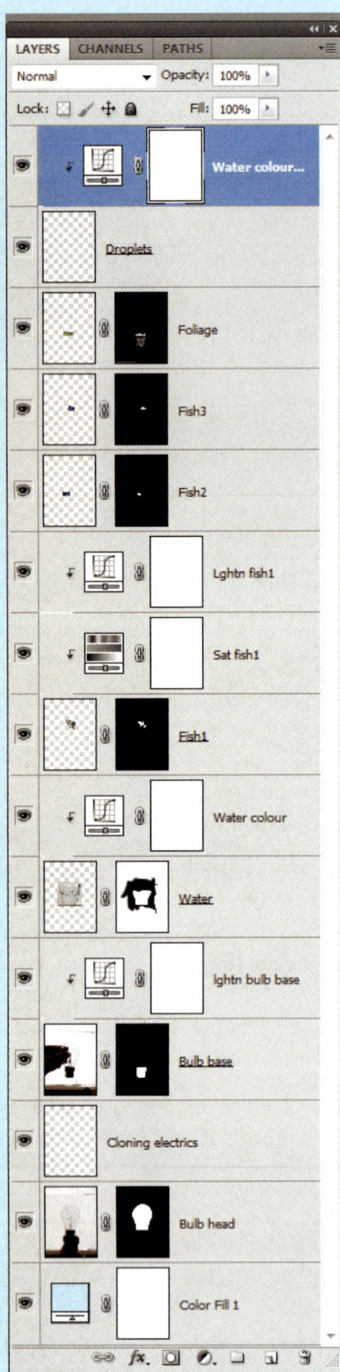
LAYERS
CHANNELS
PATHS
Normal
Opacity: 100%
Lock:
Fill: 100%
Water colour...
Droplets
Foliage
Fish3
Fish2
Lghtn fish1
Sat fish1
Fish1
Water colour
Water
lghtn bulb base
Bulb base
Cloning electrics
Bulb head
Color Fill 1

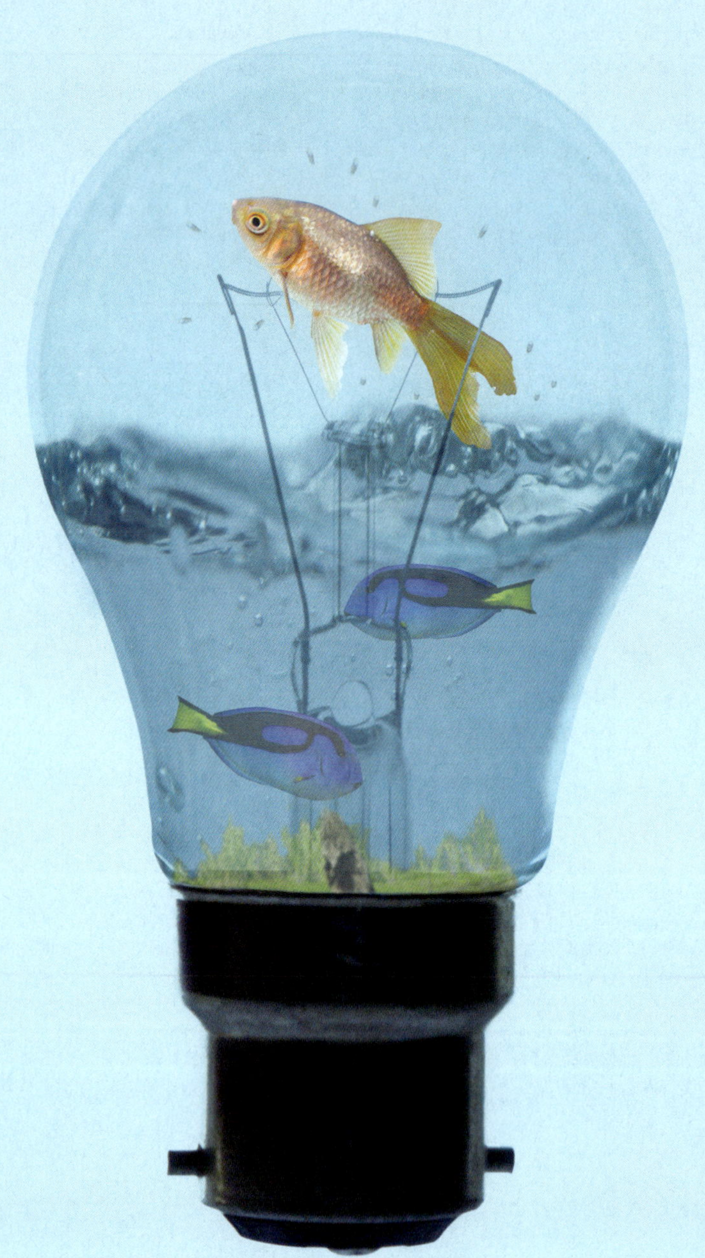

Layers: an overview

Harness the power of layers to protect data and get maximum creative control

One of the most useful analogies is to imagine layers like layers of clear acetate placed over a canvas painting. You can paint on the acetate and add to the overall look of the picture without touching the canvas below. If you decide the new work isn't so good later down the line, you can just take the acetate off and start again; all the original information is still intact. But as well as preserving our original data, layers also give us the benefit of working on this additional data independently. We might move it around using the Move tool, alter its size with Free Transform, or even make it lighter or darker using Curves or Levels. And all this work can be done independently of the Background layer, and if you have several layers with different bits of information on, you can do all that work separately on each. Imagine you start with a full body portrait. You could select each of the limbs and copy them each to their own new layer. You're now free to reshape or even recolour each limb without affecting the others. It's worth noting too that as well as pixel-based layers, there are also adjustment layers, which are special kinds of magic acetate that contain image adjustment information that affects everything below. A Curves adjustment layer, for example, might be used to brighten the Background layer; the advantage being the Background itself still remains untouched. And you can go back and alter those Curves settings at any given time.

> "Imagine layers like layers of clear acetate placed over a painting"

WHAT YOU'LL LEARN

Find the Layers palette

The Layers palette is often grouped with other palettes and accessed by clicking its tab. If you can't see it, go to Window>Layers or hit 'F7'.

Background

Every image comes with a Background layer by default when first opened up in Photoshop. It's important to keep the Background layer intact.

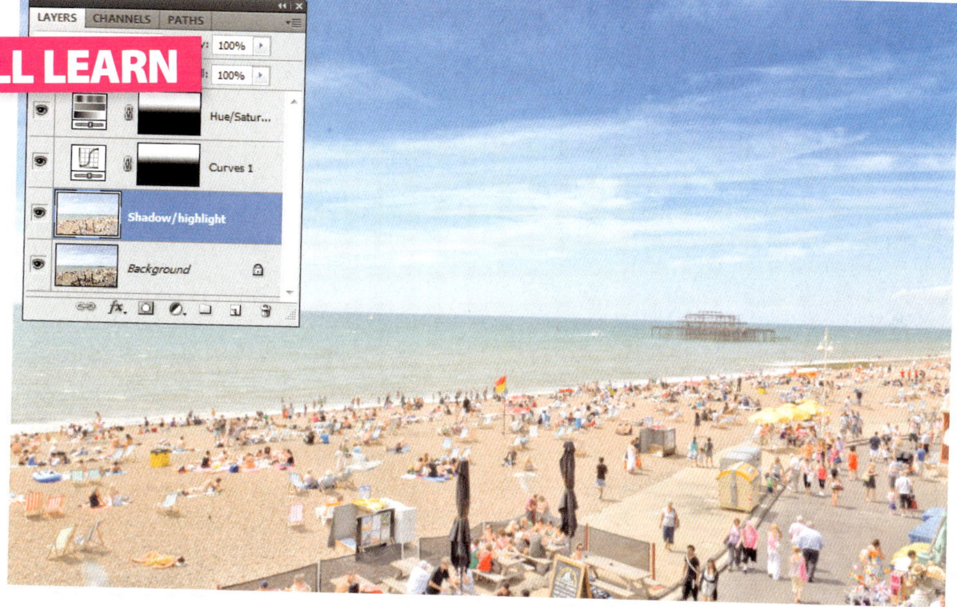

Pixel layers

The first type of layer is a pixel-based layer, containing pixel information. This might be a duplicate of the background, as in this case, or something else entirely.

Adjustment layers

In addition to pixel-based layers there are adjustment layers, such as the two found in this image. You can use their layer masks to focus the adjustments in specific places.

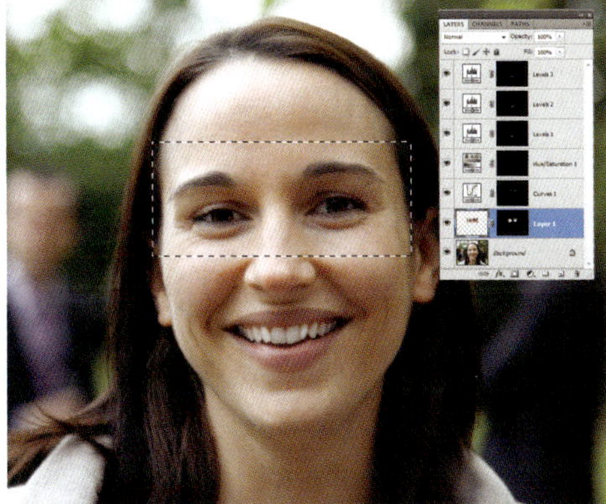

01 Copy the eyes

By copying the eyes across to a new layer, we can enlarge them slightly using a Free Transform without affecting the rest of the face.

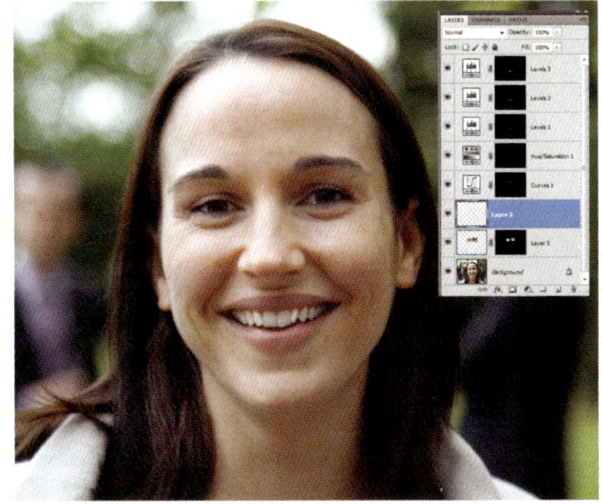

02 Blank layers

We can also use a blank layer to remove any skin blemishes by setting the Clone Stamp Tool to Current and Below. The Background remains intact.

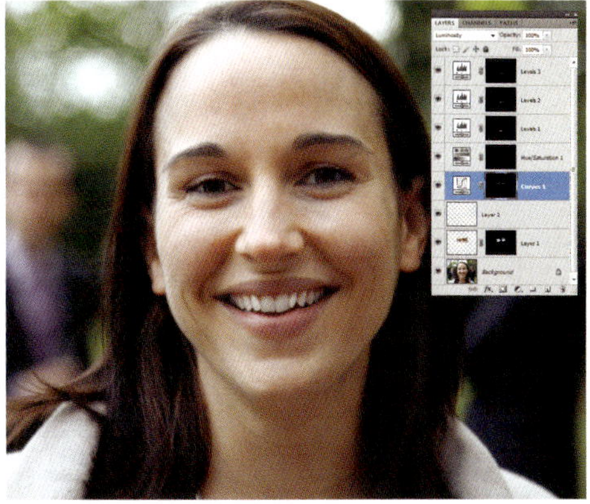

03 Adjustments

The remaining five layers here are adjustment layers, used in conjunction with layer masks to focus each adjustment to specific parts of the face.

How to use new layers

Learn how to add a new layer to preserve your Background layer and apply great retouching edits

We've already established the importance of using layers to preserve the information on our Background layer. This can be as simple as duplicating the Background layer before applying a filter effect, or adding an adjustment layer to change something like brightness or contrast. But we can also create new blank layers on top of our Background layer, allowing us to add pixel information of any kind. You create a new layer by clicking the 'Create new layer' button at the bottom of the Layers palette, or alternatively going to Layer>New>Layer. You can then add what you like on top.

There are many more applications than basic painting. With portrait photography, for example, a new layer is used to clean up any blemishes in the skin. By using the Spot Healing Brush and setting it to Sample All Layers mode, we can click over spots or moles on the skin and Photoshop will place a clean piece of skin on our new layer to replace the blemish. The Background layer still remains untouched, and the file size will be considerably less than doing the same job on a duplicate of the Background layer. Alternatively, by changing the layer blending mode to Color, we can alter any of the colours in our image by simply choosing the appropriate foreground colour and painting over the desired area. These are just two of many possible applications for new blank layer, so don't underestimate the power of this clean sheet of acetate!

"With portrait photography, a new layer is used to clean up any blemishes in the skin"

USING THE NEW LAYERS

Skin clean up

Our first new layer is used to clean up skin blemishes with the help of the Spot Healing Brush tool.

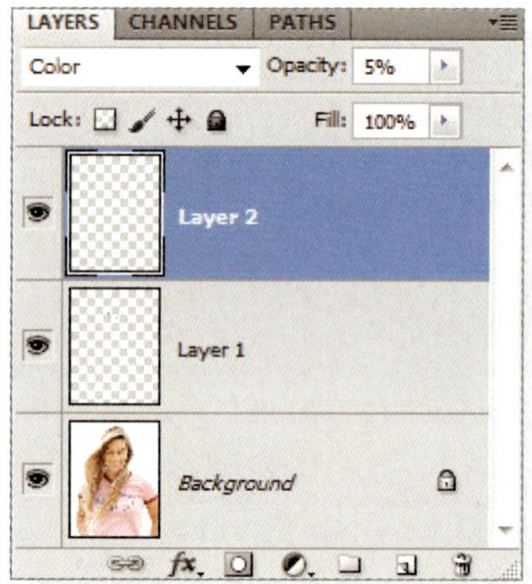

Eye colour

Our second new layer is used to alter the colour of the subject's eye, using the Color blending mode and the Brush tool.

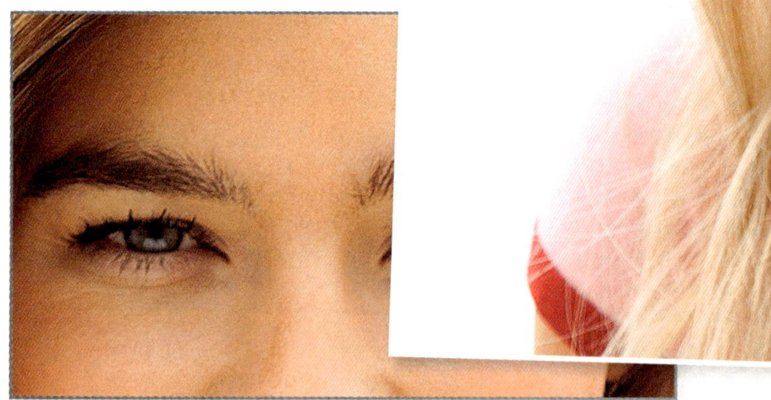

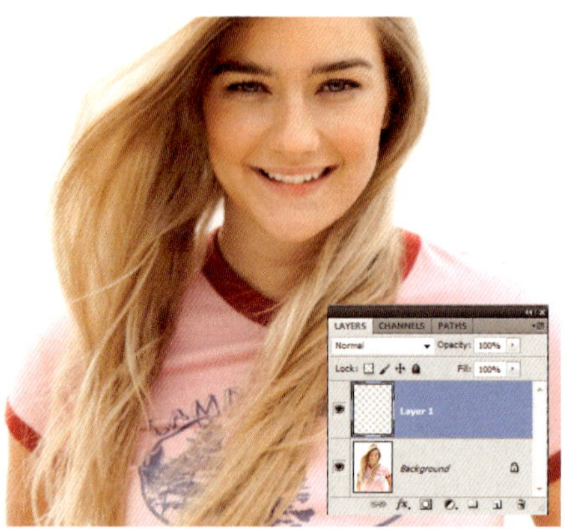

01 Create new layer

We create a new layer to start using the 'Create new layer' button in the Layers palette. We're going to use this to clean up minor skin blemishes.

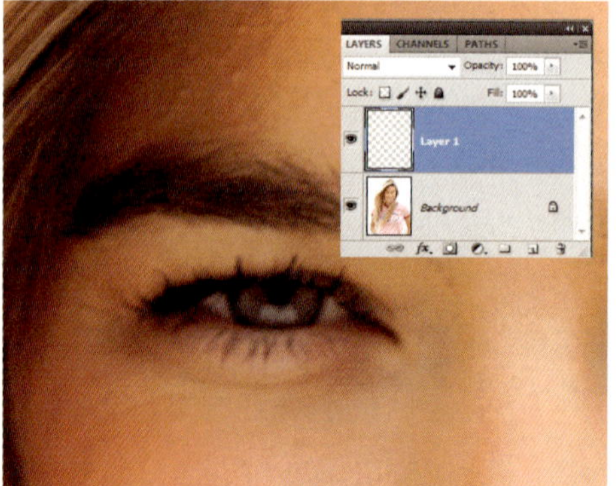

02 Set up the tool

We press 'J' for the Spot Healing Brush and set it to Sample All Layers in the tool Options bar. We zoom into the skin with Cmd/Ctrl and '+'.

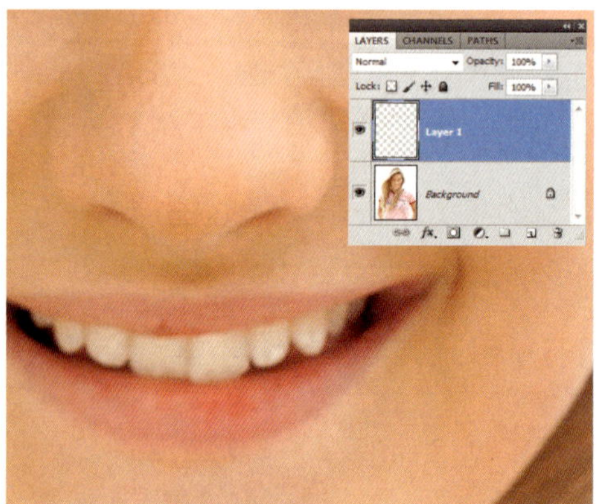

03 Remove the spots

Resize the brush with '[' and ']' keys to slightly larger than each spot, then click on each to remove them, dragging with Space to move around the image

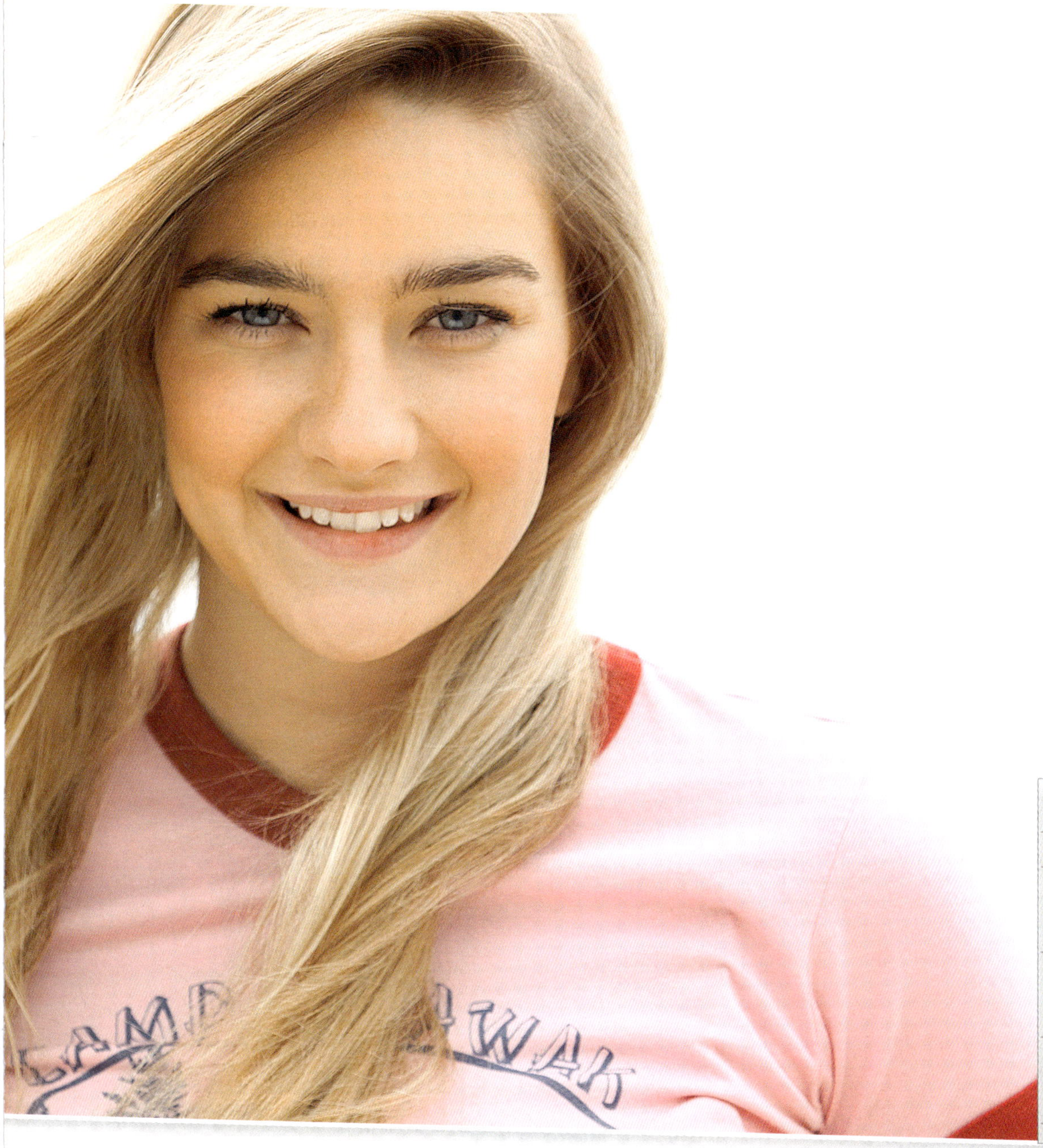

Layer blending mode

We can change the layer blending mode from Normal to Color using this drop-down menu at the top of the Layers palette.

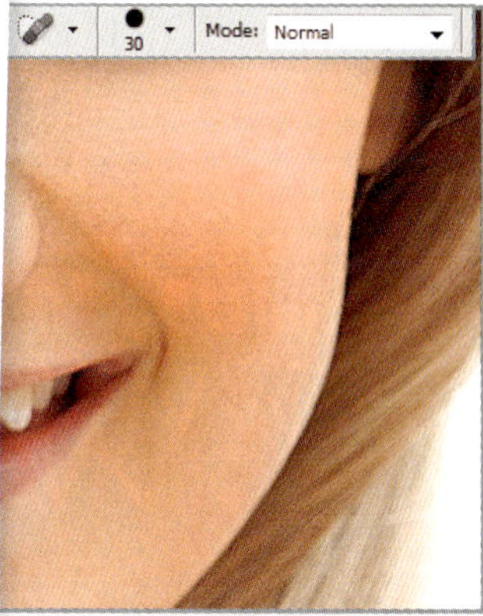

Layer strength

We can reduce the strength of the blue colour by dropping the layer Opacity using this using this drop-down menu at the top of the Layers palette.

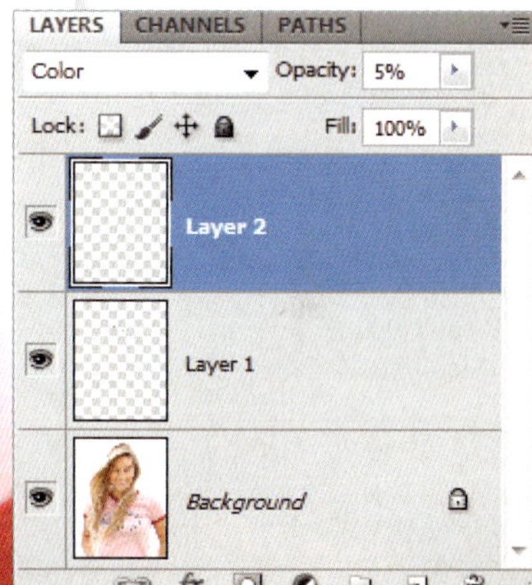

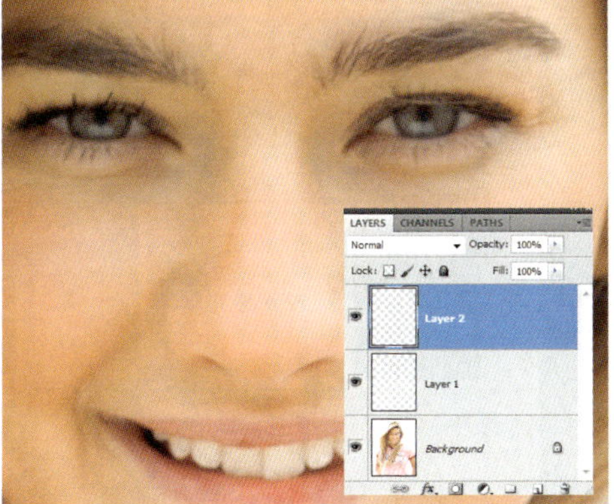

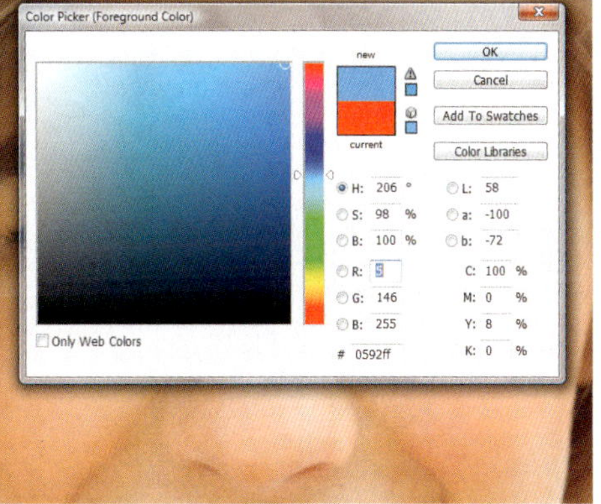

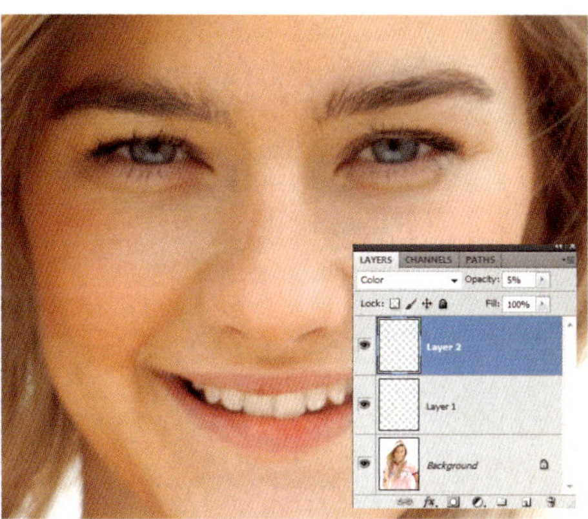

04 Create another new layer

The spots are removed but the Background layer remains intact. Next we can use another new layer to alter the eye colour. Create another new layer.

05 Change the blending mode

Change the layer blending mode to Color. In the toolbar, click the foreground colour swatch (front) and choose a bright blue from the Color Picker.

06 Change the eye colour

Press 'B' for the Brush tool and paint blue into the iris. The Color blending mode protects the detail. Drop the layer's Opacity to 5-10% for better realism.

Merging layers

Learn how to merge layers to declutter your Layers palette and save precious space

With very complex retouching edits you can sometimes find yourself totting up absolutely stacks of layers and it can all get a little confusing – even if you group or cannily colour code them. And the more layers you have, the greater the file size; to give you a rough idea, an image from a high-resolution camera with more than 15 layers can easily hit the 1GB mark.

When you take into account the fact that a decent-sized hard drive is around 500GB, you'll quickly realise that you don't have the space for too many of these images – particularly as you'll no doubt want to store all of your unedited RAW files too. The solution, in many cases, is to make a compromise between the ability to change every single one of your edits at a later date and to keep file size down and not overwhelm the eye with monstrous numbers of layers taking over the Layers palette.

If you've got an image with a large volume of layers, a good habit to get in to hunting through them and asking yourself whether any could be combined into a single layer to save on space.

Perhaps you've used one layer to correct skin on the face, and then another to reshape a body part. By merging these two layers, you've still got the option of altering the layer at a later date or removing it entirely; the only things you won't be able to do are change the blending mode independently or reposition each separately. That said, if you desperately need to make these changes at a later date, you can always copy the relevant information back to a separate layer. So don't dismiss merging layers as a dull optional extra; it's essential for space saving and keeping things simple!

> "If you've got an image with a large volume of layers, have a hunt through and ask yourself whether any could be combined"

QUICK PHOTOSHOP TIPS

Merged duplicate layer

To create a merged duplicate of everything without flattening an image, you need to select the top layer, hold Opt/Alt and go to Layer>Merge Visible.

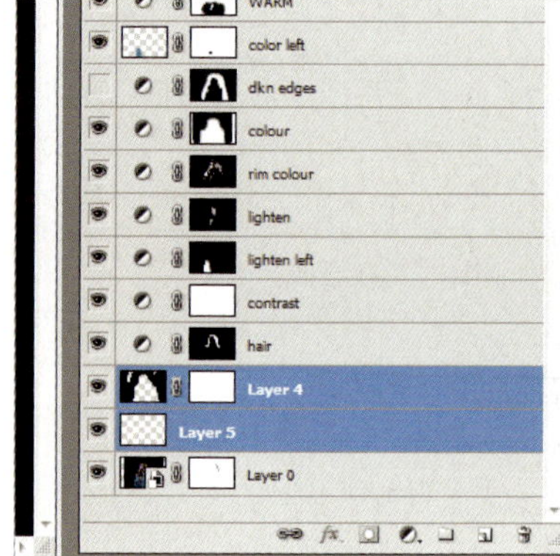

Clipping mask layers

You can spot clipping mask layers by the small down arrow icon that sits beside them. Merge them into their pixel layer if they're no longer needed.

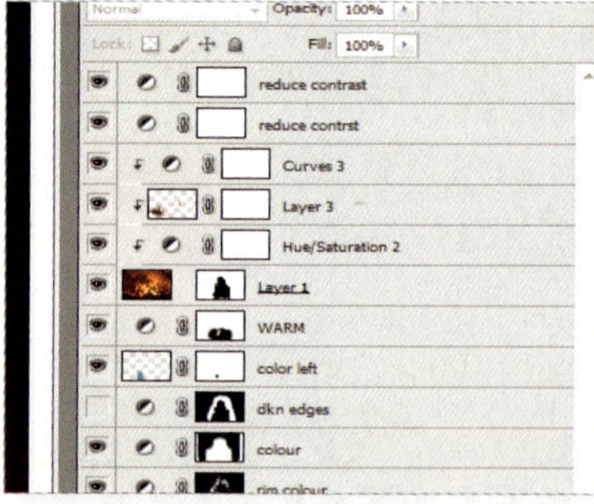

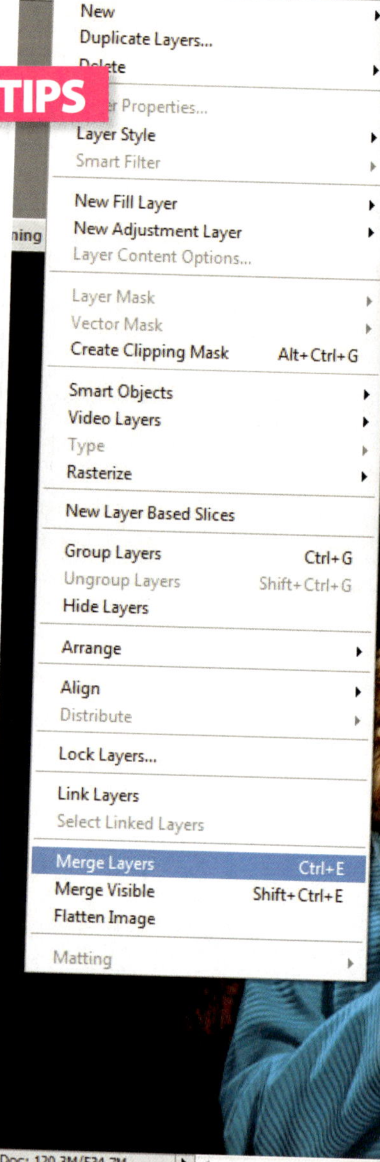

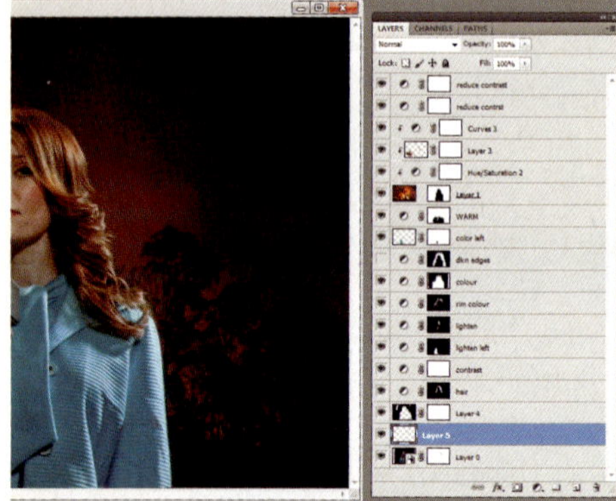

01 Examine layers

We've got quite a complex image here and we're looking to save some space. There are two pixel-based layers above the base layer ripe for merging.

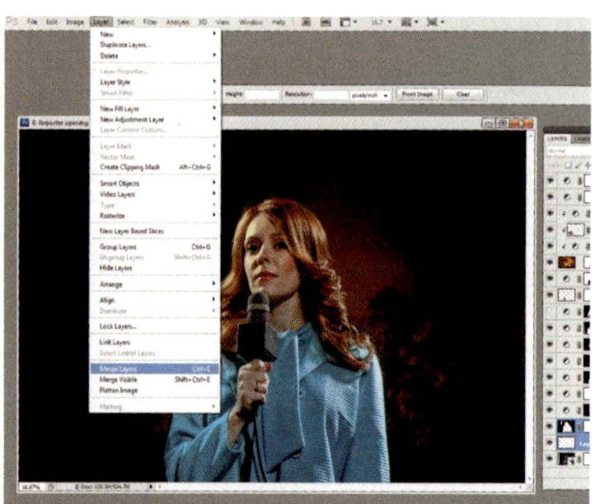

02 Select layers

We hold down the Ctrl key and click the two layers to select them both and then go to Layer>Merge Layers. They're now combined into one layer.

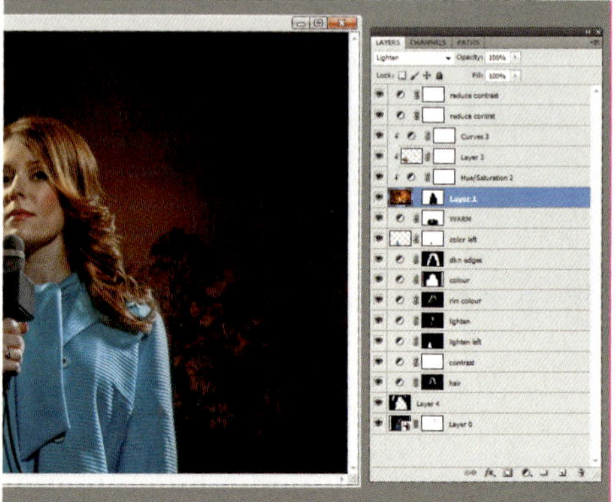

03 Merge layers

The adjustment layers above contain a lot of important data, so we leave those as they are. Instead we look at the fire background layer above.

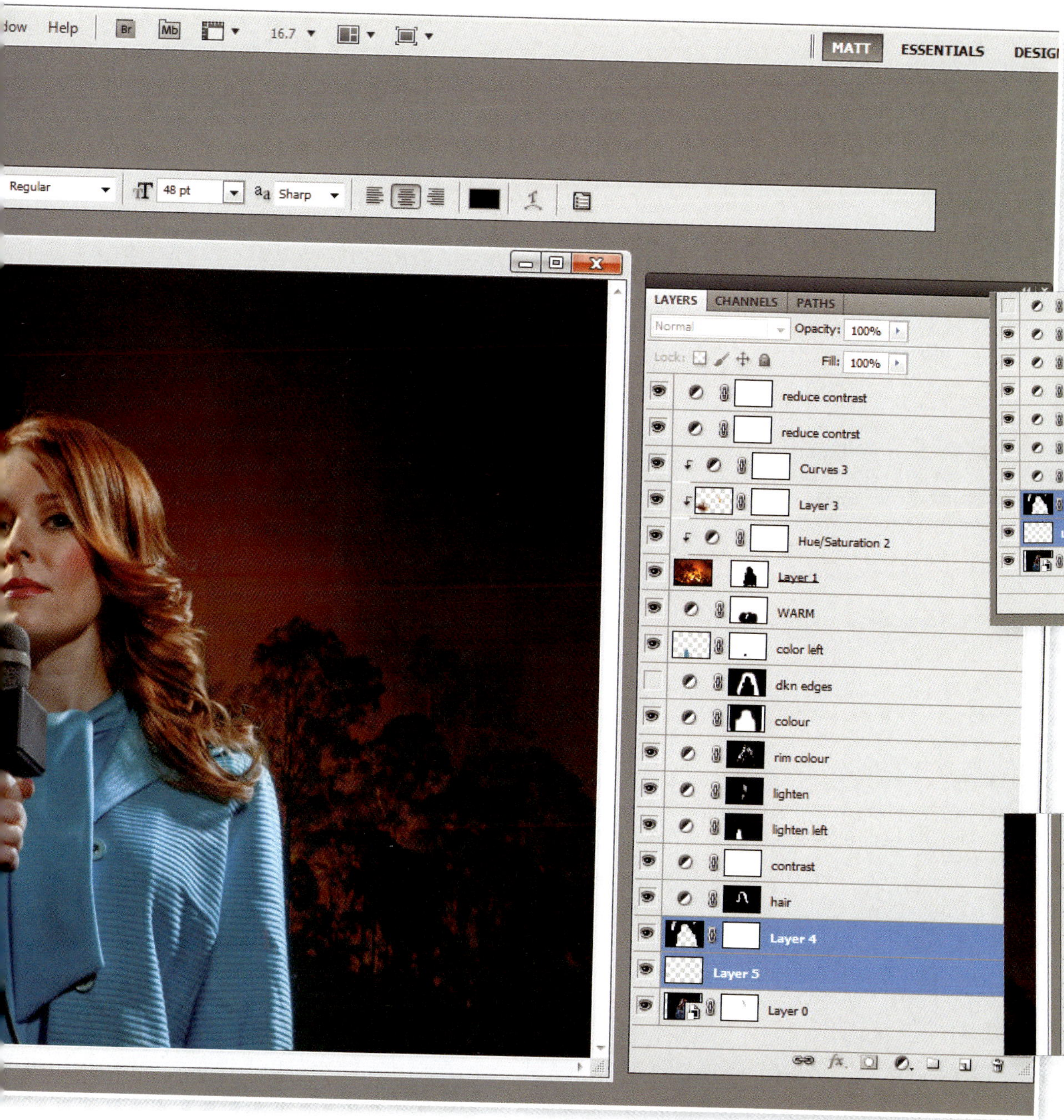

Choosing which layers to merge

In this instance, the first two layers above the background are ripe for a merge to save space. There's no need for them to exist independently.

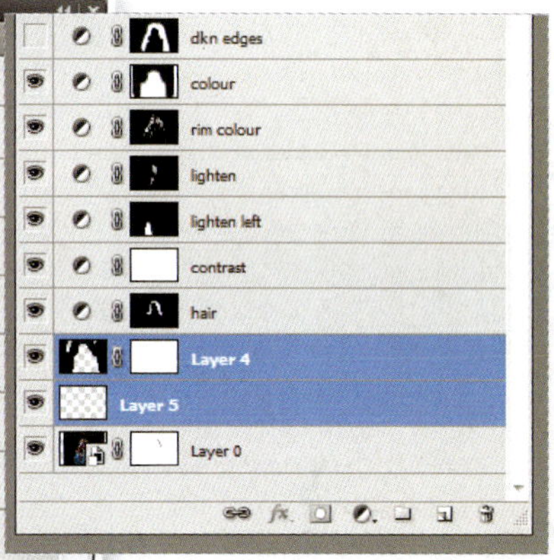

Adjustment layers

Adjustment layers should only ever be merged with pixel-based layers. If you merge them to each other only, their various effects will disappear.

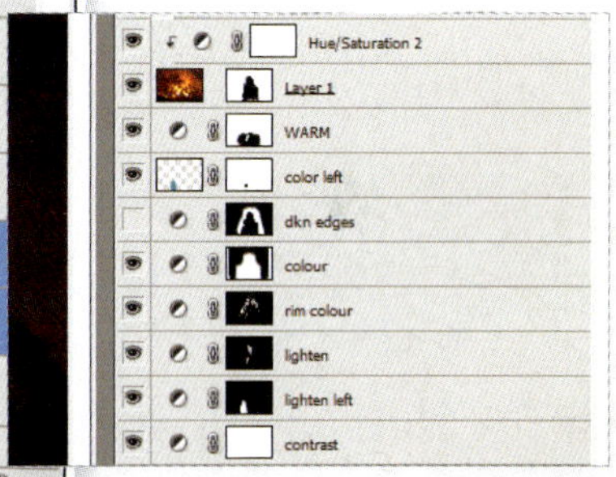

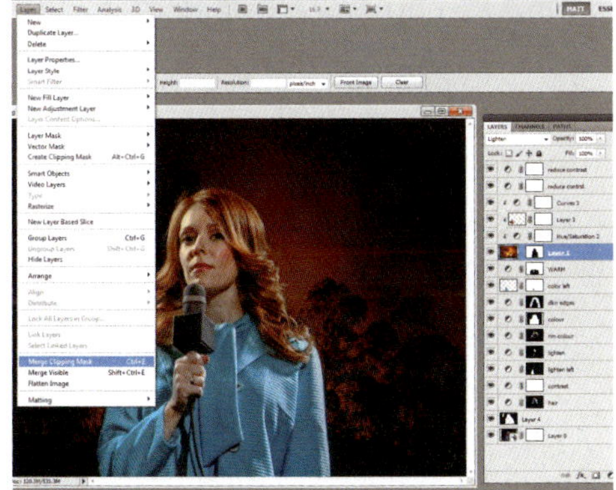

04 Merge clipping masks

This layer has three similar clipping masks above it. Deciding this fire layer is perfect for merging, we go to Layer>Merge Clipping Mask.

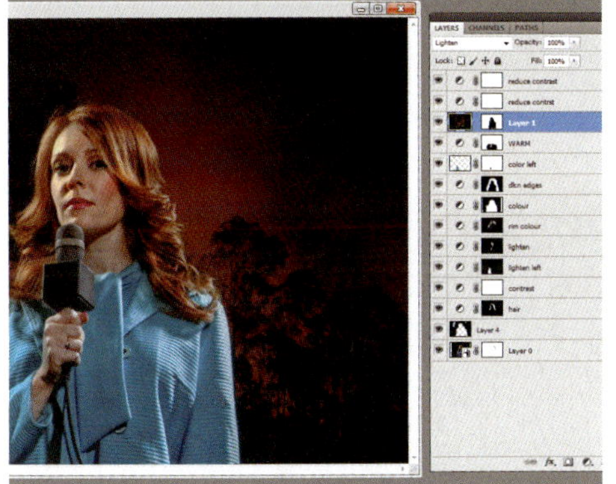

05 Prepare to sharpen

These four layers are now combined into a single layer. Finally, we want to sharpen the image so we need to merge everything without flattening.

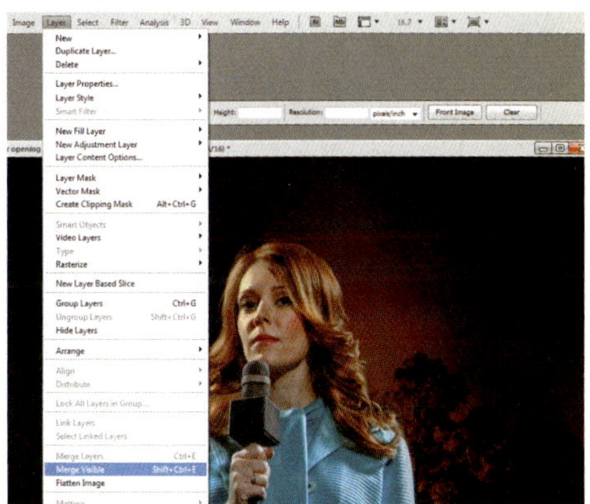

06 Merge Visible

On the top layer, hold Opt/Alt and select Layer> Merge Visible. We now have a merged layer to apply sharpening to but our work is still beneath.

Flattening layers

Learn how to flatten layers down to one single layer for web and email use

Every time you add a layer to a file you increase the total size of that file. In an ideal world this would be of no real consequence, but the fact is that our hard drives contain limited amounts of storage and there's also the time restriction involved in transmitting large files across the web; uncompressed files containing a number of layers can take several hours to transmit.

We can tackle these potential issues in two possible ways. Firstly we can try and make sure that we don't use unnecessary layers to complete a specific task; some jobs can be completed with a lot less additional layers than you might first think. The use of adjustment layers in particular can save an awful lot of space.

Secondly, we can 'flatten' our images down for the purpose of web transmission using the Layer>Flatten Image command. This merges all of our layers into one single layer for the purposes of reducing file size. In addition to this, we can use a 'compressed' format like a JPEG to cut down file size even further (a JPEG compression setting of 9 is the one to go for). A flattened image saved as a JPEG can impressively go from something like 300MB to just 2MB using this process.

The important thing to remember is that you make sure to save the layered version (non-flattened) in the uncompressed Photoshop (ie PSD) format first. That way you've got the full layered version with every shred of information that you can go back and adjust at any time if further edits are required at a later date, as well as a smaller version that you can transmit easily across the web or email to clients, etc.

"A flattened image saved as a JPEG can impressively go from something like 300MB to just 2MB using this process"

QUICK PHOTOSHOP TIPS

Save As you go

The File menu at the top of the application window contains the Save As command, which does exactly what it says on the tin, letting you save both non-flattened and flattened versions of your image at any stage. Take the time to back up your work to avoid losing it.

Flatten Image

The Layer menu at the top of the application window contains the Flatten Image command – a vital feature for when it comes to flattening layers!

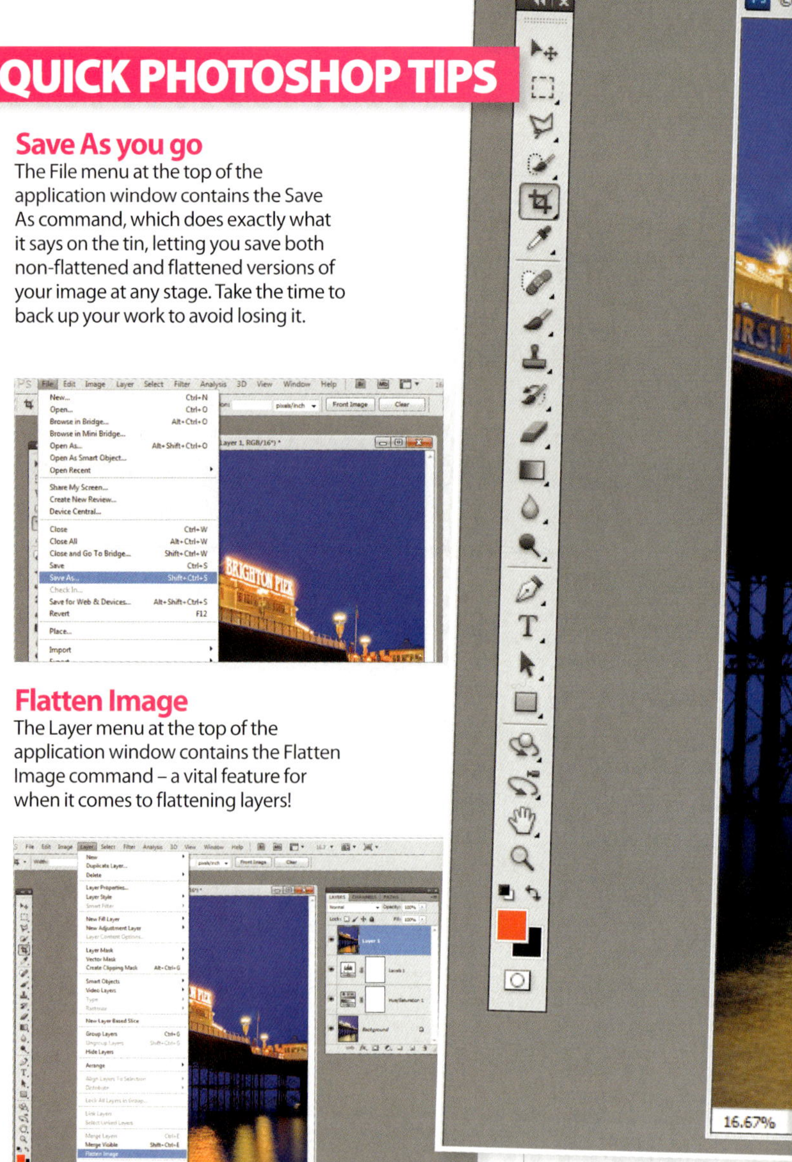

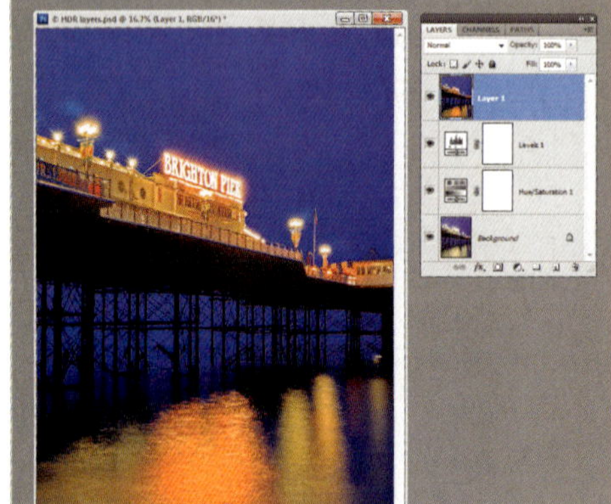

01 Start at the end

Here you can see we've completed our work. We have the Background layer, two adjustment layers and a merged duplicate layer. 137.1MB in total..

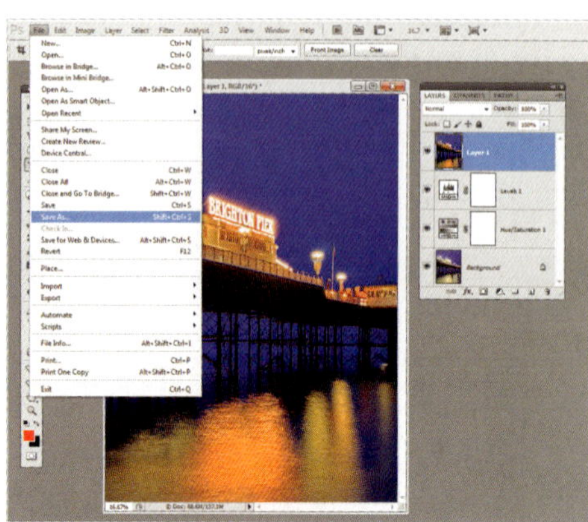

02 Save your work

We want to make sure that we save the image with all our layers on so we can go back and adjust them if need be, so we go to File>Save As.

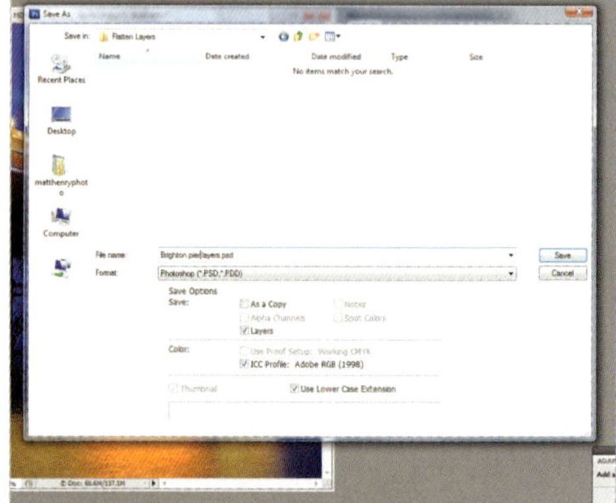

03 The name game

When the Save As dialog appears, give the image a name and select the format from the dropdown. For layers it must be the Photoshop (PSD) format.

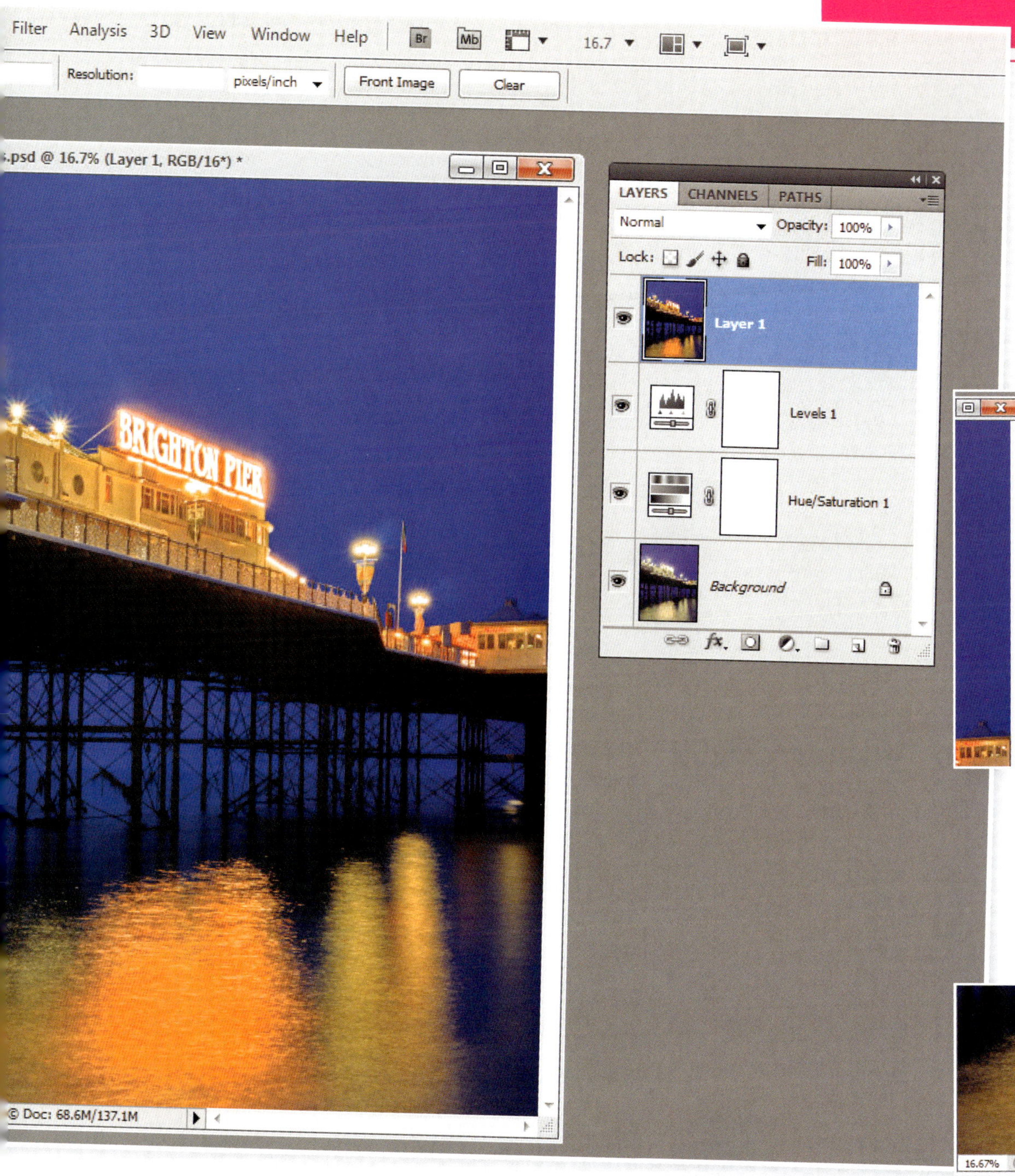

Flattening will get you everywhere

In the unflattened version, you can see all the layers in the palette. Once flattened, these layers are condensed into just a single layer.

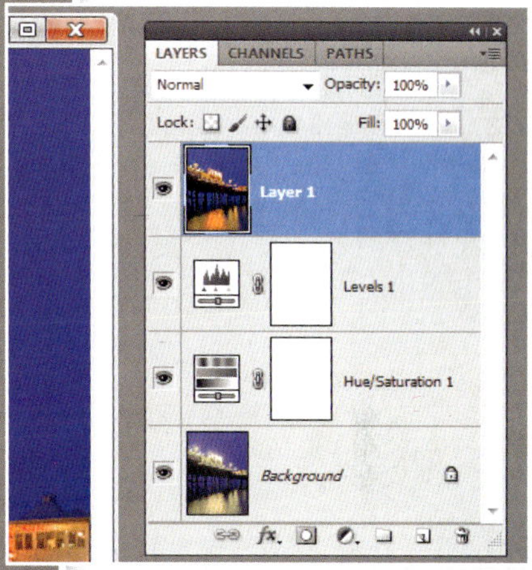

Size up your file

At the bottom of the image window you'll find two figures; the first tells you the file size for the Background layer only, while the second is the total file size including all the layers.

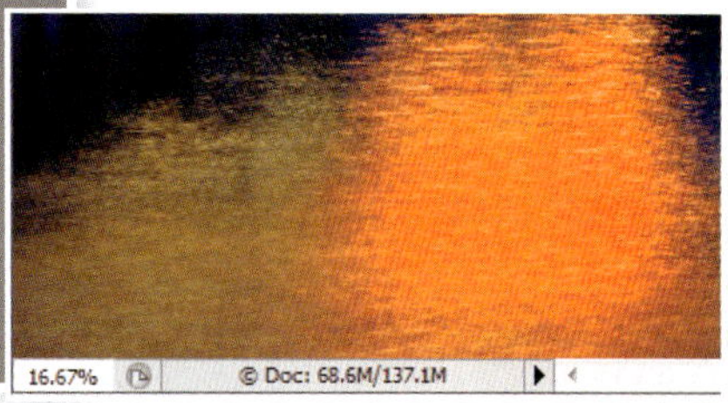

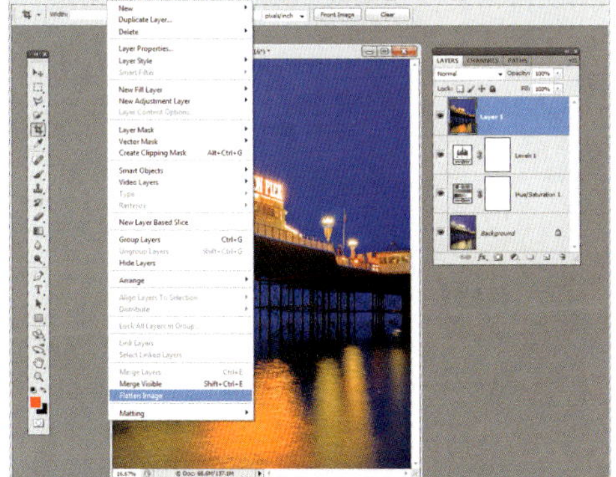

04 Size matters

With the layered file saved as a PSD, we are free to reduce the file size for email and the web. Start by flattening the layers via Layer>Flatten Image.

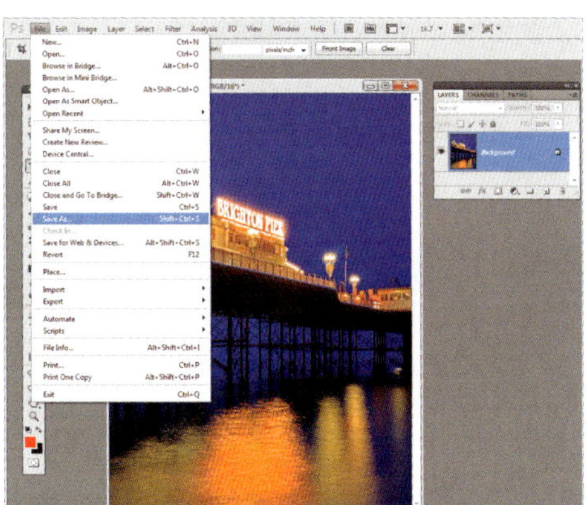

05 Slimline files

With all of our work condensed into a single layer, file size has been reduced from 137.1MB to 68.6MB. Next go to File>Save As to save the web version.

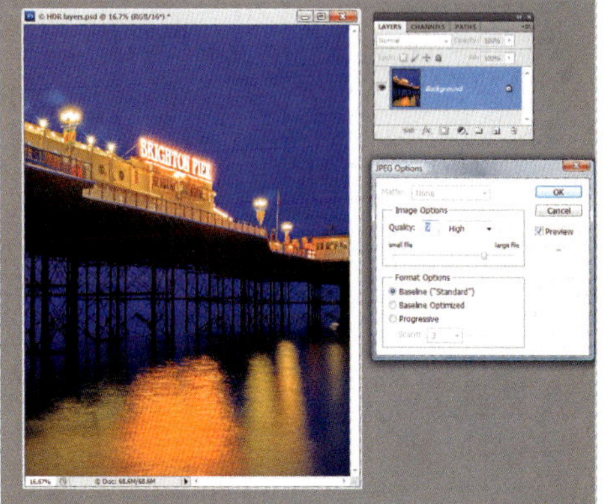

06 PSD to JPEG

We can keep the same name, but we must make sure to change the format to JPEG. Click Save and the compression dialog appears. Use a setting of 9.

Working with layers

Rename, group and colour code layers to keep your palette organised for later use

As you get a bit more proficient at using Photoshop, you'll find yourself using more and more layers. The numbers can quickly stack up and it can all become a little bit disorientating, making it vital that you keep your Layers palette nicely organised. The most important thing to do is to rename your layers, so that if you return to make edits a month or more down the line, you won't have to fiddle with each layer to work out just what it does. A name with a clear description like 'Eye colour change' saves you a lot of head scratching, so you can get right in and make the edits you need.

There are two other things that we can do to keep stuff organised. One is to place similar layers into a Group folder and the other is to make use of coloured labels. Normally one of these two options is enough to keep things ordered. There's one other advantage of using groups that goes beyond simple organisation, and that's that we can make sure adjustment layers apply only to those layers inside the group rather than everything below, kind of like a clipping mask but for more than one layer. A clipping mask you may recognise as a way of ensuring an adjustment layer only affects the pixel layer below it, and not everything else. You hold down Opt/Alt and click between the two layers to create one. To ensure that adjustment layers inside a group affect only that group, it's a matter instead of changing the default blending mode from Pass Through to Normal. It couldn't be easier.

"A name with a clear description like 'Eye colour change' saves you a lot of head scratching, so you can get right in and make the edits you need"

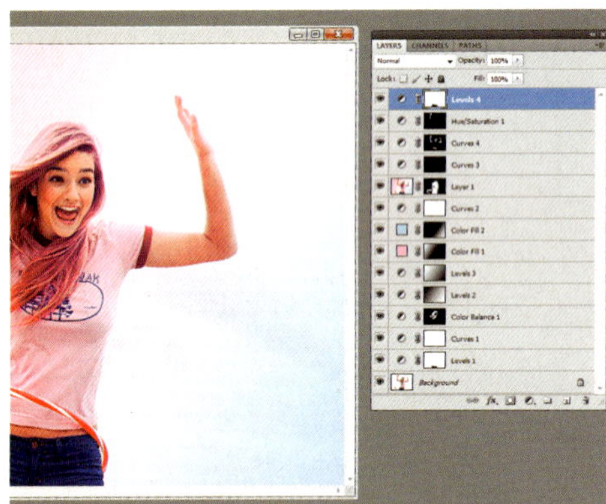

01 Confusing layers
This image has had a lot of work and, as a result, layers have really stacked up. If we opened it later, it would be difficult to work out what does what.

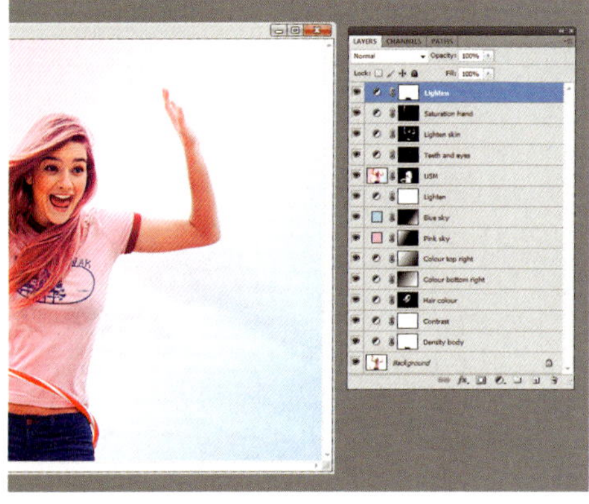

02 Rename layers
The first thing we need to do is to rename each layer appropriately. Ctrl/right-click the text and select Rename or simply double-click the text.

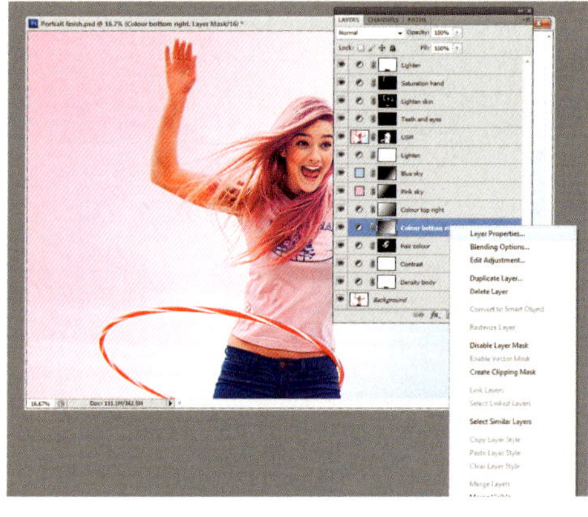

03 Colour code
The other thing we can do is colour code our layers. To do this, Ctrl/right-click the 'layer' icon and select Layer Properties from the option list.

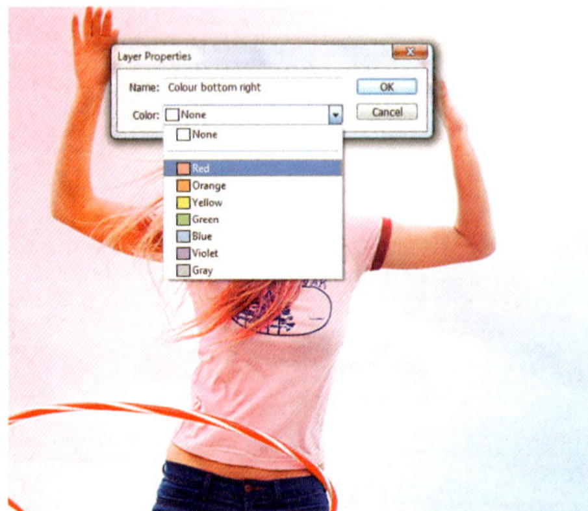

04 Select colour
When the next dialog appears, click the Color dropdown menu to get a selection of possible colours. Pick the one you want and hit OK.

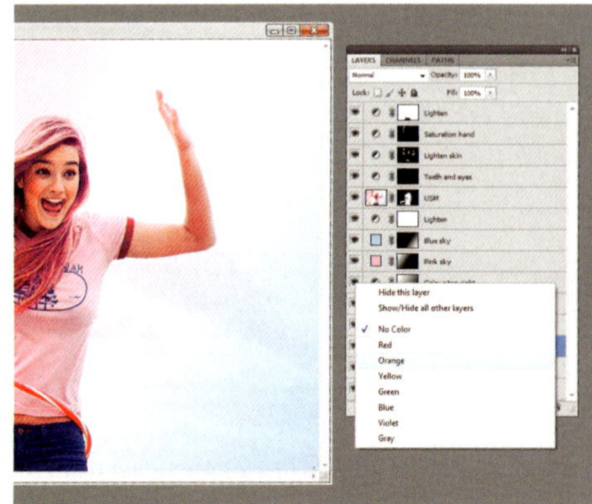

05 A shortcut
There's actually a shortcut for selecting colours that avoids the Layer Properties menu: Ctrl/right-click the 'eye' icon and select a colour from the window.

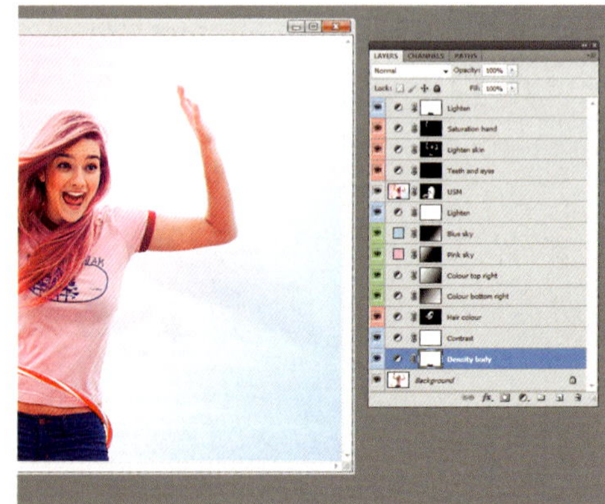

06 Devise a code
We use Blue to describe global tonal changes, Red for local tonal changes (eg eyes) and Green for any work that relates to sky colour washes.

QUICK PHOTOSHOP TIPS

Mask a group

You can add a mask to a group to localise its effects, just as you can with a layer. Select the group and click the Add layer mask button located at the bottom of the Layers palette.

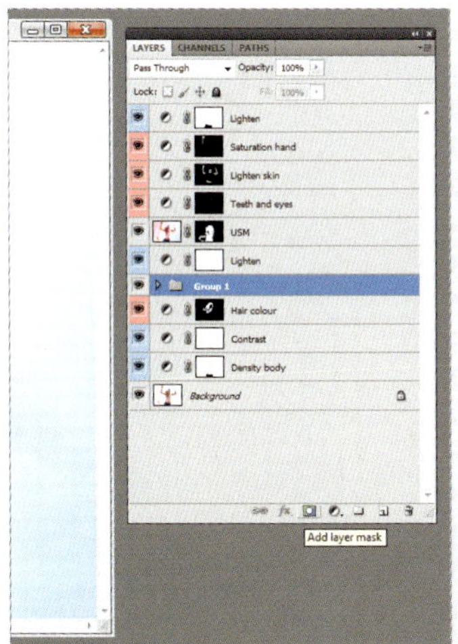

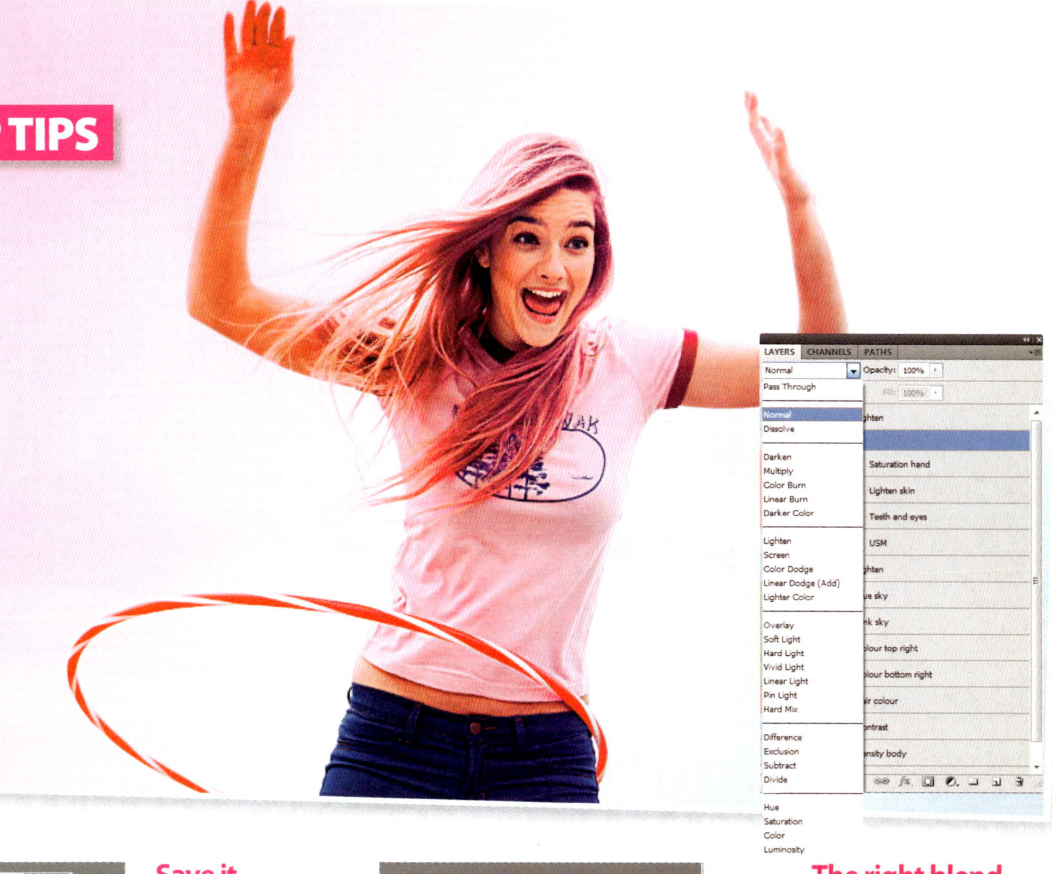

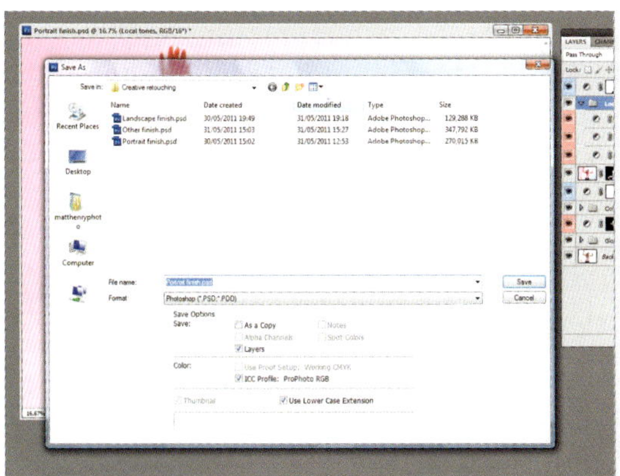

Save it right

Don't forget that to have the opportunity of accessing your layered file at a later date, you'll need to make sure that you save it in the Photoshop format (ie PSD) via File>Save As.

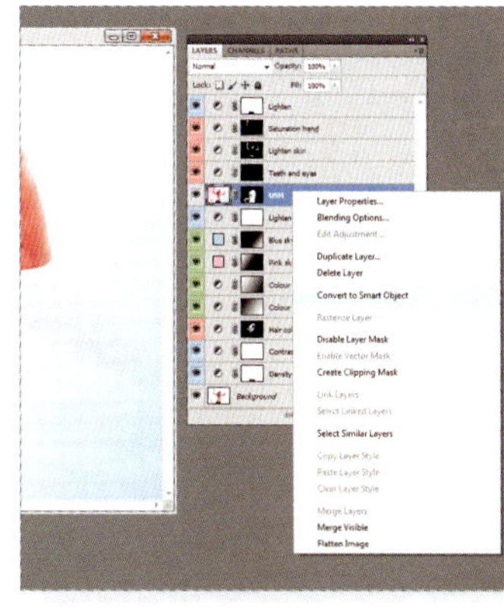

The right blend

You can ensure that an adjustment layer inside a group affects only the group layers by changing the group's blending mode from Pass Through to Normal.

Work smart

You can preserve the content of pixel-based layers by Ctrl/right-clicking and selecting Convert to Smart Object. Changes can then be reversed at any time.

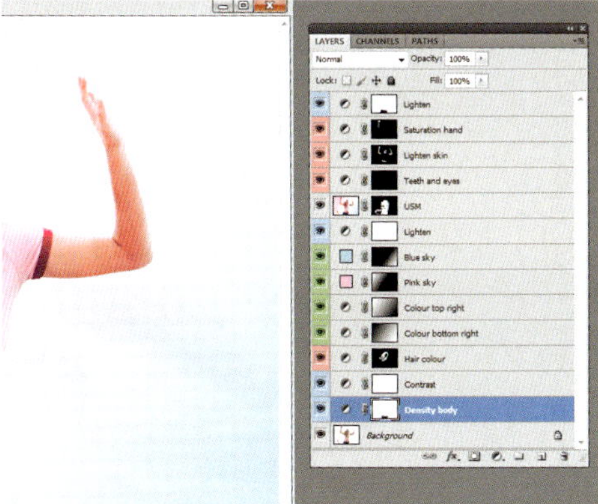

07 Grouping layers

We can also group our layers together. You can only Group adjacent layers so we'd need to change the layer order to group all of our colours together.

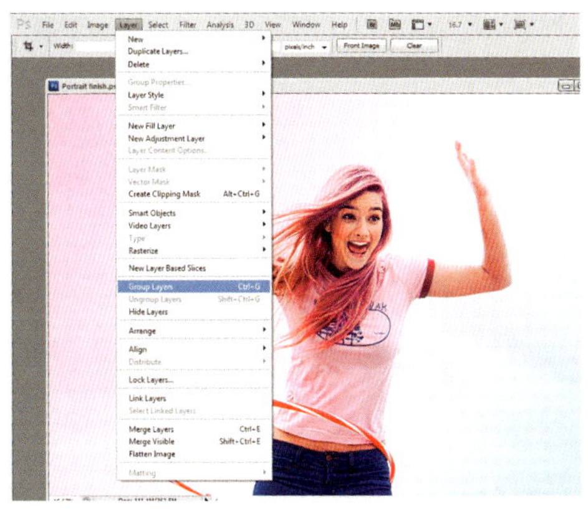

08 Select layers

Changing the layer order will alter the effects here, so we group adjacent colours only. Ctrl/right-click the first two layers and go to Layer>Group Layers.

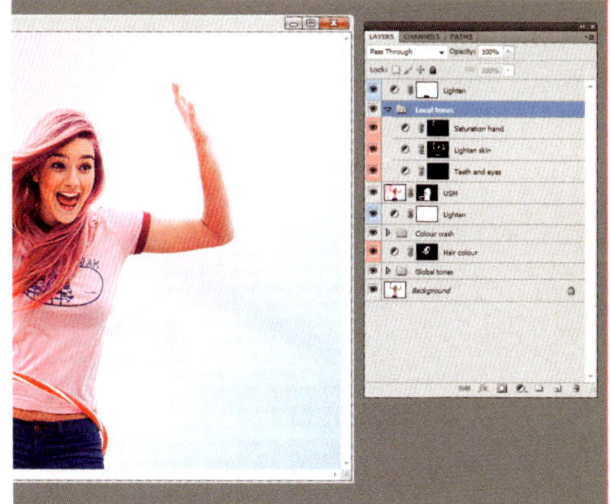

09 Rename groups

We do this for all adjacent colours. We then double-click the name of each and rename it. Expand a group at any time by clicking its triangle.

Opacity and Fill controls

Discover how to control the transparency of layers and added layer effects with the Opacity and Fill controls

Positioned at the top of the Layers palette, next to the blending mode dropdown menu, is a box called Opacity that contains a percentage figure. You can alter this value by clicking the triangle to the right and using the slider or alternatively you can click inside the figure box and enter a new amount manually. But just what does Opacity do?

Well, a layer's overall opacity determines to what degree it obscures or reveals the layer beneath it. A layer with 1% Opacity appears nearly transparent, whereas one with 100% Opacity appears completely opaque. If you think of these layers as sheets of acetate, you're essentially fading any work that you've applied onto that acetate as you drop the opacity.

There are a number of great uses for this; it can be helpful for temporarily lining up areas you've added to the image. Bring in eyes from another image, for example, and you've got to guess where they go unless you drop Opacity to something like 50%. Then you can easily see the detail behind, reposition with the Move tool before pushing Opacity back up to 100%. It can also be used to reduce the strength of an adjustment layer without having to go back into its settings. Just below the Opacity bar you'll notice a slider called Fill. This does the same thing as Opacity until you add a layer style such as Drop Shadow using the fx button at the base of the Layers palette. Dropping the Fill value reduces the opacity of pixels as per usual but doesn't touch the layer style – a great way of controlling one without touching the other.

"A layer's opacity determines to what degree it obscures or reveals the layer beneath it"

UNDERSTANDING OPACITY AND FLOW

Alter style settings

The added style is also listed underneath. You can turn visibility on and off using the 'eye' icon next to each layer and change settings by simply double-clicking the text.

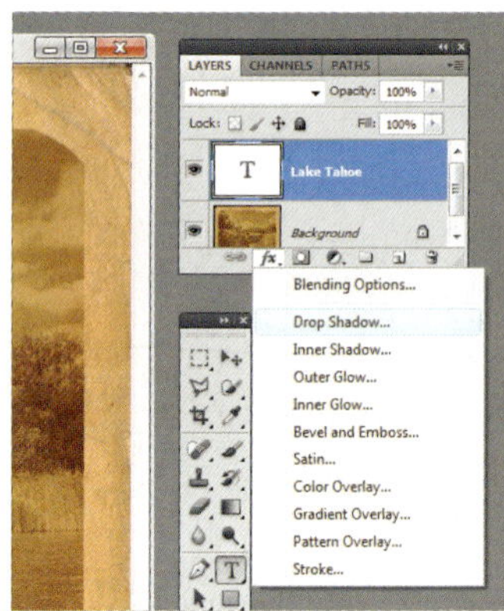

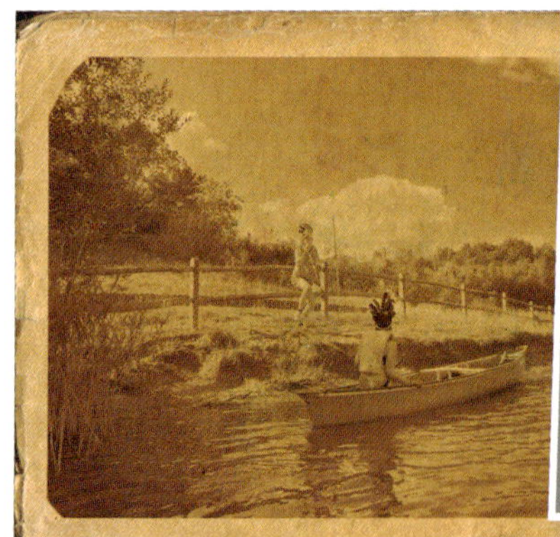

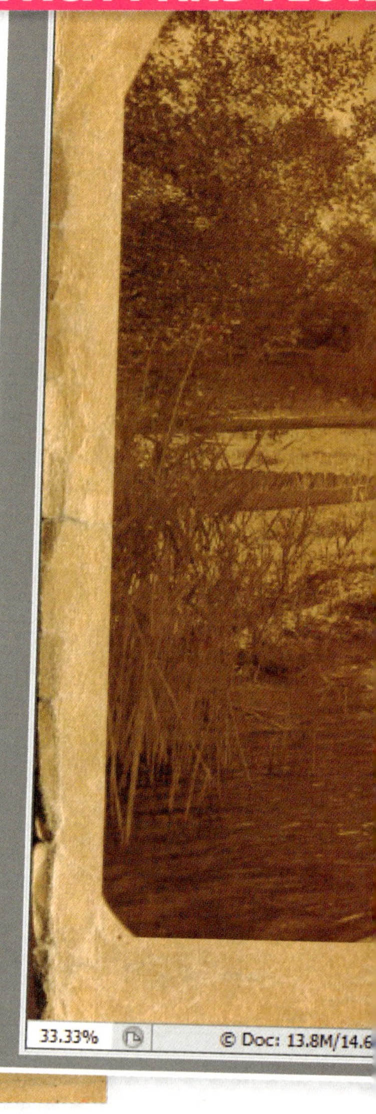

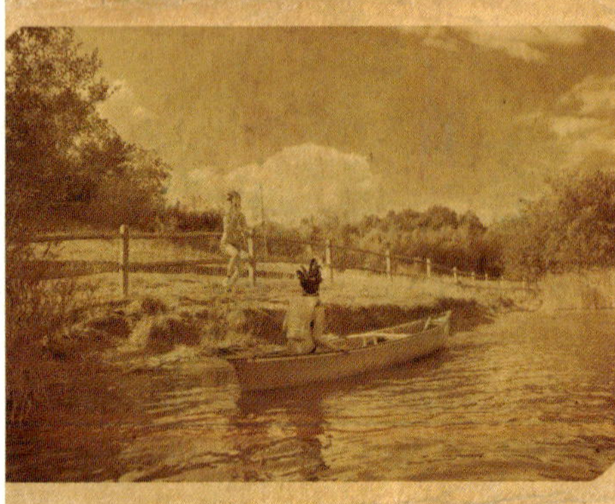

01 Add text layer

Here's an image we've turned into an antique-looking photo to which we want to add some realistic text. Press 'T' to call up the Text tool.

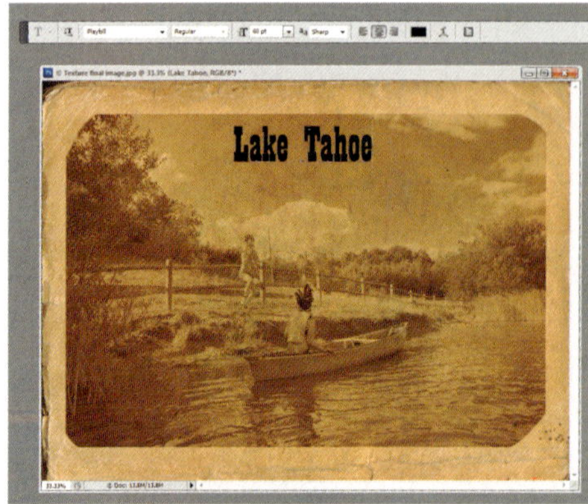

02 The write stuff

Choose a suitable font (eg Playbill), colour and font size from the Options bar, click where you want the text and type. Simply click and drag to reposition.

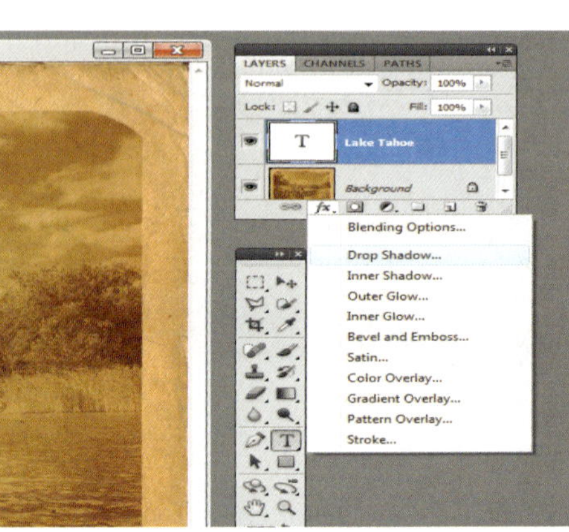

03 Drop Shadow

We want to add a shadow effect to the text to help it stand out, so we hit Enter then click the fx menu in the Layers palette and select Drop Shadow.

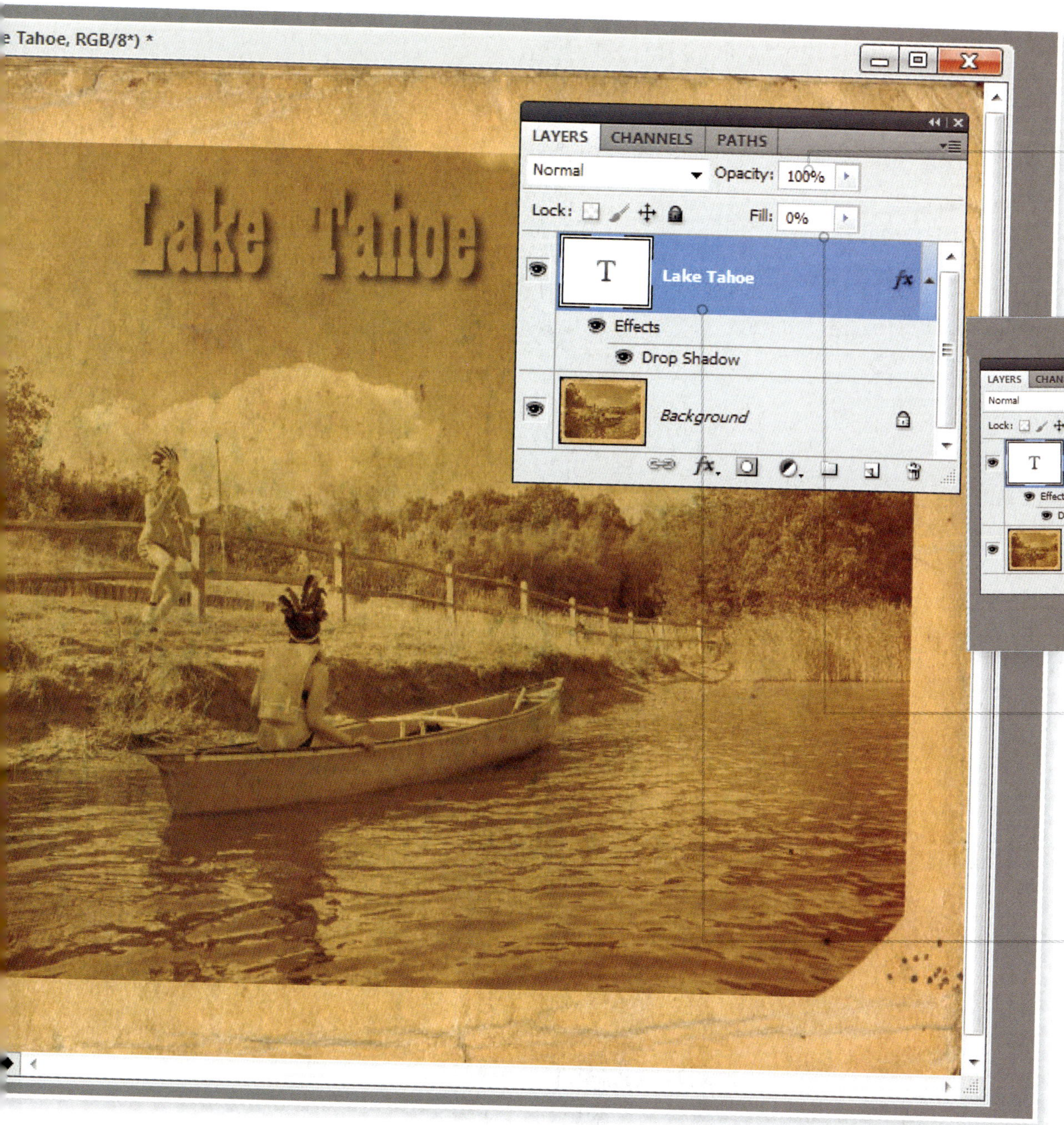

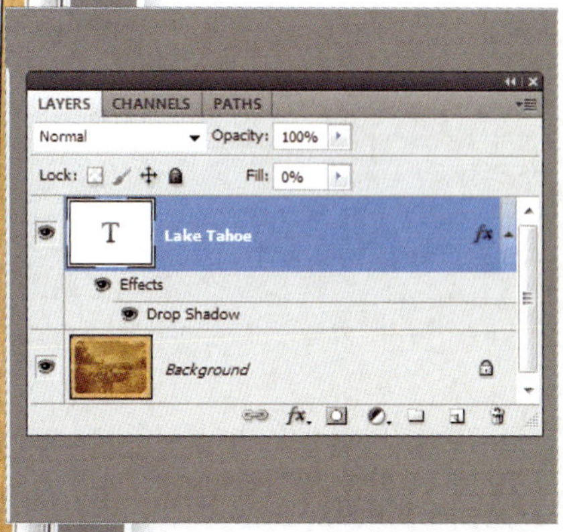

The Opacity control

The Opacity slider adjusts the opacity of the whole layer, including any added layer styles, such as Drop Shadow in the case of our image.

The Fill control

The Fill slider controls opacity in the image too, however it only drops opacity of any pixel-based information on the layer, ignoring any added layer styles.

Adding layer styles

You can apply a layer style by clicking the fx button at the base of the Layers palette. An fx icon appears next to your layer to indicate a style has been added.

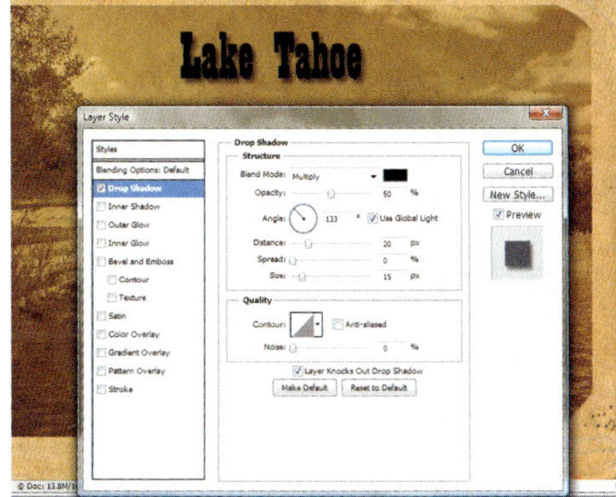

04 Shadow settings

In the Drop Shadow dialog, Angle is fine but we need to alter Distance to 20px. We use 15px Size to blur it a little and lower the Opacity to 50%.

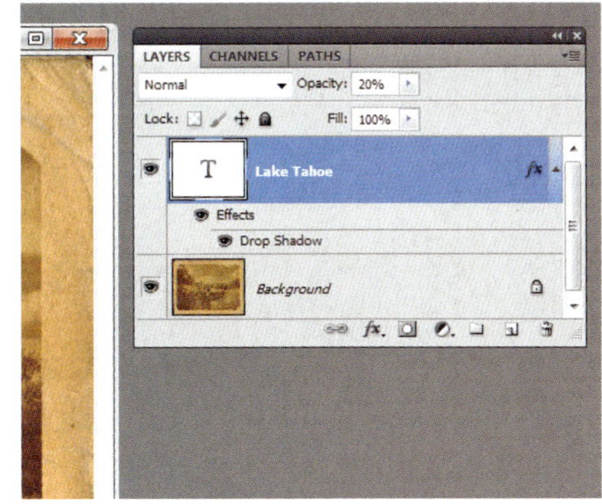

05 Opacity slider

Next we need to fade the text to make it look realistic. Dropping Opacity to 20% doesn't look great, mainly because of Drop Shadow settings.

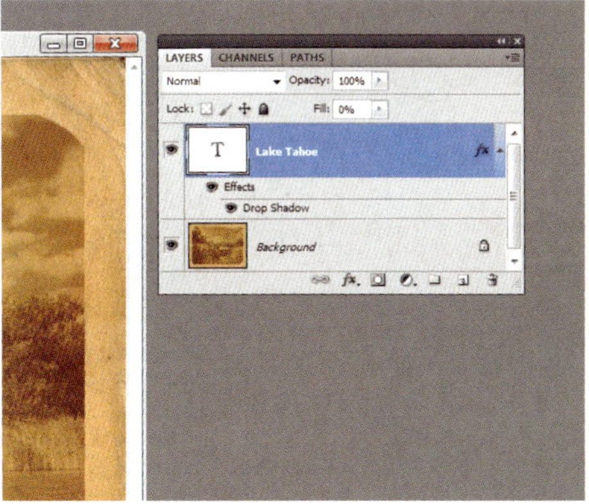

06 Fill slider

Time to try something different. With Opacity at 100%, we drop Fill to 0%, removing the text and just leaving the shadow. This does the trick nicely!

Blending modes

Unleash the power of blending modes to get total control of how your layers interact

If you can imagine layers as sheets of clear acetate laid on top of the Background layer, allowing you to add pixels where you please, then the blending mode is a little bit of magic applied to each sheet to determine just how it reacts with the information below. If you paint light red and dark red onto a new layer, for example, in the Normal blending mode, it will be light red and dark red regardless of what's underneath. However, change from Normal and the magic starts to happen. In Darken mode, for instance, only those areas of the colour darker than information below it will show up. So, to take another basic example, if you had a solid shade of midtone green underneath, only the dark red would show up; the light red is a paler shade than midtone green so will be excluded with a Darken blend mode.

Each blending mode does very different things, and there's a breakdown of how they work across pages 100-103. For the sake of description, we shall call the layer with a blending mode changed from Normal the 'blend layer', and the layer(s) affected below the 'base layer(s)'. The magic each performs is hard to describe without recourse to some complex terminology, so it's always a good idea to try out each mode on your own image. By comparing the visual results alongside the descriptions below, you can get a better sense of how each works and why. Lighten, Darken, Soft Light, Overlay, Multiply as well as Hue, Saturation, Color and Luminosity are the most commonly used with photo editing, but you can also find creative uses for the rest!

"The magic each performs is hard to describe without recourse to some complex terminology, so it's a good idea to try out each blend mode on your own image"

THE PERFECT BLEND

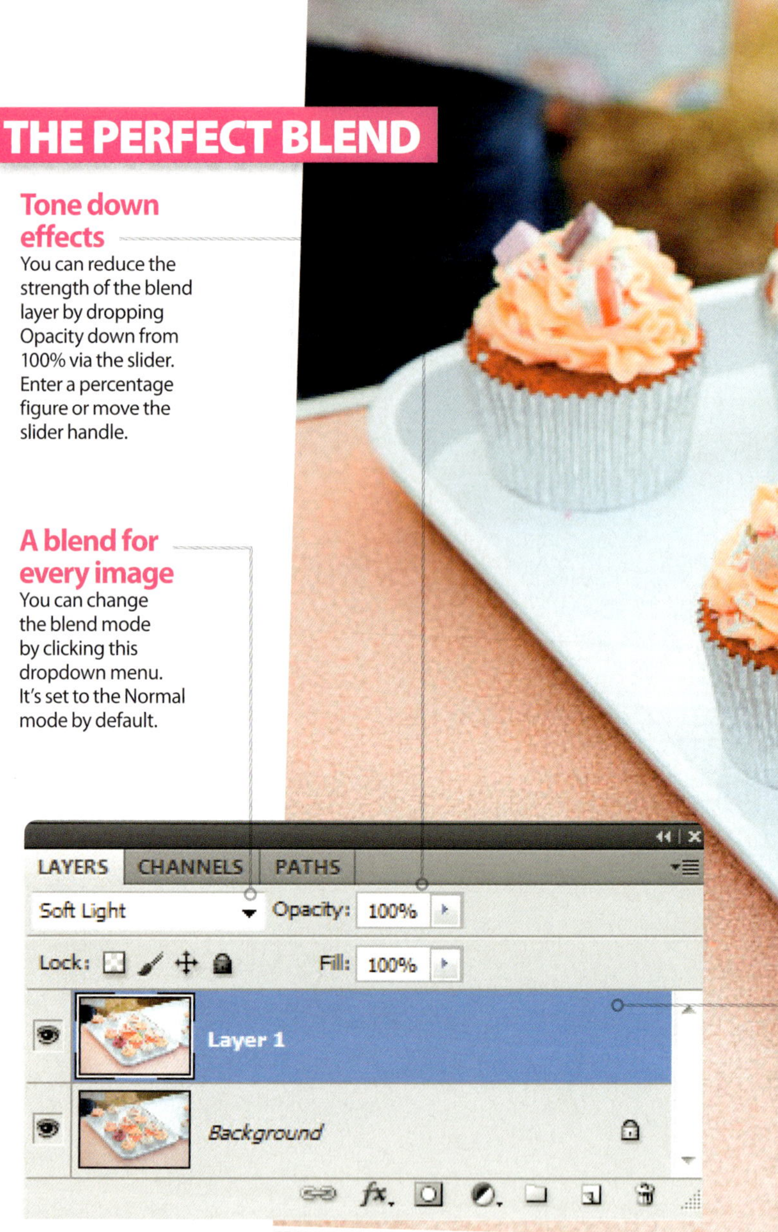

Tone down effects
You can reduce the strength of the blend layer by dropping Opacity down from 100% via the slider. Enter a percentage figure or move the slider handle.

A blend for every image
You can change the blend mode by clicking this dropdown menu. It's set to the Normal mode by default.

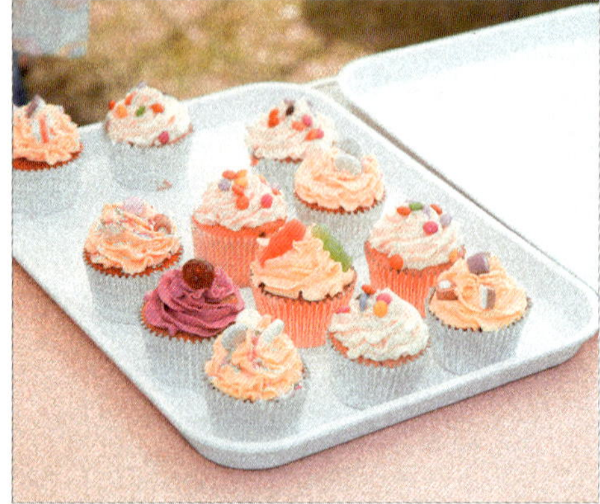

01 Dissolve

Dissolve randomly chooses pixels from the blend layer with which to replace pixels on the base layer and only starts working as you reduce the opacity.

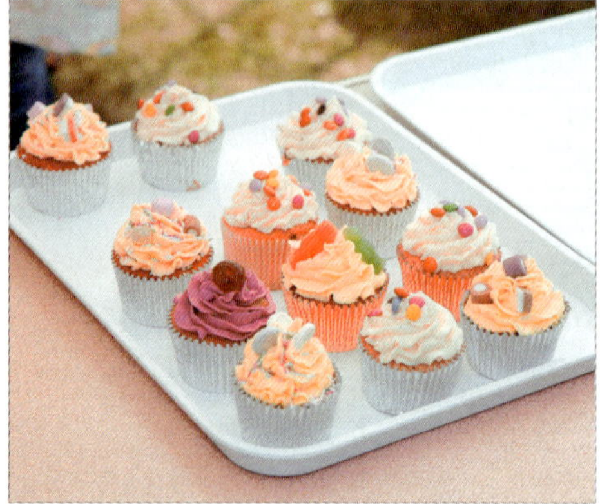

02 Darken

Darken lets through only tonal information that is darker than the base layer. Pixels darker than the base layer are replaced with lighter ones.

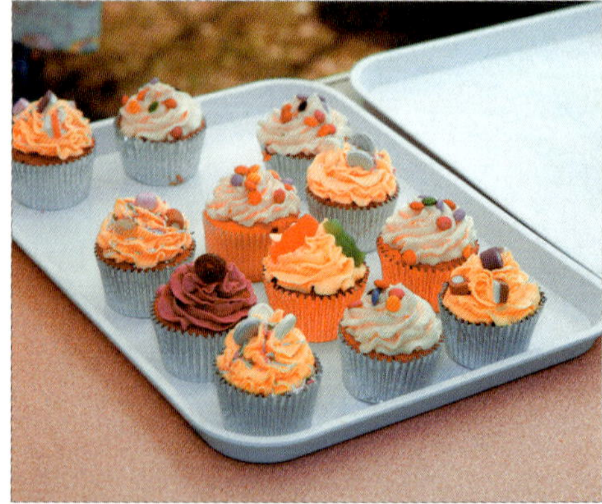

03 Multiply

This multiplies the tones of the base layer by the tones of the blend layer for more saturated results. Multiplying with white leaves pixels unchanged.

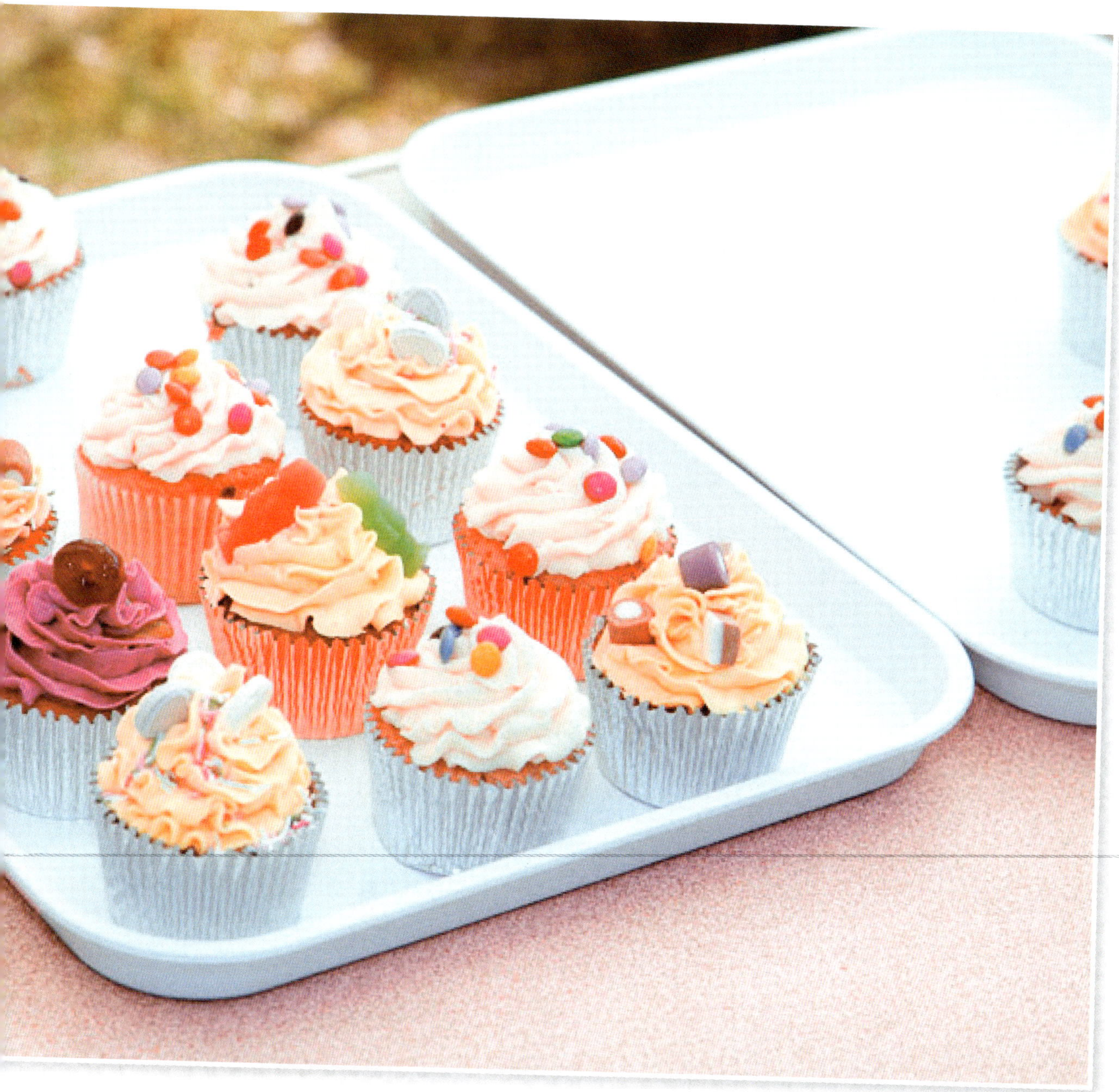

Base layer
The layer or layers below the blend layer affected by blending mode changes are known as 'base layers'.

Blend layer
The layer above with the blending mode changed from Normal is known as the 'blend layer'. The chosen blending mode affects how the blend layer reacts with everything positioned below it.

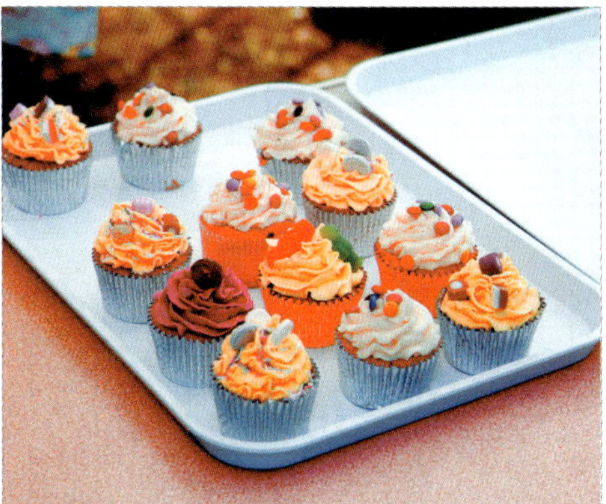

04 Color Burn
Color Burn darkens base layer tones to reflect blend layer tones by upping the contrast between the two. Once again, white produces no change.

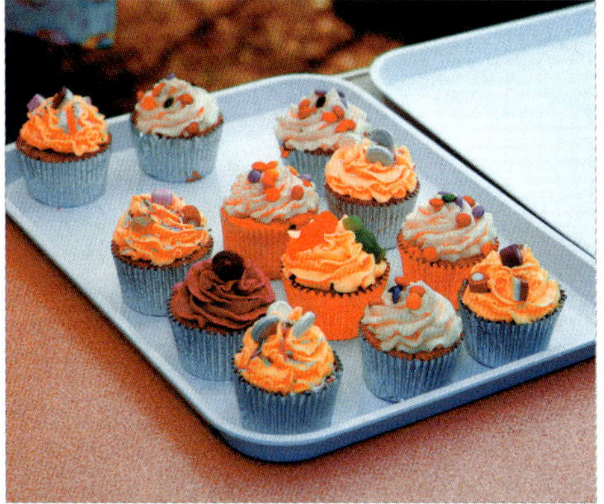

05 Linear Burn
This darkens the base layer colour to reflect the blend layer colour by decreasing the brightness, usually producing a darker result than Color Burn.

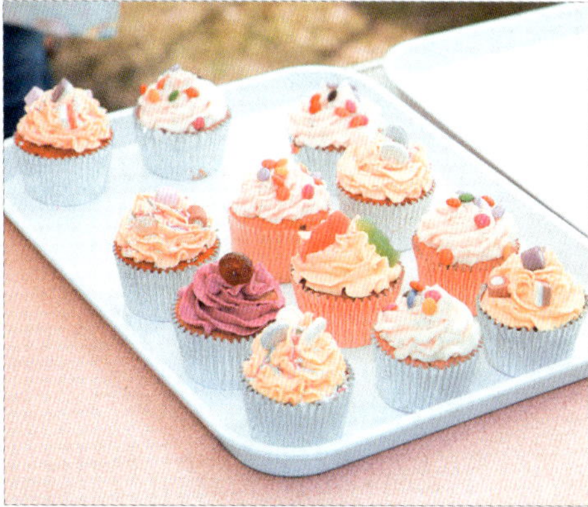

06 Lighten
Lighten only lets through tonal data that is lighter than the base layer. Pixels lighter than the base layer replace darker ones, in contrast to Darken.

More blending options Getting to know the blend modes

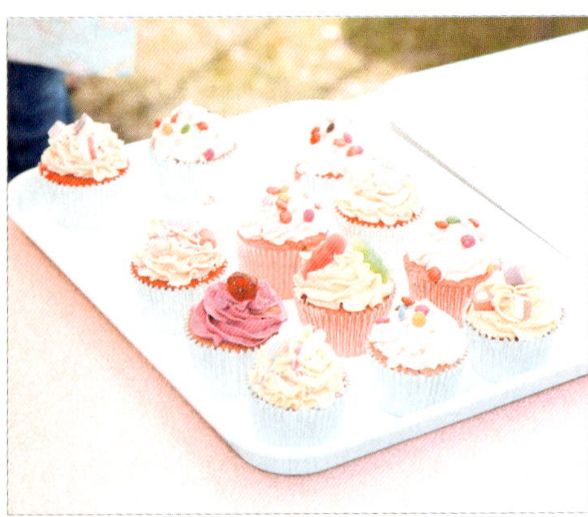

07 Screen
Screen multiplies the inverse of the blend and base layer tones. The result is always lighter. Screening with black leaves the colour unchanged.

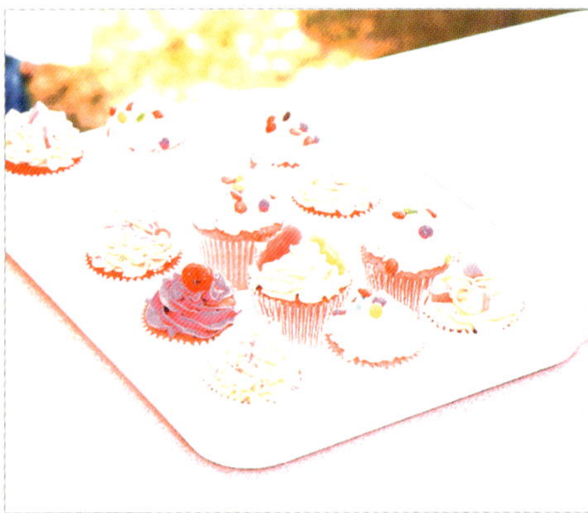

08 Color Dodge
Color Dodge brightens base layer tones to reflect blend layer tones by decreasing contrast between the two. Blending with black produces no change.

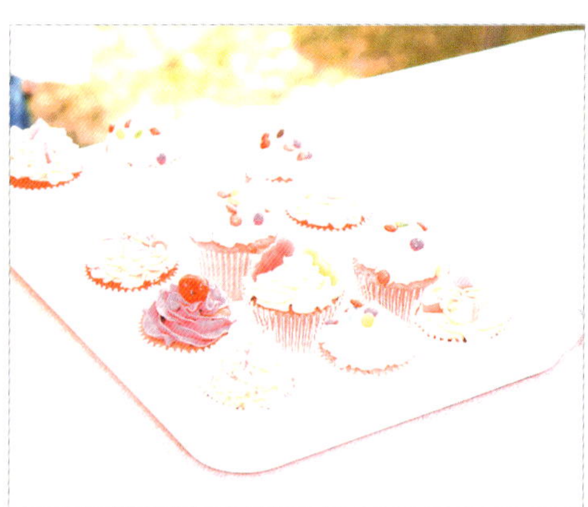

09 Linear Dodge (Add)
This brightens base layer tones to reflect the blend layer tones by increasing the brightness. It tends to produce lighter results than Color Dodge.

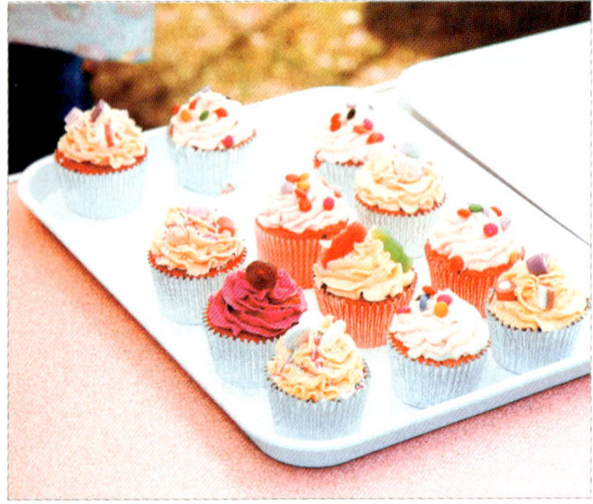

10 Overlay
Overlay multiplies or screens, depending on base layer tones. Base tonality is not replaced but mixed with the blend layer tones to reflect the original.

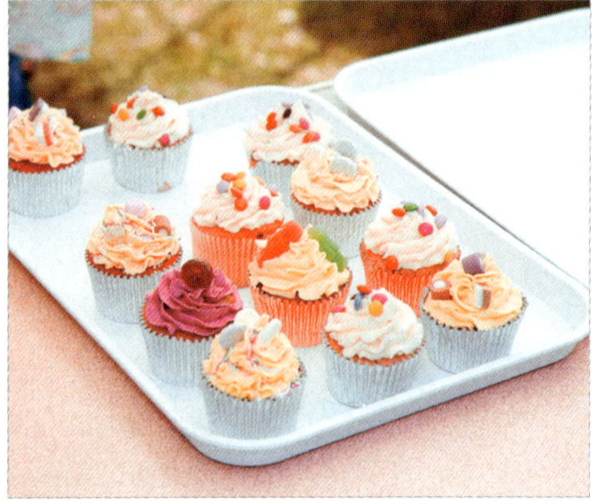

11 Soft Light
Soft Light darkens or lightens, depending on blend layer tones. Any blend layer tones lighter than 50% grey will lighten, while those darker will darken.

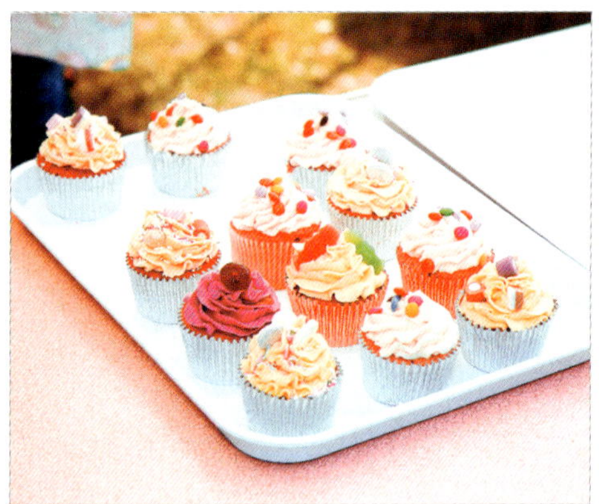

12 Hard Light
Hard Light multiplies or screens, depending on tones. Any blend layer tones lighter than 50% grey will screen, while any tones darker will multiply.

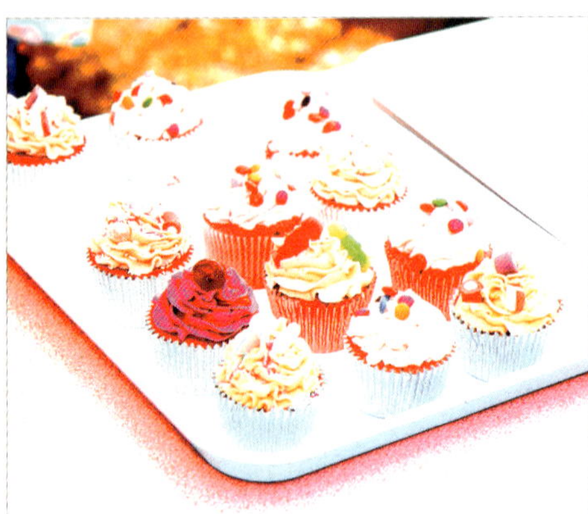

13 Vivid Light
Vivid Light lightens or darkens by increasing or decreasing contrast. Eg blend layer tones darker than 50% grey will darken by increasing contrast.

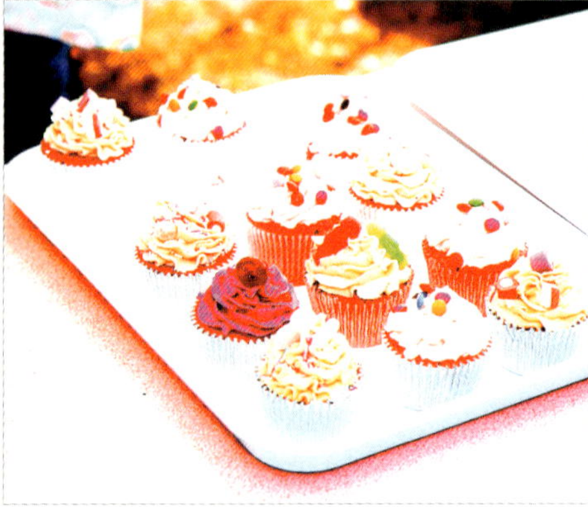

14 Linear Light
Linear Light lightens or darkens by controlling brightness. Eg blend layer tones lighter than 50% grey will lighten by increasing brightness.

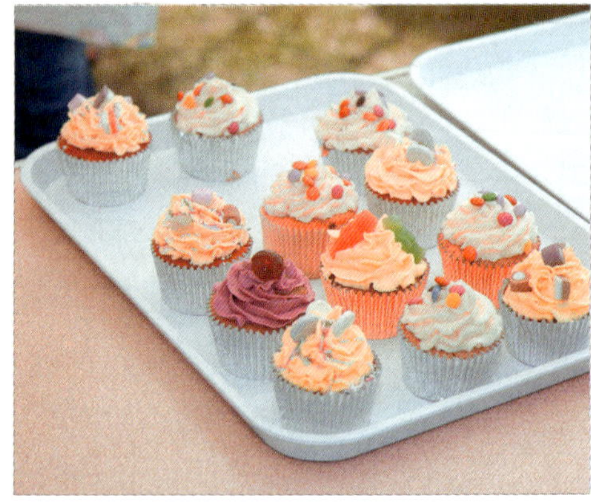

15 Pin Light
Pin Light replaces tones, depending on the blend layer. If blend layer tones are lighter than 50% grey, pixels darker than the blend tones are replaced.

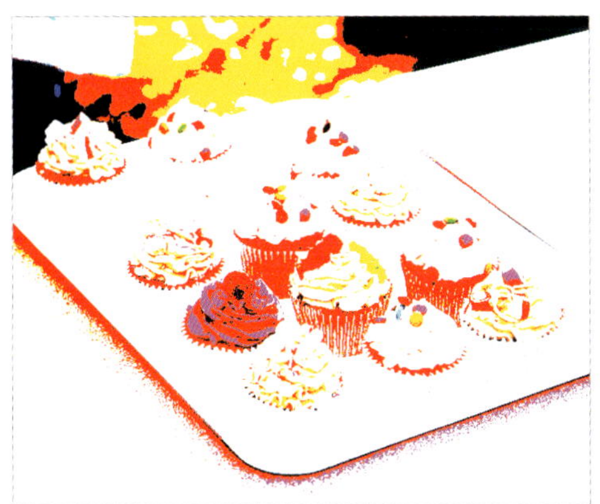

16 Hard Mix

Hard Mix gives all base layer tones a value of either 0 or 255 depending on the blend layer tones, effectively clipping colour channels and tonal detail.

17 Difference

This subtracts either blend layer tones from the base layer tones or base layer tones from the blend layer tones depending on brightness values.

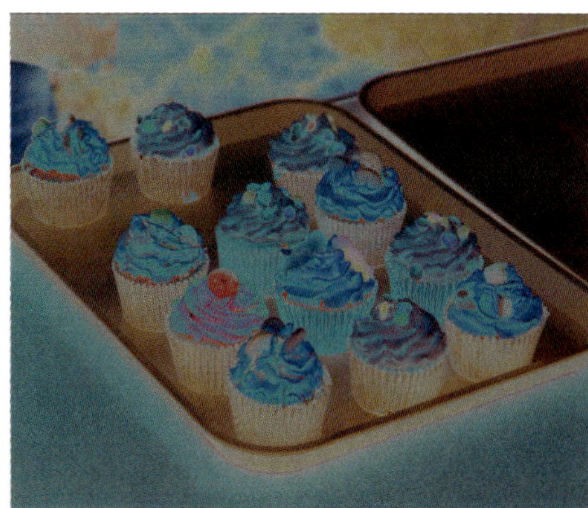

18 Exclusion

Exclusion creates an effect similar to Difference with less contrast. Blending with white inverts base colour values, while black produces no change.

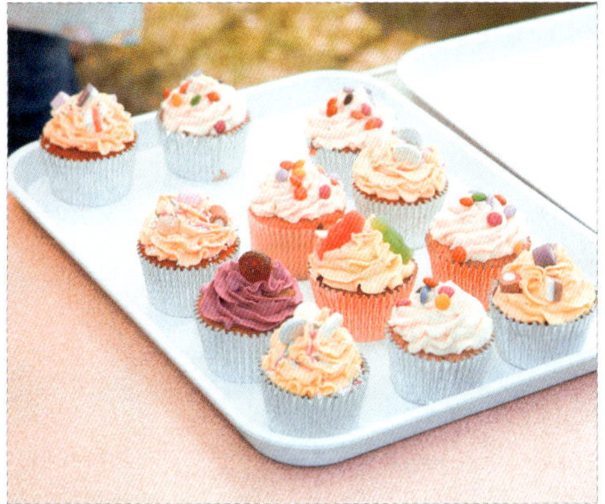

19 Lighter Color

Lighter Color compares the blend and base tones and displays the higher value tone. It does not produce a third colour, which Lighten can.

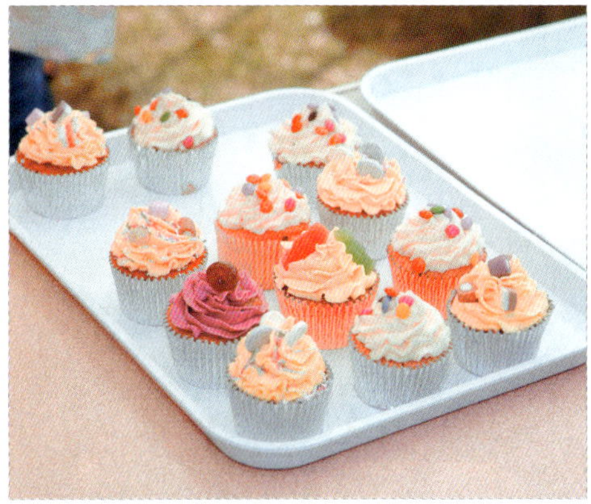

20 Darker Color

Darker Color compares the blend and base tones and displays the lower value tone. Darker Color does not produce a third colour, which Darken can.

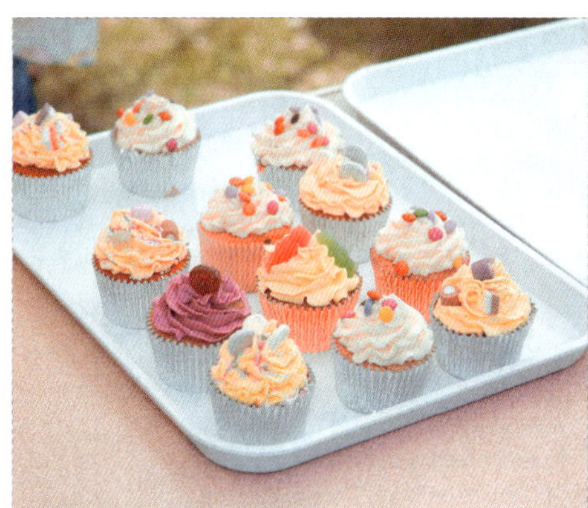

21 Hue

Hue lets through only the information on the hue (colour pigment) of the blend layer so that the luminance and saturation remain unchanged.

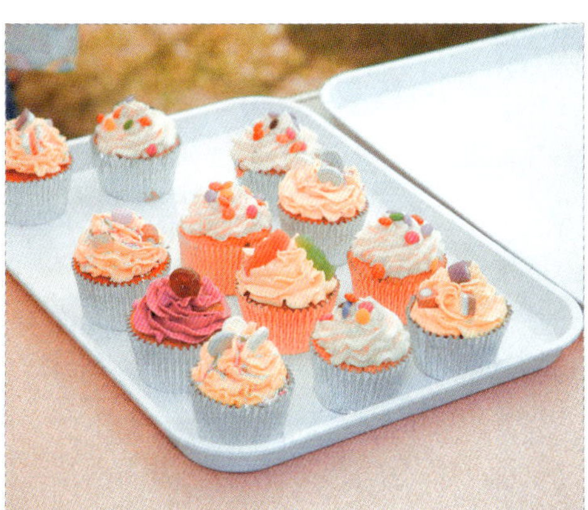

22 Saturation

Saturation lets through only the information on the saturation (vividness of colour) of the blend layer so that the luminance and the hue remain unaffected.

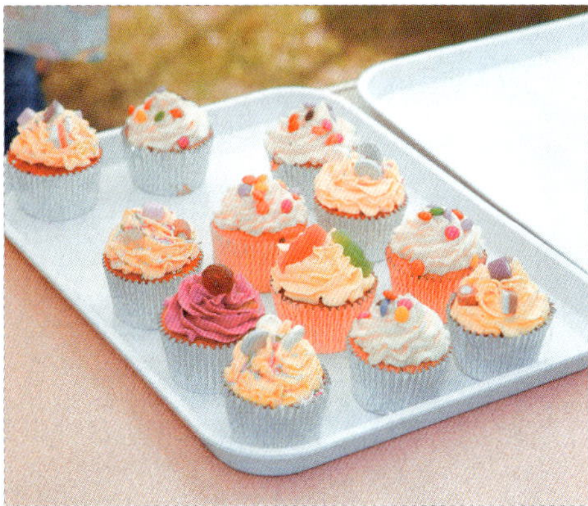

23 Color

Color lets through only the information on the hue and saturation of the blend layer so that the luminance remains untouched.

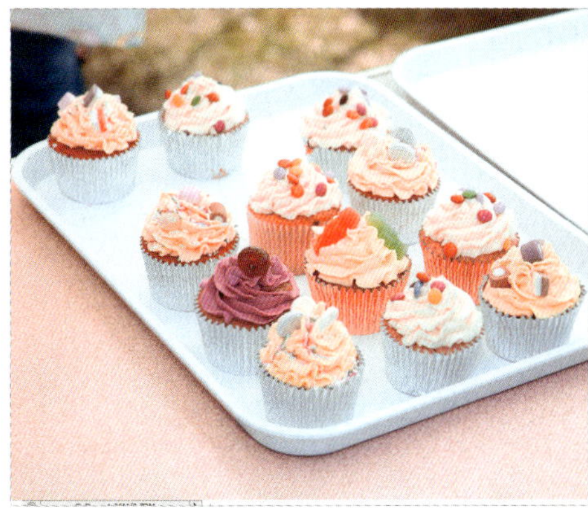

24 Luminosity

Luminosity lets through only the information on the relative luminance (lightness) of the blend layer so that the hue and saturation remain unaffected.

Retouching

Photoshop File Edit Image Layer Select Filter View Window
Clone Stamp Tool S
Pattern Stamp Tool S
CLONE OUT PROBLEMS
Use the Clone tool to fix all manner of flaws in your people pictures
Curves
Preset: Default
Channel: CMYK
OK
Cancel
Smooth
Auto
Options...
Preview
Output:
Input:
Show Clipping
Curve Display Options
Show Amount of: Light (0-255)
Pigment/Ink %
Show: Channel Overlays
Baseline
Histogram
Intersection Line
CORRECT YOUR EXPOSURES
Use Curves to dodge and burn areas of your pictures

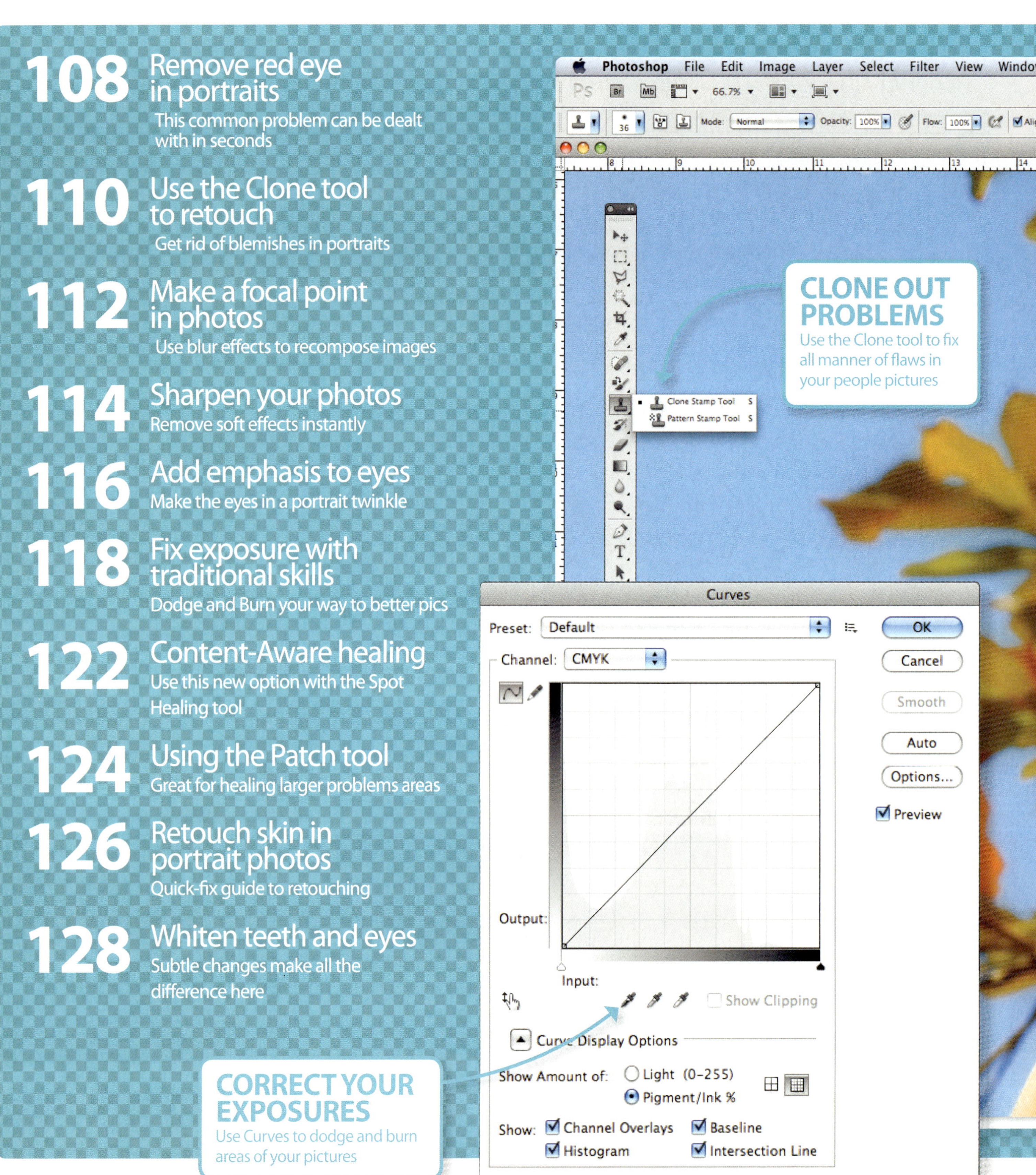

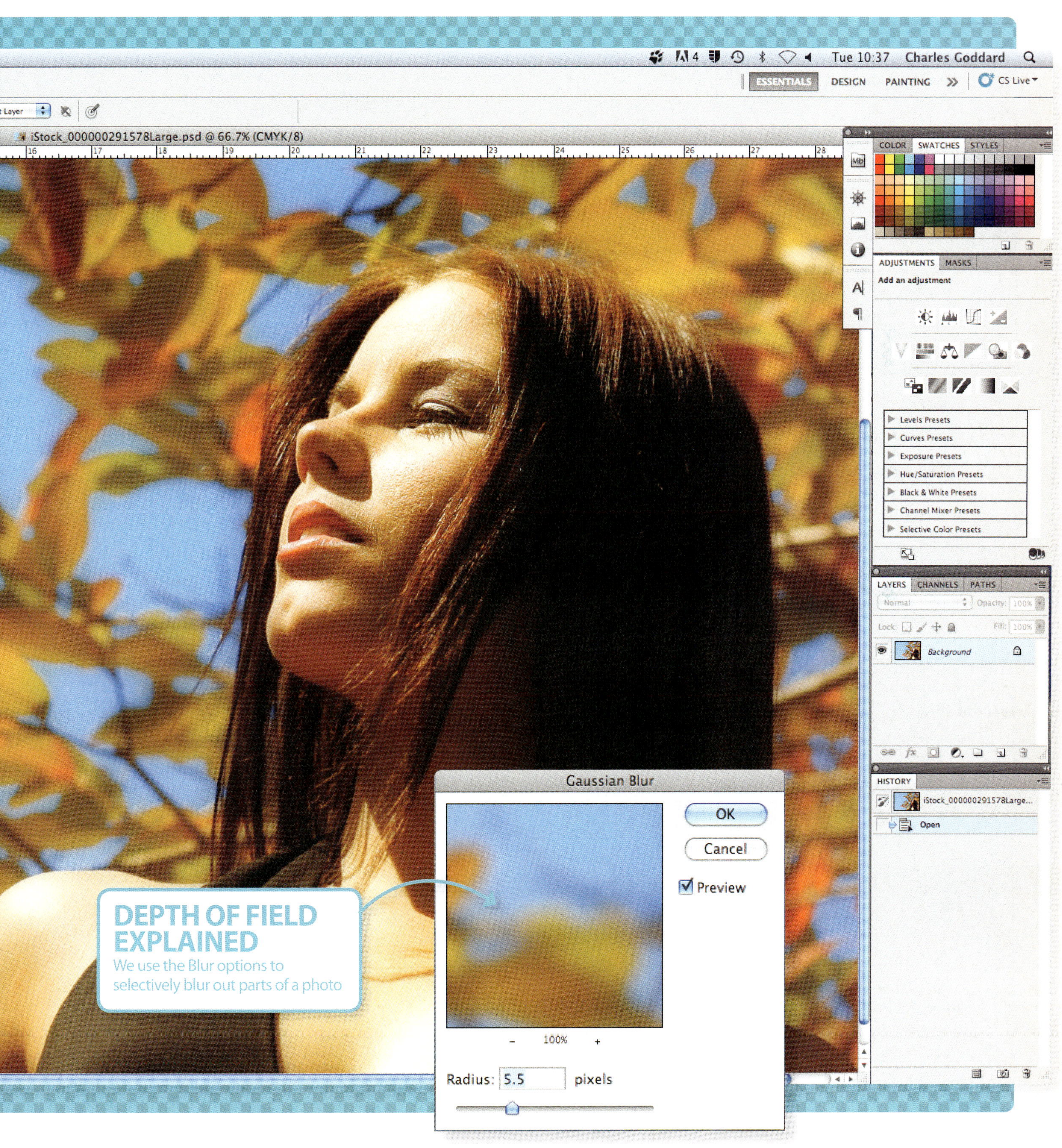

DEPTH OF FIELD EXPLAINED

We use the Blur options to selectively blur out parts of a photo

Remove red-eye in portraits

Cure the curse of red-eye in your portrait photos with the dedicated Red Eye Removal tool in Photoshop

Red eye is one of the most common flaws in portrait photos, caused by the use of flash in close-up situations and low light. If you're taking shots at a party or in a bar, you can almost guarantee that some of them will suffer. There are ways to prevent red-eye in-camera (see the side panel, right), but if the snap's already on your computer or memory card, then it's time to turn to your image-editing software for a quick fix.

All photo-editing software will have a quick fix for red eye, so it doesn't matter whether you have splashed the cash on Adobe Photoshop, or are using an older version, or even Elements – the basics are always the same. In most cases there will be a built-in one-click option for super-speedy results.

Red eye is caused by the flash from your camera. The flash light is too quick for the pupil to close, so the light passes through the eye, reflecting off the back of the eyeball and back out through the eyeball. The camera picks up this light and records it. It's red due to the amount of blood at the back of the eye, behind the retina. Red eye strength varies between people too; lighter coloured eyes show a stronger red eye effect than darker eyes. The effect is also seen in animal portraits.

Here we will show you, using the image provided, how you can use the simple controls in Photoshop to combat this natural effect.

> "All photo-editing software will have a quick fix for red eye, so it doesn't matter whether you have Photoshop or Elements"

THE ELEMENTS METHOD

Auto or manual – the choice is yours!

01 Elements offers three editing modes: Quick, Full and Guided. Both Quick and Full can be used to fix red-eye in slightly different ways. We'll start in the Quick mode.

02 In older versions of Elements, go to the General Fixes option in the right-hand panel, and click Auto next to Red Eye Fix. In newer versions, select Auto Red Eye Fix from the Enhance menu

03 Should the Auto option not clear up red eye to your satisfaction, then try entering the Full edit option instead. Locate the Red Eye Removal Tool in the left-hand toolbar to begin.

04 In the top toolbar, there is an Auto option. However, you can do it manually too. There are two settings here you can tweak to suit, but the defaults are usually fine.

05 Click and drag the tool to create a box over your first problem pupil. Let go of the mouse button, and the red eye will be removed. Repeat for all pupils in a picture.

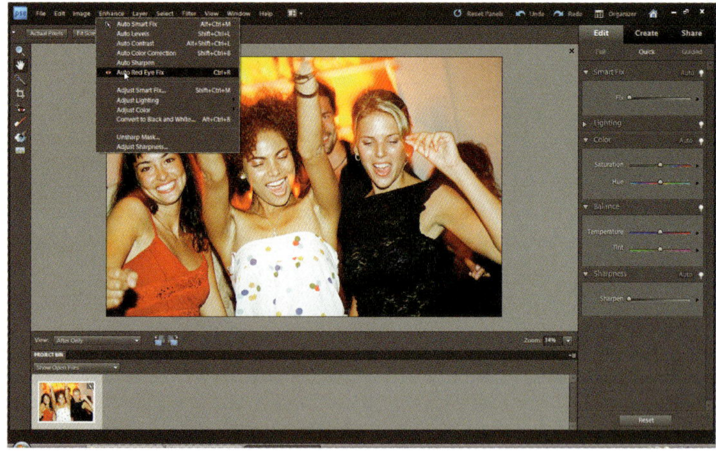

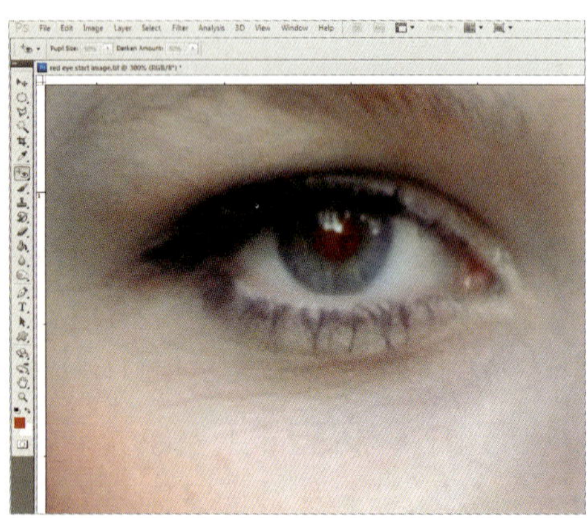

01 Load and zoom

Load the image with the problem and zoom in to the left eye. This may be around 300% depending on the file size.

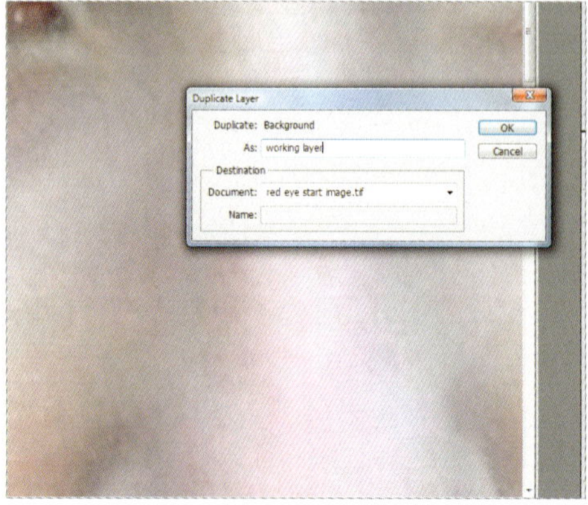

02 Duplicate

Duplicate the Background layer in the Layers palette so it can be scrapped if you need to revert back to the original.

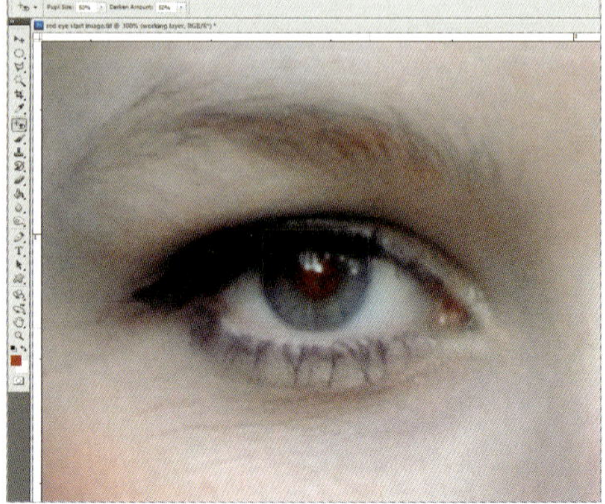

03 Use the tool

The Red Eye Removal tool is in the same group as the Healing Brush. Draw a large box covering the pupil and iris.

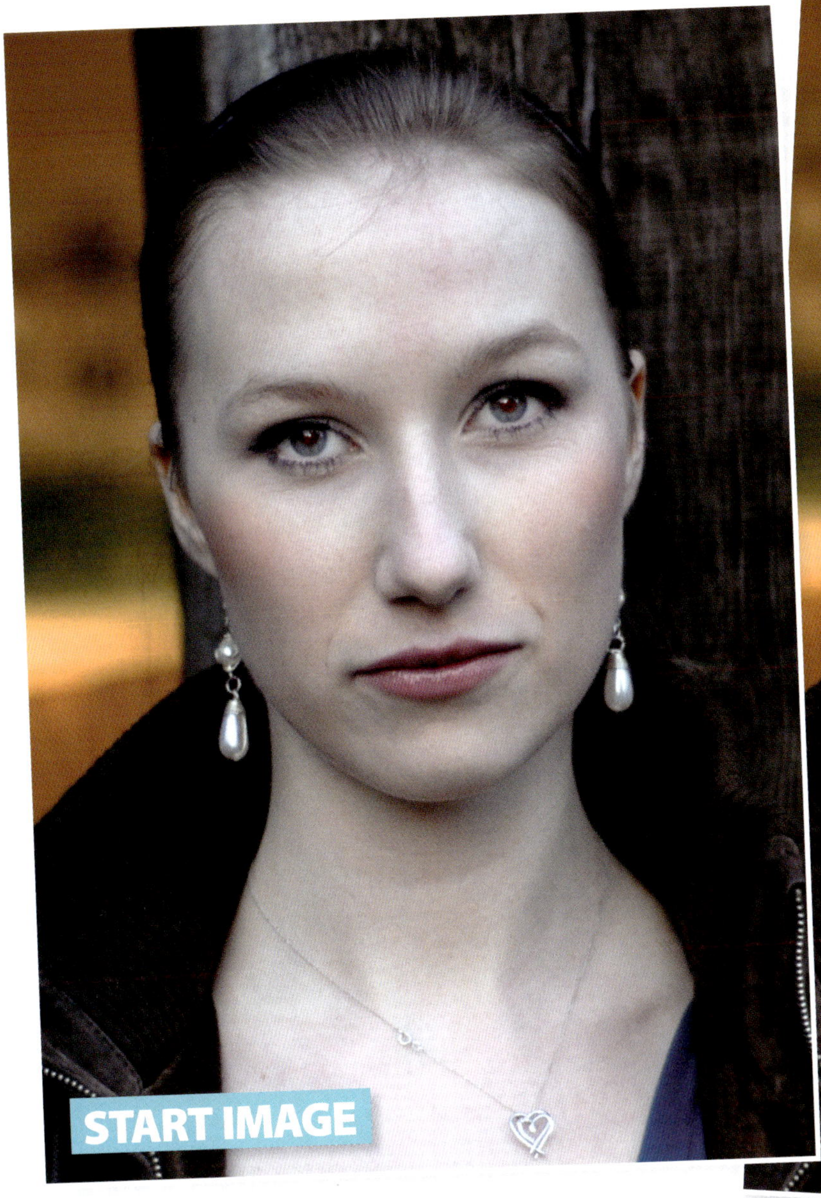

START IMAGE

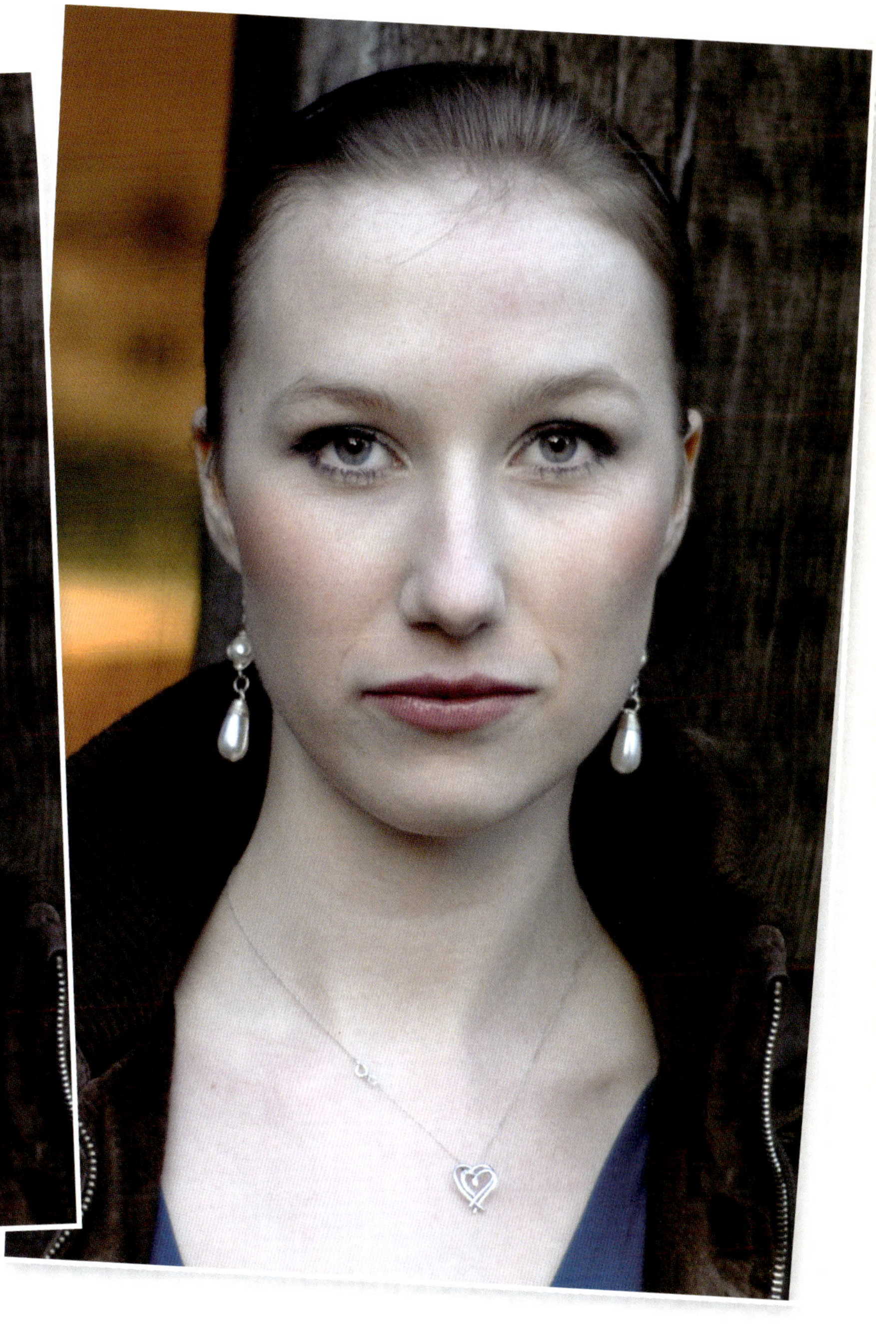

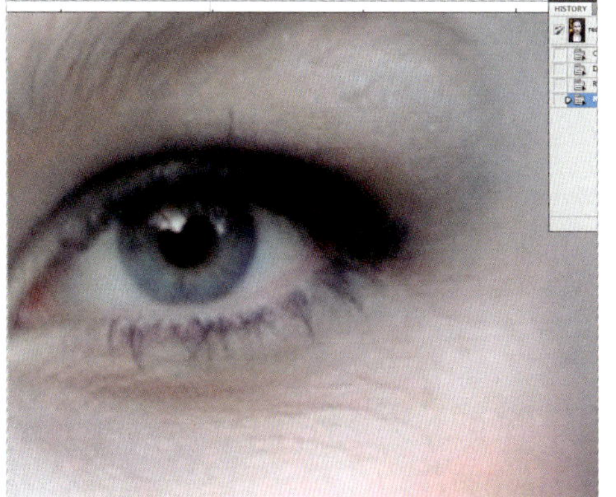

04 And repeat…

Repeat the process on the other eye and merge the layers when you're done so that you can keep the file size down.

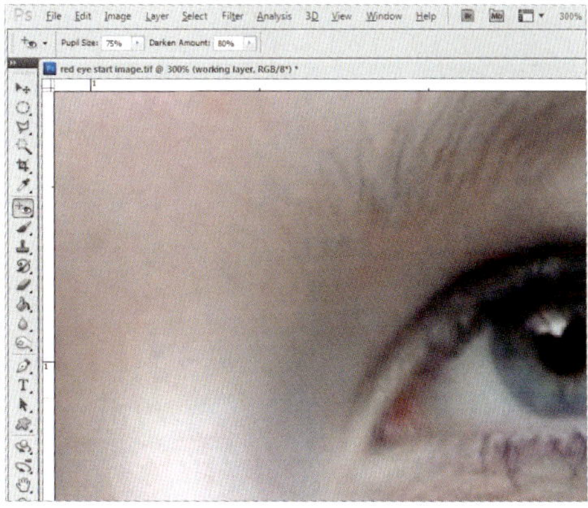

05 The options

If the eye still looks slightly red, undo the action then increase the Darken amount from 50% to 80% and try again.

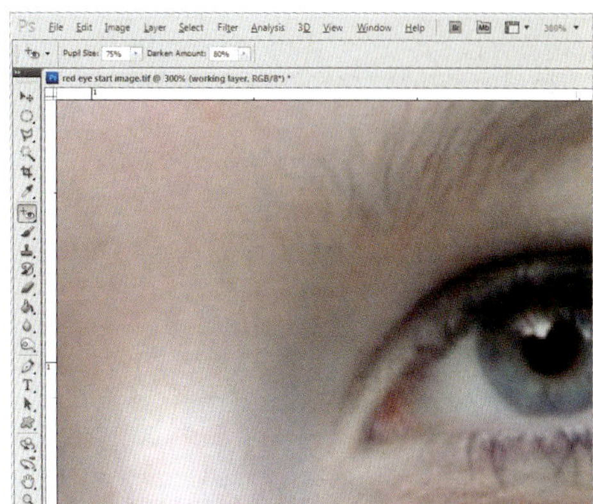

06 Tweak the result

If the effect hasn't covered all the red area then increase the Pupil Size. If there's some black bleeding into the iris, reduce the Pupil Size.

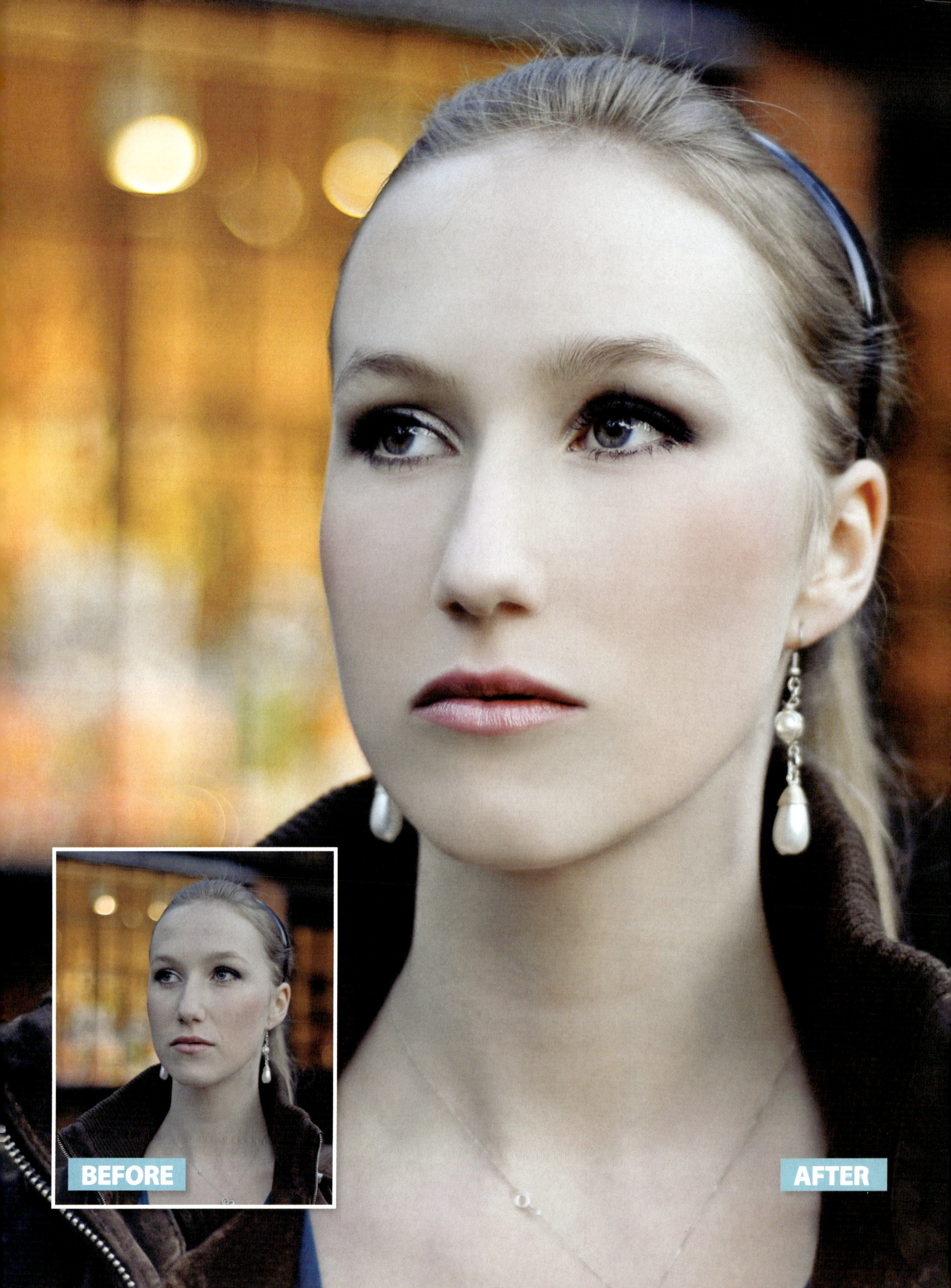
BEFORE
AFTER

Use the Clone tool to retouch

This is the Photoshop skill of using the Clone Stamp tool to clean up your photos

The art of cloning is normally concerned with making a duplicate copy of something. In the Photoshop world the idea is to clone good areas so they can be pasted over bad areas but without anyone seeing the join. In this way, it's more like a grafting procedure.

The trick is to replace the bad areas so that they blend in with the surrounding pixels and look like they were there all along. So what would you want to replace? Well, there are two applications: cleaning up faces and removing unwanted objects from scenic photos. The Clone Stamp tool can also be used to alter shapes and apply a digital diet. There are two key facets of cloning that need to be understood and addressed and they are the softness of the cloned material and the sharpness of the edge of cloning. Simply using the Clone Stamp tool with a hard edge at 100% opacity will produce circular blobs. Feathering the edge softens the effect and reducing the opacity loses sharpness. The skill is to learn what type of effect you need to apply and how to apply it.

The portrait tutorial below shows how to remove pimples and fine lines. Blending modes and when to use specific opacities is covered as well. A number of the Photoshop tools such as Healing Brush are simply variations on what you can do with the Clone Stamp, so learn take control of the process yourself.

"Replace the bad areas so they blend in with surrounding pixels"

QUICK PHOTOSHOP TIPS

Using the Lighten mode

We use the Lighten Blend Mode as spots tend to be darker than the surrounding skin area. Using the Lighten blend mode will replace the spotty pixels, but leave the edges of the brush alone so you don't get a circular effect. So, only the spot, not the rest of the skin is replaced.

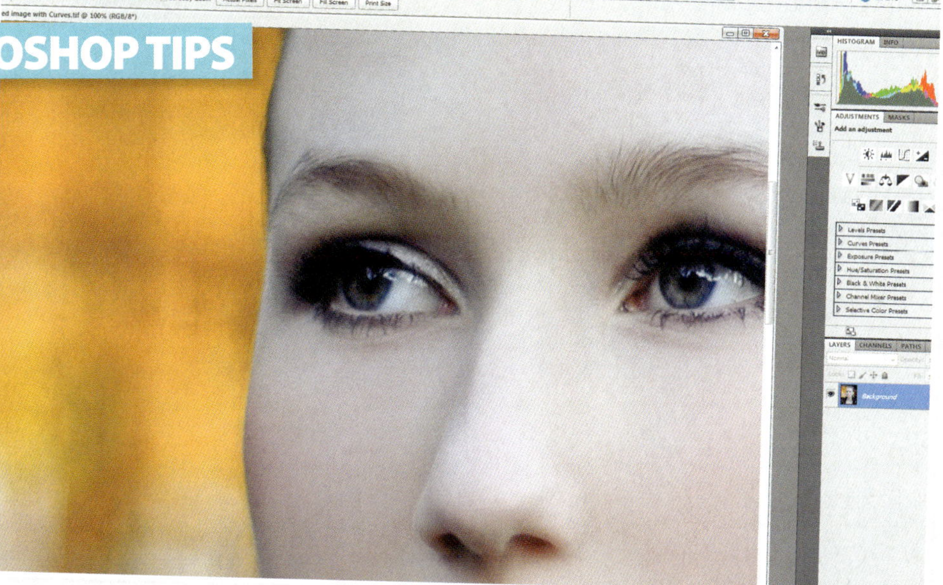

Eyebags begone!

We have decided to brighten under the eyes. Duplicate the current layer and set the Blend Mode to Lighten (as patches under the eyes are dark) but reduce the Opacity to 33%. Use a large brush and from under the eyebags, sweep upwards. The idea is to lighten the area more than remove texture. Save the image here.

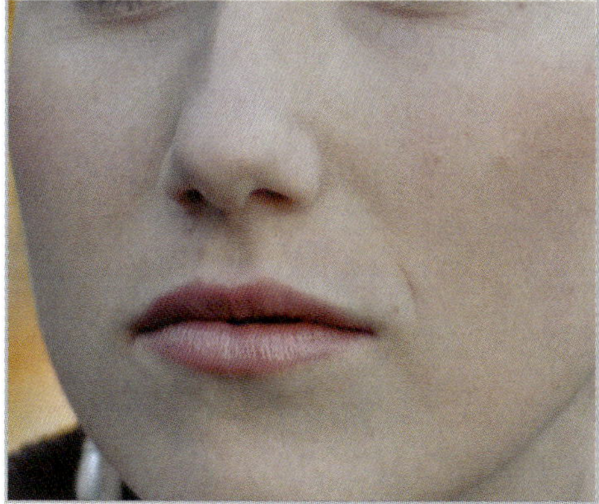

01 Spot removal

Create a duplicate layer and select the Clone Stamp, with Opacity at 100%, the Blend Mode set to Lighten and a brush size larger than the spots.

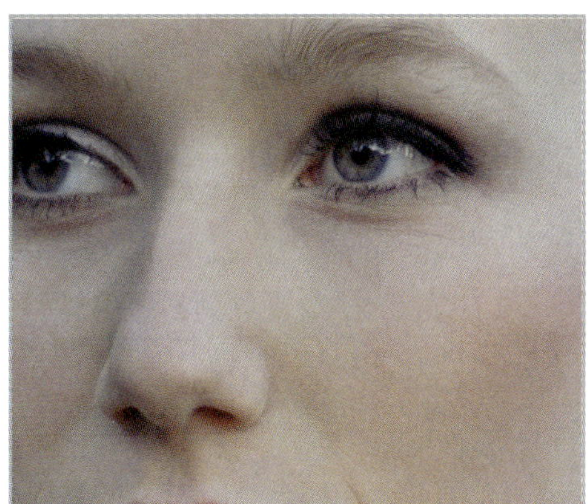

02 Take them out

Opt/Alt-click on a clean area of skin close to the spotty area. This will sample that area and cover the spot with it.

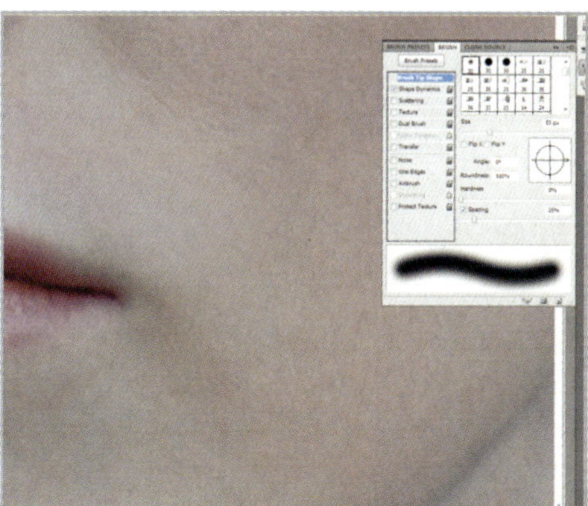

03 And repeat

You can repeat this for all the other blemishes, as well as wrinkles, dark areas eyebags, lip bleeding, and much more!

Make a focal point in photos

Quickly fix distracting backgrounds with the Gaussian Blur filter, helping to bring the focus to the main subject

Getting close to a subject can make for a wonderful photo, and can make a real impact. The aim is to have one object nice and crisp, with a blurred background sitting quietly behind. Most digital cameras these days will have a dedicated Macro mode, which helps to achieve this effect, however these are not foolproof.

All too often, the background can end up distracting the eye so that what should be the centre of attention is lost. An easy way of sorting this is to blur the background even more, faking a new depth of field. This involves selecting the background and then setting a Gaussian Blur to work.

There are lots of blur options in Photoshop, but this one works perfectly when trying to create this kind of effect. Our butterfly image is lovely to start off with, but the leaf that it's on is rather large and overbearing. Our aim is to softly blur this out, leaving the butterfly itself pin sharp and eyecatching.

You can try this method out on any of your images to practise the effect, however each image will need slightly different settings. We give the values that we used in the step by step below, so you can use these as a starting point. If the effect looks too strong, then try lowering the Amount of the Radius, until you are happy with the result.

In order to perform the blur on just the background, we need to make a selection of the area that we want to blur – take a look at our dedicated Selections section, starting on page 156.

"Our aim is to softly blur the leaf, leaving the butterfly itself pin sharp and eyecatching"

HOW WE ACHIEVED THE EFFECT

Selections

We will go into selections in more detail later in the book, but it is essential to know how to only work on the background in this project. We use the Magnetic Lasso tool, which you can draw around an object and it will find the edges automatically.

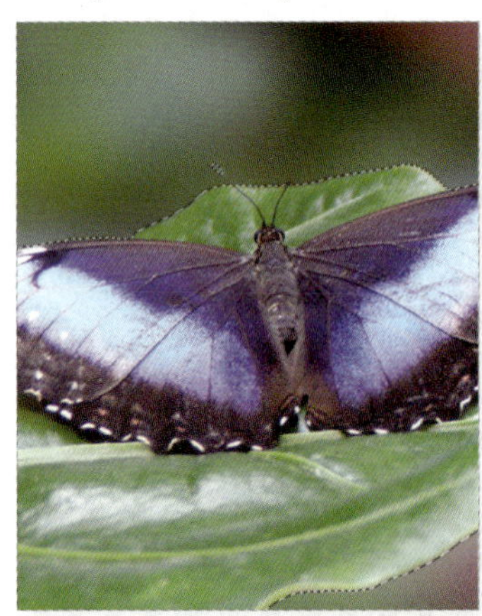

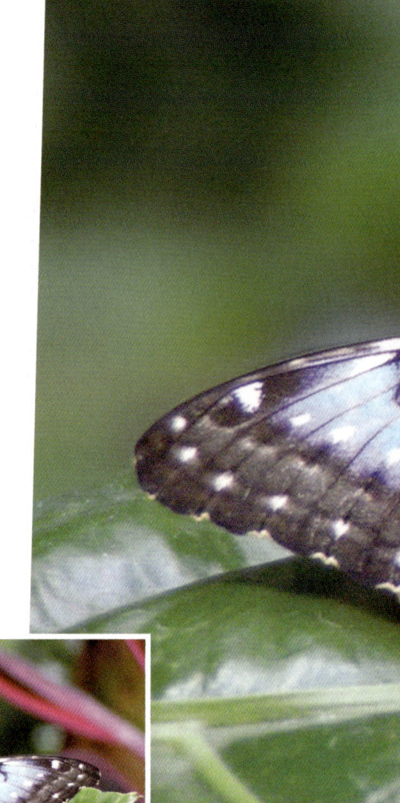

START IMAGE

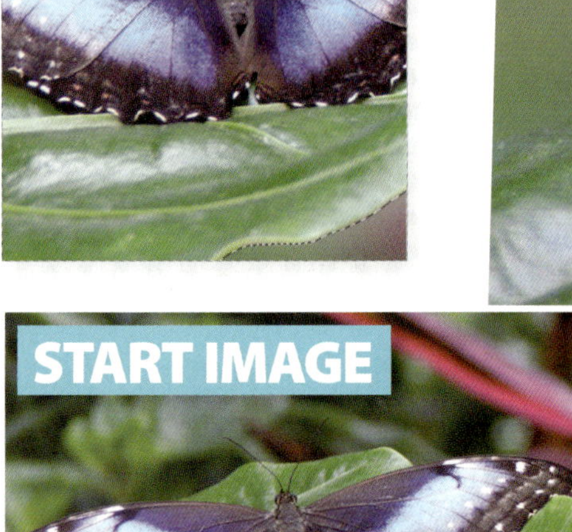

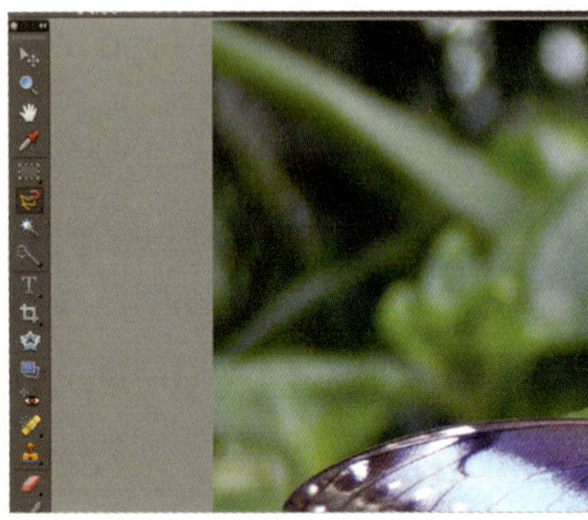

01 Select the background

We are going to use the Magnetic Lasso tool to select our background. Pick it from the toolbar and then go up to Feather in the top Options bar.

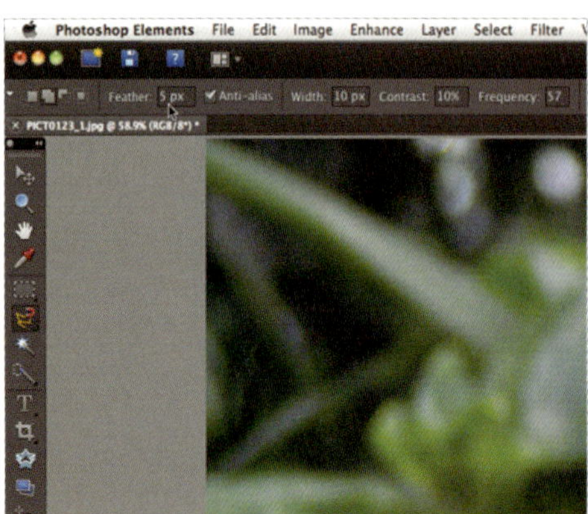

02 Set the Feather

Enter a setting of 5 as this will soften the selection edge so there isn't a harsh line between the blurred area and the sharp part of your image.

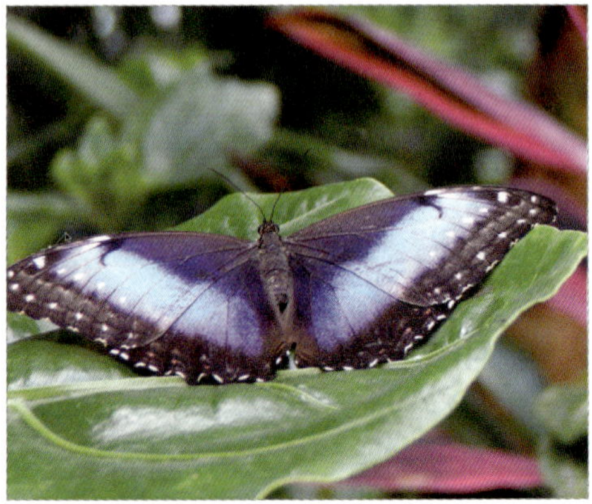

03 Draw around the object

The Magnetic Lasso clings to the edges. Click on the butterfly's leaf and drag the tool around it and the butterfly before moving out to the edges.

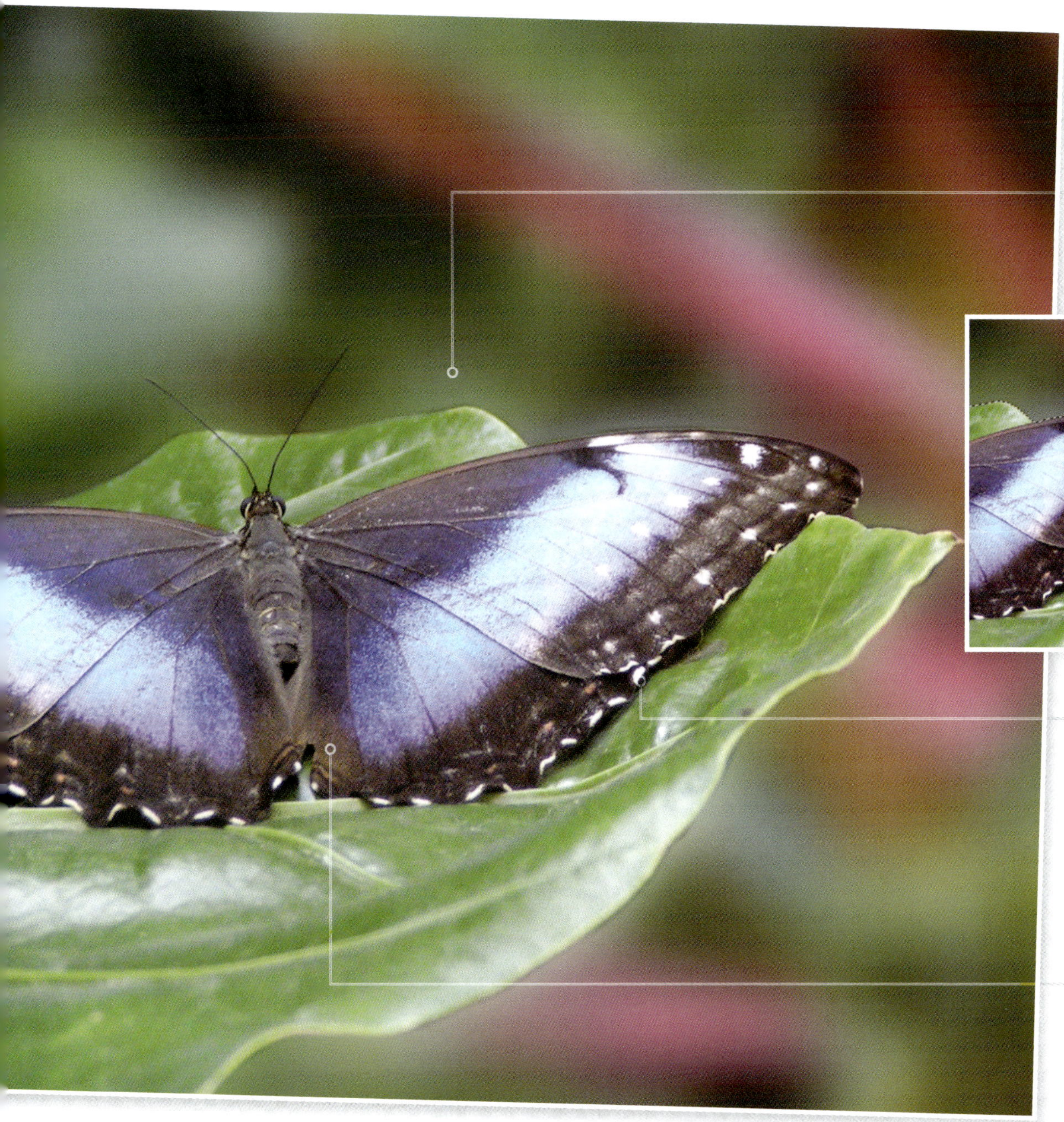

Blurred background

We have applied the Gaussian Blur to just the background of the image, which makes the butterfly really stand out, improving the photograph.

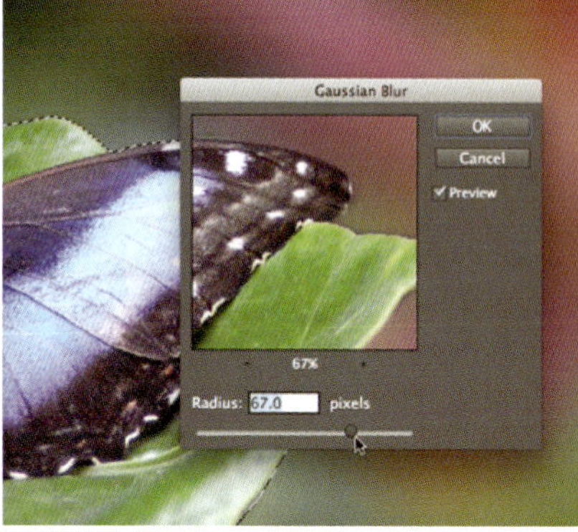

Feathering

We have used the Feather control to help soften the line between the bit that we blurred and the bit that we didn't. If we hadn't done that, then we run the risk of making it look as though the butterfly is stuck onto the background – stopping it from looking photorealistic.

Sharp subjects

The aim of this project is to ensure that the main subject – in this case the butterfly – appears perfectly sharp, which it does as soon as the background has been blurred.

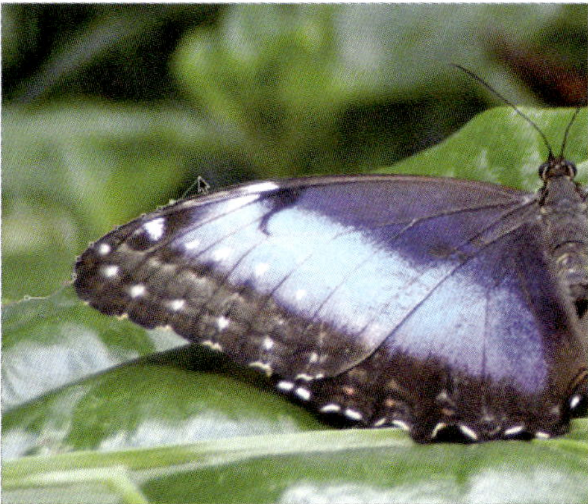

04 Tweak away

You need to select the background. If your selection line goes astray, just hit the Backspace button on your keyboard to undo the last shape.

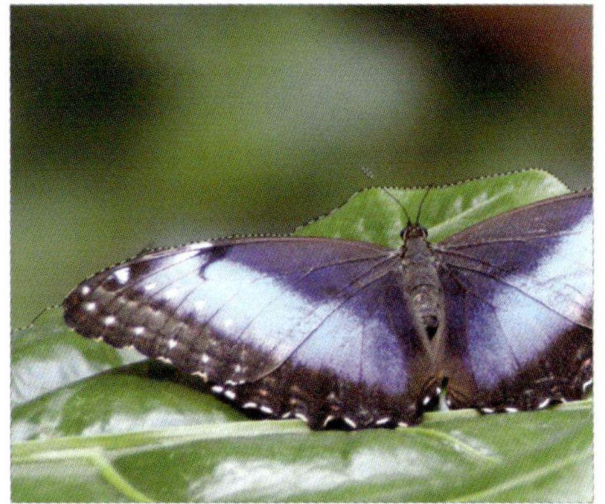

05 Final selection

Draw all around the background until you get to the first point you made. A little 'o' will appear next to the Magnetic Lasso icon.

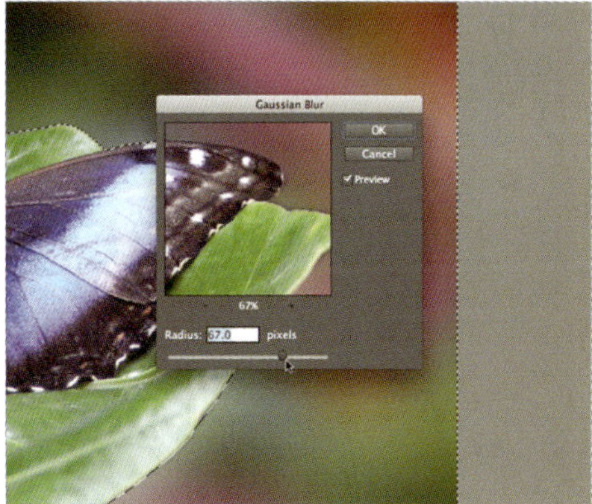

06 Now blur

Go to the Filter menu and pick Blur>Gaussian Blur and enter a setting of 67. Press OK, then go to Select>Deselect to see the final result.

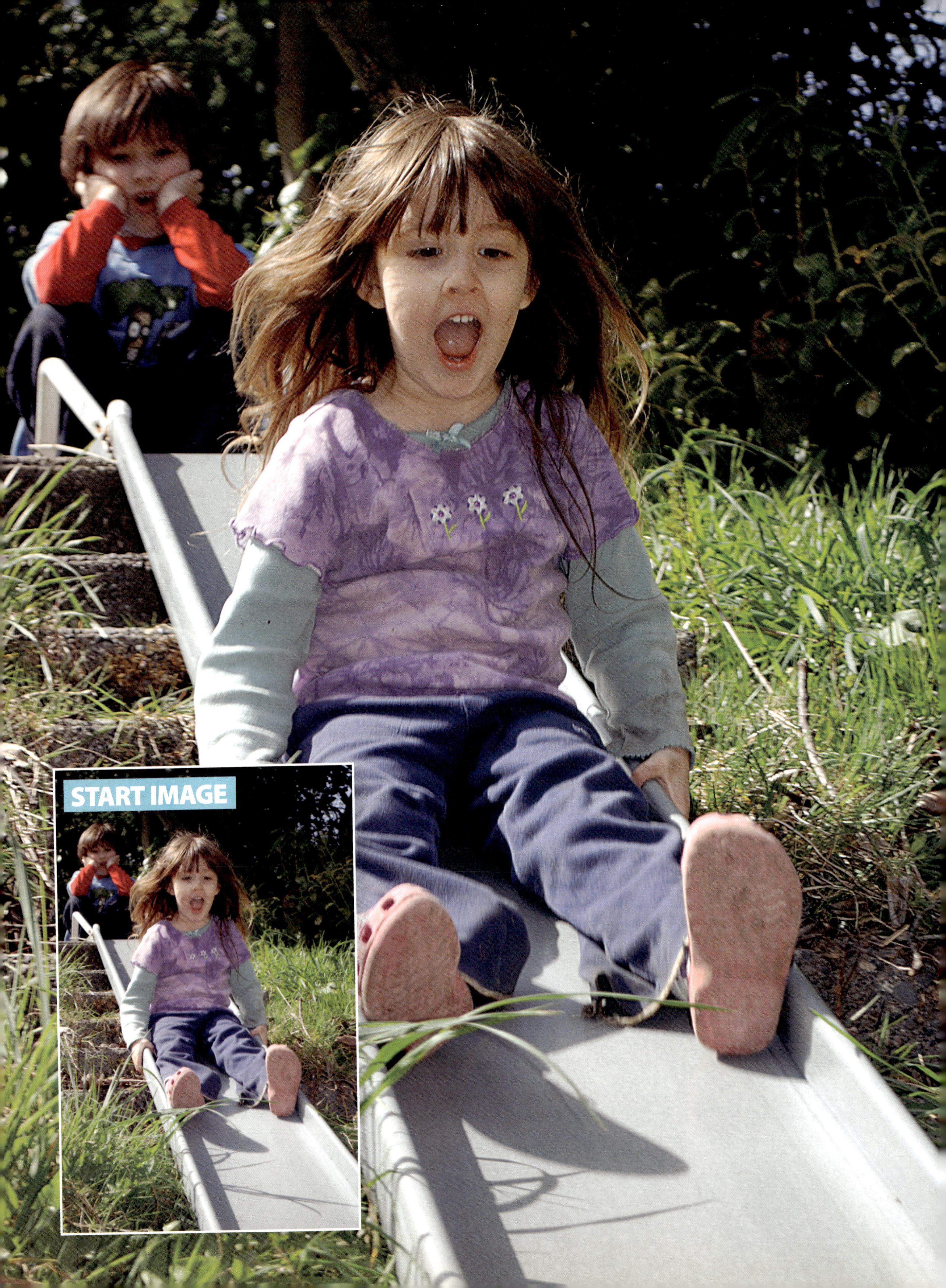
START IMAGE

Sharpen your photos

We show you how to fix camera blur using the Unsharp Mask filter

Camera blur is an extremely common problem and if you are like us, you will have your fair share of images that aren't a sharp as you'd like. Luckily, Photoshop and Photoshop Elements have a whole host of tools to help you to correct this flaw. You can use the Sharpen filters (see the Filters section of this book) or you could use the Sharpen tool to selectively sharpen certain areas of an image for effect, however there is a quick and easy method, which is what we are going to be looking at in this mini tutorial.

Whether you have Photoshop or Photoshop Elements you have at hand a nifty way of dealing with blurring problems in the shape of the Unsharp Mask filter. It seems strange that something called 'unsharp' actually does the opposite, but that's just one of Adobe's little quirks! It's easy to access the tool by going to either the Filter menu or the Enhance menu, depending on which version of Photoshop you are using.

You control the tool using a series of sliders in the dialog box that comes up and the Preview window means you can see exactly what effect the edit is having. It works by emphasising the object edges in an image, tricking the eye into thinking that the image is crisper than it is. This transforms soft, blurry images into crisper renditions of themselves.

We're going to show you quickly and easily how to use the Unsharp Mask for yourself using a typical image, which is blurred thanks to the motion of the child coming down the slide – we have provided this image to practise on.

> "Transforms soft, blurry images into crisper renditions"

THE UNSHARP MASK

FINDING THE TOOL

Click the Enhance or the Filter menu, depending on which version of Photoshop you are using, then select the Unsharp mask option from the dropdown list.

DIALOG BOX

This is the Unsharp Mask box that pops up, which has all of the tools that you need to sharpen your image to perfection using a selection of sliders.

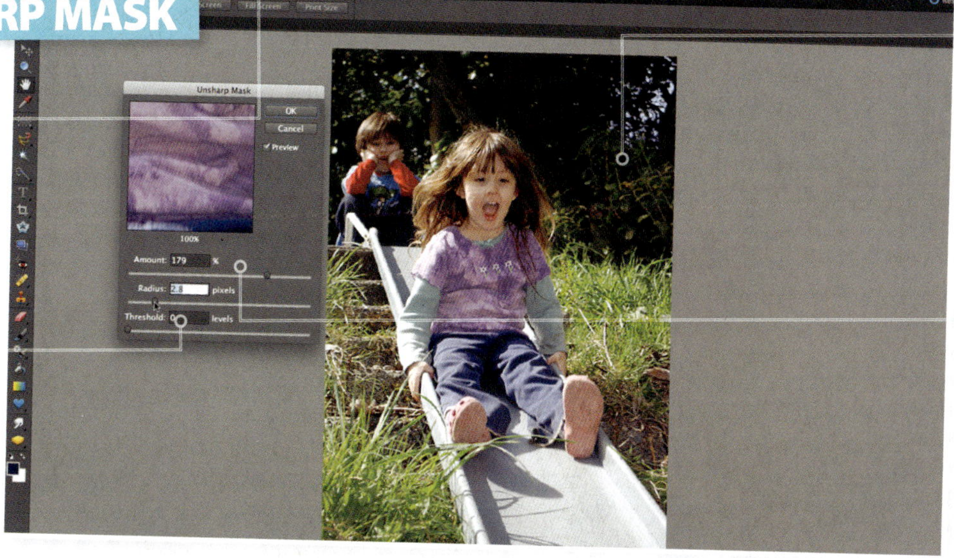

Preview

Make sure that Preview is ticked so that you can see the changes as you make them on your photo. The window in the dialog box lets you zoom in closer to see what's happening.

Amount

Experiment with the Amount control to change how strong the effect of the filter is. To keep it realistic try and use the lowest value possible for the effect that you want.

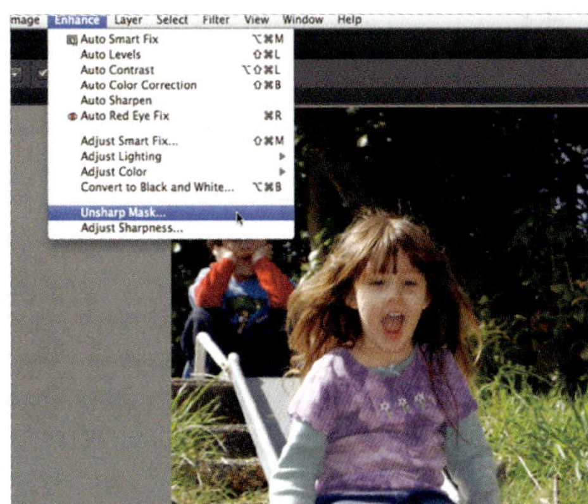

01 Open the command

In Photoshop, go to Filters>Sharpen>Unsharp Mask; in Elements go to Enhance>Unsharp Mask. Make sure the little Preview box is checked.

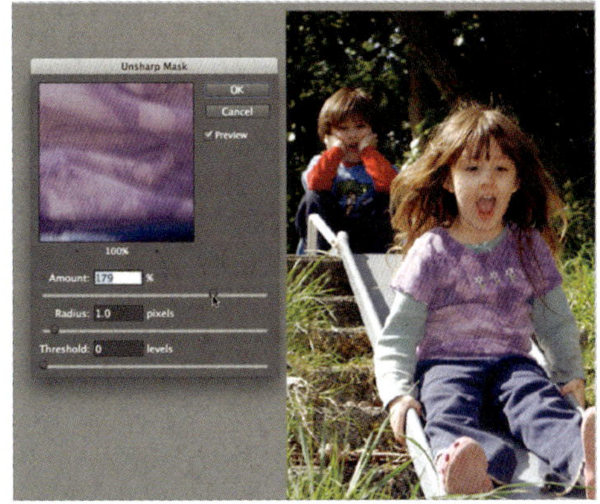

02 Set the Amount

This sets how intense the sharpening is – move to the right to increase the intensity. We have a bit of work to do here with this image, so move it to 179.

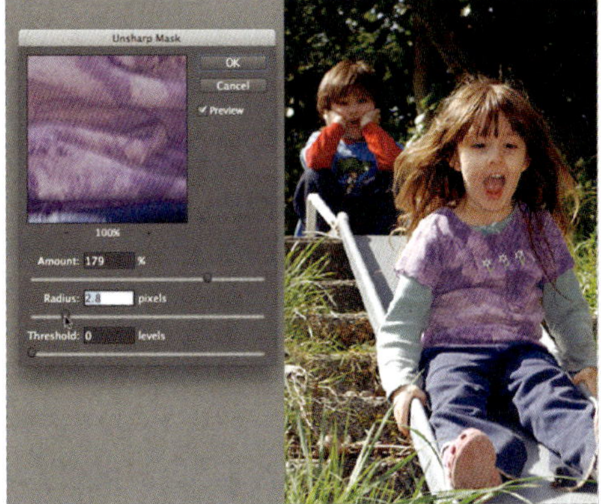

03 The Radius

The higher the setting, the more extreme the effect. We used 2.8. Threshold calms the edit down but a setting of 0 was all that was needed here.

Add emphasis to eyes

Use Dodge and Burn tools to give the eyes a sparkle and lift your portraits from good to great

It's well known that a person's eyes are the windows to their soul and it is one of the first things that we look at in any portrait photo. As such, it really pays to look closely at your subject's eyes and see if they could be improved, so as to stop anyone looking at the image in their tracks. On these two pages, we have a very quick way to draw more attention to the eyes in a portrait image.

For this task we've used two tools: Burn and Dodge. These are sat together on the Toolbar so you can find them quickly. For each you can set the Strength using the slider in the Tool Options bar at the top of the interface, and we suggest starting with a low Strength and building the effect up by brushing over the area more than once. Also, both tools use a brush to apply, so you can make the brush hard or soft, small or large, to fit your needs.

The Burn tool is great for deepening shadows, which in turn makes the highlights stand out and it is the first step for us in making the eyes of our subject really impress. But to really create a polished effect, the Dodge tool is the perfect way to add that all-important sparkle.

You can try this quick fix out on any portrait image, though you may need to play with the settings to get exactly the right look.

"The Burn tool is great for deepening shadows, which makes the highlights stand out"

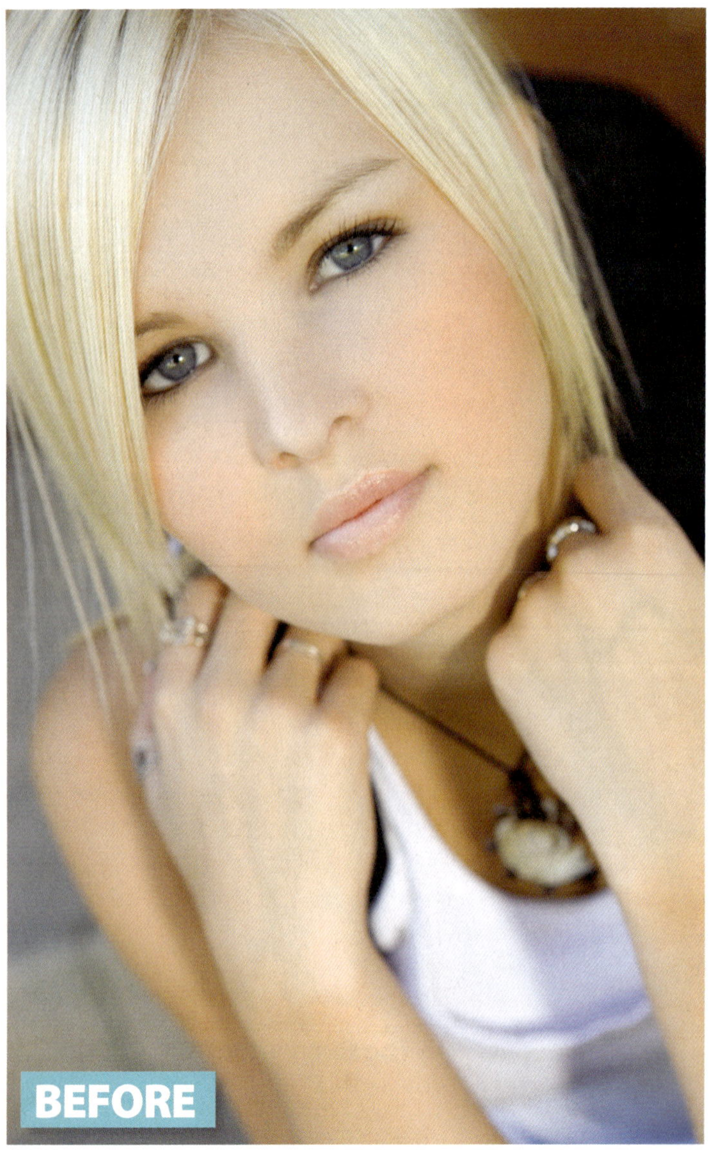

BEFORE

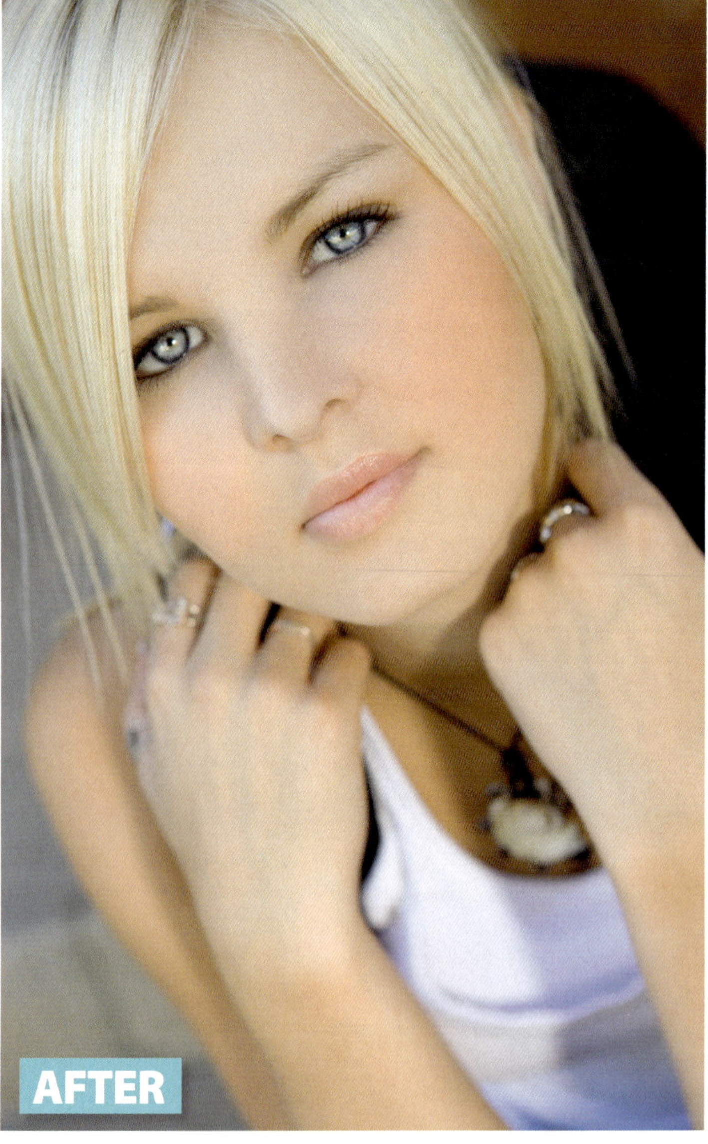

AFTER

WHAT WE HAVE DONE

The original photo

This is a lovely photo to begin with, but if you look at the eyes they are quite dark and they don't really draw the viewer in. Look at your image both up close and zoomed out to ascertain the amount of work that needs to be done to fix the image. Here we want to lift the coloured part of the iris, darkening the outer edges to help the colour stand out.

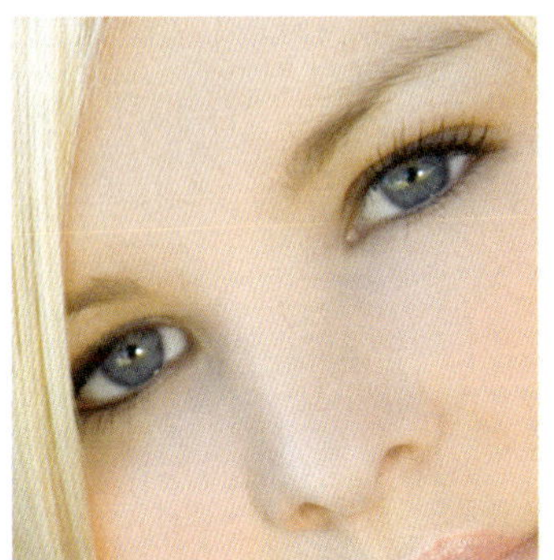

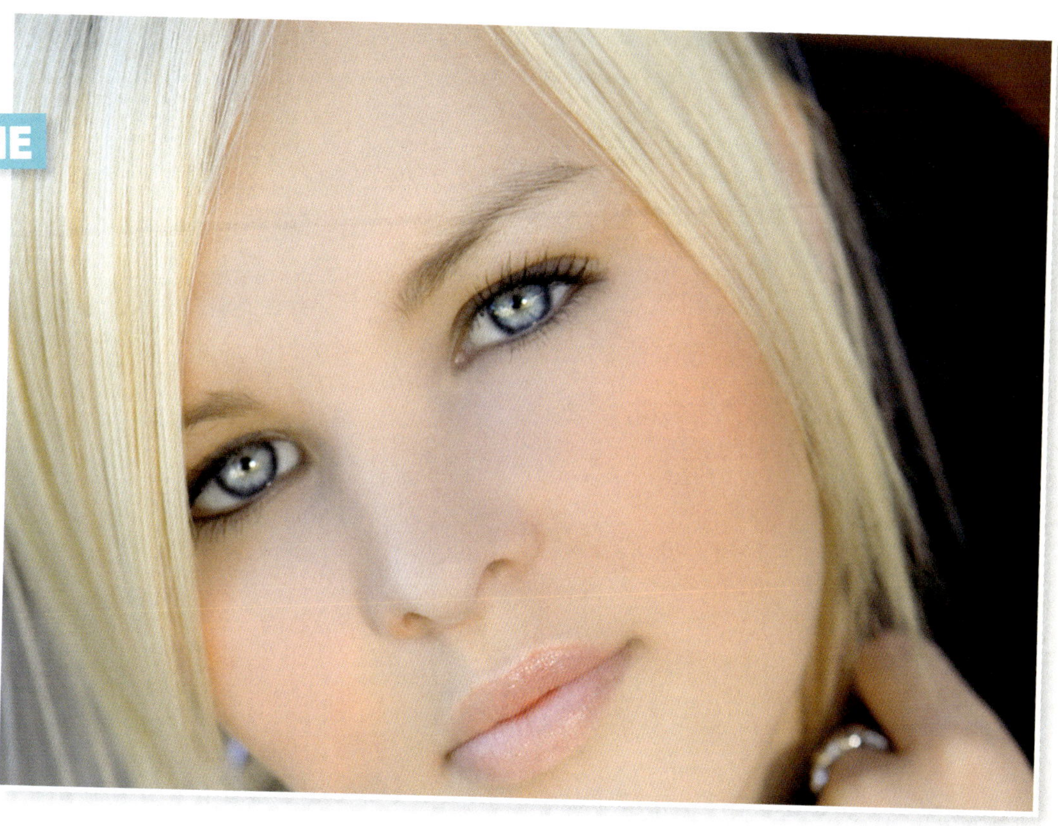

Duplicate

In all retouching tasks it pays to work on a duplicate layer in case anything should go wrong. Do this by going to Layer>Duplicate Layer, by dragging the original layer's thumbnail to the New Layer icon at the bottom of the Layers palette, or use the shortcut Cmd/Ctrl+J.

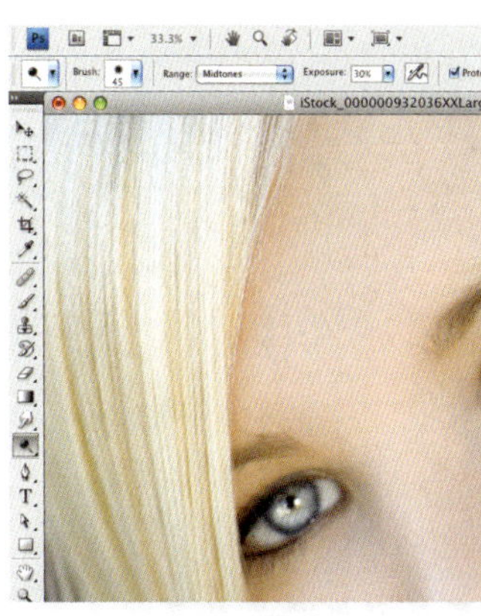

Range

You can choose to work on the Midtones, Highlights and Shadows separately. We work on the Shadows with the Burn tool and the Midtones with the Dodge tool here.

Tool Options bar

If you look at the top of the interface with the Dodge or Burn tools selected, you will see a set of options that enable you to choose the brush size, the strength, the range and whether to Protect Tones.

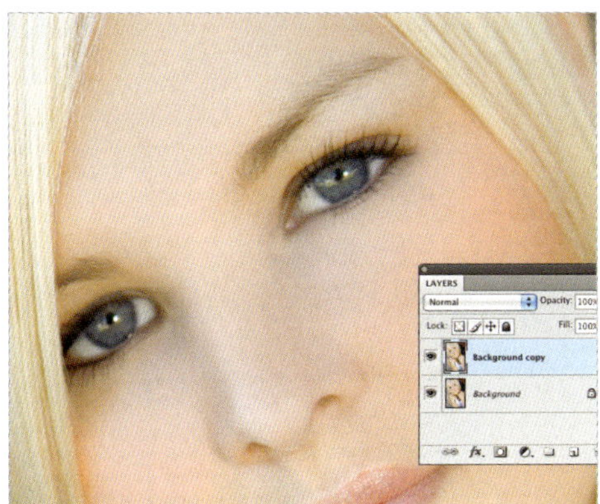

01 Non-destructive editing

To edit non-destructively, drag the image's layer onto the Create New Layer button in the Layers palette to duplicate.

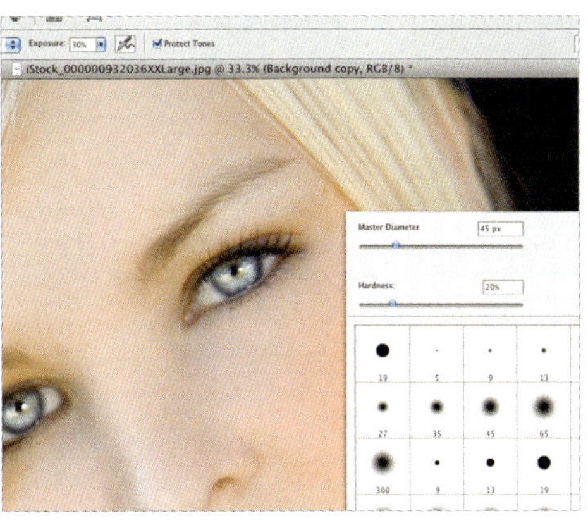

02 Lighten

Pick the Dodge tool. Set its size to cover the iris, Hardness to 20%, Range to Midtones, Exposure to 30%, and tick Protect Tones. Softly paint the iris.

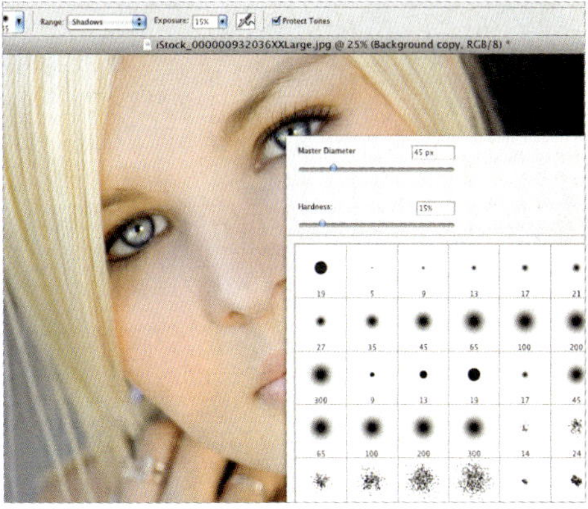

03 Darken the edges

Select the Burn tool and set it to 15% Hardness, Range to Shadows and Exposure to 15%. Apply the brush to the outside edge of the iris.

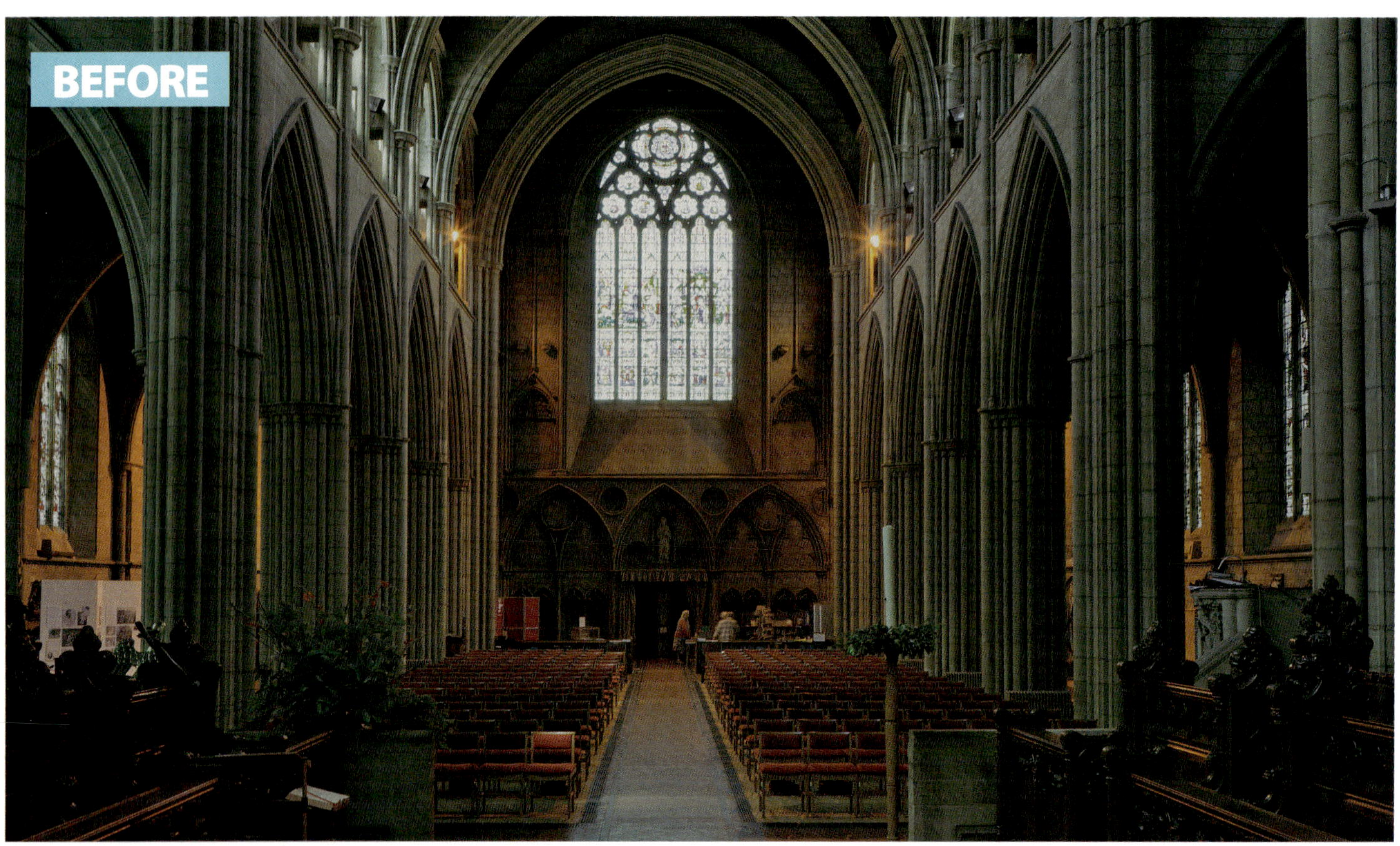
BEFORE

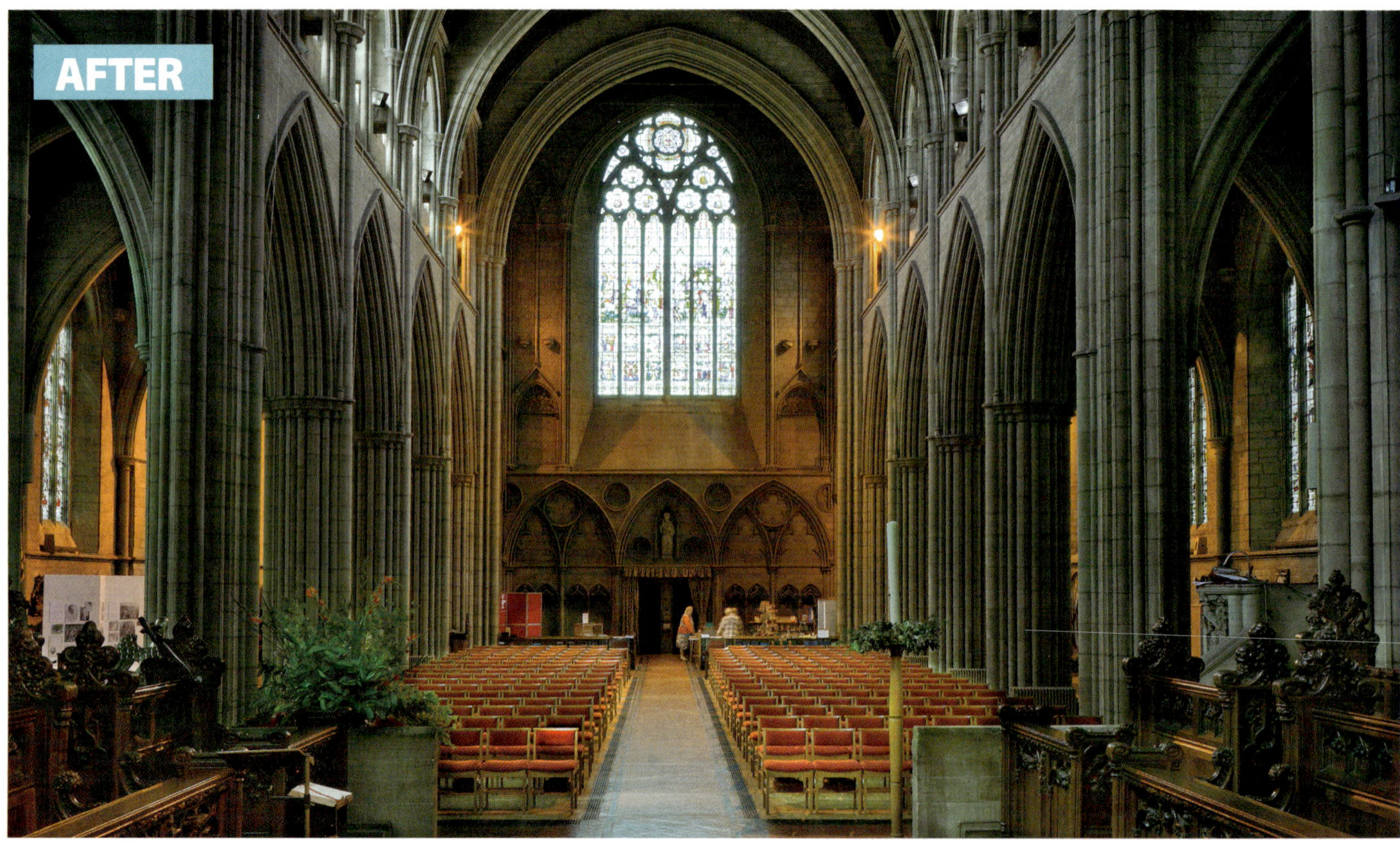
AFTER

Fix exposure with traditional skills

Use adjustment layers to emulate the traditional practice of dodging and burning

Dodge, Burn and Sponge are three tools packaged within Photoshop that should spend most of their time locked in the cupboard under the stairs. They're destructive, meaning that if you use them directly on a pixel-based layer, you've only got the Undo command should you decide that you've made a proper mess or aren't happy. And as you'll probably already know, this means undoing everything else you've done in the process, some of which might be perfectly good work.

A better, non-destructive method is to use adjustment layers and their masks (you may want to check out the dedicated section on this starting on page 130) Separate Curves layers can be used instead of Dodge and Burn, and separate Hue/Saturation layers can be used as an alternative for Sponge . The layer mask allows you to apply these edits to specific parts of the image just as you would with those naughty Dodge, Burn and Sponge tools, but this time all your work is recorded on the layer mask and undone at any time by simply brushing with black instead of white. Nothing else you do will have been affected, allowing you to be more creative and experimental.

But why should you dodge, burn and alter saturation in the first place? Well, quite often the lighting or tones that nature provides aren't always the most beautiful. Dodging can draw attention to pivotal details while burning is great for knocking back elements that are better hidden. Saturation is great for focusing the eye to the centre of the frame, and used together they're a formidable, image-editing team.

WHAT YOU'LL LEARN

More light
We will look at how you can enhance the lighting in your images to brighten the shadows and make more of the highlights.

Detail revealed
What's so great about this technique is that rather than losing detail through editing, we're actually going to reveal more of it.

Image brightened overall
The whole image is given a boost to make the most of all the enhancements that we have made.

Saturate colour
The HDR-type feel comes from the fact that the colours are boosted to just past the point of photoreal, creating a striking, eyecatching piece of art.

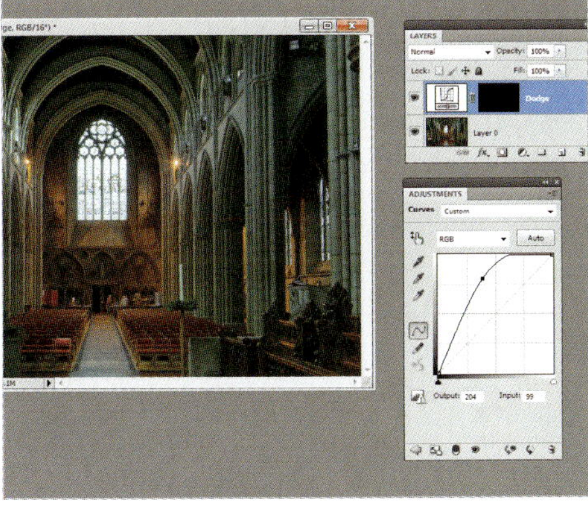

01 Add a Dodge layer

Add a Curves adjustment layer. Push the Curve up hard and invert the layer mask using Ctrl/Cmd+I to Hide All. Double-click the layer and name it 'Dodge'.

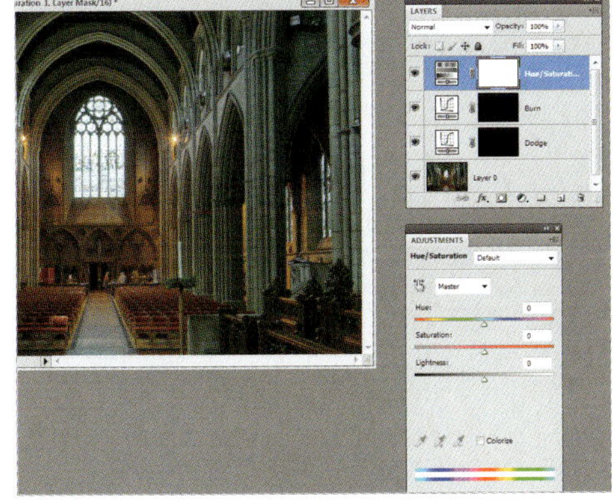

02 Add a Burn layer

Add a second Curves layer, this time pulling the Curve down hard. Invert the layer mask and name it 'Burn'. Add a Hue/Saturation adjustment layer.

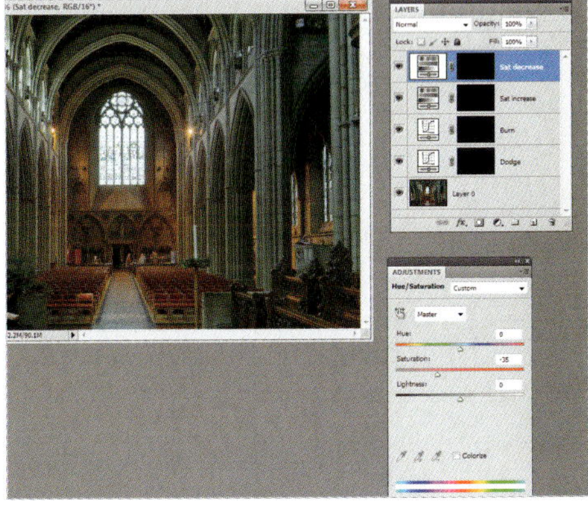

03 Saturation layers

Make Saturation +35 and invert the mask. Rename 'Sat Increase'. Add another Hue/Saturation layer (Saturation = -35). Invert and name it 'Sat Decrease'.

Let's get dodging… …and burning

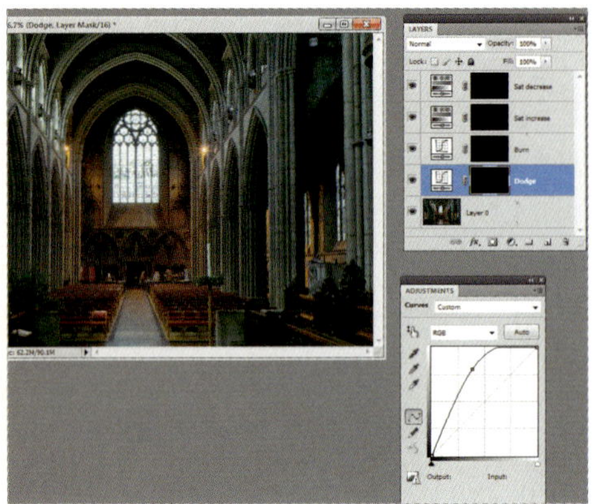

04 Set up the Brush tool
Press 'D' to reset the colour palette and 'B' to access the Brush tool. Set it to 0% Hardness. Click the Dodge layer mask to make it active.

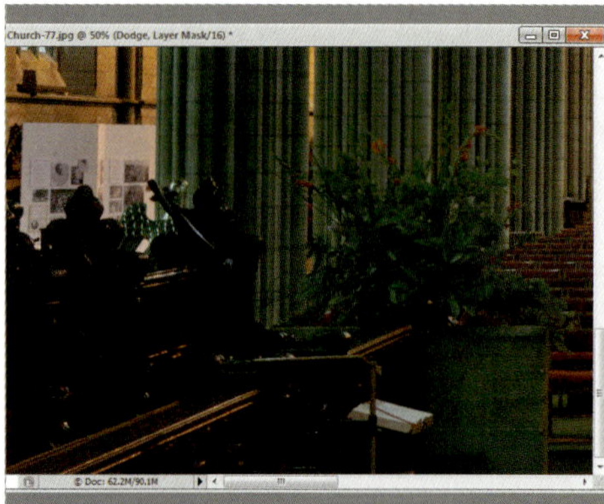

05 Zoom in
Ctrl/Cmd and '+' to zoom in to the pews. Resize the Brush tool appropriately with '[' and ']' and press 3 to set the brush Opacity to 30%.

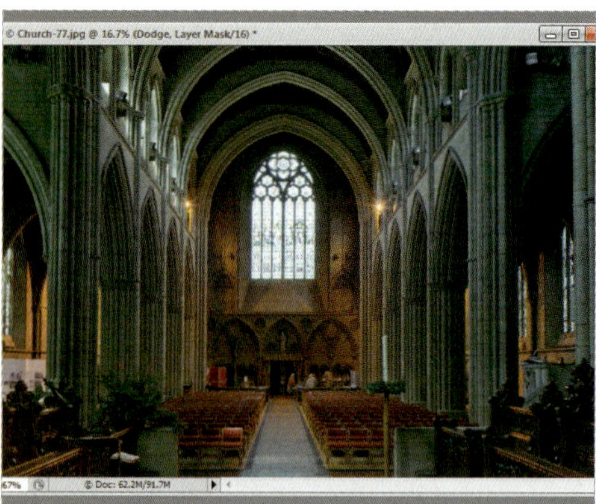

06 Dodge to balance tones
Brush over the pew area as many times as necessary to lighten it to match the lighter pews on the right of the image. .

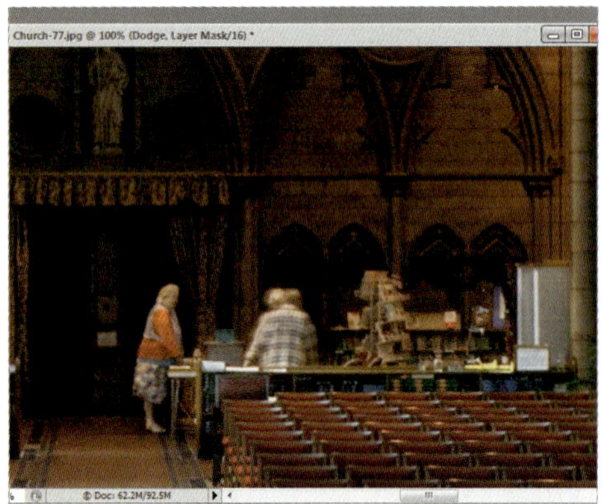

07 Dodge people
We're going to use dodge to draw attention. Zoom in on the people and the stall in the background and brush over them as needed.

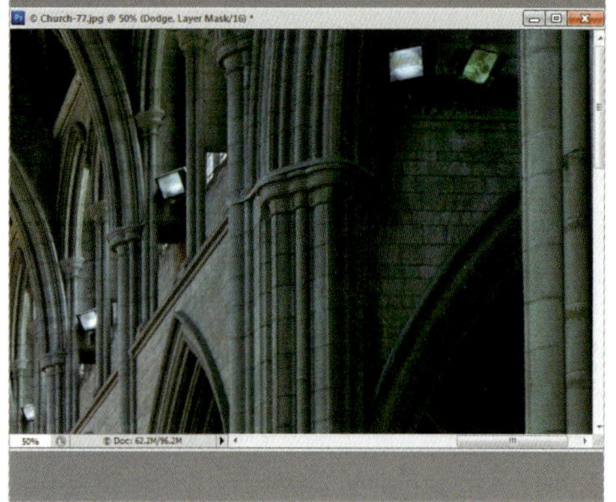

08 Dodge the details
Work around the rest of the image in the same way, picking out areas to lighten. The dark areas of the arches are a good idea, for example.

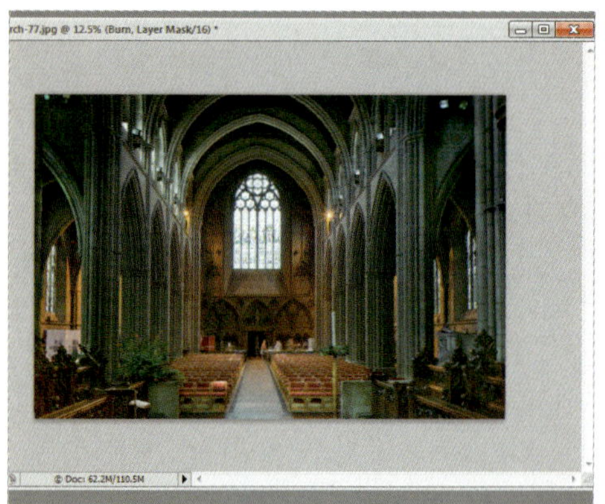

09 Burn corners
Click the layer mask on the Burn layer. We're going to use a very large brush, again at 30%, to darken the top-right and top-left corners.

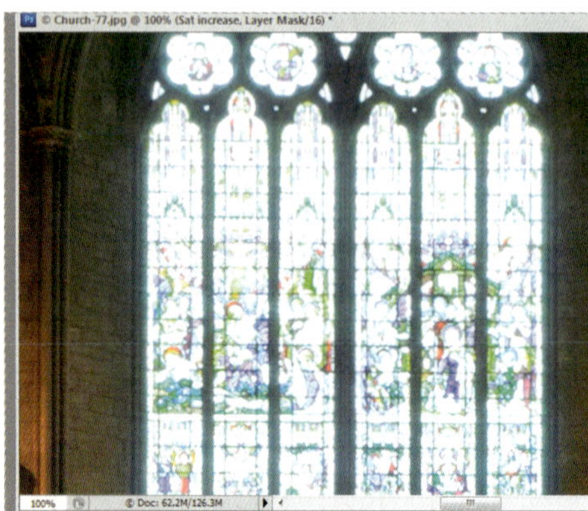

10 Burn windows
Press 0 for 100% brush Opacity, size the brush very small and zoom in on the stained glass window. We want to work over all the detail in the glass.

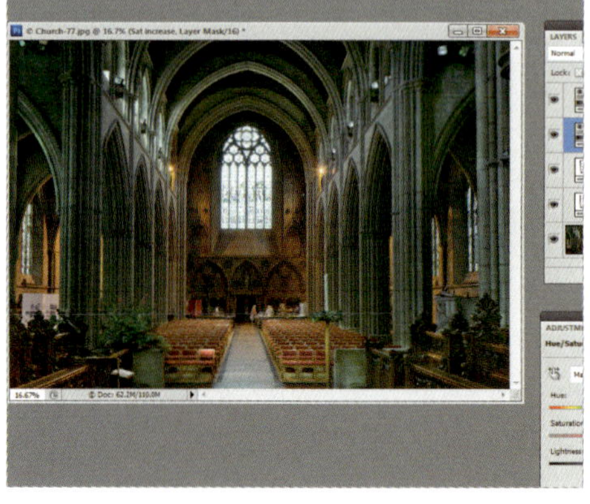

11 Sat increase
Click the Sat Increase layer mask. Stay at 100% brush Opacity as we know we want to increase the colour by the same initial setting of +35.

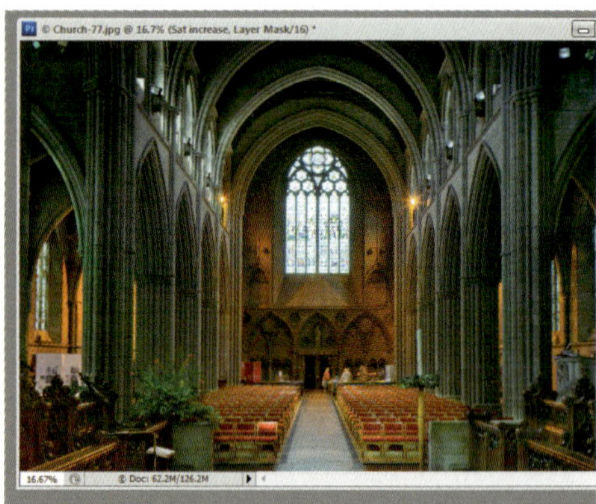

12 Brush the colour in
Work over the people, pews, the foliage, the stained glass windows and any areas with orange light as well as the whole of the back wall.

QUICK PHOTOSHOP TIPS

Dodge and burn in colour

Traditionally dodging and burning were techniques used on monochrome images. The process of removing colour already affords a sense of unreality so adjustments to tonality tend rarely to bother the viewer. Colour imagery provides greater expectations of reality, as it's viewed as being that much closer to an authentic reproduction of the world. This means dodging and burning, as well as colour saturation changes, tend to have a much stronger impact on the eye, appearing to drive a scene more towards a cartoon or hyperreal mood. If you're trying to maintain a semblance of photographic reality, you'll need to be very conservative with your adjustments and focus them on larger areas rather than details. If you want to go for the cartoon look, however, strong adjustments in lots of small areas are the way to go for a stylised effect.

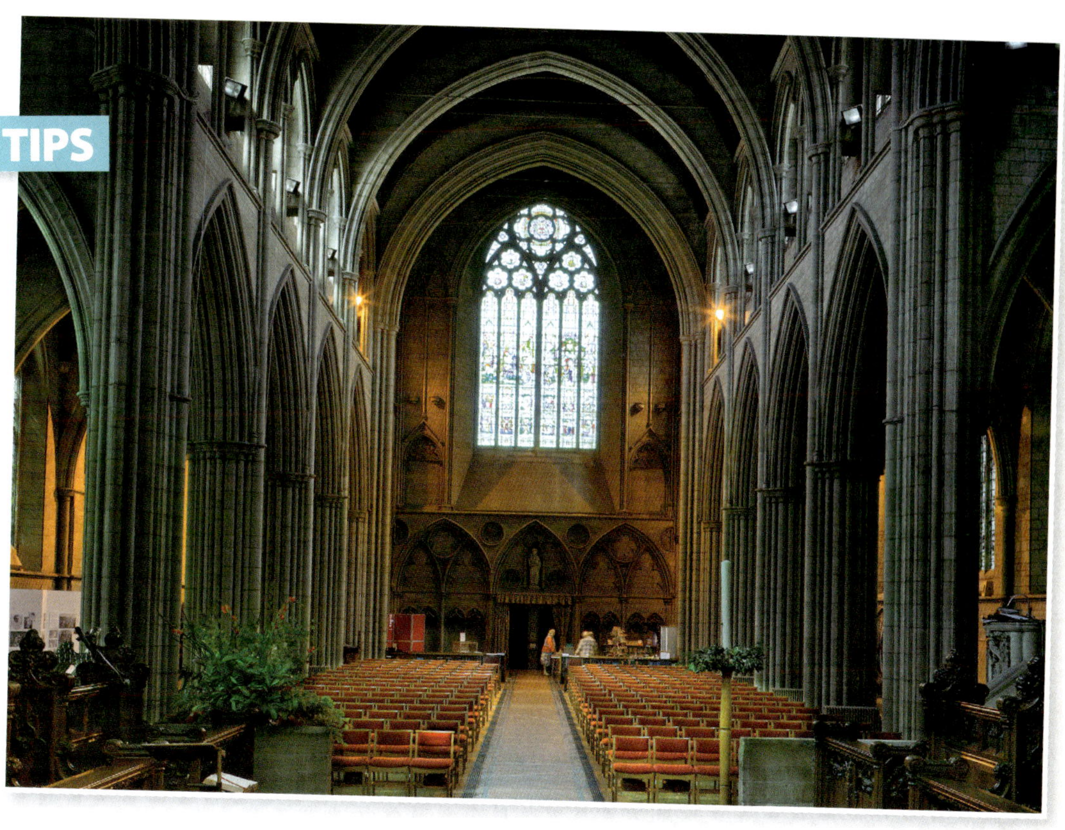

Converging verticals

When shooting large structures, you're going to have to point your camera upwards and this means that the verticals are going to lean inwards. Correct this by running Edit>Transform> Perspective on a duplicate of the Background layer.

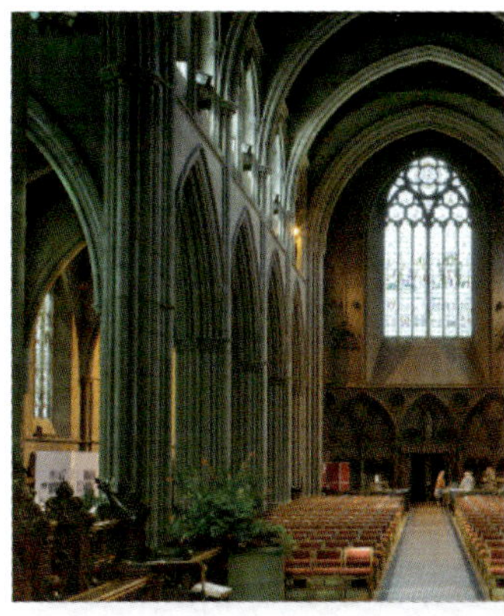

Burning for the corners

If you're using dodge or burn layers to correct large areas rather than small details, you need to use a very large brush for a more graduated effect. Zoom far out and pull the edges of the window to reveal an area outside of the canvas, then work with the brush edge for subtlety.

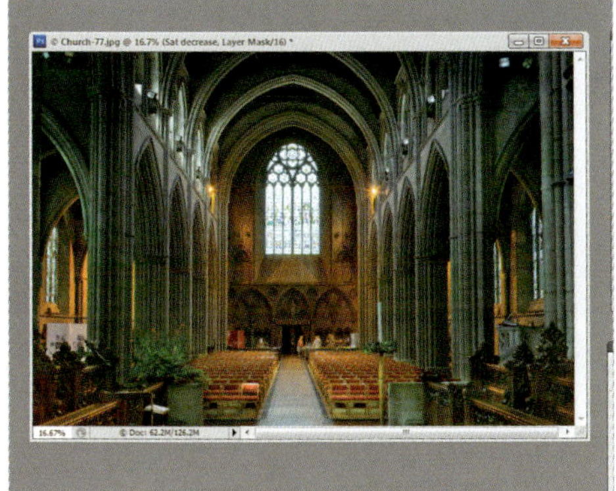

13 Sat decrease

Click the Sat Decrease adjustment layer mask. Again, we can work at 100% here as -35 is a pretty good setting for our work.

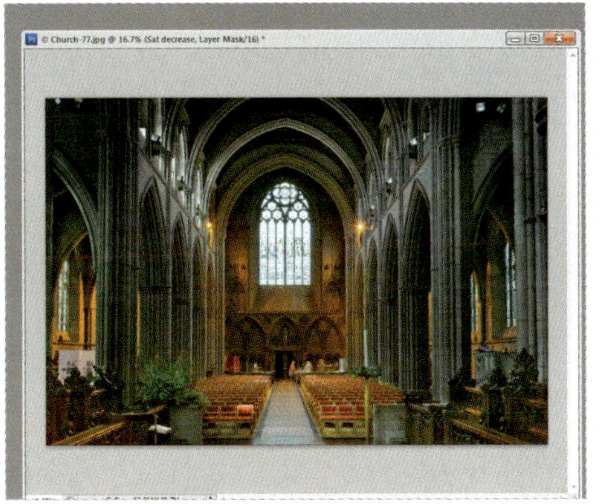

14 Brush the colour out

Resize the brush to suit and carefully brush the adjustment into the stone walls to knock back the colour to suit the scene.

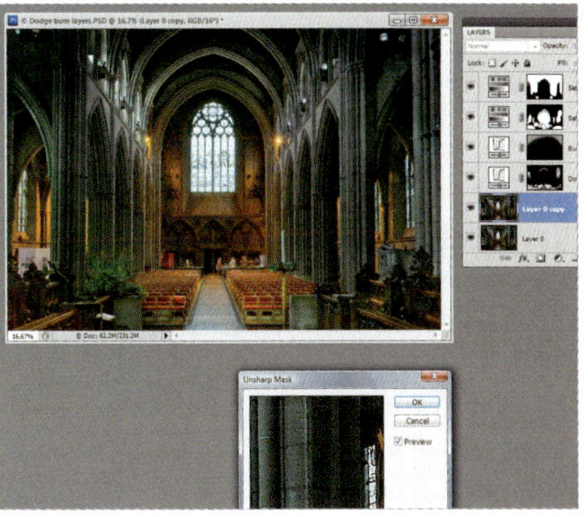

15 Sharpen to finish

Finish by running the Unsharp Mask filter on a duplicate of your Background layer. A Radius of 0.5 pixels with 300% Amount is good here.

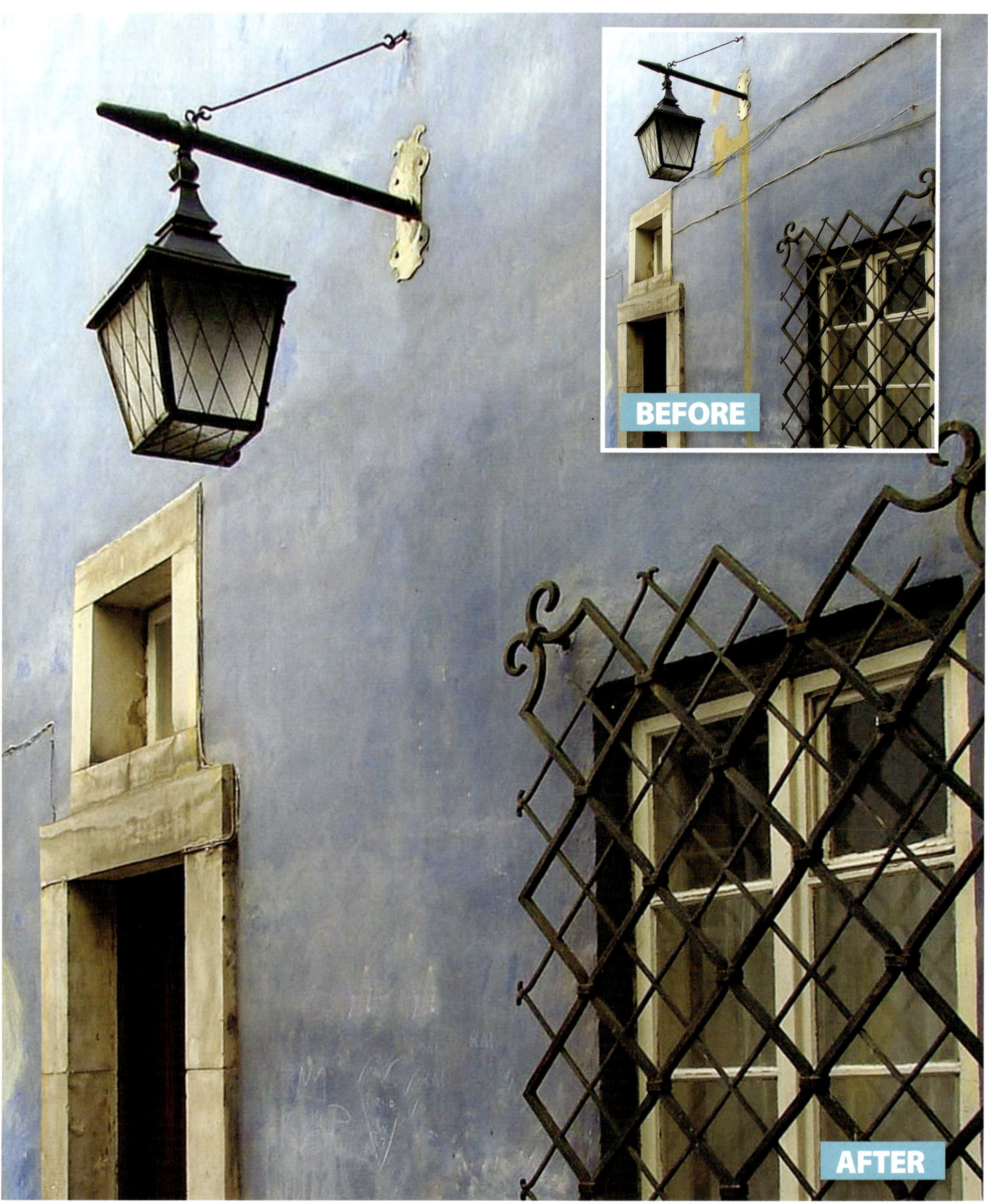
BEFORE
AFTER

Content Aware healing

This is the Photoshop skill of using the Clone Stamp tool to clean up your photos

As well as Content-Aware Fill, which was introduced in CS4 and we look at in detail on page 176, you also have the option to use the Content-Aware algorithm as an extra feature in the Healing brush tool if you are using CS5 onwards. While the Fill option is great for tackling quite straightforward retouching jobs, the Healing brush options give you a far greater degree of control. Before, the Healing brush only gave the option of 'Proximity Match', which sometimes gave rather patchy, blurred results, but now it's almost like painting with actual image elements.

No matter whether it's a beach scene, fields, skies or even rippled water, you'll find that the new Content-Aware Healing brush can cope with it in a completely seamless way,. Using Content-Aware technology via the Spot Healing brush tool is perfect for those more complex retouching tasks, where the retouching can be guided by simply brushing the particular blemish away. Even with the Content-Aware option, the way you actually use the Spot Healing brush tool hasn't changed at all, but as you'll see in the walkthrough, the results certainly have!

"Using Content-Aware technology via the Spot Healing brush tool is perfect for those more complex retouching tasks"

IN PROGRESS

CS5 users only

This amazing tool option was only introduced in CS5. If you have an earlier version, then you will need to use the Clone Stamp tool instead (see page 110).

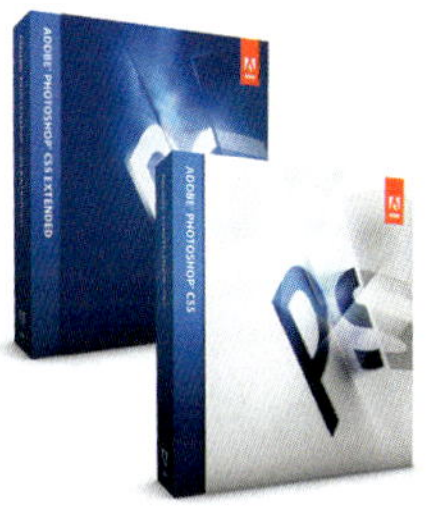

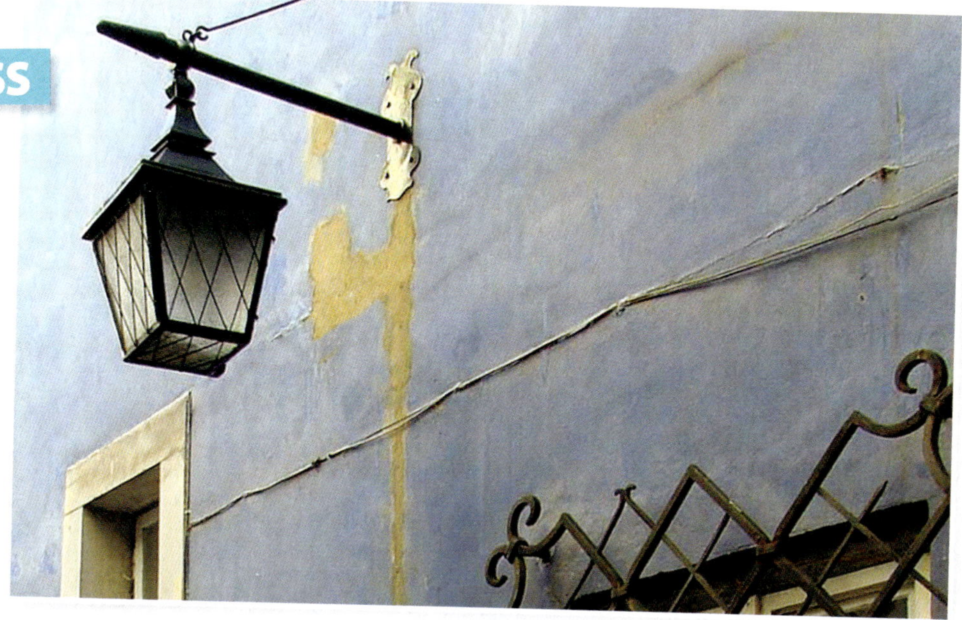

Careful brushing

You'll be amazed at the difference you'll see as a result of the Content-Aware option being used. With some careful brushing, you'll quickly produce perfect results.

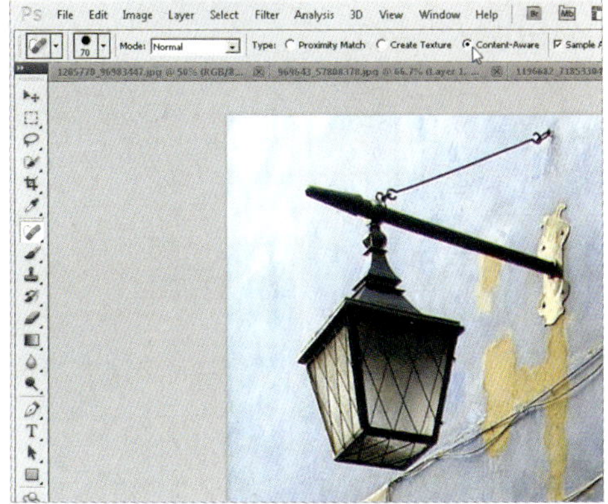

01 Choose Content Aware

Choose the Spot Healing brush tool and choose the Content-Aware button in the Options bar. If you're on a separate layer, check Sample All Layers.

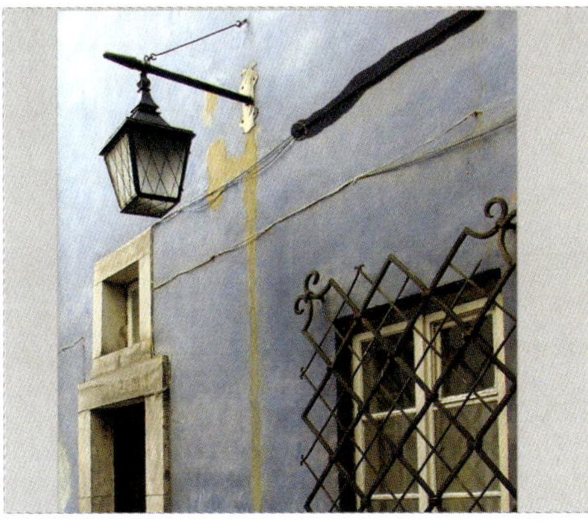

02 Size your brush

Make sure to size your brush so it's just a little bigger than the area you want to clone away. Now begin to brush over the offending blemish.

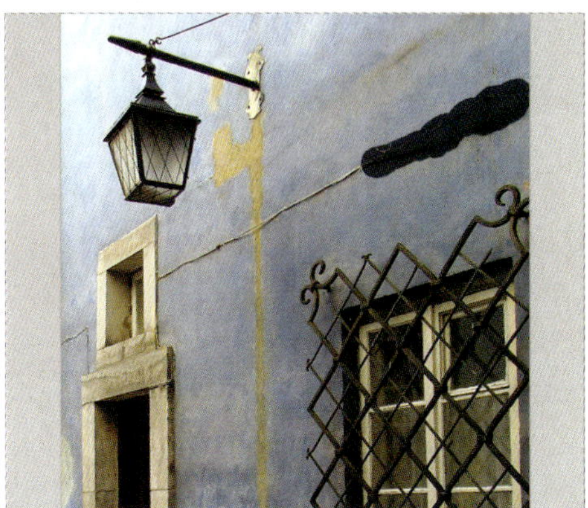

03 Short strokes

Try to cover the blemish in a single stroke. Actually scrubbing a 'pool' with the brush to cover an object will work better than using short strokes.

Using the Patch tool

Image repair has never been easier, thanks to this great tool, which lets you clear up larger flaws in seconds

The Patch tool is incredibly easy to use, and is perfect for restoring and repairing any parts of your photos that are damaged or blemished.

This tool is a Photoshop staple, and has been around since version 6.0 of our favourite app. It's the ideal option for quick image edits, as it enables you to replace large or small selections from your images with equally large or small portions of replacement image information.

The Patch tool is tucked away in the toolbar, sharing space with the Healing brush, and can be accessed by holding the cursor down on the small black arrow and activating the fly-out menu. Once the tool is selected, three options are added to the top menu bar: Source, Destination and Use Pattern – in this guide, we will be concentrating on the first two options, as they are the ones that you are most likely to use over and over again.

There are a few methods available to repair your images using the Patch tool. First, you can choose to select the 'bad' part of your image and move this selection around the photo to find an acceptable portion to put in its place. Alternatively, you can select a good part of your image first, and then move this to cover or 'patch' the unsightly part. Finally, if you don't have enough image to patch up the problem area, you can opt to patch the problem spot with a pattern fill, combining the texture of your pattern with the underlying colours present in your photograph.

> "This tool is a Photoshop staple, and has been around since version 6.0 of our favourite app"

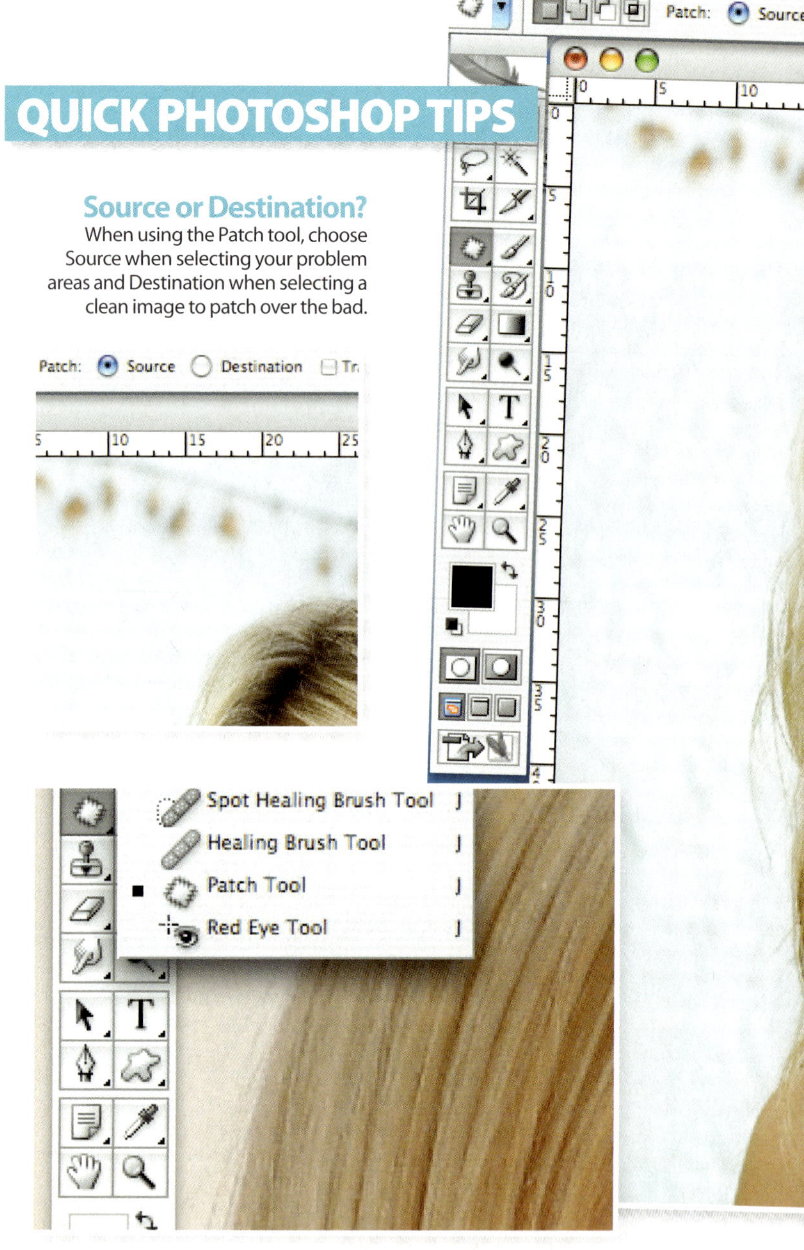

QUICK PHOTOSHOP TIPS

Source or Destination?
When using the Patch tool, choose Source when selecting your problem areas and Destination when selecting a clean image to patch over the bad.

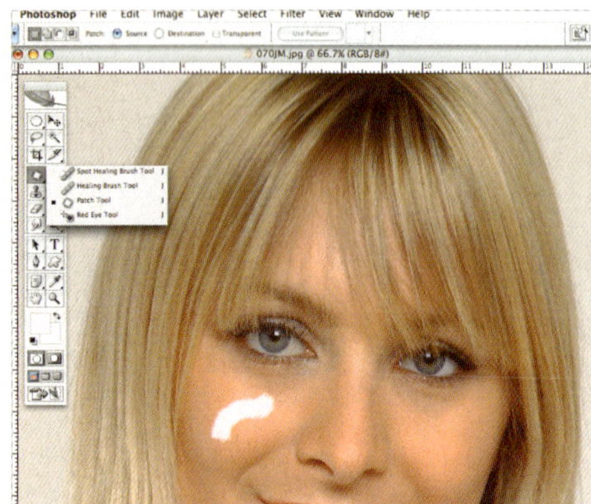

01 Getting ready
Open your start image and activate the Patch tool (in the toolbar along with the Healing brush). Notice the options that appear in the top toolbar.

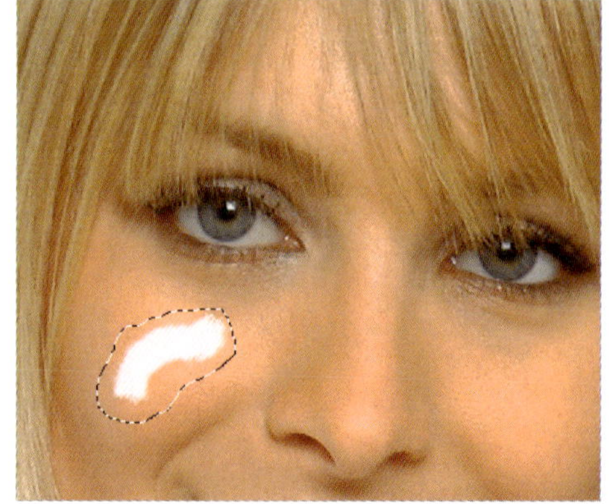

02 Select a source
Your source point is the area that needs fixing. Pick the Source option in the top toolbar and select the area just as you would when using the Lasso.

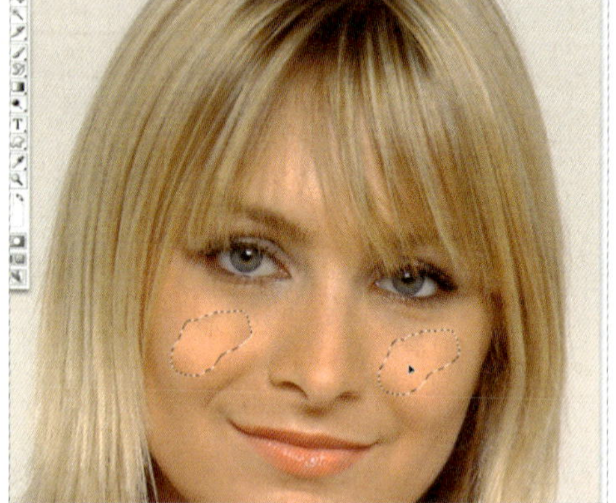

03 Drag 'n drop
Place the cursor in the centre of the selection. Now drag it to another area of your image that can be used to patch up the blemish, then release.

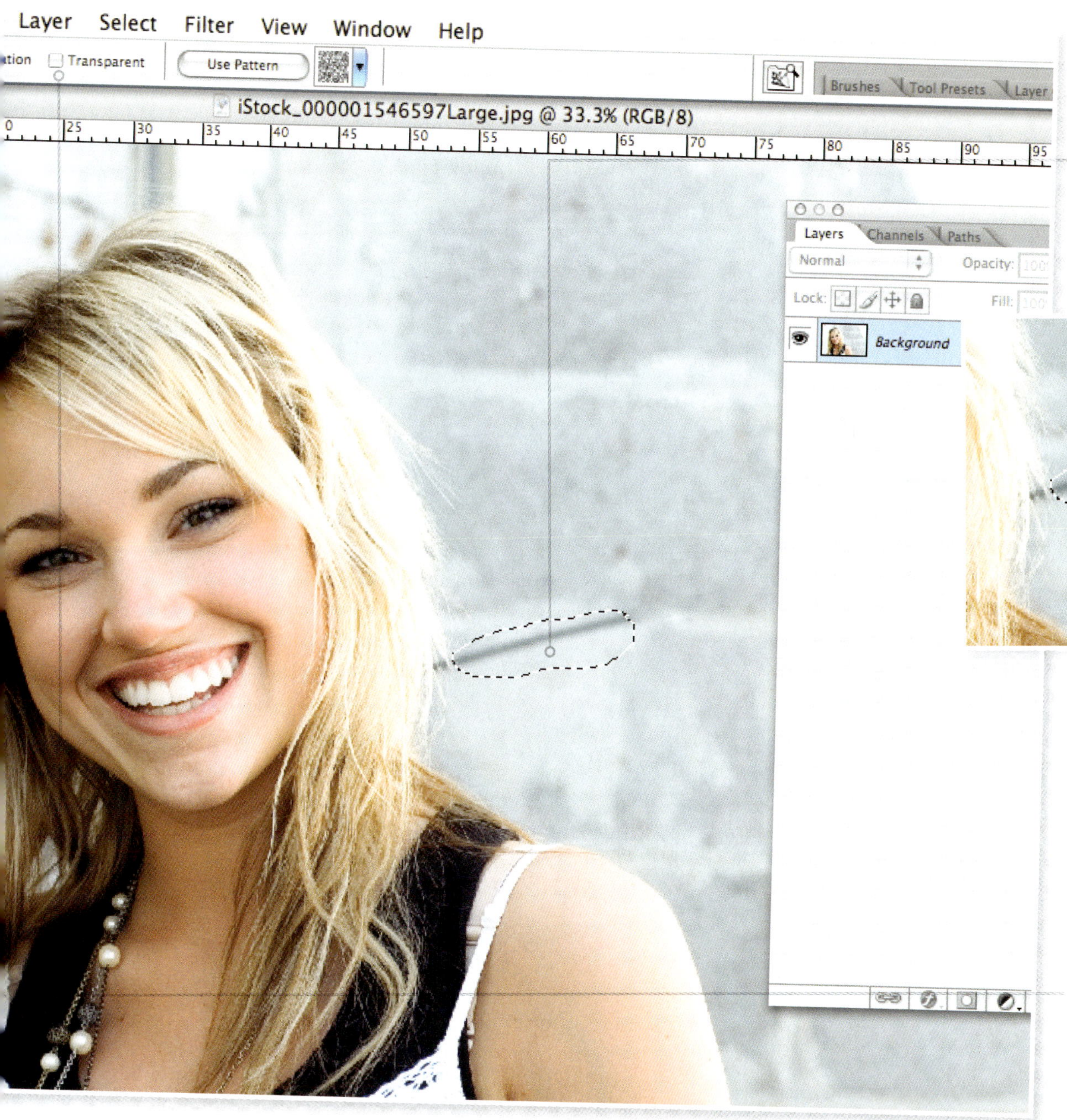

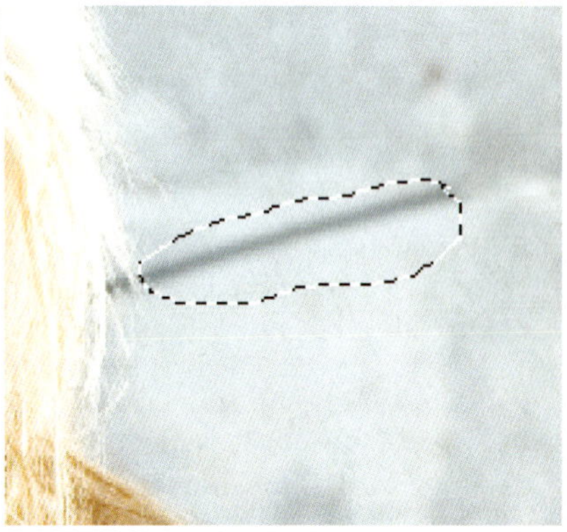

Patch tool

This tool shares the same well as the Healing brush on the toolbar. To access the tool, just hold down the cursor over the small black arrow and the fly-out menu will appear.

Smudge tool

For a quick touch-up to the seams of your patchwork, try opting for something like the Smudge tool to help soften the edges.

Transparent

For a very subtle bit of patchwork, try opting for the Transparent feature on the top toolbar. This gives a much less exaggerated effect – perfect for that barely there look.

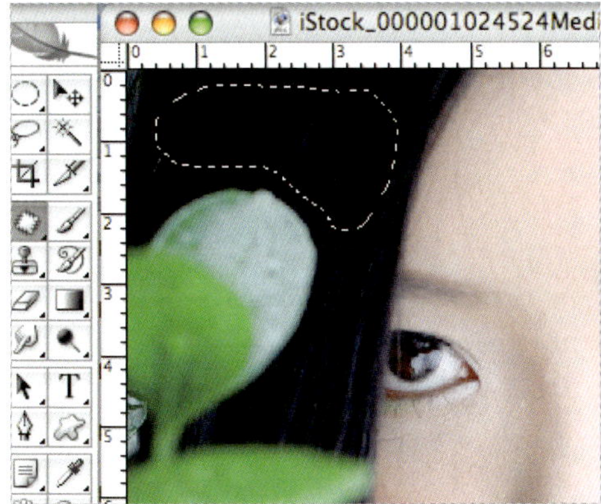

04 Patch the bad bits

You can also do the opposite, and select a clean part of your image first, then drag this over the blemish. Simply hit 'Destination' instead of 'Source'.

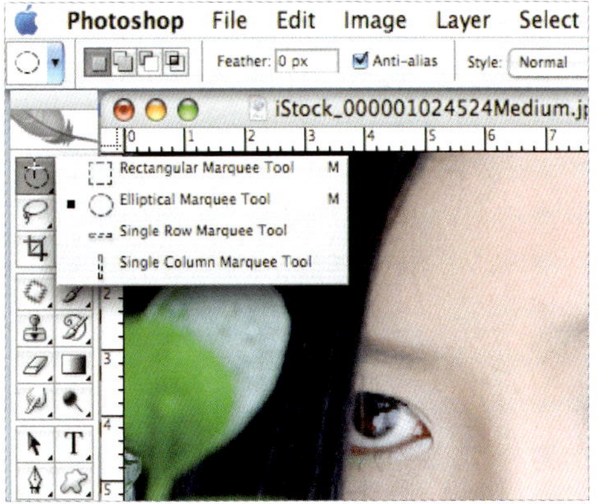

05 Making selections

You can also make a selection with your favourite Selection tool first and activate the Patch tool next. This is a more controlled way of doing things.

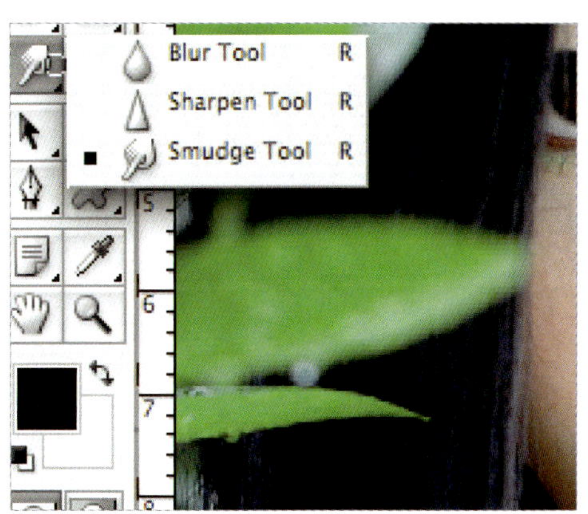

06 Hide the patchwork

You can hide the fix using the Smudge tool. Turn the Strength down to 20%. Work at the edges of your new patch and watch it blend in.

Retouch skin in portrait photos

You don't need complicated techniques to retouch portraits, as we show you with the Spot Healing Brush and Patch tools

One of the most popular uses of Photoshop is to retouch images – Everyone wants to look good in pictures! We aren't talking intensive cosmetic surgery here, just a few healing swipes to make portraits really sparkle. And both Photoshop and Elements have some really simple tools to help you do this.

The easiest, and most useful, is the Spot Healing Brush tool. With this you do nothing more than click on an area for it to magically disappear. Obviously there are a wealth of complex measurements running in the background, but your task is just a simple click. This is perfect for things like isolated spots, freckles, moles and the like.

If there are a few blemishes in the same area, then you can use the Patch tool. This is found in the same place as the Spot Healing Brush tool, but you have to click and hold on the Spot Healing Brush icon to reveal more tools hidden underneath. The Patch tool is one of these and it has the icon of a plaster to identify it. This isn't quite as straightforward as the Spot Healing Brush tool, but you can learn it quickly. You draw around the area that needs retouching by clicking your mouse button and dragging. This makes a selection. Next, click on your selection and drag it to a clear area of skin. The Patch tool then replaces the blemished area with the clean skin as if by magic! We have supplied the start image for this tutorial so that you can try it out for yourself.

"We aren't talking intensive cosmetic surgery here, just a few healing swipes"

RETOUCHING ADVICE

Retouch 101

There is a slight problem with the retouching tools being so simple to use, and that is that you can get easily carried away with them! The secret of good retouching is to leave some character intact, so don't remove all of the flaws, just the ones that annoy you the most.

Photoshop File Edit Image

Spot Healing Brush Tool J
Healing Brush Tool J
Patch Tool J
Red Eye Tool J

START IMAGE

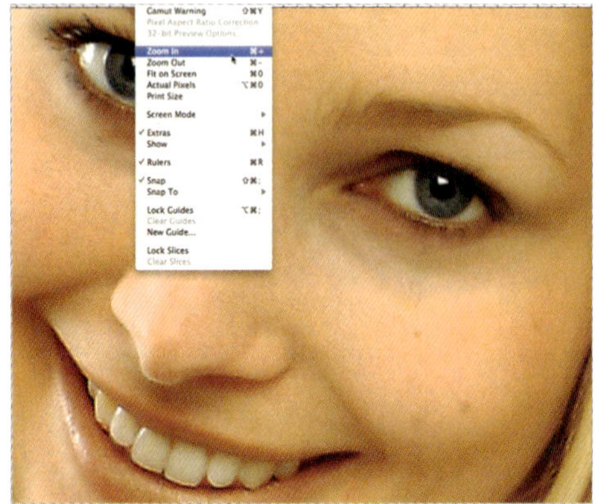

01 Zoom into the image

It's really important that you can see what you are doing. Go to View>Zoom In. It's worth learning the shortcut: Cmd/Ctrl and +.

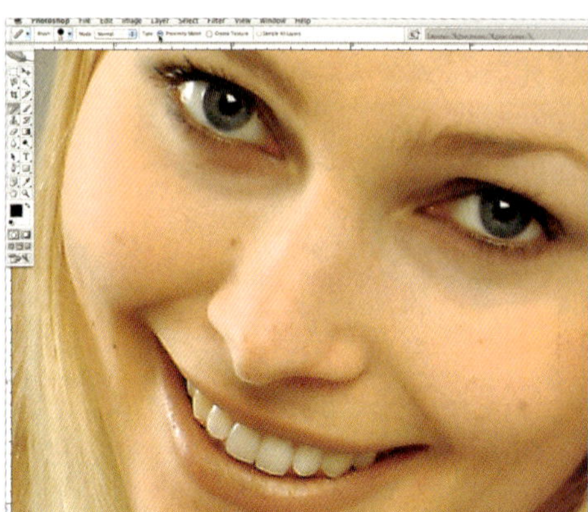

02 Spot cleaning

Let's start with the Spot Healing Brush. Click the icon that looks like a plaster. In the top Options bar make sure Proximity Match is selected.

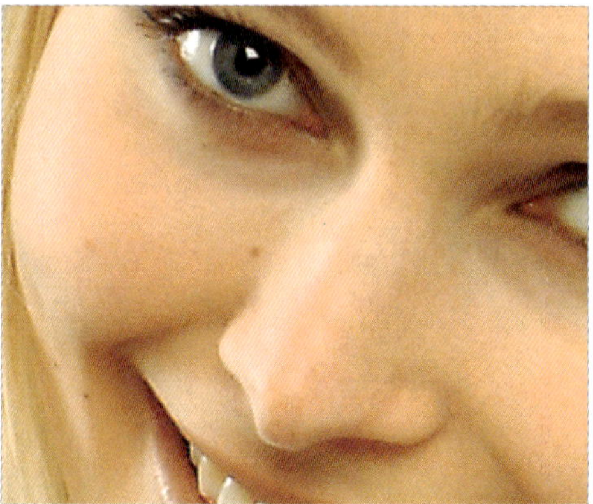

03 Click to fix

This is best for areas that can be erased in one click. Go to the top Options bar and click the brush icon. Pick a brush slightly larger than the area to remove.

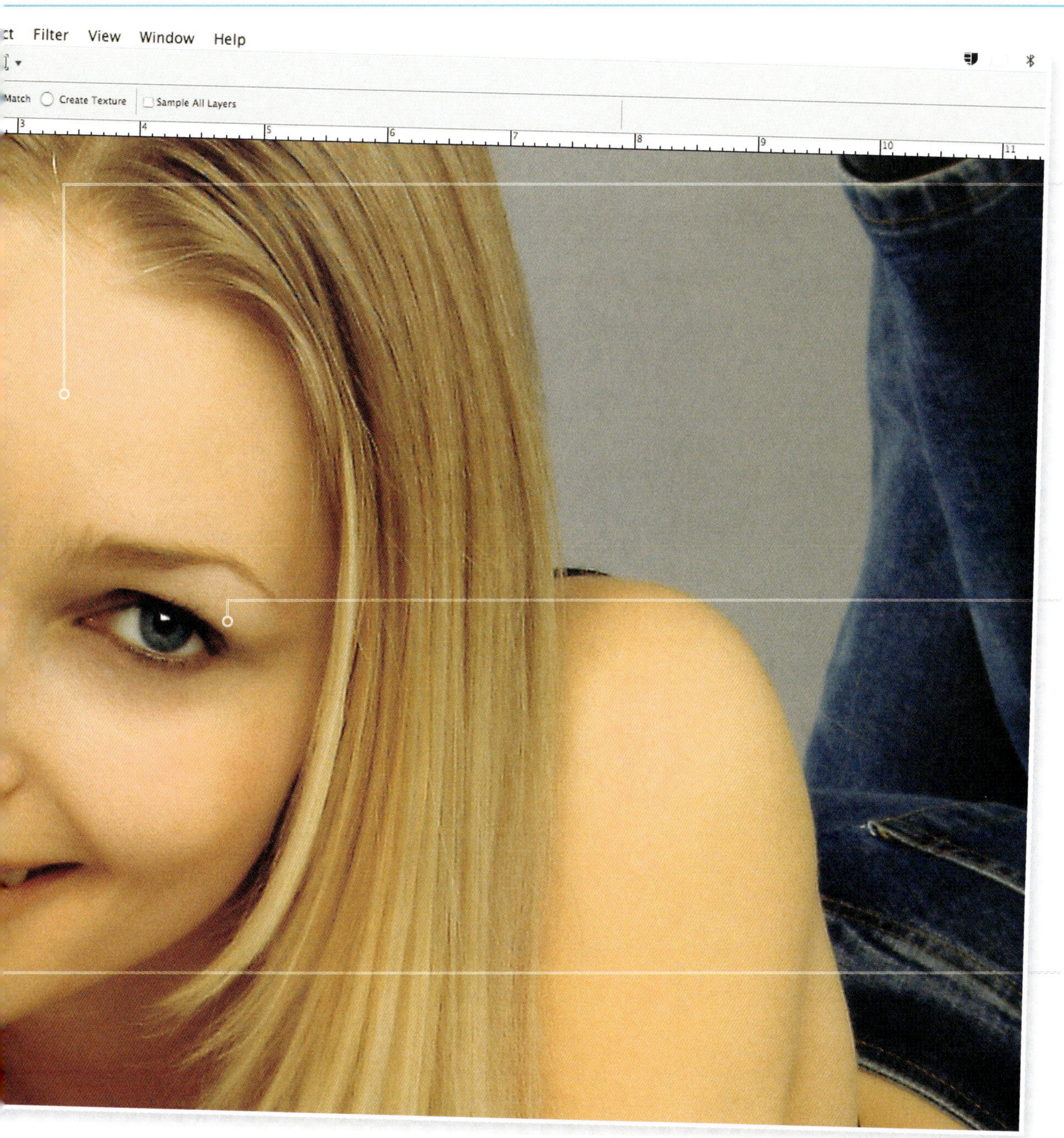

Small blemishes

Our model had a few blemishes on her forehead. These benefited from a blast of the Patch tool, as it was a simple case of drawing around one area, dragging to a 'good' area for it to replace the offending part.

Eye treatment

The Patch tool was also used to make light work of the bags under the eyes. We didn't do too much here, just enough to remove the darkest pixels. The technique was exactly the same as for the blemished areas.

One-click wonder

The Spot Healing Brush is fantastic for very small areas that need to be erased. It really is just a case of clicking once for the edit to take place. Just make sure you have Proximity selected in the Options bar.

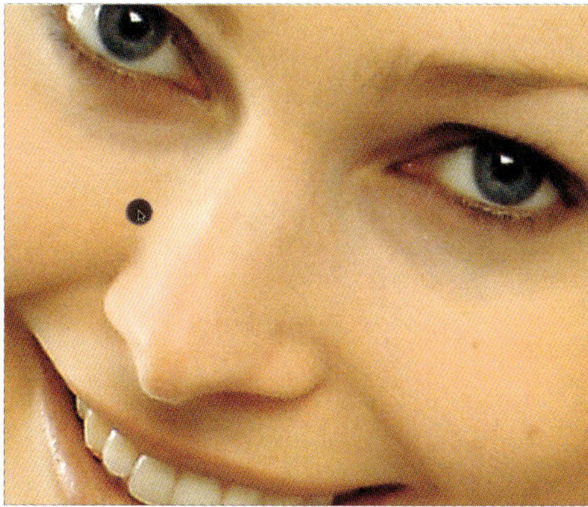

04 Mole begone!

Click on a mole and let go. You will initially see a black mark where you clicked, but then that will disappear… along with the mole.

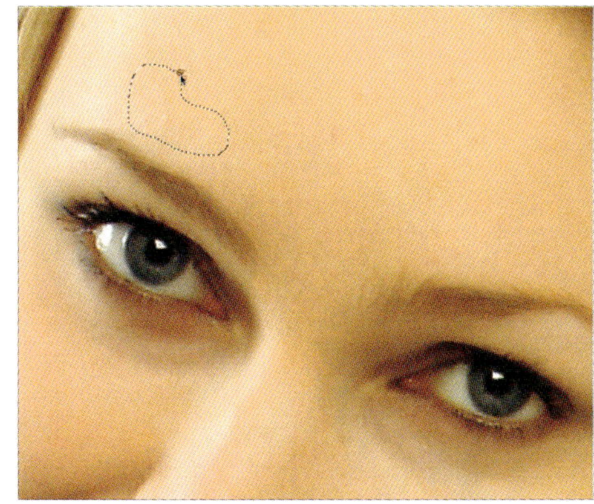

05 Patch tool

Click and hold the Spot Healing Brush icon. Pick the Patch tool. Make sure that Source is chosen in the top Options bar. Draw around a blemished area.

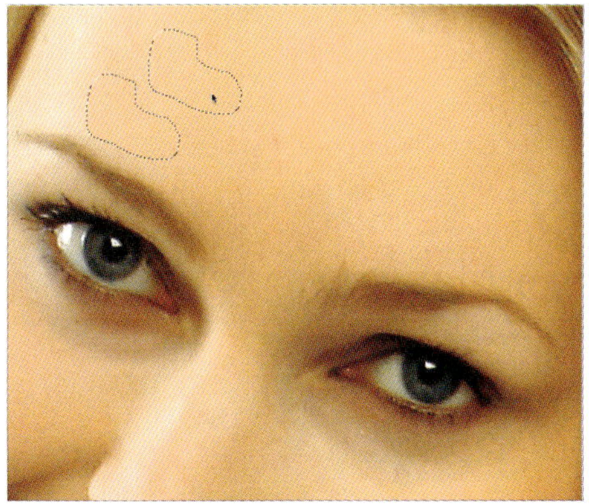

06 Now drag

Move your cursor over the selected area and click and drag it to a clean area. You will see the blemished area be replaced by the new section.

Whiten teeth and eyes

Lighten and colour correct teeth and eyes with precision Curves and Levels adjustments

The eyes are always the first thing we're drawn to in a portrait, and this fact is something of a double-edged sword for Photoshop folk. On the one hand you can improve any portrait quickly and easily by retouching these most important facets. On the other hand, bad retouching will obviously be just as quick; there's nothing like overly white eyes to send the viewer packing! So the message here is clear – do it, but do it well and leave it looking natural.

The same goes for lightening and whitening teeth, another good method of improving your portrait, although you can usually get away with a shred more work than is possible for eyes. In both cases, once you've done your work, it's good practice to zoom out and try reducing the opacities of the layers involved by half. Then ask yourself if you're sure that isn't enough before changing it back. If you're convinced the person has white teeth and eyes, but they're not going to blind your viewer, it's time to stop!

The techniques we're applying are a little more sophisticated than the standard Dodge and Burn approach. We're using a three-point Curves adjustment to make tonal changes to the pupils and whites of the eyes, while ensuring that the iris remains untouched (it receives a more suitable method of lightening via Hue/Saturation later on).

And for teeth, we can target individual colour channels with a Levels adjustment layer to get them perfectly white and neutral. Both methods can produce natural results.

QUICK PHOTOSHOP TIPS

Colour management

We're doing our colour work by eye, so it's important that you have your monitor calibrated and profiled using a dedicated device to ensure that your monitor is displaying colour accurately. If you haven't invested in one of these gadgets yet, you can use the Color Sampler tool (see opposite) and focus on the numbers to produce your neutral white instead.

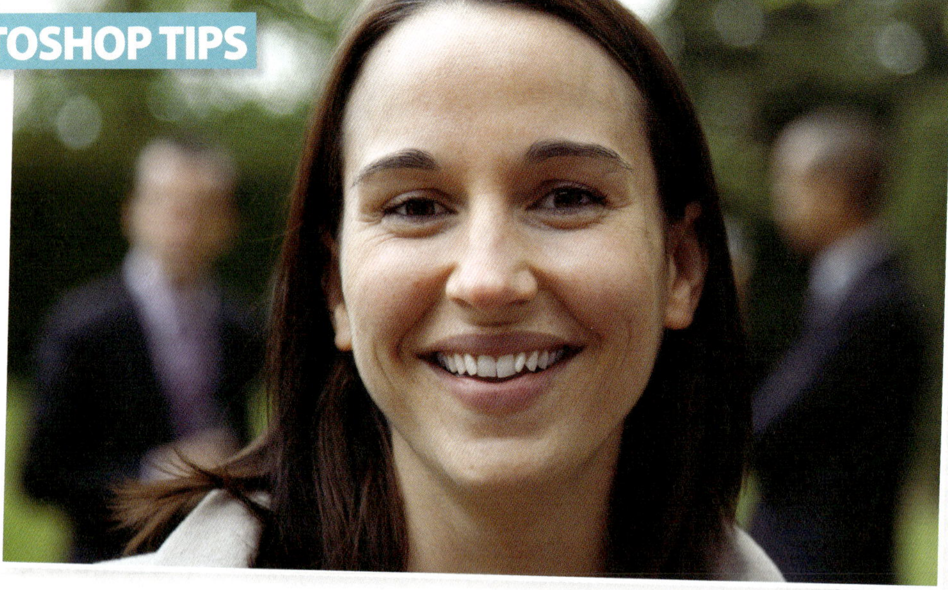

Precision colour correction

If you want to get an absolutely neutral white, you can use the Color Sampler tool (I). Click in three different teeth areas to produce three sample points, then work the Blue and Red sliders in each Levels layer until the values of Red, Green and Blue are all as close as possible. The values are displayed in the Info palette (Window>Info) – focus on the second set of numbers.

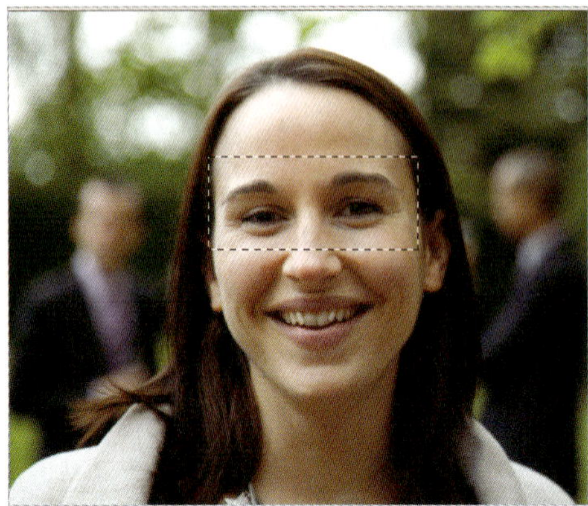

01 Select the eyes

Select the Rectangular Marquee and select around both eyes. Float this to a new layer using Ctrl/Cmd + J. Remove any unsightly veins with the Clone Stamp.

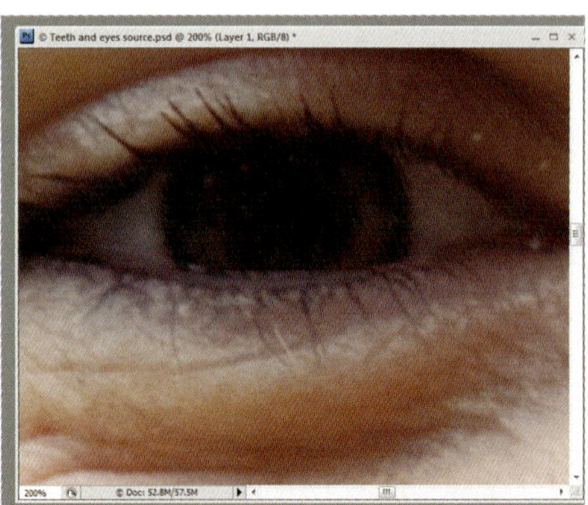

02 Clone out veins

Use Opt/Alt to source clean areas, then brush over the veins. It's important to source as close as possible to the destination points.

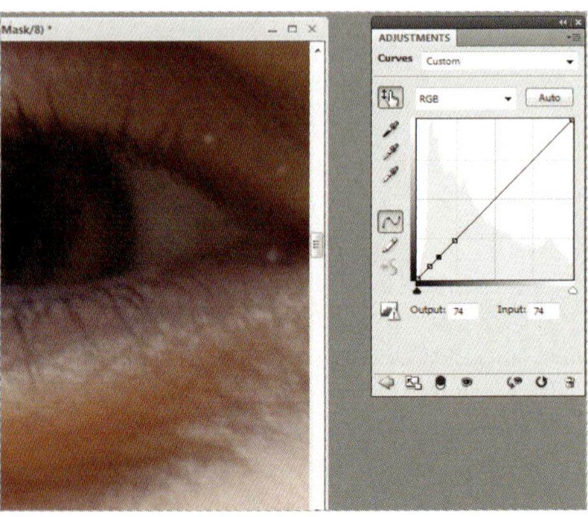

03 Set up a Curves adjustment

Add a Curves adjustment layer and click the button with the finger pointing up. Click the white of the eye, again on the iris and once more on the pupil.

It's all white... The inexpensive Hollywood smile solution

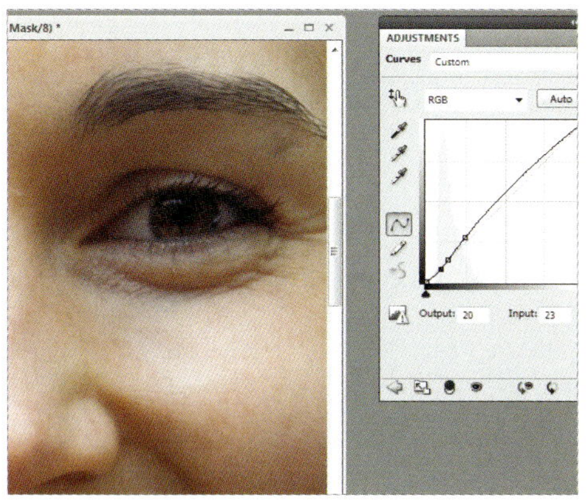

04 Paint into eyes
Drag the pupil point down and the whites up. Leave the iris point. Invert the mask with Cmd/Ctrl+I, then use a white brush to paint the eyeballs in.

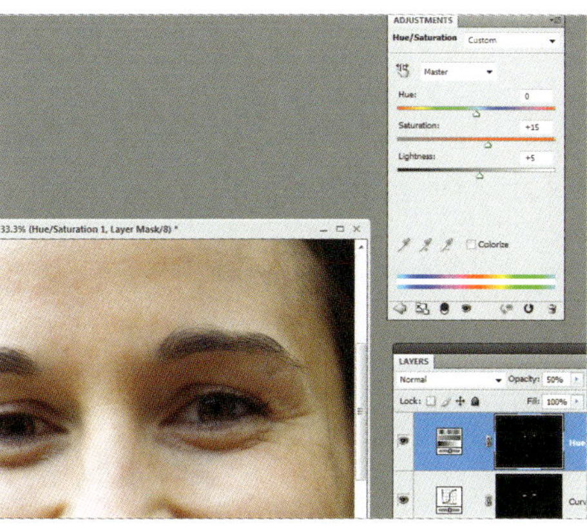

05 Bring out the colour
Add a Hue/Sat adjustment layer, boost Saturation by +15, Lightness to +7 and then invert the mask with Ctrl/Cmd+I. Paint into the pupil with white.

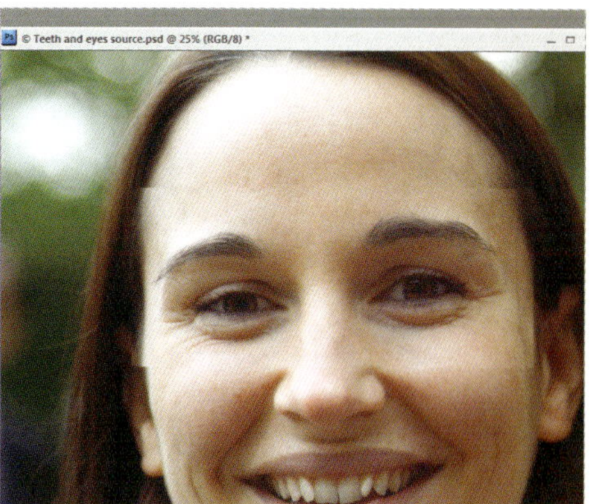

03 Enlarge the eyes
Ctrl/Cmd-click on the eye layer and the two adjustment layers and hit Ctrl/Cmd+T for a Free Transform. Enter 103% in the Width and Height.

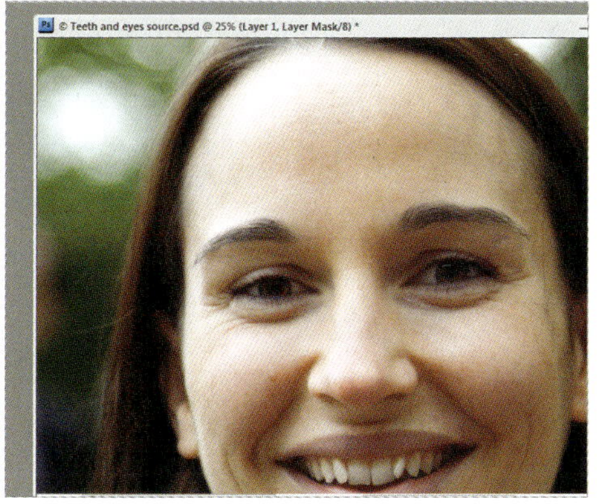

07 Brush the mask
Add a layer mask to the eyes layer, invert it and paint in the eye areas (including eyelids, lashes and eyebrows) using a soft white brush.

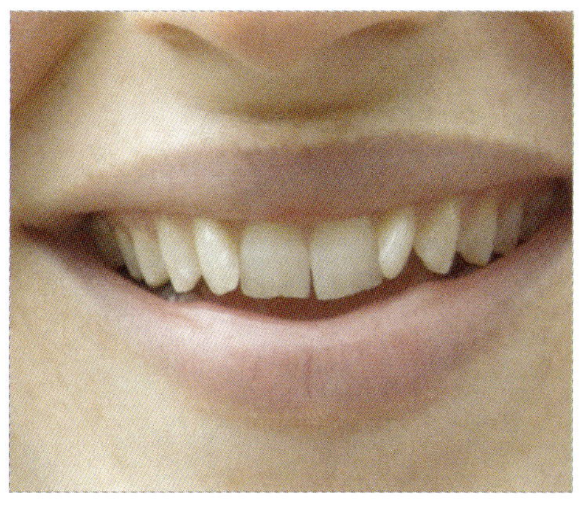

08 Levels adjustment layer
Zoom into the teeth. Add a Levels adjustment layer. Move the middle slider left to around 1.50. Now invert the layer mask with Ctrl/Cmd+I to Hide All.

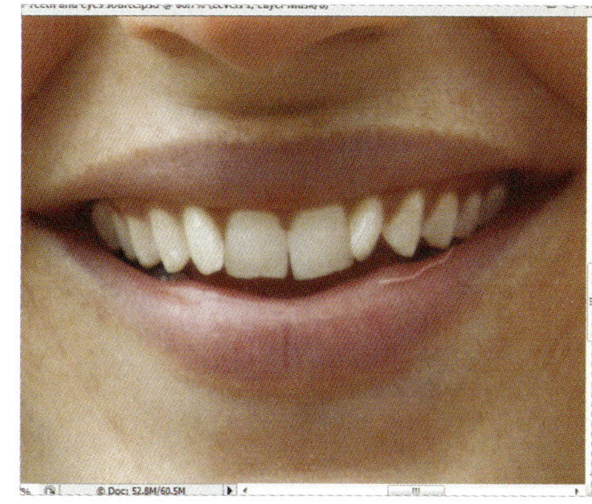

09 Brush into teeth
Take a white brush and carefully brush into the teeth. Toggle layer visibility on and off to check you haven't missed any bits.

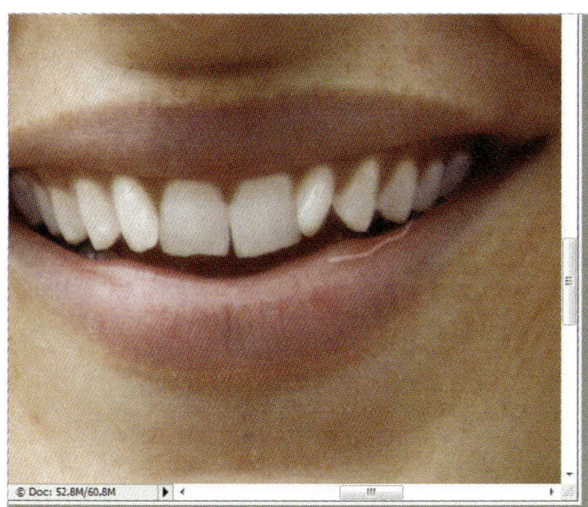

10 Reduce yellowing
Ctrl/Cmd-click the layer mask to load its selection and add a Levels adjustment layer. Select Blue in the Levels menu and move the middle slider left.

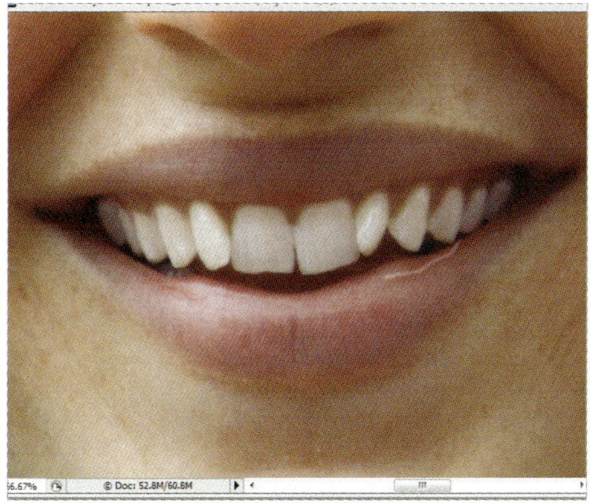

11 Knock back the blues
Knock blue areas back by brushing over with a black brush set to around 30% with the layer mask selected. Work over until you get a neutral white.

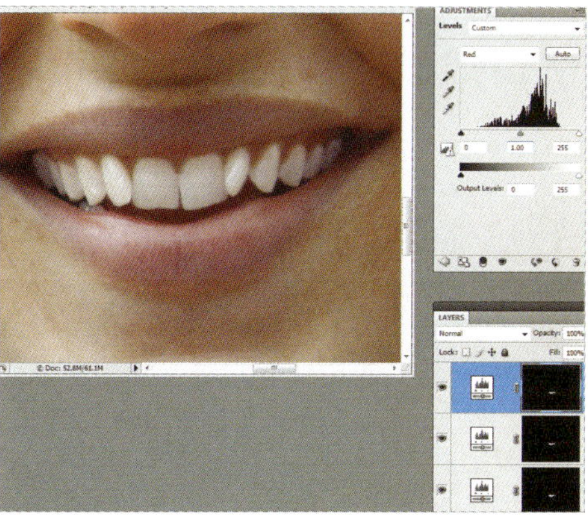

12 Reduce opacity
Reduce the opacity of the first lightening Levels layer if the effect looks too strong. You can alter the opacity of the colour removal layers too.

Adjustments

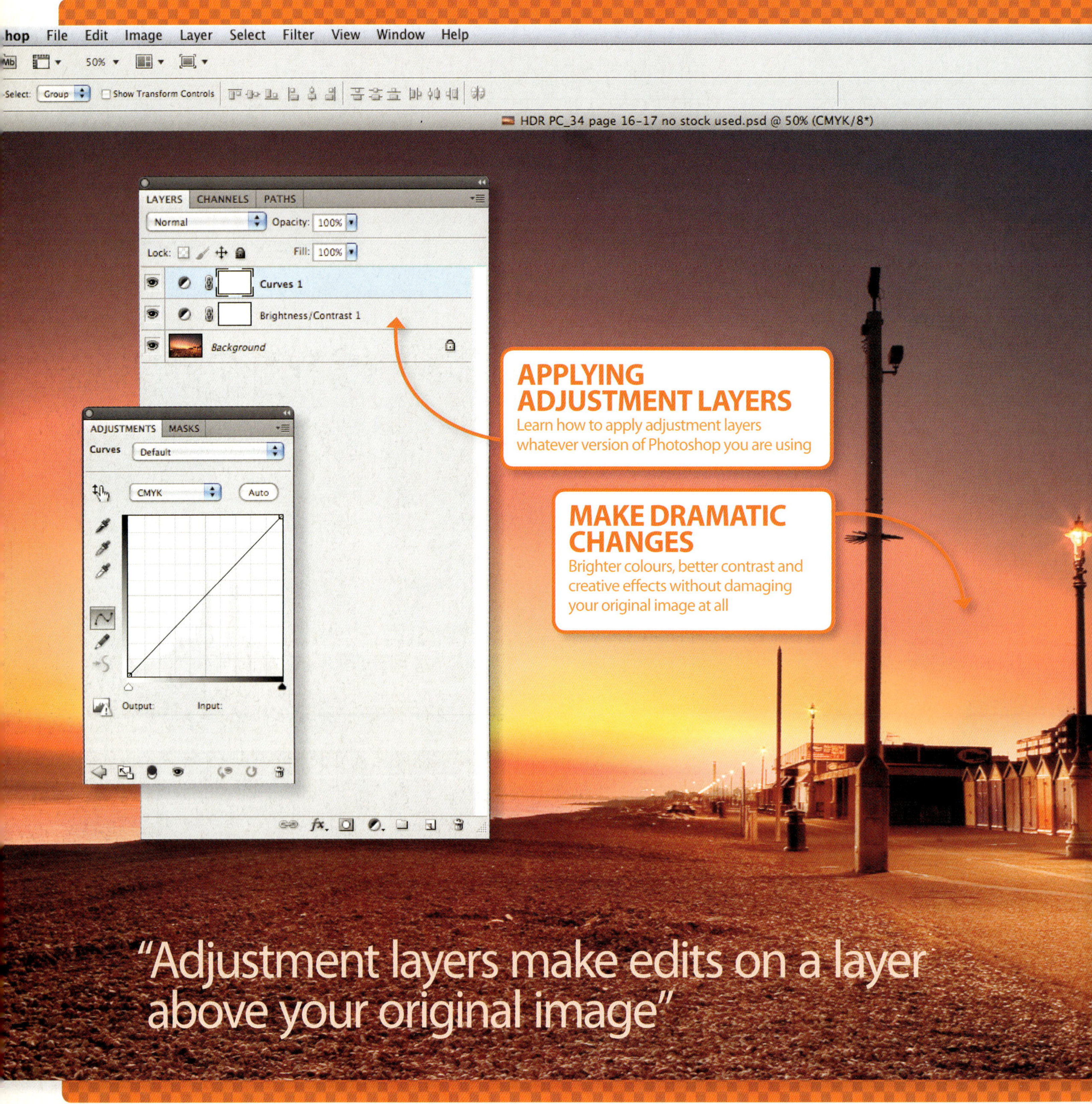

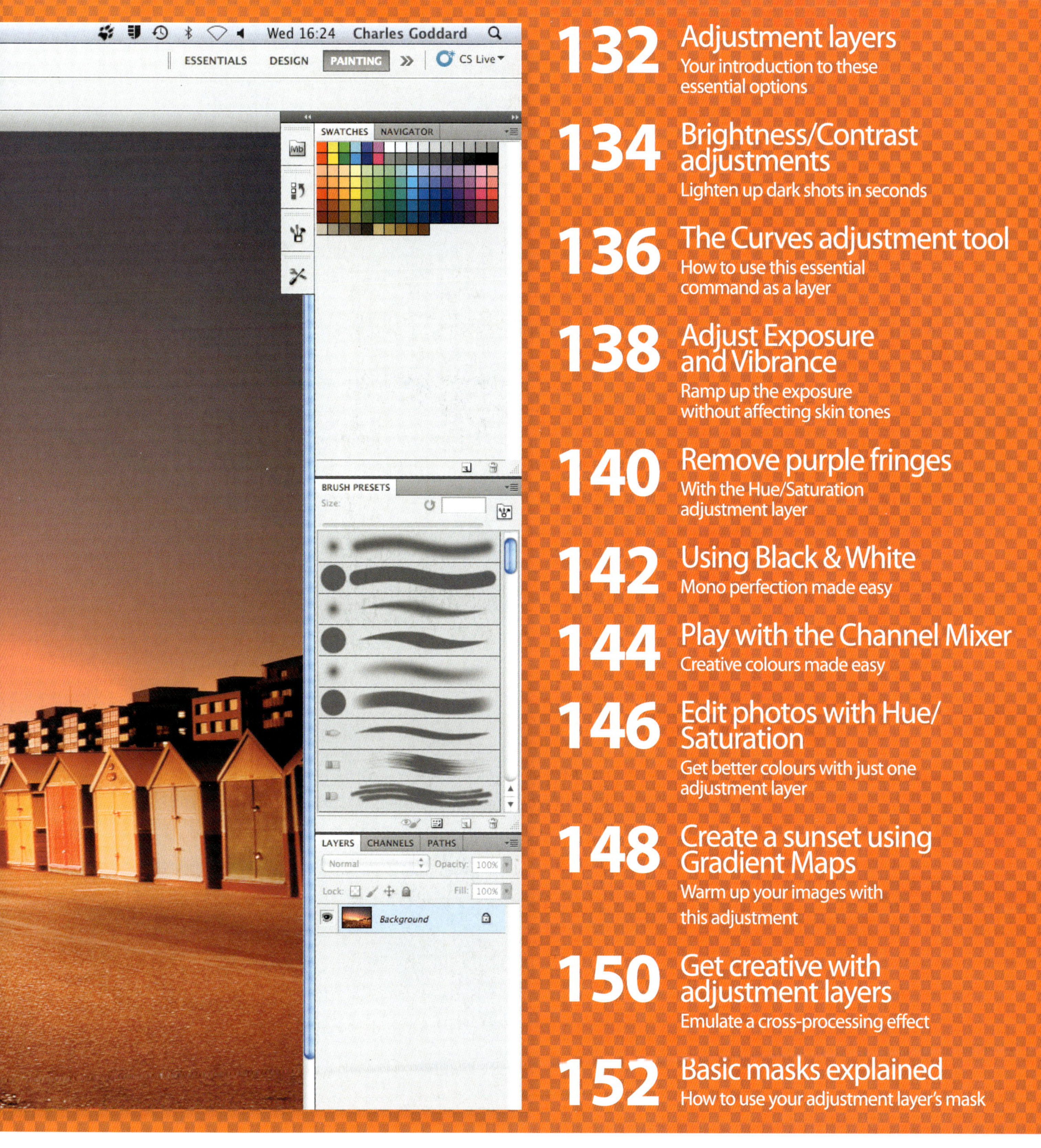
Wed 16:24 Charles Goddard
ESSENTIALS
DESIGN
PAINTING
CS Live
SWATCHES
NAVIGATOR
BRUSH PRESETS
LAYERS
CHANNELS
PATHS
Background

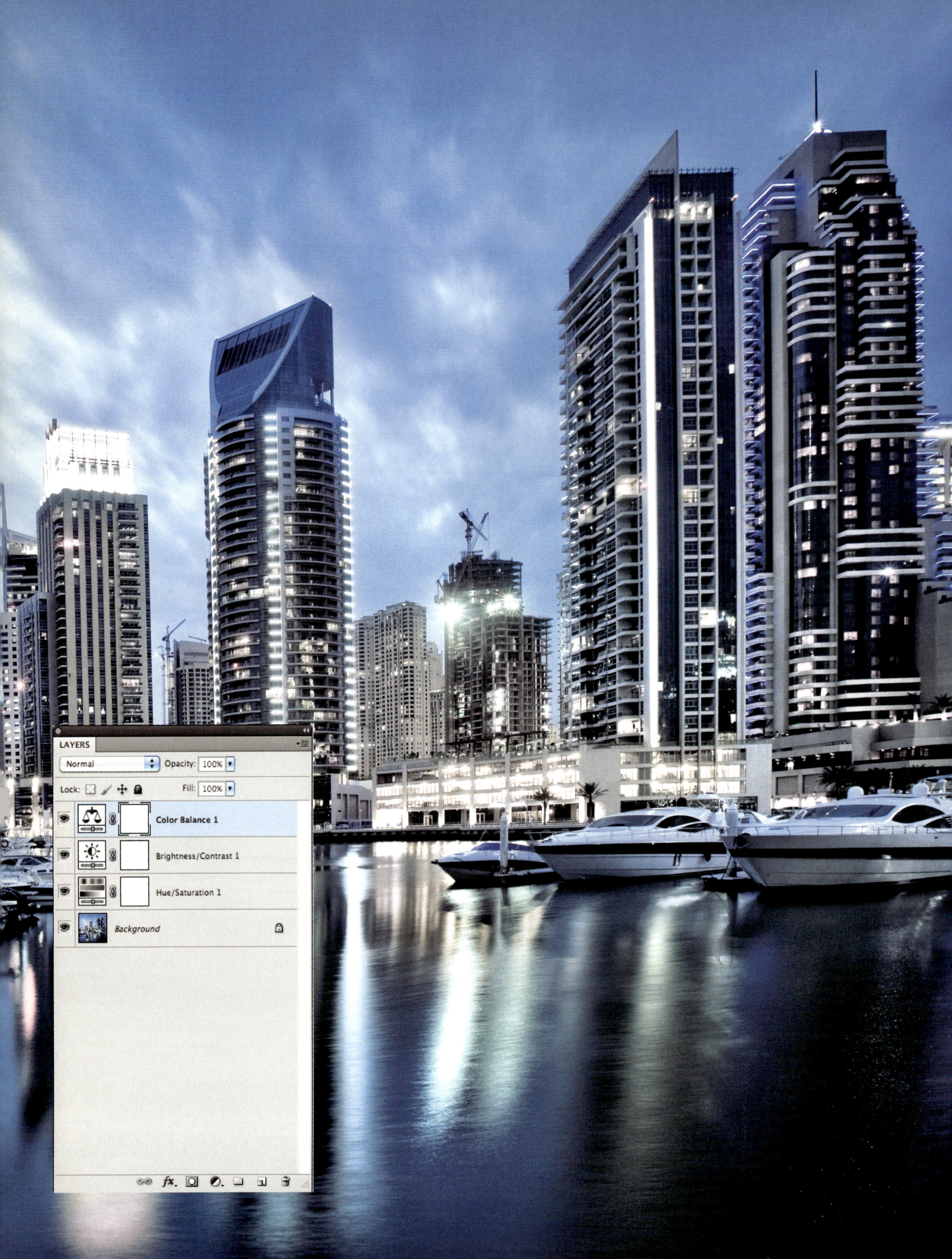
LAYERS
Normal
Opacity: 100%
Lock:
Fill: 100%
Color Balance 1
Brightness/Contrast 1
Hue/Saturation 1
Background

Adjustment layers

Find out how you can make major edits to your photographs that don't ruin the original image, and can be re-edited at any time

Adjustment layers are worth using whatever it is you are working on, but they are especially useful for retouching tasks. Because so much depends upon you creating a natural effect, being able to refer back to the original photo is extremely useful, especially if you need it to bring back information that has been lost through editing.

In case you aren't familiar with them, adjustment layers make edits on a layer above your original image. If something goes horrendously wrong, you can simply delete the adjustment layer and return to the original. Adjustment layers can also be edited at any stage, so if you decide part way through an edit that you need to alter the adjustment, it's easy to do so without affecting your later tweaks.

Adjustment layers also preserve image quality, as each time you edit a pixel value directly, you lose a bit of information. This doesn't happen with adjustment layers. There are various types of adjustment layers but the most useful ones for retouching are the Levels one and the Curves one, which are among the first that we will be looking at in this section.

Here we take a look at the Adjustment Layer menu options, which are accessed from the Layer menu. However, as you get used to using them, it is much easier to click the little button at the bottom of the Layers palette, which looks like a half-black, half-white circle. When you click on this, the same list of options will pop up and you just click on the one that you want.

If you have CS4 or CS5, there is a dedicated Adjustments panel too, which has icons for all of the adjustment layers available and you can simply click on those instead to add them to your project. You can also directly edit the settings for the adjustment layer at the same time. Let's have a look closer at adjustment layers.

"If you decide part way through an edit that you need to alter the adjustment, it's easy to do"

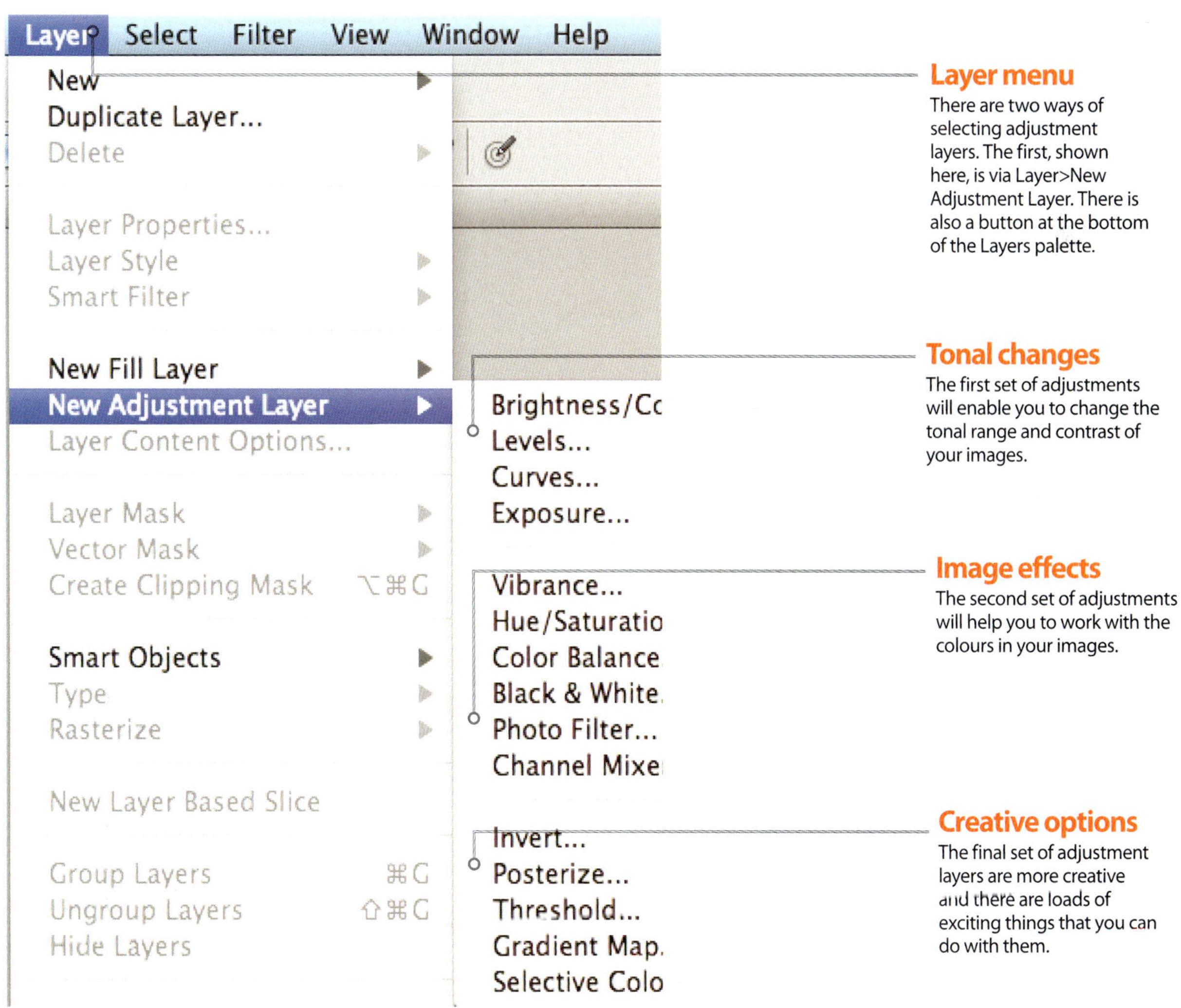

Layer menu
There are two ways of selecting adjustment layers. The first, shown here, is via Layer>New Adjustment Layer. There is also a button at the bottom of the Layers palette.

Tonal changes
The first set of adjustments will enable you to change the tonal range and contrast of your images.

Image effects
The second set of adjustments will help you to work with the colours in your images.

Creative options
The final set of adjustment layers are more creative and there are loads of exciting things that you can do with them.

Brightness/Contrast adjustments

Breathe some life back into your images with this super-simple and effective adjustment

Some of the adjustment layers do what they say on the tin, but that doesn't make them any less effective or essential. We have covered the Brightness/Contrast controls briefly in the Basic Corrections section of this book, but here we are going to look at how they can be applied as an adjustment layer.

Getting the Brightness and Contrast values spot on can mean a lot of trial and error. If you get it wrong as a normal adjustment you have to hope that a quick Cmd/Ctrl+Z will undo the change so you can start again.

But what if you come back to an image and want to do more lightening on it? With adjustment layers, as long as you save a layered version of your work, then you can do just that. This is great if you are printing images, as sometimes you might find that your printer darkens or lightens prints and you will need to play with the controls over and again to get perfect prints. Adding an adjustment layer is so simple, that it really is the best solution when editing the fundamentals of your photos.

As you can see from our sample images below, there is a significant amount of lightening that has been carried out, and yet the final image looks natural. Use the sliders subtly and you can emulate this result. You may need to do further post-processing after this command has been applied, depending on the final result.

"What if you come back to an image and want to do more to it?"

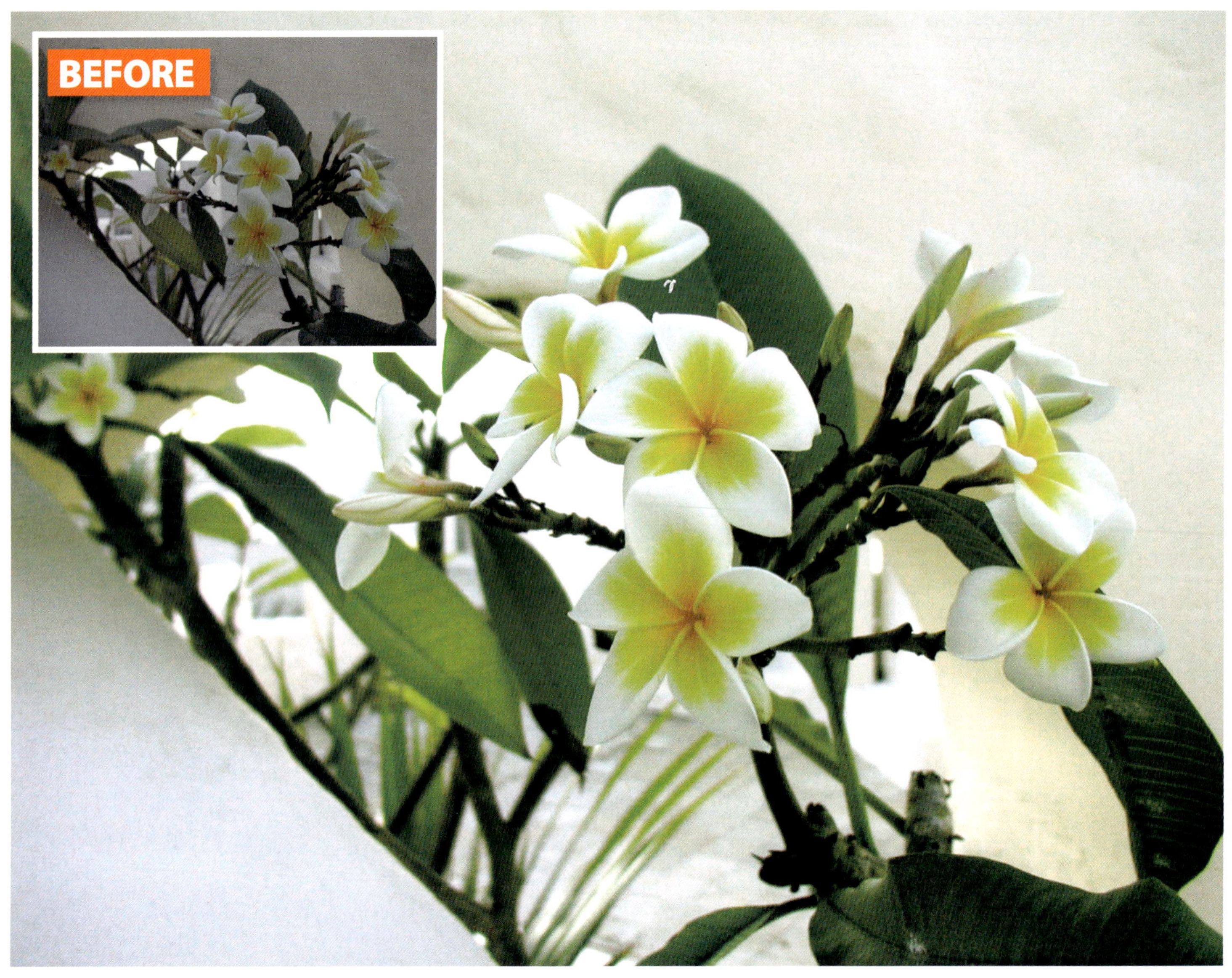

QUICK PHOTOSHOP TIPS

Using Eyedroppers

There are three Eyedroppers in this dialog box, for selecting the White Point, Black Point and Mid Point. To use, click the one that you want and then click on your image in the area you need. For the White Point, click the area that should be the most white in your image, for example, and the image is adjusted around this.

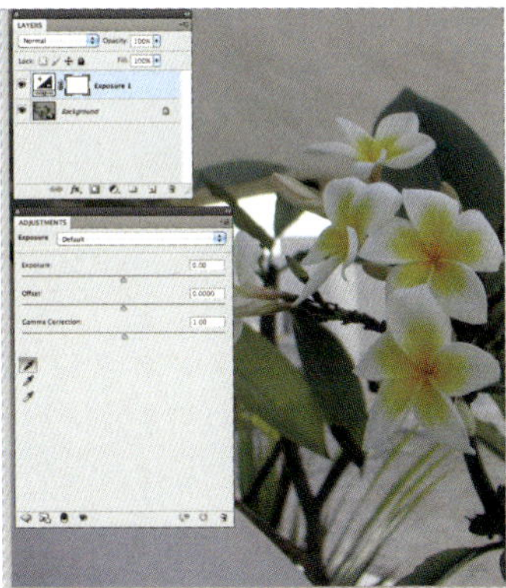

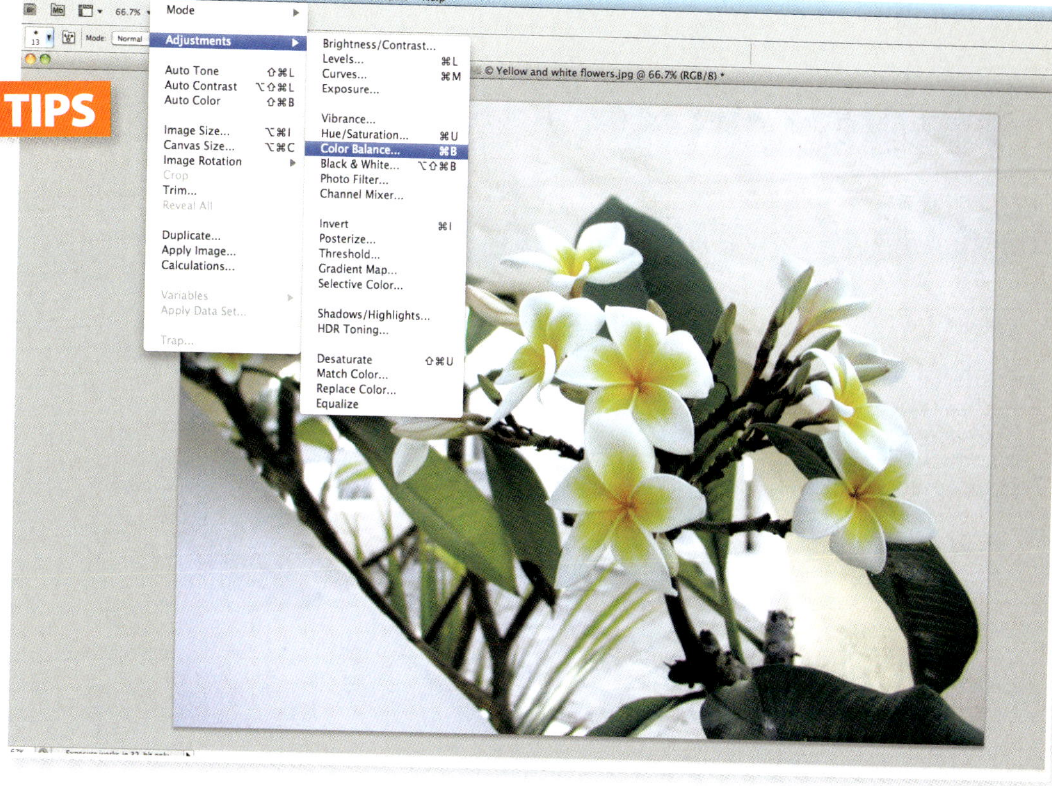

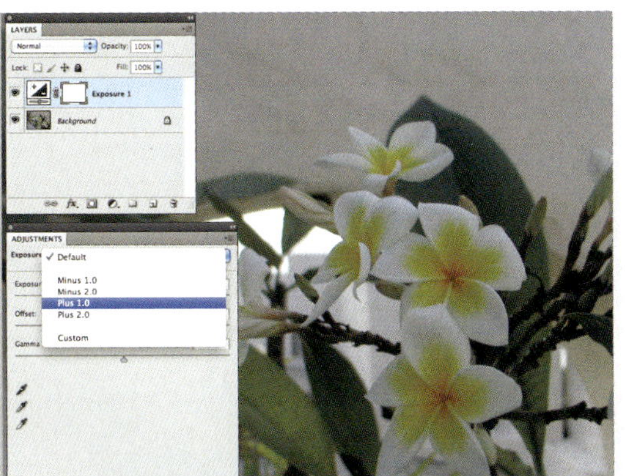

Presets

There are a couple of Presets built into this adjustment layer. These allow you to quickly push the exposure up or down, and they work just like the exposure controls on cameras. Try a couple of these out before you start as they give you a good base to work from.

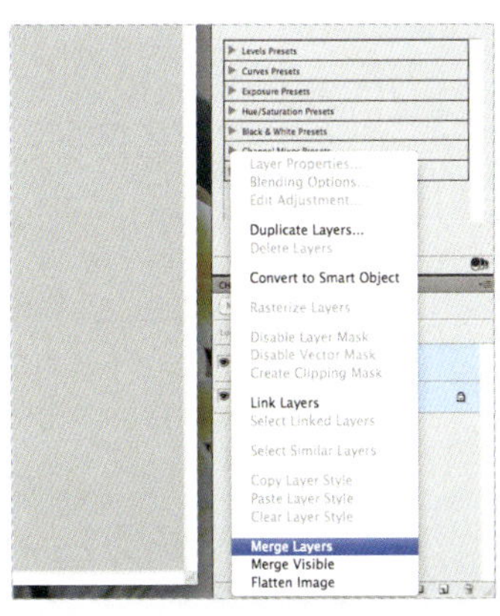

Color Balance

After finishing our image we found that there was a slight magenta hue, which we decided to correct using Image>Adjustments>Color Balance and push the Magenta-Green Slider toward Green.

Merge layers

When we are happy with the effects of our adjustment layer, we choose to merge the adjustment with the original layer – only do this if you don't need to re-edit at any point in the future.

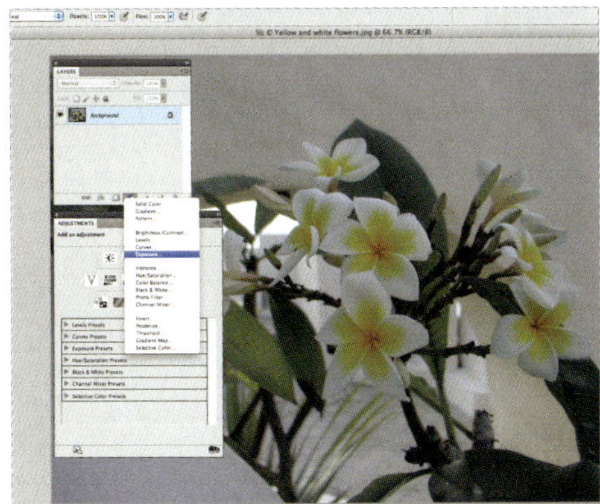

01 Add the adjustment

We are selecting the adjustment directly from the Adjustments palette, but in older versions use the icon at the bottom of the Layers palette.

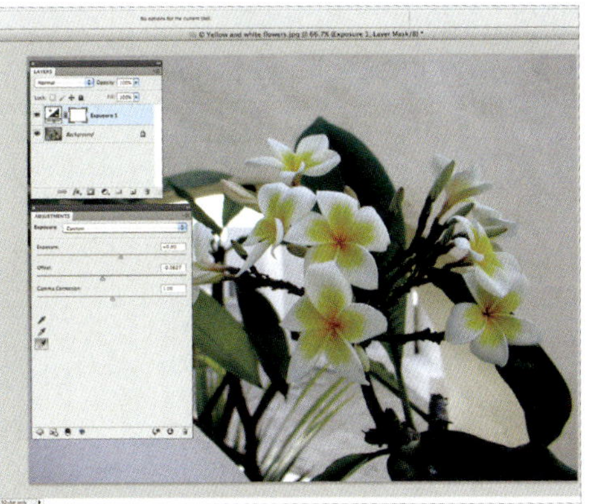

02 Start tweaking

You can use the sliders to help boost the Brightness and the Contrast of your image easily with the effect shown immediately.

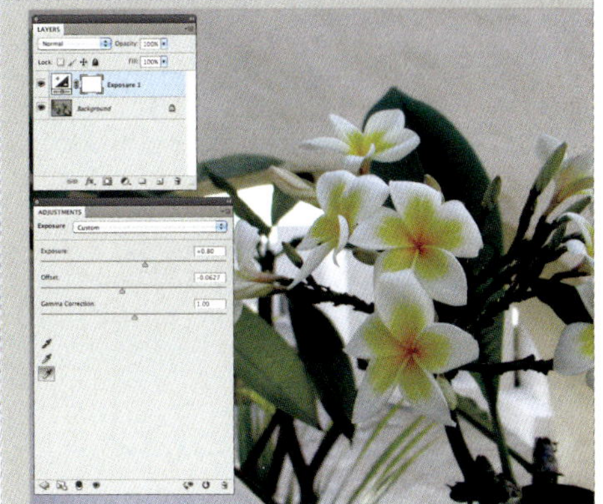

03 Eyedroppers

The Eyedroppers allow you to set the black and white points in the image, which give you an automatic correction.

The Curves adjustment tool

The Curves tool is a powerful Photoshop feature that when properly applied can transform contrast, colour and tonal range

The Curves tool in Photoshop is deceptive. To the Photoshop beginner its graph-like appearance can be intimidating, bringing back memories of early maths lessons. However, it's a powerful tool that can be used to adjust tonal ranges, change colour levels, alter exposure, boost contrast and even create some less conventional photo effects.

Although the Curves tool is not as intuitive as some of the other features in Photoshop, the basic functions are simple and dramatic results can be easily achieved. We have had a look at it in the Color & Tone section, but this tool really comes into its own when applied as an adjustment layer. In the Layers palette, hit Create New Fill Or Adjustment Layer and select Curves. Adjustment layers let you make changes without degrading the original. It also means you can continue to edit a Curves adjustments by double-clicking the adjustment layer. If the changes aren't wanted, you can revert to the original by deleting the layer.

In this tutorial we will demystify the Curves graph, and in doing so show how you can make practical improvements to your images. We'll look at understanding the graph and at exactly what happens as the line changes shape. We'll reveal tips and tricks to make editing your image quick and easy. We will also look at editing the colour channels to recover and boost lost colour. The Curves tool has many more facets than might at first be obvious, and we'll introduce you to as many as we can on these pages.

"The Curves tool has many more facets than might at first be obvious"

QUICK PHOTOSHOP TIPS

Channel

This drop-down menu allows you to select which channels to edit. You can edit the master (labelled RGB or CMYK etc) or individual colour channels. When editing individual colours, the curve affects the selected colour and its opposite colour.

Bezier/Pencil tool

There are two ways of changing the path of the curve. The common way is to use anchor points to create a smooth Bezier curve; this makes it easy to get consistent realistic results. The Pencil tool allows you to be more creative and get some interesting effects, but the results are hard to reproduce accurately.

Eyedropper tool

Use the left-hand Eyedropper tool to set the dark pixel limit, and the far right Eyedropper tool to set the highlight limit. The middle Eyedropper tool can be used to alter the colour balance. Experiment with these to find your optimal settings. The beginner however, may wish to leave these and adjust the curve manually.

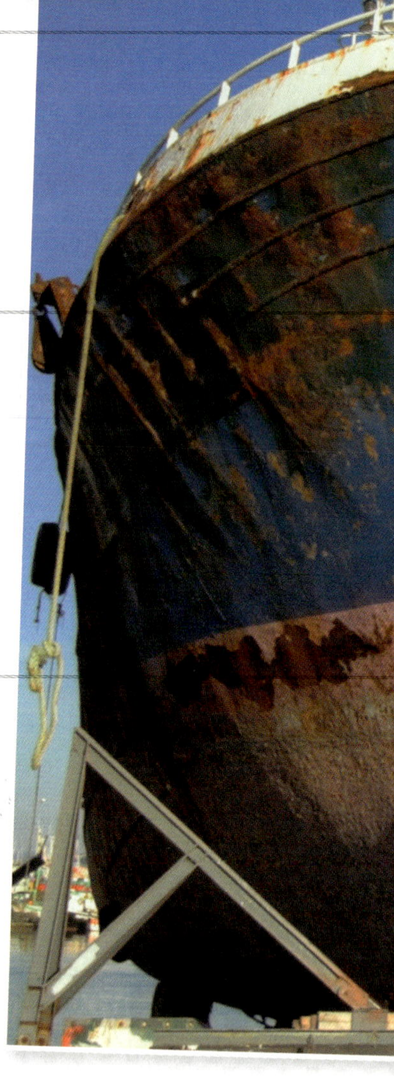

01 Try in mono
Try using Curves on black-and-white images, as the final image corresponds to the info that Curves use: shadows (black), midtones (grey) and highlights (white).

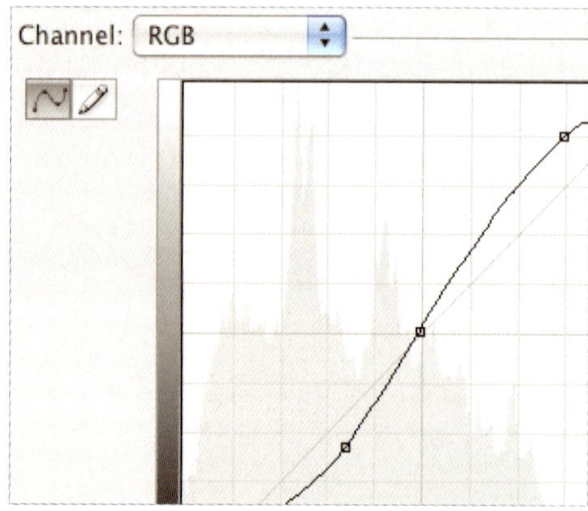

02 Colour channels
Curves allow you to edit separate channels. When a channel is selected, the curve affects the density of the colour, eg red and its opposite, cyan.

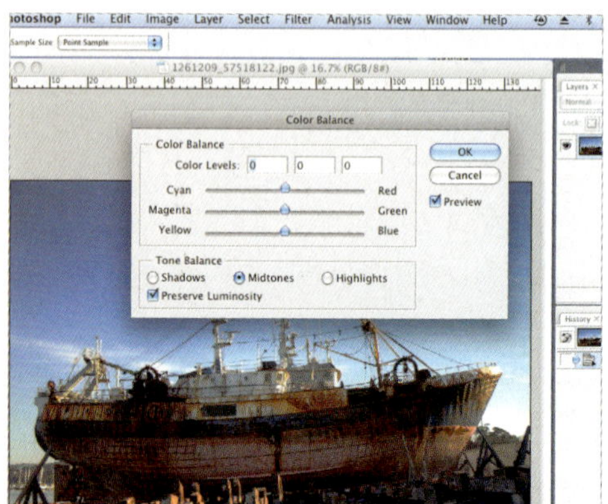

03 Using channels
Moving the curve upwards increases the red in the image; moving it down increases the cyan. The Color Balance tool uses the same principle too.

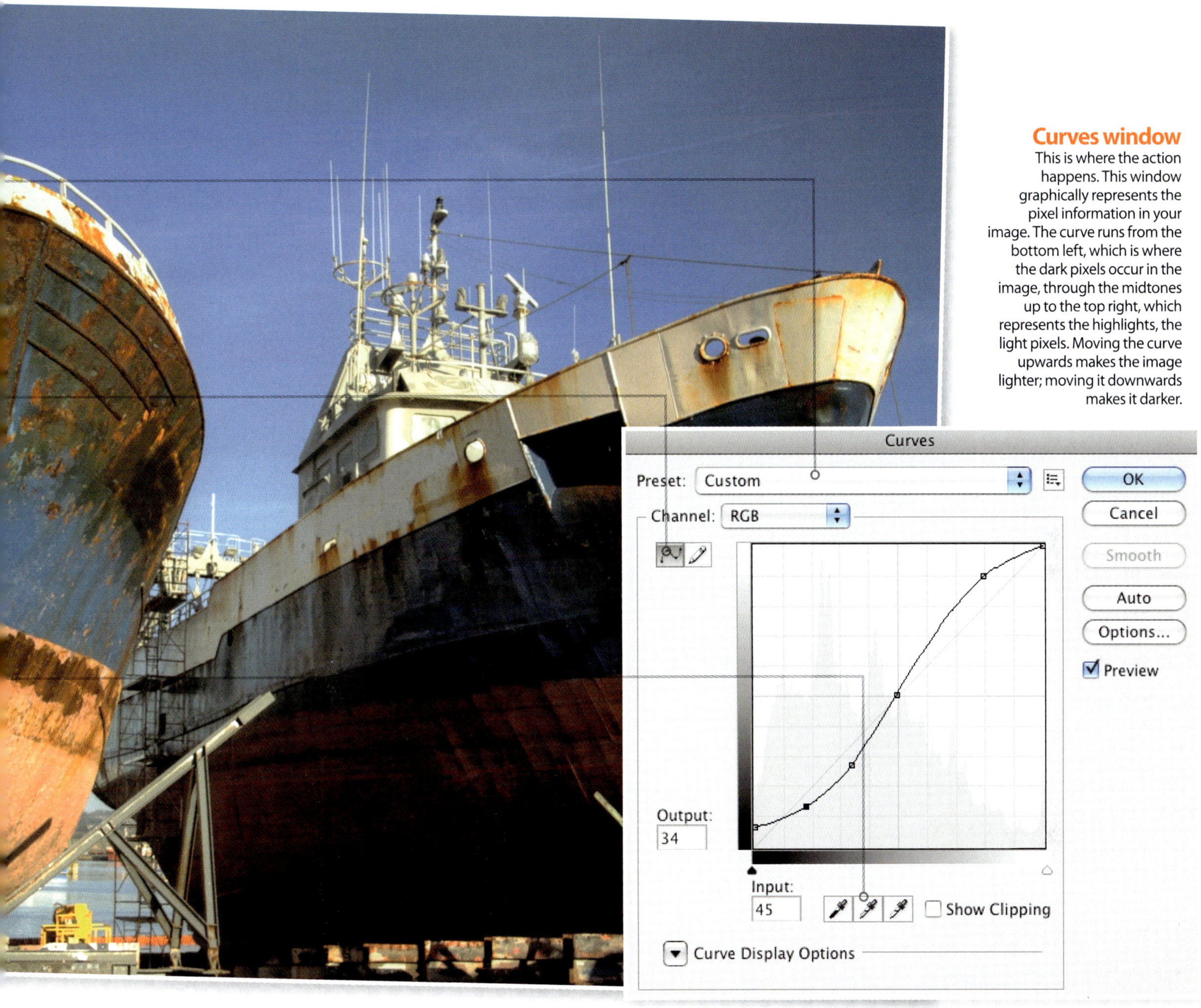

Curves window

This is where the action happens. This window graphically represents the pixel information in your image. The curve runs from the bottom left, which is where the dark pixels occur in the image, through the midtones up to the top right, which represents the highlights, the light pixels. Moving the curve upwards makes the image lighter; moving it downwards makes it darker.

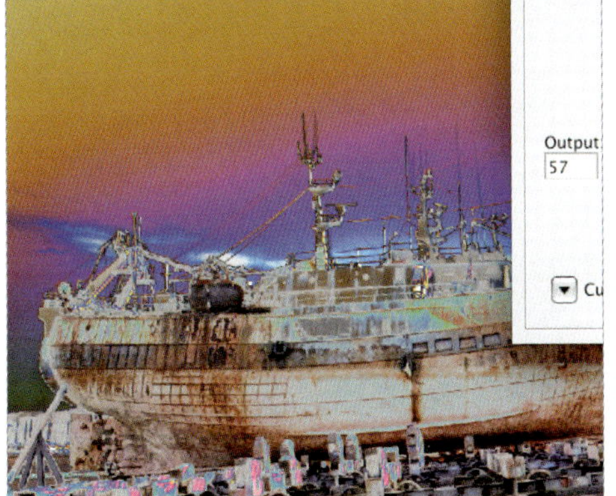

04 Crazy results

To avoid the crazy effects make sure there are no flat spots. These occur when the curve follows a horizontal line across the graph.

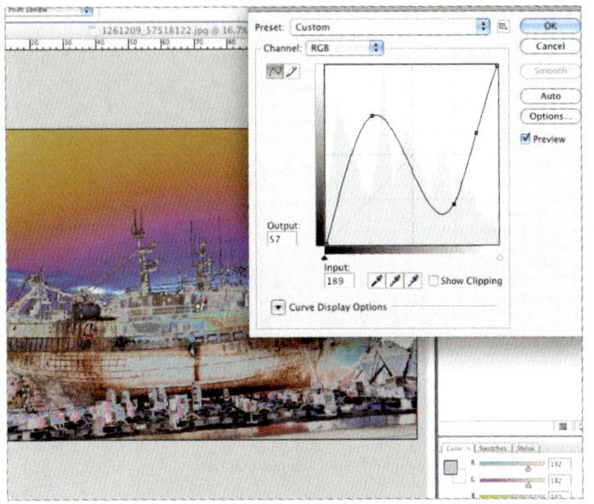

05 Rule number 2

The second way to keep images natural, is to make sure that the curve doesn't go beyond the horizontal to create a downward curve.

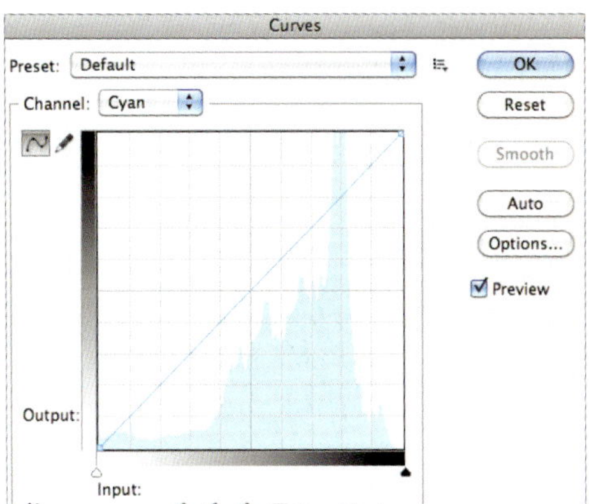

06 Quick reset

Hold Opt/Alt and the Cancel button will change to Reset. Hit this and the curve reverts to its original settings. This works in most PS dialog boxes.

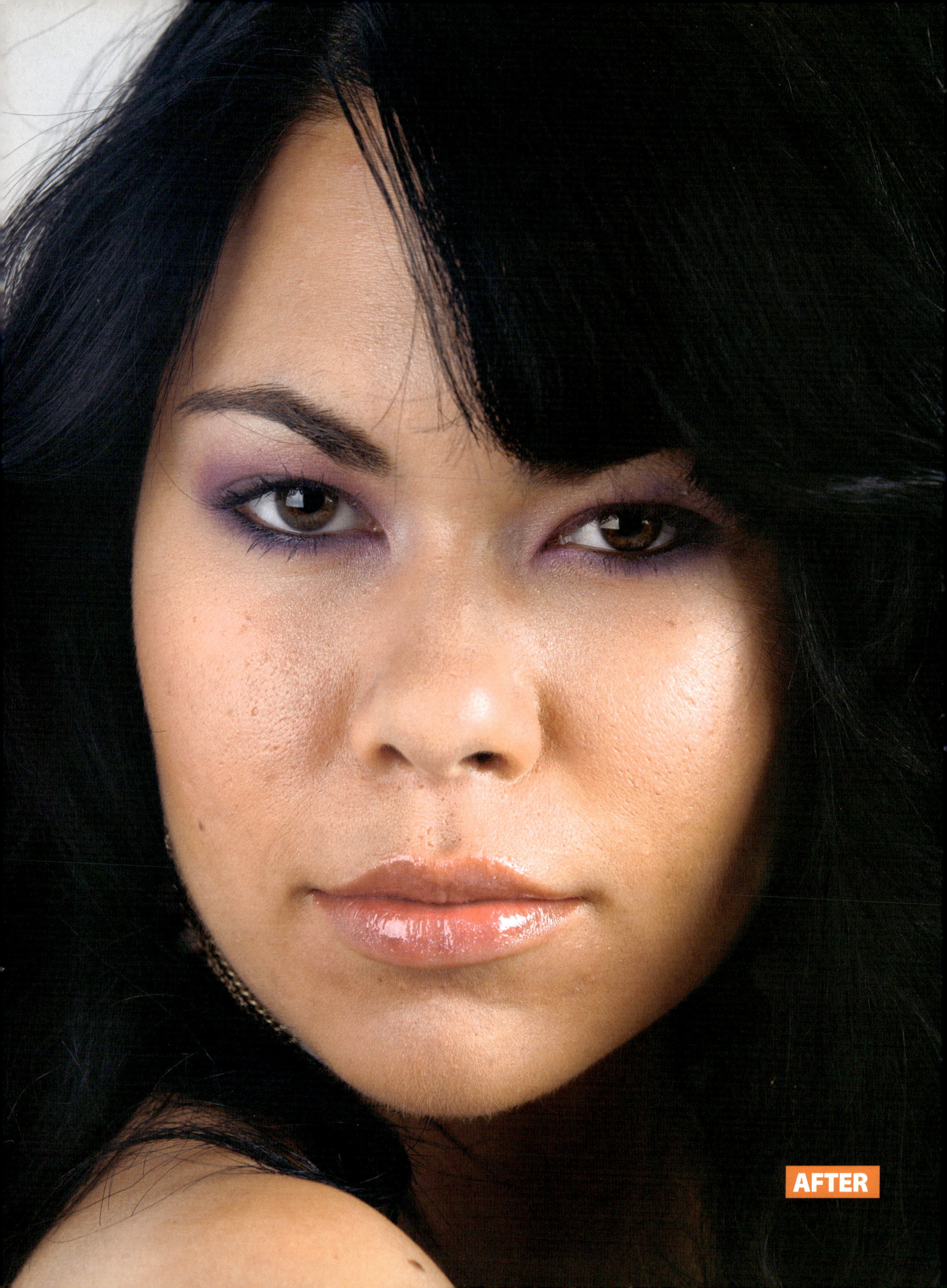
AFTER

Adjust Exposure and Vibrance

Use these tools to lighten your images intelligently for spot-on exposure levels

One of the main problems with portrait images is that you can find the need to lighten and brighten them but you still want them to look realistic. Luckily, adjustment layers are perfect for this, as if you make a mistake, you haven't harmed the original photo and you can go back in and adjust the settings at any time.

For our image here, we are going to use a combination of adjustment layers. First, we are going to add an Exposure layer, which is designed, as the name would suggest, to alter exposure problems. We want to boost the highlights in this image, so we are using the Exposure slider and moving it to the right to lighten the whole image. As with any image-editing project, subtlety is usually the key, so push the slider just a little at a time. You can try playing with the other sliders too, to get exactly the effect you want.

Next, we want to boost the colours. We could use the Hue/Saturation command, but this changes the saturation across the whole image and, in portraits, this can leave you with rather unbecoming orange skin – not the look we're going for here! Instead, we will use Vibrance, which is reasonably new to Photoshop (from CS4 onwards). This intelligently alters the saturation of colours in an image, by only saturating less saturated areas and leaving parts that already have good saturation as they are. Again, use the slider in small increments to ensure that the result remains realistic.

"Vibrance intelligently alters the saturation of colours in an image"

WHAT YOU'LL LEARN

Exposure
Our start image is on the dark side and the highlights are not pronounced enough. We will use the Exposure adjustment layer option in order to correct this.

Vibrance
Use Vibrance to saturate your image only in the areas that need it. This is much better than using Hue/Saturation on portrait photos.

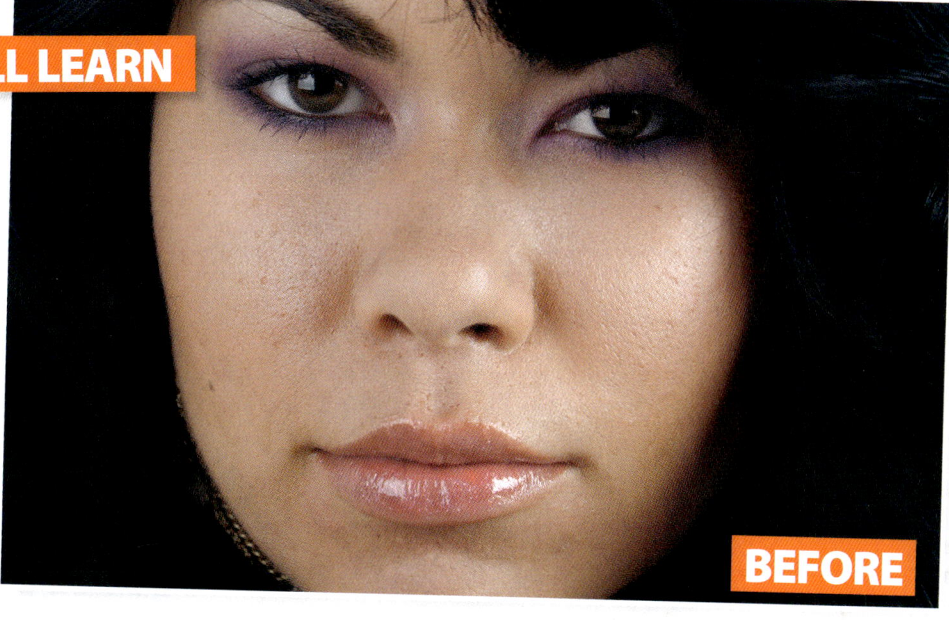
BEFORE

Skin
We need to lighten and brighten the skin, but we don't want a shiny, orange result. This is why it pays to be subtle with enhancements – start small and you can always add more.

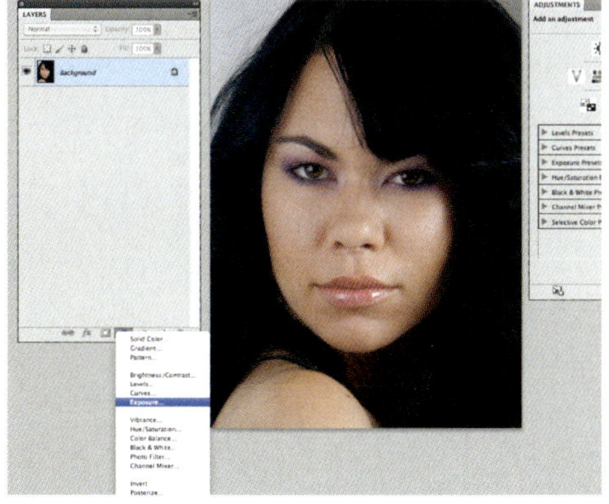

01 Add an Exposure layer

Click on the Create new fill or adjustment layer button at the bottom of the Layers palette, and scroll down to the Exposure option.

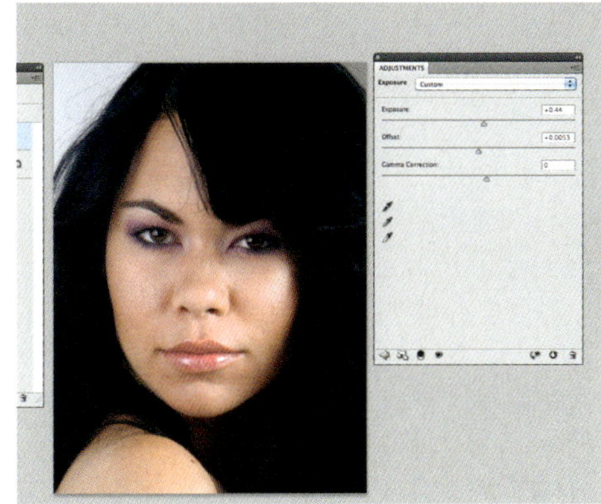

02 And adjust…

Use the various sliders in the Adjustment palette (in CS4 onwards) – or the popup menu (pre-CS4) – to get an evenly exposed image.

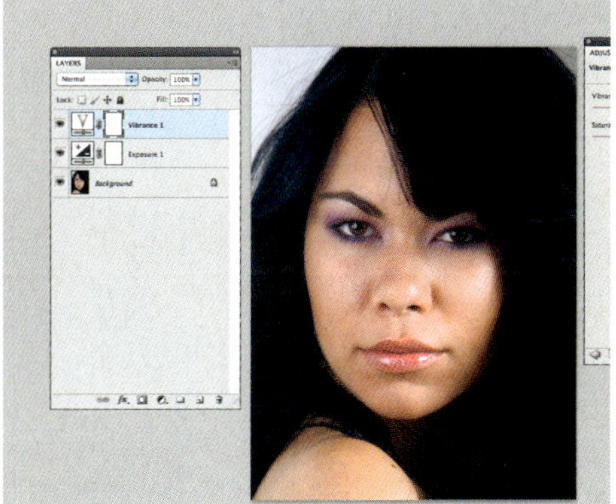

03 Vibrance

In the same manner, select the Vibrance adjustment layer (only found in CS4 onwards) and tweak your image's colours to perfection.

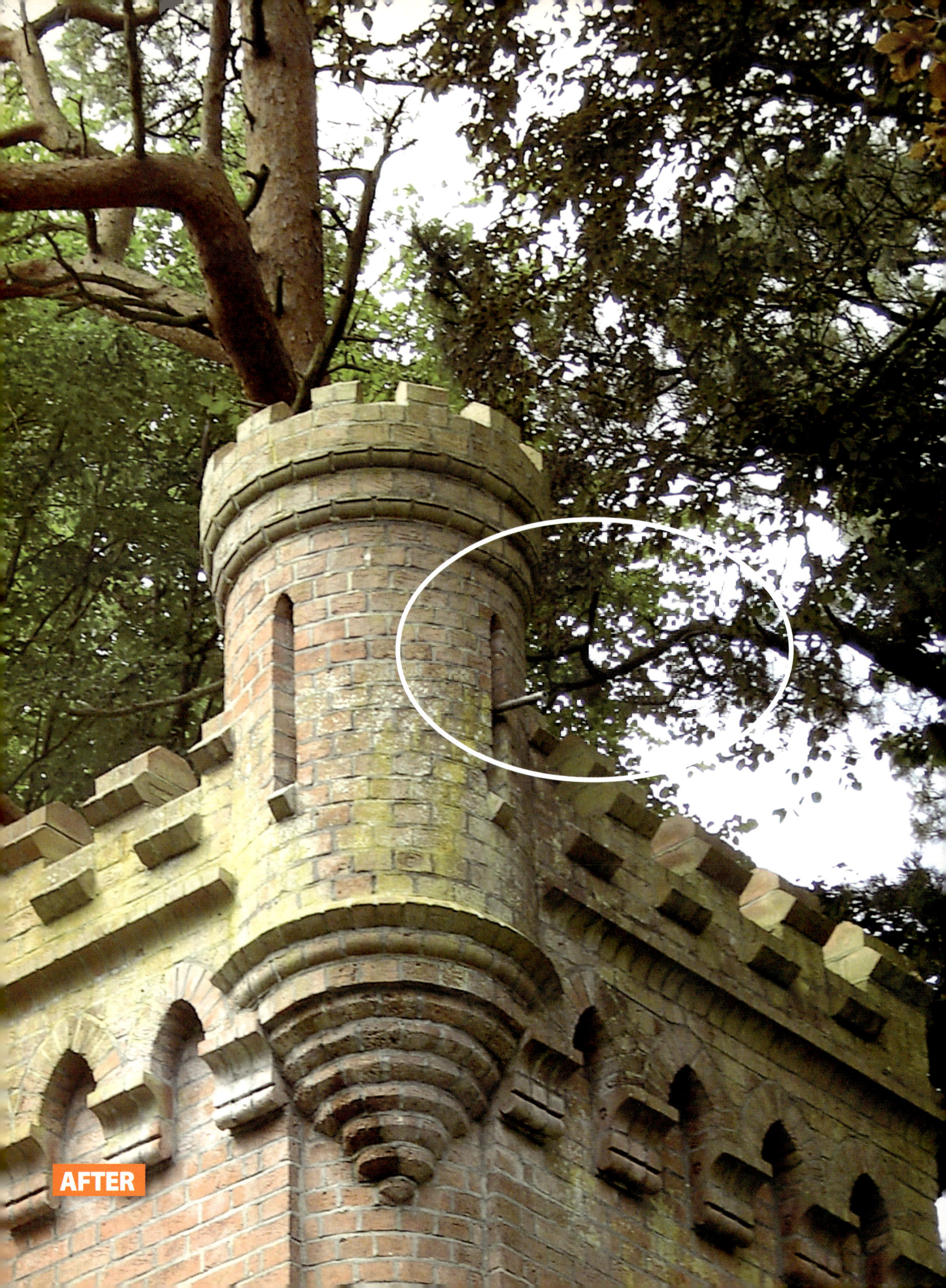
AFTER

Remove purple fringes

A quick and easy way to clean up a common photographic problem

Purple fringing occurs in high contrast areas of photos, and gives the edges of dark subjects a nasty, fuzzy purple outline. It's commonly seen in photographs of trees against bright, overcast skies. This is a problem that occurs with many cameras, but thankfully it's quick and easy to fix in Photoshop.

This phenomenon is more technically called chromatic aberration and while purple is the usual flaw, there are other forms of colour spill. Luckily, this tutorial can be tweaked to be used on any kind of unwanted colour spill. We will be doing this using a few simple Hue and Saturation adjustments.

We will be applying the adjustments to an adjustment layer so that we can carefully control the colour changes. With the image that we are using here, you can only really see the purple fringing when you zoom right in, however there is no other purple in the image, so our adjustments will do more good than harm to the image. Should you have this flaw in images that have other areas of purple, you will need to use the mask that comes with the adjustment layer. To do this, click on the white thumbnail to the right of your adjustment layer thumbnail and select a black brush.

Paint over any areas in your image that you don't want the adjustment applied to and they will revert back to the original colours in the start photo on the layer underneath.

"Purple fringing is quick and easy to fix in Photoshop"

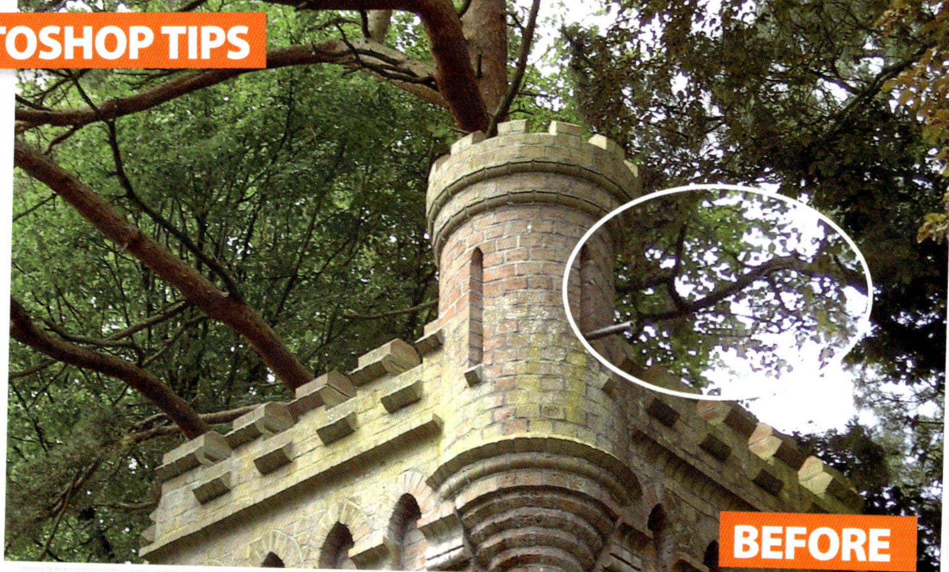

QUICK PHOTOSHOP TIPS

Purple fringing vs purple colours

You might find that you have images with purple fringing that also have purple colours in the scene. If you do this tutorial on those, then all the purple areas will be affected. Using a mask is a great way of protecting other purple areas in your shot.

Zoom in

Find problem areas in your photographs by zooming in. You can see the purple fringing in the before shot here, but not in the after shot, zoomed into to the same degree.

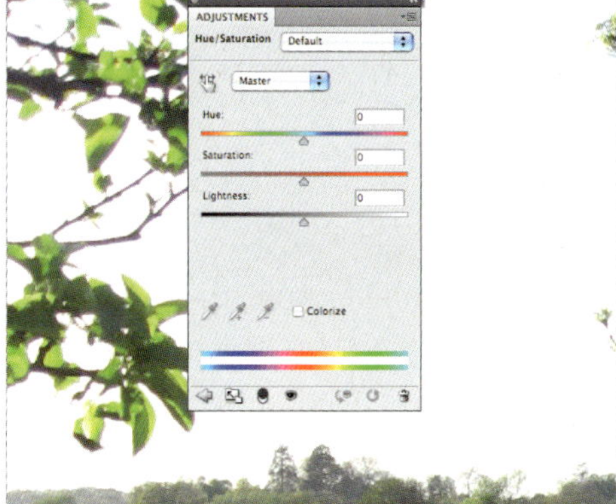

01 Adjustment layer

Go to Layer>New Adjustment Layer>Hue/Saturation. A new dialog box will appear on your screen containing eyedroppers and sliders.

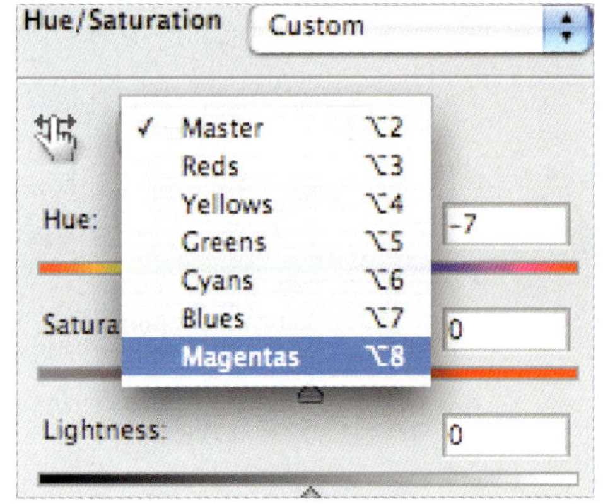

02 Match your tones

Using the drop-down menu, select Magenta. This is the closest match to the purple that fringes the foliage. Only these tones will be affected.

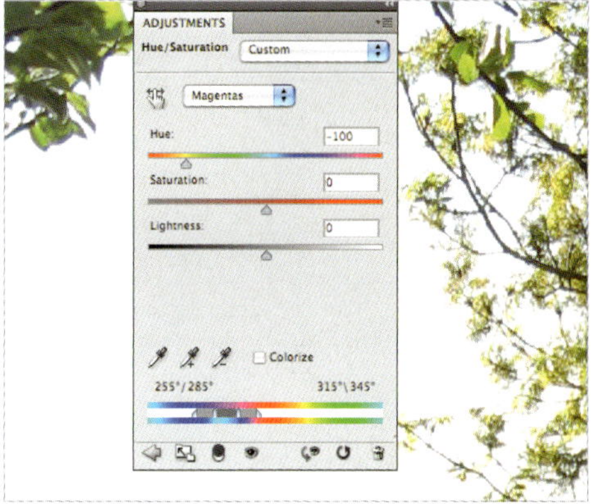

03 Slide it

Drag the Hue and Saturation sliders to the left and see the purple disappear. The 'fringe' still exists, but it's replaced with a more natural colour.

Using Black & White

Get creative with your colour photos by adding a little monochrome magic – we show you how!

Black-and-white photography has always been popular. Perhaps this is due to the fact that it works with almost any kind of image. Portraits, landscapes and abstracts in particular, take on a whole new feeling when they are turned into a monochrome representation.

Of course, there are always exceptions. Images need to have a good contrast between the light and dark tones, as you would otherwise have a great expanse of grey that's just not overly appealing.

Using the Black & White adjustment as an adjustment layer gives you endless control over the conversion of your photos. As well as a whole host of Presets that give you instant results, you can target each channel that makes up the image independently. It takes a bit of getting used to when you're playing with the Reds in a black-and-white image, but each colour looks different in mono, so it is worth playing with your images to see how they can be adapted.

As well as using the sliders, there is a little hand icon with a double-ended arrow underneath. Click on this icon, then click and hold on an area in your image that you want to adjust. Photoshop will determine which channel is most prominent in that specific area and as you slide your mouse back and forth, the relevant slider will go up and down too. A really convenient and easy way to ensure that the tonal range of your black-and-white images is as close to perfect as possible.

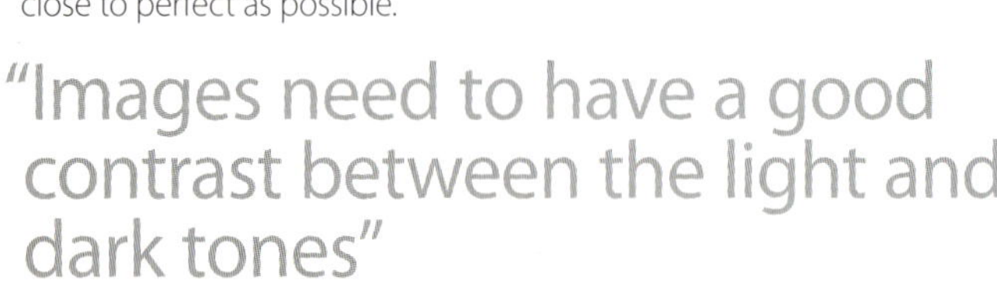

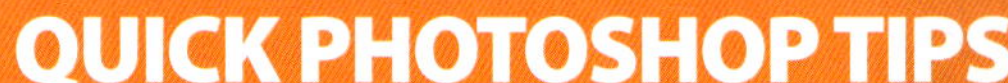

Using Presets

There is a list of Presets for every adjustment layer available. You can simply click on any of these to instantly apply them to your photos. You can also see the Presets as a drop-down menu at the top of each adjustment's individual dialog boxes.

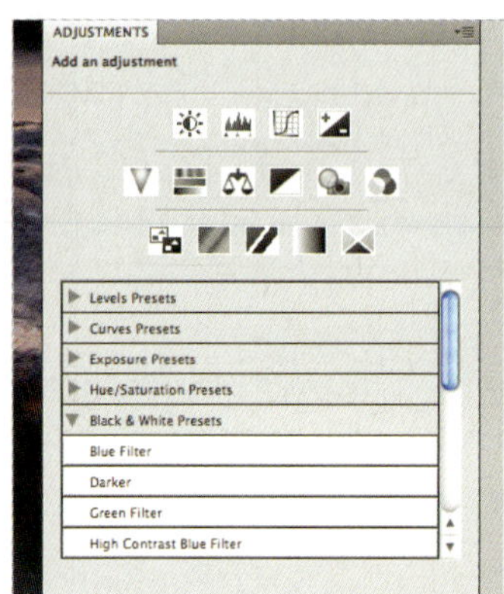

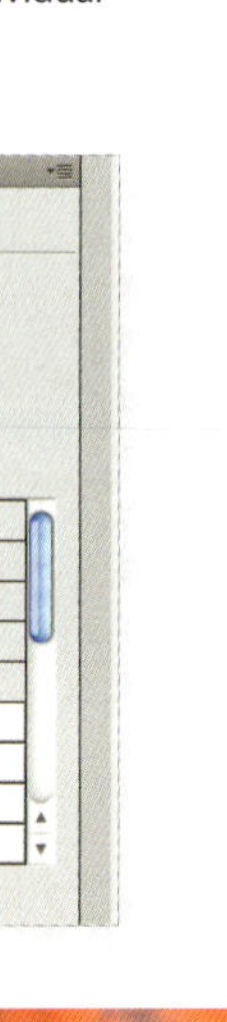

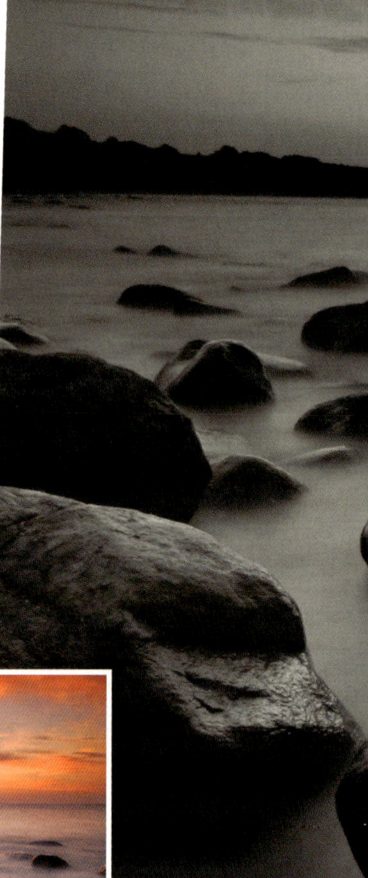

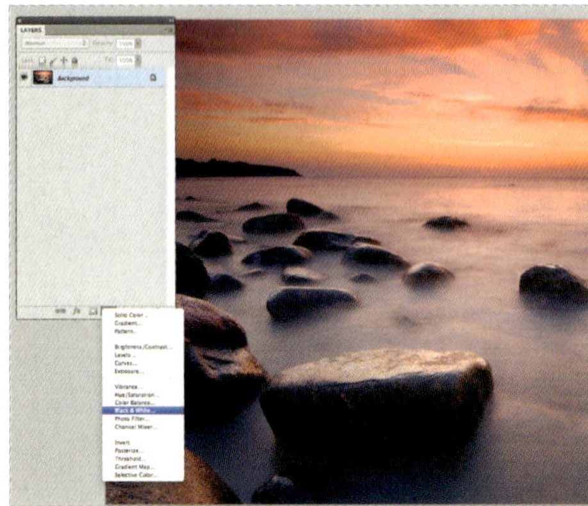

01 Option 1
You can click on the black and white circle icon in the Layers palette to quickly apply the Black & White adjustment layer

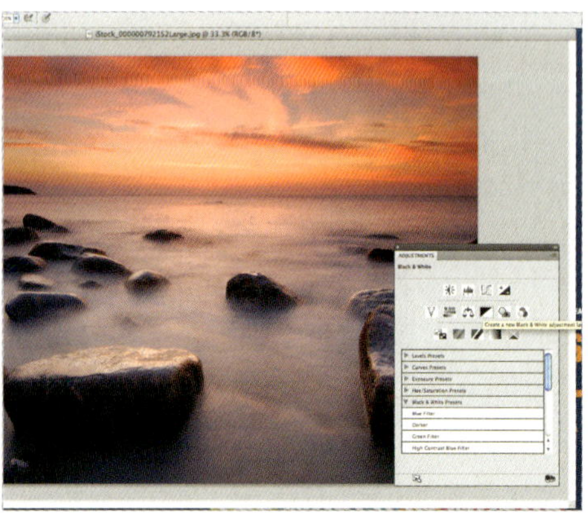

02 Option 2
If you have CS4 or CS5 then you can use the Adjustments palette instead. The Black & White adjustment is the half-black, half-white square.

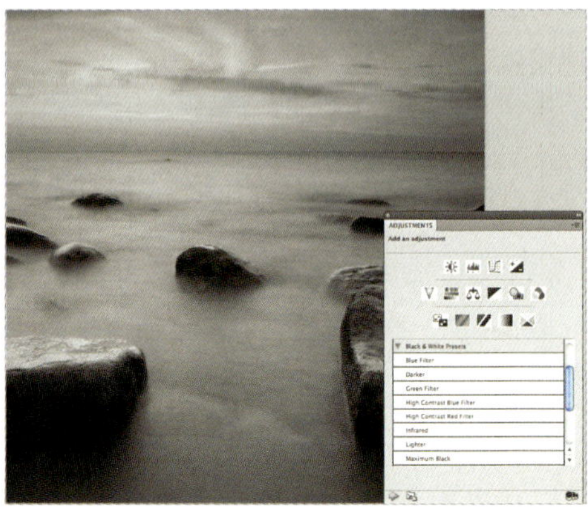

03 Presets
The Presets are a good place to start, so go through all of them and find the one that best suits your image.

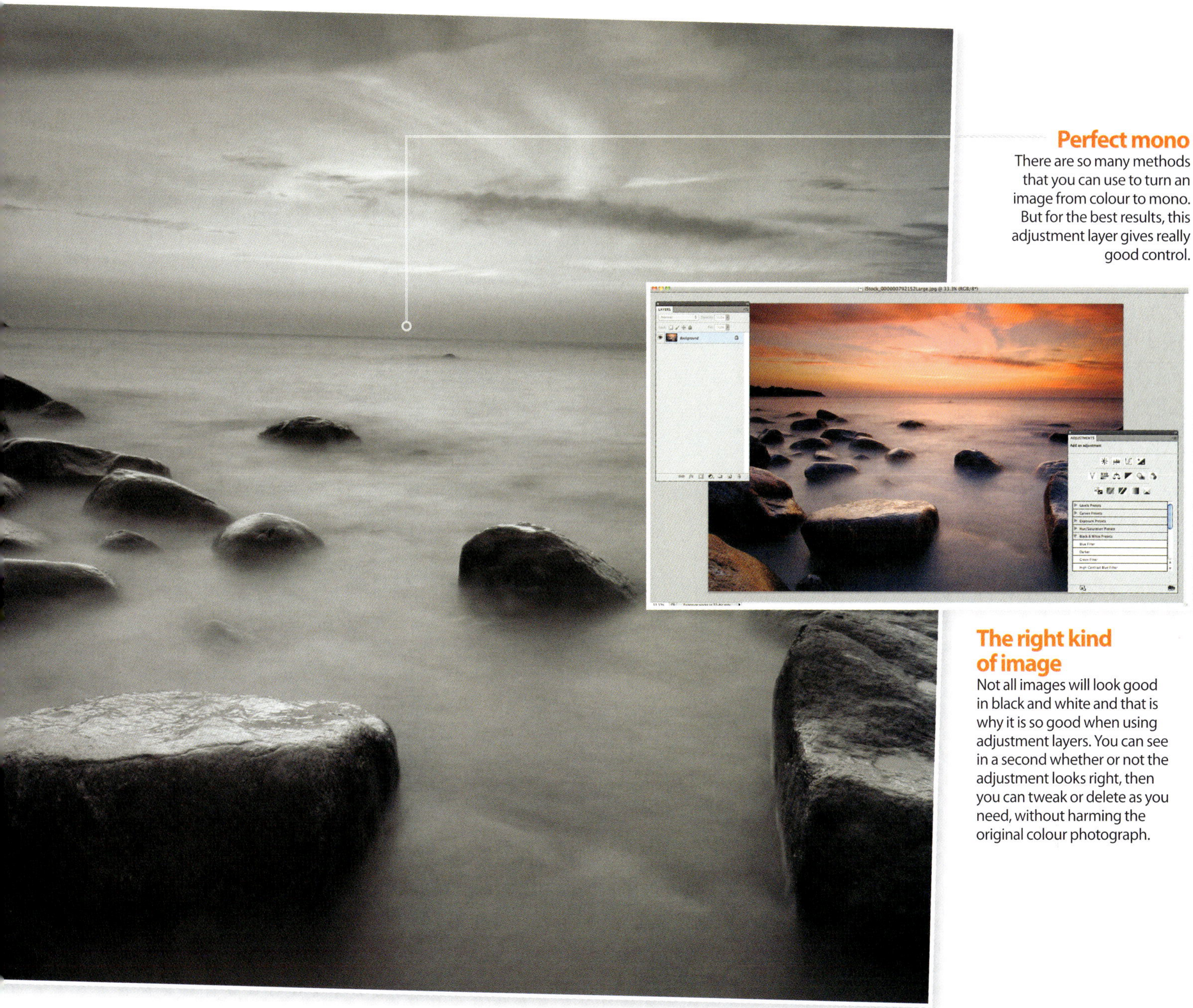

Perfect mono

There are so many methods that you can use to turn an image from colour to mono. But for the best results, this adjustment layer gives really good control.

The right kind of image

Not all images will look good in black and white and that is why it is so good when using adjustment layers. You can see in a second whether or not the adjustment looks right, then you can tweak or delete as you need, without harming the original colour photograph.

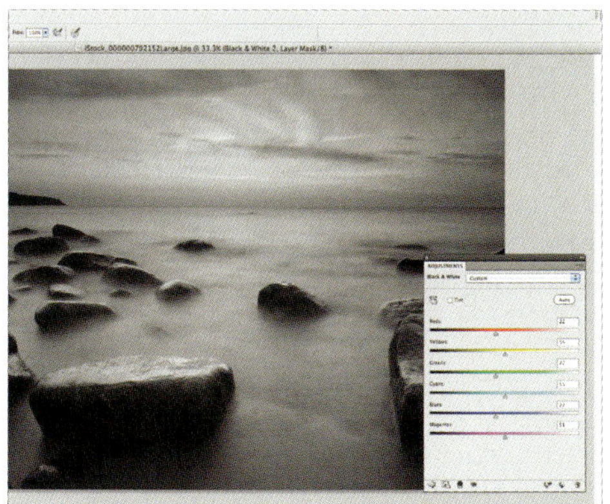

04 Customise

Now you can start tweaking the sliders to get the right balance of 'colours' in your image. Trial and error works best here.

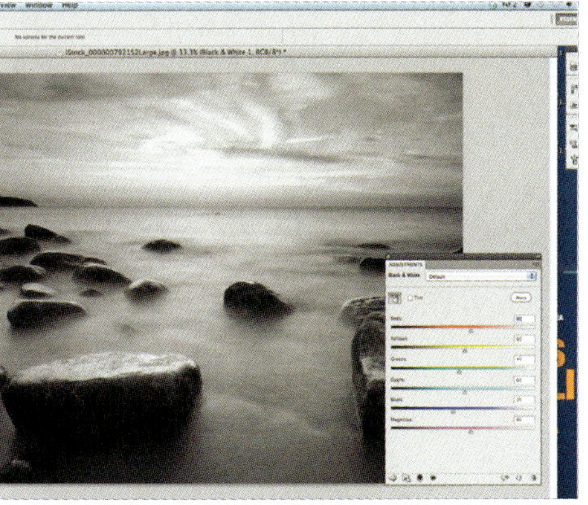

05 Precise control

There is a little hand icon here, which you can use to click on a part of the image you want to edit and then slide along your image to adjust,

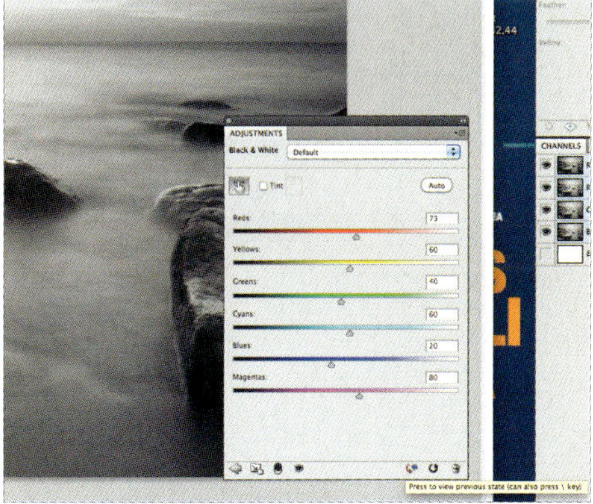

06 Check the edit

Using the little icon shown in the screenshot, you can click to see the image before its conversion to compare the result with the original.

Playing with the Channel Mixer

From magical monochromes to crazy colour combinations in one tool. Start playing with channels the easy way

The Channel Mixer can sounds complex, thanks to that one word, 'channel'. We don't really cover channels in this book, as they are used in more complex Photoshop projects. However, the Channel Mixer can give great results, even without understanding what a channel really is. In essence, a channel shows how much of one colour there is in your image as a greyscale representation. So, if you were to look at the Red channel, for example, the areas that are black are completely red, and the areas that are white have no red. Shades of grey cover the tones in-between.

Before CS4 and CS5, the Channel Mixer was the best way to convert images to black and white, as it gave you a lot more control over the results than using the Grayscale image mode, for example. When you add a Channel Mixer adjustment layer, you can tick the little Monochrome box to convert the image, and then use the sliders to fine-tune the image to perfection. Even though we have the Black and White adjustment layer option in CS4 onwards (see page 142), it doesn't mean that the Channel Mixer should be discarded.

There are plenty of reasons that you might want to use it. In our guide here, we look at using it to boost colours in an image selectively, as well as creating crazy clashing colour effects; try a couple of different mixes and you can easily put them together into an Andy Warhol-style artwork.

"Can give great results, even without understanding what a channel really is"

USING THE CHANNEL MIXER

Going mono

Channel Mixer is still a great way to create monochrome images. If you don't have a version of Photoshop that has the Black and White adjustment, then use the Channel Mixer instead and you get many of the same benefits.

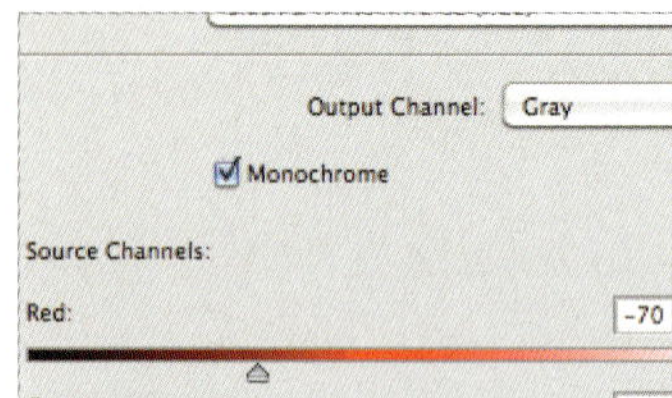

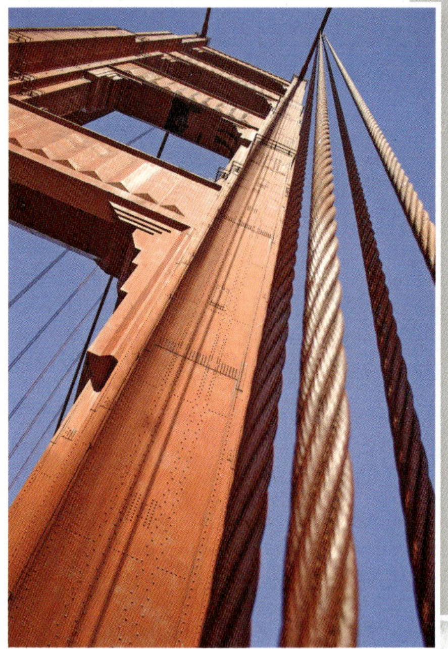

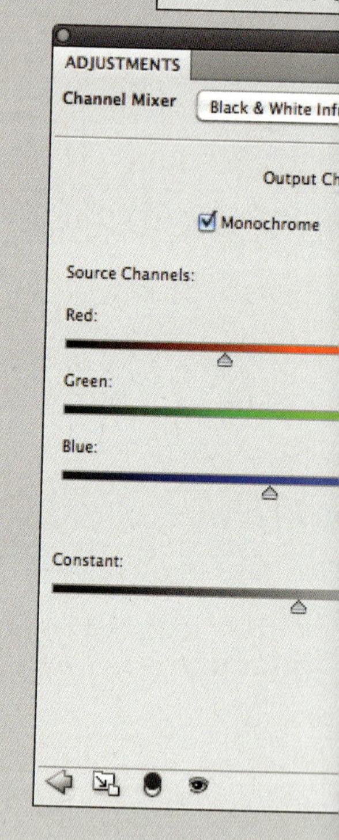

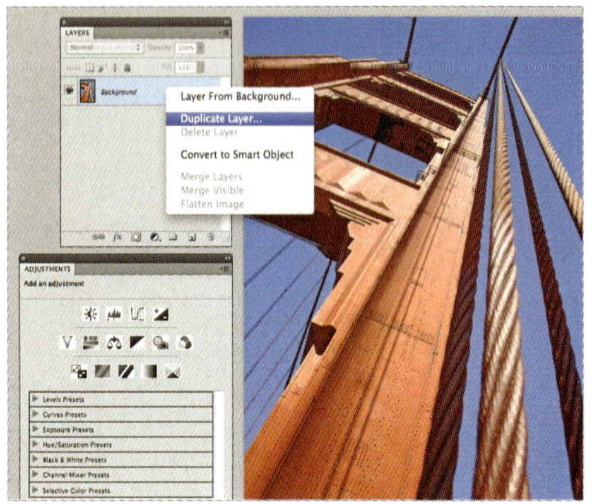

01 Duplicate

Even though adjustment layers are non-destructive, we prefer to make a Duplicate layer to play with. This saves 'unlocking' the Background.

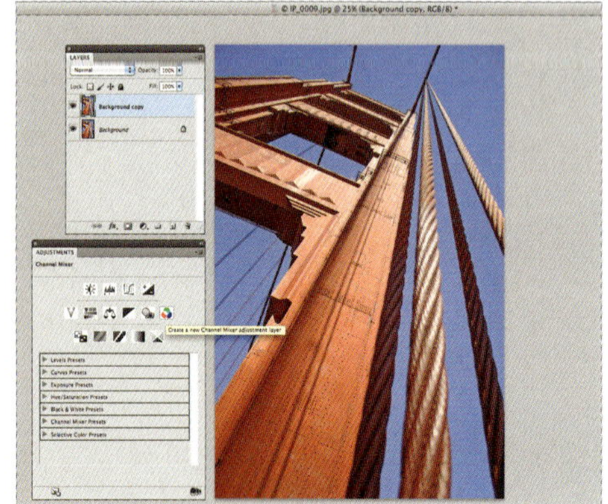

02 Channel Mixer

Add a Channel Mixer adjustment layer using the options in Layers palette or directly from within the Adjustments palette in CS4/CS5.

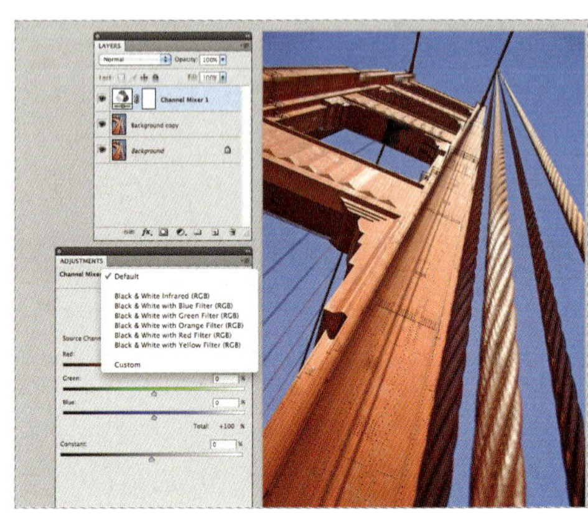

03 Presets

There are a number of presets available. These are mostly different Black and White options, as this used to be a popular use of the Channel Mixer.

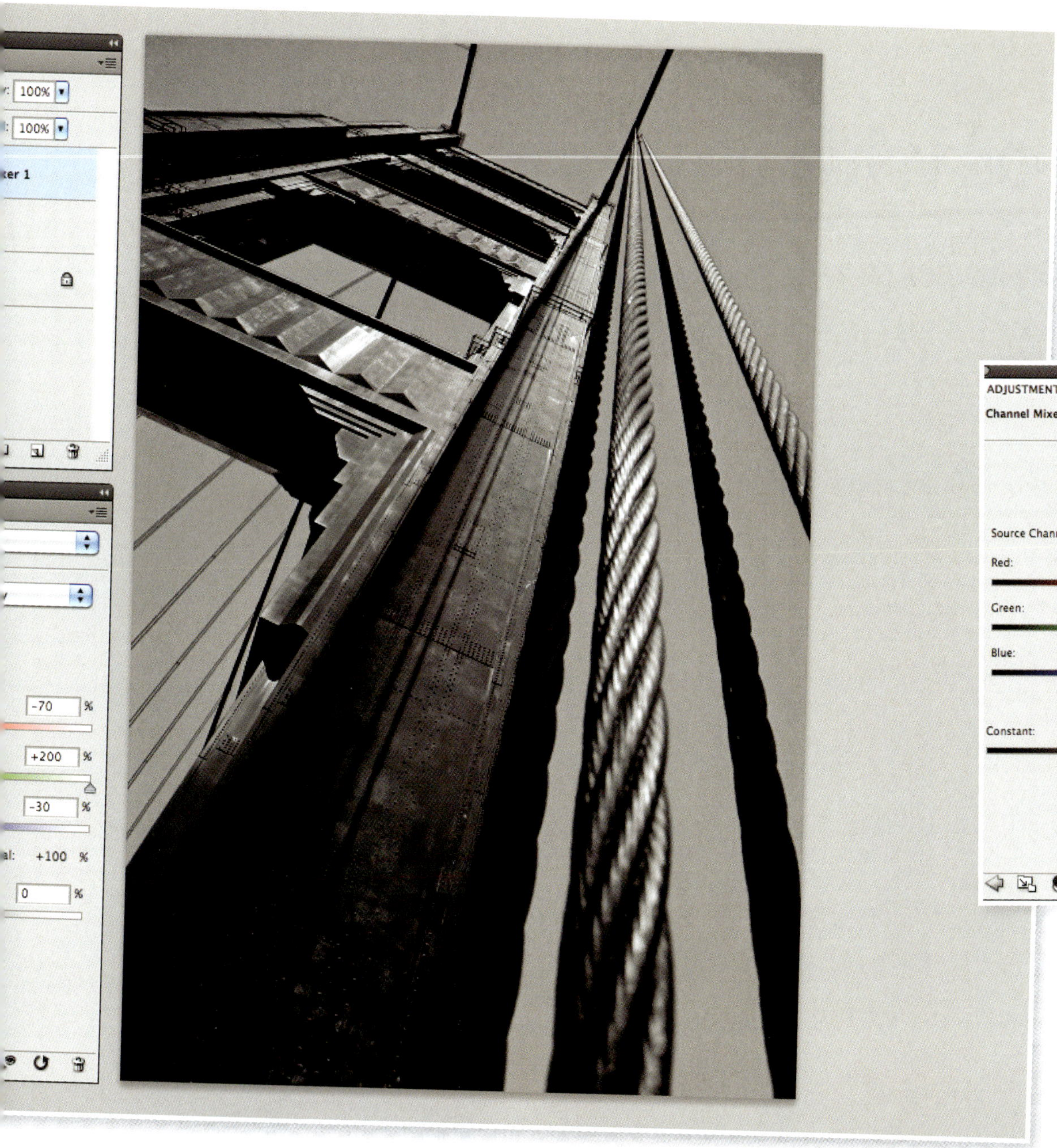

Adjustment layer

When you add the adjustment layer, it shows up in the Layers palette above your currently active layer. Double-click on this to view the Channel Mixer dialog at any time to make changes to the settings.

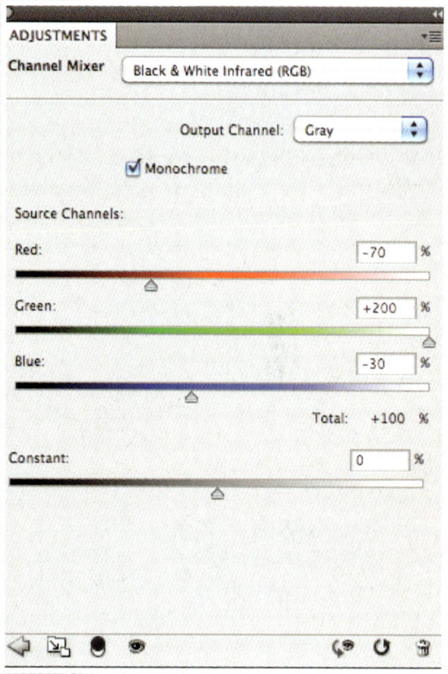

Adjustments palette

If you have CS4 or CS5, then this is the Adjustments palette, from which you can hit the icons to add new adjustment layers. If you don't have these versions, then when you add an adjustment layer in the usual manner, a dialog box will pop up with the same options in it.

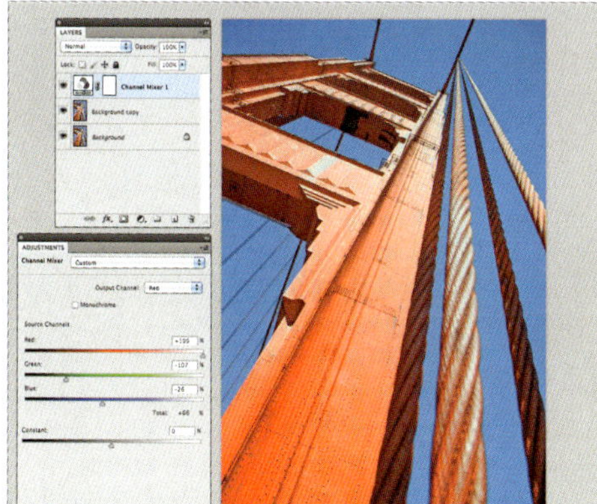

04 Boost the colours

Here we target the Red channel (in the Output Channel drop-down) and push the Red slider to maximum to make the bridge more saturated.

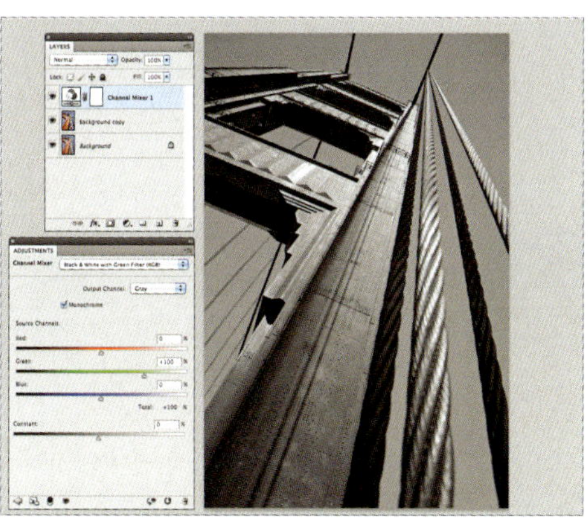

05 Monochrome

You can tick Monochrome manually and then play with the sliders to give the best contrast for good black-and-white results.

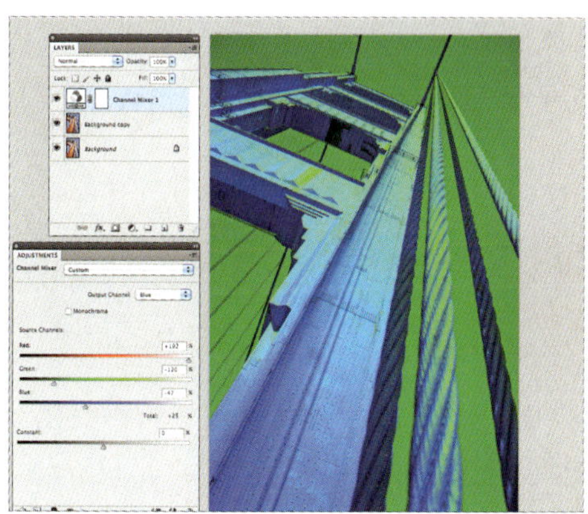

06 Crazy colours

Go crazy with the Channel Mixer and you can create almost pop-art effects by pushing certain channels to their maximum and dropping others.

Edit photos with Hue/Saturation

Do more with this dialog box by using it as an adjustment layer when editing image colours

Photoshop offers many different ways to control colour and tone in your images, but one of the absolute best is the Hue/Saturation command. Found under the Image>Adjustments menu or applied as an adjustment layer, the Hue/Saturation command allows you to alter the hue, saturation and brightness.

You can apply the changes over an entire image or target specific colours. It is this level of control that makes the command so powerful – if you have an image that's basically okay but one shade is letting it down, you can target the colour and improve it.

You control the edits by either moving sliders or entering numbers. There are three bars that control the hue, saturation or lightness, and these are in place whether you alter an entire image or just specific colours. You can also use the command to create monochrome and duotone effects, opening up the creative possibilities even more. We're going to look at all the controls in these pages and show you how they can be used to create perfectly coloured images.

As we're looking at adjustment layers, make sure that you use this method to apply your Hue/Saturation command, as you can make as many changes as you like without harming the original photo at all. You can try this out with any image to get used to the controls.

"You can apply the changes over an entire image or target specific colours"

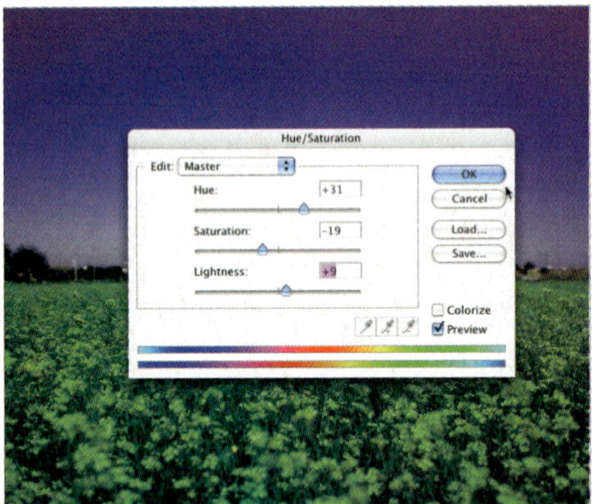

01 Assess the problem

Have a look at the image and work out what needs doing. It might be that using the sliders on the Master setting will work.

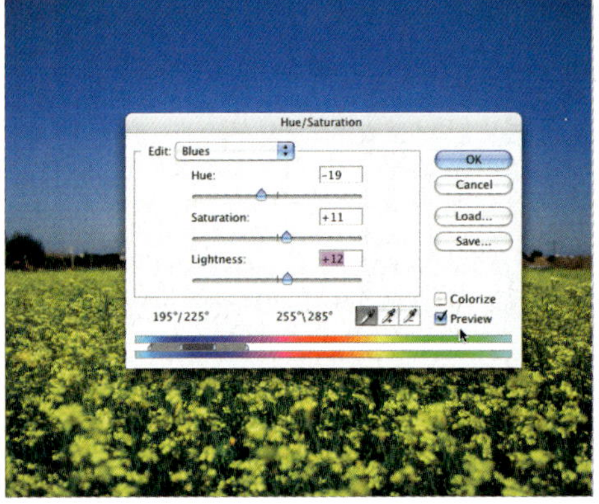

02 Blue sky

The sky is very dark. By selecting Blues and moving the Hue slider left, things are improved. Moving the Saturation slider right also brightens things up.

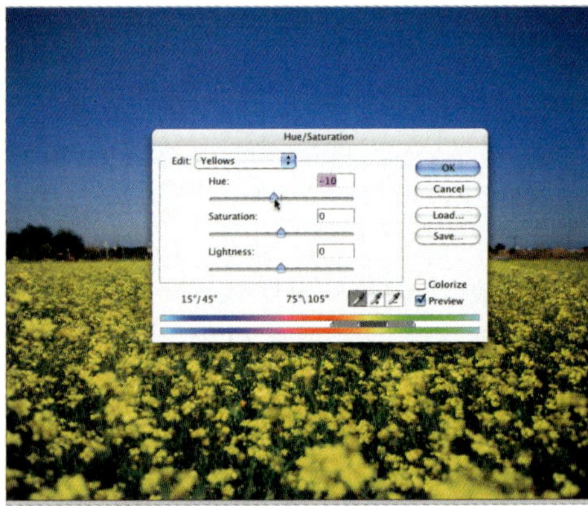

03 Not so mellow yellow

We want striking yellow flowers. This calls for Yellows to be set as the colour range. Moving the Hue slider left brightens things considerably.

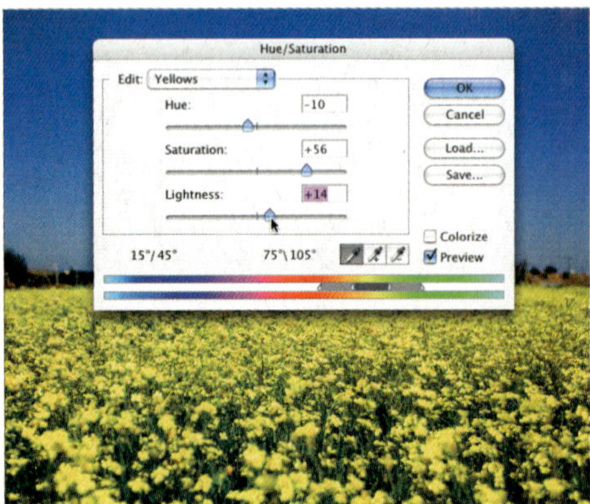

04 Boost some more

It's time to boost the effect even more. This involves moving the Saturation slider to the right. We also moved the Lightness slider to the right.

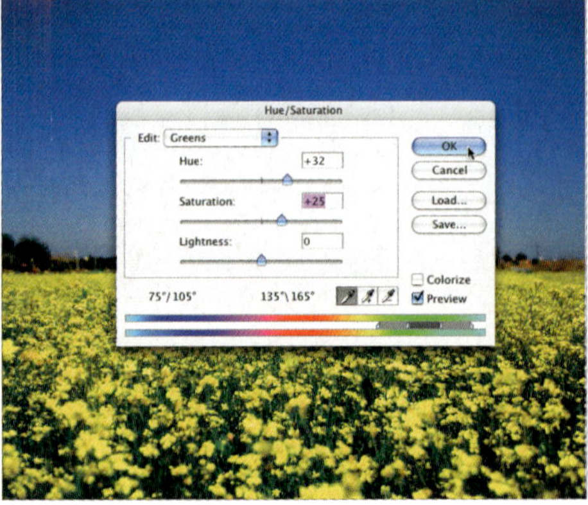

05 The final touch

The other colour that needs attention is green. It just needs the Hue and Saturation sliders to be moved to the right for the effect to improve.

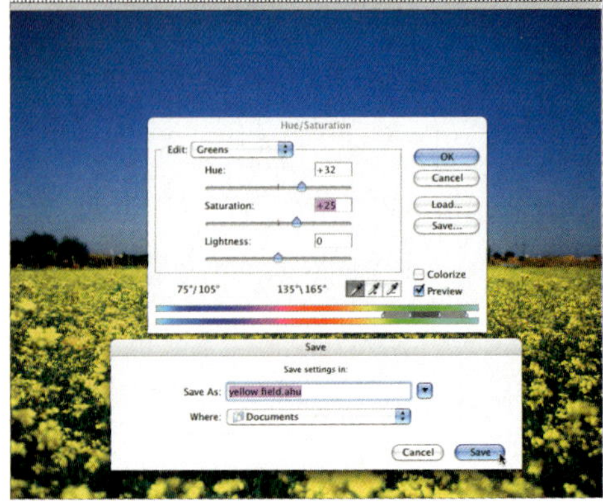

06 Save for a rainy day

If you have a collection of similar-coloured images, it's worth saving your settings. Click Save, name your settings and then save. Use Load to retrieve.

QUICK PHOTOSHOP TIPS

Preserve the original

It's a good idea to use a Hue/Saturation adjustment layer because then you know the original is safe and you can go back and edit it at any time

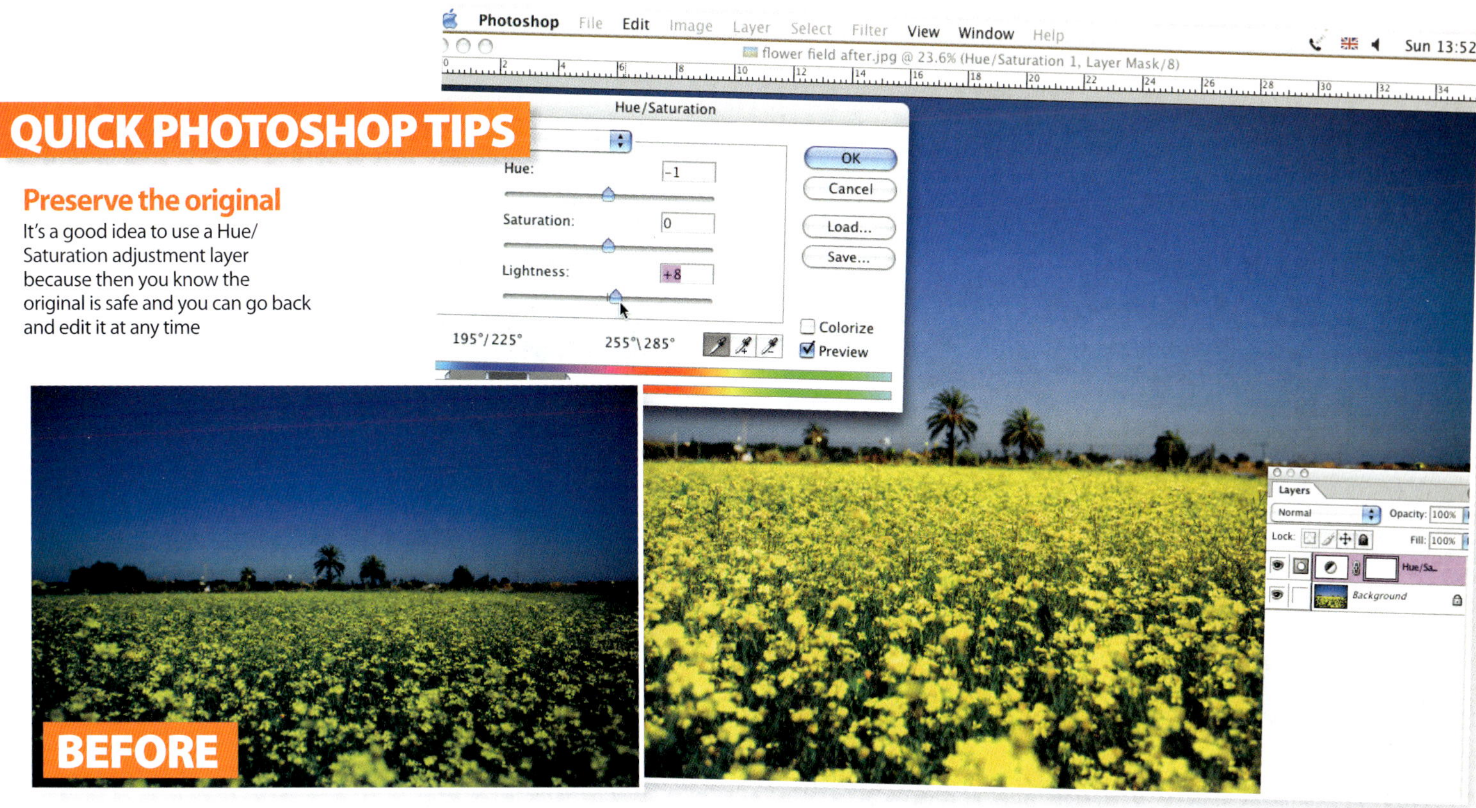

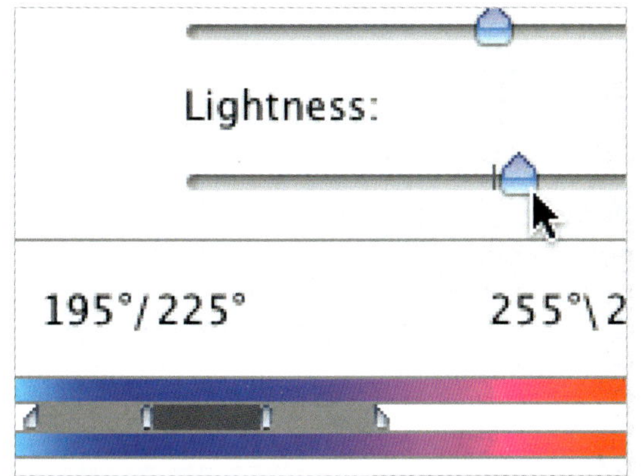

Control the parameters

When you target a specific colour, you are given the option to set how far you can tweak it. By moving these parameters, you can incorporate more hues than set by default

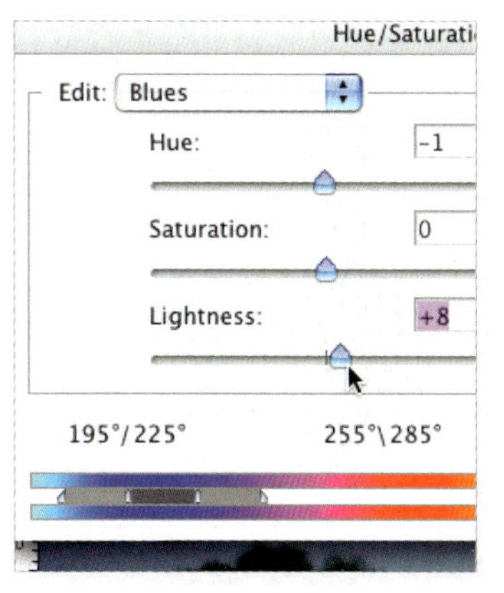

Slide edits

Control how the Hue/Saturation dialog works by using these three fields. You can enter values to make edits, but the best way is to move the sliders

Preset tones

In addition to editing the entire image, you can select preset tones from this menu and concentrate just on one colour. This makes image editing far easier

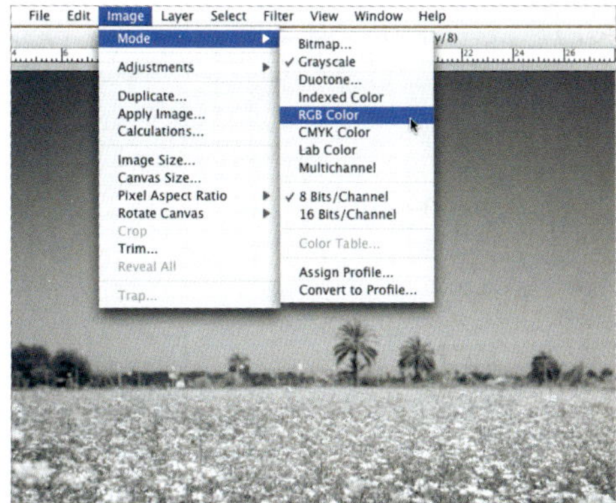

01 Colour greyscale

If you have a greyscale Image, begin by going to Image>Mode and pick RGB. Open up the Hue/Saturation dialog box and tick the Colorize box.

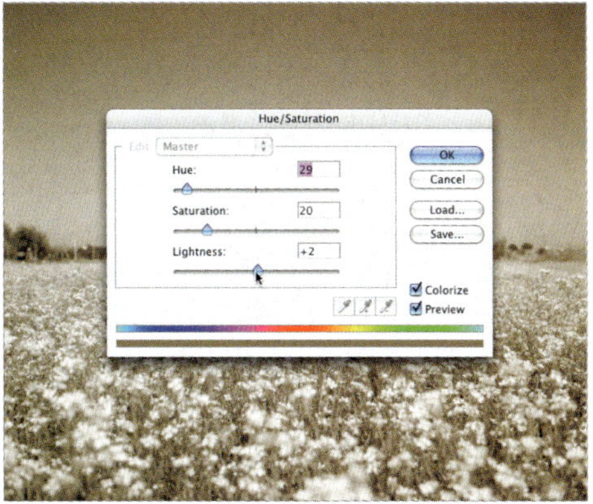

02 Colorize

If your foreground and background colours are black and white, the image will tint red. If not, it'll have the hue of your foreground colour.

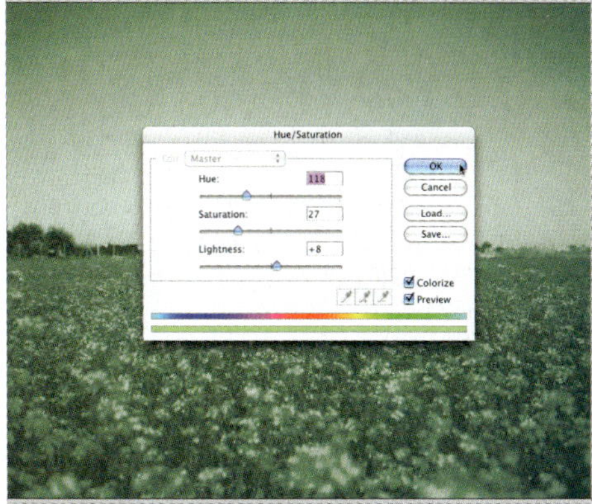

03 Colour images

With a colour image open, hit Colorize. Your image will take on a duotone look, which can be altered by moving the Hue slider.

Create a sunset using Gradient Maps

Intensify colour in your sunset photos with this non-destructive method

The Gradient Map option makes it possible to change colours in an image while retaining the individual highlights and shadows. In this tutorial we've used a gradient map to enhance our image of a sunset that's not quite captured the vibrancy of the light hitting the clouds and water's surface. They are simple to apply, and work effectively when combined with Photoshop's blending modes.

Gradient Map is an option under the adjustment layers option in the Layers palette. The maps can be used with options such as Curves to intensify highlights in an image. The trick with the adjustment layers lies with their individual masks, which appear every time you create a new one.

The Gradient Map, as its name suggests, creates a gradient with multiple colours that covers your image to account for every subject and light source. For this sunset effect, we've created a gradient with the colours red, orange and yellow, and then we let the adjustment layer do the hard work for us. It's also a great way to change a normal scene into a more fantasy-based image, by applying odd colours that you wouldn't normally expect to see.

Although there are many ways to change the tone of your image in Photoshop, the Gradient Maps option is one of the easiest and is nondestructive. Grab any landscape image in your collection to give this a go today!

> "Change colours while retaining the individual highlights"

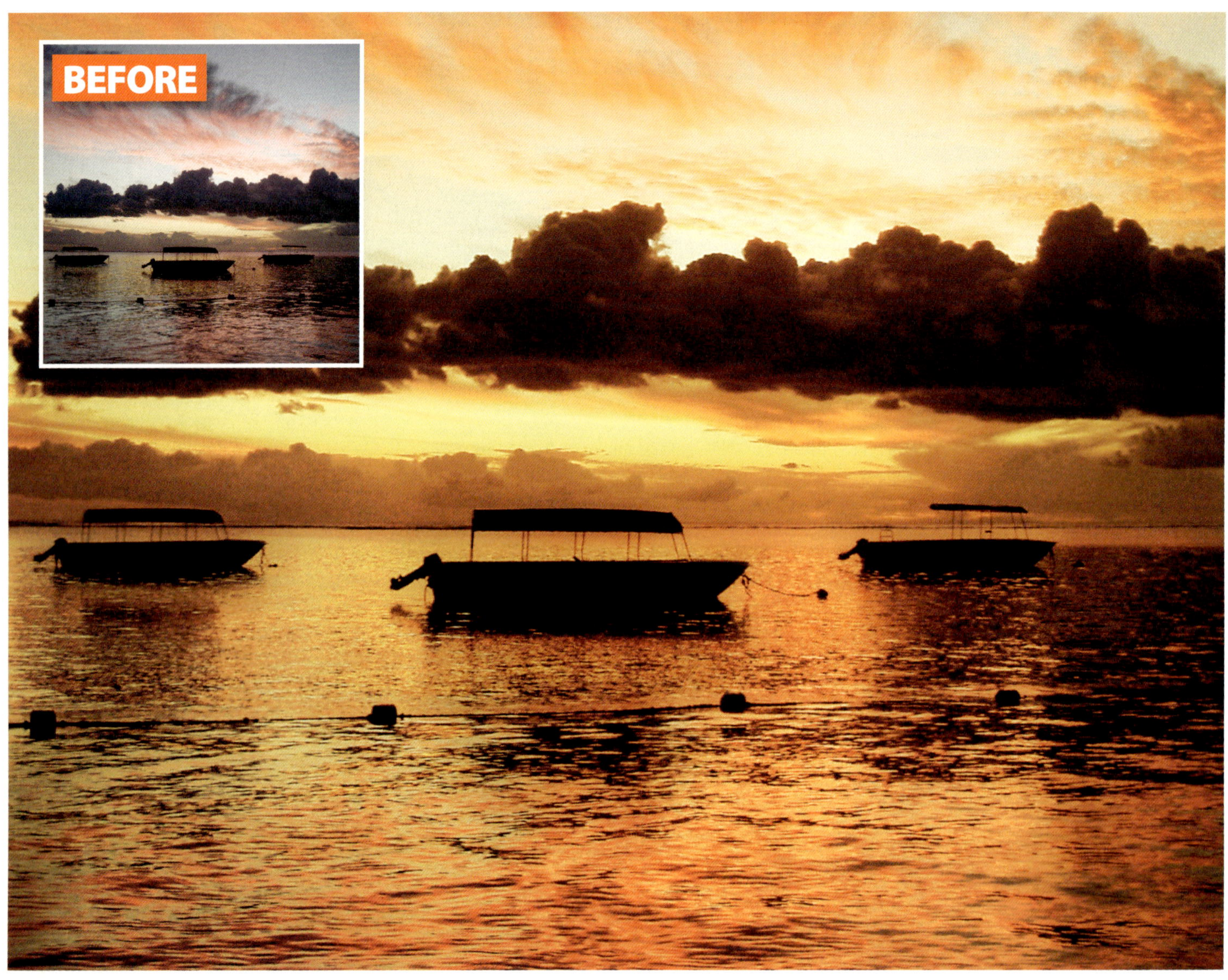

Add warmth to sunset images

With Gradient Maps and blending modes

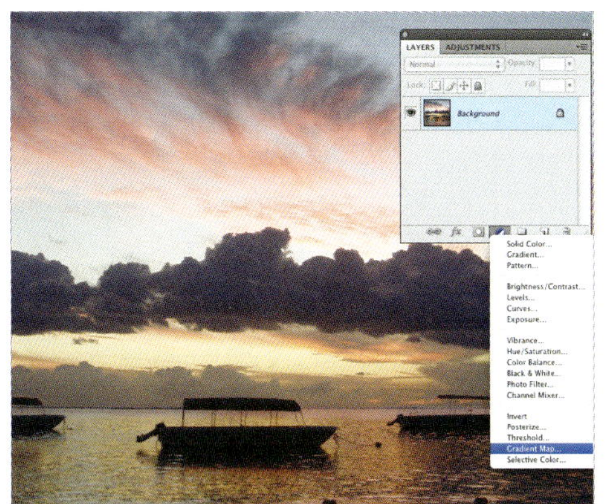

01 Find the Gradient Map

Click the Create New Adjustment Layer button in the Layers palette, and select Gradient Map to add an adjustment layer.

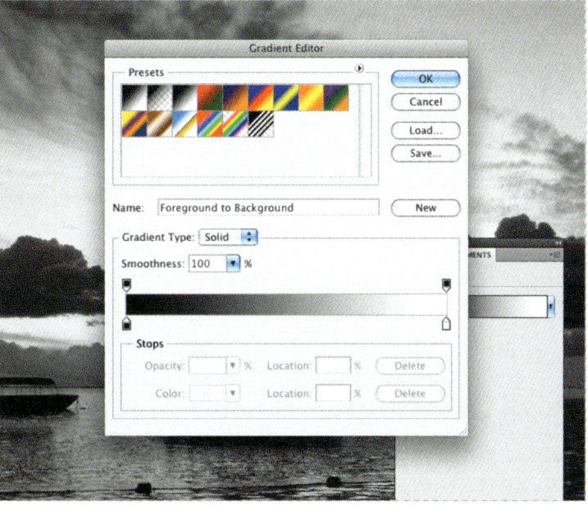

02 Gradient Editor

The image turns to black and white. Double-click on the left thumbnail on its layer to open up the Gradient Editor dialog box.

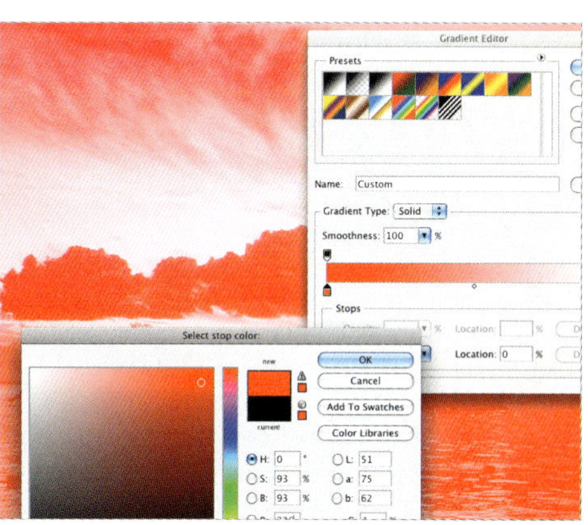

03 A splash of red

There are two squares on the bottom side of the gradient's colour bar. Double-click on the bottom left square and choose a warm red.

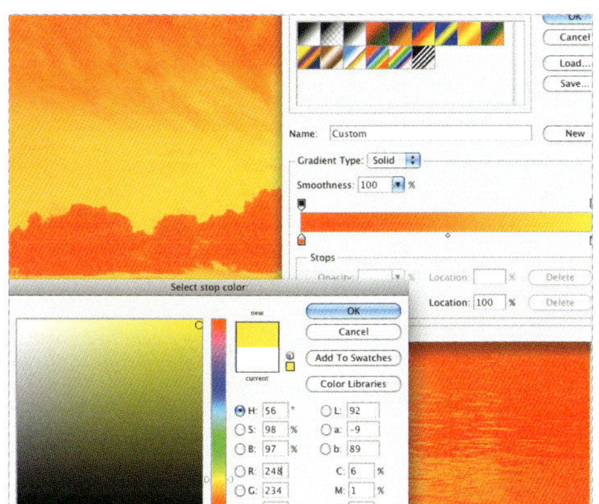

04 A tint of yellow

Double-click on the far right square. Select a bright yellow and hit OK. The colour bar now has orange as the midtone, with red and yellow either side.

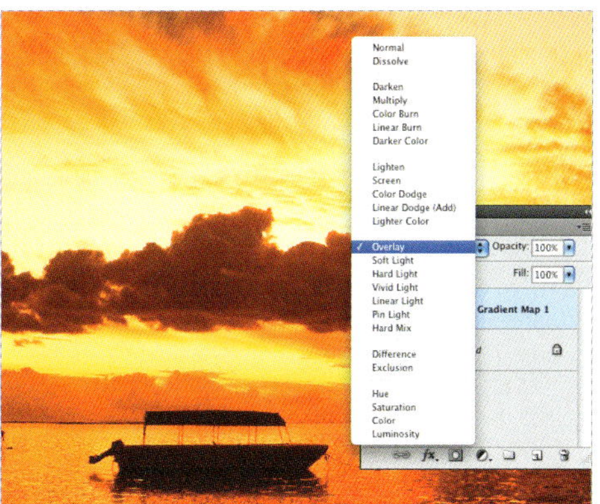

05 Blend

Hit OK to apply the mapping. In the Layers palette, change the blending mode to Overlay. This boosts the sunset's contrast.

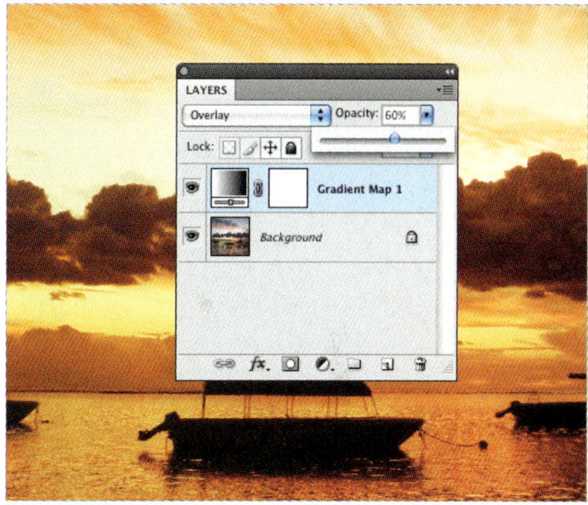

06 Tweak settings

To reduce the harshness of the Gradient Map, use the Opacity slider in the Layers palette. Reduce its value to 60% to make the sunset subtle.

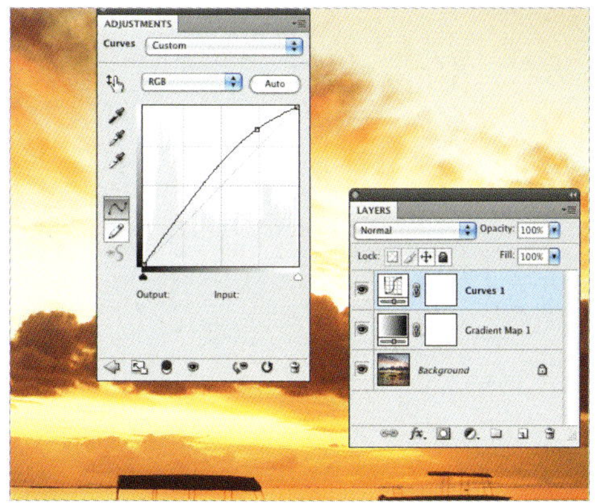

07 Add some shimmer

Click on Curves in the New Adjustment Layer list. Now pull the top of the line upwards in the Curves dialog box to give the image more brightness.

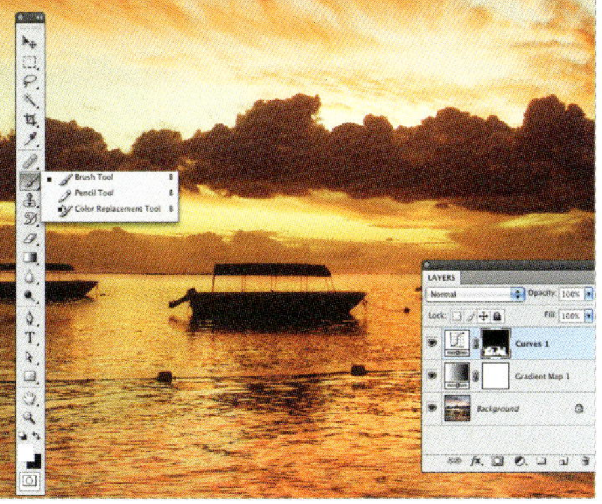

08 Paint in light

Select the white thumbnail on the Curves layer, and go to Image>Adjustments>Invert. Use a black Brush to paint over the water.

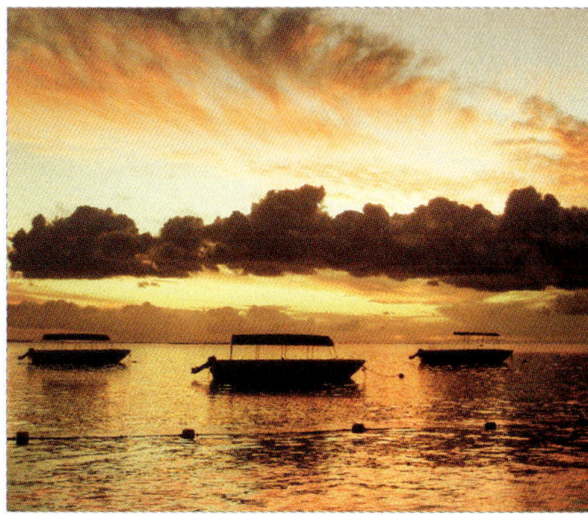

09 And we're done!

You should now have an image that looks like this, but the beauty of adjustment layers is that you can go back and change settings as you go.

Get creative with adjustment layers

Emulate a cross-processing effect

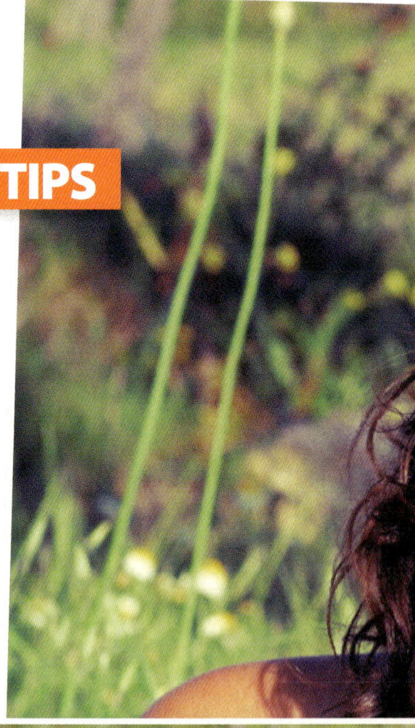

QUICK PHOTOSHOP TIPS

Picking a start image

While you can try out this technique on any image that you like, it tends to work particularly well on vibrant portraits. Landscapes don't have the same impact, and images that have a low tonal range to start off with, can end up looking washed-out rather than cross-processed. Luckily, it is so easy to do that you can play with a few images to find the ones that work from your own collection.

Most likely to have been discovered by mistake, the cross-processing effect was originally created by running a roll of colour negative film through the wrong processing chemicals. A waste of chemicals, we hear you say? This surprisingly wasn't the case, as the results showed rather pleasantly peculiar colour variations and hues, especially noticeable in the shadow tones of the image.

A sense of realism is still present, but with a shift of artistic meaning. This is perhaps why it stuck in the minds of traditional artists throughout the Seventies and into the Nineties, and now it's been reincarnated using Photoshop. Luckily, we don;t have to get our hands dirty with chemicals any more and you can try this effect out on any image. It takes just a few minutes to do, but the result is largely down to personal preference. Therefore, through the use of adjustment layers, it's possible to go back time and again until you get the result that you want. In this guide we will be using more than one adjustment layer, both the Curves and the Brightness/Contrast options. This just goes to show how endlessly versatile the adjustment layer options can be and how you can get amazing effects by simply layering up a few. As long as you save the layered version, then you will have all your edits ready to be tinkered with to your heart's content at any point in the future.

> "The results show rather pleasantly peculiar colour variations and hues, especially noticeable in the shadow tones of the image"

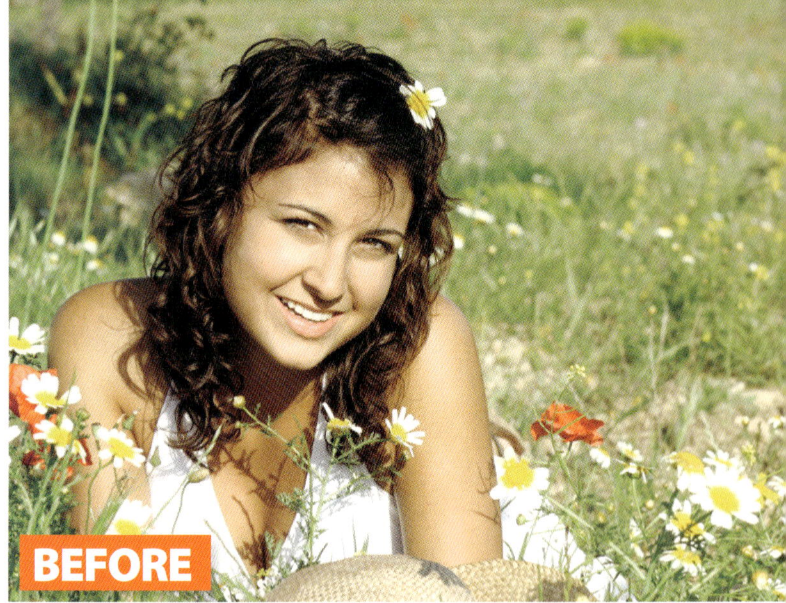
BEFORE

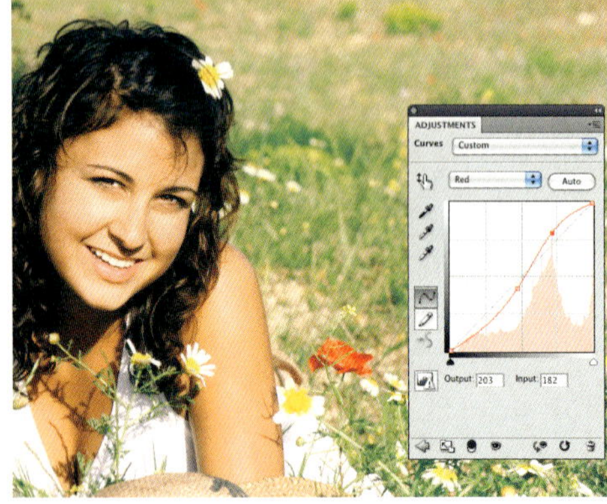

01 Apply red

Go to Layer>New Adjustment Layer>Curves. Select the Red channel, and create a narrow S shape by dragging the line of the graph.

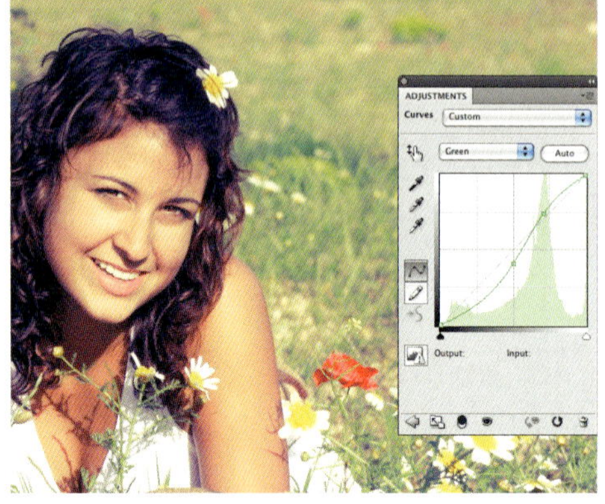

02 Adjust green

Select the Green channel and apply a similar S shape The more the curve is moved, the more contrast and colour will be added to your image.

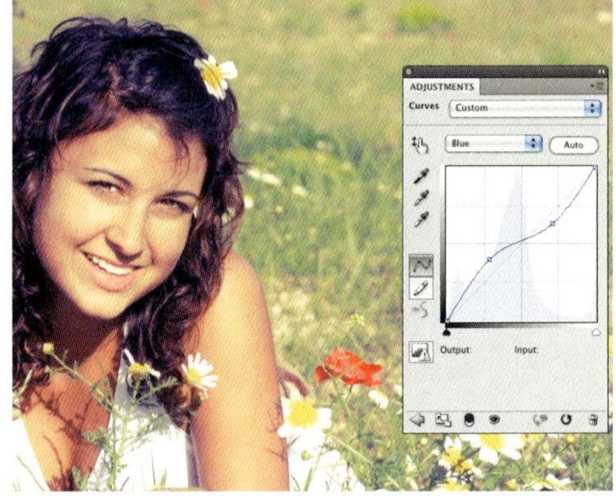

03 Increase blue

Select the Blue channel and apply a reverse S shape. This gives the shadows in your image a tint of blue, distinctive in cross processing.

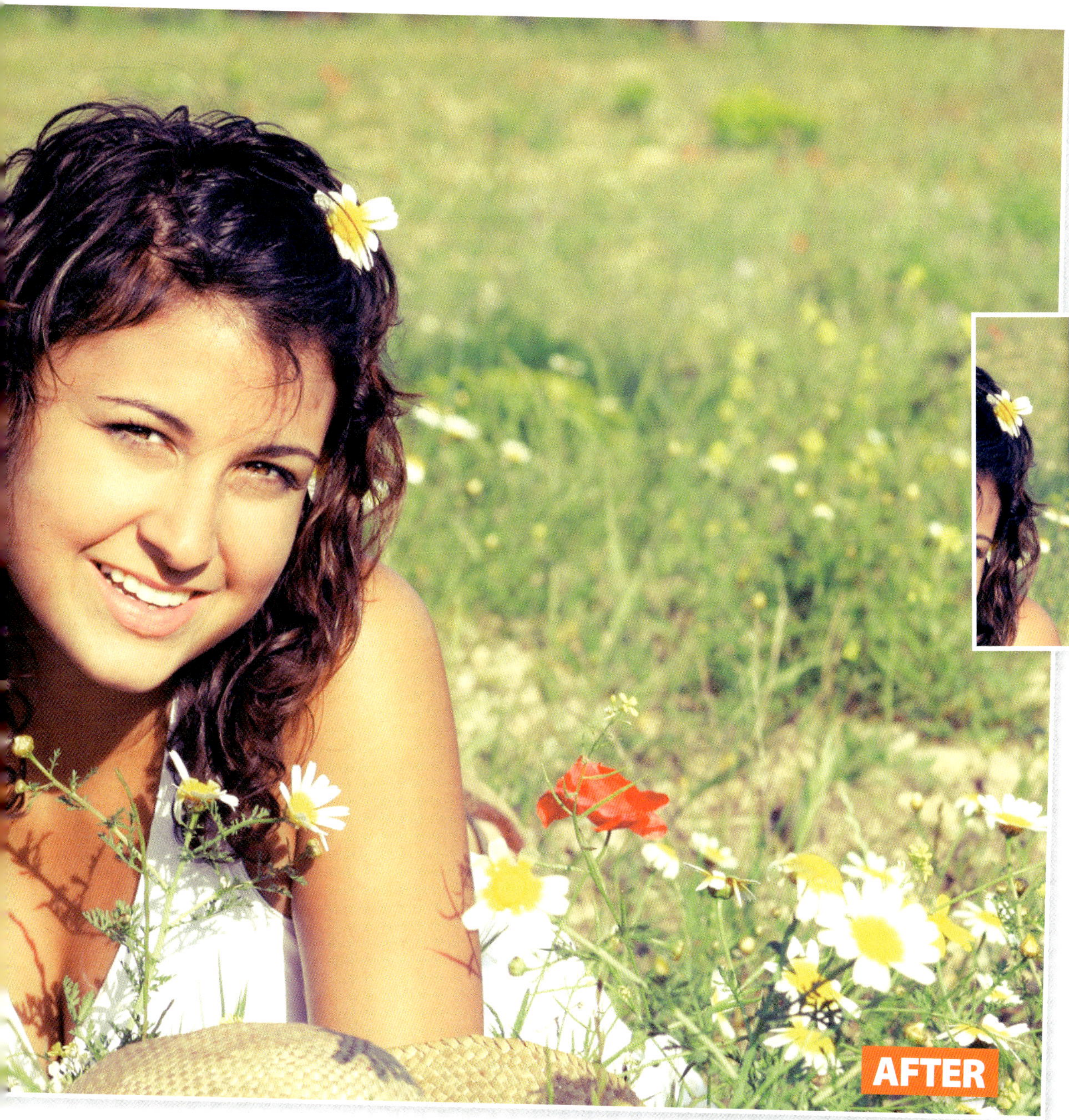

AFTER

Blending modes

We use a Color blending mode here, but it's easy to cycle through the many options to find one that works for you. It's all about giving it a try!

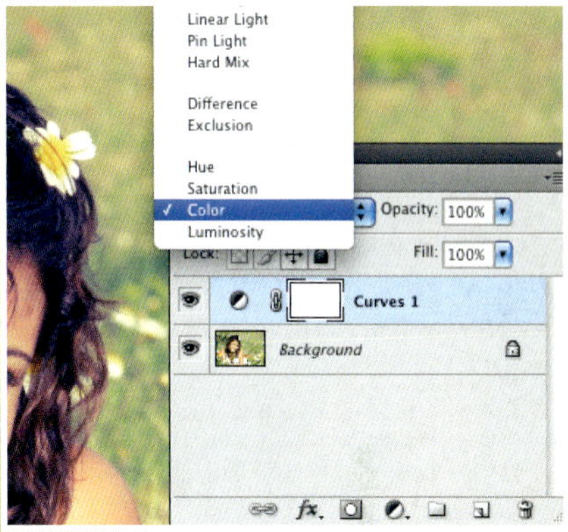

Bleach it

Our cross-processed image still looks natural, but some effects go a lot further. You can bleach the image out to give it a vintage vibe, simply by lowering the contrast with Curves. You can also try upping the green for a very Seventies, retro feel.

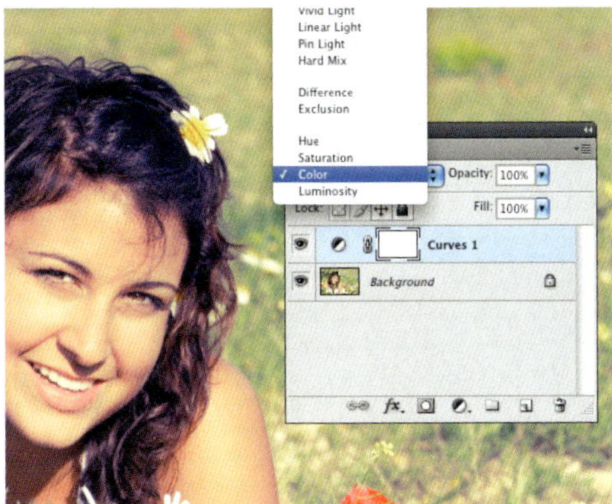

04 Apply a blend mode

Change the blending mode to Color. If the colours need tweaking, click back on the adjustment layer to edit the RGB channels separately.

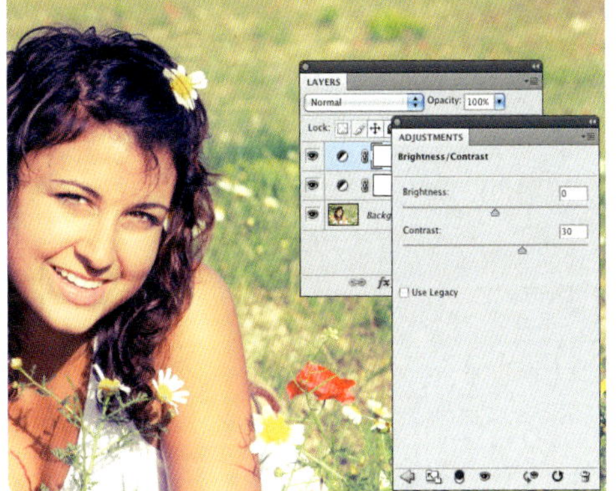

05 Boost contrast

Add a Brightness/Contrast adjustment layer and increase the Contrast slider to 30. This gives your image the authenticity needed.

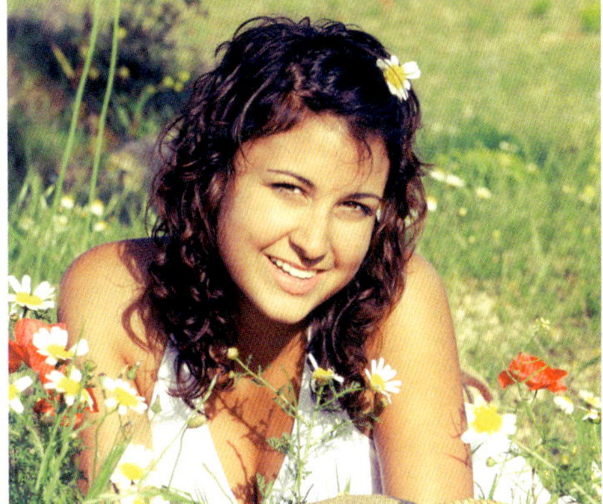

06 The result

Your final image should have the colour variations and tonal range expected from a cross-processing photograph; if not, go back and make tweaks.

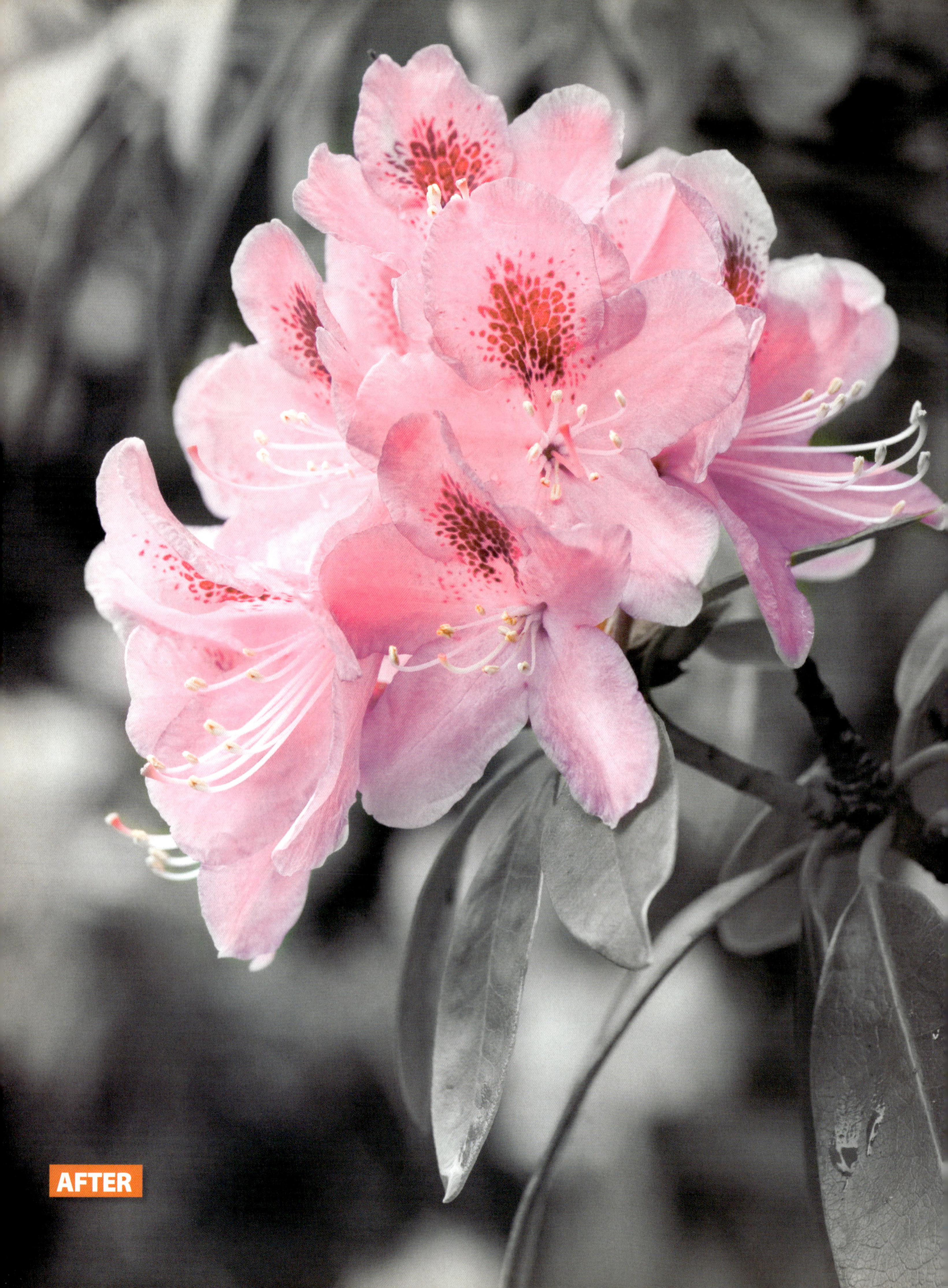
AFTER

Basic masks explained

Your adjustment layer comes with its own mask – but what does that mean?

We have made reference to masks throughout this book, but they are generally used for more complex projects. However, even as a beginner, it is worth getting to grips with the basics of masks, as every time you add an adjustment layer it comes preloaded with its own mask.

A mask essentially controls what parts of your adjustment can be seen, and what parts can't. So, for example, if you wanted to lighten just the sky in a landscape image, you would apply a Curves adjustment layer as usual and then use the mask to make sure that only the sky is targeted.

This is done using brushes, but only in black or white colors. Black brushes are used to hide areas that you don't want to be affected by the adjustment, and white areas are used to show areas that you want the adjustment applied to. If a mask were all black, then nothing on the adjustment layer would be visible, and vice versa with an all-white mask. By default, you are given an all-white mask when you apply an adjustment layer, so that everything you are doing is applied to the whole image.

Like adjustment layers, masks are editable and you can go back in and refine them at any time in the future. We have put together a very simple use of masks here, but have a play with them and you will soon pick them up.

> "Masks are editable and you can go back in and refine them"

QUICK PHOTOSHOP TIPS

Masks and selections

There is an even easier way of applying an adjustment layer selectively. If you know you want just the sky affected, then select that first using any of the methods in the Selections section of this book. Then, with the selection active, hit the adjustment layer button. As if by magic, your selection is used to create a mask from the outset, with everything black bar the selected area.

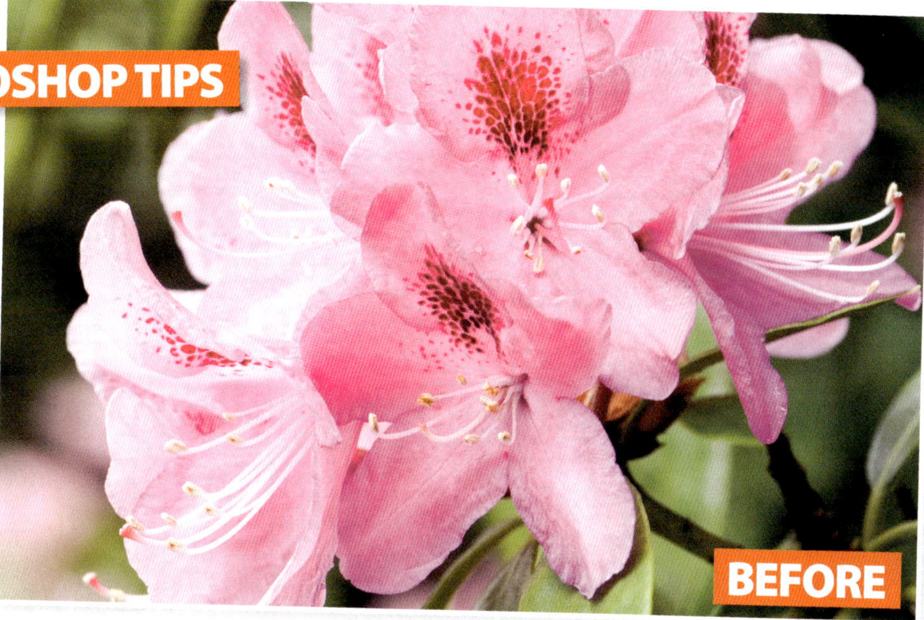

Selective colouring

There is a dedicated Selective Color Adjustment layer, but for the purposes of showing you how to use the adjustment layer masks, we're using the Black & White adjustment option instead.

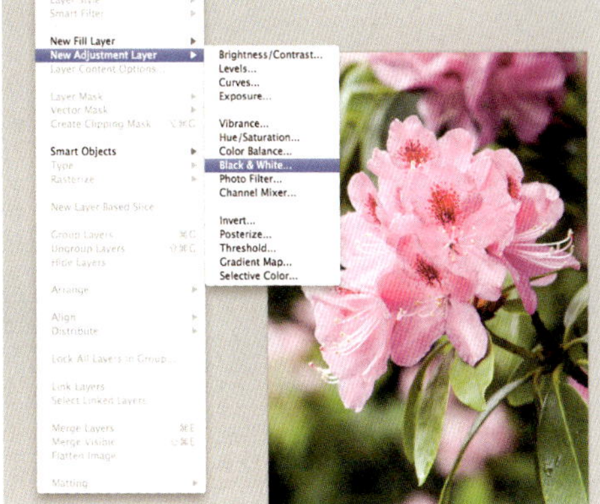

01 Adjustment layer
Apply a black-and-white adjustment layer in your preferred manner, from the Layers palette or the menu options.

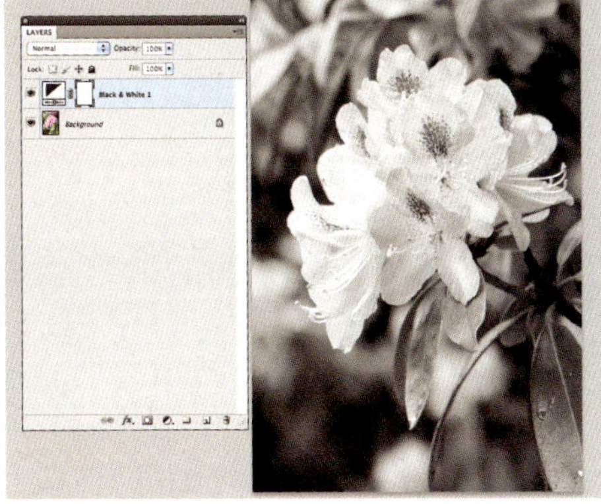

02 The mask
The empty white box next to the adjustment layer thumbnail is your mask. Make sure that your brush is set to black (hit 'D' to reset colours).

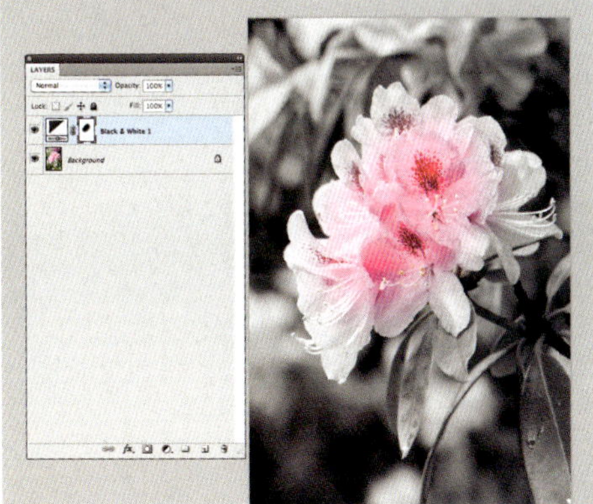

03 And paint...
Now use your brush to slowly paint over the areas that you want to remove from the adjustment, using small brushes around the edges.

Selections

"Selections enable you to isolate parts of an image if you only want to edit that layer"

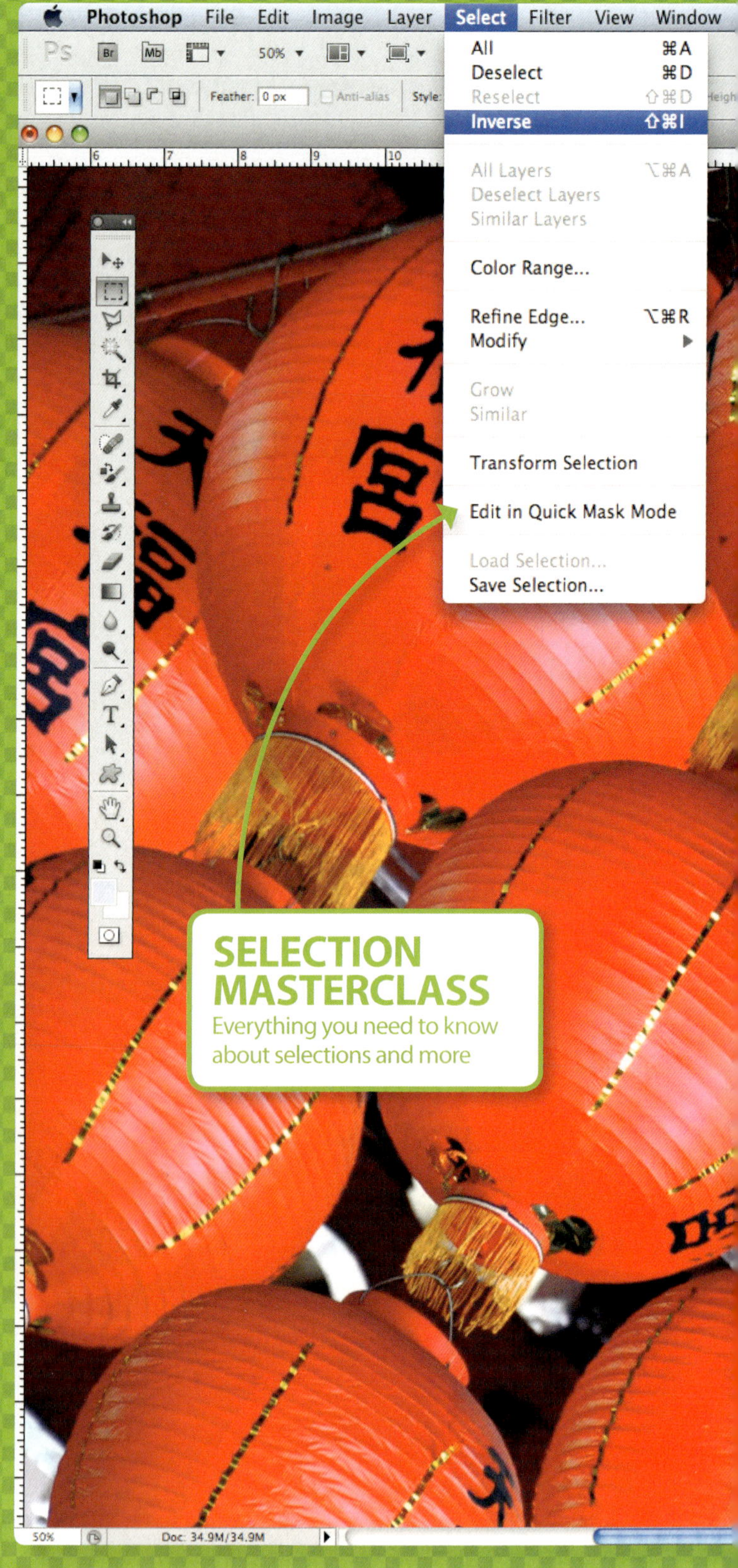

SELECTION MASTERCLASS
Everything you need to know about selections and more

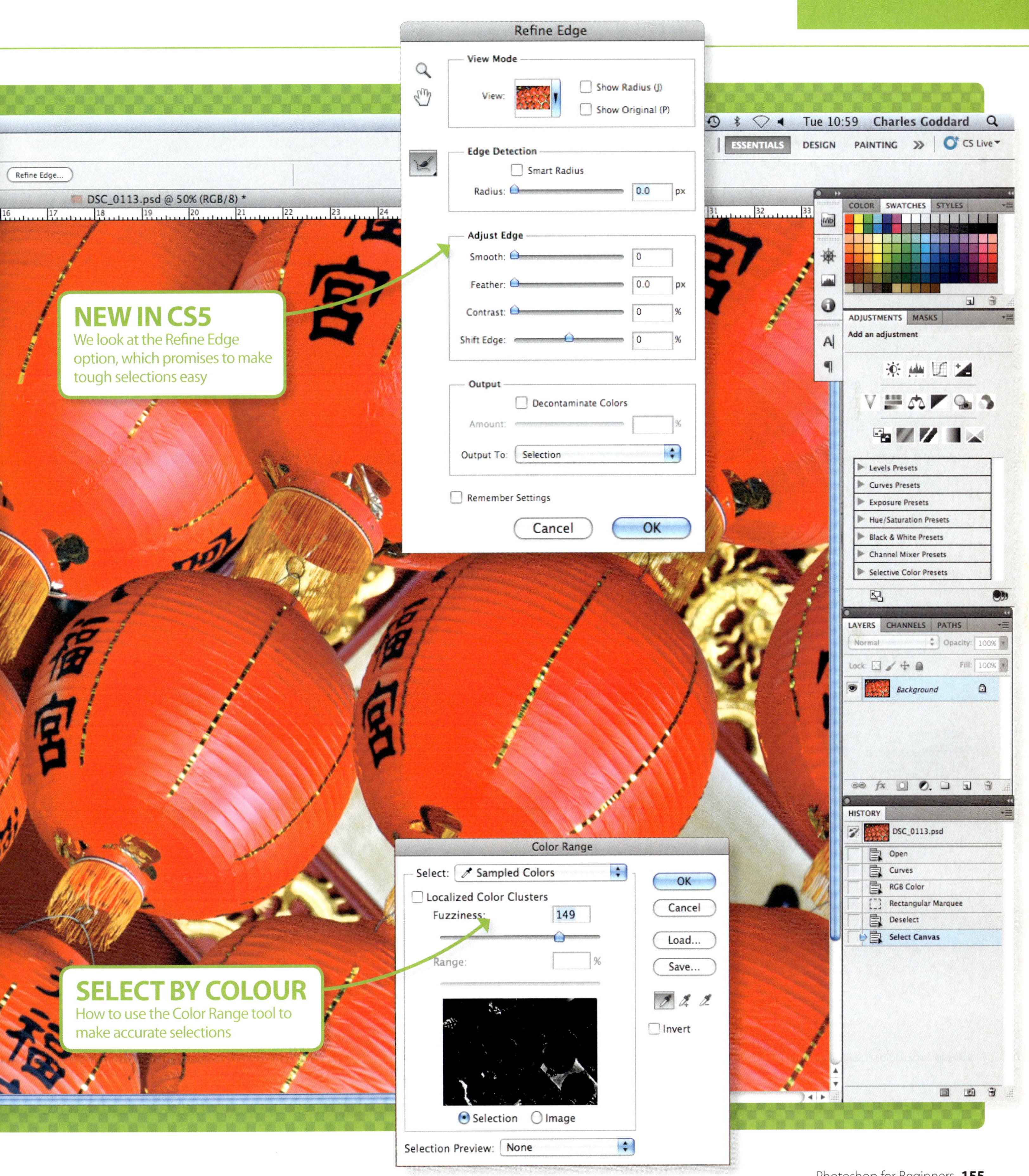
NEW IN CS5
We look at the Refine Edge option, which promises to make tough selections easy
SELECT BY COLOUR
How to use the Color Range tool to make accurate selections
Refine Edge
View Mode
View:
Show Radius (J)
Show Original (P)
Edge Detection
Smart Radius
Radius:
Adjust Edge
Smooth:
Feather:
Contrast:
Shift Edge:
Output
Decontaminate Colors
Amount:
Output To:
Selection
Remember Settings
Cancel
OK
Color Range
Select:
Sampled Colors
Localized Color Clusters
Fuzziness:
149
Range:
Load...
Save...
Invert
Selection
Image
Selection Preview:
None
DSC_0113.psd @ 50% (RGB/8) *
Refine Edge...
Tue 10:59
Charles Goddard
ESSENTIALS
DESIGN
PAINTING
CS Live
COLOR
SWATCHES
STYLES
ADJUSTMENTS
MASKS
Add an adjustment
Levels Presets
Curves Presets
Exposure Presets
Hue/Saturation Presets
Black & White Presets
Channel Mixer Presets
Selective Color Presets
LAYERS
CHANNELS
PATHS
Background
HISTORY
DSC_0113.psd
Open
Curves
RGB Color
Rectangular Marquee
Deselect
Select Canvas

Selections in Photoshop

Whether it's controlling which area to edit or having fun by cutting up images, selections are a vital skill

When working with both digital photos and graphics, you may need to select from the background or surrounding areas. Selections enable you to isolate parts of an image, either because you only want to edit that area or maybe because you want to move it to another document or layer.

One of the benefits of having multiple tools at your fingertips is that you decide how intensive your selection is. The choices range from you clicking in areas and letting Photoshop decide where to select, up to you creating the selection edge using the Pen tool and paths. Which is a good time for us to say that we aren't actually going to cover the Pen tool here. While it is a lot easier to use than its reputation suggests, it can be daunting and it isn't an option for Elements users. The methods we have chosen to look at are the Marquee tools, the Lasso tools, the Magic Wand, Color Range and Quick Selection tool. Different versions will have other options, but these are a good base to start with and will provide easy and accurate selections. We'll be looking at these in more detail throughout this section of the book.

The most impressive thing about the selection tools is how flexible they are. Once you've chosen your method, you can modify the way it performs by moving to the Options bar and choosing either the Add To, Subtract From or Intersect selection modes. By clicking these after you've made your main selection, you can use the tool to add or remove specific parts from it. It's also possible to determine how harsh or soft edged your selection is by entering a value into the Feather box to blur the boundary.

We will also take a quick trip up to the Select menu and have a look at the options in there. You'll find some of the tweaks already mentioned, in addition to more wholesale selection methods that can be useful for building up compositions.

SELECTION TOOLS IN DETAIL

Lasso tool family

The Lasso tool family consists of three members – the Lasso, Polygonal Lasso and Magnetic Lasso tools. All of these are Selection tools with greater precision than Marquee tools and the Magic Wand tool. You can also use the keyboard shortcut 'L' to access this tool at any time. It is the same in both Elements (right) and Photoshop (below).

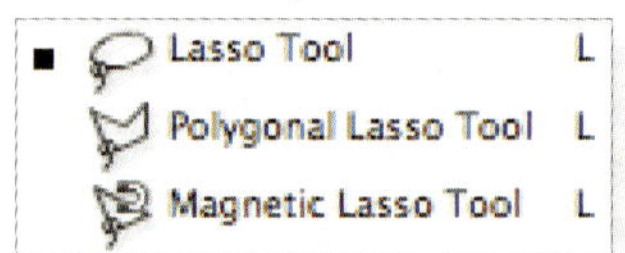

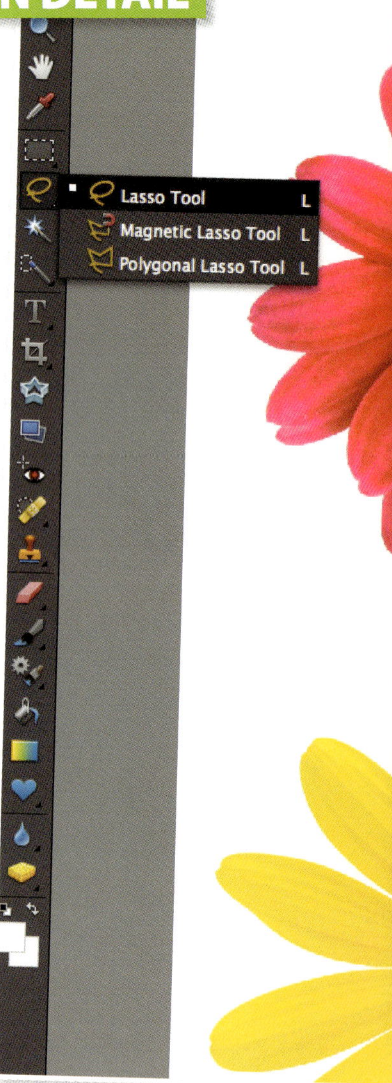

Marquee tools

The Single Column or Row Marquee tools offer easy ways to achieve selections in a straight vertical or horizontal line. The Elliptical Marquee tool creates elliptical selections and the Rectangular Marquee tool produces square and rectangular selections that are great for cropping photographs. Make the width proportionate with the height by selecting Fixed Aspect Ratio from the Style menu or choose Fixed Size to specify a set selection width and height and then make the selection. Elements only has the Rectangular and Elliptical options.

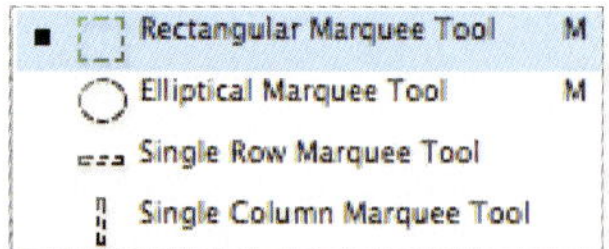

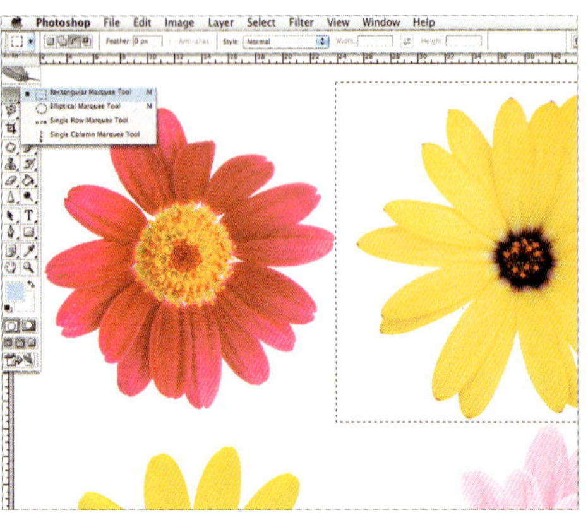

01 Marquee tools
This group of tools work by clicking and dragging to make the selection. There are a number of different options, which we will explore later.

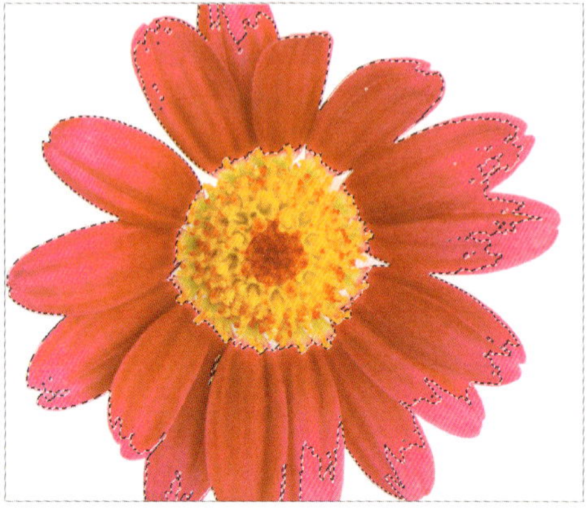

02 Magic Wand
Magic Wand automatically creates a selection for you. All you have to do is pick a colour, and the tool will select that, plus similar adjacent colours for you.

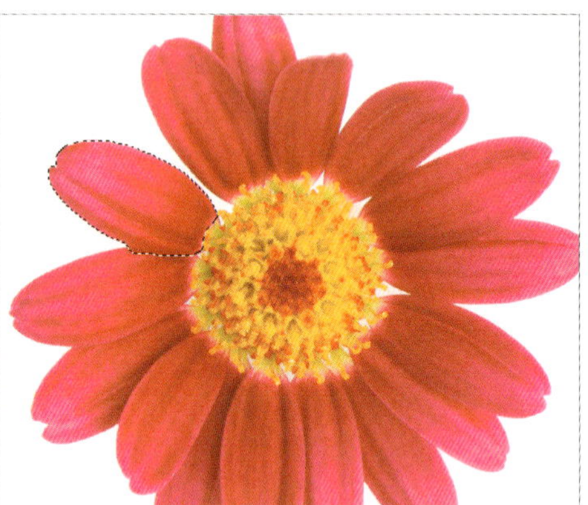

03 Quick Selection
With this tool you make selections by 'painting' the area you want to select. The tool automatically expands and finds defined edges of the image.

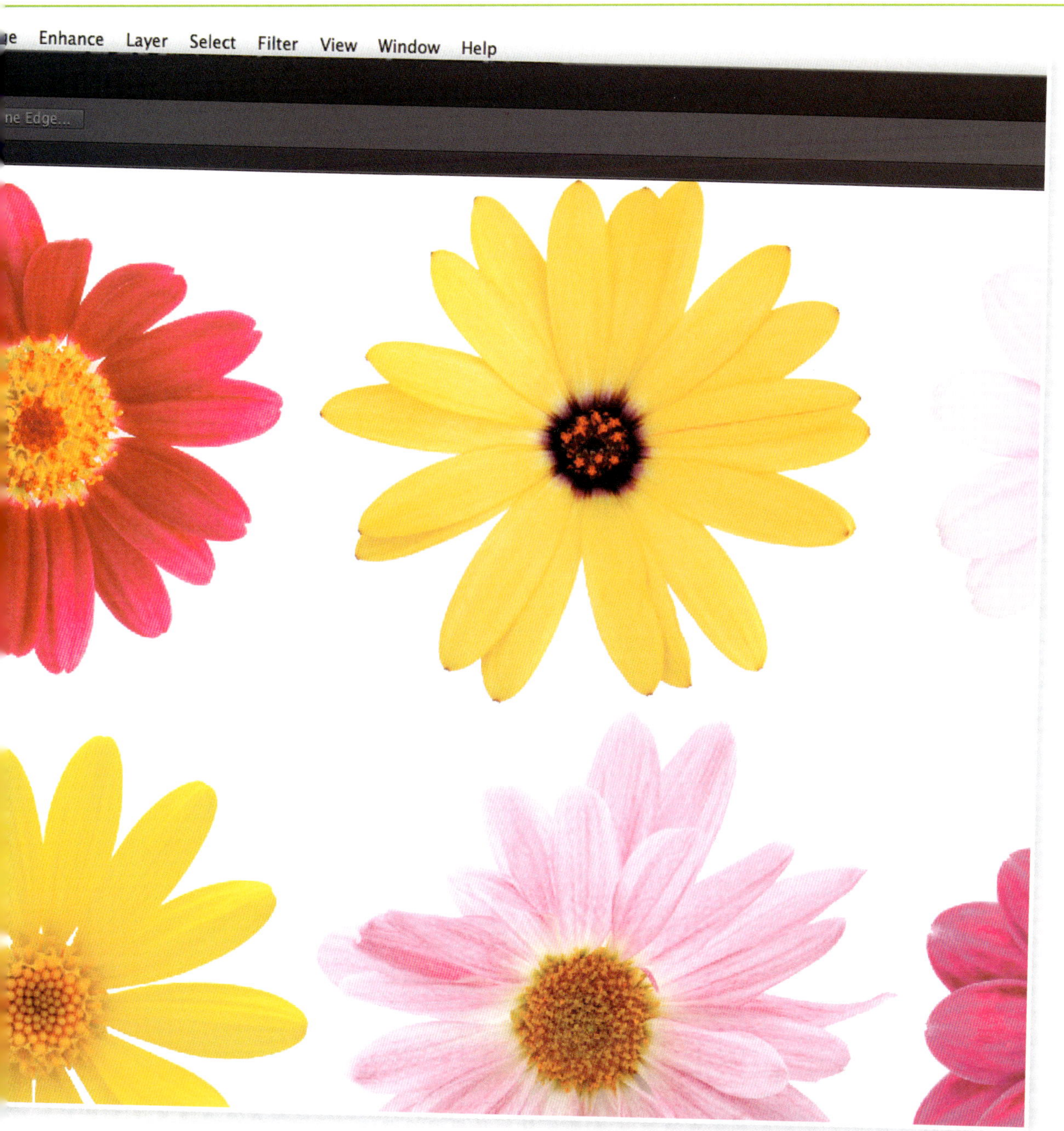

Lasso tool

The Lasso tool allows you to trace out areas to select using a click and drag method. Release your mouse button to create the selection borders. You can also hold down the Shift button to add to your selection. Or you can hold down Cmd/Ctrl and click and drag to deselect unwanted areas.

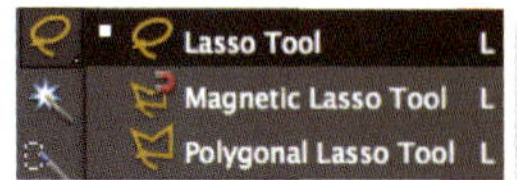

Polygonal Lasso

The Polygonal Lasso tool works best when creating selections with straight edges. Click on the start point (no need to hold the mouse button). Drag the tool to the next point, and click again. Continue until you get back to the start point – the pointer will have a little 'o' next to it. Click again to close the selection.

Magnetic Lasso

The Magnetic Lasso is a smart tool that 'senses' the edges of an object by its colour contrast. Click and drag (you don't have to hold down the mouse) around the portion you wish to select, and the lasso will automatically 'stick' to the shape. The pointer will have a little 'o' when you return to the start point. You can adjust the tool's sensitivity by tweaking its Width and Edge Contrast settings in the top menu bar.

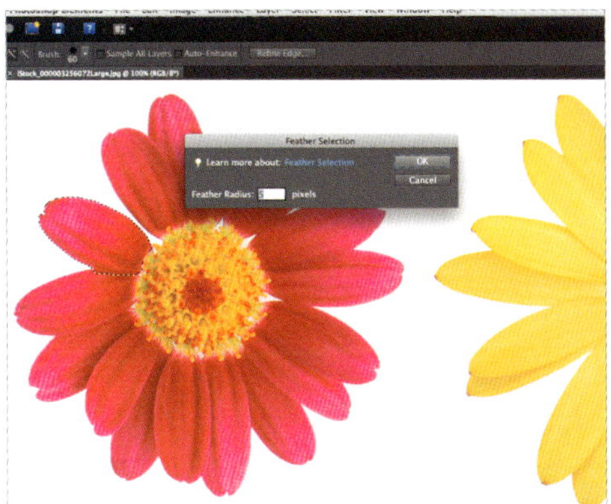

04 Selection options

Achieve a gradual transition between the inside and outside of a selection using feathering. Enter a value into the Feather box in the Options bar.

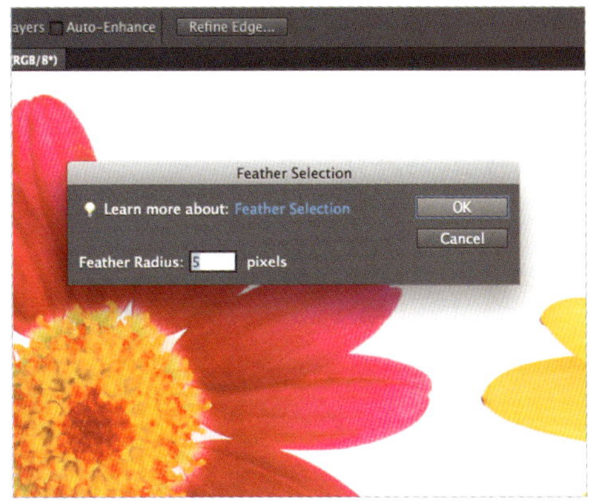

05 Feathering

This is measured in pixels, and the greater the value, the more subtle the transition between pixels and less obvious the harsh edge is.

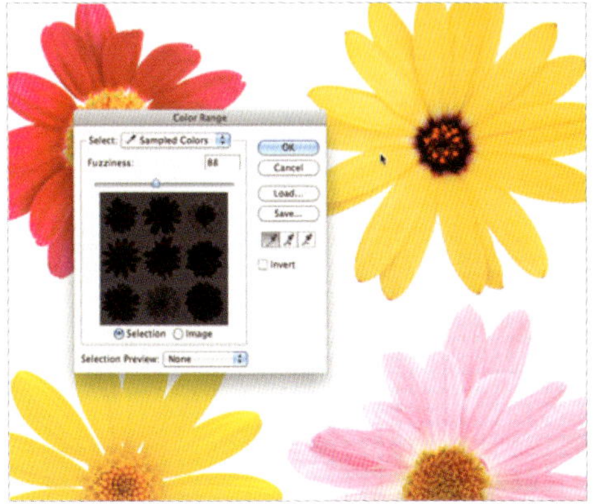

06 Color Range

Found in the Select menu (although not present in Elements) Color Range allows you to select a specific colour in an image.

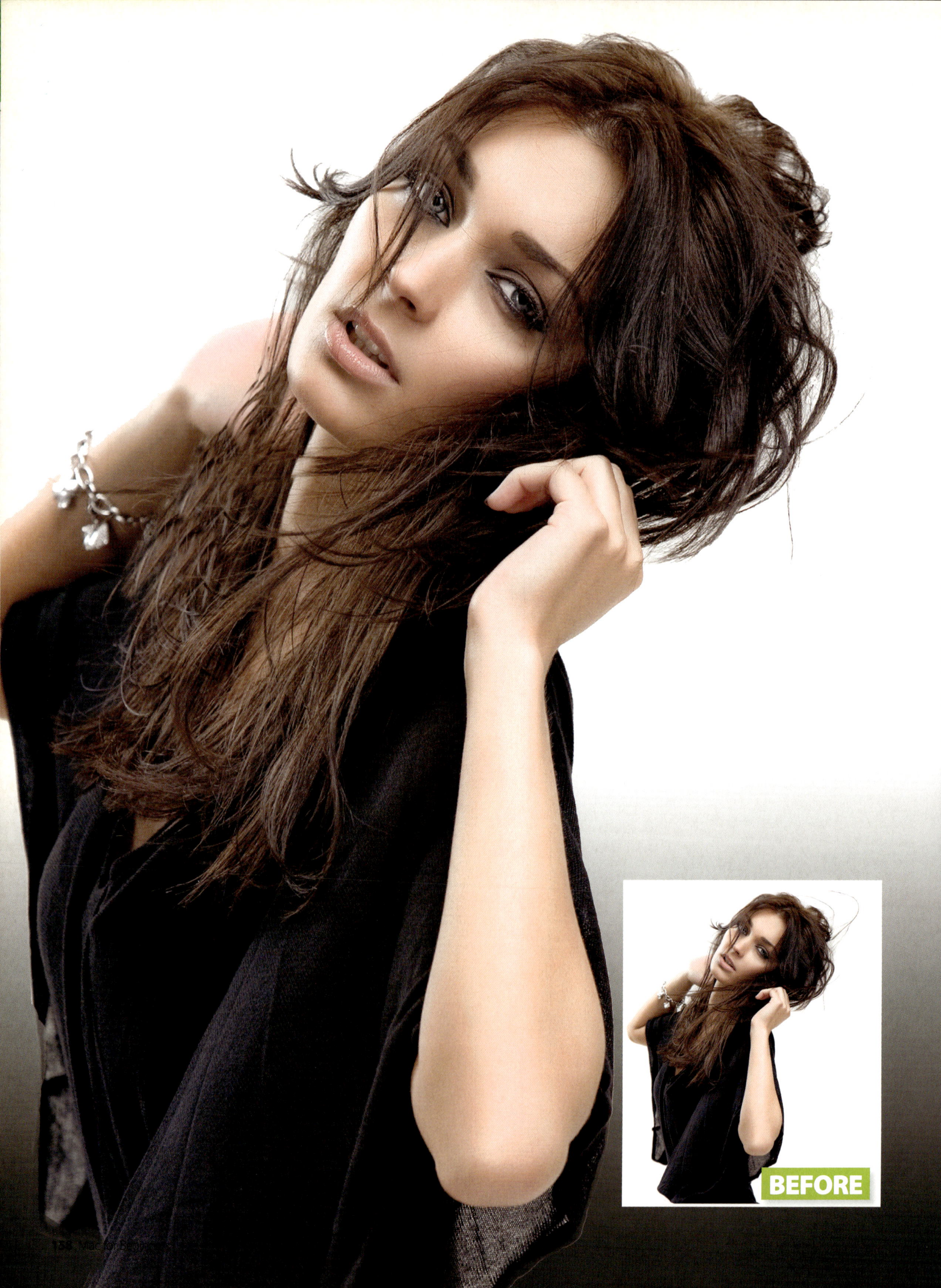
BEFORE

Making a magic selection

Discover how to the Magic Wand can make selections in a flash

The Magic Wand is the ideal tool when dealing with objects that have an irregular edge which is hard to manually select, or an image that has a lot of the same colours. It can either select the part of the image you want, or the area outside the part you want and the selection can be inverted. This quick fix tutorial will show you what effect options such as Tolerance, Anti-alias and Contiguous selection have on the process.

In the tutorial we take a look at how the Magic Wand can work even on images where there are a lot of similar colours, which is why we need to go into the fiddly settings in the main Options toolbar to get the most accurate selection. However, if you have an image with a perfectly definite background, then the Magic Wand can be a one-click tool. For example, in the main image (opposite), the model is very clearly defined against the white background. This means that when we select the Magic Wand tool, it will automatically select the background without any trouble. We can then hit Backspace to delete the background and input a brand new one.

This method opens up loads of creative options. You can create simple photo composites, or, as shown with the flower tutorial below, you can create a kind of 'out-of-bounds' effect, which makes the flower look as if it is jumping out of the frame. We have supplied the start flower image for you so that you can practise for yourselves.

"Ideal for dealing with objects that have an irregular edge"

QUICK PHOTOSHOP TIPS

Zoom in

If you are cutting out a selection it's worth zooming in to check the edges. If they are too rough it can either need smoothing, modifying or anti-aliasing, which feathers the edges. Click on the Refine Edge button to access the various options

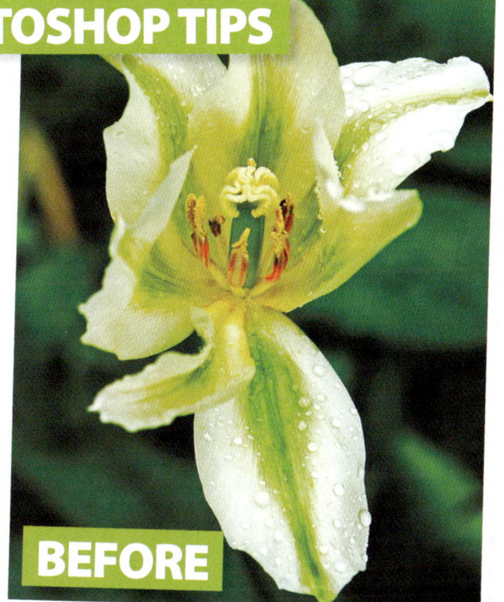

BEFORE

AFTER

Contiguous

The Contiguous setting means that it includes similar colours that are next to the ones selected. This is the setting we want for this image. because there are similar colours in the middle.

Precision advice

If areas that are not wanted become selected, hold Opt/Alt and click on them to deselect, then reduce the Tolerance. Go to Select> Modify>Smooth and enter a value of 1px to help smooth out any rough edges.

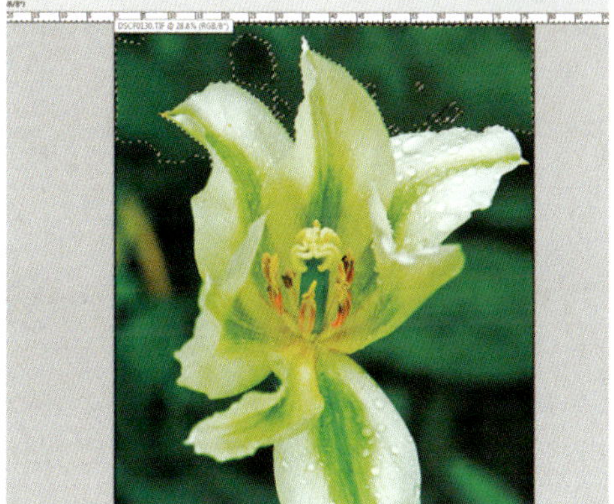

01 Set the Tolerance

Load the image and select the Magic Wand tool. It works by selecting areas of similar colour based on the Tolerance setting. Click outside the flower.

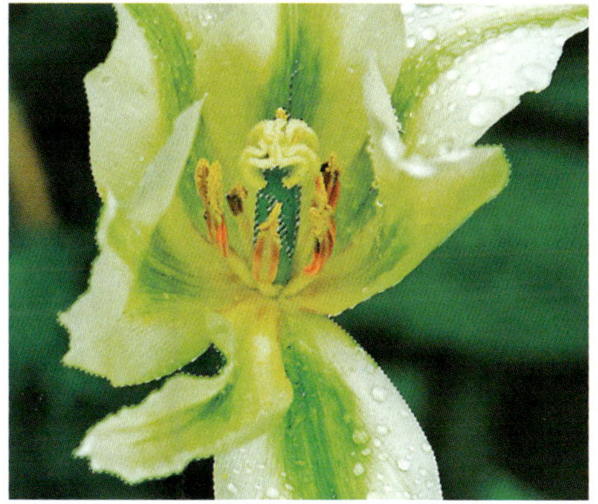

02 Contiguous colours

Tick the Contiguous box. If this is unticked, similar colours are select wherever they are. Hold down the Shift key and click in areas not selected yet.

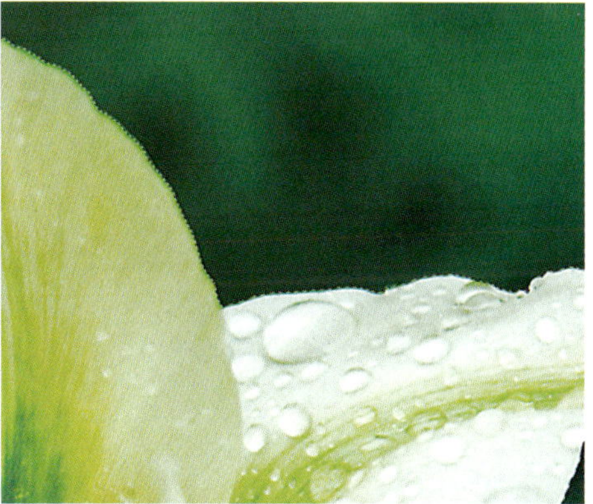

03 Zoom in

Until you zoom in to 100%, you won't see small areas that have been missed by the Magic Wand. Hold down Shift and click on these.

The Smart Brush tool in Elements

Photoshop Elements users have the power of quick selection and adjustment layers in this valuable tool

The Smart Brush tool's menu of presets is bursting with useful effects that can be added to your images at the click of a mouse. Located in the Full Edit area of the Elements interface, the Smart Brush tool's presets are arranged into groups to suit different images and different workflows. These include options for portraits, landscapes and black and white conversions. The tool works through a combination of adjustment layers and layer masks, and with each brushstroke the layer mask in the Layers palette changes.

The white area of the mask represents the parts of the image that the effect has been applied to and the black shows the sections of the photograph that have been protected from the preset. The original image is always safe as the effect is applied on a completely separate adjustment layer. As you are painting on an effect, think of the Smart Brush as you would the normal Brush tool and adjust the settings using the top Options bar. For example, when working on a more detailed area, it makes the job easier if the brush size is reduced.

When aiming for a subtle effect it is advisable to ensure the Hardness is low. We have summarised some of the presets but explore the full menu to see which best suit the types of images you are working on.

"The tool works through a combination of adjustment layers and layer masks"

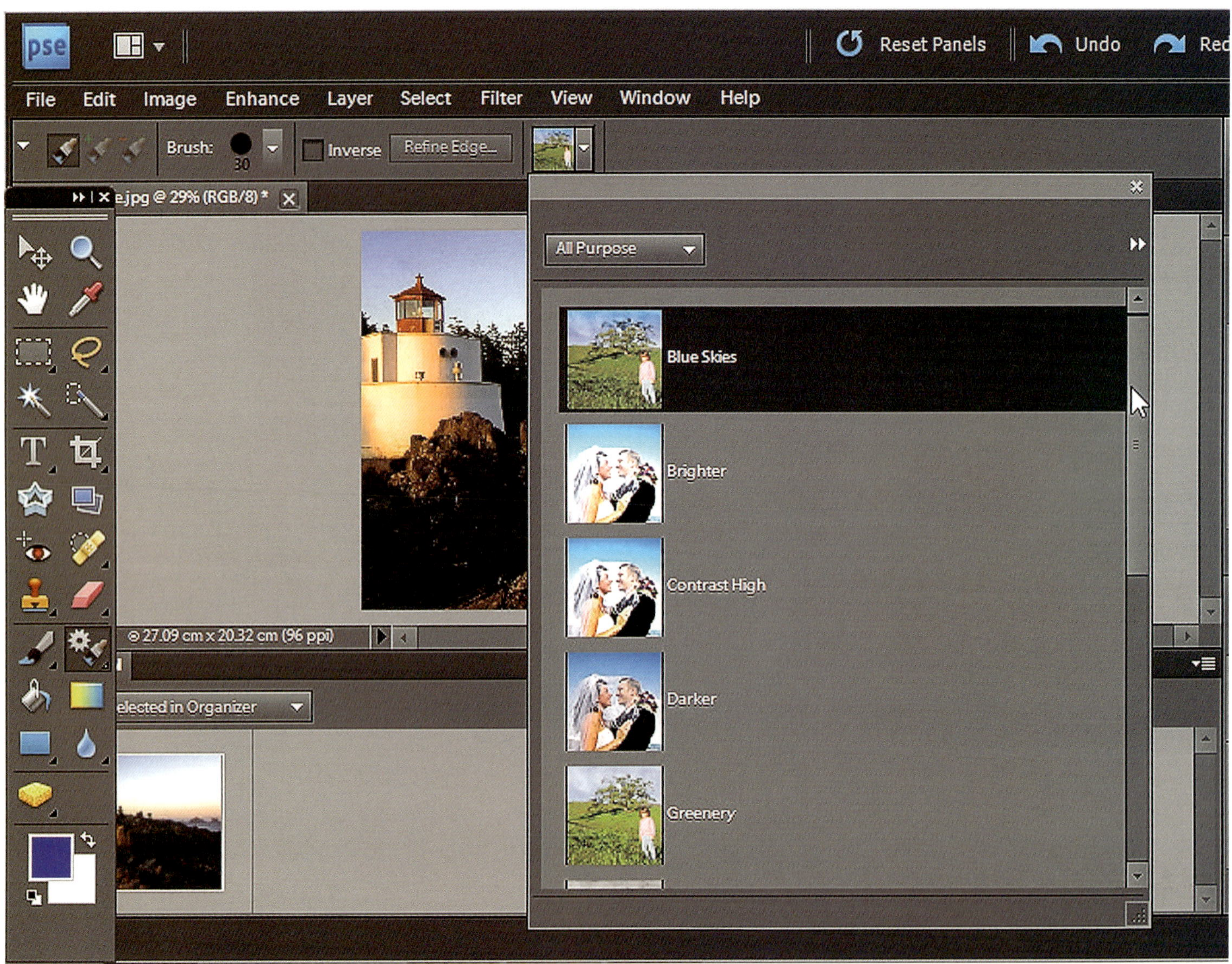

WORKING WITH SMART BRUSHES

Brush alteration

When using the Smart Brush tool you are painting an effect with a brush. Different types of brush are needed for different photos, therefore. To customise the tool in terms of size, hardness and spacing, click on the arrow beside Brush to open the Brush Picker. More options become available when the Detailed Smart Brush tool is being used.

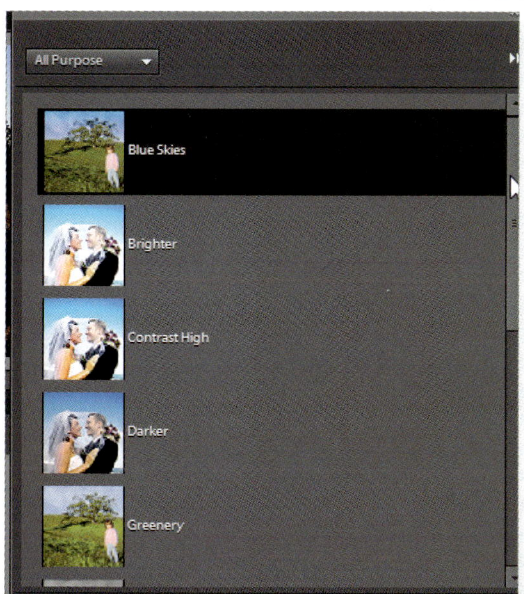

Preset perfection

Once either the Smart Brush or Detailed Smart Brush tool is chosen, the Presets button will appear in the top Options bar. Clicking on the arrow to the right presents a fly-out menu of different preset groups which each contain a selection of effects.

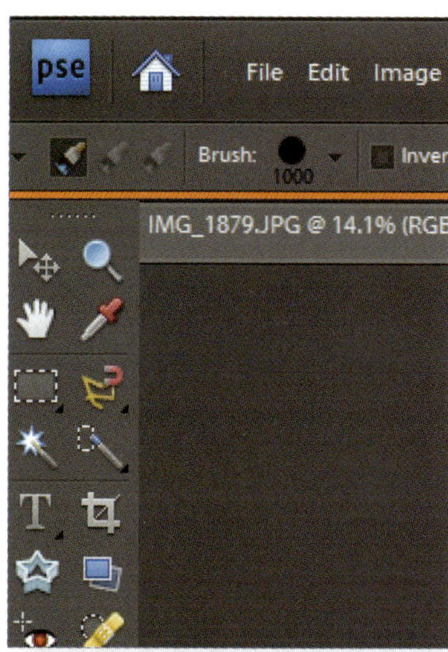

Snappy selections

The three tabs in the top left of the Options allow the type of selection to be chosen. Initially, New Selection will be chosen, but after the first brushstroke is made, this changes to Add to Selection. If you need to undo brushstrokes, select the Subtract From Selection option.

Use on filters

If the edge of the area that has been painted over needs to be adjusted, click Refine Edge. Now, by adjusting the settings in the dialog box that appears, it is possible to smooth the edge of the selection, contract it, expand it or feather it to make it softer.

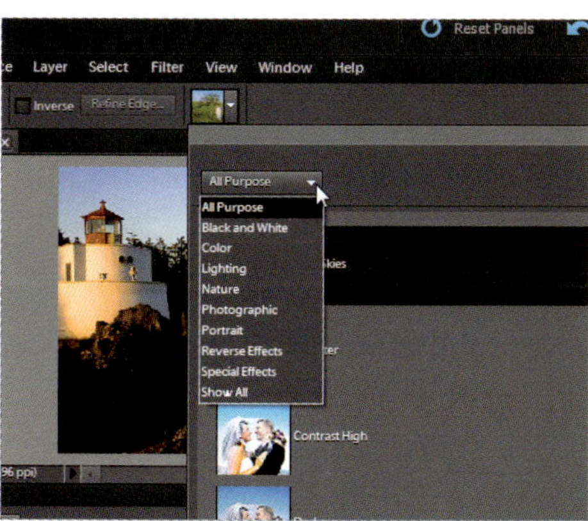

01 Find a preset brush

There are loads of different Smart Brushes available, and you can filter these using this drop-down menu at the top into different categories.

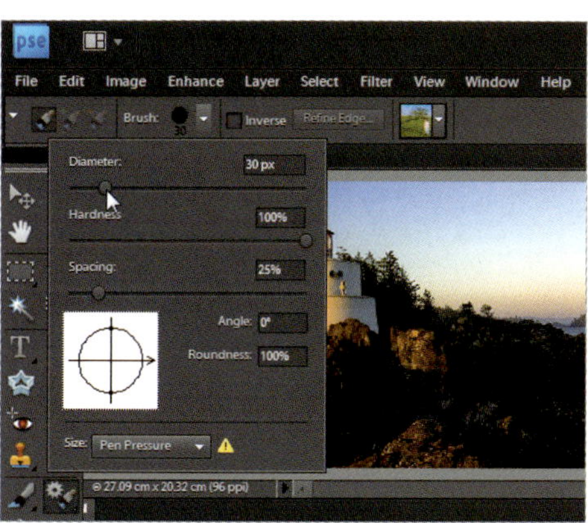

02 Set the brush

Select the brush that you want to use and how soft or hard you want it to be. Start painting over the area you want to select and adjust.

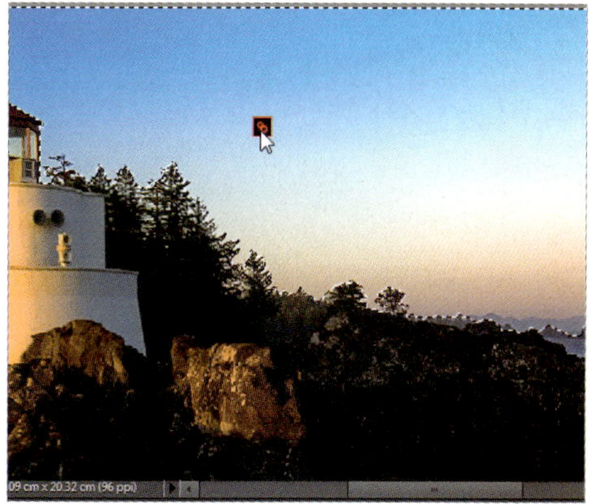

03 Selection made

Your selected area will be automatically altered, but you are left with the marching ants. You can click on the red icon to activate the selection at any time.

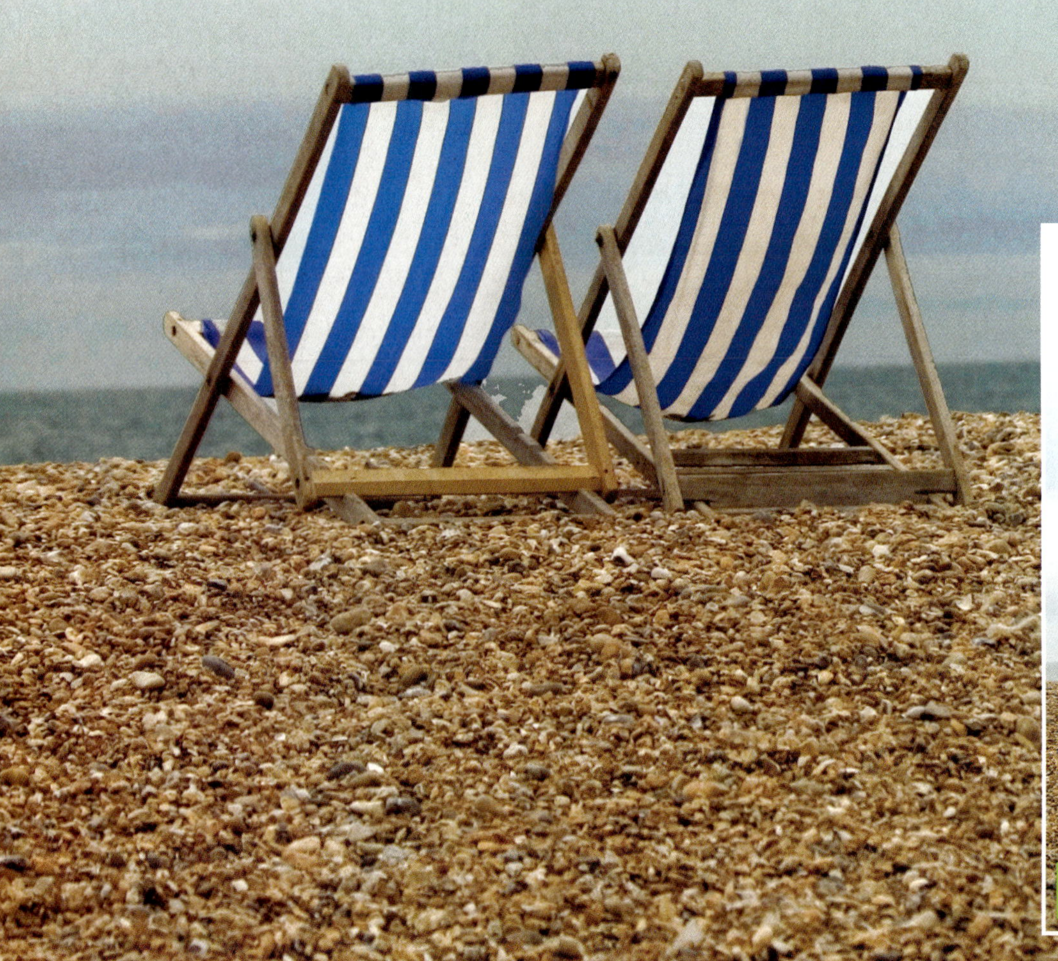

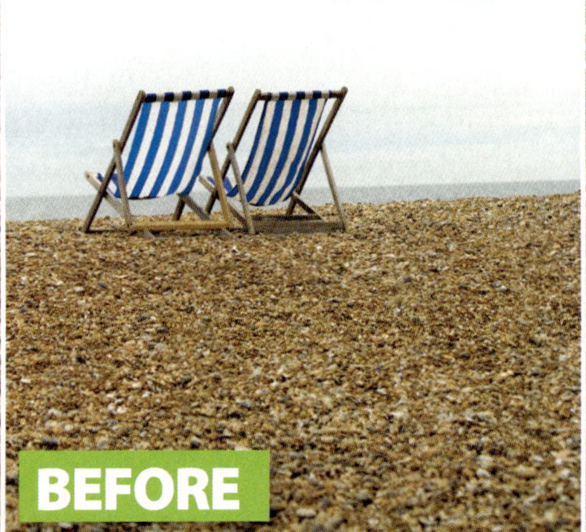
BEFORE

Select and enhance skies

Use the Blue Skies Smart Brush in Photoshop Elements

There are so many presets for the Smart Brush tool that it is hard to pick just one to look at in more detail. We have gone for the Blue Skies preset, as it is one of the most common fixes that people want to make. You might have a lovely composition and a perfectly exposed subject, but the sky is just a wash of grey. This simple tool eradicates that in seconds, and it does it in a very clever way too.

Smart Brushes are definitely smart, as they use a complex combination of adjustment layers and masks. We cover this in more detail on page 131 onwards, but essentially an adjustment layer is a layer that applies an effect over an image but not affecting the original image itself. The mask then isolates just the parts that need the adjustment to be made to. In our case, we only want the sky to go bluer.

To do this, we select the Blue Skies preset from the Smart Brush options. Now you can set a brush to paint the selection on with. It's best to go for a softer brush that will help the new sky blend in, and one that is quite large. The Smart Brush looks for areas of similar colour, so it makes an intelligent selection of just the sky area. Now you can paint over the area and your selection and adjustment will be made.

"You might have a lovely composition, but the sky is just a wash of grey"

SMART SELECTIONS

Active selection

Once you have applied a Smart Brush, your selection remains active just as if you had used a selection tool.

Red icon

This little icon denotes that a selection has been made. Even if you deselect the area, this icon remains, and you can click it to reactivate the selection at any time.

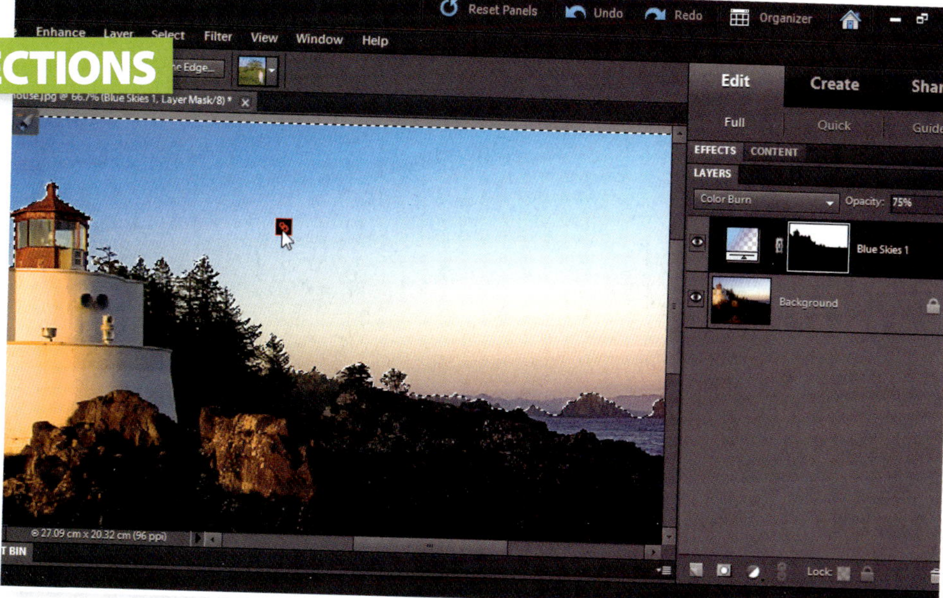

Layer and mask

Essentially a Smart Brush adds an a adjustment layer, which is nondestructive, meaning that the original image is still intact. The selection area is then masked so that nothing else is affected by the adjustment.

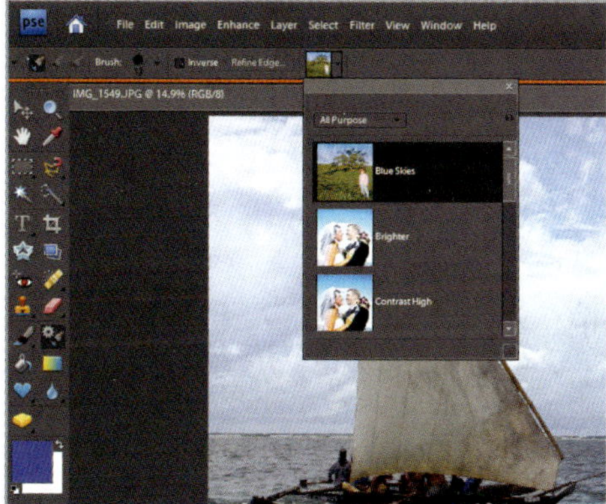

01 Select a preset

Select the Blue Skies preset from either the All Purpose, Nature or Show All groups by clicking on the top-right arrow of the Options bar.

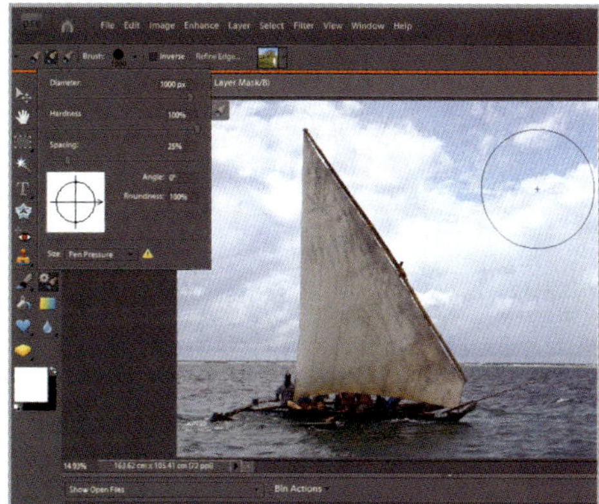

02 Customise the brush

Adjust the size of the brush to suit the image you are painting the effect onto. Click the arrow beside Brush and reduce the Hardness slider.

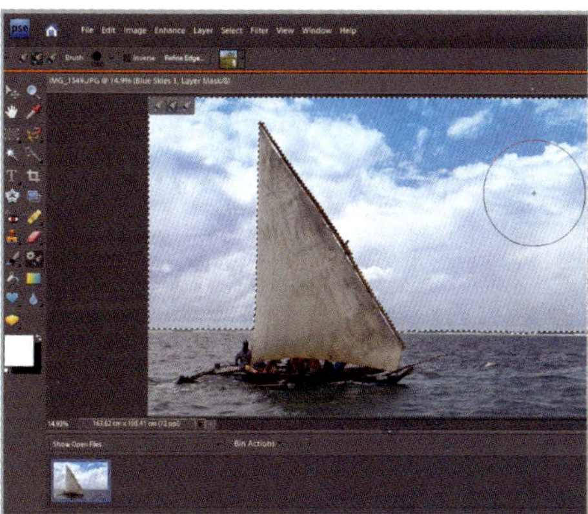

03 Paint the drab sky blue

The Smart Brush works in a similar way to the Quick Selection tool, so by roughly painting over the sky, the effect will work to the sea.

The Smart Brush options

Now you know what the Smart Brushes do, find out here how you can tweak them to suit your images

The Smart Brush tool does a pretty good job of things on its own, but it is not fixed. There are still a number of edits that you can make to ensure that your selections are pixel perfect.

For example, the brush that you choose to use makes a huge difference on your selection areas. If you use a soft, large brush you can cover large areas quickly but with no harsh edges, perfect for skies. If you are playing with fiddlier blemishes when retouching, then you can use a small hard brush to target the area very accurately.

Once you have done this, Elements will create a selection for you on the area that you want to select. However, you may have a number of areas that are not connected but need the same adjustment. You can use the tools at the top of the interface to add to the current selection, meaning you can target multiple areas in one go. You can also delete from the selection too, if Elements has included things that you don't want touched.

When the selection is almost right, then you can use the Refine Edge options to add a feather so that the selection adjustments will blend in better with the photo, so that the retouching is not obvious. Here we take a look at some top tips for when using Smart Brushes.

"There are still edits that you can make to ensure that your selections are pixel perfect"

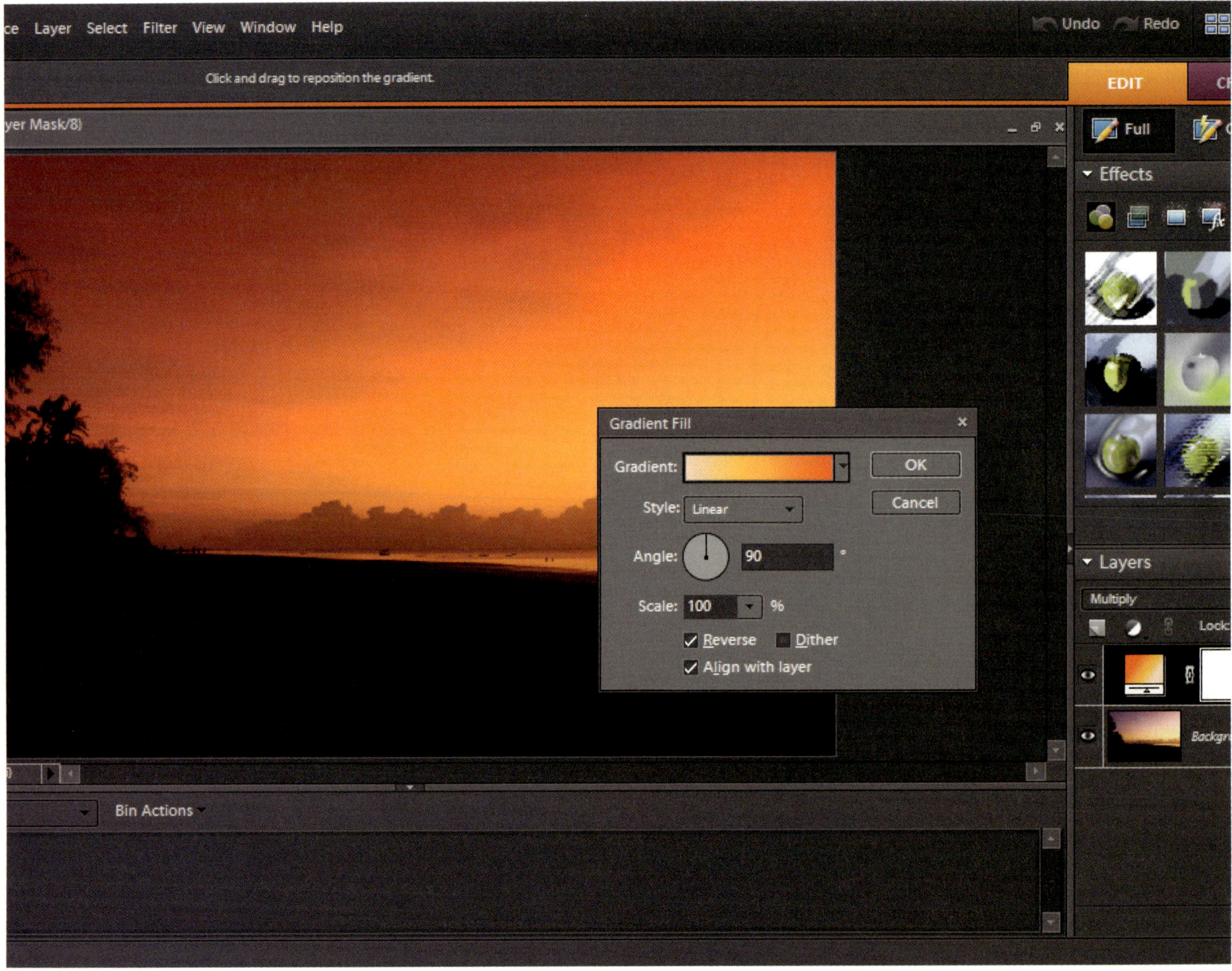

QUICK PHOTOSHOP TIPS

Adjust your tool options

The type of image you are working on has an impact on the settings that you should choose for the Smart Brush tool. In the Options bar, once you have selected the Smart Brush, there are different ways you can adjust the way it is used. For example, it is advisable to use a smaller size of brush when working on more detailed areas.

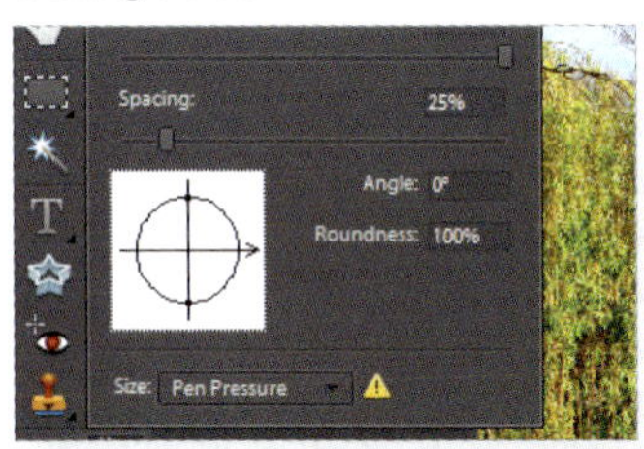

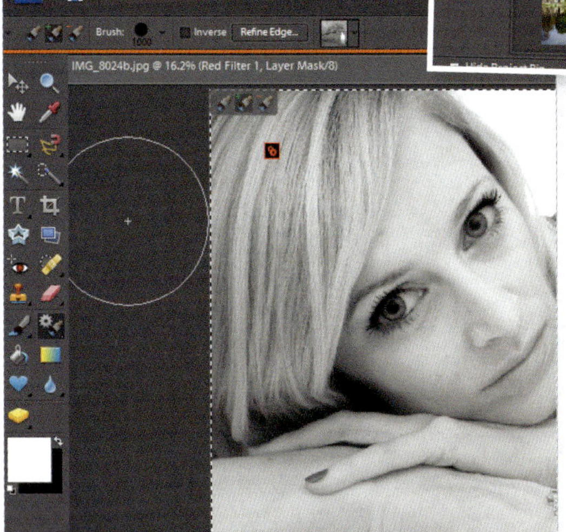

Getting smart

One of the most convenient preset groups is black and white, which allows users to opt for different types of effect from Cold Tone through to High Contrast Red Filter. However, an equally useful black and white preset – Reverse Black and White – can be found in the Reverse Effects set. This enables areas of an image to be painted over to remain in colour while the rest is desaturated to make elements stand out.

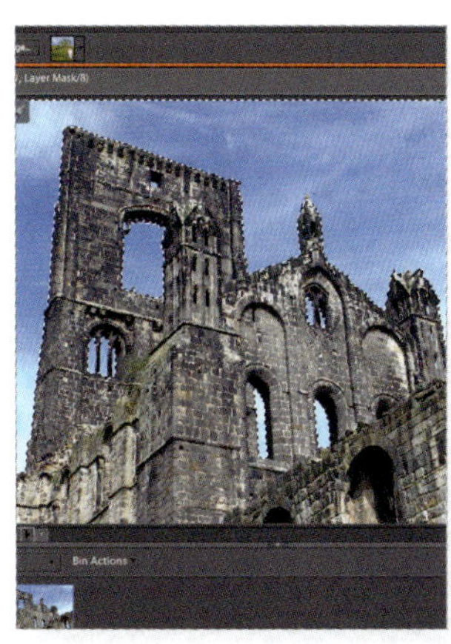

Selection skills

In the top left there are three different brush options for making selections with the Smart Brush tool. Clicking the 'New selection' option allows you to paint on the photo to make a selection which your effect will be applied to. If you have already painted with the Smart Brush and want to add the effect to more areas of an image, use the 'Add to selection option'.

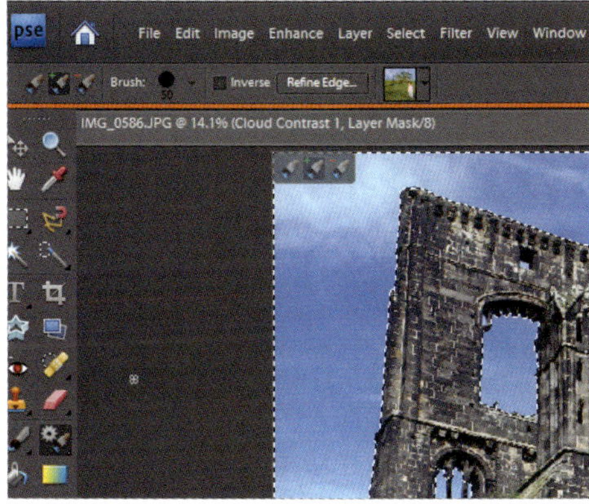

01 Refine Edge

Once a selection has been made you can make it more accurate by clicking on the refine Edge button at the top of the interface.

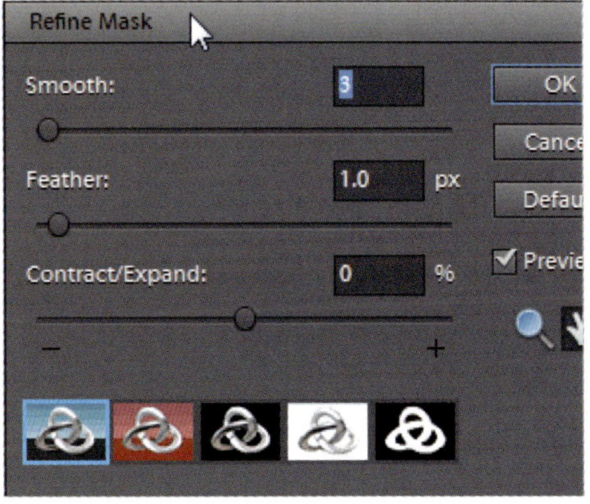

02 Settings

Now you can smooth the selection or feather it so that the selection blends more effectively into the rest of the scene.

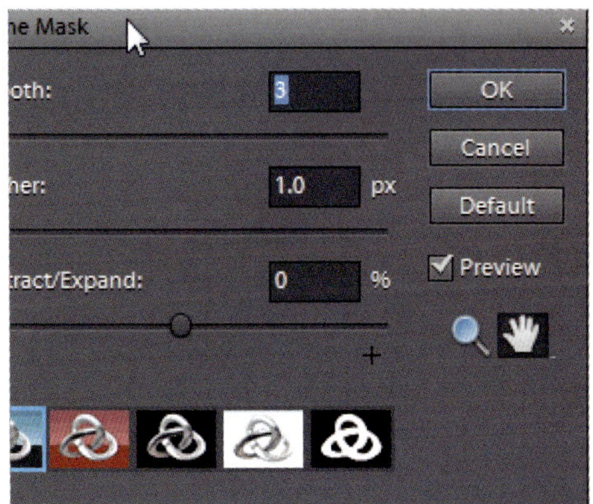

03 Apply

Use the Preview text box to check your selection and when you are happy, just click on OK to return to the main interface.

Marquee tool masterclass

Use the Marquee tools to give your images an exciting new look and lease of life

The Marquee tools are a group of basic shapes used to make a selection. They are very simple to use but have endless possibilities. The Magic Wand or the Quick Selection tools quickly introduce marching ants around a subject, whereas the Marquee tools have transformable dimensions, which can be a set size, perfectly round or a row of pixels, depending on the intended use.

Not only that, but essentially being a selection, a marquee can have a layer mask attached to it and even a touch of feathering around its edges to soften its effects. Or it can be mixed in with a stew of marquee selections to create interesting and varied shapes.

There are four Marquee Selection tools in all, starting with the Rectangular Marquee and followed by the Elliptical, Single Row and Column tools. They are all represented on your image as dotted lines and can be used to cut out an area, revealing the layer underneath. They are like ordinary shapes but with no fill colour, so you can customise their contents with whatever you like, for example an adjustment or filter.

Have a read through of this dedicated guide to understand the difference between the Marquee tools and what they can offer the creative Photoshop user. There is lots of fun to be had with a little experimentation so let's get started!

> "There is lots of fun to be had with a little experimentation"

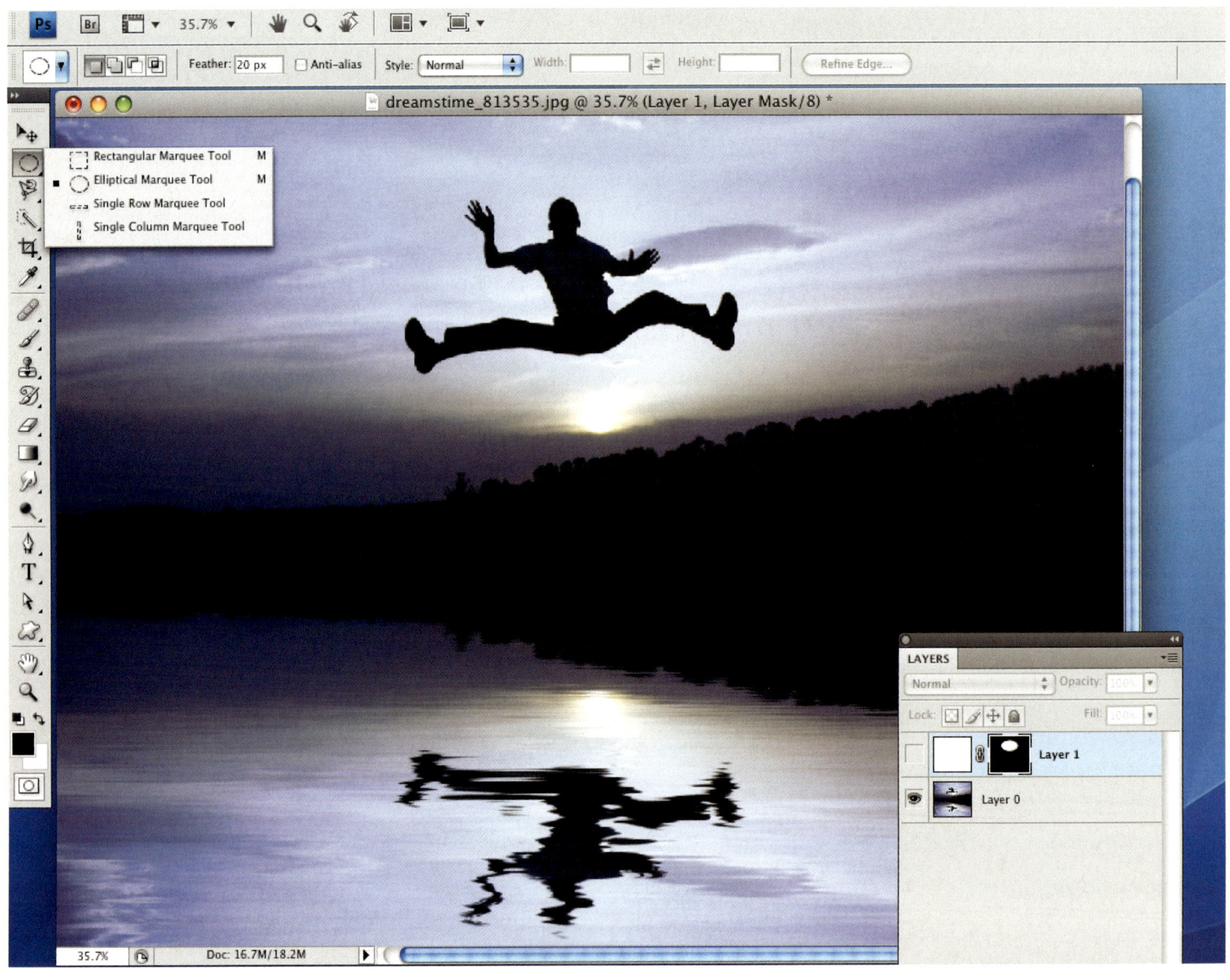

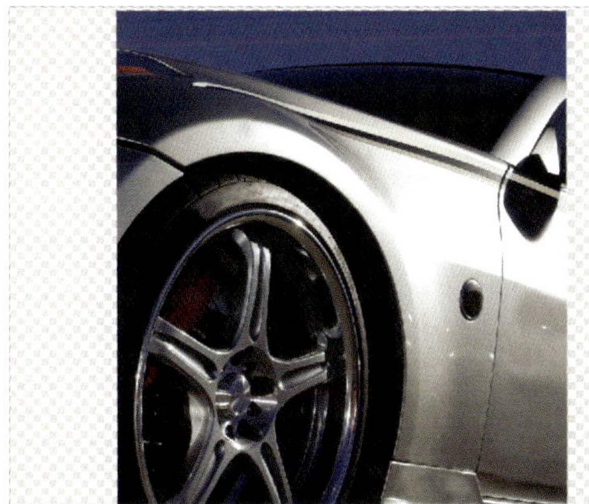

01 A rectangular window

Draw a rectangular border with this, and you can soften its edges, bend its shape or even make it a mask on a layer.

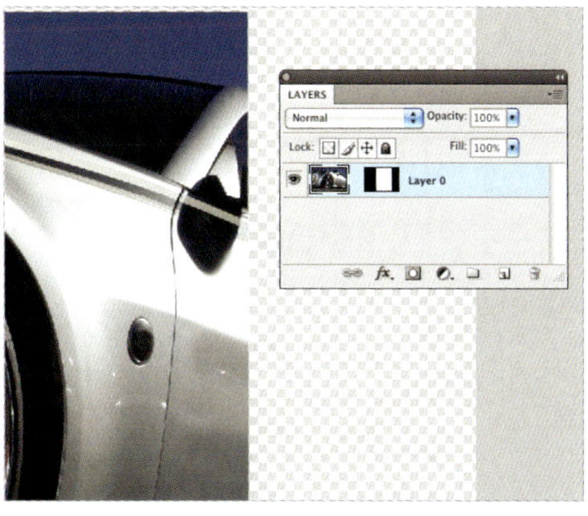

02 Add a mask

To combine a layer mask with the Rectangular Marquee tool, draw your rectangle on an editable layer and click the Add Layer Mask button.

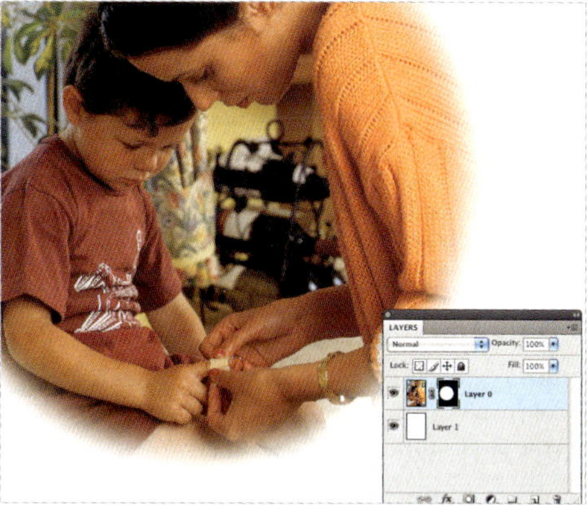

03 Carefully frame an image

On a new layer at the bottom of the layer stack, go to Edit>Fill and choose White. Select the Elliptical Marquee tool with a 50px Feather.

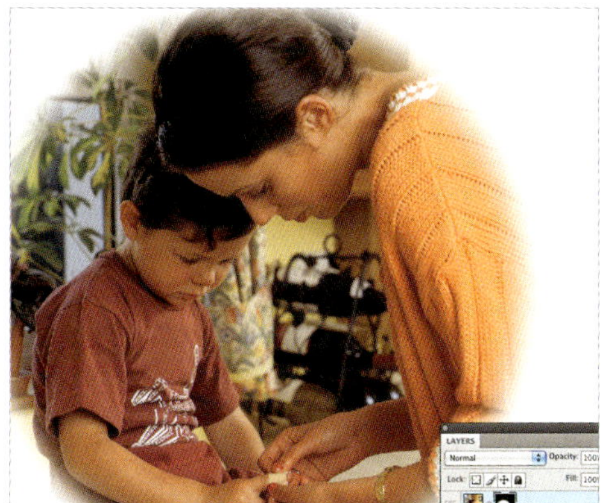

04 Make the mask

Hold the Shift+Opt/Alt keys to draw a perfect circle over the subject in your image. Select the original layer and click on the Add Layer Mask button.

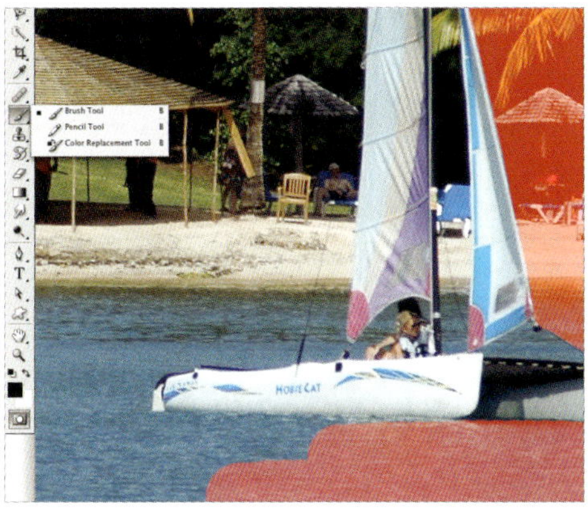

05 Quick Mask mode

Press Q with the selection active. A red opaque layer coats everything outside the selection. With the Eraser and Brush tools, paint or remove this.

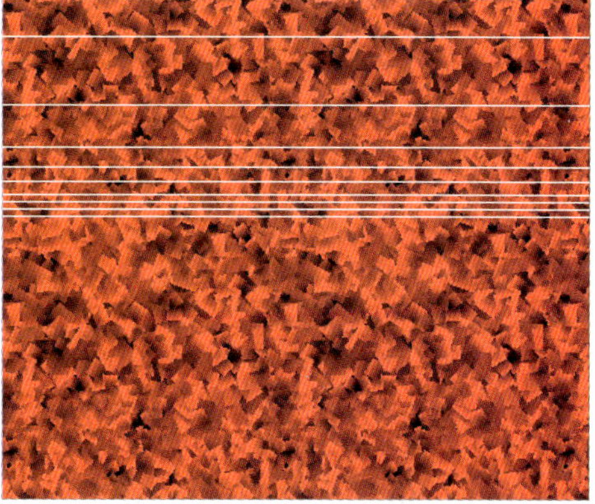

06 Selecting pixels

In the Marquee set of tools there are the Single Row and Single Column tools. With one selected, click anywhere on your image to apply a selection.

Make a stroke

Use the Marquee tools in order to make a stroke

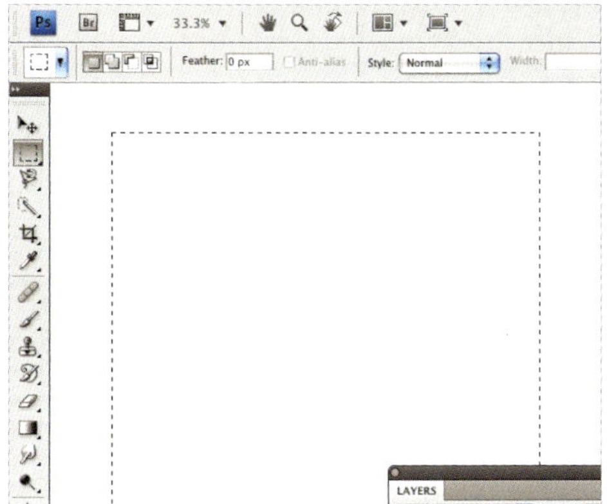

01 Pick your tool

Choose one of the Marquee tools and draw the shape. So that the stroke doesn't affect the image underneath, create a new layer.

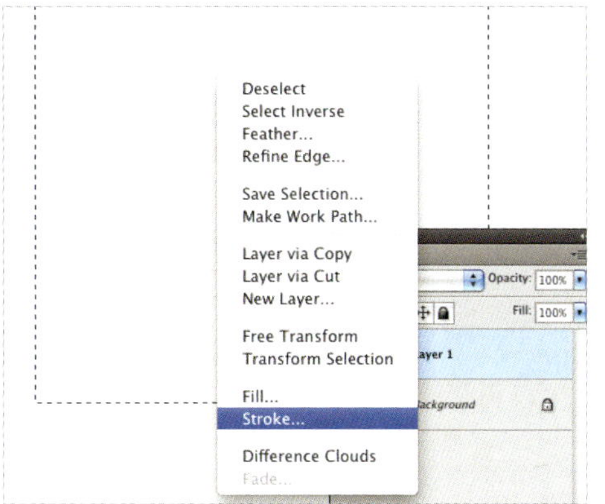

02 Stroke options

Ctrl/right-click inside the selection to open a list of editing options. Select the Stroke option, and a separate dialog window should pop open.

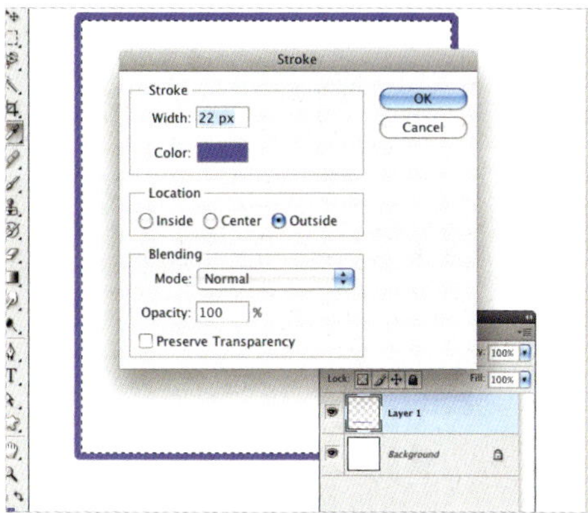

03 Set up the stroke

Work your way through the menu, setting up Width, Color, Location and Blending. The stroke can be placed inside, central or outside the marquee.

Understanding Quick Mask

Discover this versatile tool, which is great for making selections easily and quickly – hence the name!

The Quick Mask mode is one of the most versatile tools you are likely to find within Photoshop's expansive toolbox. Its primary use is for isolating areas that you want left untouched by any adjustments or tweaks, and it is easy to get to grips with.

Quick Mask mode has been around since Photoshop 6.0 and offers a fantastic alternative to the traditional Selection tools. If you find yourself more partial to using the Paintbrush rather than the fiddly Pen tool, then this could well become your ideal selection method.

The Quick Mask mode is activated by clicking on the square icon that contains a white circle. This is situated at the bottom of the Toolbar alongside the Standard mode (a white box with a white circle). For instant access, you can simply hit the letter 'Q' on your keyboard and Quick Mask mode activates or deactivates.

This is a fantastic feature to help in the creation of a whole host of effects. Use it to create quick and easy vignettes for your portraits, paint a Quick Mask on specific colours to achieve amazing selective colouring results, or simply use it to protect an area from an image adjustment you're about to perform.

If you've never used this feature before, we're certain it will be in constant use from this day forward!

"Use it to create quick and easy vignettes for your portraits or achieve amazing selective colouring results"

QUICK PHOTOSHOP TIPS

Dialog

Hit Match Color and this box appears. Use the drop-down Source menu to select your source image. Ensure Preview is checked to see the change, and use the Luminance, Color Intensity and Fade sliders to adjust.

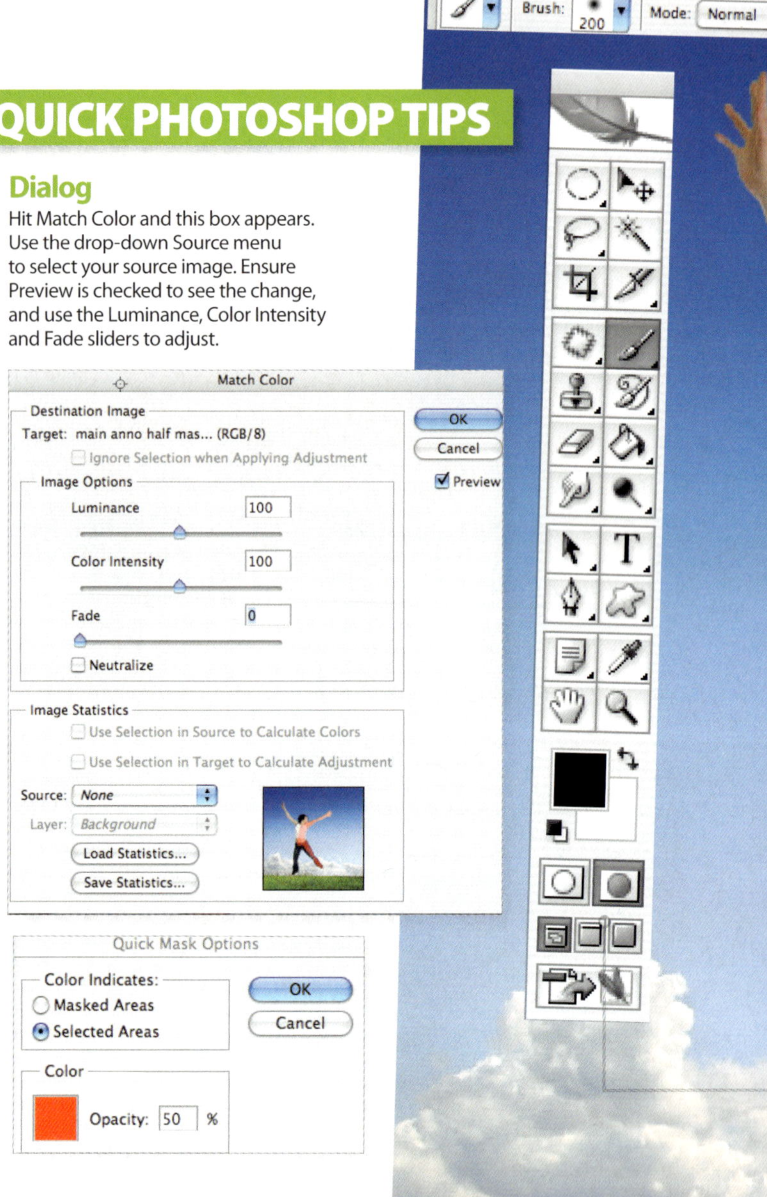

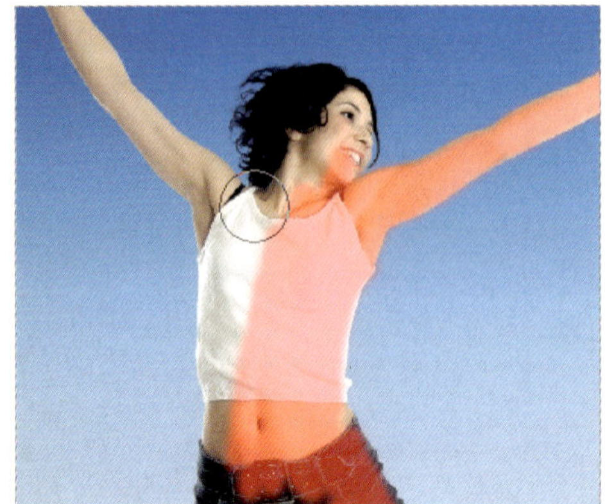

01 Quick Mask

The Quick Mask mode is a fantastic way to select objects or people within a scene. It's not as fiddly as the Pen tool and is easily erased..

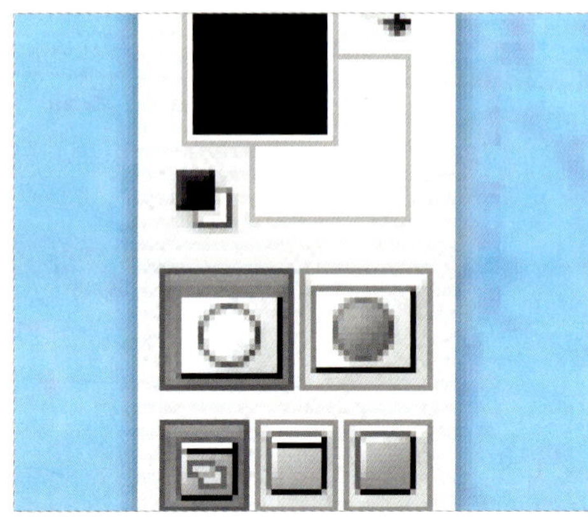

02 Activate

Open up an image in Photoshop and hit 'Q' to select the Quick Mask mode. You can also activate it by choosing the grey box with a white circle.

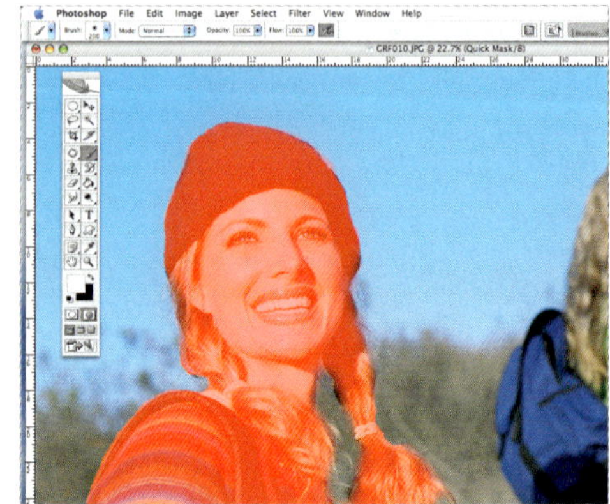

03 Brush it on

Select the Brush tool and choose a suitable size. Paint over everything you don't need, using the Eraser if you make any mistakes.

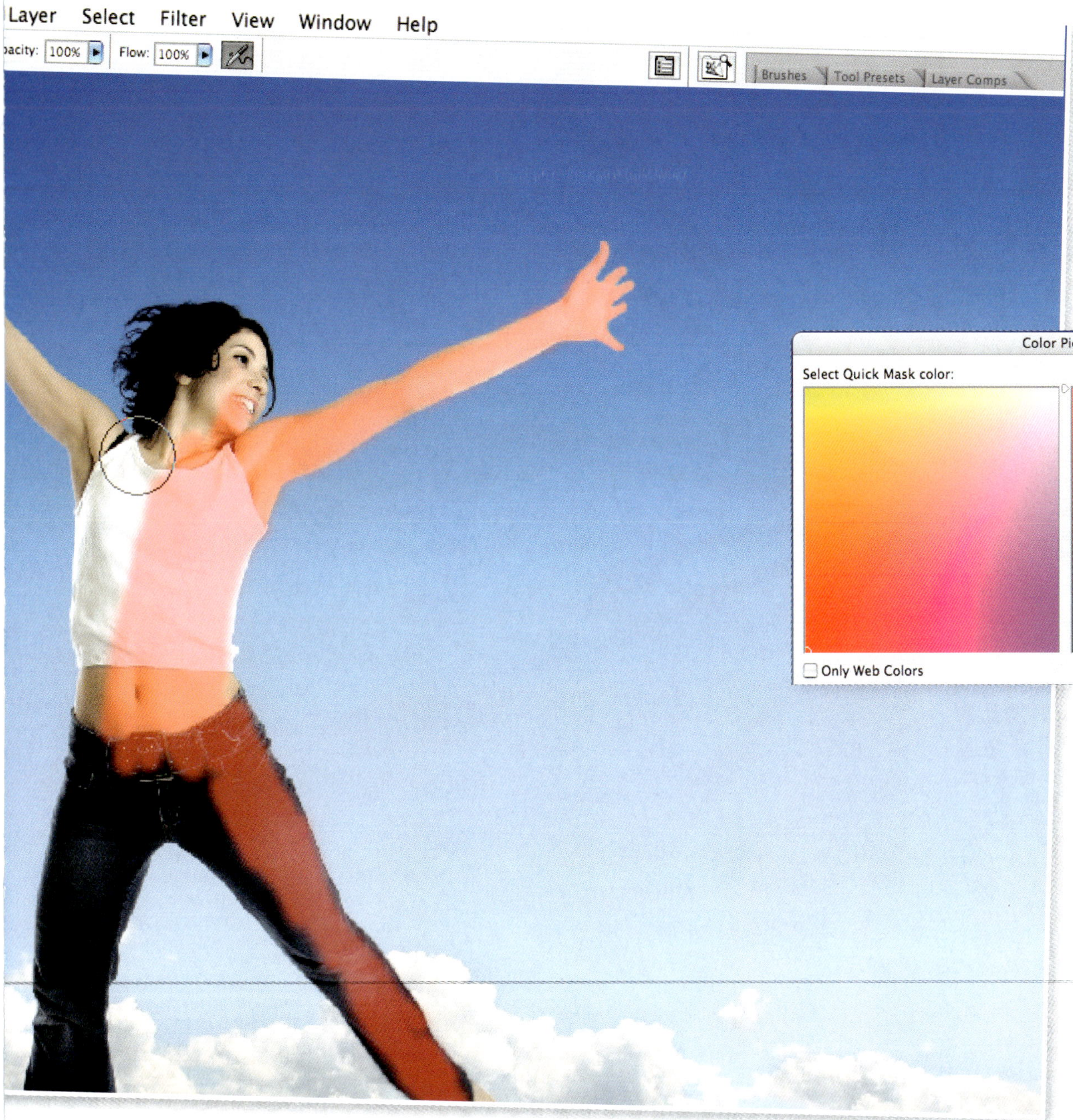

Colour your mask

If the colour of your mask is too similar to the colours within your image, double-click on the Quick Mask icon. Now click on the Color swatch and select a colour. You can adjust the opacity here as well.

Get control with brushes

You can use any brush to apply a Quick Mask. We recommend you use a soft brush for details such as hair and fur – this will give you a softer, more subtle selection.

Settings

To reverse the way the mask operates, just double-click on the Quick Mask icon and select Masked Areas (masked areas are black) or Selected Areas (masked areas are white).

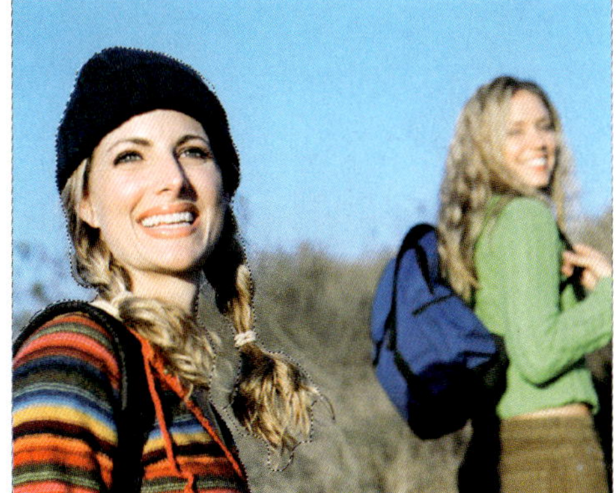

04 Enjoy

Deactivate the Quick Mask by hitting 'Q'. You'll have an isolated selection highlighted by marching ants. You are now free to do anything you like with this!

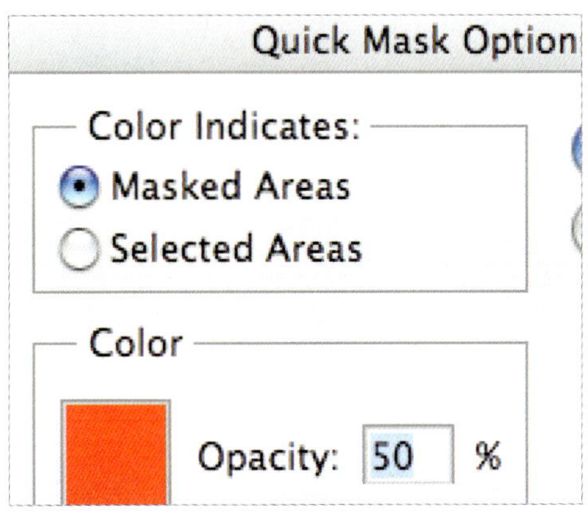

05 Colour change

The colour of the mask can often be hard to see. Double-click on the Quick Mask icon and a dialog box will appear. Choose a mask colour here.

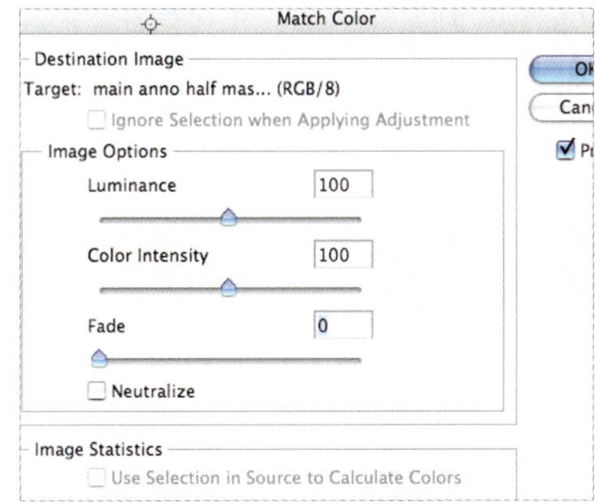

06 Match Color

The Match Color tool is found in Image>Adjustments>Match Color. Ensure that both your images are open in Photoshop first.

Refine Edge in Photoshop CS5

Complex selections are suddenly a lot easier to manage with this essential addition to Photoshop

Refine Edge is a fantastic little tool to play with in Photoshop. It means that even complete beginners can cut out complex objects, like hair and trees perfectly, with little hassle.

You can easily create a simple, rough selection around the subject that you want to cut out, and then use Refine Edge to perfect it. There are loads of options to play with, but controls like Smart Radius and Decontaminate Colors mean that Photoshop can do most of the hard work for you.

As well as being far more intelligent than previous versions, Refine Edge now gives you a choice of output destinations once you've perfected the selection. One of the most useful is New Layer With Layer Mask, because this gives you a super-accurate layer mask based on your selection that you can continue to work with manually as needed. You can also choose to output to a new layer with transparency, or even a completely new document.

Another way you can use the Refine Edge command is directly on an existing mask via the Masks panel. In this form you'll find the Refine Edge technology labelled as Mask Edge, and you'll find all the same powerful controls at your fingertips. Our short tutorial will get you started.

"Refine Edge is a fantastic little tool… even complete beginners can cut out complex objects like hair and trees perfectly"

USING REFINE EDGE

Smarter edges

The results of this new Edge Detection technology are truly remarkable, but to realise just how much difference it makes it's useful to see a direct comparison between the mask generated by the initial rough selection we made (left), and the mask itself after applying the new features of the Refine Edge command (right). You can see the before and after masks below, and easily see the level of hair detail you can achieve with just a couple of clicks.

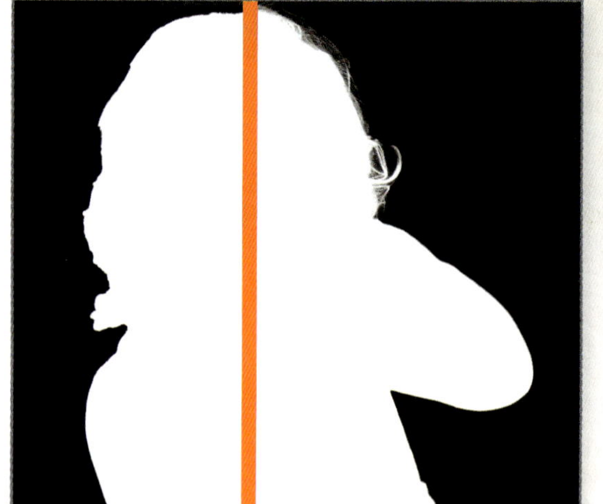

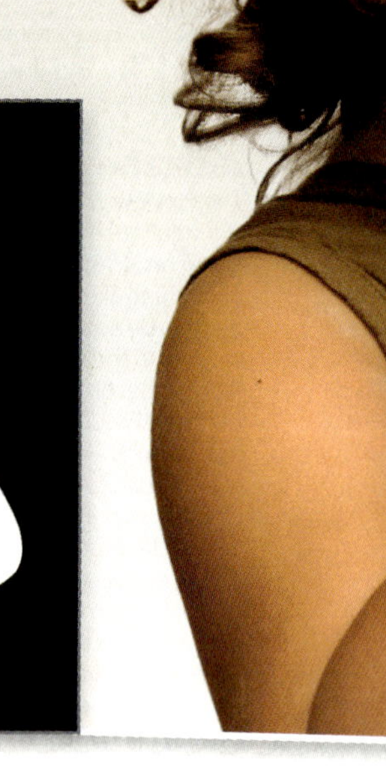

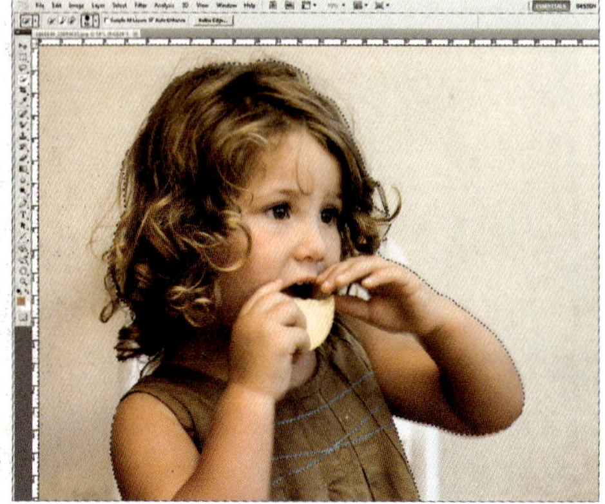

01 A quick selection

First make a rough selection of the subject. Thanks to the new technology, this selection doesn't have to be that accurate.

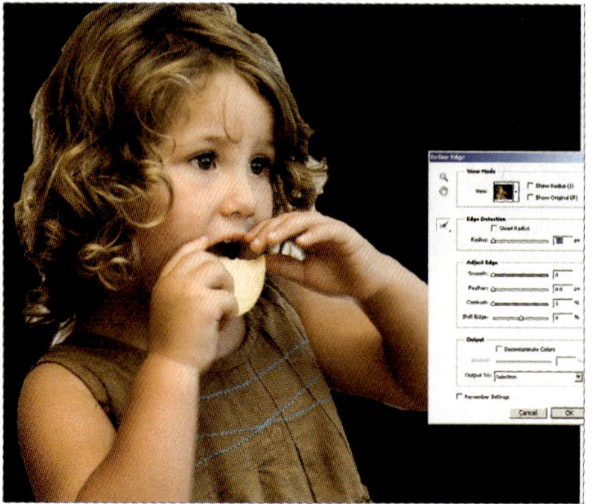

02 Invoke Refine Edge

Hit the Refine Edge button if your Selection tool is still active, or otherwise go to Select>Refine Edge. The Refine Edge dialog appears.

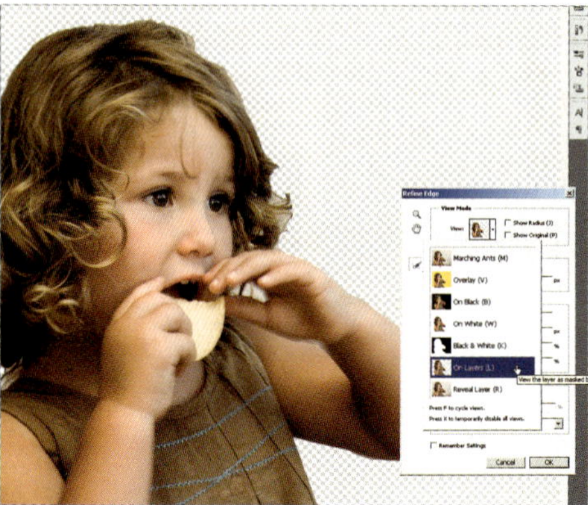

03 View modes

In the Refine Edge dialog you can pick one of many View mode. These help you to judge the quality of your hair mask.

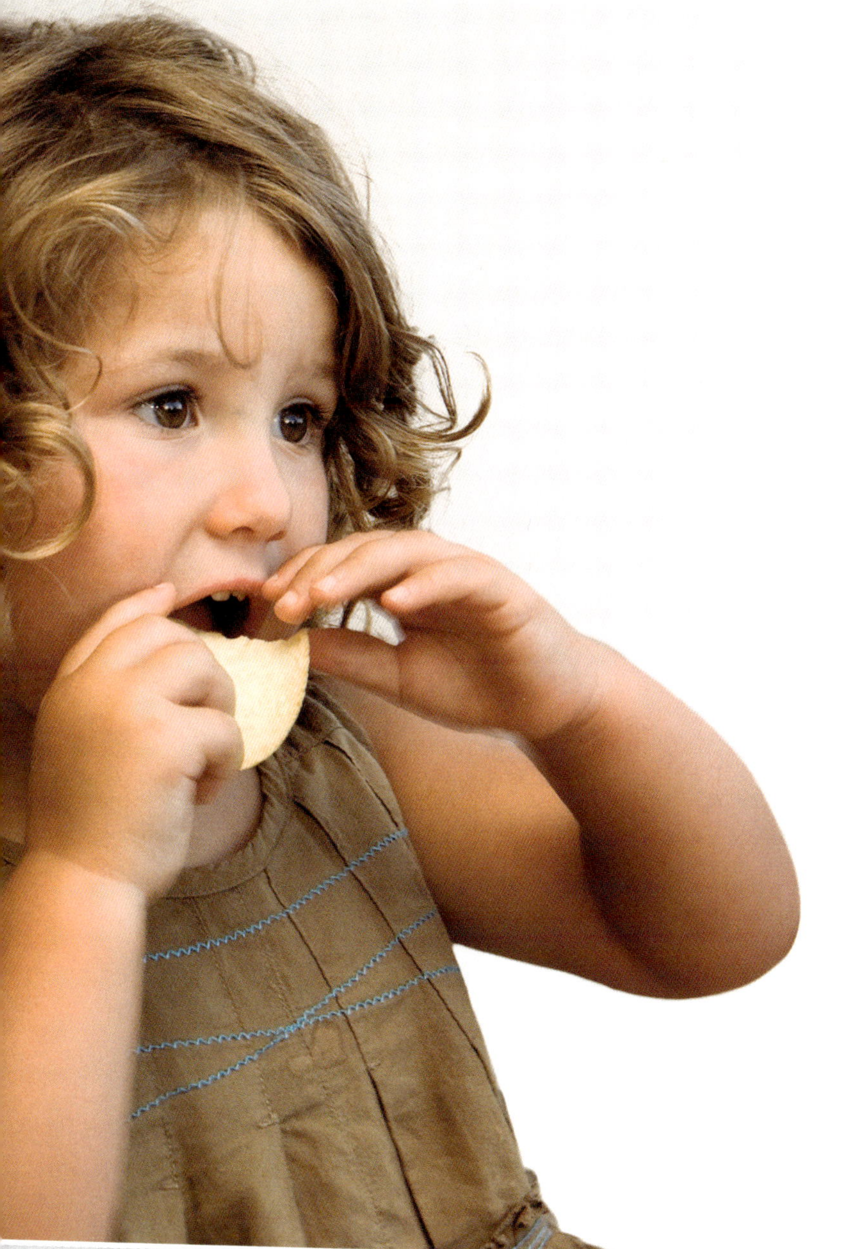

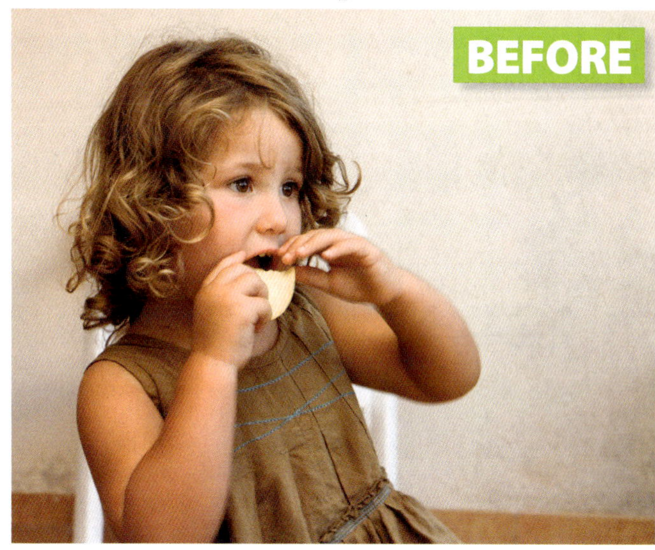

BEFORE

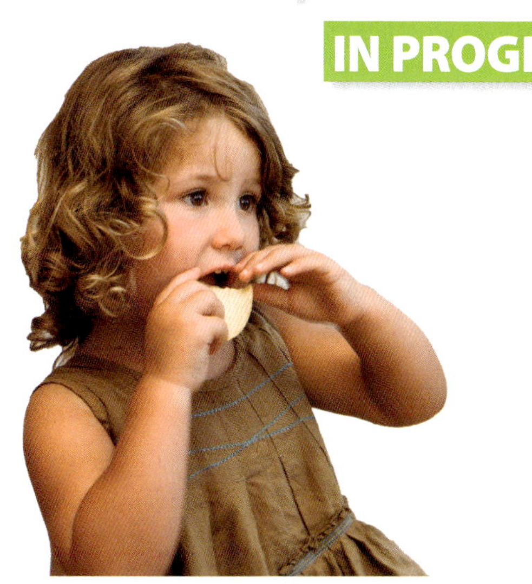

IN PROGRESS

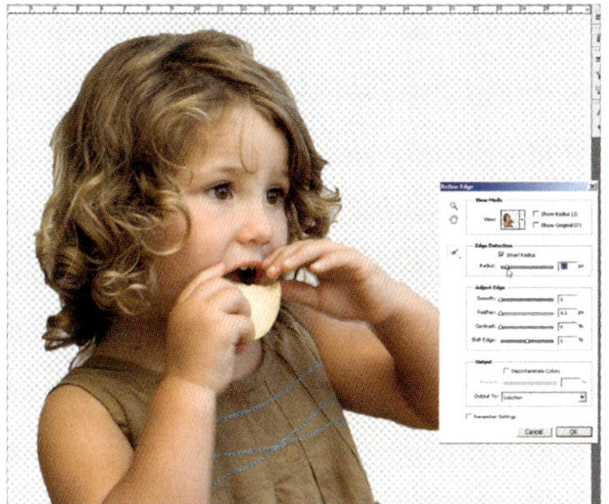

04 Smart Radius

Adjust the selection for the other edges (not the hair). Check Smart Radius and adjust the Radius slider. Choose Output To Selection and click OK.

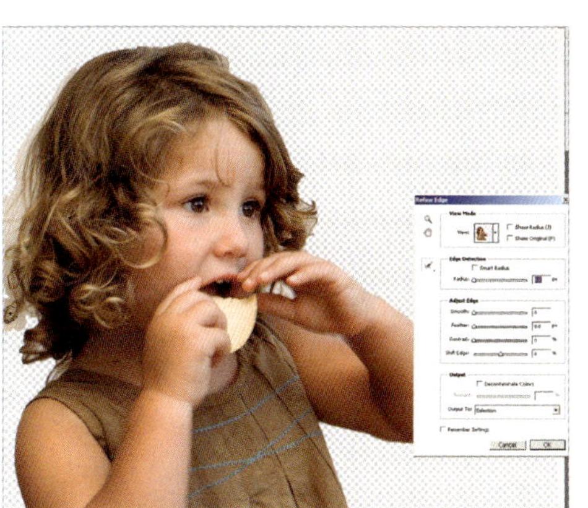

05 Hair magic

Go to Select>Refine Edge again. Choose your View mode and click on the Refine Radius tool. Use this tool to simply brush over wispy strands of hair.

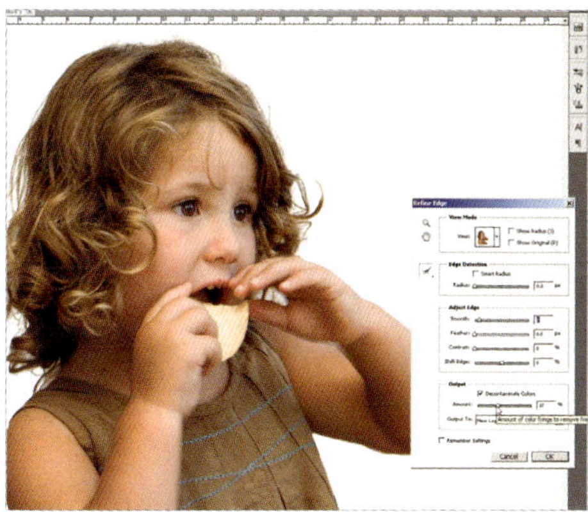

06 Decontaminate

Any remaining colour fringes around the edges of the extracted subject can be removed using the Decontaminate Colors option.

Replace dull skies with selections

Don't let your skies be a washout – simply add a better one from another image

Even with an amazing camera and a masterful handling of its controls, there's little that can be done about bleak skies.

You know the ones we mean – those pale grey expanses typical of drizzly days. Because the skies are so bleak, there is nothing for Photoshop to hang onto in order to make a fix. So the best option in this case is to just replace the sky with a better one. It sounds a tad drastic but is actually very easy to do. Once you try it, you'll find yourself doing it again and again, meaning you won't lose an otherwise decent photo to bleak horizons.

It is always worth having a handy supply of sky photos on your computer for such occasions, so if it's a nice day and you are out and about with your camera, then consider taking a few shots of just the sky so that you can slot them into duller snaps and give them a new lease of life.

In order to make the selecting on the sky easiest, try to only snap the sky… otherwise you will have to cut out any distracting elements like birds, planes and the tops of buildings, adding to your workload.

What we are going to do in this project involves the use of layers. We have a whole section on layers in this book, which starts on page 82. We only use two layers here: one for our original image and one for our new sky. By showing just the sky in one layer, and just the house and gardens in the other, we can blend the two together easily.

"You won't lose an otherwise decent photo to bleak horizons"

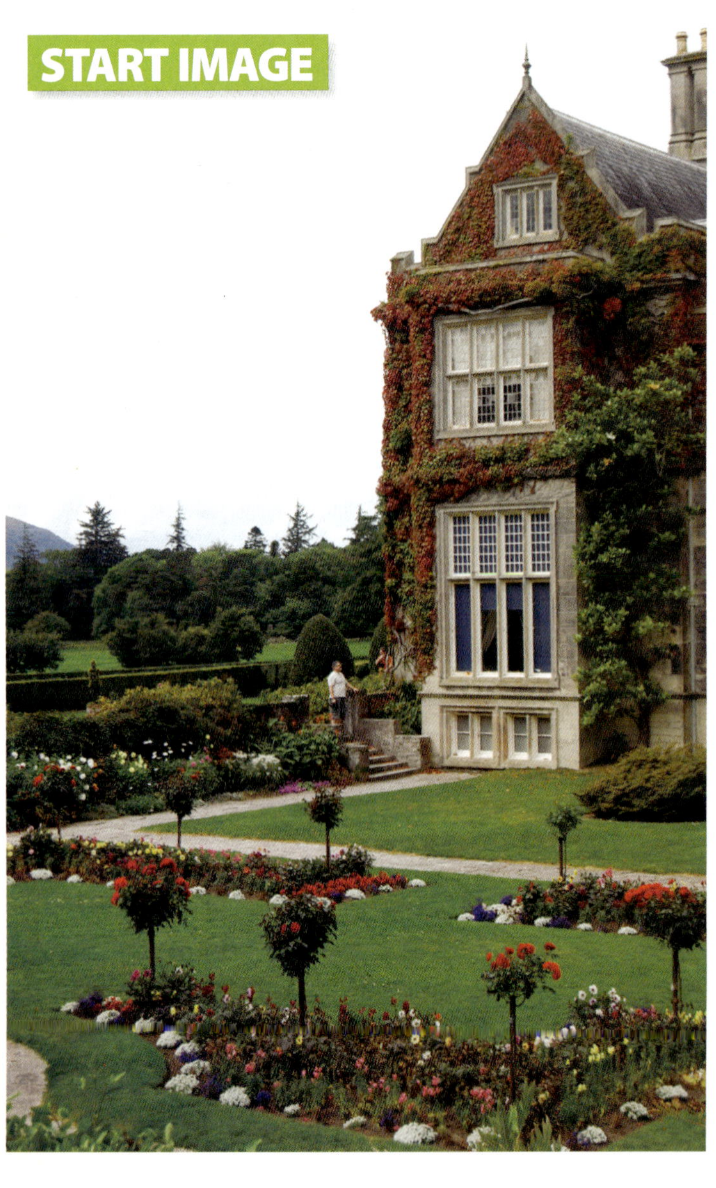

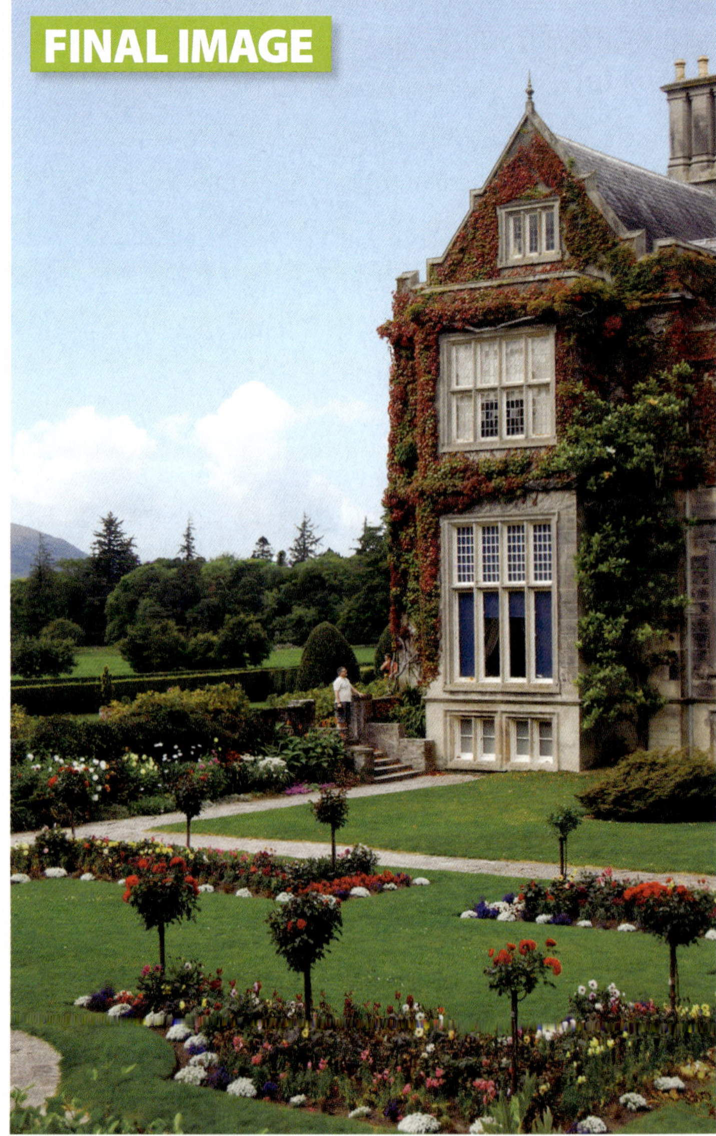

New sky in minutes

Master our essential, steps to improve your shots

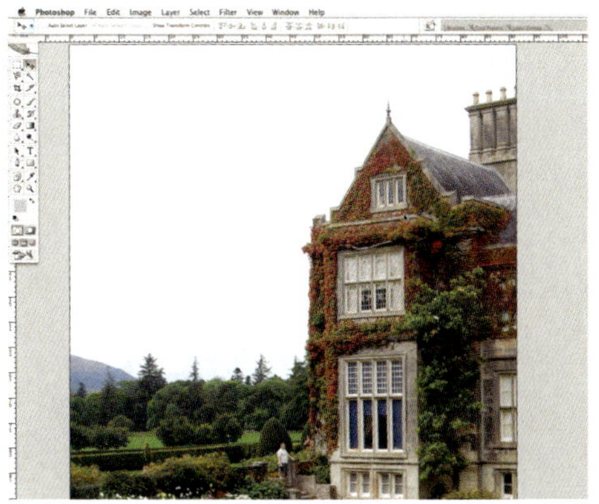

01 The problem

Here we have an image that was taken on a typical British summer day! The overall colours are good, but the sky is extremely washed out.

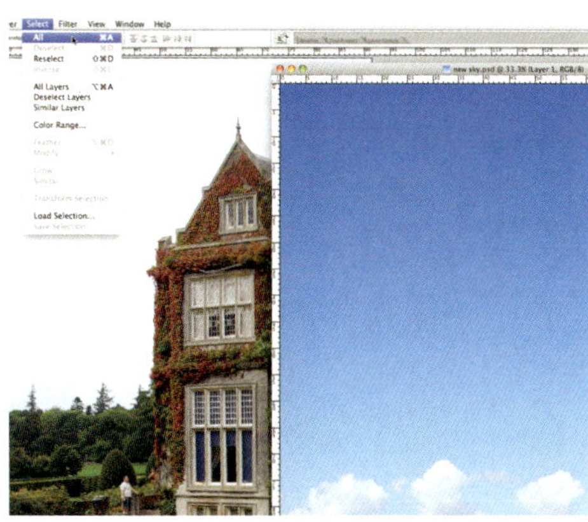

02 Get a new sky

Find a new sky image with better colours. Open this up by going to the File>Open. Go to the Select menu and then scroll down to All. Click to accept.

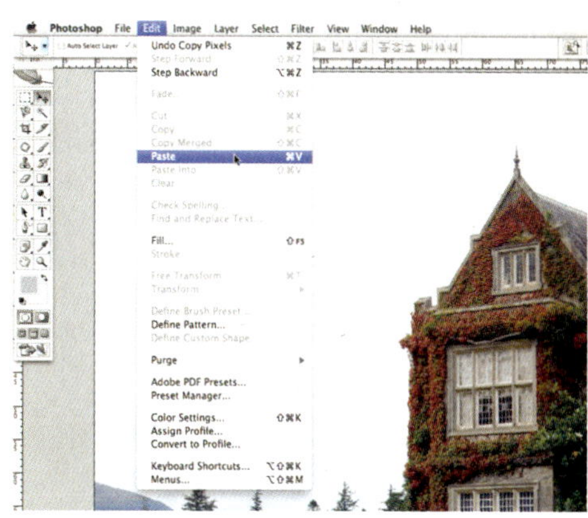

03 Paste

You will see some shimmery lines appear around the edges of the sky. Go to Edit>Copy. Now go back to the original image and go to Edit>Paste.

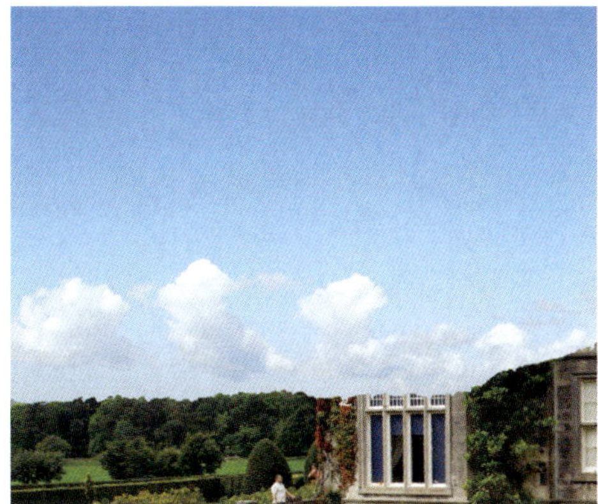

04 Lining up

Your new sky will appear over the original image. Select the Move tool and move the sky up and into position. Now look at the Layers palette.

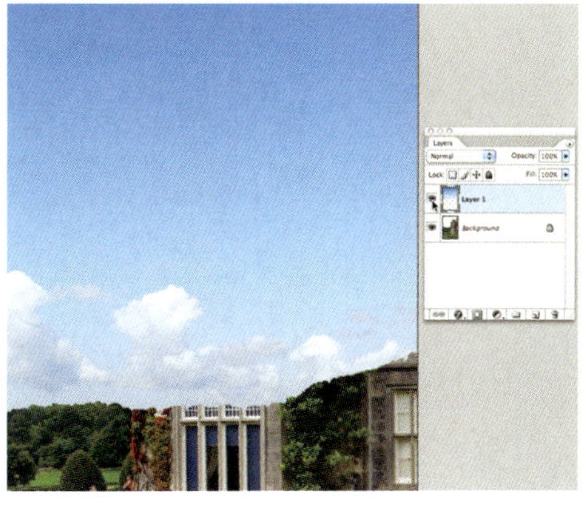

05 Some layer work

The sky is sitting above the original photo. Click the eye icon next to the sky layer to make it invisible and then click on the Background layer.

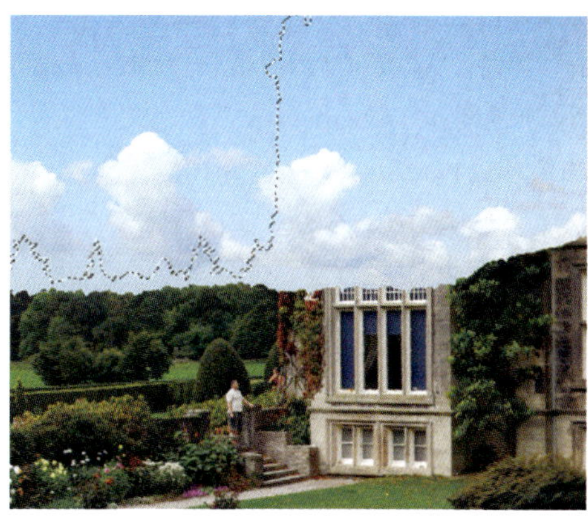

06 Magic selection

Pick the Magic Wand tool and set the Tolerance to 52%. Click on the sky area. Go to the Layers palette, click on the new sky layer and click the eye icon.

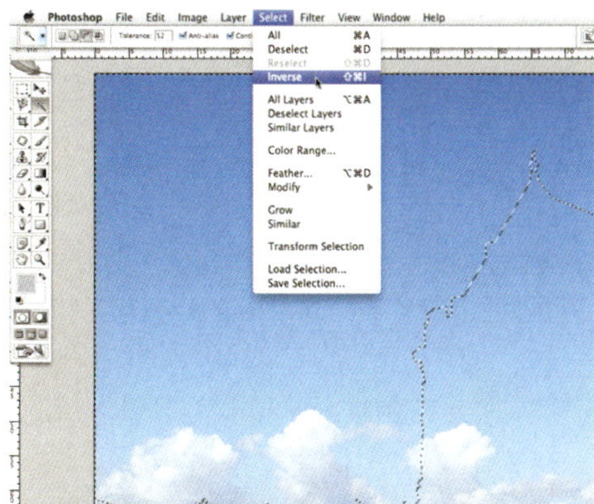

07 Inverse selection

Go to the Select menu and click on Inverse. This selects everything but the sky (ie the house and the grounds). .

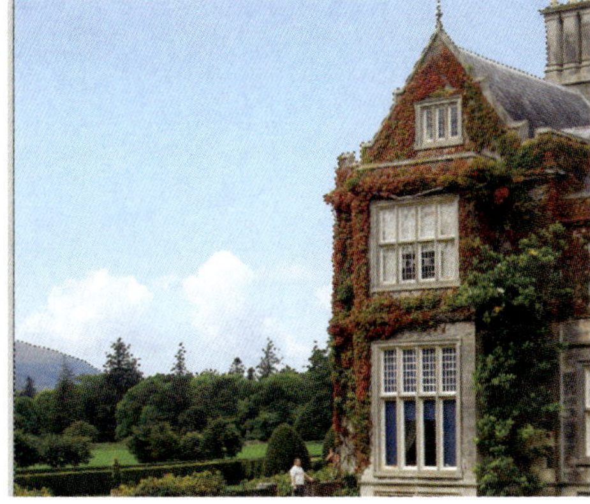

08 Tie it together

Press the Backspace or Delete key. The house will magically disappear and you can see the new sky in its new setting.

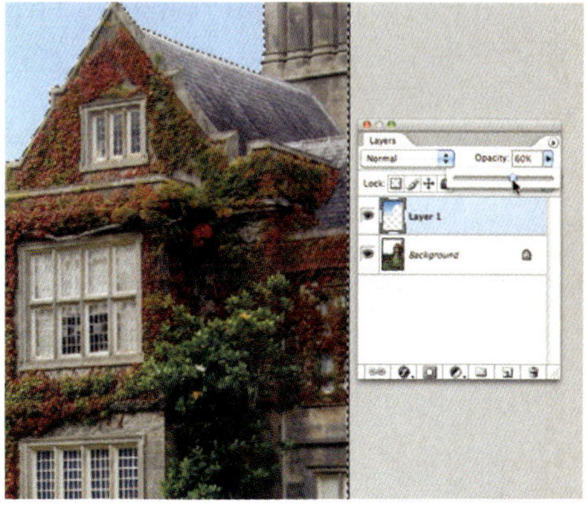

09 Finish it up

At the moment it looks a little too bright, so go back to the Layers palette, make sure you are on the sky layer and drag the Opacity slider.

The magic of Content Aware Scaling

Content Aware Scaling is one of the greatest things to have appeared in Photoshop. Let's look at some scaling magic!

We've all been there. You have the perfect shot, but the proportions are simply all wrong for your current project. Normally you'd be presented with just two options. You could crop it, but then you'd lose a lot of the image itself – more often than not, a lot of the background areas that you liked so much when you saw the image through your camera's viewfinder.

Or you could scale it via a transformation, but when you need to change the proportions of the image you run the risk of distorting it beyond all recognition. In short, you've really no way of keeping everything as it was in the image except change the images proportions – until now!

In Photoshop CS4 and CS5, Content Aware Scaling has brought a smile to many a photographer's face, because it allows you to change the proportions of an image without distorting the subject within the image at all. Essentially, Content Aware Scaling will intelligently scale the low detail areas of an image such as the background elements, while leaving the main subject remarkably intact and unchanged.

Notwithstanding the fact that this function is truly impressive, on some images it needs to be used carefully and with a good deal of thought – so over these two pages we're going to give you the lowdown on the Photoshop CS4 wonder that is Content Aware Scaling.

Photoshop Elements has the sam technology in it, but it is under a slightly different name. It is called Recompose, and you use it by painting in green over any areas that you want yo keep in the photo without distortion. You can then intelligently scale the image without unwanted distortion. Give it a go and you will be surprised at just how accurate this tool is.

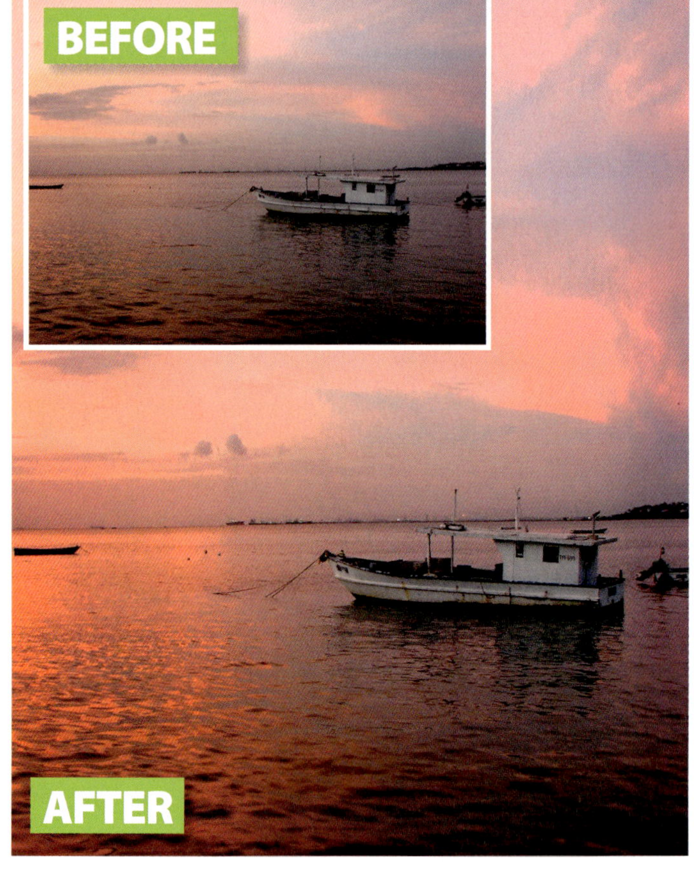

"It allows you to change the proportions of an image without distorting the subject at all"

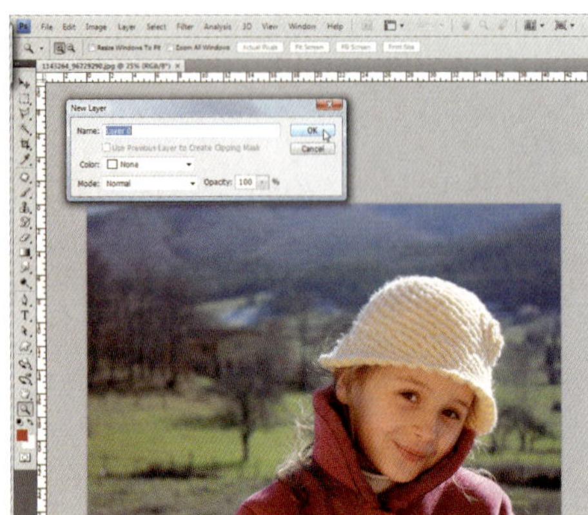

01 Scaling portraits

Content Aware Scale command has a feature that can help scale faces. Promote your image to a layer by double-clicking the Background layer.

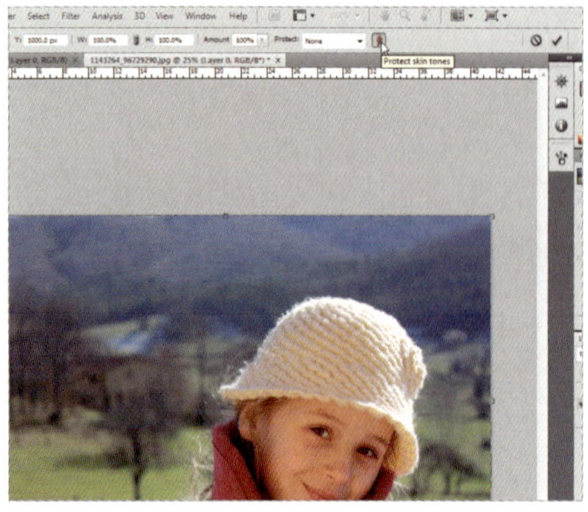

02 Protect skin

Go to Edit>Content Aware Scale. We want to protect the girl's face from distortion. Do this via the Options bar: 'Protect Skin Tones'.

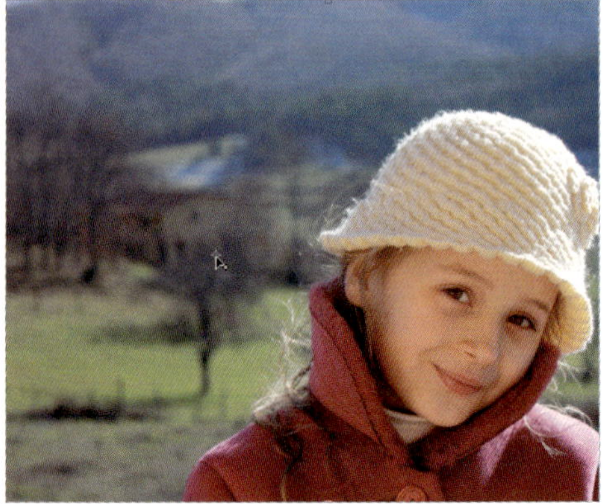

03 Anchor point

In the centre of the Transformation bounding box, you'll see a tiny circle. This is the anchor point so move this away from the centre of the face a little.

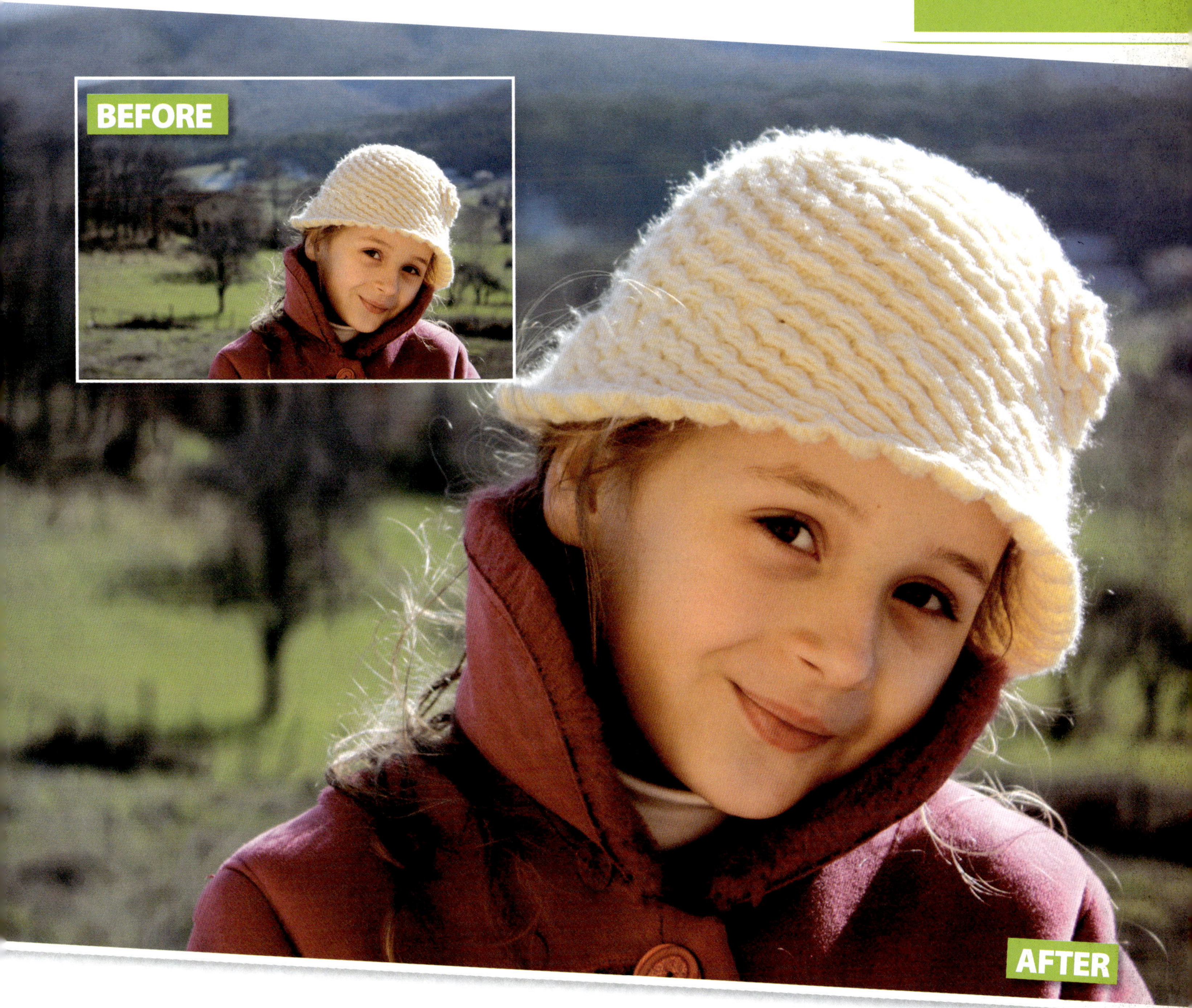

BEFORE

AFTER

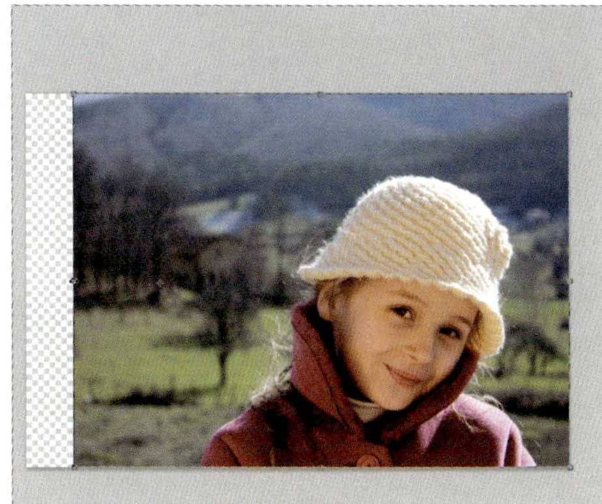

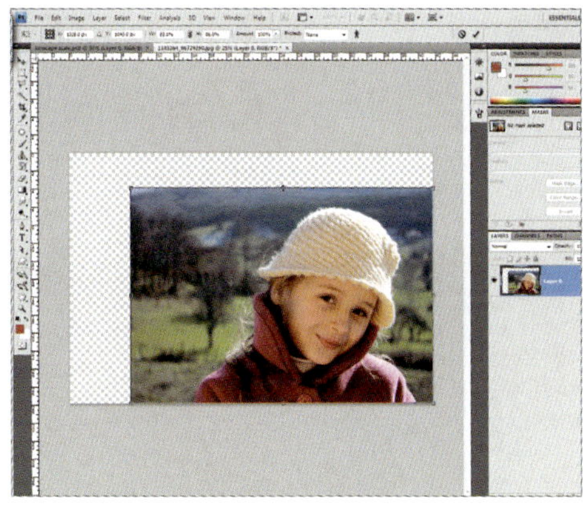

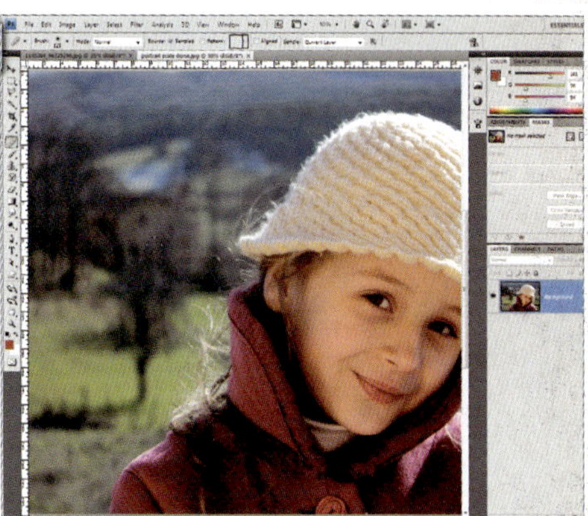

04 Bit by bit

Now just move the left-hand handle a little way to the left before hitting Enter to commit the transformation to the image.

05 More scaling

Return to Edit>Content Aware Scale and drag the side handle in a little more. You can now start to move the top handle down to reduce the height.

06 Cleaning up

You'll sometimes find some ragged pixelation at the extremes of the transformation area. Use the Healing Brush tool with a soft brush to correct.

Photomontage techniques

Combine your favourite photos to produce stunning results as you tackle your first photomontage

Photomontage refers to the process of compositing two or more separate images together to produce one final piece of artwork, a common use of both Photoshop and Photoshop Elements for those who want to get more creative with their work.

There's no doubt that it's one of the most popular projects performed in Photoshop and other image-editing software packages. The ability to combine images to produce a single new piece of artwork appeals to all genres and is also very easy to do.

This is a great technique for the Photoshop newcomer, as you can make a photomontage as simple or as complex as you wish. Here we'll cover the basic techniques involved – and it's up to you how far you take your artwork. Within this two-page guide, we will introduce the concept of blending images into one another using simple masks and gradients. We'll also talk about the use of Selection tools and all the cheats to give your photomontage a polished look. This includes the Smudge and Blur tools for tidying up jagged edges, as well as the Clone Stamp tool for covering up any unsightly gaps.

All these tips can be applied to a variety of projects, so we encourage you to gather all your favourite photographs and start experimenting with your own photomontage style today.

> "It's one of the most popular projects performed in Photoshop and other image-editing software"

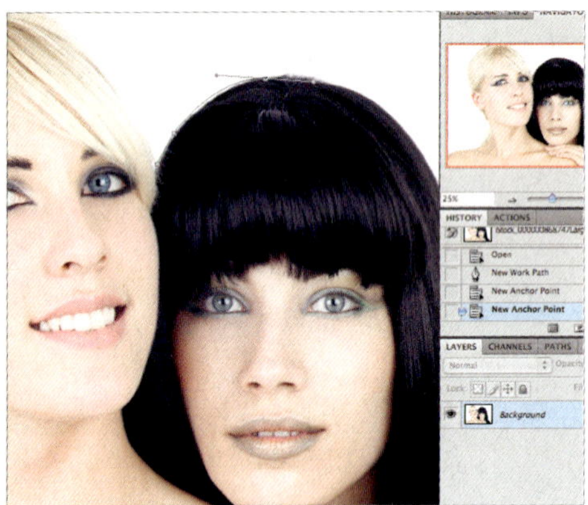

01 Isolate your objects

For subjects on high-contrast backgrounds or with easy edges to select, the Lasso tool offers some good options for simple selections (see page 166).

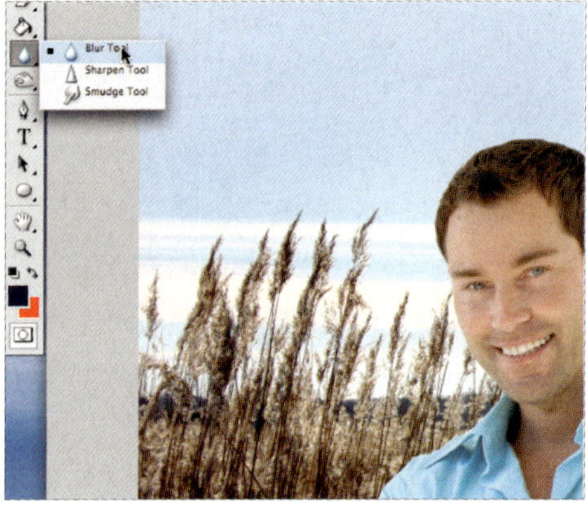

02 Cutting out hair 1

Try selecting the model with the Lasso or Pen, then use the Blur and Smudge tools to blend in the hair edges for a smooth finish.

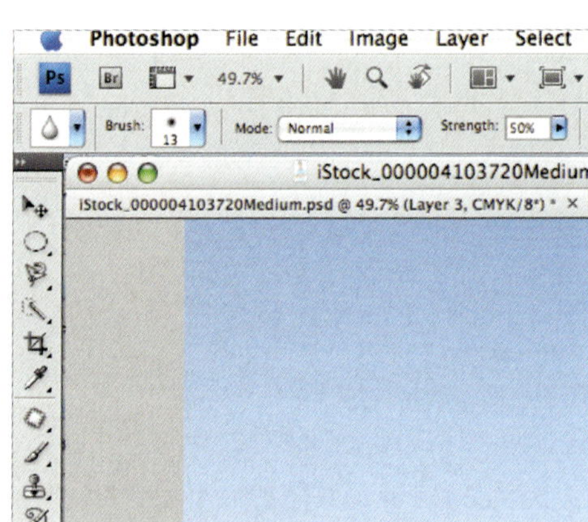

03 Cutting out hair 2

For a convincing finish, use a low strength and build up the strokes lightly, stroking the edges of the hair so it blends into the background.

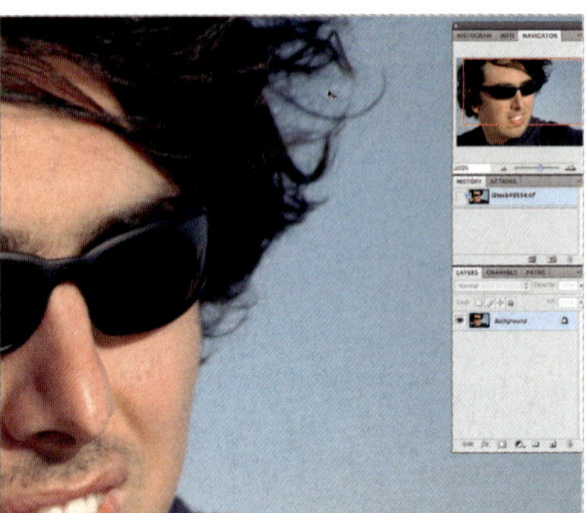

04 The Clone Stamp tool

Use the Clone Stamp over any empty spaces in the hair, which look a bit unnatural. Sample an area of good hair by pressing Alt/Opt and clicking.

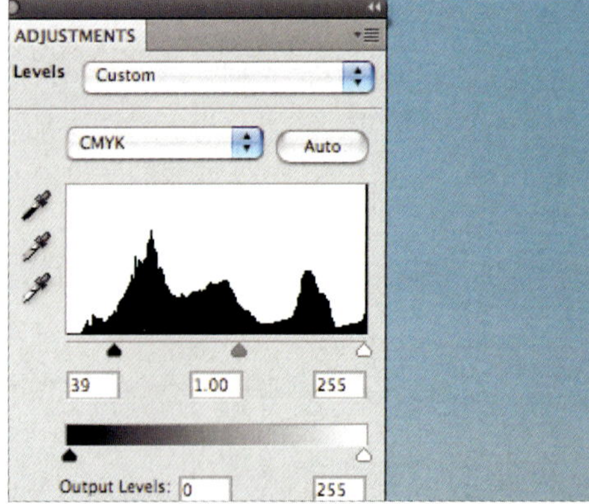

05 Perfect lighting 1

A simple way of getting the right lighting is setting the Levels on each layer to match one another. Add the Levels as adjustment layers.

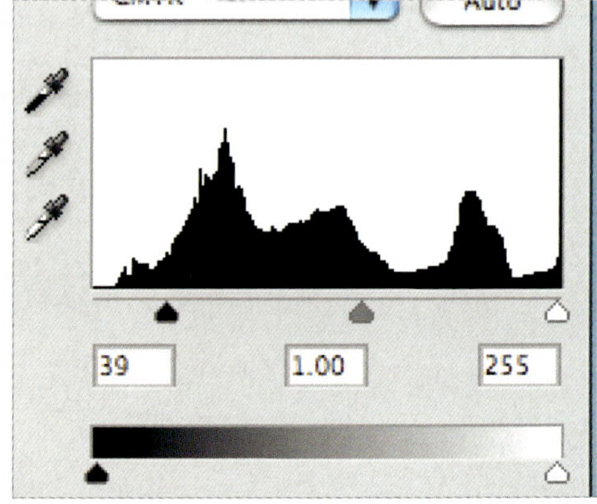

06 Perfect lighting 2

Use the sliders to alter the shadows, midtones and highlights. Match the tones of your background and subject so they look like they belong together.

QUICK PHOTOSHOP TIPS

Perfect hair

To make any remaining original background vanish, use the Stamp tool. Lock the girl layer (in the Layers palette) and select the Stamp toolset at 20% Opacity. Sample a good section of hair and lightly paint over any hair area where the background is showing through.

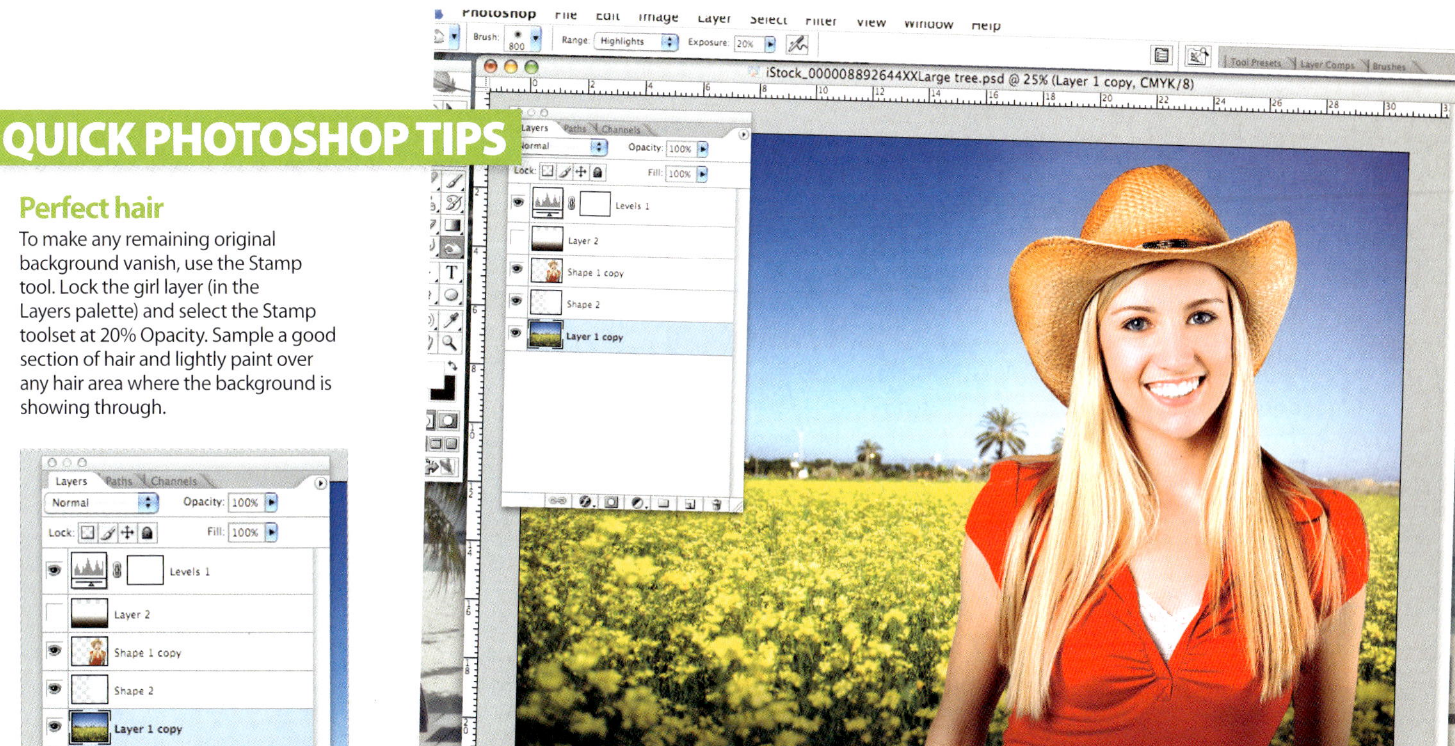

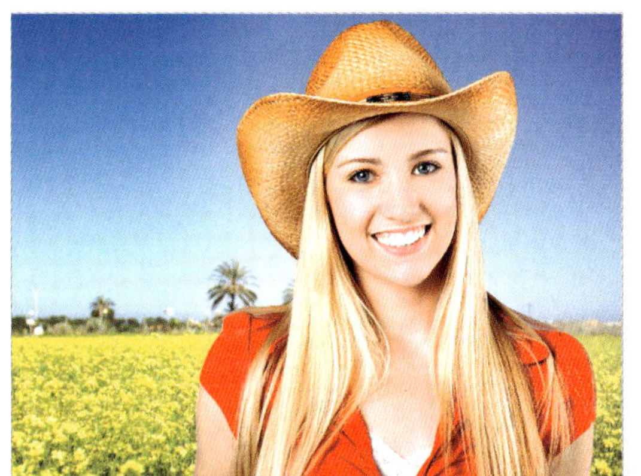

Extra light

In this example we have added some light behind the girl to try and even up the lighting. Using the Ellipse tool an oval shape was created, then the shape layer was rasterized. A Gaussian blur of 130 pixels was set. The layer blend mode was set to Luminosity and the opacity lowered.

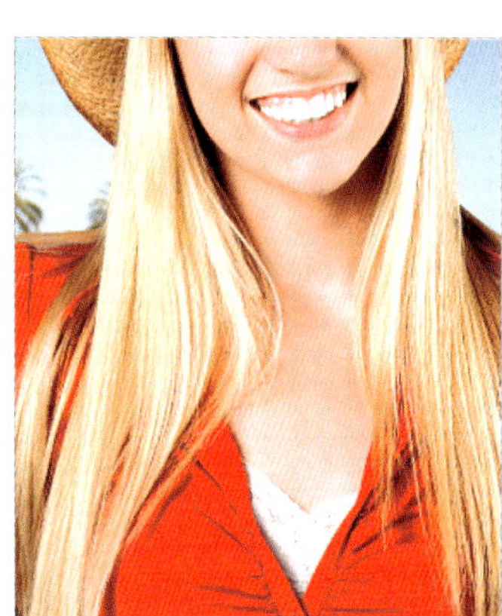

Levels

The two photos had Levels adjustments separately, then a Levels adjustment layer was added to bring the photos together.

Final hair touches

To make the hair look natural now it's been cut out, use the Smudge tool, which is hidden in the toolbar. Lower the tool's strength to 90% and reduce the Brush Size to between 1-3 pixels.

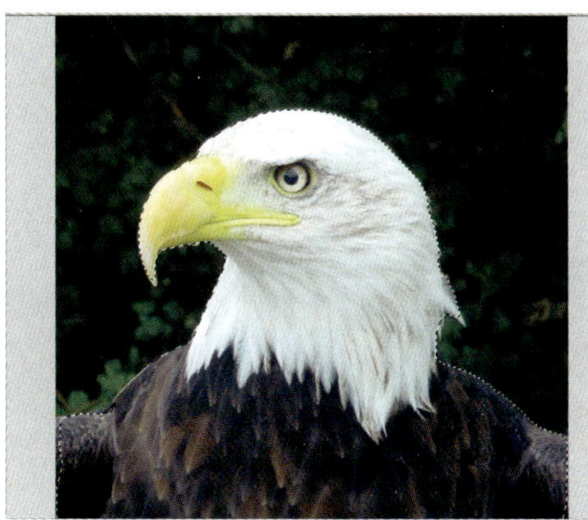

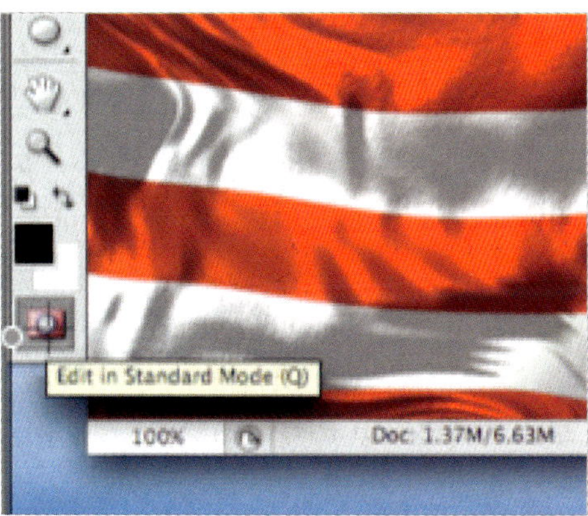

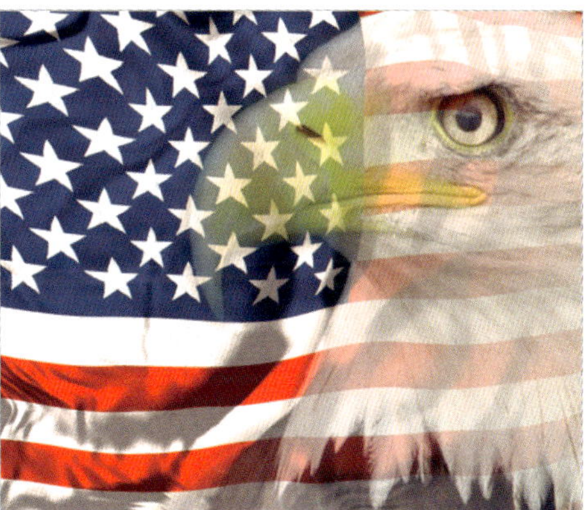

01 Select your object

Use the Magnetic Lasso to isolate an object. Copy the selection (Ctrl/Cmd+C) and paste it onto a new layer in your background image (Ctrl/Cmd+V).

02 Mask It

Go to Edit>Transform>Scale and resize the image. Ensure the object layer is active and hit Edit In Quick Mask (circular icon in a rectangle).

03 Add gradient

With the Gradient tool with Linear Gradient checked, drag a line from left to right. Hit Edit In Quick Mask again. Hit Delete; the images will blend.

Brushes

"Brushes are divided into categories that you can swap between them at your desire"

DIGITAL PAINTING TRICKS

Turn your photos into paintings with this dedicated section, breaking down all the tools you need

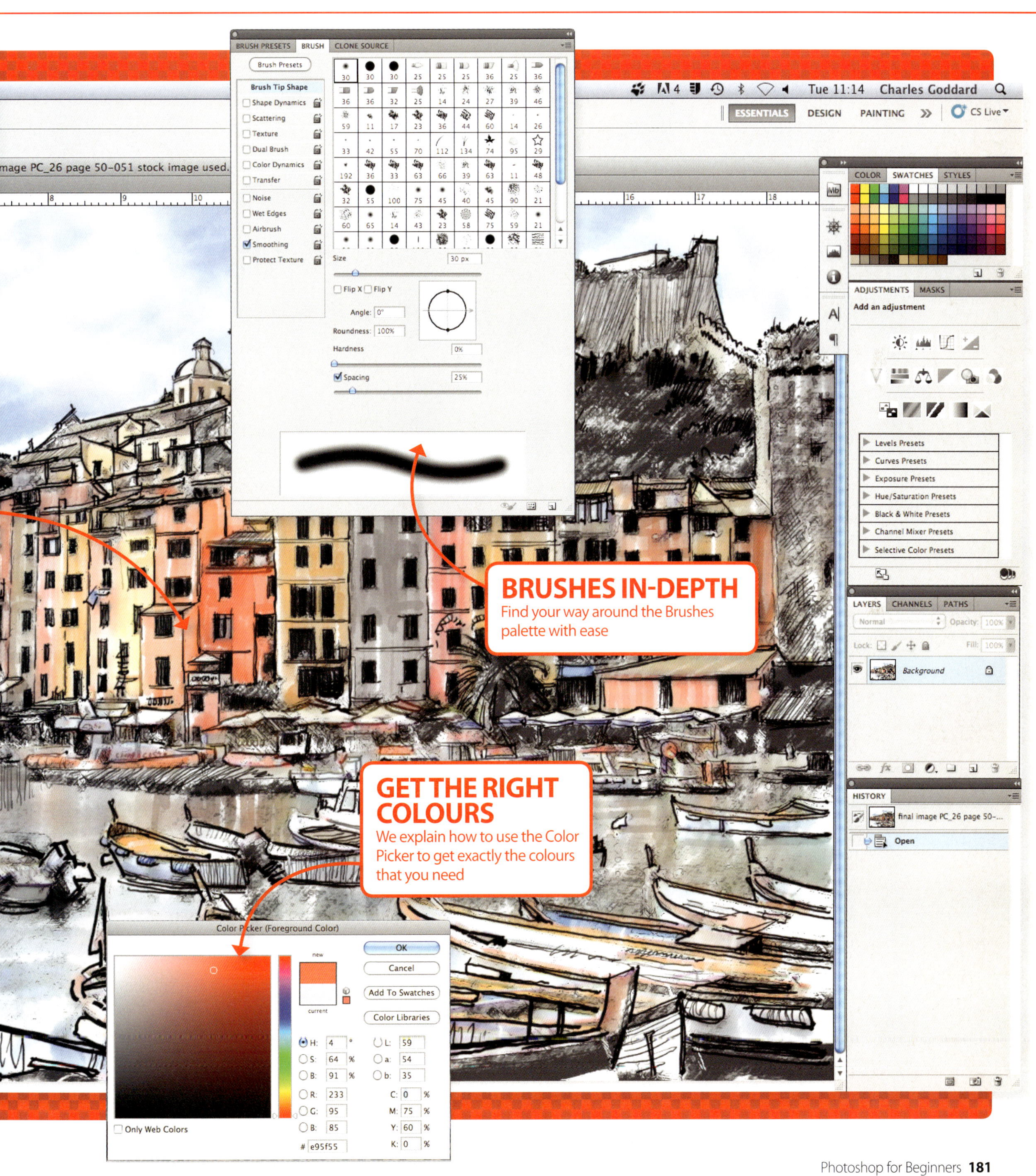
BRUSHES IN-DEPTH
Find your way around the Brushes palette with ease
GET THE RIGHT COLOURS
We explain how to use the Color Picker to get exactly the colours that you need

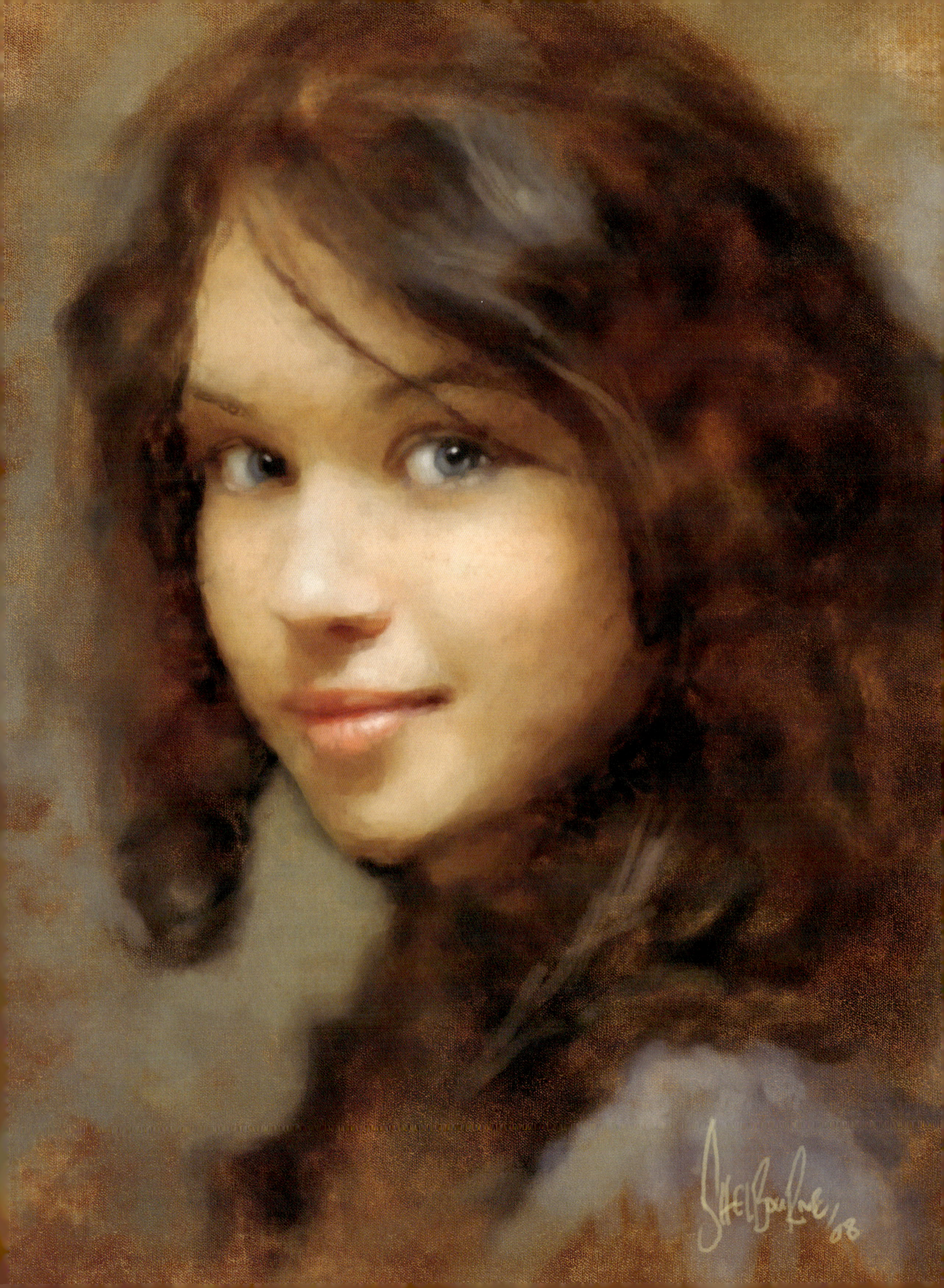

Brush tools overview

A guide to some of Photoshop's best Brushes

If you're new to Photoshop, looking at all of the brushes on offer may be a bit daunting, but don't worry; our guide will point out some of the more interesting brushes built into Photoshop to help get you started.

Simply put, the Brush Tool allows you to paint in Photoshop. When you click on the canvas it draws a stamp of the brush head. When you drag the cursor it repeatedly re-draws the brush head to form a brush stroke. Changing the Brush Tip Shape by selecting any one of Photoshop's numerous Presets on offer will change the style of your brush strokes.

Photoshop's brushes are divided into categories that you can swap between at your desire, or you can append multiple sets together. The categories are broken down into the Sets so that brushes of a similar nature are grouped together for ease of use. Some of the groups have more to offer than others, but we'll get to that in a moment. When you've found your favourite brushes you can create your own set with the Preset Manager located in the Brush Preset Palette Options. For easy access, you can also save your most used brushes with specific changes in the Tool Presets Tab.

Although you can use all of Photoshop's brushes with a mouse, they're much more effective, intuitive and, frankly, more fun when used in conjunction with a graphics tablet.

A useful time saver when using brushes is to use the ']' and '[' keys to increase and decrease your brush size; it's much more efficient than changing your preset or dragging the Size slider around in the Toolbar.

"Photoshop's Brushes are divided into categories that you can swap between at your desire"

FIND YOUR WAY AROUND THE BRUSHES PALETTE

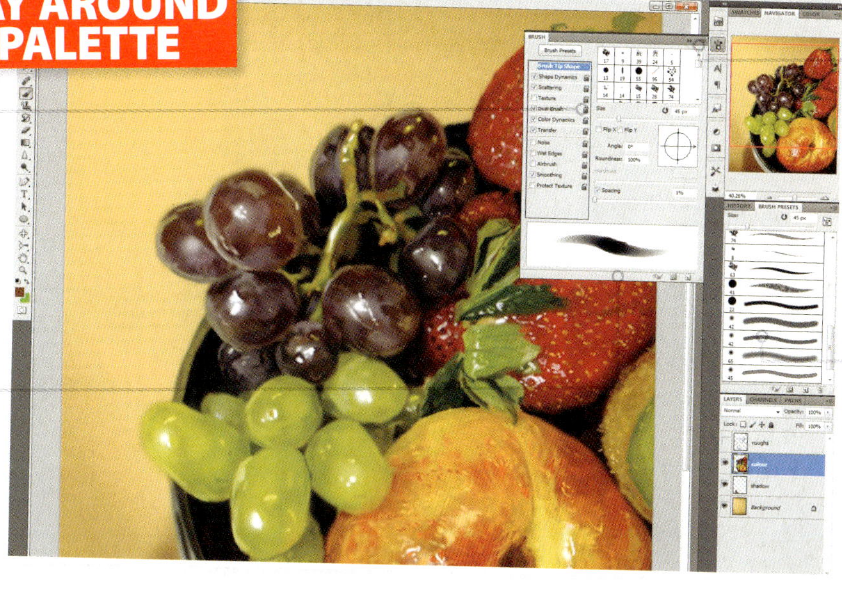

Fixed settings

The lower half of the left-hand column contains options that have no alterable settings, you can simply choose whether to have them activated or not.

The stroke thumbnail

An extremely useful resource that displays a thumbnail preview of what your brush stroke would look like using the current settings. Change a setting and the thumbnail will alter accordingly.

The Settings section

The top-right section is where you can tinker and experiment with any brush's settings to your heart's content. Even changing one setting can drastically alter a brush's behaviour and appearance.

Editable settings

The top half of the left column displays all of the brush options categories that can be altered manually. Clicking on a category displays its particular settings with a series of sliders and drop-down menus.

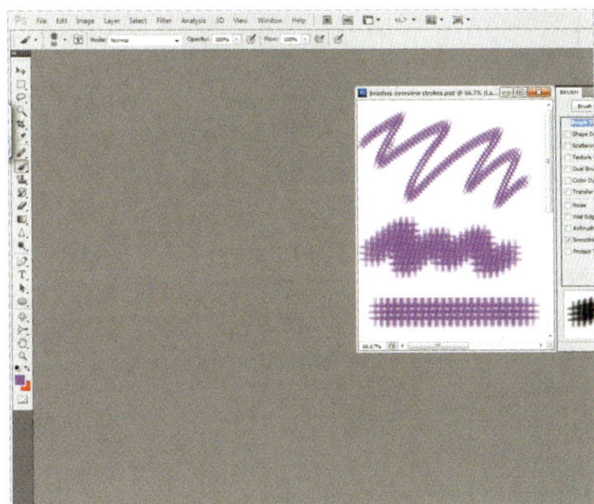

01 Assorted Brushes

Assorted Brushes offers an eclectic array of brushes that you may find occasional use for, but there's probably not any that you'll frequently return to.

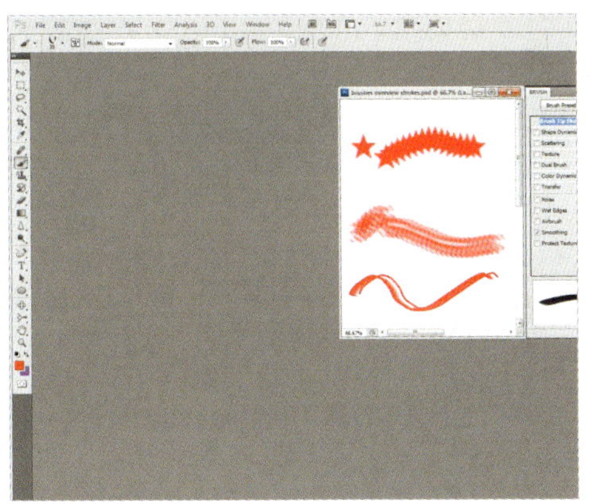

02 Assorted Brushes

Although presets like the 'Star Brush' are fairly basic, there are some decent texture brushes in this set that are worth your attention.

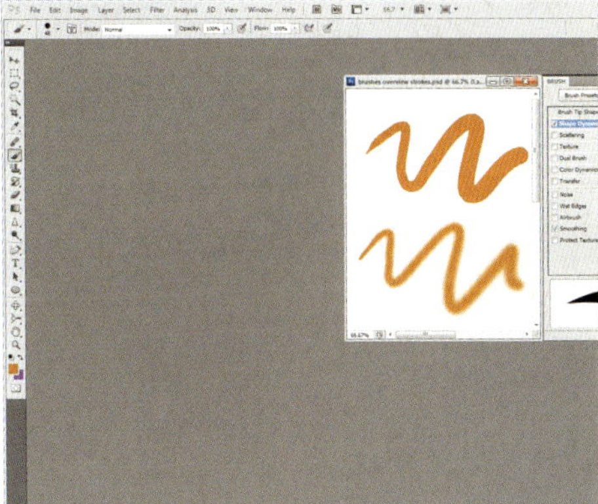

03 Basic Brushes

A fairly limited category, Basic Brushes offers a hard-edged 'mechanical pencil' brush and a 'soft-edged pencil' brush at numerous sizes.

Best brushes Get the most out of Photoshop's brushes

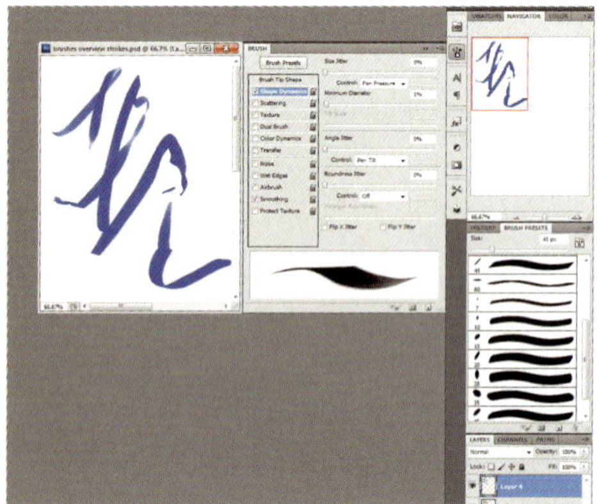

04 Calligraphic Brushes

The Calligraphic Brushes set contains a number of brushes tailored to emulate calligraphic nib shapes. Set the Angle Jitter to 'Tilt' for maximum effect.

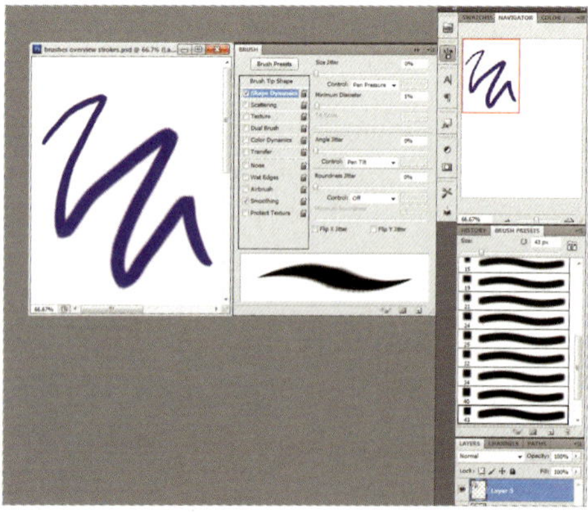

05 Drop Shadow Brushes

Drop Shadow Brushes provide brushes of both round and square varieties with feathered edges to render shadows with a soft edge to them.

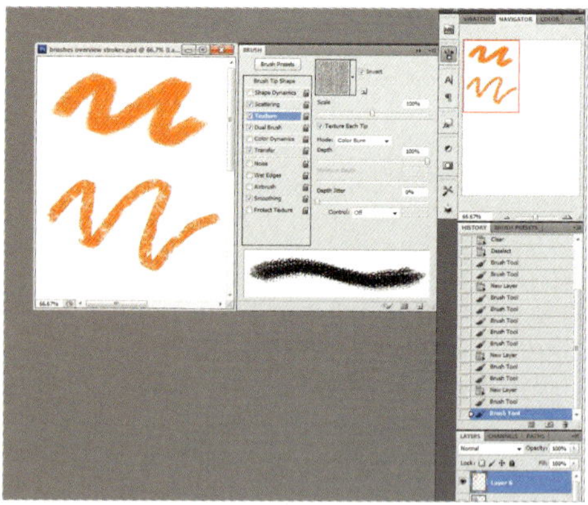

06 Dry Media Brushes

A great set of brushes that emulate traditional media such as pastels and charcoals. A great place to start if you want to create custom brushes.

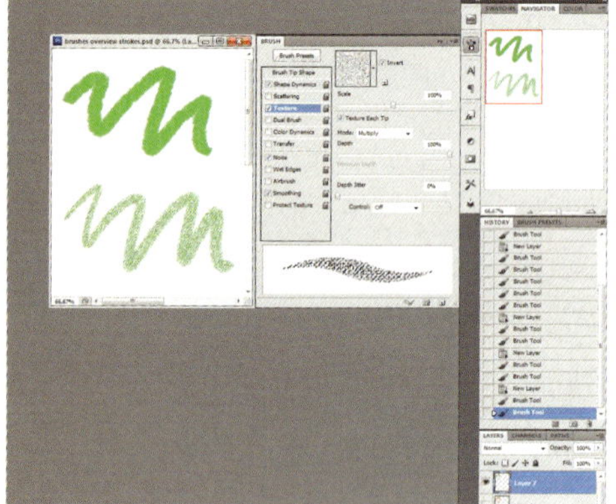

07 Dry Media Brushes

Most of the brushes here make use of many of the attributes you can alter in the Brushes Palette, such as adding Texture and Dual Brush functionality.

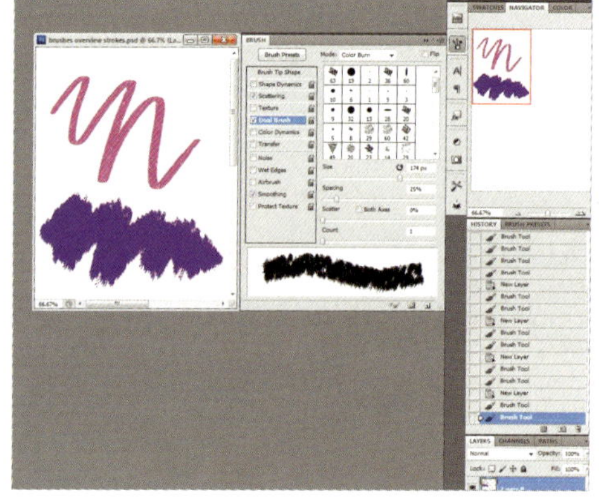

08 Dry Media Brushes 2

By looking through the Brushes Palette settings you'll get an idea of why these brushes behave the way they do, which will help you make your own.

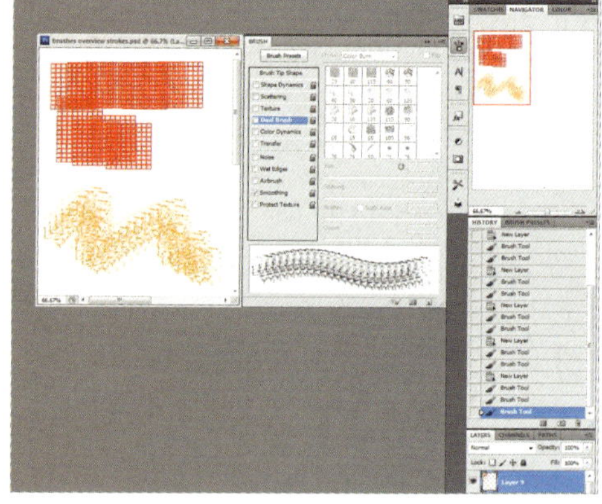

09 Faux Finish Brushes

With brushes like Plastic Wrap and Sea Sponge this set appears quite limited, but playing around with the settings makes them a lot more versatile.

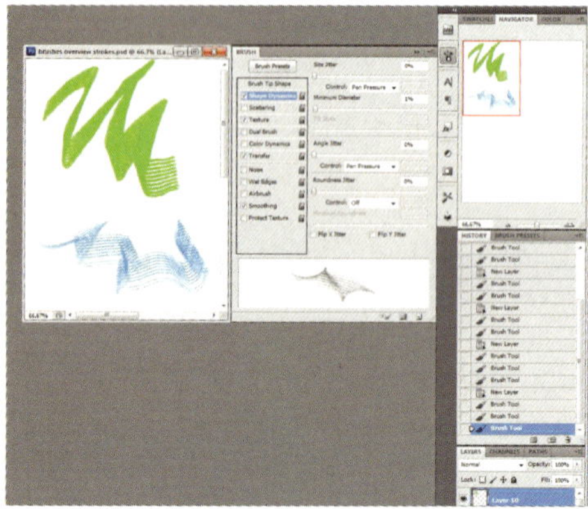

10 Faux Finish Brushes 2

Toy with the settings of the Texture Comb brushes; with a little experimentation you can create some very expressive brushwork.

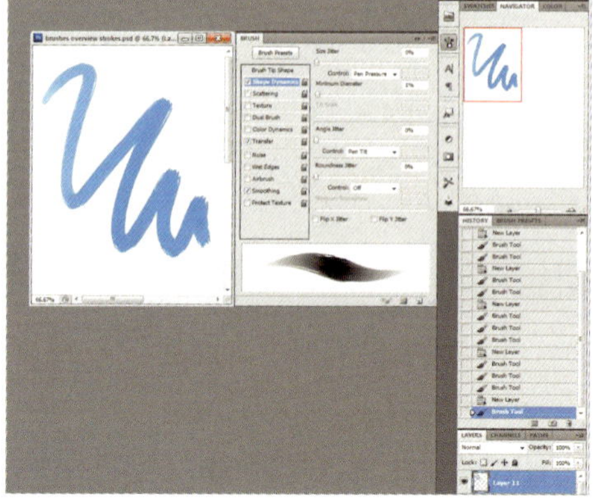

11 Natural Brushes

Natural Brushes includes Stipple and Spray brushes. The Stipple brush works well with Angle Jitter set to Pen Tilt and Opacity set to Pen Pressure.

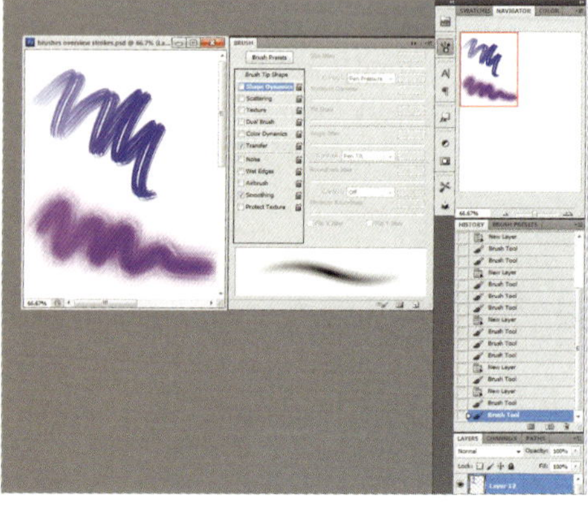

12 Natural Brushes

The Spray brush works like the Airbrush but has a faint stippling effect so the result is more textured. Set the Opacity to Pen Pressure for best results.

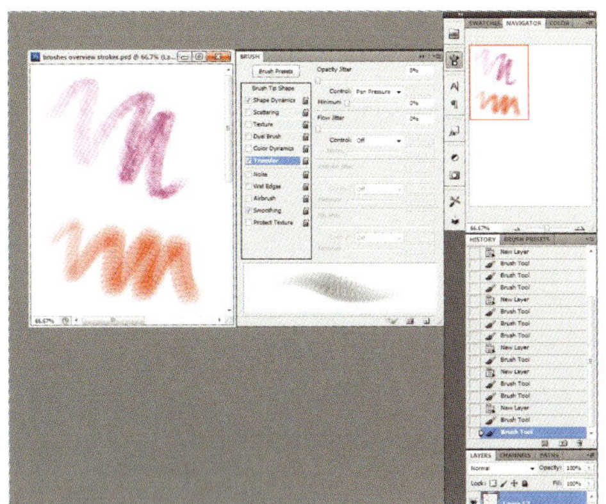

13 Natural Brushes 2

Natural Brushes 2 collects brushes that have textures built into them. Chalk and Pastel effect brushes are well represented here.

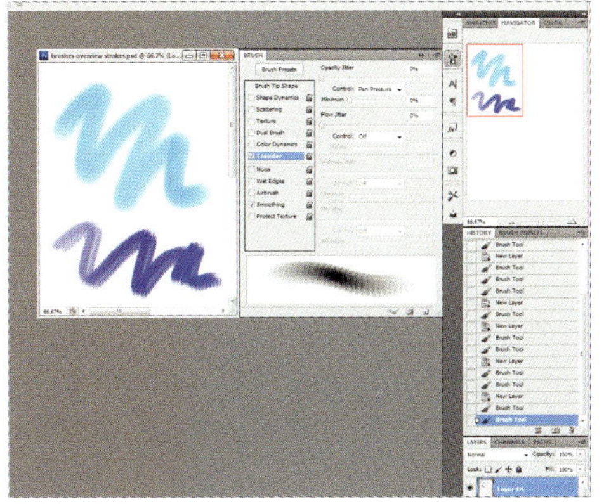

14 Natural Brushes 2

To get a natural build-up effect set Opacity and Flow to Pen Pressure. Set the Blending Mode to Multiply in the Toolbar to enhance it even further.

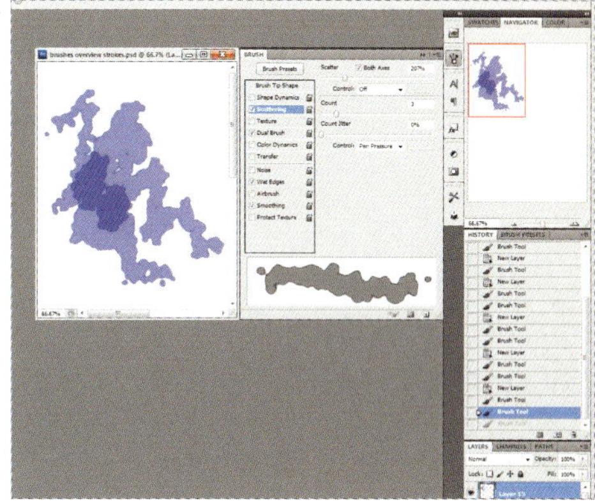

15 Special Effect Brushes

Other than Drippy Watercolor, which has some painting application, the brushes here are fun but slightly gimmicky.

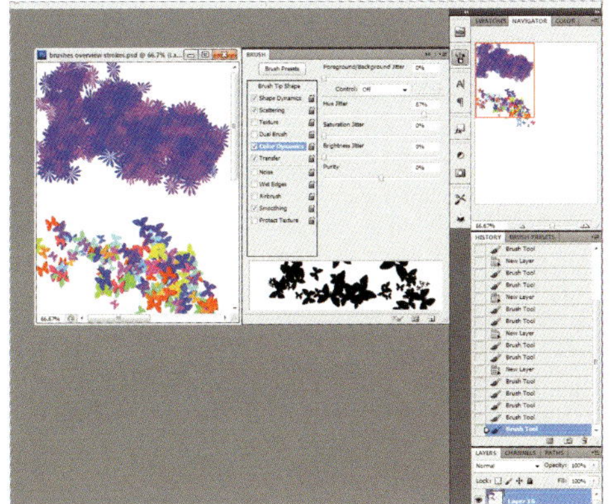

16 Special Effect Brushes

The Azalea brush switches Foreground/ Background colours, while the Butterfly brush's high Hue Jitter randomises them.

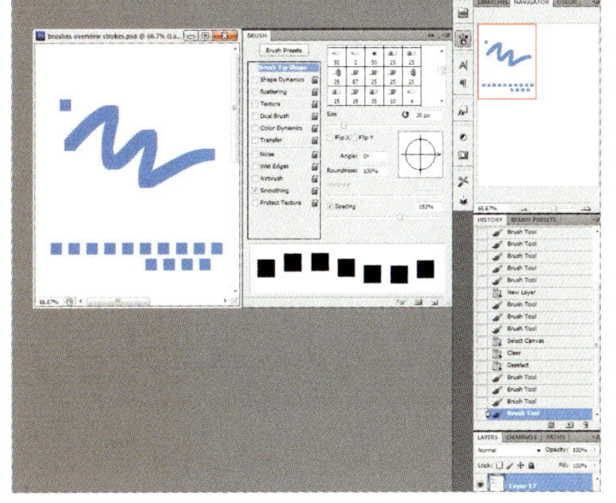

17 Square Brushes

Square Brushes is misleading; there is really just one brush here supplied at a number of different sizes. Its brush work is surprisingly pleasing, though.

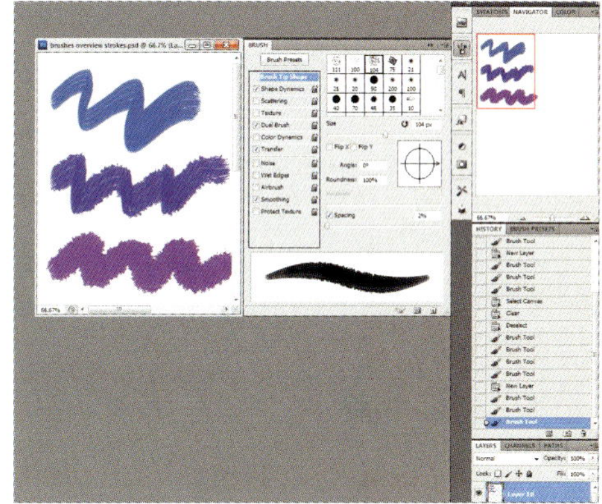

18 Thick Heavy Brushes

The Thick Heavy Brushes set features five bristle effect brushes that will add a little texture to your brush work.

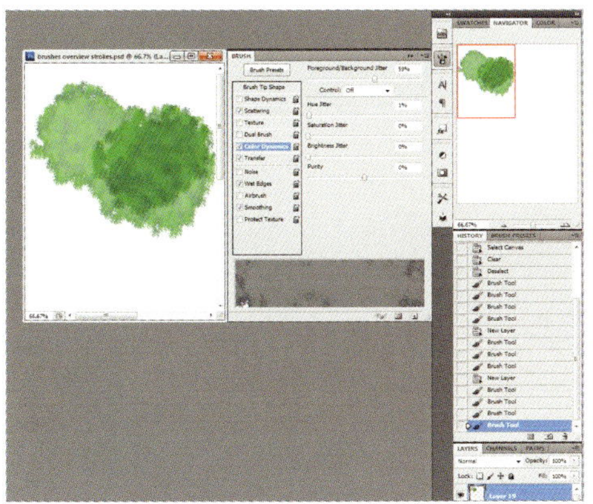

19 Wet Media Brushes

Wet Media Brushes includes a superb selection of assorted brushes. As well as watercolour brushes there are also ink, oil and dry brushes.

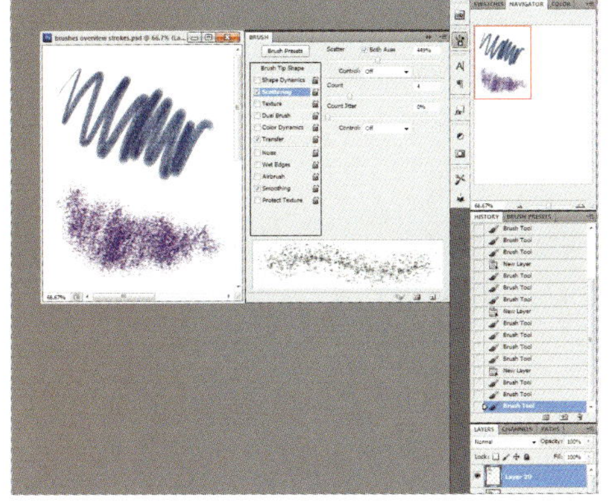

20 Wet Media Brushes

There are a number of Brush Tip Shapes employed in the Wet Media Brushes section, which makes the effects of each one noticeably different to the last.

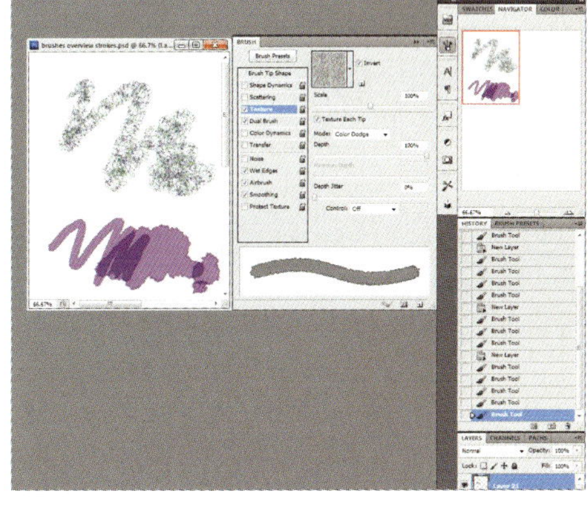

21 Wet Media Brushes

The variety of styles in this category is impressive; most use Textures and at least one other feature. The watercolour brushes use the Wet Edges option.

New brush controls in CS5

Get Photoshop's most authentic painting experience yet with its new Bristle brushes engine and Mixer brush

If you're into painting digitally, Photoshop CS5 has a whole stack of exciting new features for you in the form of Bristle brushes. Photoshop's brushes have always been versatile but Photoshop CS5 features a revamped brush engine that completely changes the playing field. Your brushes will act much more like traditional paint brushes.

So what's the difference? The Bristle brushes have virtual bristles that react to tilt and pressure sensitivity in a much more advanced way than you'll be used to. With standard brushes, when you pushed down hard on your stylus you just got the biggest possible stamp of your brush, when you push down with a Bristle brush the bristles actually splay out on the virtual canvas just like an actual paint brush, giving you more expressive brush strokes. There's more scope for variation with Bristle brushes than Photoshop's old static brushes

As if the Bristle brushes weren't enough, Adobe then threw in the Mixer brush. The Mixer brush uses the Bristle brush functionality to pick up the digital paint that you've already laid down on the canvas and lets you alter and mix the colours you have on each individual bristle; essentially you have all of the fun of painting with all of the editing options of Photoshop!

With the 'mix mode' drop-down menu you can quickly change the wetness, paint load and mixing levels without having to tweak each individual setting, which makes painting feel quick and natural. Ooh, and did we mention 'non-destructive painting'? Let's have a look at what CS5's new painting engine has to offer…

> "Essentially, you have all of the fun of painting with all of the editing options of Photoshop!"

A VISUAL GUIDE TO THE NEW CS5 PAINTING LAYOUT

A handy guide to help you visualise your brush

The preview box displays the exact angle that your brush is tilting so you can see the position and shape that your brush will make on the canvas.

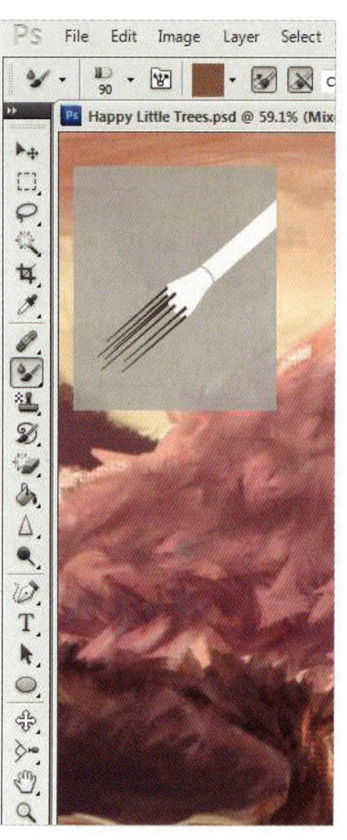

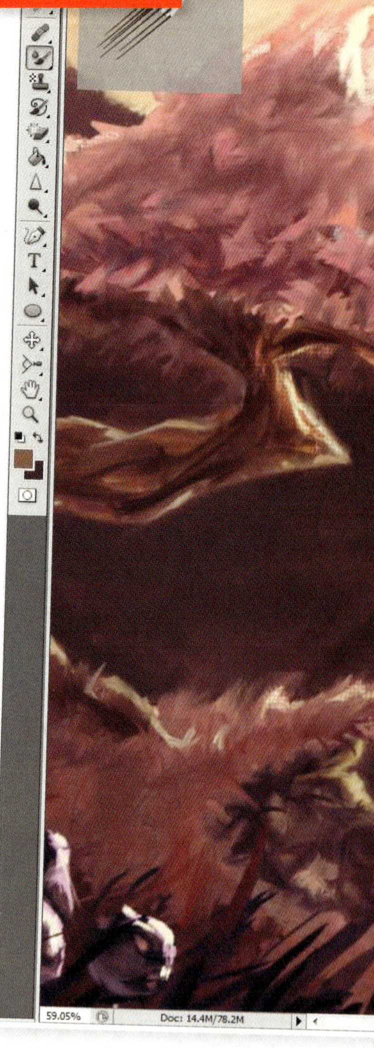

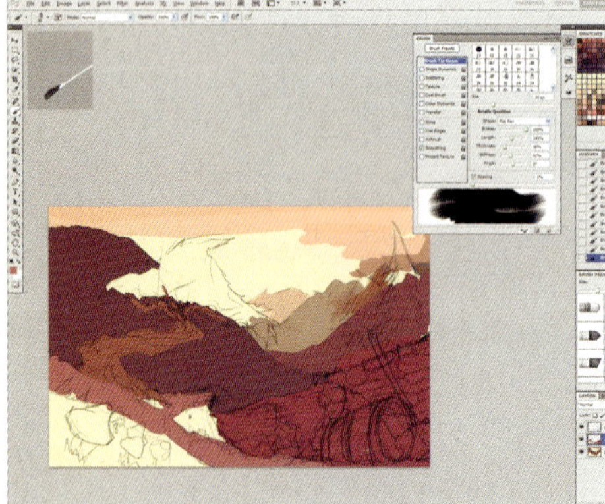

01 Quickly lay out flat colours

Select Flat Fan brush, tilt your stylus so you're painting with the side of the brush. Set the bristles to long and Stiffness to low to get broad strokes.

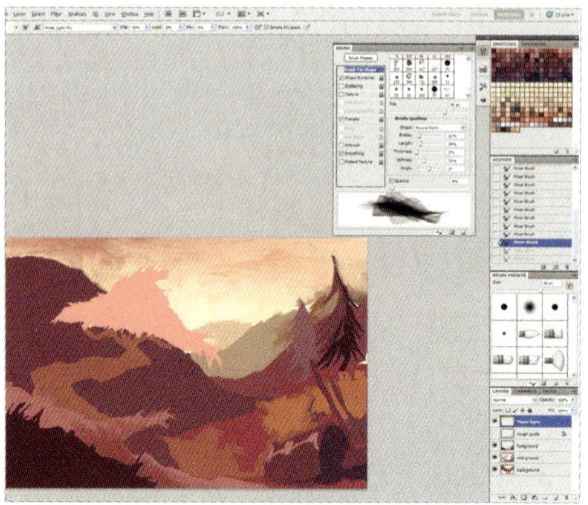

02 Non-destructive painting

Create a New Layer above your flat colours. Select Mixer brush and tick 'Use All Layers'. The colours will now blend without affecting the layer below.

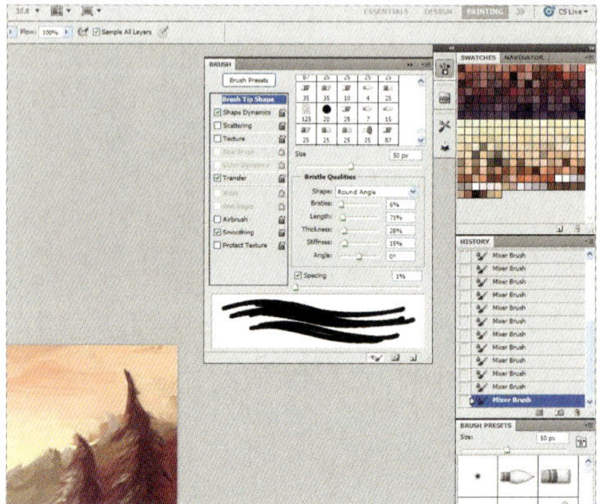

03 Brush work with less bristles

Paint the more detailed areas with obvious brush work; make the brush strokes more visible by lowering the bristle count.

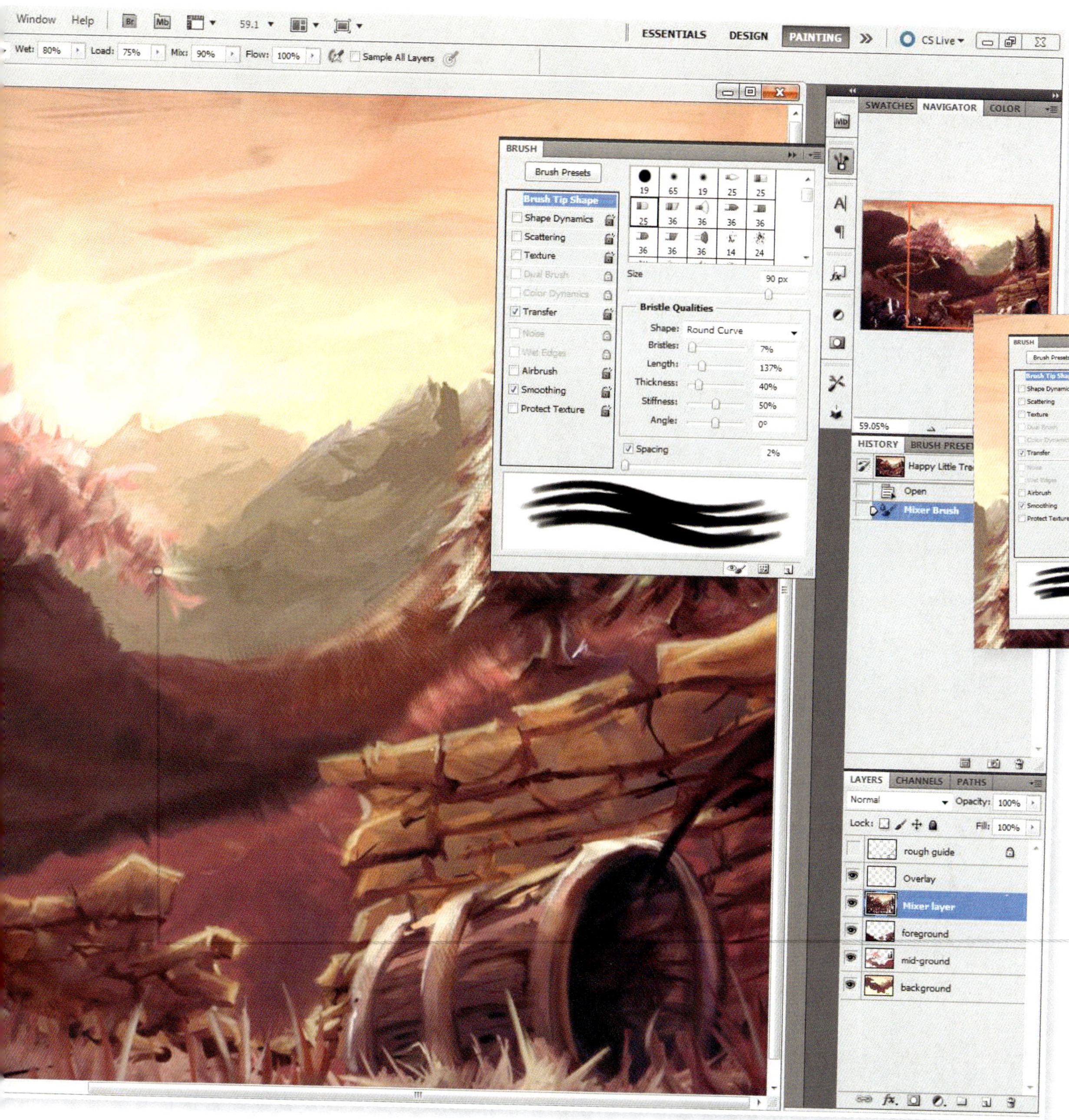

Choose your brush

Shape gives you a drop-down menu with the various brush shape presets. You can choose from a Round Point brush to the Flat Fan and every major style is represented.

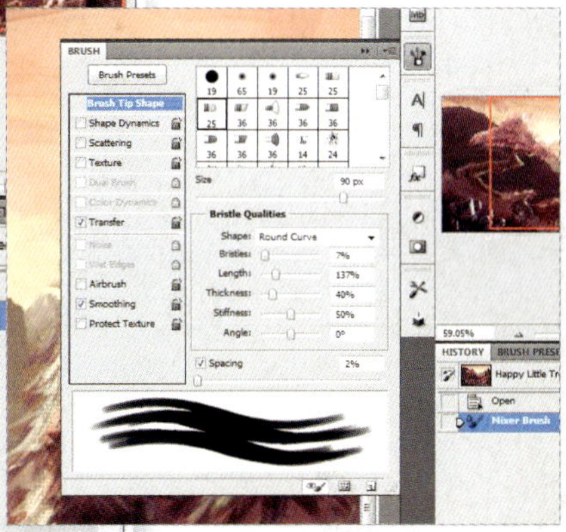

Bristles affect brush strokes

The Bristles setting affects the actual number of bristles in the brush, a high percentage will make for a smooth brush stroke whereas reducing the percentage allows you to see the individual bristles more easily.

Choose controlled or expressive brush strokes

The Stiffness setting affects the rigidity of the brush; a high percentage will make the brush stroke predictable, a low setting allows the bristles to move freely, giving expressive strokes.

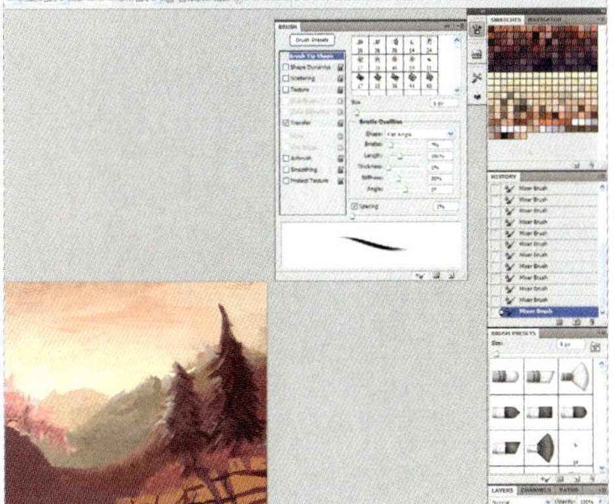

04 Add defined details

To add more defined details reduce the Wetness to 0 so none of the colour underneath is picked up and set the Load of your brush to 100%.

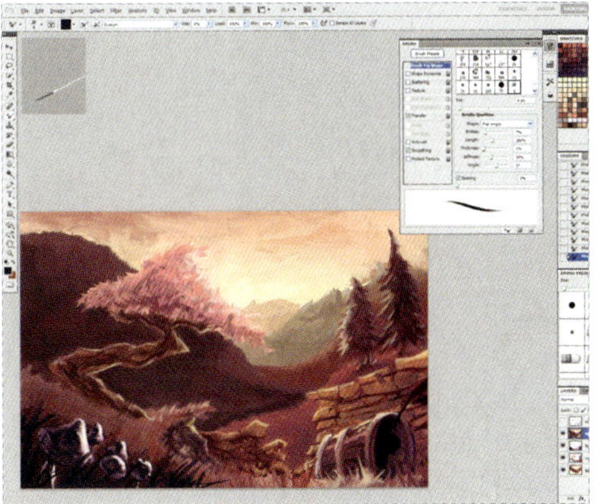

05 Blend and refine

Blend in and refine your details with your paint Load set to 100% and 1% Wet. Even 1% Wet will pick up lots of underlying colour.

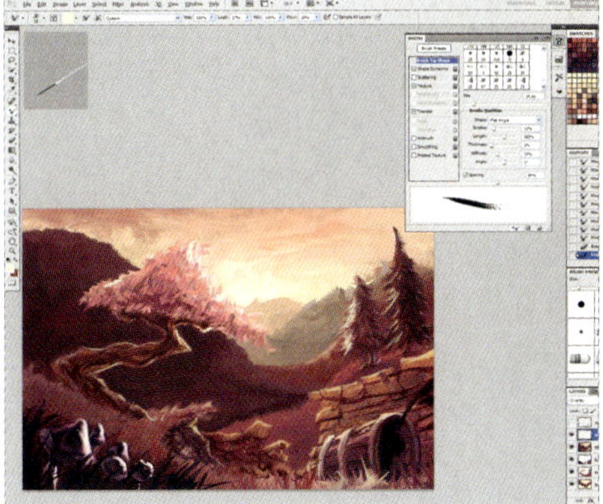

06 Finishing touch

Finish by painting where the Sun's light hits the elements in the image on a layer set to Overlay; use a light yellow with settings: Wet 100%, Load 27%.

Building a better brush

Don't just rely on brushes 'from the box'; create your own custom brushes to suit your painting style

Although Photoshop comes with an array of impressive brushes built in, they're barely the tip of the iceberg; Photoshop's brushes are capable of much more. When you start to alter their settings by clicking on the Brushes tab you'll see just how versatile they can be.

When digitally painting, it's best to work with a graphics tablet. Using a pen stylus will allow you to make the most of Photoshop's brushes with settings like Flow and Opacity.

To customise brushes you'll need to access the Brushes Palette (press F5). The Brushes Palette is where you control every aspect of the brush tool, and although the number of aspects at your control can be a little daunting at first glance, keep persisting and you'll soon be customising brushes like a pro.

You can choose the brush you want to customise by clicking the Brush Presets to bring up a brush stroke thumbnail preview. When you've selected the brush you want, you have a number of options. Clicking on Brush Tip Shape will display the stroke your current brush will make. Here you have the options to change the X and Y axis of the brush head, the Angle, Roundness, Hardness and Spacing.

You can add texture to your brushes, or use Dual Brush to combine two brushes and come up with a completely new third brush. You can even add Scattering to a brush which is great for painting things like leaves and foliage.

"Using a pen stylus will allow you to make the most of Photoshop's brushes"

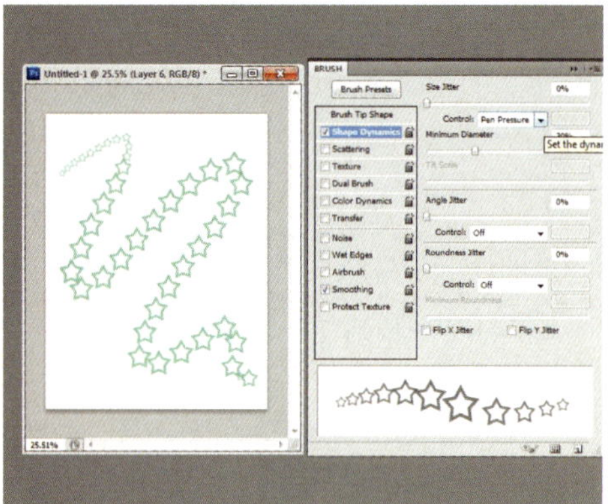

01 Size
Custom brushes will have their Size Jitter set to 'Pen Pressure', but you can set the Minimum Diameter of the brush head to maintain a brush's appearance.

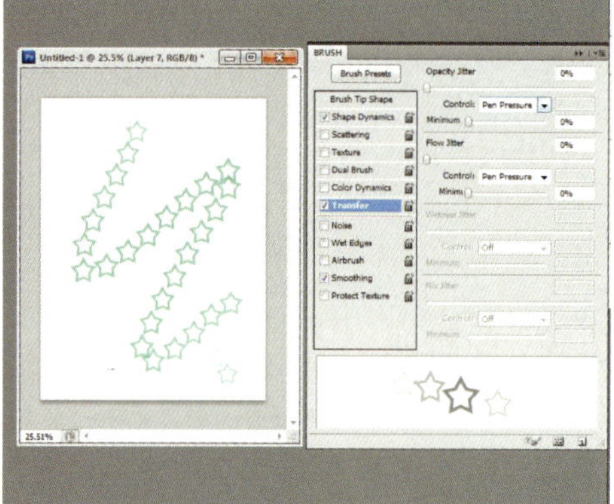

02 Other Dynamics
Adding the Flow and Opacity Jitter to the settings to Pen Pressure in conjunction with the Size Jitter will make your brushes feel more natural.

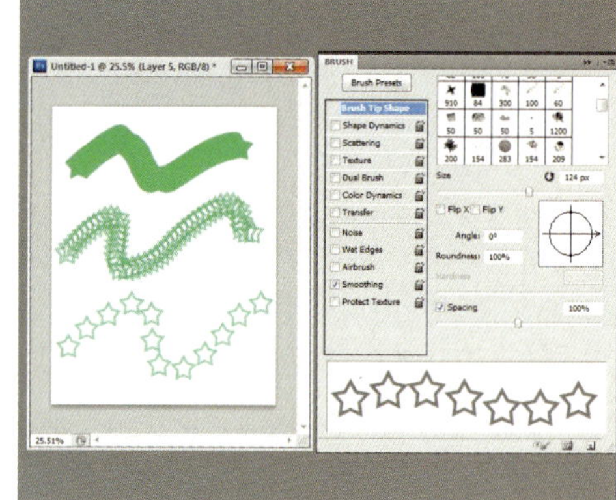

03 Spacing
Changing the Spacing of a brush tip can drastically alter it. The three strokes here are drawn with the same brush, but the Spacing is 1%, 25% and 100%.

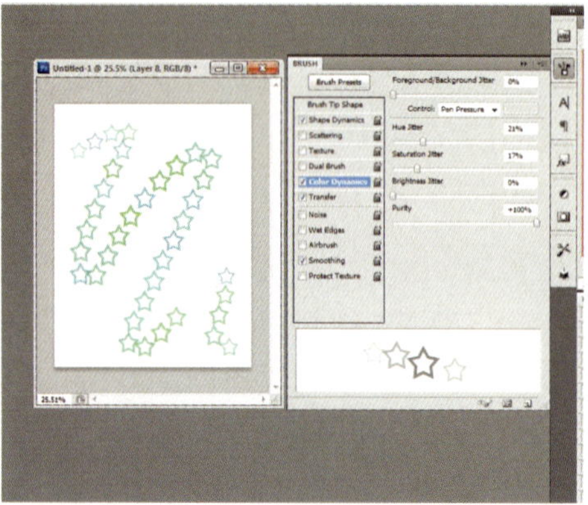

04 Color Dynamics
Use two different colours in one brush stroke by setting the Foreground/Background Jitter Control to Pen Pressure.

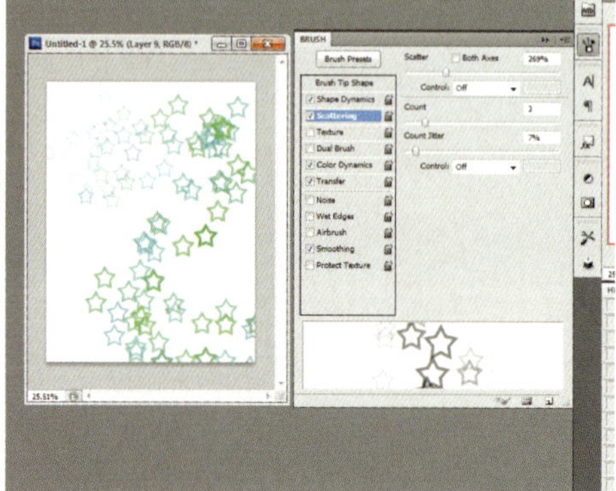

05 Scattering
Scattering multiplies the number of times the Brush Tip Shape is drawn in a brush stroke and scatters them along the line you've drawn.

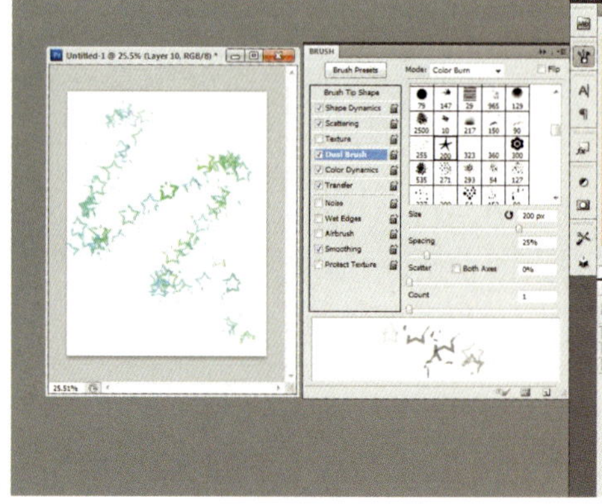

06 Dual Brush
Dual Brush combines two Brushes together with often unpredictable results. Experimentation is the key here.

QUICK PHOTOSHOP TIPS

Intuitive brush sizes

Click on the 'Shape Dynamics' tabs and set the Size Jitter to 'Pen Pressure'; your brush size will increase when you apply more pressure to your stylus

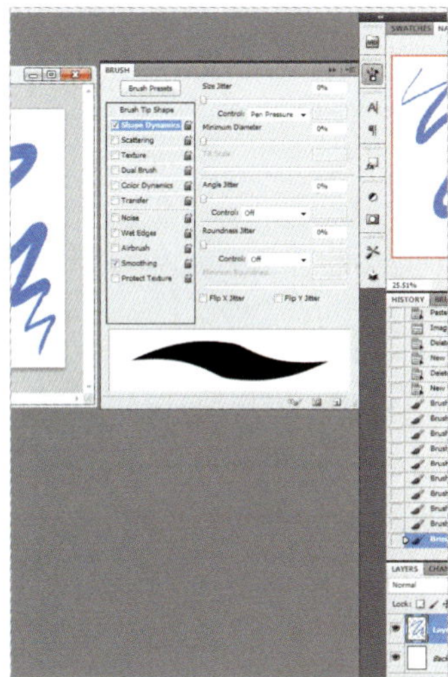

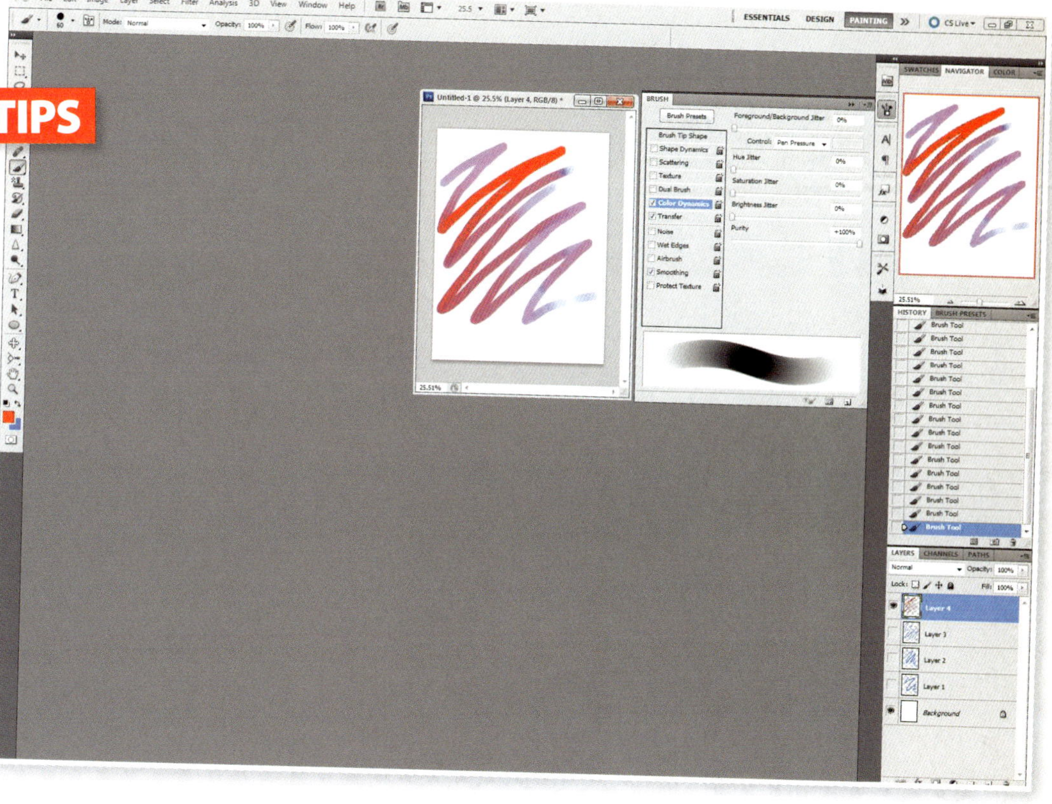

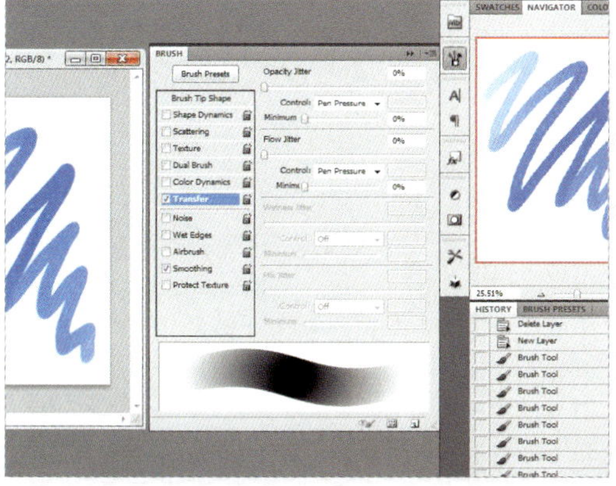

Tablet Options: Other Dynamics/ Transfer

For intuitive brush strokes, set both Flow and Opacity Jitter to 'Pen Pressure'. This will result in the harder you push down on your stylus, the more opaque the brush stroke becomes

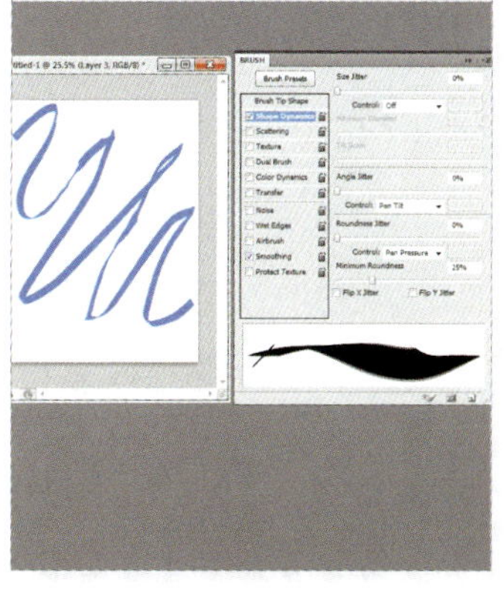

Change colours in one stroke

Set Color Dynamics to 'Pen Pressure' and apply light Pressure to start painting with the background colour, apply more pressure and the colour of the brush stroke blends into the Foreground colour

Alter a brush by tilting your pen

Certain tablets will have the ability to understand how you're tilting your stylus. Setting the Angle Jitter to 'Pen Tilt' takes advantage of this; Photoshop will alter your brush strokes accordingly

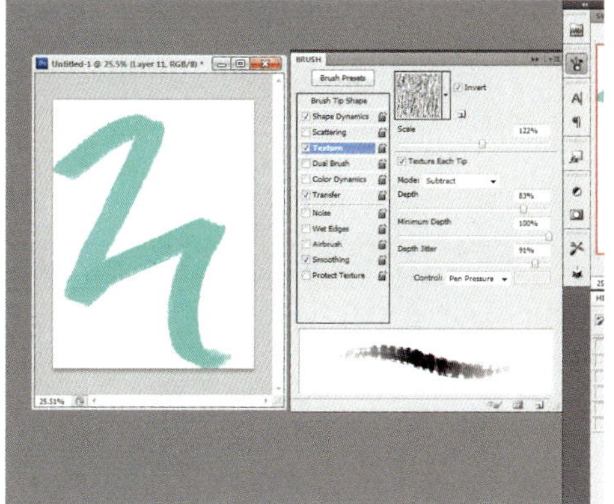

07 Texture

If you're not so keen on the digital look, make your Brushes look more like natural media by adding a Texture to it that affects the Brush Tip Shape.

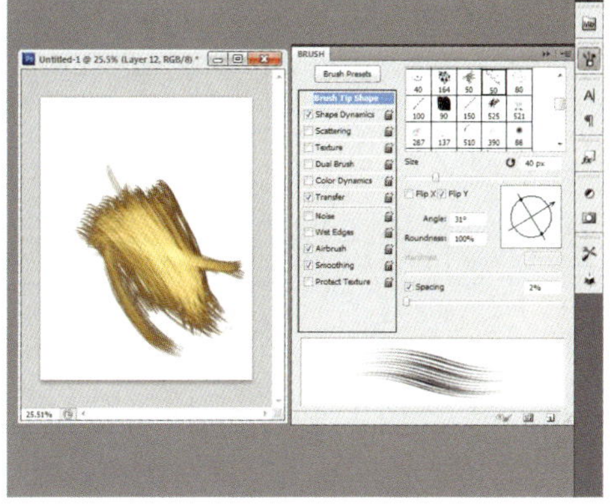

08 Change Blending Modes

You can set a brush's Blending Mode to Screen to make every stroke lighter than the first, which works great for rendering things like hair or grass.

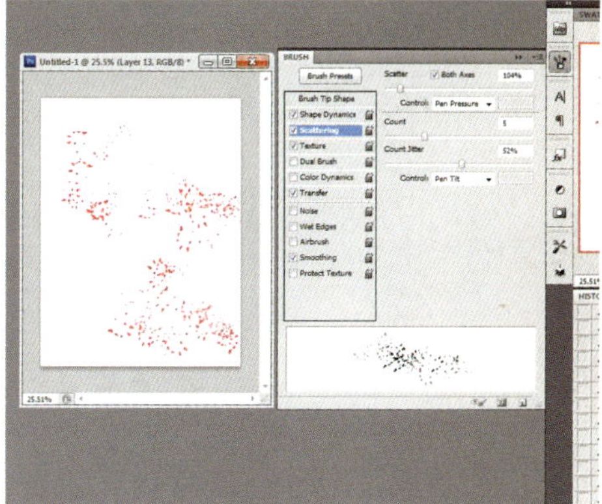

09 Spatter Effects

Spatter brushes are a great way of adding a messy look. Make sure to alter your brush's Scattering and Angle options for a randomised appearance.

Using tools with brushes

A lot of the tools in Photoshop use brushes; here's our quick guide to the most popular ones

Understanding how Photoshop's brushes work isn't just important to people that want to paint digitally, the knowledge will help you in photo editing and pretty much any Photoshop-related task. All of the tools we look at here can be used with any Brush Tip Shape you have in your Brush Library because they all work with Photoshop's Brush Engine.

No matter which of the Brush Engine-based tools you use, whether it's the Clone Stamp, History Brush or Smudge Tool, you'll be able to alter the options in two specific areas in your Workspace: the Toolbar and the Brushes Palette. The Brushes Palette can be opened by pressing F5 and contains the same brush-editing options regardless of which tool you are currently using.

The Toolbar is positioned directly below the Main Navigation Bar in Photoshop. Unlike the Brushes Palette, the settings available here are tool specific, you'll get a different selection of settings when the Eraser is selected than you would if using the Blur Tool.

Common elements in the Toolbar that each tool shares are the display of the Brush Tip shape and size and the brush's Blending Mode. There will also be an icon to enable your graphics tablet to override controls set in the Brushes panel.

Opacity and Flow are common settings to see in the Toolbar when using a brush-based tool and are helpful for controlling the strength of a brush's impact if you're using a mouse instead of a pressure-sensitive tablet.

"Opacity and Flow are helpful for controlling a brush's impact"

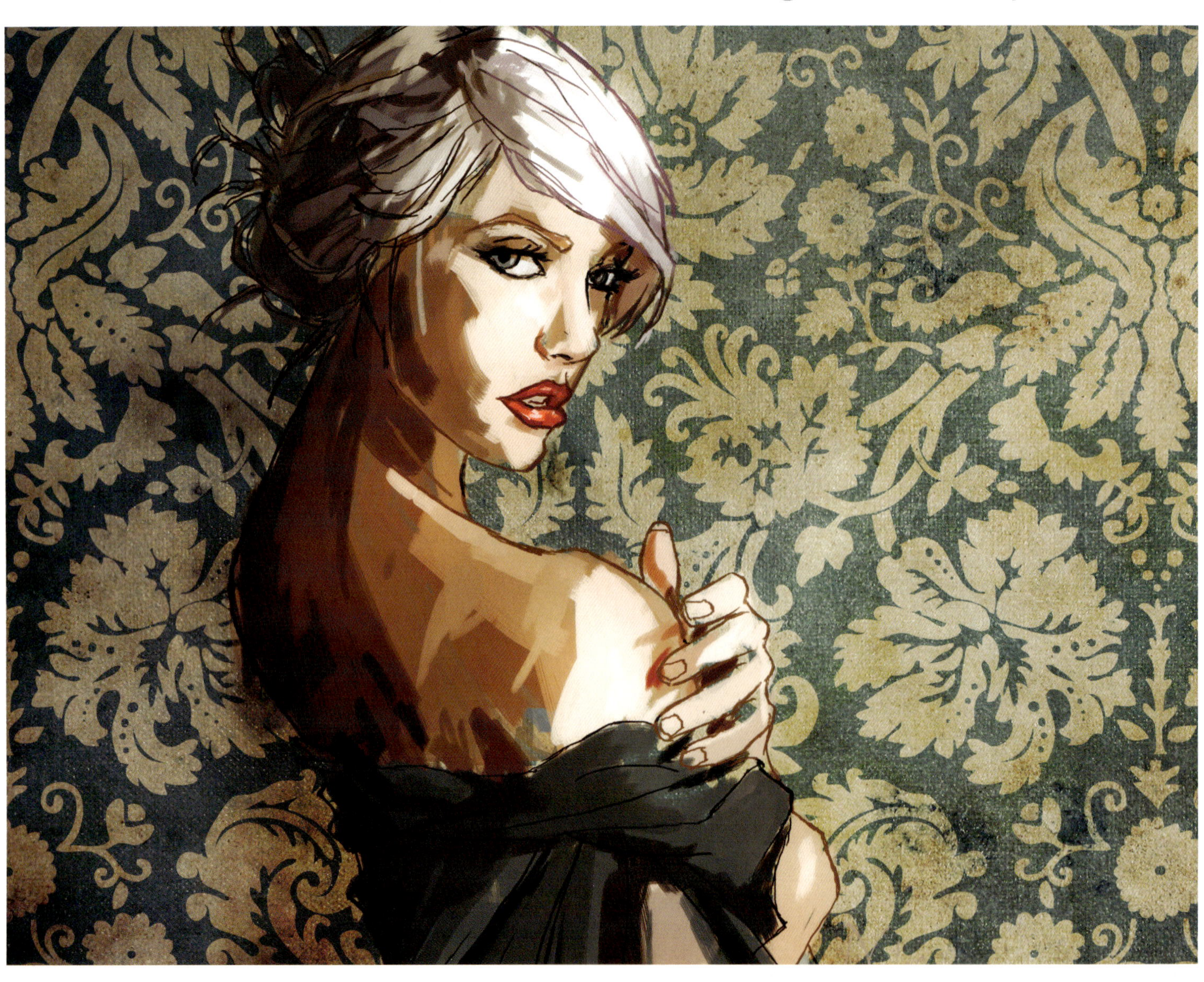

Popular brushes The various brushes and what they do

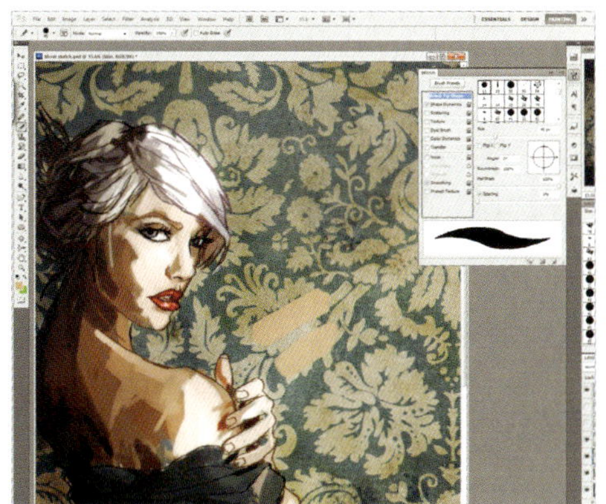

01 Hard Mix

The Pencil and Brush are almost identical but the Pencil creates hard-edged Aliased strokes and the Brush makes smoother Anti-Aliased brush strokes.

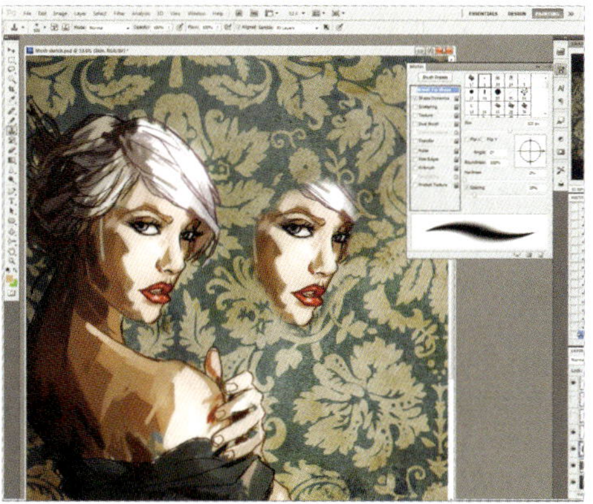

02 The Clone Stamp

Hit Alt to select an area that will be duplicated when you use the brush elsewhere on the image. Clone from All Layers or just the current Layer.

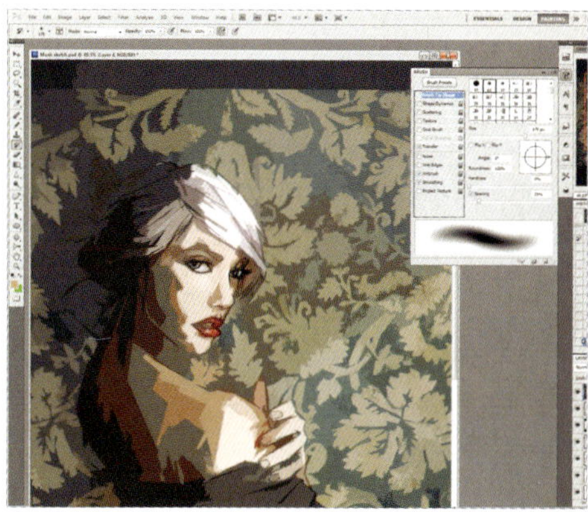

03 History Brush

The History Brush lets you fix mistakes and apply Filters; any area you paint on reverts to a previously defined state by using info from the history palette.

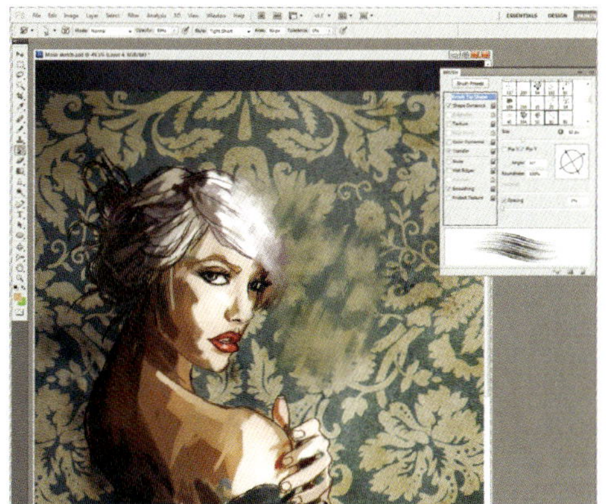

04 Art History Brush

A customisable special effects brush that gives you a pseudo-painterly effect superior to that of using a Filter by dragging your cursor over a photo.

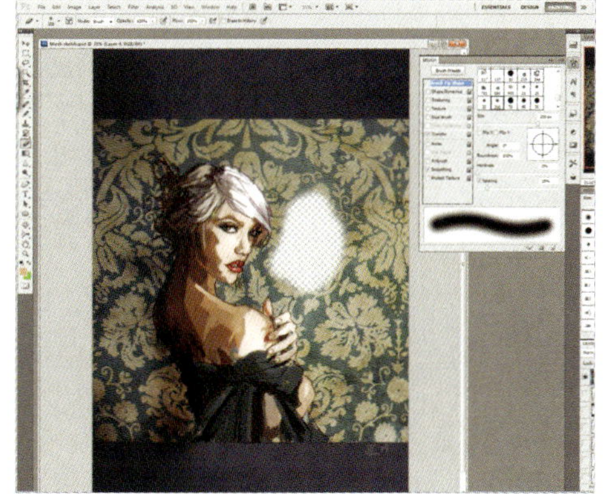

05 Erasers

Used for both corrections and special effects, changing your brush type and Opacity will give you a range of appearances to remove solid pixels.

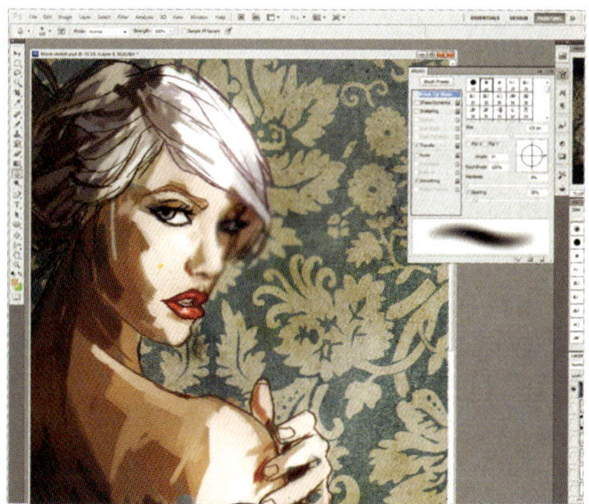

06 Blur

The Blur tool allows you to blur small areas such as wrinkles or spots. Use with restraint to avoid an obviously over-blurred image

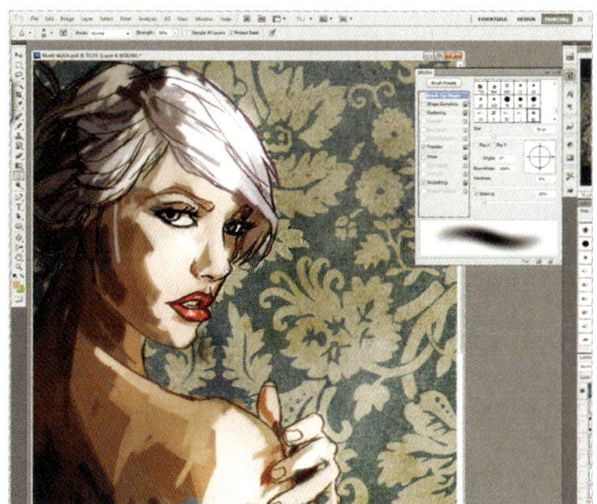

07 Sharpen

The Sharpen Tool increases the Contrast of any pixels you paint over it with to make the images appear crisper.

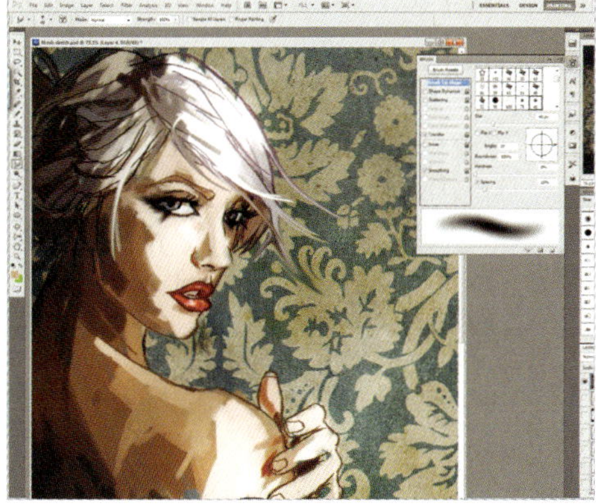

08 Smudge

The Smudge tool smears your paint across the canvas. The higher the Pressure level, the more of the paint will be removed from the canvas.

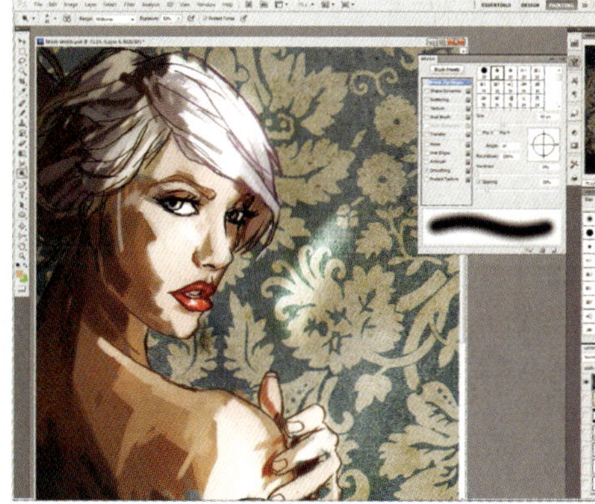

09 Dodge and Burn

Dodge and Burn lighten or darken any area you move the brush over. You can change their Range to affect Highlights, Midtones or Shadows.

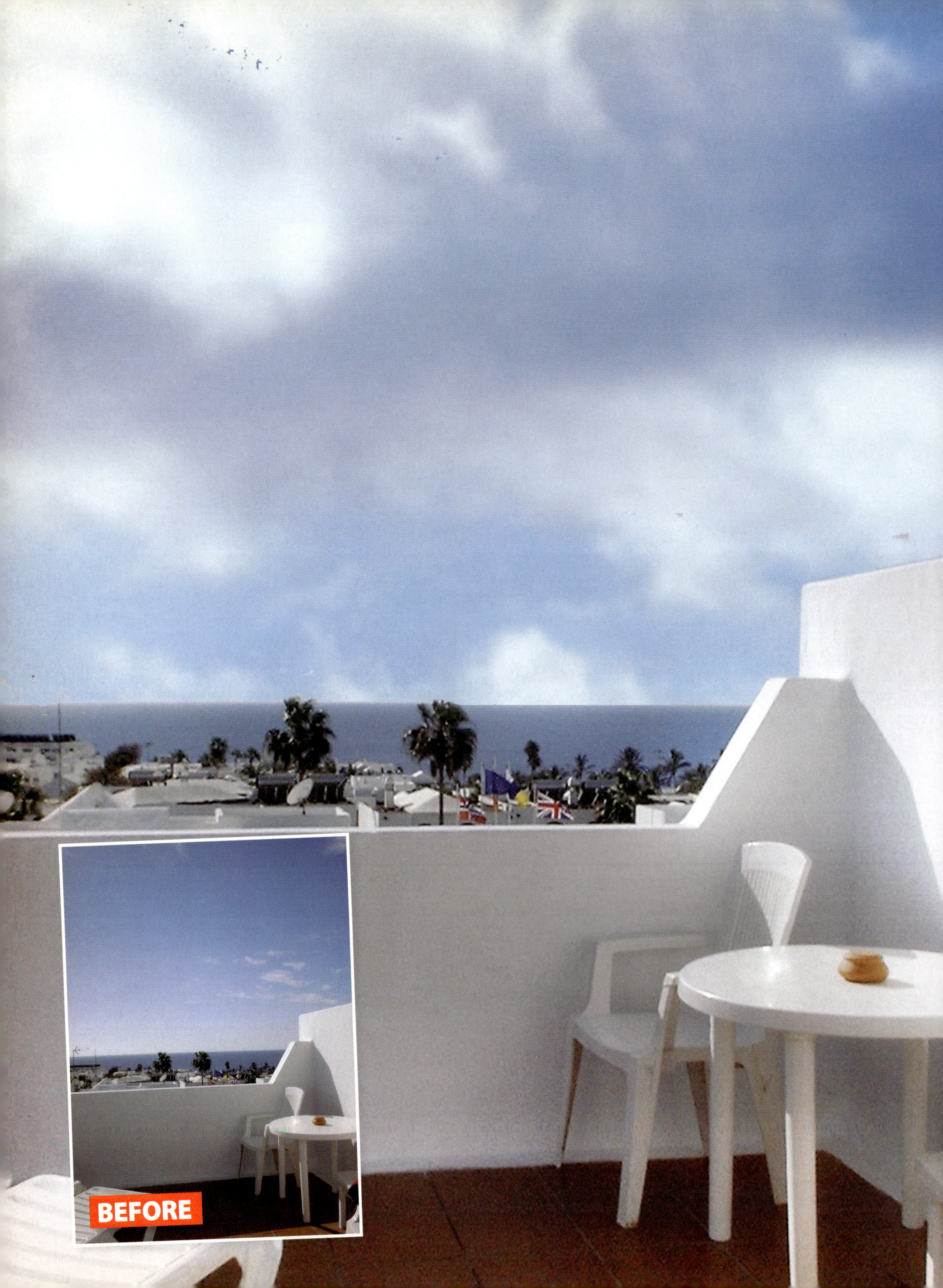
BEFORE

The multi-faceted Eraser tool

An easy-to-use tool with some great time-saving features that you can use for both correction and effect

The Eraser tool, as you've probably guessed, erases pixels, but as with everything in Photoshop, that's just scratching the surface.

There are three modes to choose from with the Eraser; 'Brush' which gives soft, anti-aliased edges, 'Pencil' which makes hard-aliased edges and block which gives you a square brush. You can make the effect more subtle by altering the Opacity of the Eraser in both Pencil and Brush modes, and you can also affect the Flow in Brush mode.

Nestled in the Eraser's flyout menu are the Background Eraser tool and the Magic Eraser tool. The Background Eraser is a useful time-saving device, although it won't magically erase a background as the name suggests. The Background Eraser samples the colour in the middle of the cursor at the moment of clicking, then as you drag the brush across the image it erases every pixel of the sampled colour leaving other colours untouched. Be careful not to move the centre of the cursor over a new colour as that new colour will be sampled and Photoshop will assume you want to erase it as well. If you are erasing similar colours you can alter the tolerance of the Background Eraser tool so Photoshop will only erase very specific shades.

The Magic Eraser tool erases all colours within a defined tolerance setting, you just need to click once and all of the surrounding colour will be erased without needing to drag the cursor.

"The Background Eraser is a useful time-saving device"

WHICH ERASER EFFECTS SUITS YOU?

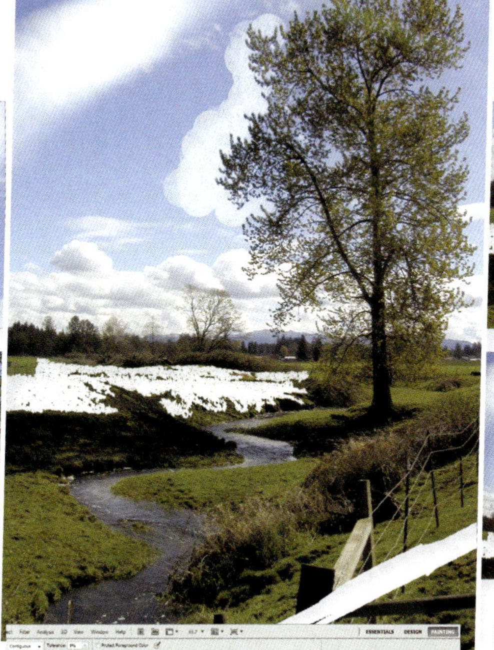

Smooth erasing

Using an airbrush Eraser set to 50% Opacity with Pen Pressure enabled will give you a subtle faded edge that you can easily control to make smooth transitions.

Erasing backgrounds

The Background Eraser makes complicated tasks like erasing the sky from a behind a tree seem easy thanks to its intelligent continuous colour sampling.

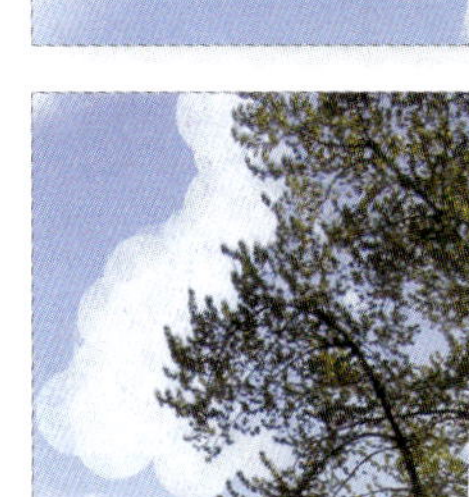

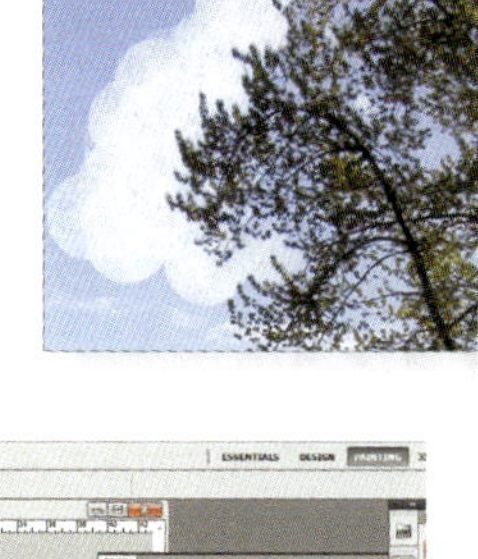

One-click quick erasing

The Magic Eraser is excellent at quickly removing large areas of similar colour, just one click and all contiguous areas of similar colour are erased.

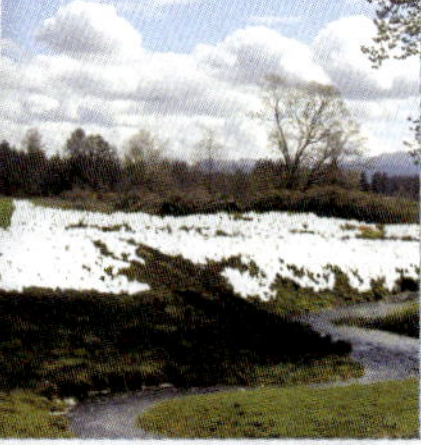

Bold erasing

Sometimes you don't need your Eraser to be subtle or clever; if you just want a nice clean brushstroke to eliminate pixels you really can't beat using the Eraser Brush tool.

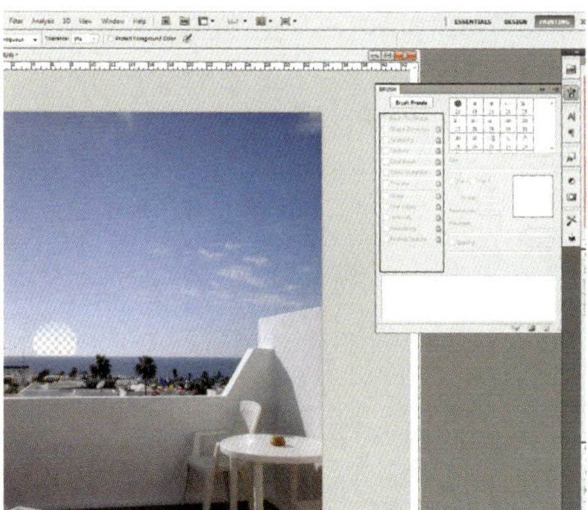

01 Click and drag

Select the Background Eraser, set Sampling to Continuous and Tolerance to 9%. Click and drag to erase the sky where it meets the sea.

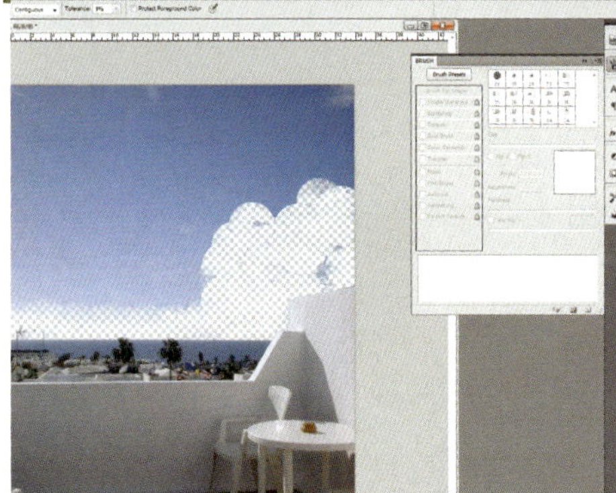

02 Remove the sky

Drag the cursor to erase the sky, leaving the sea and balcony intact. Once it's separated you can use the Magic Eraser to delete the remainder of the sky.

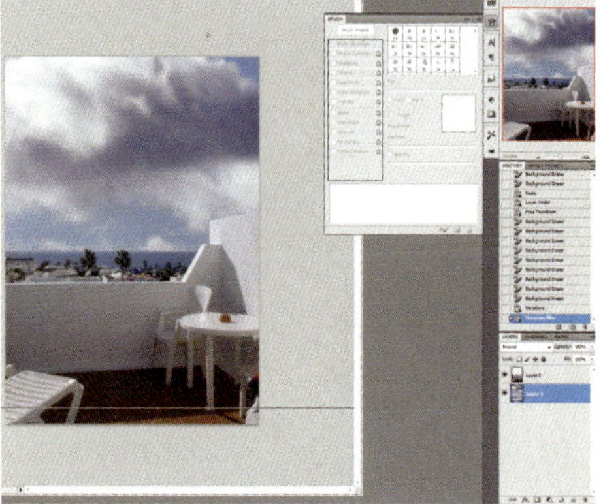

03 Change the sky

With the sky erased, you can copy and paste in the contents of a different image in the layer below what you were working on to change the scene.

Make Art History

Get painterly effect brushstrokes just by using the History palette then dragging your brush over a photo!

The Art History brush gives you a paint brush effect, allowing you to make your photos appear as if they had been painted digitally. Much like the History brush, the Art History brush tool uses a history state (designated by you by clicking in the left column in the History palette) as a source to work from. However, where the History brush simply recreates the data, the Art History brush uses the data in conjunction with your choice of brush options to create an artistic style paint brush effect with your brush strokes, allowing you to turn a simple photo into a more expressive work of art just by simply dragging the cursor over the image.

While the end result won't look like it's been painted traditionally, using the Art History brush tool will look more authentic than simply using a Filter on a photo as there are several ways to customise the effect of the tool to create attractive images. You can alter the size and type of stroke as well as its Opacity and the Blending mode it uses. There are ten options to choose from in the Style drop-down menu; it's worth playing with them to see what effects they have on the brushwork.

The Art History brush tool is more successful when set to "Pen Pressure" in Other Dynamics in the Brushes palette to make the effect more subtle. Although you can stick to a simple round brush head when using the Art History brush, you'll get much more exciting and unpredictable results if you change the brush to use a more unconventional brush like a spatter brush.

"The Art History brush uses the data in conjunction with your choice of brush options"

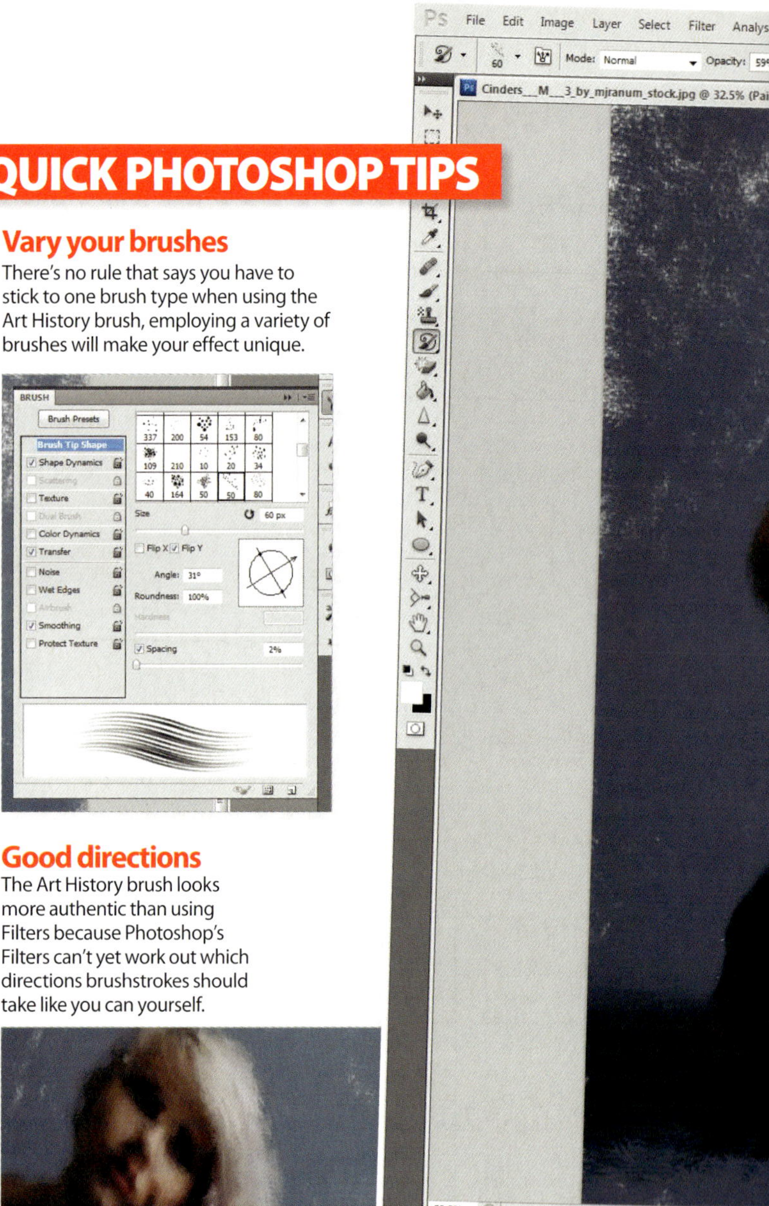

QUICK PHOTOSHOP TIPS

Vary your brushes

There's no rule that says you have to stick to one brush type when using the Art History brush, employing a variety of brushes will make your effect unique.

Good directions

The Art History brush looks more authentic than using Filters because Photoshop's Filters can't yet work out which directions brushstrokes should take like you can yourself.

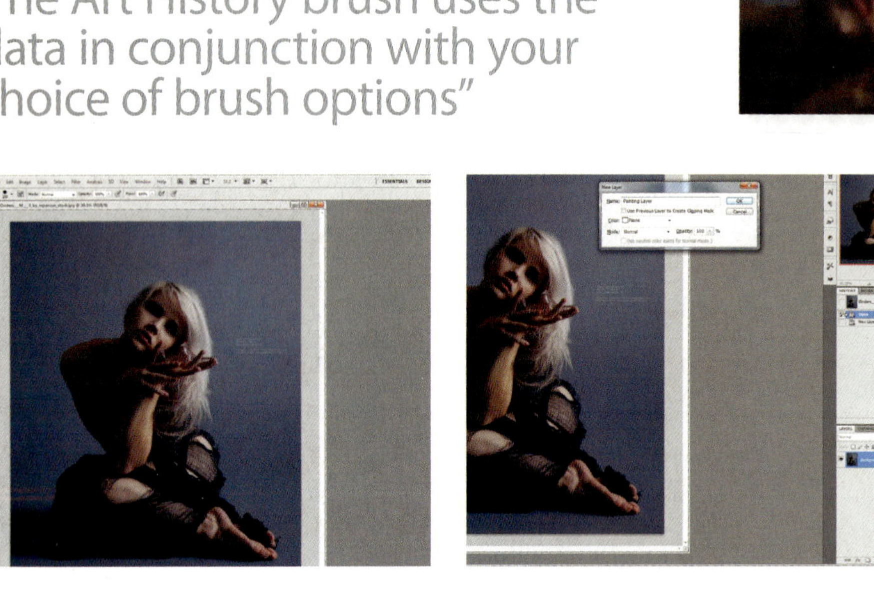

01 Making history

Open the image you want to work from and go to the History palette. Click in the left column box to use this as the source for the tool.

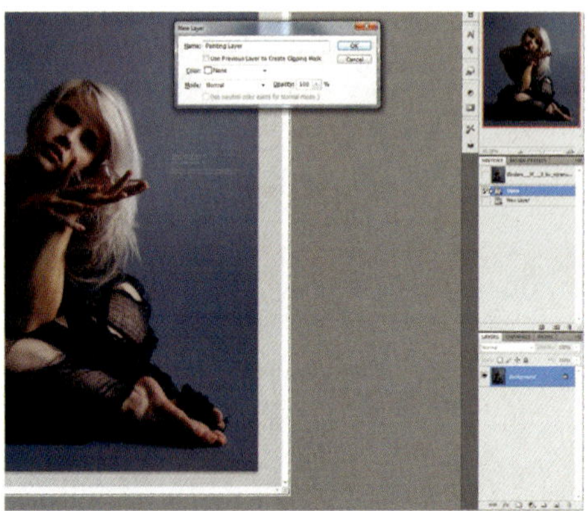

02 Create a new layer to paint on

Creating a new layer to work on will keep your original photo safe; click on the small piece of paper in the Layers palette to create a new layer.

03 Fill the canvas

Select the Paint Bucket tool and fill the canvas with white. Select the Art History tool by clicking and holding on the History tool flyout menu.

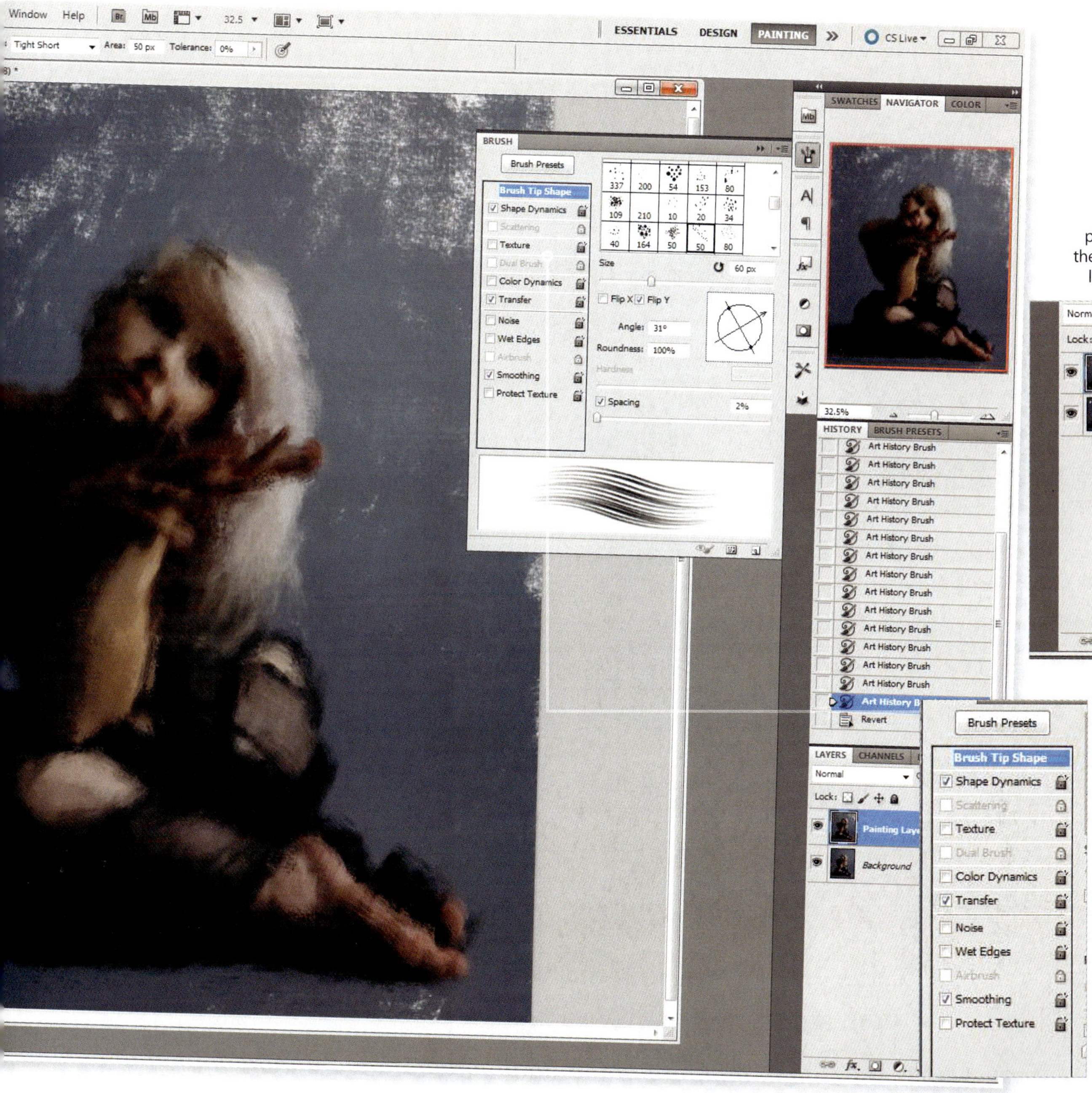

Paint on a new layer

Painting on a new layer not only protects the original photo but you can also lower the Opacity of your painting to let the photo bleed through.

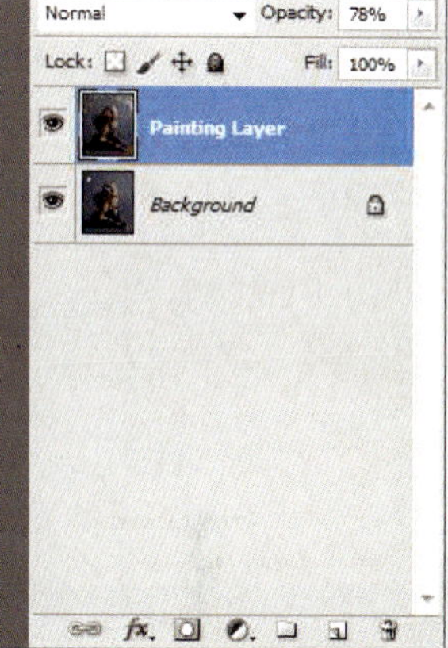

Experiment with the Style menu

Each of the ten options in the style Menu offer a different method of creating brushstrokes which will give different results depending on your custom Brush and the Brush's size.

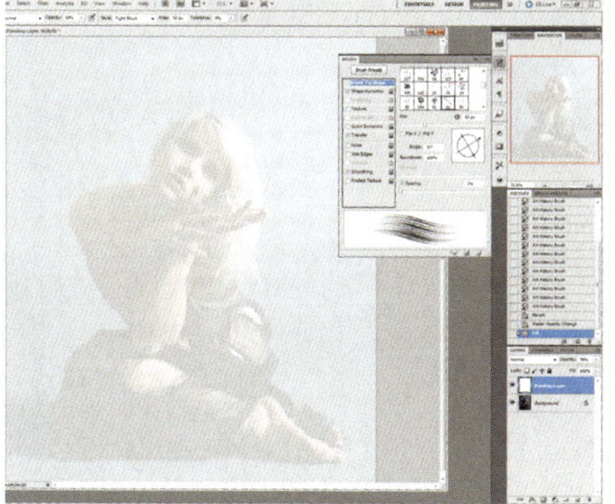

04 Give yourself a guide

Lower the Opacity of the white layer by dragging the Opacity slider in the Layers palette so you can view the original picture and use it as a guide.

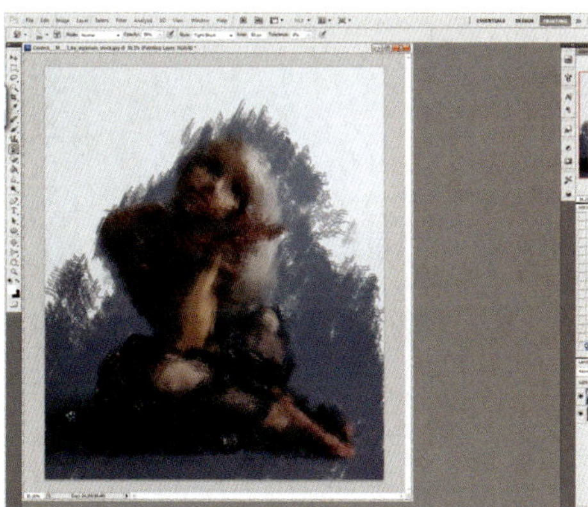

05 Start painting

Using broad brushstrokes, 'paint' in the details. Make the directions of your strokes follow the form of the photos to make it look like you painted it.

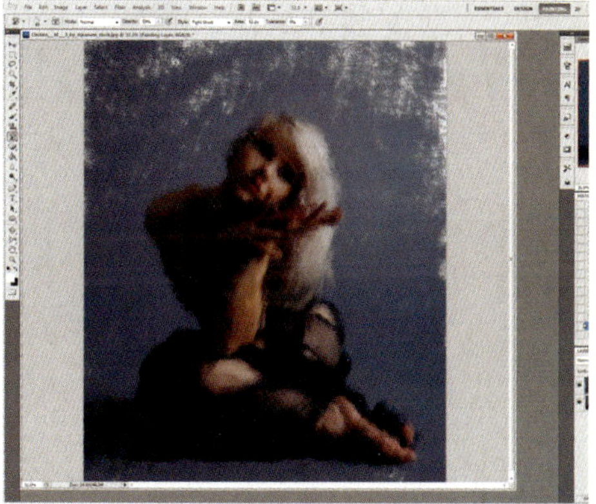

06 Adding in the detail

Reduce the size of your brush to retrace over the more detailed areas to bring some of the detail back and raise the Opacity back to 100%.

Use the History tools in Photoshop

Use Photoshop's History Brush tool to move parts of your image through time and correct those mistakes you hadn't noticed you'd made!

Want to change history? Meet Photoshop's answer to Doc Brown's DeLorean: the History Brush tool! While not quite as flashy as a time-travelling car, it's a lot more reliable and doesn't require you to have a working flux capacitor!

The History Brush tool is one of the most useful and overlooked image editing features in Photoshop; it reverts any part of an image back to a previous state without affecting the rest of the image. You can edit your photo as a whole and then use the History Brush to restore your chosen areas back to their original appearance. It has many applications, not only the aforementioned selective image editing. If you've ever had one of those annoying "Uh-oh, I hadn't noticed I'd changed that!" moments, the History Brush tool can be used to correct unintentional changes you may have made to areas of an image. All you have to do is locate the last point the section was correct in the History palette and set the source by clicking in the small column on the left of the History palette, then 'turn back time' and fix your mistakes by painting the image back to how it used to look with the History Brush tool.

You can brighten or darken with the History Brush by selecting the current state as the source then setting the History brush's Blending mode (in the toolbar) to Screen (to lighten) or Multiply (to darken). The tool will then use the existing information to re-draw a brighter or darker version.

"It's a lot more reliable and doesn't require a working flux capacitor!"

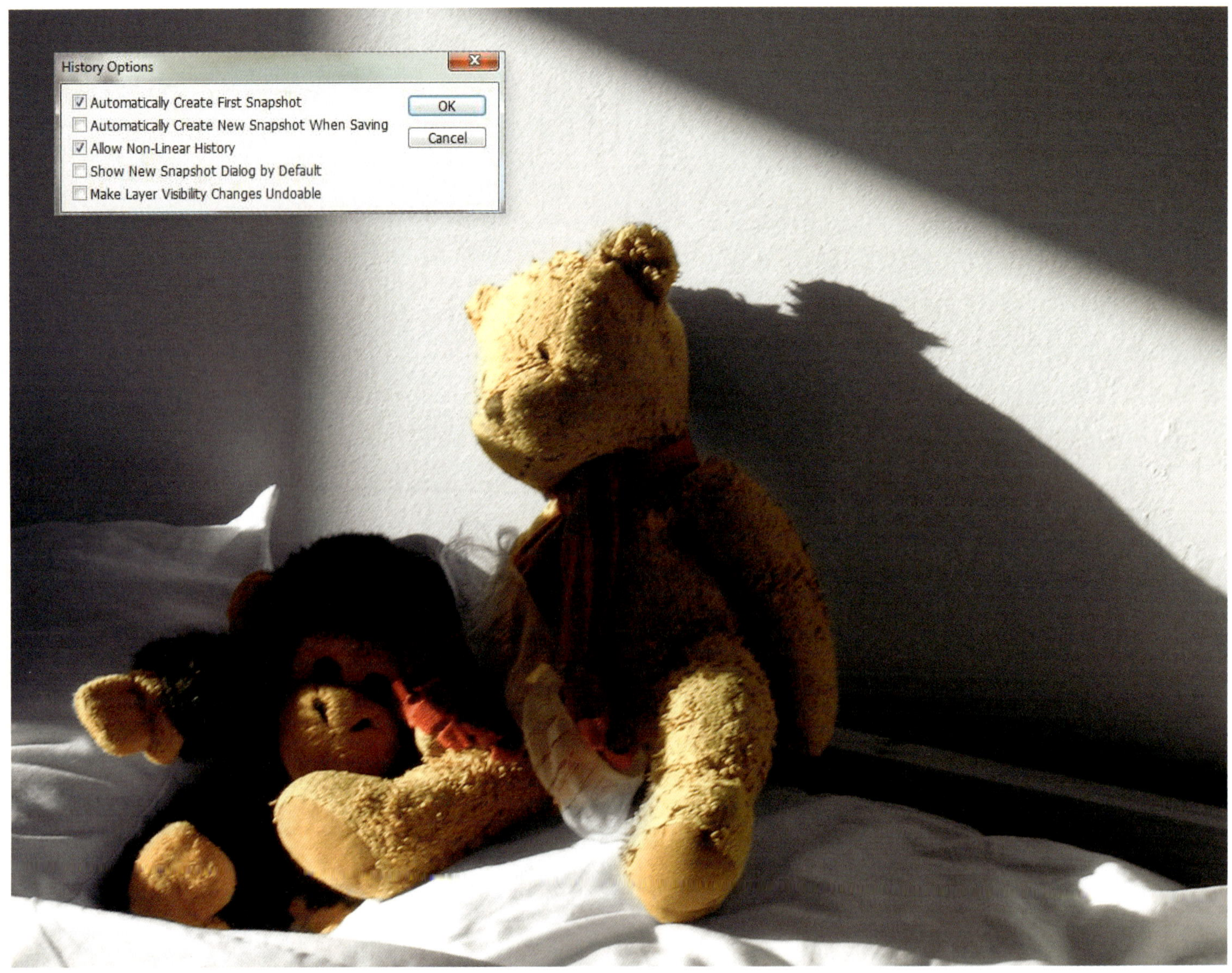

QUICK PHOTOSHOP TIPS

Bring things back quickly

Sometimes it's quicker to mask off the area that you want changes to remain intact and use a large brush to revert the remainder of the image.

Fading through time

You can change the opacity of the strokes you have just applied by going to Edit>Fade immediately after using the History Brush tool.

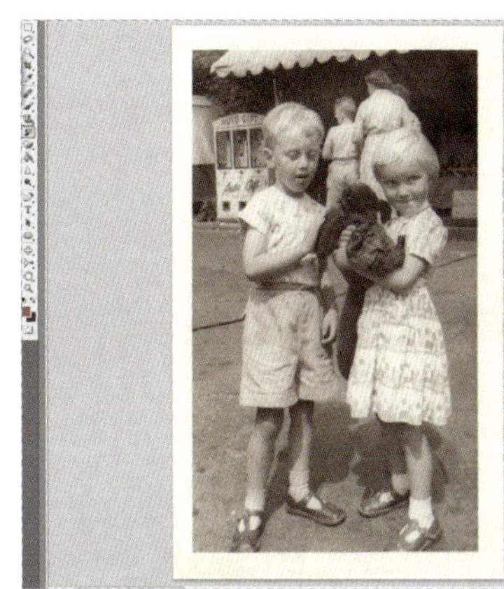

Paint from an alternate future!

Ticking 'Allow Non Linear History' in the History palette menu lets you make changes from based upon a state that you have since undone!

Use on filters

Useful filters like Dust & Scratches blur an entire image. If you only need a small section changed, use the History Brush to undo the filter on the relevant areas.

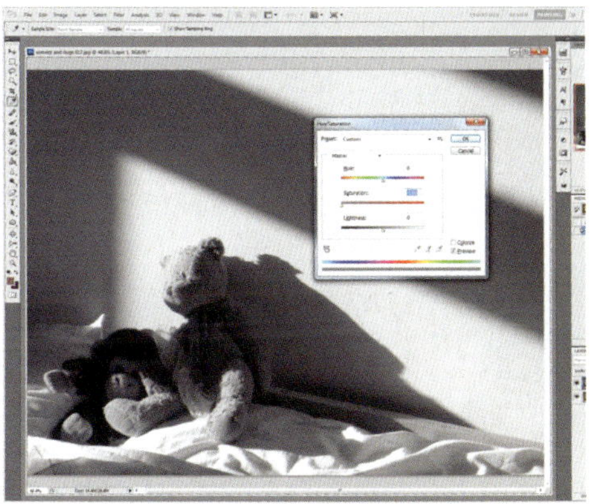

01 Applied to a whole image

Open your image and go to Image>Adjustments> Hue Saturation. In the box move the Saturation Slider to the left to desaturate the image.

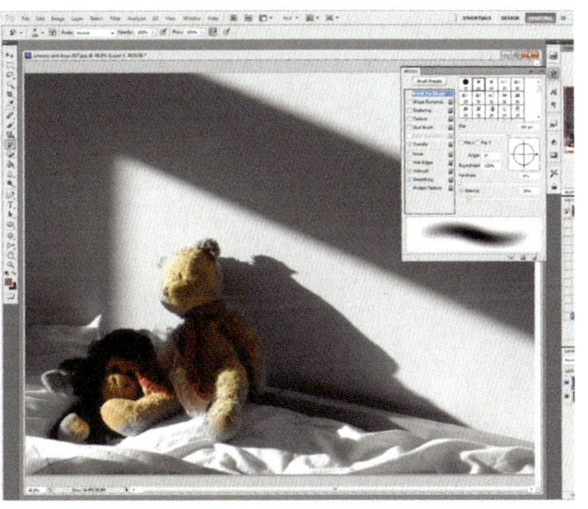

02 Quickly bring back the subject

Press 'Y' to select the History brush and select a large Airbush with its Opacity set to Pen Pressure in the Brushes tab to bring back most of the subject.

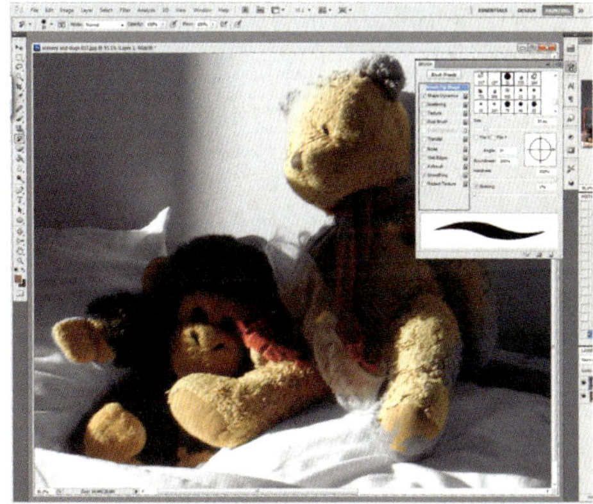

03 Tidy up the edges

Switch to a smaller hard-edged brush to bring back the edges of the subject so the background is still desaturated and the subject is in colour again.

The Color Picker uncovered

Add a little colour to your life and choose from the millions of shades available with Photoshop's Color Picker

There are millions of different shades to choose from in Photoshop and the Color Picker makes selecting the perfect one a breeze. You can set the hue used for not only the foreground and background colour but other design elements such as text. As well as offering control over the precise tint used, the Picker can make sure that the colours chosen are part of the web-safe palette or are chosen according to specific colour systems.

Selecting using the Picker is simple. First you need to get in the right colour spectrum by moving the vertical slider. The shade can then be fine-tuned in the large colour box. Photoshop lends a hand by displaying the current and new colour that has been chosen in the boxes for you to compare. Within the Color Picker there are a range of different colour modes such as RGB, CMYK and Lab, and if you don't want to choose a colour by eye you can enter values into one of the colour modes' sets of boxes. For example, entering 22 in R, 58 in G and 215 in B in the RGB colour mode area creates a bright blue.

If you are lucky enough to have Photoshop CS5, then there are a couple of Color Picker options available, which use the same principle, but in an even-easier-to-use setup.

We will go through the main points of the standard Color Picker over these two pages, but have a go for yourself to see just how easy it is to get to grips with.

"It displays the current and new colour that has been chosen in the boxes for you to compare"

QUICK PHOTOSHOP TIPS

Choose your hues

A whopping 256 levels of saturation make up the large colour square from left to right. It also has 256 levels of lightness and darkness from the top to the bottom. Clicking lower in the square with the Hue or Saturation button selection adds more black to a shade.

01 Additive and subtractive

RGB is additive colour: if red, green and blue are combined at full strength white is produced. When C, M, Y and K are combined they produce black.

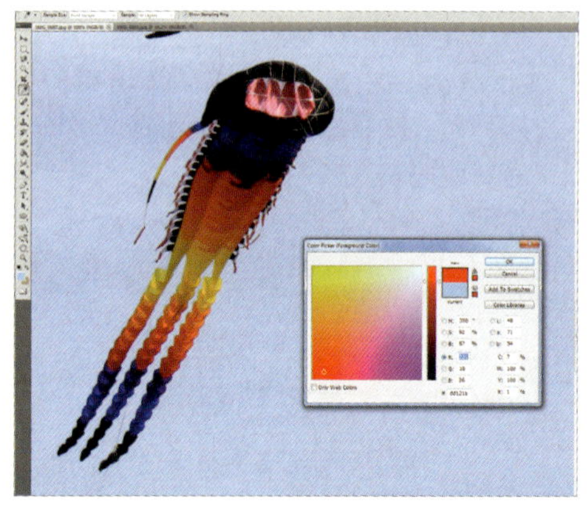

02 Primary colours

RGB mode refers to the three colours or channels of red, green and blue. It is the way that monitors show colour; making it suitable for video display.

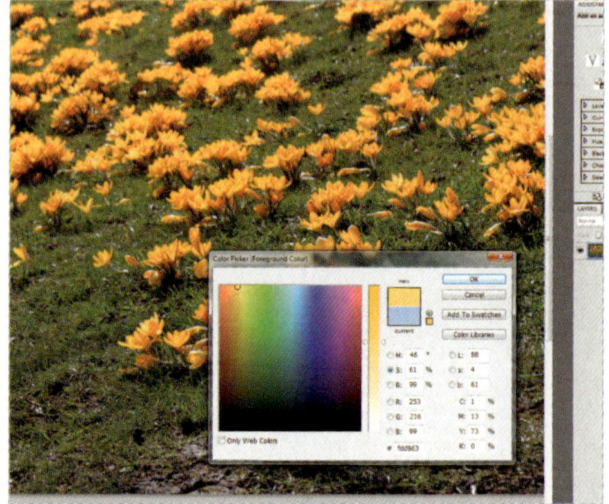

03 Amazing hues

The HSB colour space in Photoshop is selected by default when the Color Picker opens. It stands for hue, saturation and brightness.

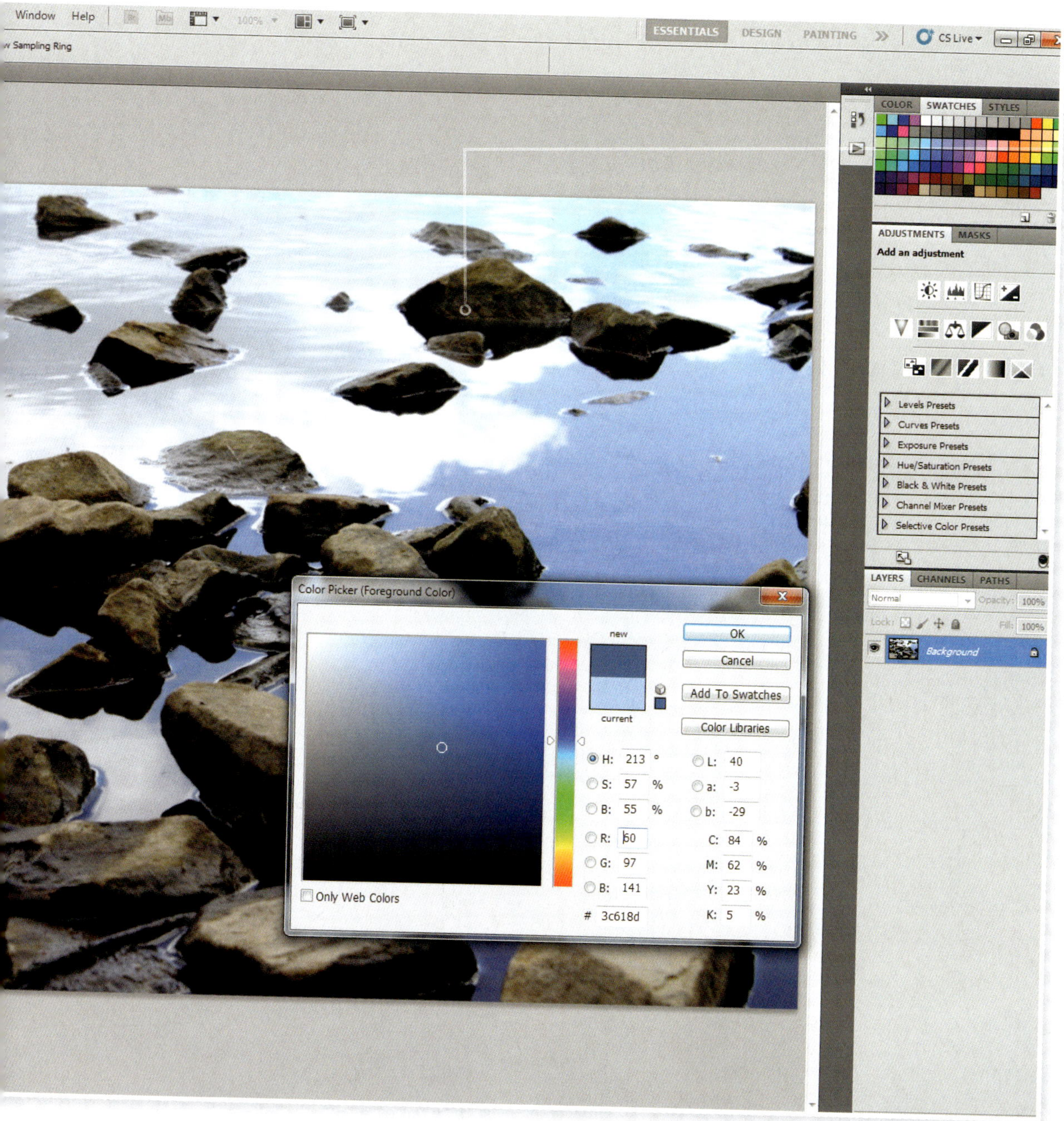

On the safe side

When the box beside Only Web Colours is checked, the Color Picker will be restricted to only displaying shades that are within the Web-safe palette which is made up of 216 different colours.

Red alert

A triangle with an exclamation mark appears if a colour is non-printable within the CMYK colour space and Photoshop displays the closest colour within CMYK's range. A small cube pops up if a colour is not Web-safe. Clicking the colour swatch that appears below the alert will change it to the closest match.

Slide it about

To change the colour in the main colour window, use the colour slider. Located to the right of the large colour square, the rainbow-coloured slider also offers 256 different hues. Clicking on an area of the slider or dragging its arrows changes the colour in the large square.

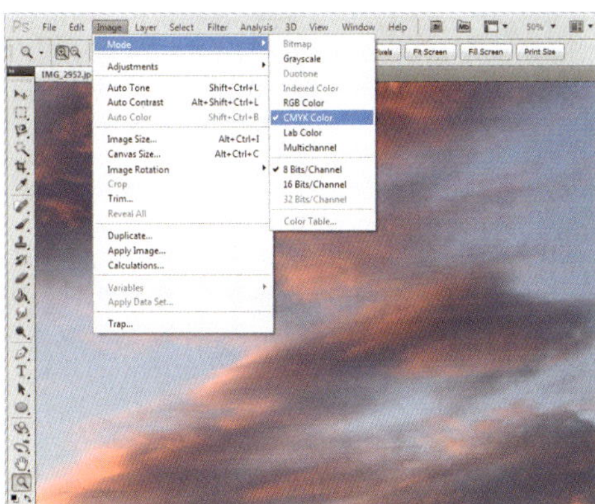

04 Perfect printing

CMYK is the standard mode for pro printing. It stands for cyan, magenta, yellow and key colour (or black).

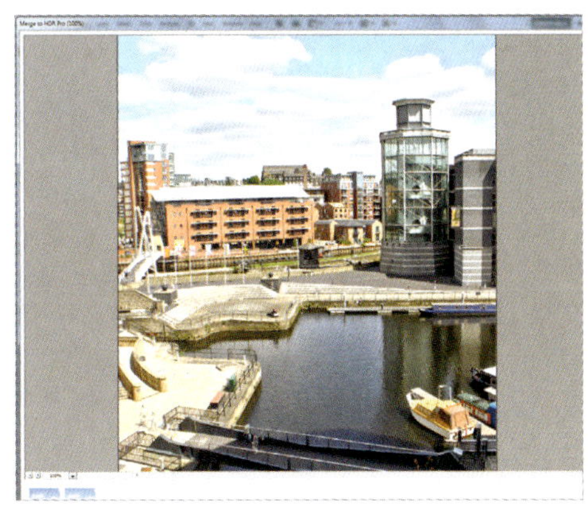

05 HDR Color Picker

Photoshop Extended users are able to enjoy the HDR Color Picker which allows colours to be selected and viewed to use in 32-bit HDR images.

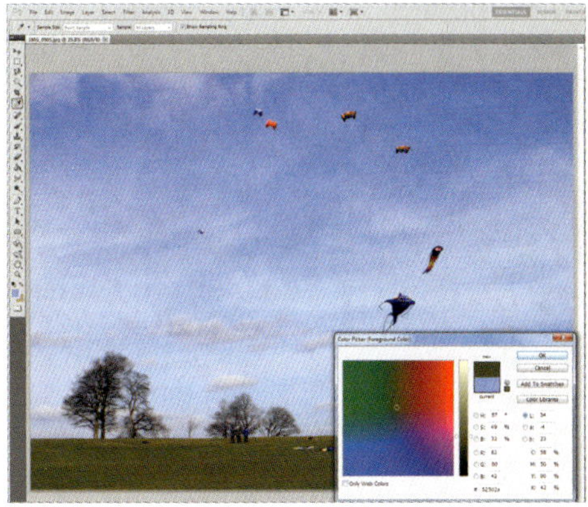

06 Like the eye

The Lab mode is the only device independent Photoshop mode which means it should print or display the same on any printer or monitor.

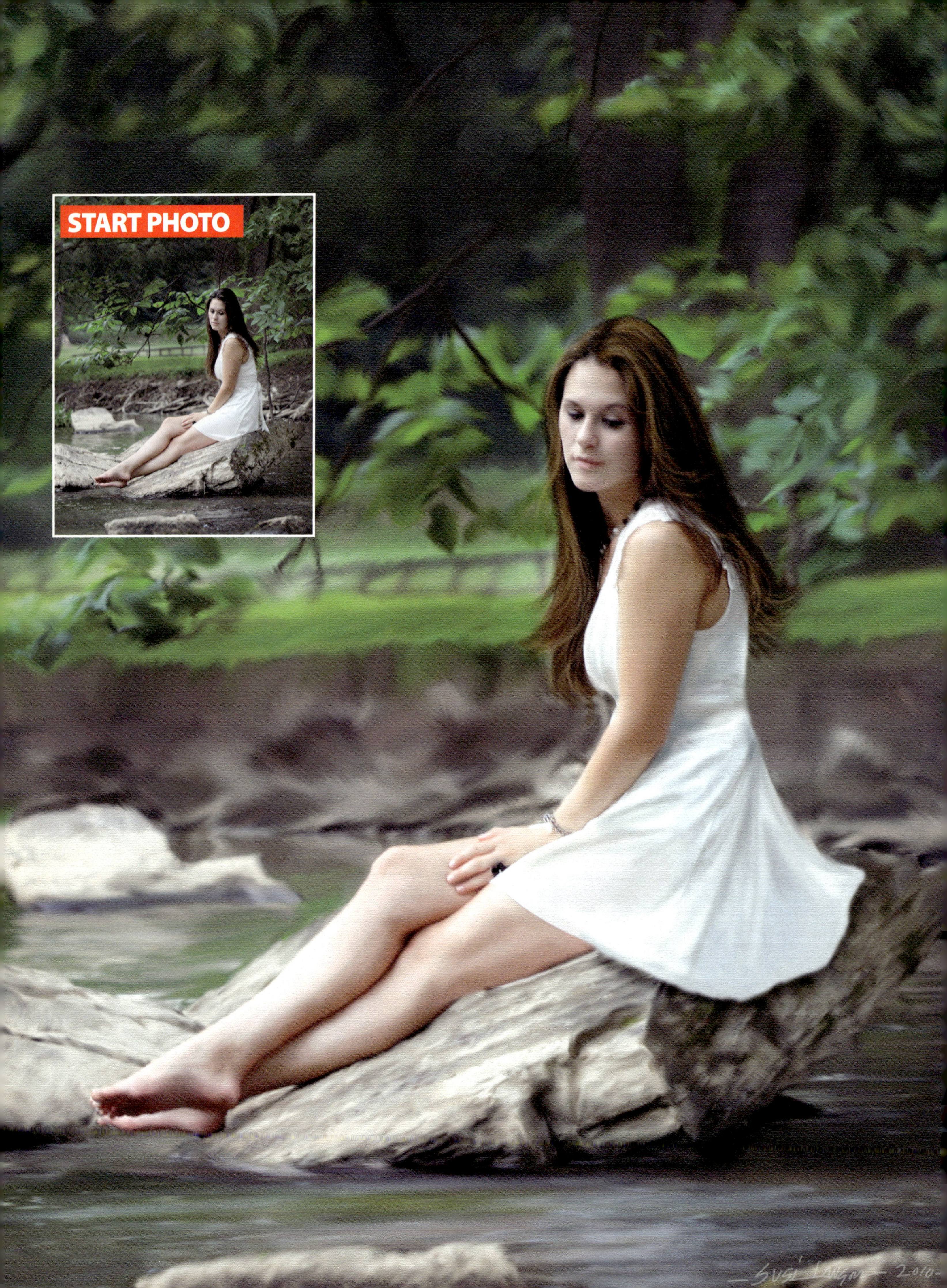
START PHOTO

Photo to painting with Smudge

A straightforward look at creating an oil portrait using this hidden gem of a tool

The Smudge tool is an easy way to try your hand at 'oil' painting, so this lesson begins with how to smudge directly over a scenic portrait and paint the entire image using only the Scatter brush.

You will work from background to foreground, which is the same process as a traditional artist. Working this way also enables you to paint over any overflow as you move towards the foreground.

You will also use the traditional brush strokes called 'hatching' and 'cross hatching' to create a nice painterly effect. Towards the end of this lesson we will switch to more difficult techniques using the Stipple brush for the hair and the Soft Round brush to paint 'free form' and add more hair, extend the dress and add sunlight to the trees. We know many of you will want to stop after the smudging ends, but we want to urge you to continue! There's a lot of fun to be had with painting freehand. You can make as many layers as you need to experiment every step of the way. Anytime you are not happy with the way things are going, just use your Eraser tool or delete the layer and start anew.

The main objective of this lesson is for you to experiment and practice to develop the skills you need to feel satisfaction in the final results. Once you've tried it a few times, we guarantee you will be up all night painting!

"Once you've tried it a few times, we guarantee you will be up all night painting!"

WHAT YOU'LL LEARN

Smudge wonder

An effective way to achieve an oil look is to use the Smudge brush. It is a quick way to get the look you want while being straightforward.

Realistic effects

The Spatter brushes are a good choice for smudging as their effect changes with brush size and pressure and can master either skin, hair or nature. Experiment!

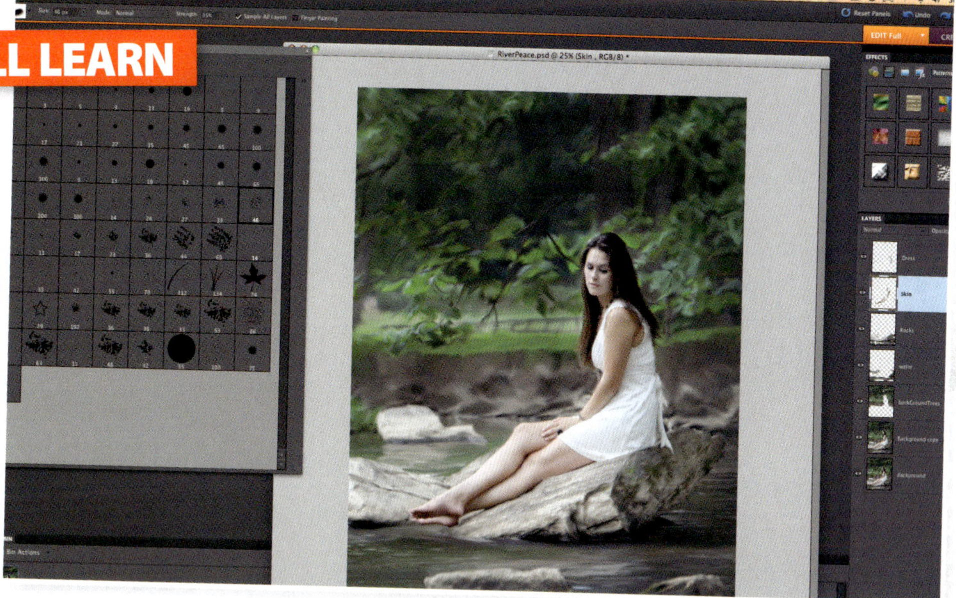

Keep it real

'Hatching' and 'Cross Hatching' is an effective brush stroke to use as it gives a nice painterly effect and can preserve form as long as care is used in changing directions.

Easy water

Painting water is quite simple, use a long swift stroke from left to right. Just be sure not to distort any nearby elements as you paint.

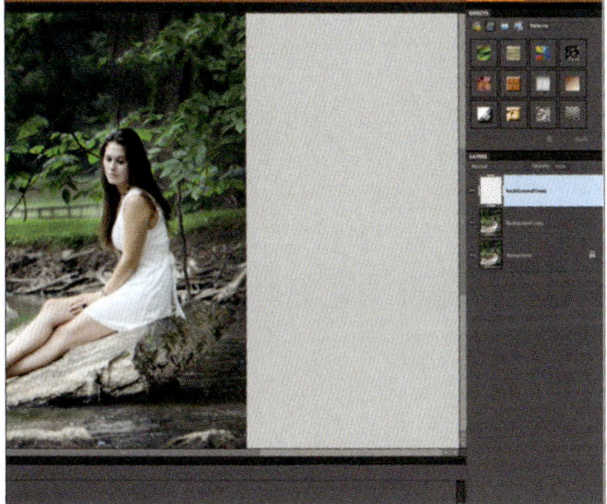

01 Getting started

Open your picture and make a copy. Make a new layer and name it 'Background Tree'. Make sure Sample all Layers in the top menu bar is selected.

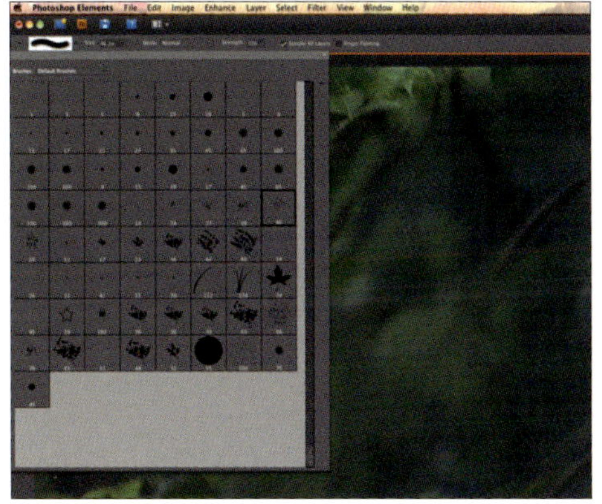

02 Painting in the old hatch style

Select the Smudge tool and the # 46 Scatter brush. At 50% Strength paint moving the brush back and forth in a consistent direction.

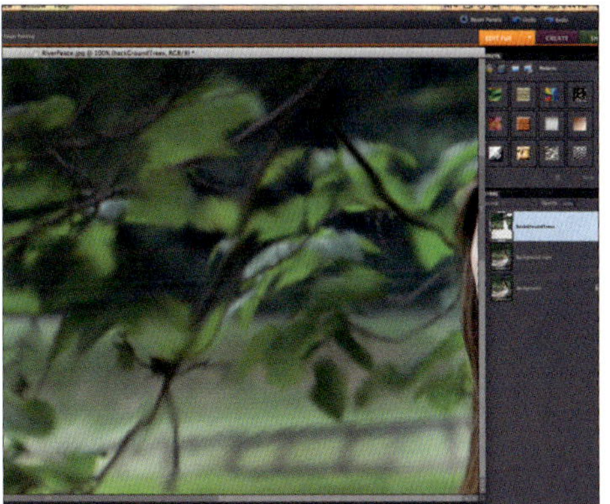

03 Change directions

Keeping on the same layer, change your 'hatch' stroke direction while painting the leaves so they are not completely lost in the background.

Painting details

Let's start to flesh it out!

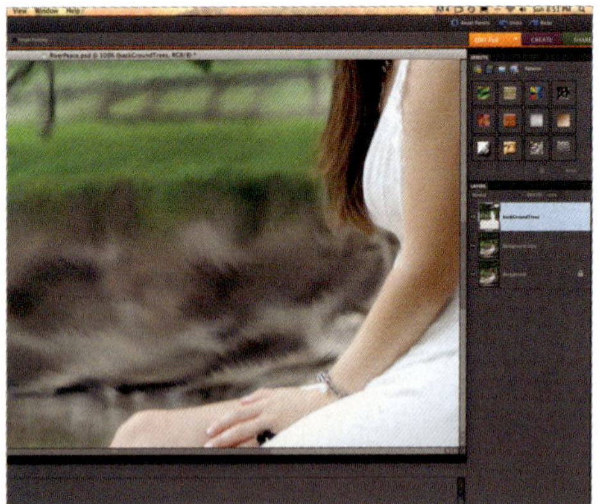

04 Paint with flare

We are now 'cross hatching' the river bank. Feel free to express your self by adding more pressure to your stylus or changing stroke directions.

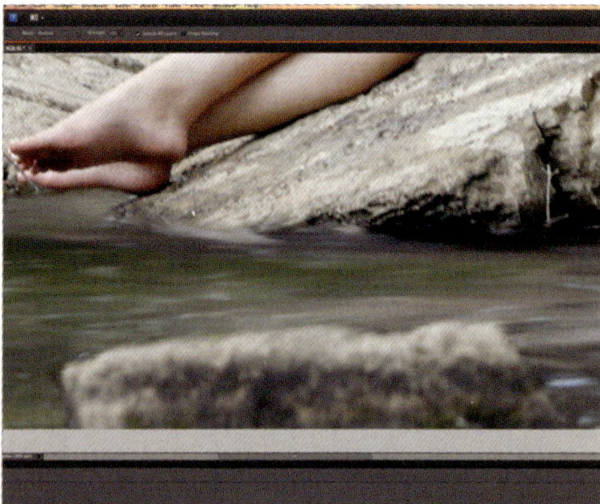

05 Painting water

Make a 'water' layer and zoom in close with a larger brush. We will now use our brush from side to side in a horizontal stroke.

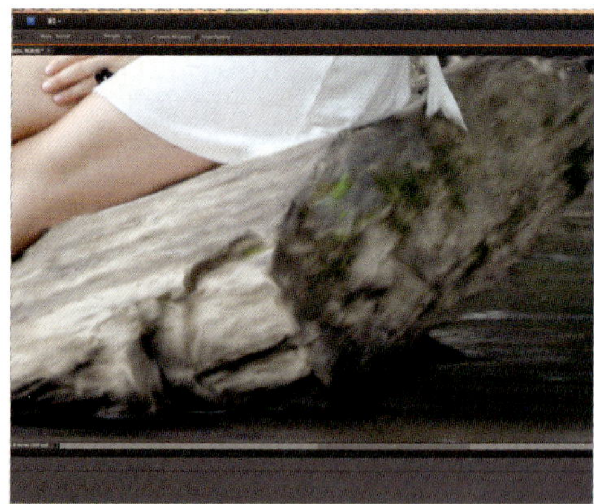

06 Rock painting

Make a 'Rock' layer and using a medium size brush, zoom and use hatching and cross hatching strokes to preserve the natural form of the rock.

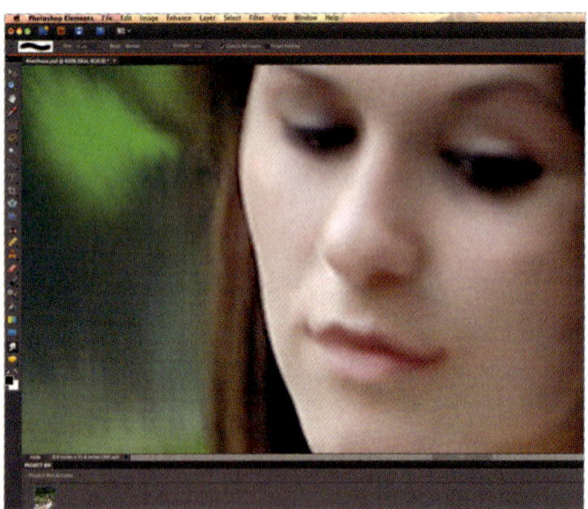

07 Painting the skin

Create a new layer called 'Skin'. Decrease the brush Strength to 35% and use a smaller brush around 15 pixels. Carefully go over all the skin area and dress.

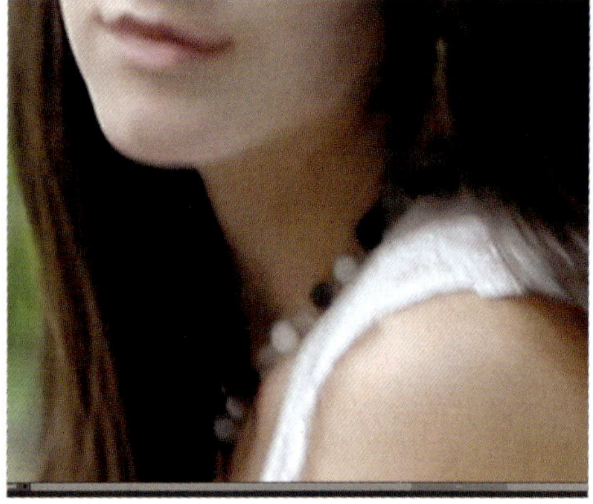

08 Painting in the round

For round objects don't use the hatch stroke, as you want to preserve their shape and paint using a careful circular motion.

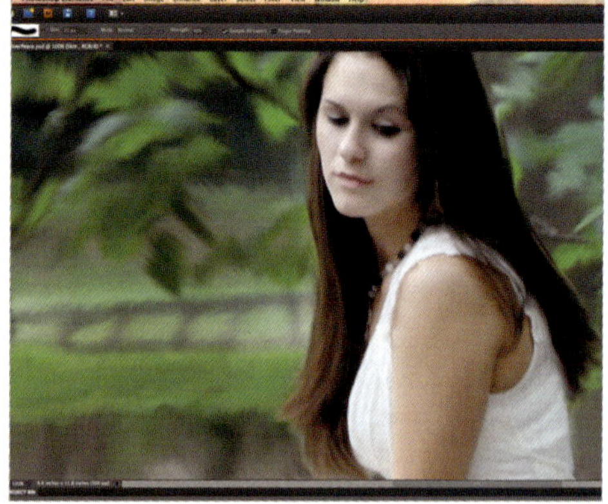

09 Painting hair

Make a new layer called 'Hair'. Zoom in close at 50% Strength and vary your brush size as you work. Paint as if you were actually brushing her hair.

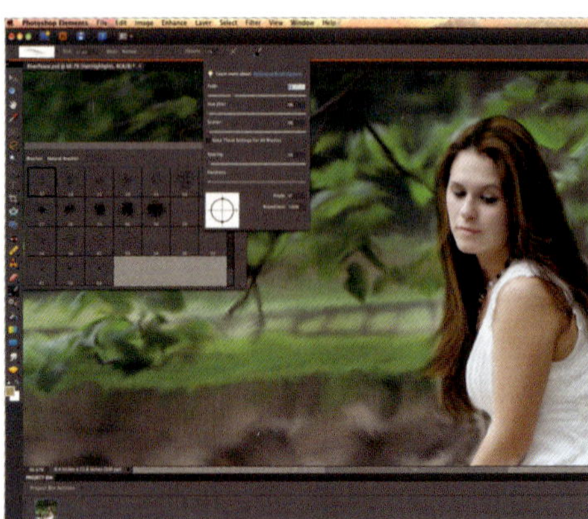

10 Switch from Smudge to paint

Change to the paint brush (Stipple from Natural Brushes, Strength 50%) and click on the Brush icon to change the Fade to 65%.

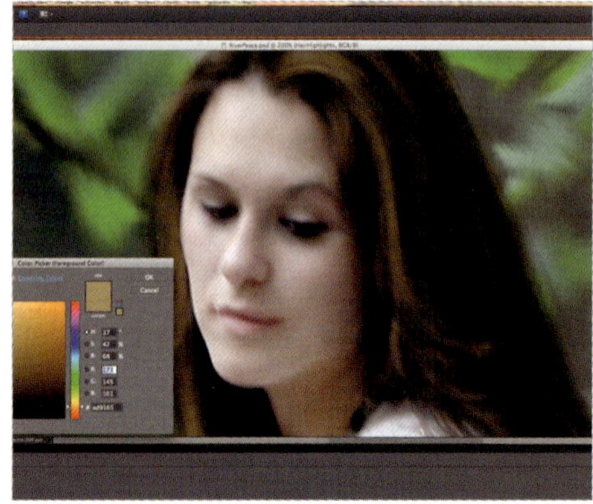

11 Paint the hair

Make a new layer called 'Hair Highlights'. Choose a golden yellow-brown colour and begin painting in highlights. Take care to vary the colour.

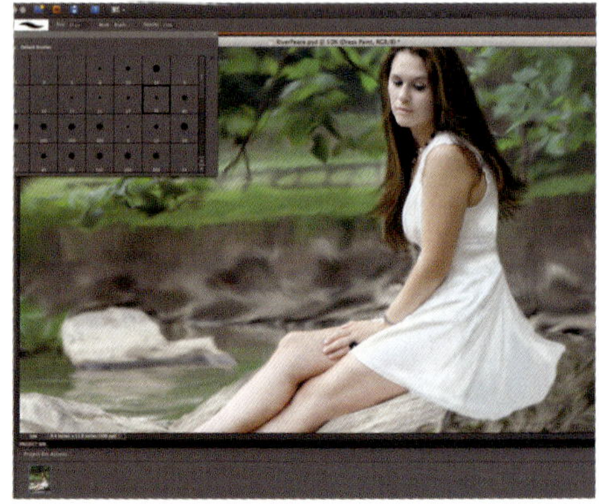

12 Painting the dress

Choose a Soft Round brush at 100%. Paint directly over the dress extending it over the rock behind her. Opt/Alt-click to sample colours.

QUICK PHOTOSHOP TIPS

Use the Clone tool

Sometimes the Clone tool is faster than painting over an unwanted area. We used the Clone tool to remove the dress bow. Sample a nearby area as a source and make sure the brush is a soft one so there are no hard edges. You can go back and smudge to remove any repetition of unwanted patterns.

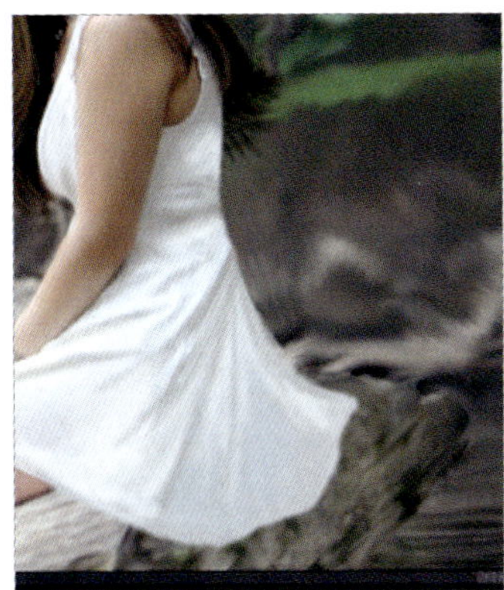

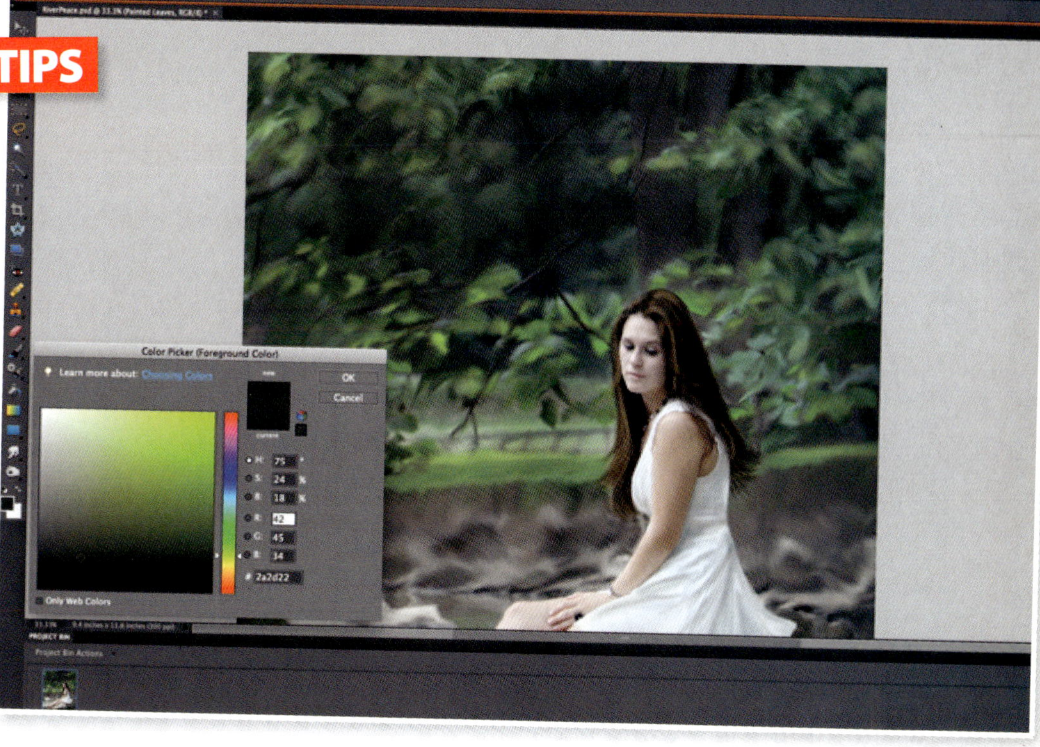

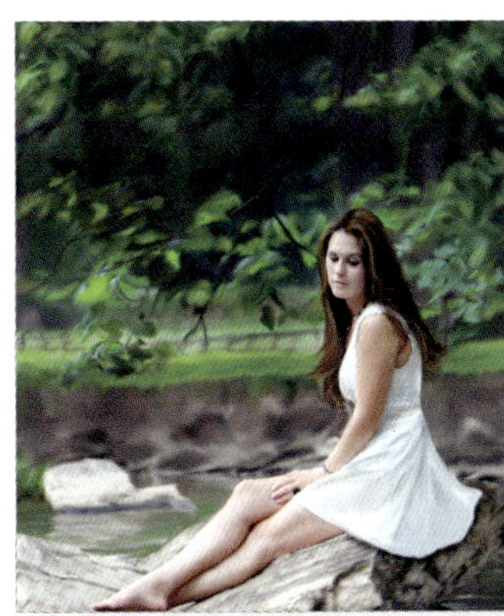

Done in Elements

We have done this tutorial in Photoshop Elements to show that you don't have to have the newest Photoshop CS5 to be able to get creative with your photos. However, you can follow the exact steps in any version of Photoshop.

Colour choices

When you start using the standard brush rather than the Smudge tool, you can use the Eyedropper in the Toolbar to click on the original photo to sample the colours.

Paper texture

To get the final look that we have here, find a crumpled paper texture or similar and place it over your painting, lowering the Opacity and playing with the blending modes to get the final effect.

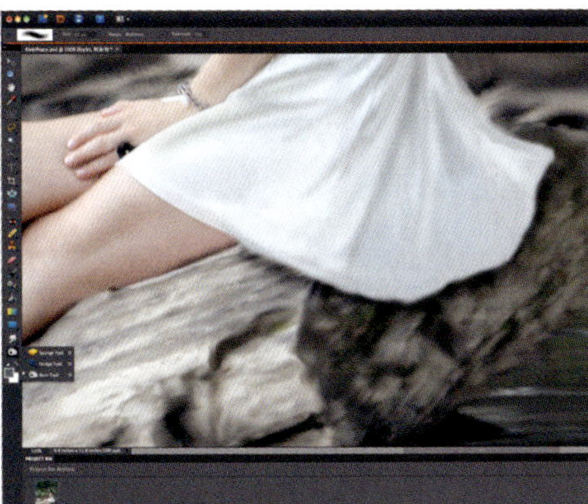

13 Casting a skirt shadow

Go back to the 'Rock' layer, choose the Burn tool and burn the area around the skirt so it looks as though there is a shadow on the rock.

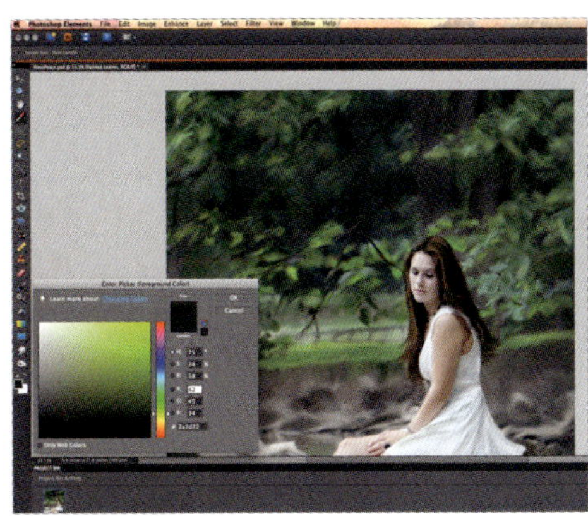

14 Sunlight in the trees

Make a new layer called 'Painted Leaves'. Bring up the Color box and choose a pretty yellow/green. Select a Soft Round brush at 50% Strength

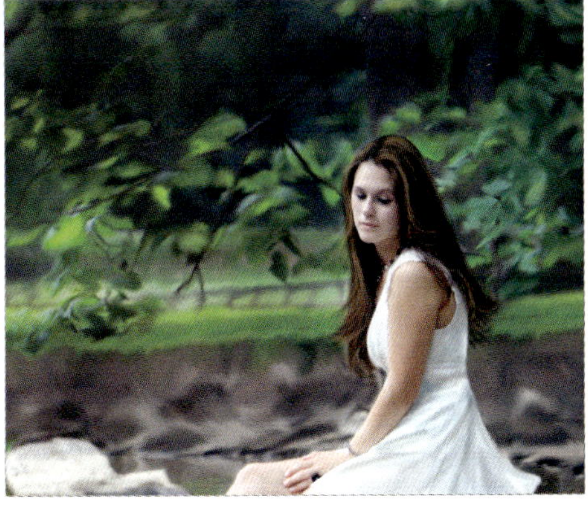

15 Final touches

Paint sunlight over the existing leaves varying direction and size. Adjust the layer for a more subtle effect.

Filters

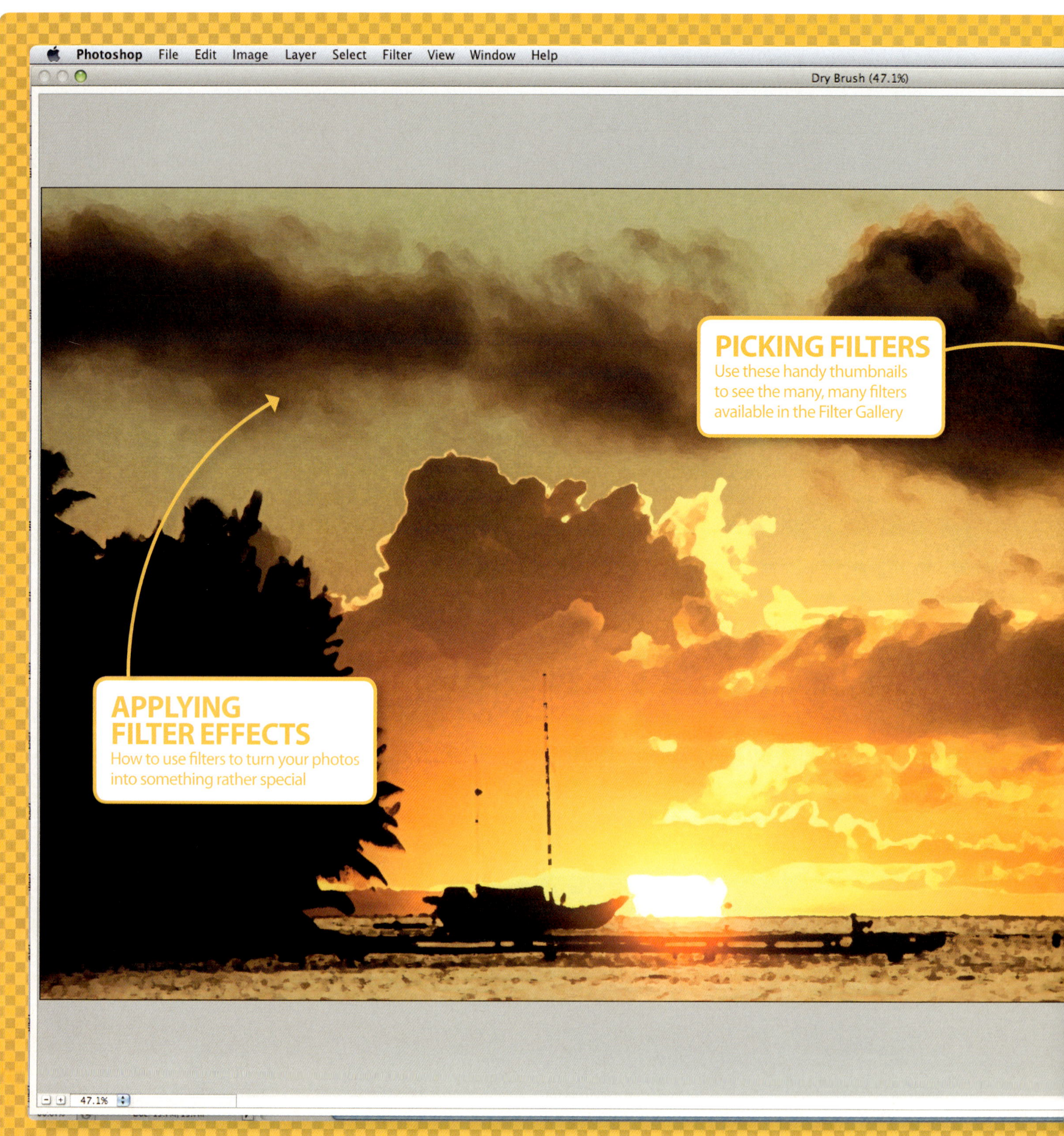

Photoshop File Edit Image Layer Select Filter View Window Help
Dry Brush (47.1%)
PICKING FILTERS
Use these handy thumbnails to see the many, many filters available in the Filter Gallery
APPLYING FILTER EFFECTS
How to use filters to turn your photos into something rather special
47.1%

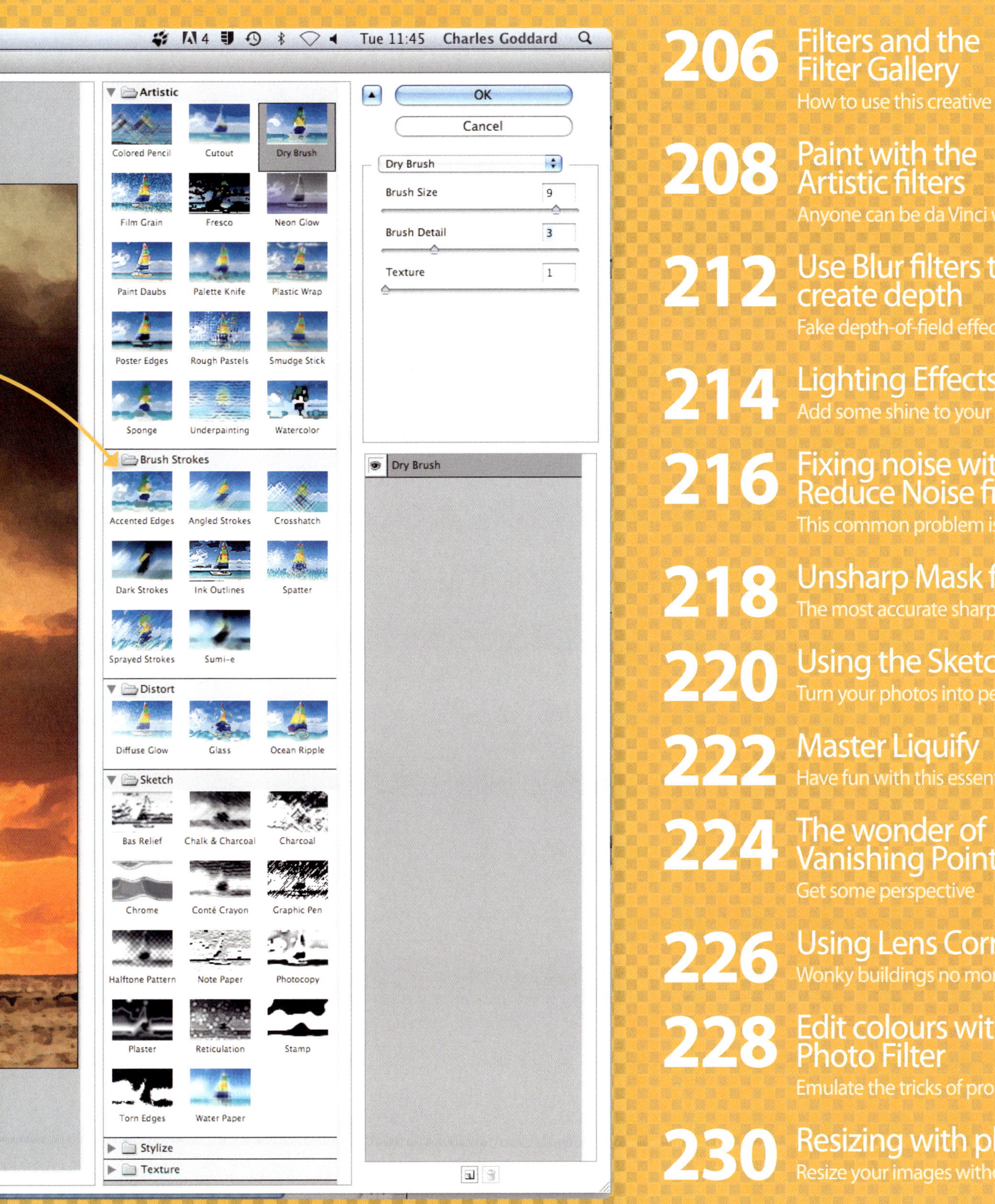
Tue 11:45 Charles Goddard
Artistic
Colored Pencil
Cutout
Dry Brush
Film Grain
Fresco
Neon Glow
Paint Daubs
Palette Knife
Plastic Wrap
Poster Edges
Rough Pastels
Smudge Stick
Sponge
Underpainting
Watercolor
Brush Strokes
Accented Edges
Angled Strokes
Crosshatch
Dark Strokes
Ink Outlines
Spatter
Sprayed Strokes
Sumi-e
Distort
Diffuse Glow
Glass
Ocean Ripple
Sketch
Bas Relief
Chalk & Charcoal
Charcoal
Chrome
Conté Crayon
Graphic Pen
Halftone Pattern
Note Paper
Photocopy
Plaster
Reticulation
Stamp
Torn Edges
Water Paper
Stylize
Texture
OK
Cancel
Dry Brush
Brush Size 9
Brush Detail 3
Texture 1
Dry Brush

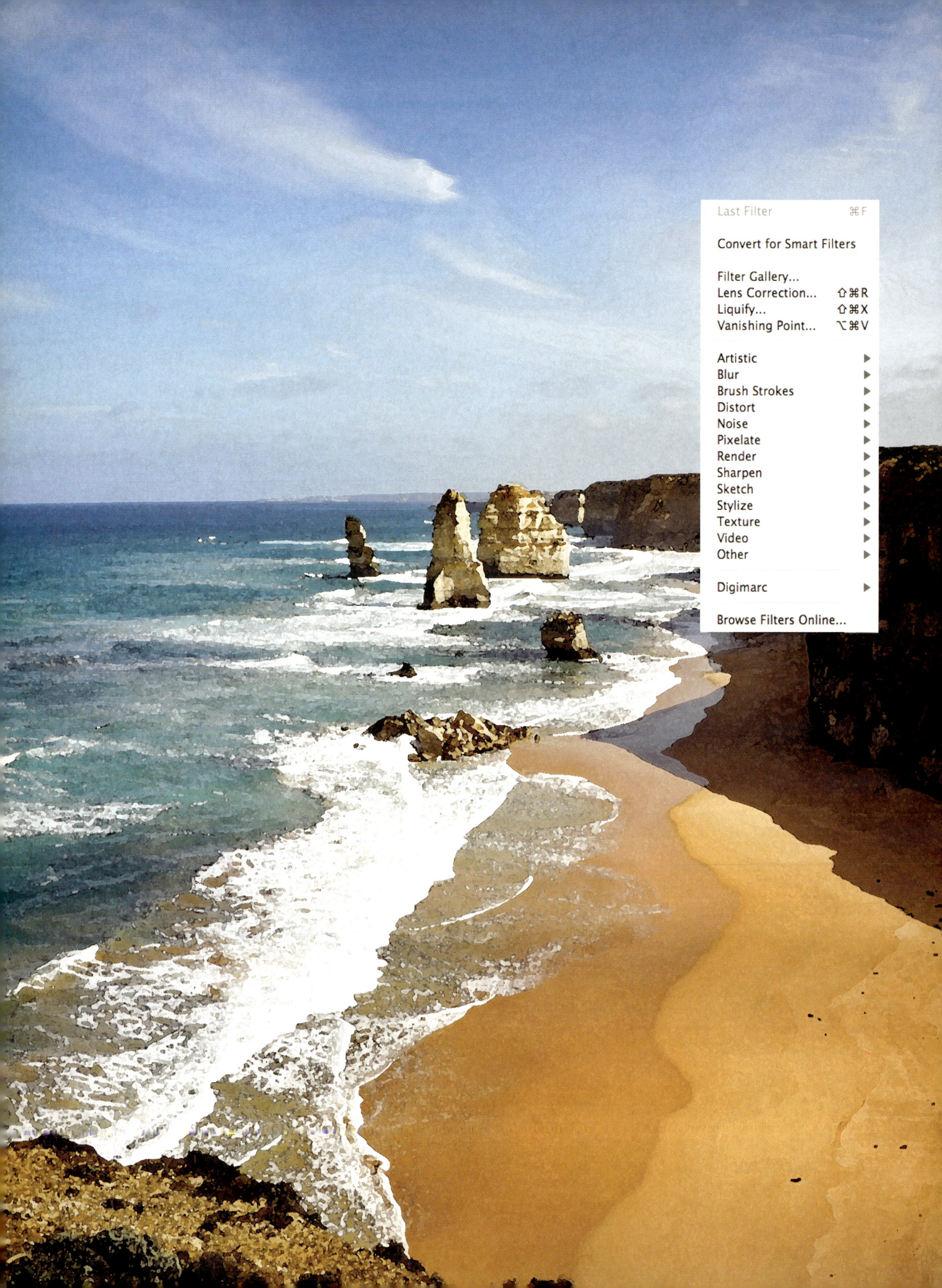

Last Filter ⌘F
Convert for Smart Filters
Filter Gallery...
Lens Correction... ⇧⌘R
Liquify... ⇧⌘X
Vanishing Point... ⌥⌘V
Artistic
Blur
Brush Strokes
Distort
Noise
Pixelate
Render
Sharpen
Sketch
Stylize
Texture
Video
Other
Digimarc
Browse Filters Online...

Filters and the Filter Gallery

In this introduction, we give you an overview of Photoshop's Filter Gallery so that you can start experimenting with the available options

Filters have a bit of a bad reputation for producing cheesy effects. And yes, while it is possible to turn your photos into garish caricatures, this is true of any Photoshop tool. Every tool can be taken to an extreme, when in most cases, subtlety is key.

Accessed via the Filter menu in Photoshop, the Filter Gallery is a quick way to start playing with all the available filters. Your photo is in the main preview window and to the right are a whole host of thumbnails with different effects. These are all categorised into genres like Sketch, Blur, Artistic, etc, but even if you pick any one of these from the Filters menu, then you will still be taken to the Filter Gallery – you can change your mind again and again, as your changes are not applied until you hit the OK button.

Each filter will also have a set of custom settings for you to play with the in the far right-hand palette. These are usually sliders that can enhance and strengthen the effect, or tailor the way that the filter is applied. Again, this is down to experimentation and as it's so easy to do, why not? It's even possible to add multiple filters on top of each other, again using this far right palette. When you apply a filter, it is listed here with a small eye next to it, the same as the Layers palette. You can add a new 'layer' using the controls at the bottom of this panel, to which you can apply another filter effect. YOu can then turn filter layers on and off using the eye symbol, or click and drag to move them higher or lower in the filter stack.

This whole section is dedicated to the many filters available, but we don't have the space to get through all of them – there are so many! However, we encourage to spend some time in the Filter Gallery, getting to know the options and the effects, and we're sure you will find a few favourites in there too!

"We encourage to spend some time in the Filter Gallery, getting to know the options"

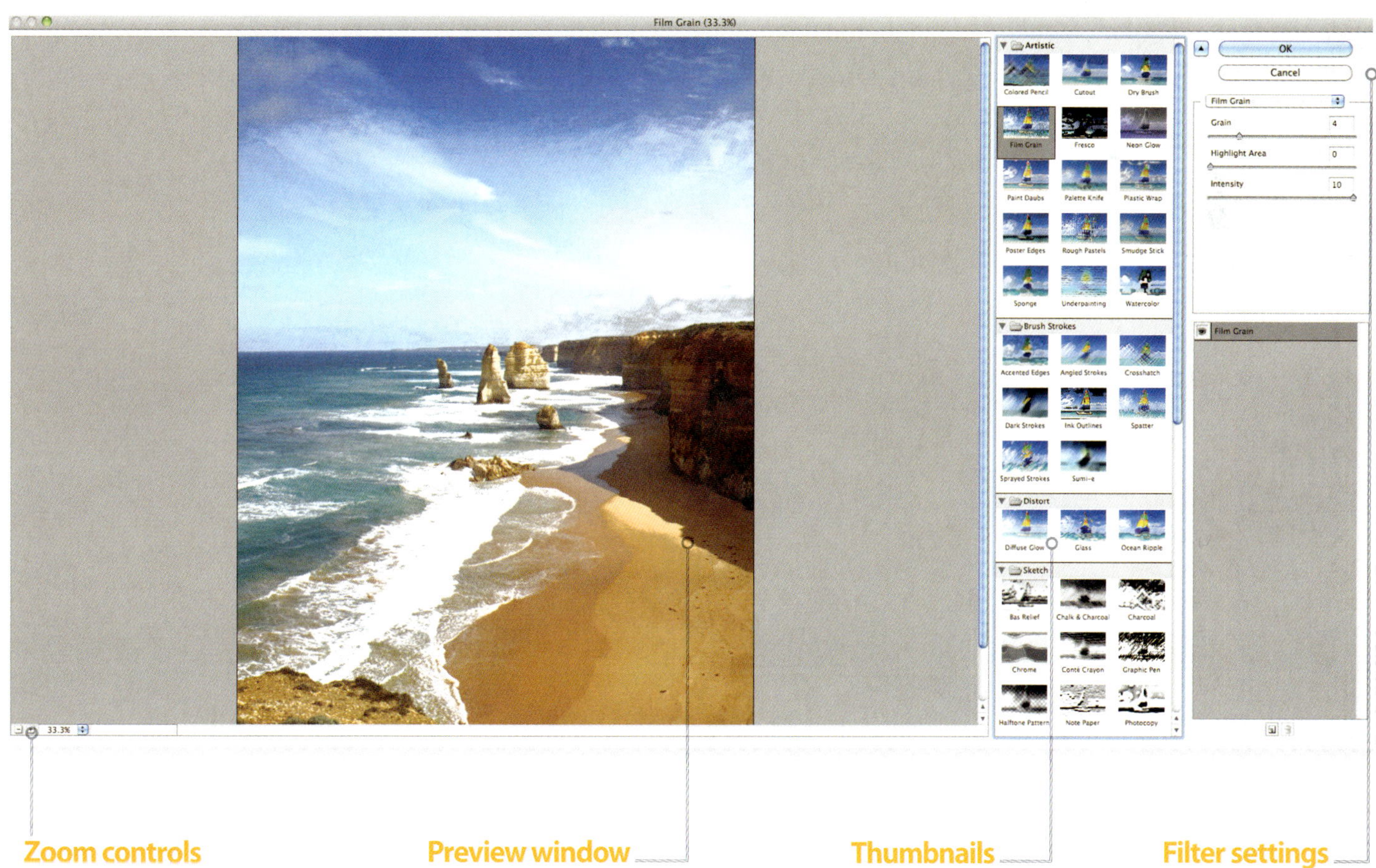

Zoom controls
Use these controls to zoom in and out of your image, so that you can check that you are happy with the details as well as the overall effect.

Preview window
This is your image with whatever filter you have selected applied so you can see what the effect will look like before hitting OK.

Thumbnails
These thumbnails give you a quick preview of each and every filter in the Filter Gallery. Click one to apply to the image.

Filter settings
Here you can control the strength of the filter being applied. In many cases other include brush size and as well.

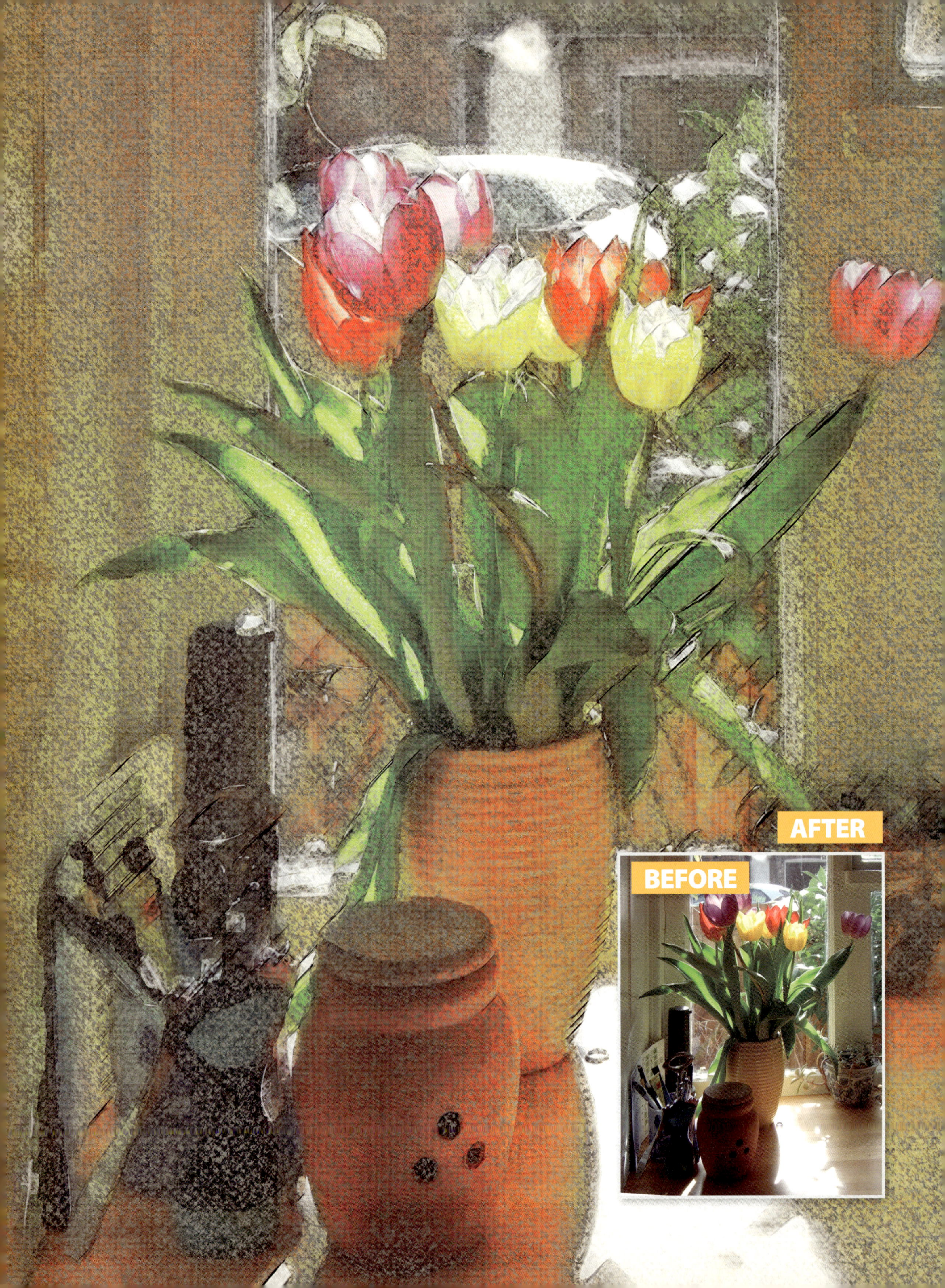
AFTER
BEFORE

Paint with the Artistic filters

You don't have to be a digital da Vinci to paint in Photoshop. Try using the stock filters to mimic natural media effects

There are many Photoshop users who would love to be able to paint digitally, but don't have any artistic training and are nervous about using brushes. Well, the good news is that if you use Photoshop's stock filters intelligently you can produce convincing and effective natural media-style paintings without ever lifting a single brush!

That's exactly what we're going to demonstrate here, directly from a photographic start image. The key is to overlay different filter effects via various layers, and use the power and subtlety of layer blending modes.

Many Photoshop filters are pretty clumsy and mechanical when used in their raw form, but when you combine them they can be very effective indeed, and it's important to remember that you can even use these filters on layer masks – as we'll do here a couple of times to add a dose of much needed natural media-style textures. We're going for a mixed media effect here, which will give the impression of loose painterly areas of liquid colour contrasting with chalky areas, working together to create a very painterly effect.

When you're experimenting with filters, the Filter gallery (Filter>Filter Gallery) is a nice, quick way to browse through the various filters available. Ideally, you should use this project as a start point. Adapt it to use some of the other filters that we'll be pointing you towards, and you will be able to transform photos into your own unique, natural media-style filter paintings.

> "You can produce convincing and effective paintings"

THE FILTER GALLERY

Preview
The main window shows a preview of the image with the filter applied. This is not set in stone until you click the OK button, so play around to get the right look.

Settings
Each filter has a bunch of settings that can be changed to customise the filter. These are usually in the form of simple sliders.

Effect thumbnails
The little boxes on the right-hand side give you a preview of each of the filters available. Click to apply to your image.

Categories
The filters are split into a bunch of different categories. We are only looking at the Artistic filters, but other pages in this chapter will cover more options.

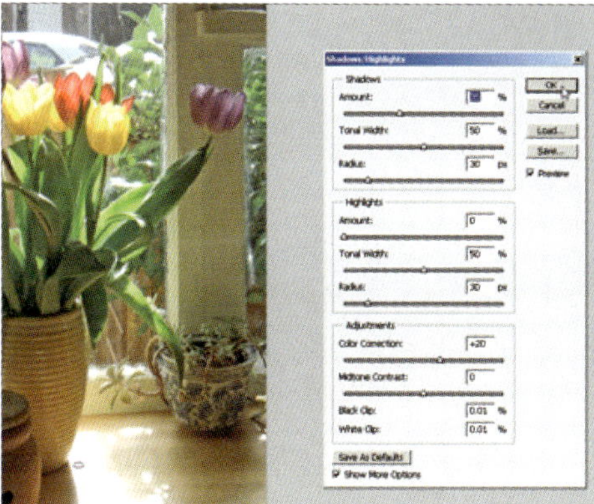

01 Start off

Open the start image, brighten it using Image>Adjustments>Shadows/Highlights. Make two duplicates of this layer (Hit Ctrl/Cmd-J twice).

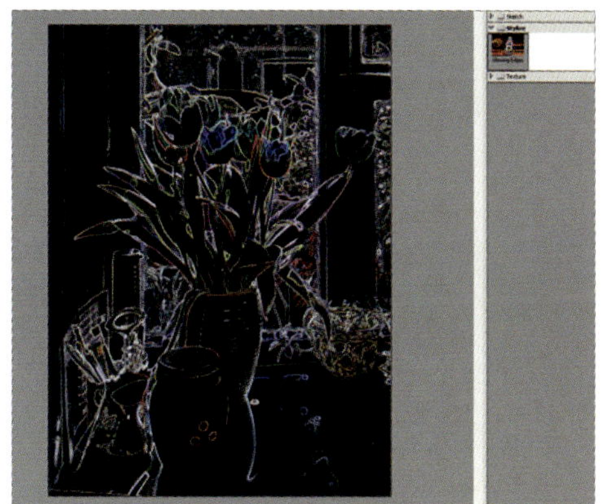

02 Glowing edges

On the second layer Edit>Fill using colour '#72684c'. On the upper layer go to Filter>Stylize>Glowing Edges (Width: 2, Brightness: 13, Smoothness: 7).

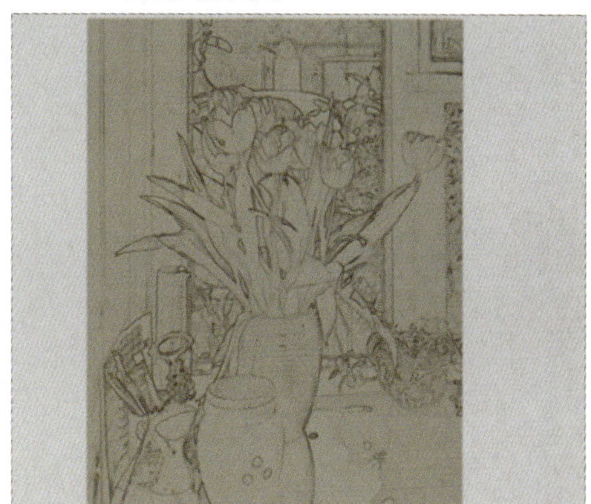

03 Small adjustments

Go to Image>Adjustments>Invert, then Image>Adjustments>Desaturate. Set the blending mode to Soft Light, Opacity 45%. Duplicate this layer..

Working through the filters Getting to the nitty gritty

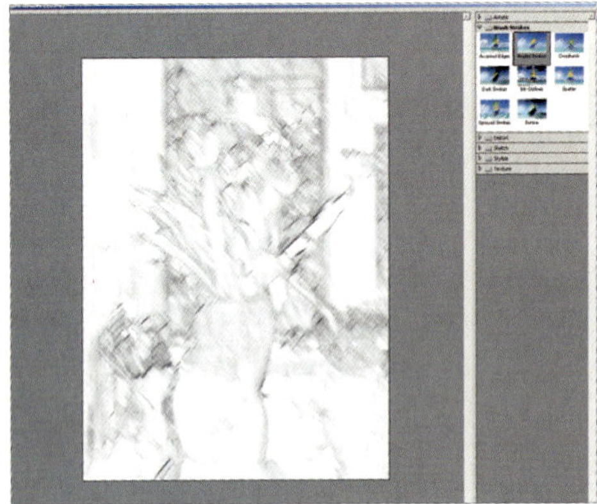

04 Angled strokes

On the duplicate, go to Filter>Brush Strokes>Angled Strokes (Direction Balance 72, Stroke Length 50, Sharpness 3). Duplicate and set to Multiply at 100%.

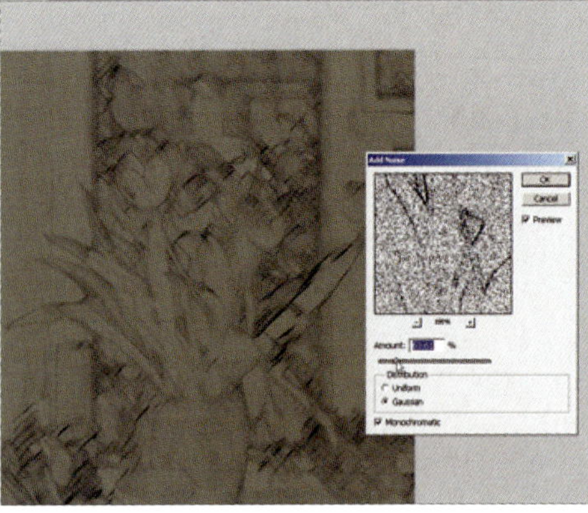

05 Make some noise!

Return to the layer below the current one and go to Filter>Noise>Add Noise. Choose Gaussian, Monochromatic and an Amount of 65%.

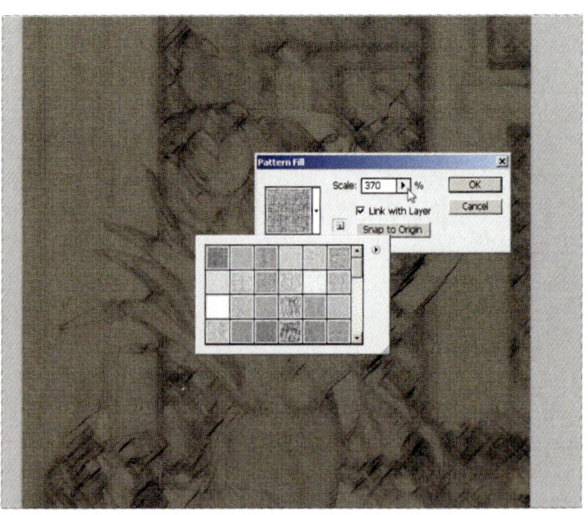

06 Paper patterns

On the top layer go to Layer>New Fill Layer>Pattern. From Artist Surfaces choose Heavy Weave. Set Scale to 370%. Set the layer mode to Soft Light at 25%.

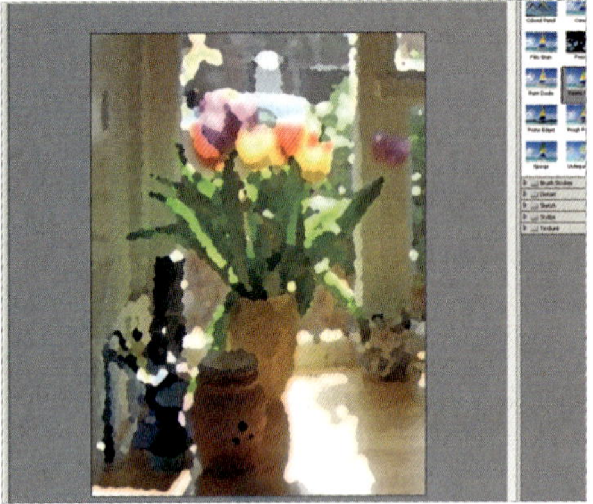

07 Paint with a Palette Knife

Duplicate the Background layer. Drop this above the filled layer. Go to Filter>Artistic>Palette Knife (Stroke Size 41, Stroke Detail 3, Softness 3).

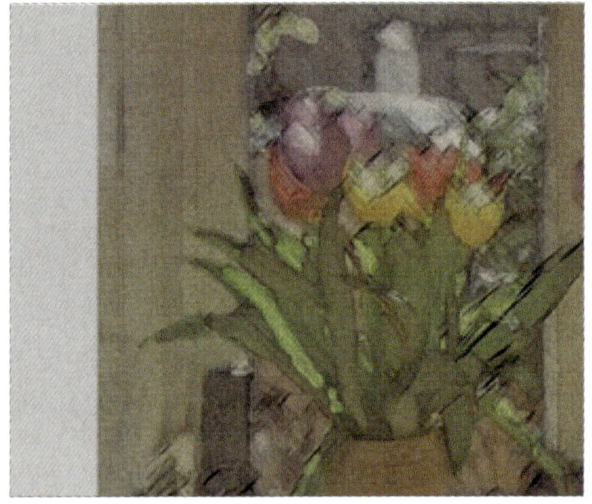

08 Layer mask

Go to Layer>Layer Mask>Reveal All. Click on the layer mask thumbnail in the Layers panel and go to Edit>Fill, choosing 50% Gray for Contents.

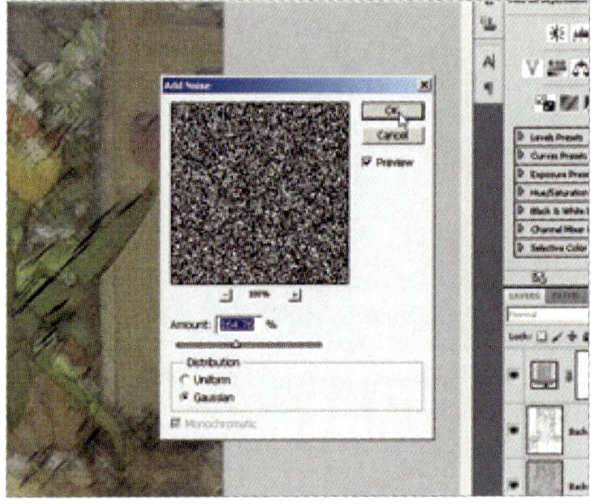

09 Final noise

Go to Filter>Noise>Add Noise (Gaussian, Monochromatic, Amount 160%). Go Filter>Blur> Gaussian Blur, using a Radius of around 3.

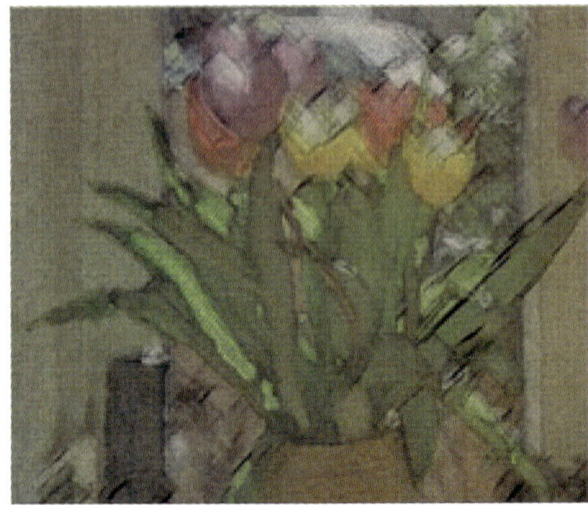

10 Getting gritty

Still on the layer mask, go to Image>Adjustments> Levels. Drag the Black and White sliders beneath the Histogram closer together to increase contrast.

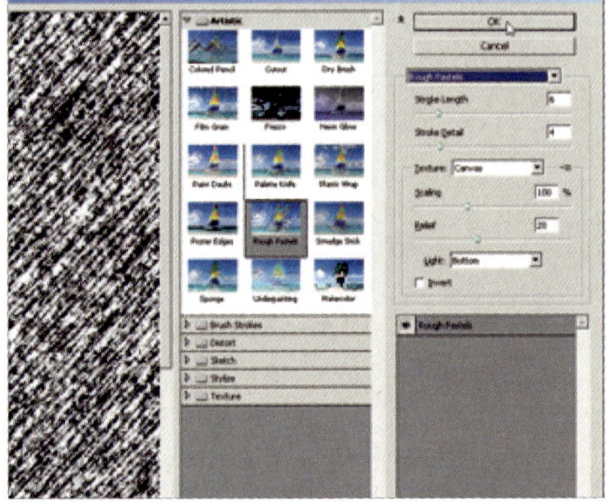

11 Glowing edges

Go to Filter>Artistic>Rough Pastels using the screenshot settings. Set the layer blending mode to Overlay, Opacity 92%.

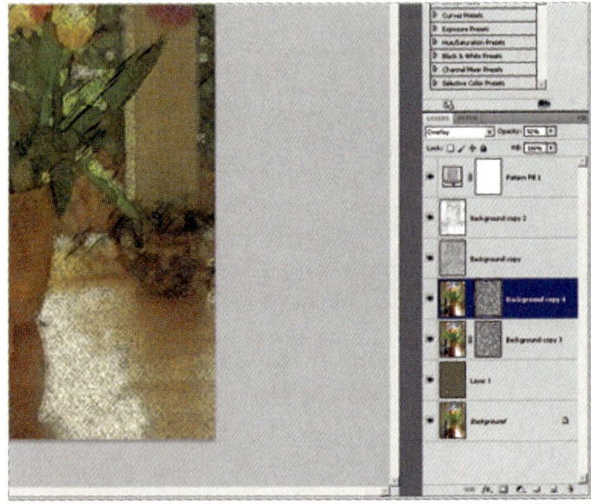

12 Crosshatch

Duplicate this layer. On the copy, click the link between image layer/layer mask thumbnails to unlink them

More filter fun Keep layering them up for a realistic effect

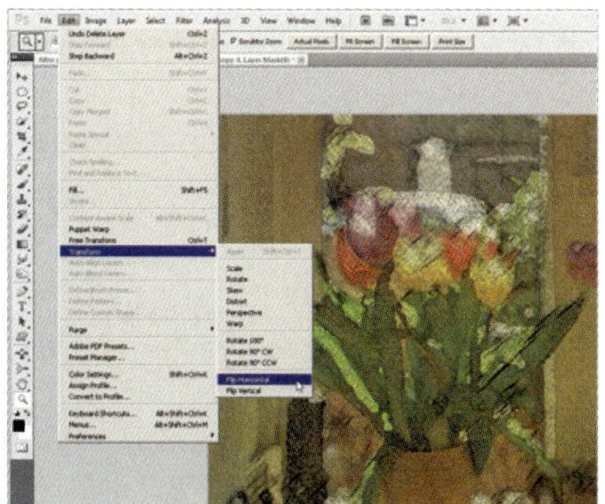

13 And flip

Click the layer mask thumbnail and go to Edit>Transform>Flip Horizontal to flip the direction of the strokes and add more chalky details.

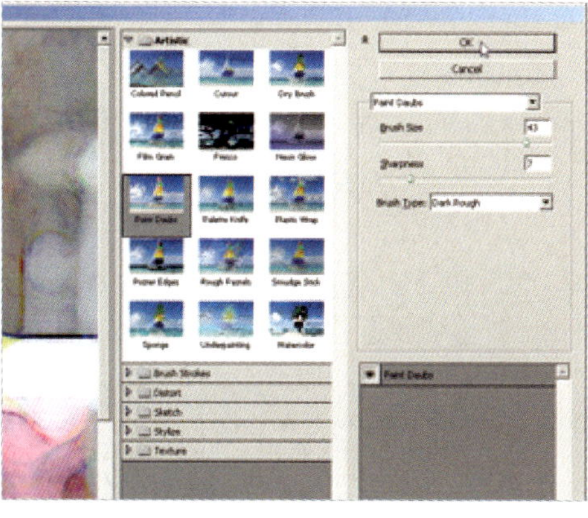

14 Paint Daubs

Duplicate this layer and set to Color Dodge at 43%. Click on the image thumbnail and go to Filter>Artistic>Paint Daubs with the settings shown.

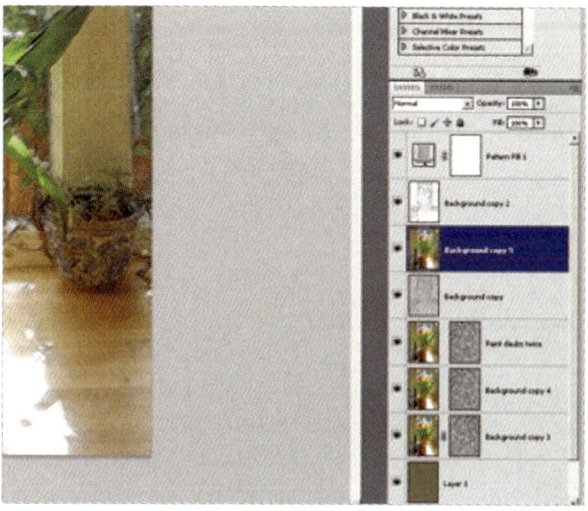

15 Super selections

Return to the original background layer and duplicate it. Drag this layer up the stack and drop it between the two line drawing layers.

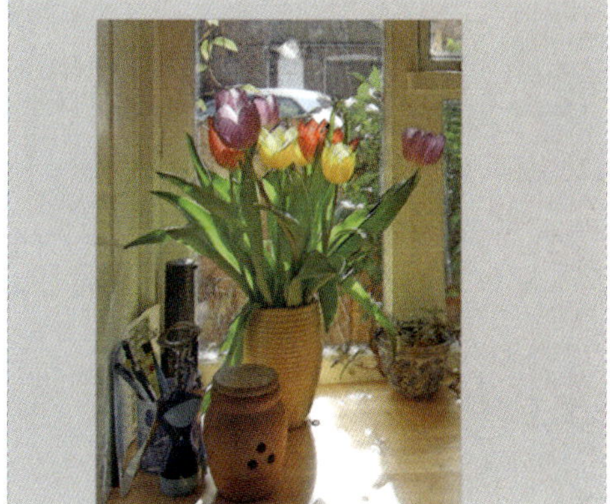

16 Eyedropper

Now choose the Eyedropper tool and click in one of the red flowers to sample the colour, then go to Select>Color Range.

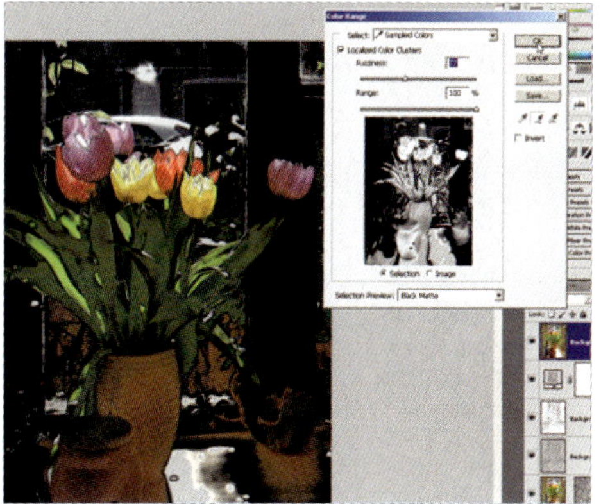

17 Feeling fuzzy

Choose the '+' Eyedropper. Set Fuzziness to 75% and choose Black Matte for Preview. Click around the very brightest parts of the flowers.

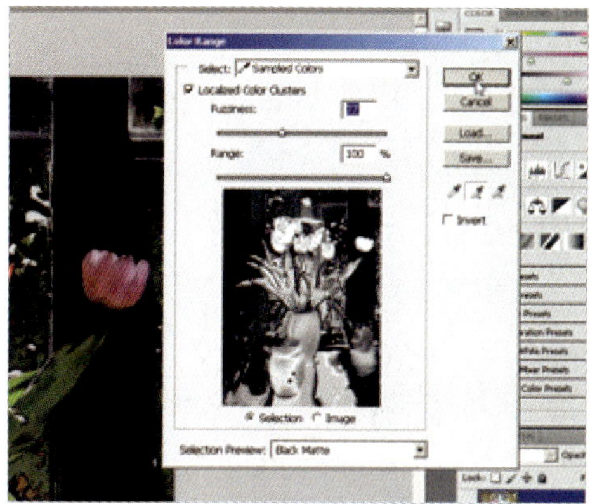

18 Delete

Click OK to exit the dialog box and go to Select>Inverse. Hit the Backspace key to clear the unwanted areas.

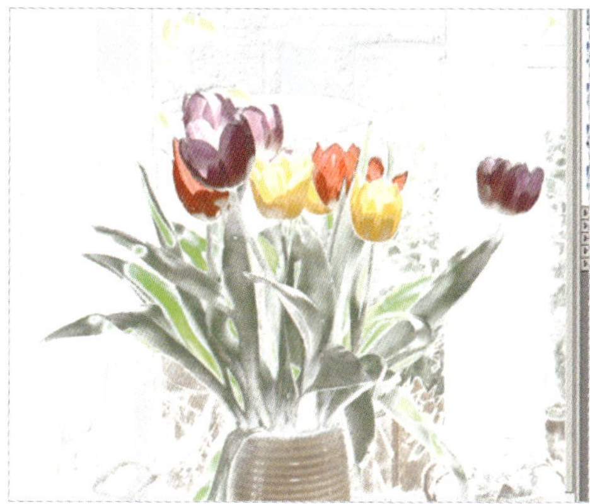

19 Use the Dry brush

Go to Select>Deselect and set the blending mode to Luminosity. Next, go to Filter>Artistic>Dry Brush. Use Brush Size 7, Brush Detail 8, Texture 2.

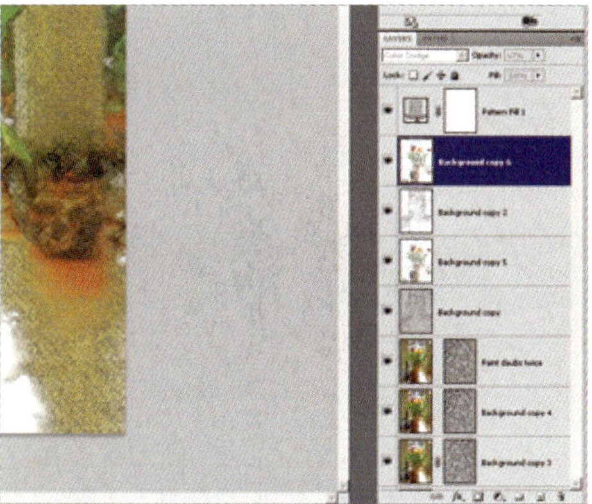

20 Turning it up

Duplicate this layer for the final time and drop the copy directly below the Pattern Fill layer. Set the blending mode to Color Dodge at 0%.

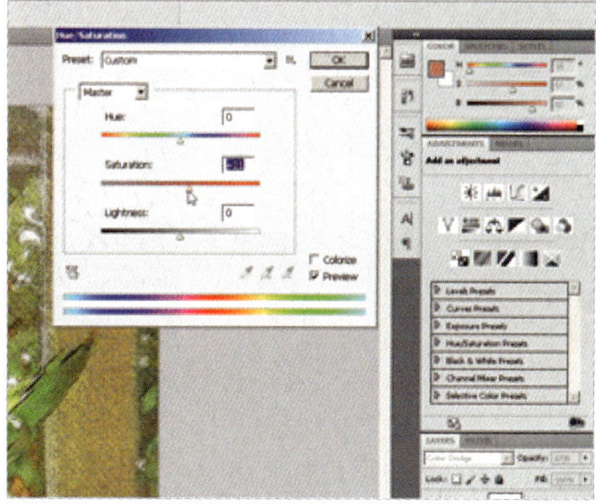

21 And finally…

Tweak the saturation of these last two layers via Image>Adjustments>Hue/Saturation, modifying the Saturation slider as required.

Use Blur filters to create depth

We look at Photoshop's multitude of Blur options and show you which ones to use and when to use them

Depth of field happens naturally in all cameras, but if you don't own a camera with a flashy lens or manual controls it's much harder to achieve – and this is where Photoshop comes in.

The idea of the effect is very simple – to blur different parts of the image in order to make one subject stand out over the rest. To better understand this effect, imagine a blurred image with every object indiscernible from the next. Now picture an invisible wall in focus, cutting across your image, and whatever this wall touches is made pin-sharp. It's a gradual effect and fades out at the closest and furthest points away from the eye.

The effect works better in images with close foregrounds and interesting backdrops. It also works well with close-up photos, and here we've used Photoshop's Lens Blur filter to transform this picture of a flower with a depth of field effect. As well as actually applying the blur selectively, we have changed its composition so that it makes a greater impact. The petals are softly blurred, but the centre of the flower is kept in sharp focus.

We also give you some advice to using blur on portrait images to help soften the skin. The trick with any of the Blur filters is knowing which one to use with which task. Experimentation is the key, but make sure that you always work on a copy of your original photograph.

"Here we've used Photoshop's Lens Blur filter to transform this picture of a flower with a depth of field effect"

QUICK PHOTOSHOP TIPS

Soft focus

To make the effect a little easier on the eyes, reduce the contrast of the Overlay blend mode by lowering the Opacity of the layer to 80%. For the final touch we need to soften the image more. Go to Filter>Blur>Motion Blur and give it a Distance of 20 pixels and change its Angle to 0 degrees. Although this blur is mostly to add movement to an image, it works wonders for softening images of people.

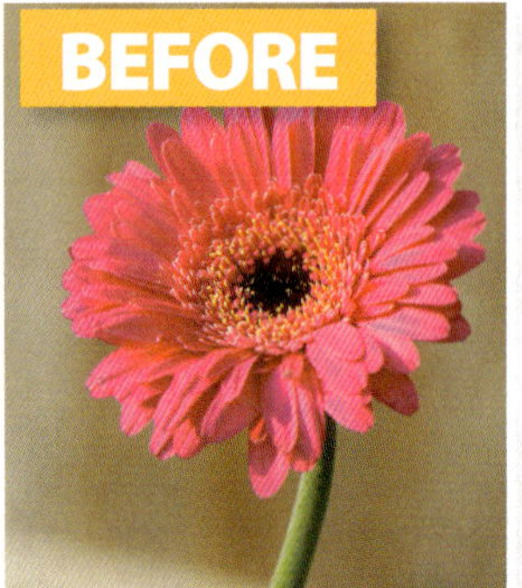
BEFORE

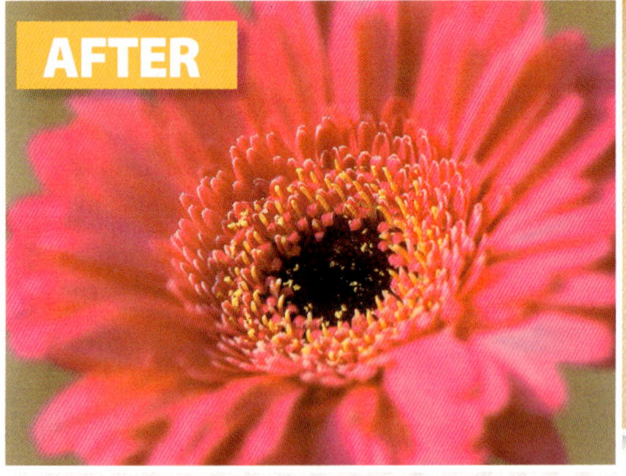
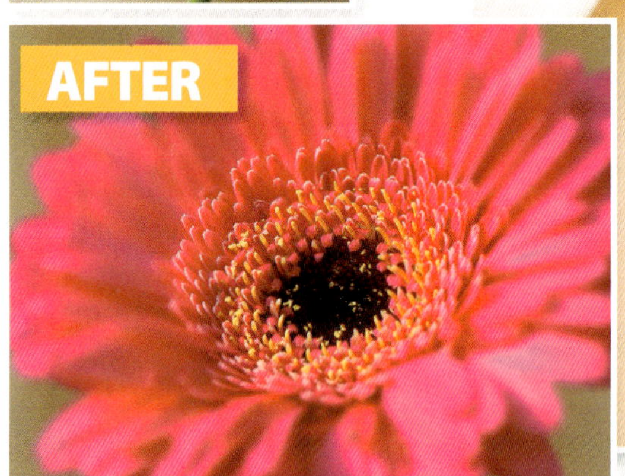
AFTER

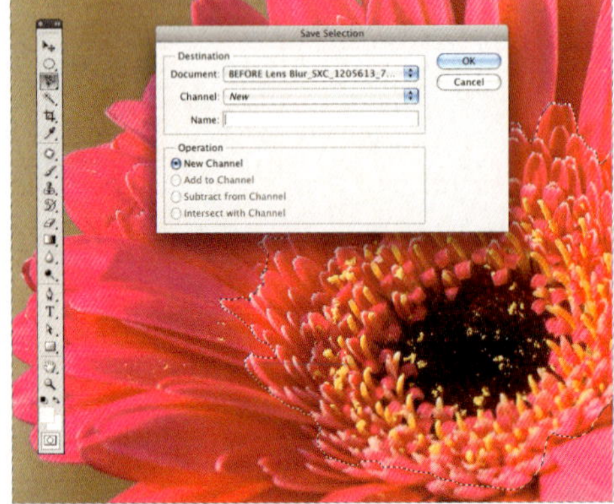

01 Make a selection
With the Magnetic Lasso, make a selection around the middle of the flower. Ctrl/right-click and choose Save Selection to create 'Alpha 1' in the Channels box.

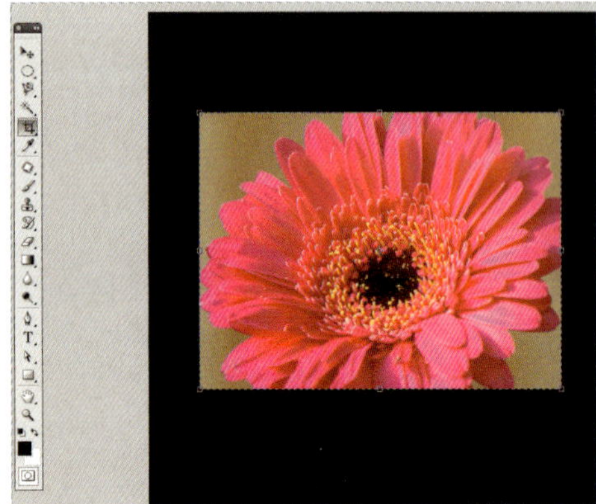

02 Compose
Hit Cmd/Ctrl+D to deselect. Using the Crop tool, cut out the surrounding area to give the strongest composition. We removed the background.

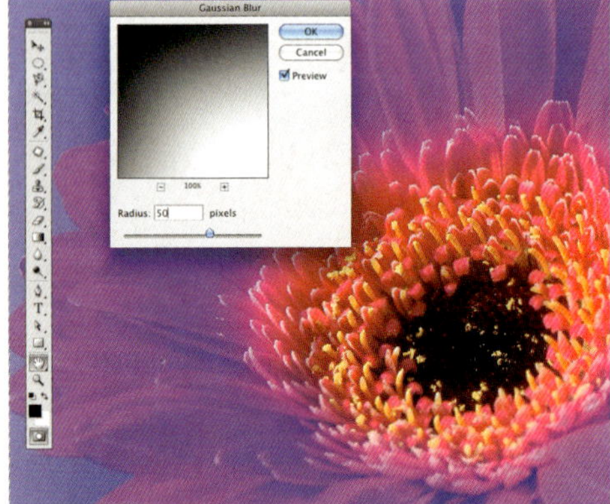

03 Add your blur
Cmd/Ctrl-click the thumbnail of the Alpha 1 layer. Click the Quick Mask box in the toolbar. Head to Filter>Blur>Gaussian Blur and set Radius to 50px.

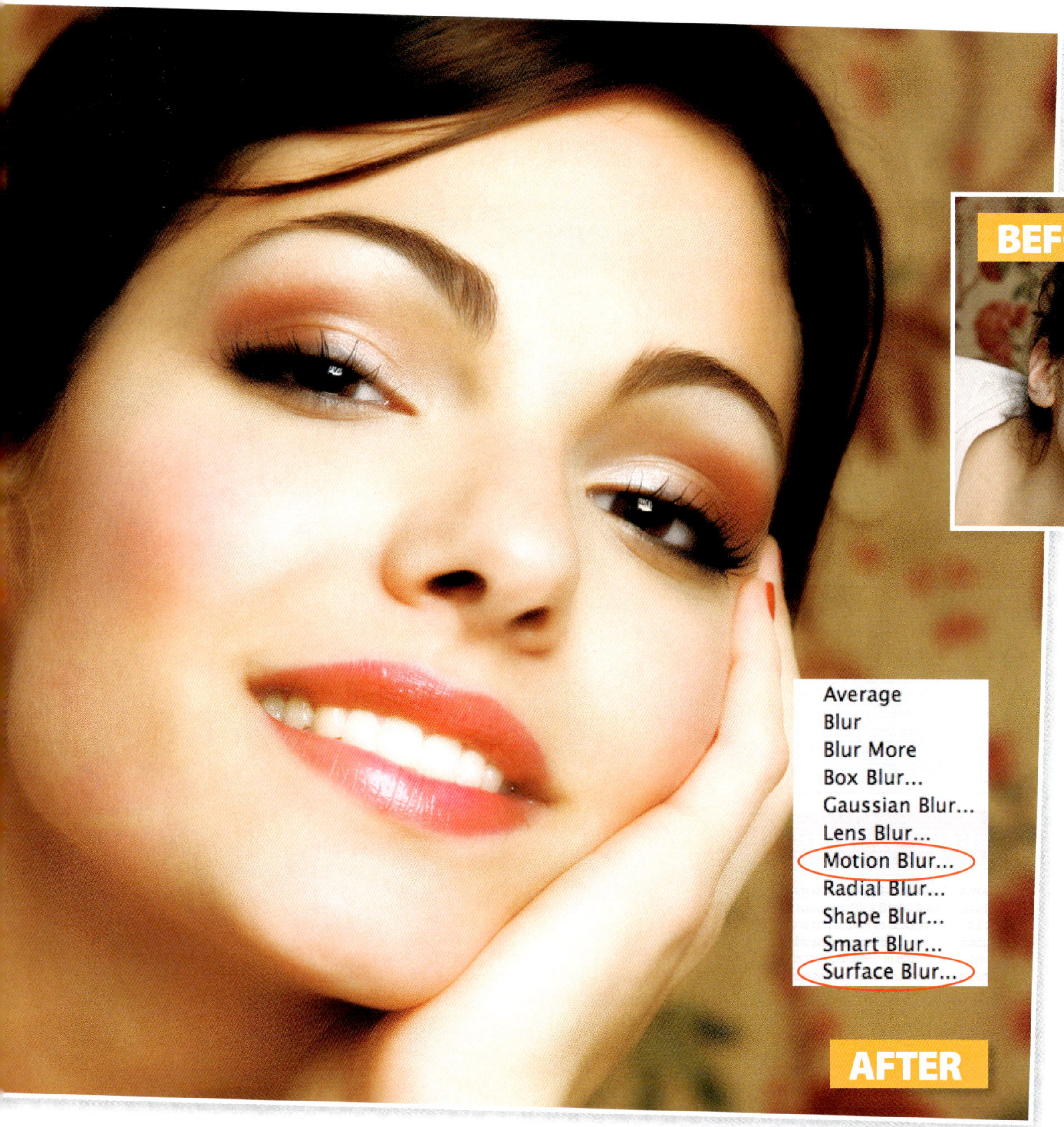

BEFORE

Average
Blur
Blur More
Box Blur...
Gaussian Blur...
Lens Blur...
Motion Blur...
Radial Blur...
Shape Blur...
Smart Blur...
Surface Blur...

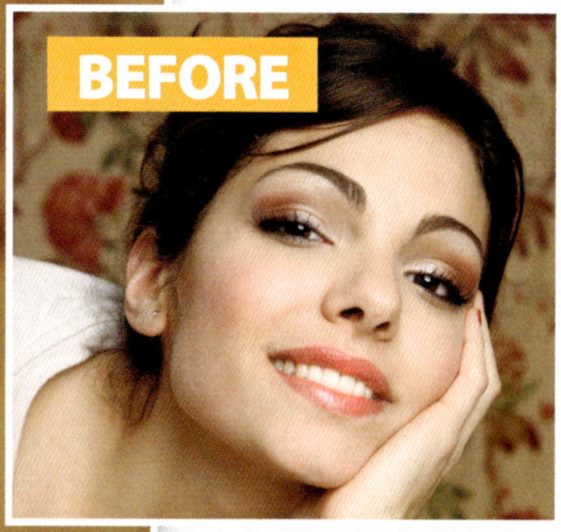

AFTER

Overlay blending

To add more contrast and impact to the soft focus effect, go to the Layers palette where you should have the duplicated layer with the blur applied. Drag this layer onto the Add New Layer button to duplicate it again. On the new duplicated layer, go to the list of blend modes in the Layers palette and add the Overlay option. Your image will now look bolder and punchier.

Surface Blur

We recommend using a portrait image for this effect. Duplicate the image layer to make adjustments non-destructively and head to Filter>Blur>Surface Blur. This only works in CS versions and above; for earlier versions use Noise>Median instead. In the Surface Blur menu set the values 15 for Radius and 30 for Threshold.

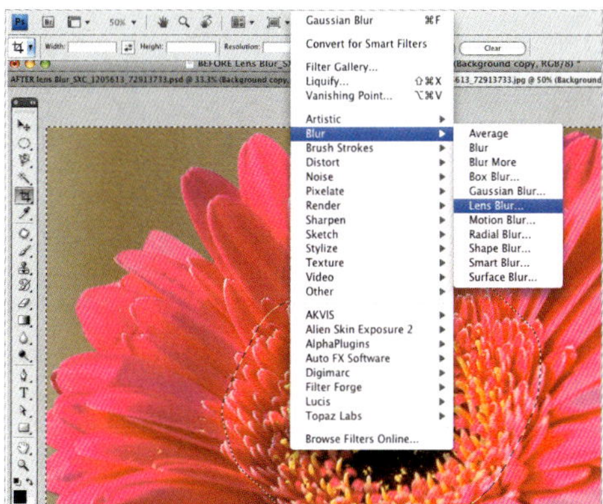

04 Blur some more

Hit 'Q' to return to the normal view. Go to Select>Inverse, then Filter>Blur>Lens Blur. If your version doesn't have this, try the Gaussian Blur filter.

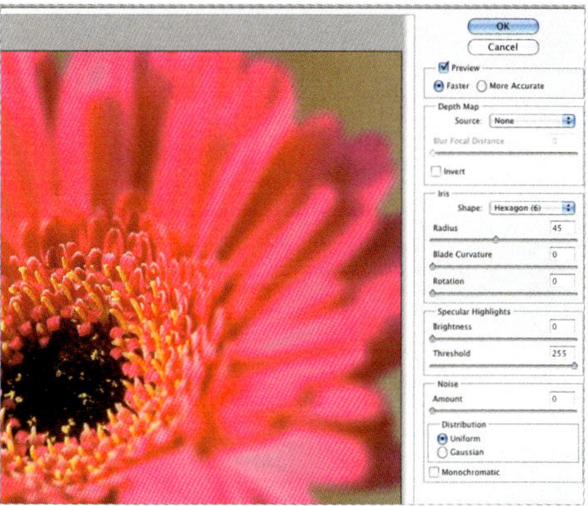

05 Set the Radius

Tick the Preview button. In the Iris section of the menu, set Shape to Hexagon and change the Radius value until you're happy.

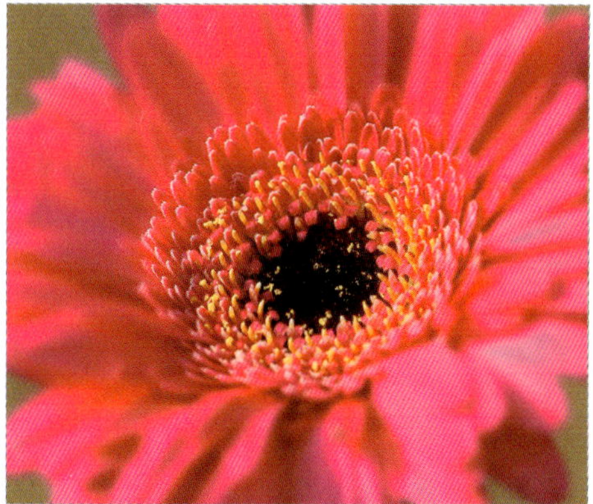

06 And you're done!

The blur effect is now complete, so try it on your own images. Bear in mind the values will change depending on the image.

Lighting Effects filter

In the dark about this filter's capabilities? Allow us to light the way for you with this handy guide

The Lighting Effects filter is an intuitive tool that, unsurprisingly, allows users to apply a plethora of lighting effects to their images. This set of applications can be taken at face value, seemingly standard and crudely presented in most creative projects.

In fact, the functionality and power of the Lighting Effects filter, when applied constructively, can provide tremendous results. Couple these with digital photography, and users are presented with a wonderland of creative opportunities. Once you've accessed the dialog box, the Style drop menu instantly provides you with 17 separate options, counting Default. These include Soft Omni, Flashlight, Flood Light and 2 O'clock Spotlight.

Application is effortless and a live preview is ever-present in the Preview window to monitor treatment. Utilising the control nodes, users can alter the lighting direction and location. This filter also includes a highly efficient set of property options that allow users to measure and edit the intensity of common light effects such as exposure, ambience and the amount of surface reflection. All of these can be deployed to enhance and pinpoint selected image areas.

The key with this filter is in keeping it subtle. A gentle spotlight can really lift your image, but go crazy with too many lights and harsh settings, and you will cheapen your image. Still, a lot of this filter is down to trial and error, and personal preference.

"The functionality and power of the Lighting Effects filter can provide tremendous results"

QUICK PHOTOSHOP TIPS

Real-time

The Preview window is quite essential when applying effects in the lighting Effects dialog box. It shows live alterations at all times. By holding Alt/Option and dragging, you can also duplicate light sources here.

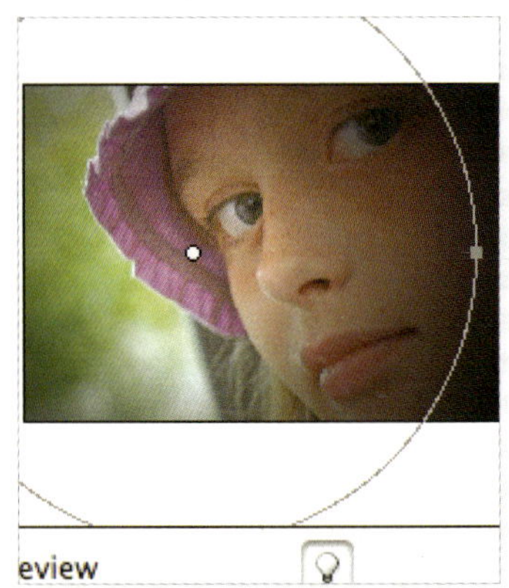

Add to what's there

You can use Lighting effects with other applications to enhance and create image effects such as moonlight, sunrise and sunset. Try opening a sunny image then duplicating the image. Select the Lighting Effect filter, applying a Spotlight in the appropriate 'o'clock' position. Set this to a yellow tone, set an Orange Properties tone and apply the desired settings. Clicking OK, apply a Soft Light blend mode. Create a new layer and apply an Orange Foreground to Transparent gradient, top to bottom, applying a Linear Burn. Lower Opacity to get the desired effect.

01 3D text effects

Cmd/Ctrl-click the text thumbnail and click the Create a New Channel icon in the Channels palette. Activate the channel and apply a Gaussian Blur.

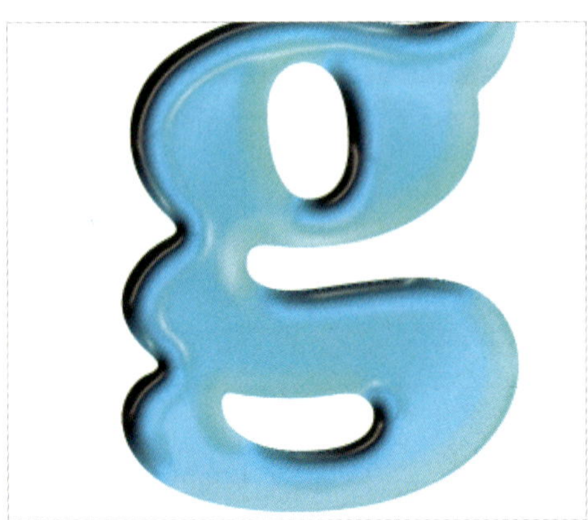

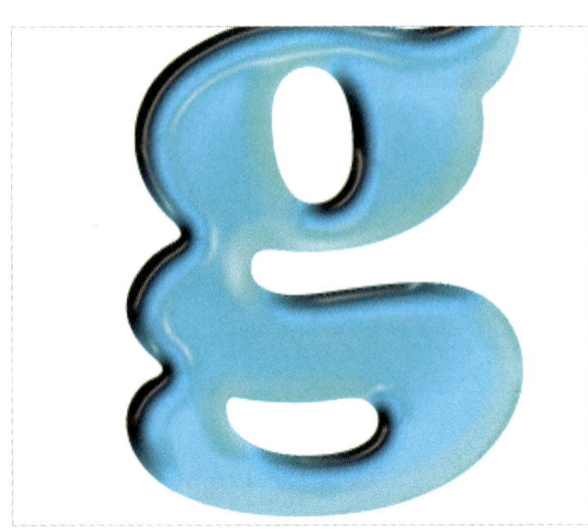

02 Text lighting

Select Lighting Effects. Set Texture Channel to Alpha 1 and apply a Direction light either side of the font. Set Exposure: 25, Ambience: 42.

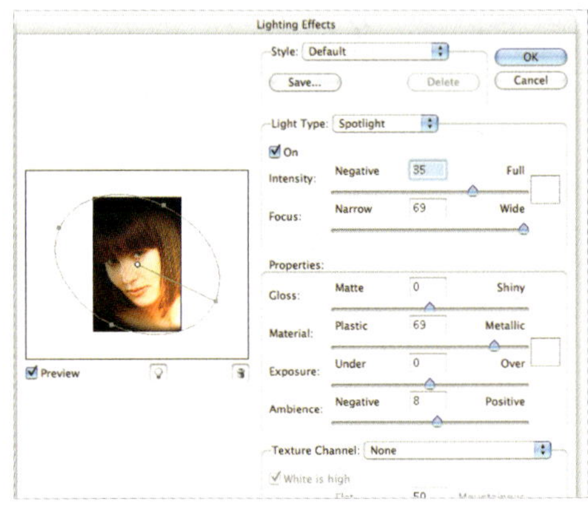

03 Spotlight on you

Spotlight is probably the most used of the Light types, creating a realistic hotspot effect, fading as it moves further from the source.

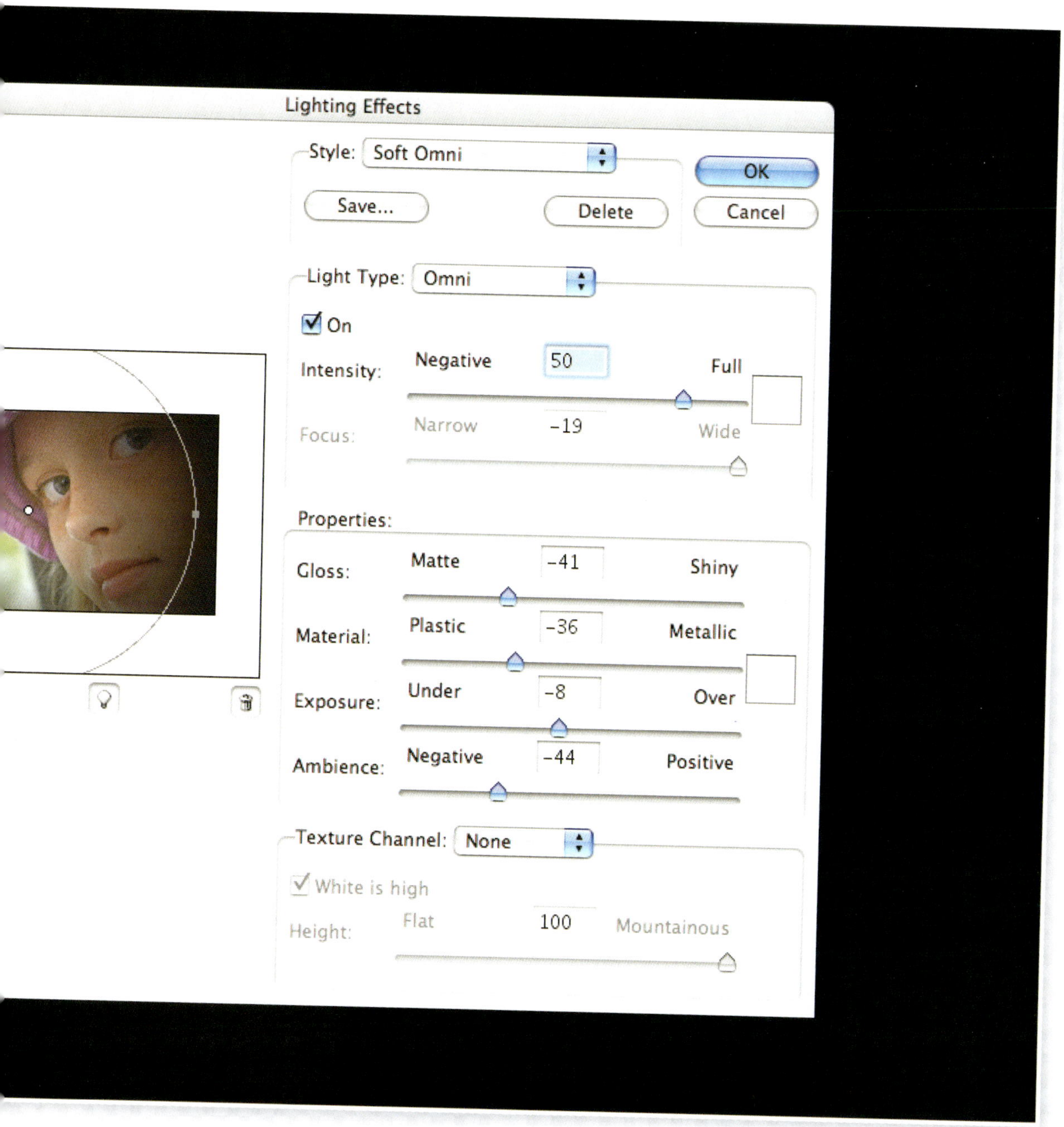

Ambience

Ambience acts as a light diffuser in your image. It combines with the lighting, so the more negative the value the more it removes, and the more positive the more it uses only the light source.

Reflect on it

The material determines which is more reflective: the light itself or the object on which it's cast. Plastic reflects the light's colour; Metallic the object's colour.

Get exposed

Understanding the functions of the properties is essential. Exposure works by increasing (positive values) or decreases (negative values) light across the image. A value of 0 has no effect.

Shiny surface

Gloss determines how much the surface of the image reflects light from Matte (low reflectance) to Glossy (high reflectance), much like it does on actual paper surfaces.

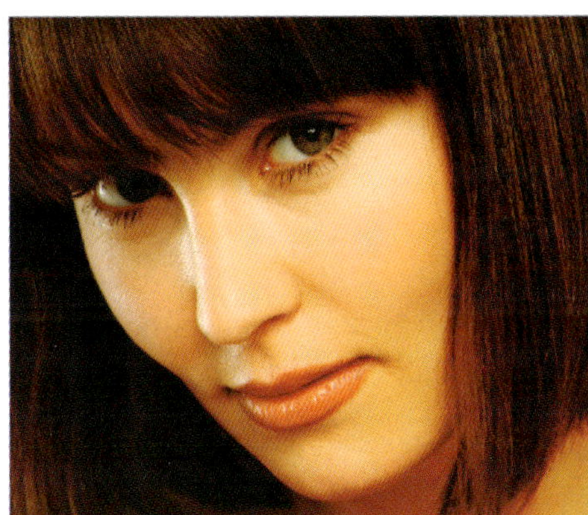

04 Blending modes

Try duplicating the layer before applying the lighting effect – and a Soft Light or Overlay blend mode creates good effects.

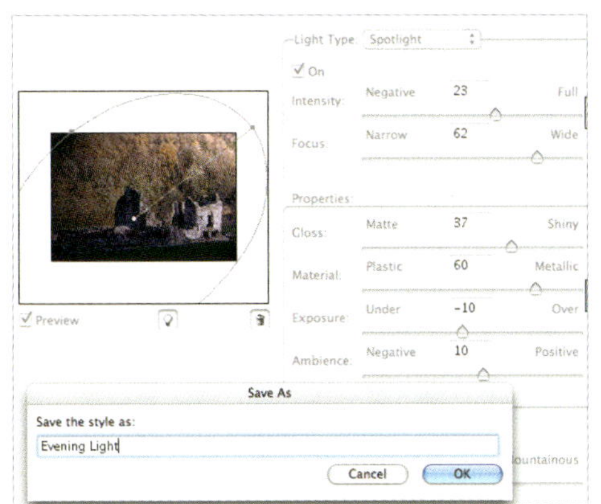

05 Options

There is a way to save and reapply effects at any time. Select Save in the Style options. Name it, and it will be added to your presets for the future.

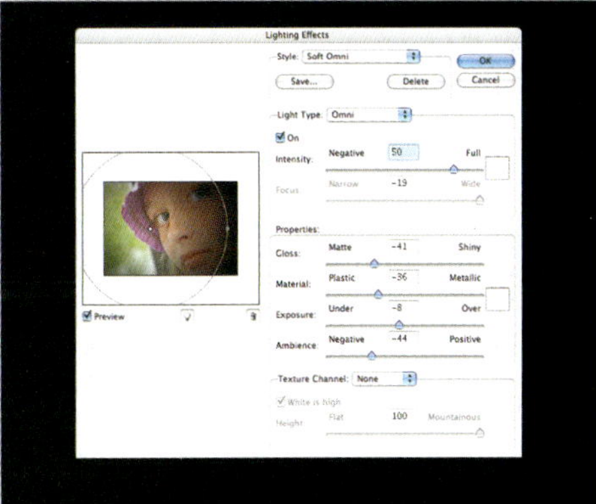

06 RGB only

The Lighting Effects filter will only operate in RGB Color mode. Use View>Proof Setup and apply Working CMYK to see a preview of how it looks.

Fixing noise with the Reduce Noise filter

Discover a clever technique for sorting noise caused by bad lighting conditions or a high ISO

Often when we go out we take along our moderately powerful compact cameras that fit neatly into our pockets or bags, we point and shoot and we come back with hundreds of photos.

Among these we may see one photo that really catches our eye. The trouble is that sometimes due to the nature of digital cameras and the shooting conditions the photo was taken in we may have a great amount of noise. Noise comes in three different flavours – colour noise, luminance noise and JPEG artefacts. Luckily for us we can reduce (although not completely remove) noise using a Photoshop filter called Reduce Noise.

Colour noise can be seen as small red, green and blue dots within our photos. Luminance noise is probably far more recognisable as actual noise – this consists of small black, white and grey dots. JPEG artefacts are blocky and make the image look as though it is low resolution. If you have a more expensive DSLR camera you can combat noise by first shooting in RAW and secondly setting your ISO to a lower number, the results from a DSLR are often very impressive.

Sadly this filter was introduced by Adobe in Photoshop CS2 so users of earlier versions will not be able to use this tutorial. Instead, you could try small amounts on blur on a duplicate layer. We have provided the image that we used here for you to practise on.

"We can reduce noise using Photoshop's Reduce Noise filter"

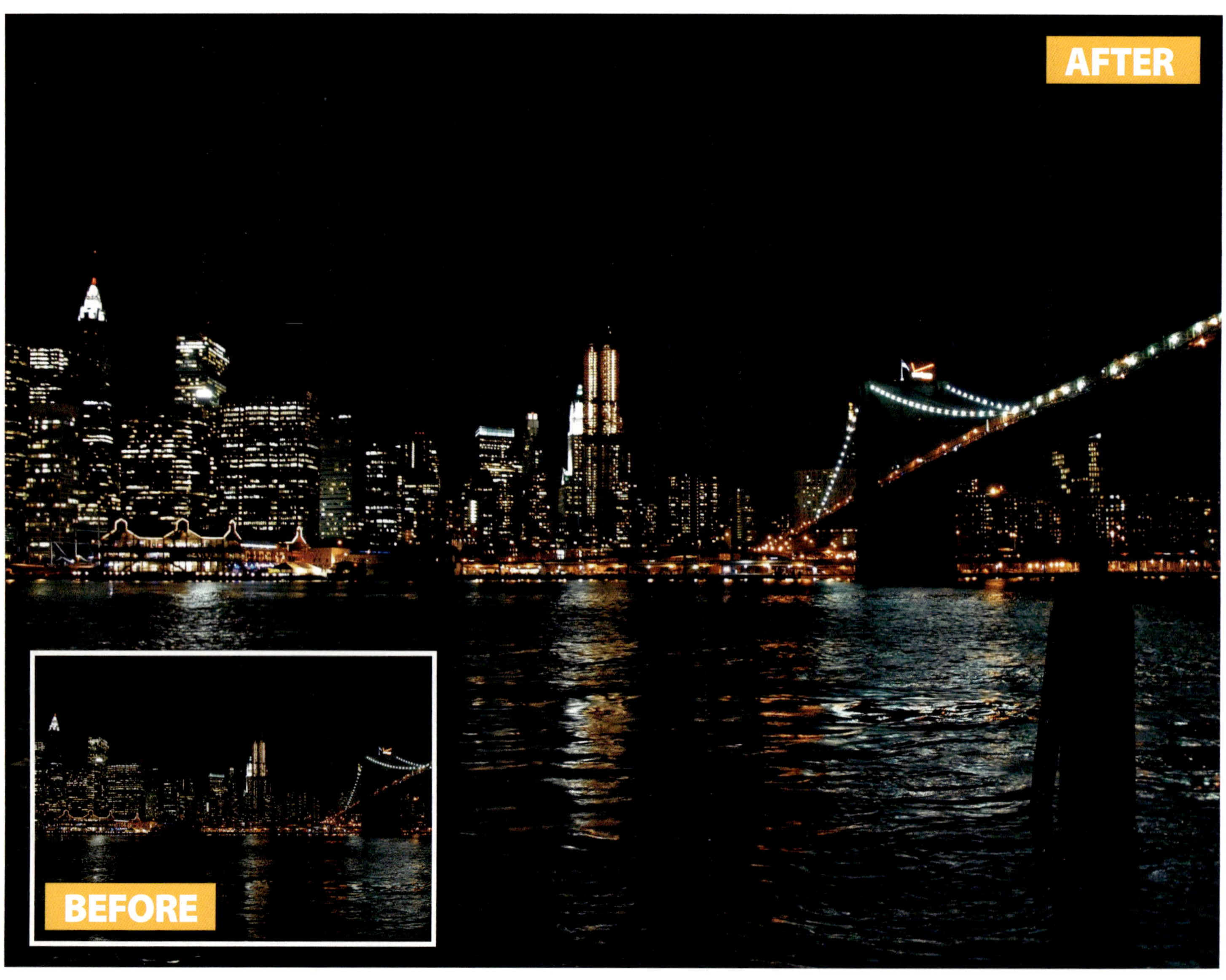

Reduce noise in photos Without losing details or texture

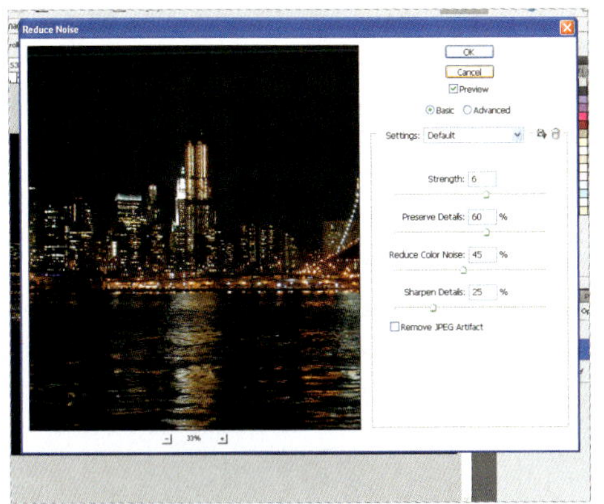

01 Get started

Open your start image. Start things off by duplicating the Background image and naming it 'RGB Noise'. Go to Filter>Noise>Reduce Noise.

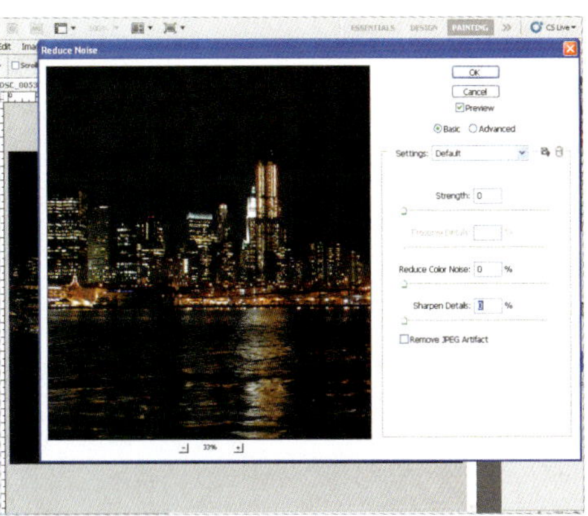

02 Set to 0

Make sure you are in Basic mode. Next reduce all the sliders to 0 and make sure Remove JPEG Artifacts has no tick.

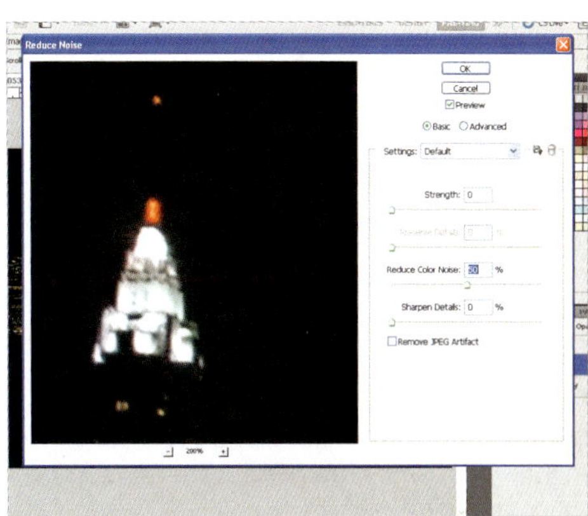

03 Reduce RGB noise

Find a spot that has lots of lights. Zoom into 200% then increase the Reduce Noise slider. We set ours to 50% but this will be different for each photo.

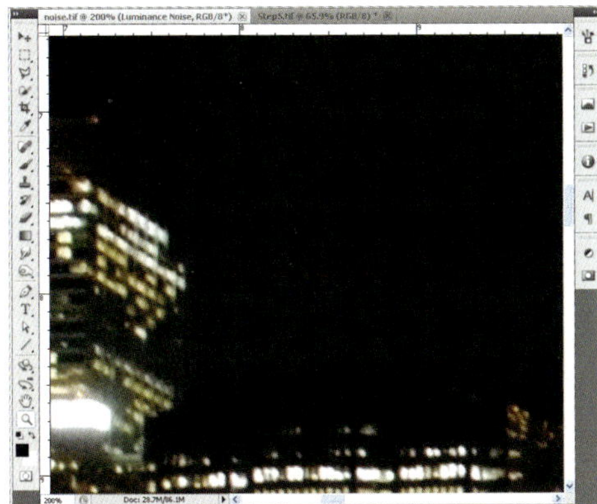

04 Luminance noise

Luminance noise is seen as black, white and grey dots. Copy the 'RGB Noise' layer to a new layer and name it 'Luminance Noise'.

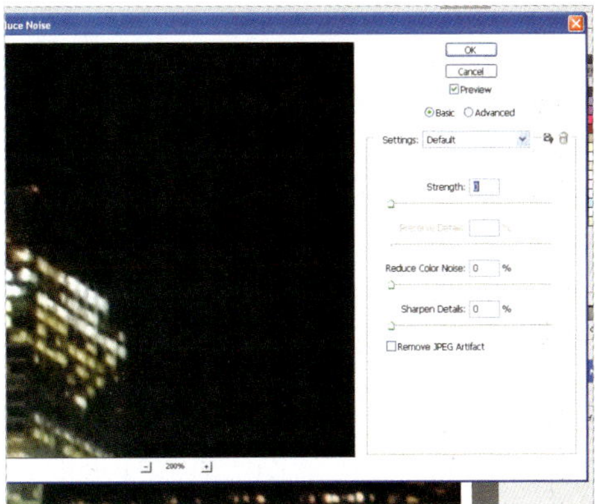

05 Back to the filter

Make sure you are on the new layer and access the Reduce Noise filter. We will now reduce the luminance noise by moving the Strength slider.

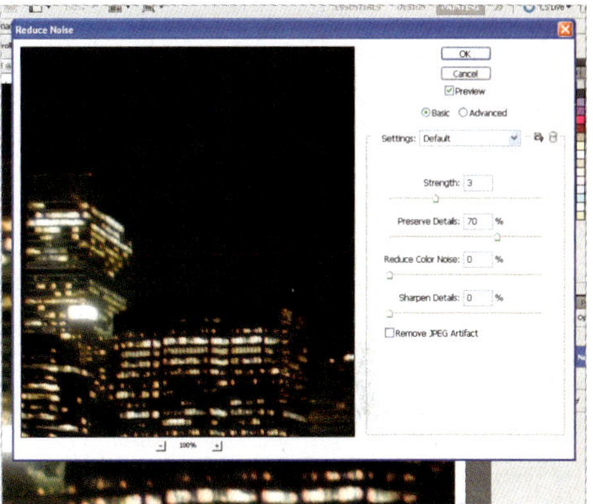

06 Strength in numbers

Move the Strength slider gradually up. We have to be careful not to destroy the details, so we also increase the Preserve Details slider.

07 Channel hopping

We can reduce noise further using the filter's Advanced options. Create a copy of the 'Luminance Noise' layer and name it 'Channels'.

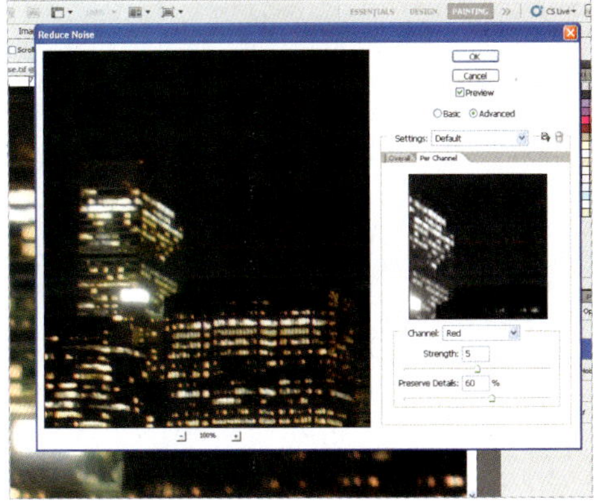

08 And filter once more…

Load the filter again and click Advanced. Click on Per Channel. Now you can edit the noise by channel independently.

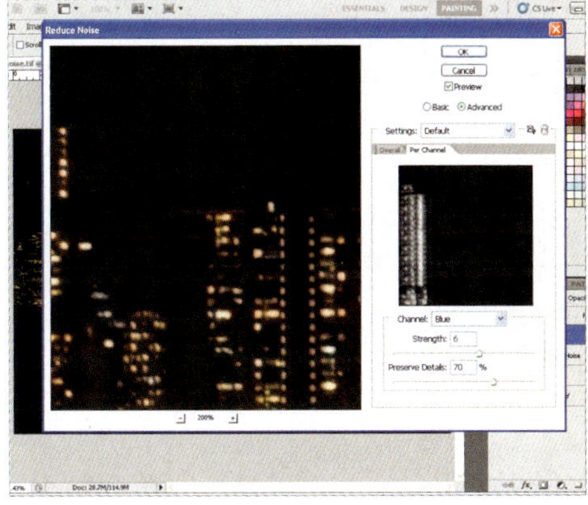

09 Final settings

We set Red and Green's Strength to 2 and Preserve Details to 60%, and Blue's Strength to 5 and Preserve Details to 70%.

Unsharp Mask filter

Achieve control over your sharpening with this handy filter from Photoshop's Filter menu

Almost every image can benefit from a touch of sharpening, and it's usually a process that is best performed after all other image-editing has been completed.

When you sharpen images in Photoshop, you are increasing the contrast between neighbouring pixels. This gives your image a sharper appearance, especially when viewed at full size. Zoom in, and the sharpness isn't so apparent.

Sharpening is something that should be applied in moderation. A heavy hand can cause your image to look pixelated and harsh. Photoshop offers a host of sharpening methods under the menu option Filter>Sharpen. The majority of filters apply sharpening to the entire image, which is not always preferable. For a more localised and controlled sharpening effect, Photoshop has a secret weapon called the Unsharp Mask filter.

It's a bit of a strange name for a filter that sharpens, but learning to use it will help you to perfect your portrait and landscape shots with just a little know-how.

Here we will discuss the benefits of this special sharpening filter and how to use it effectively. Unsharp Mask comes with three adjustment sliders to help fine-tune the sharpening effect you want to create: Amount, Radius and Threshold. With a little practice you'll be able to control these sliders for an impressive sharpening effect.

> "With a little practice you'll be able to control these sliders for an impressive sharpening effect"

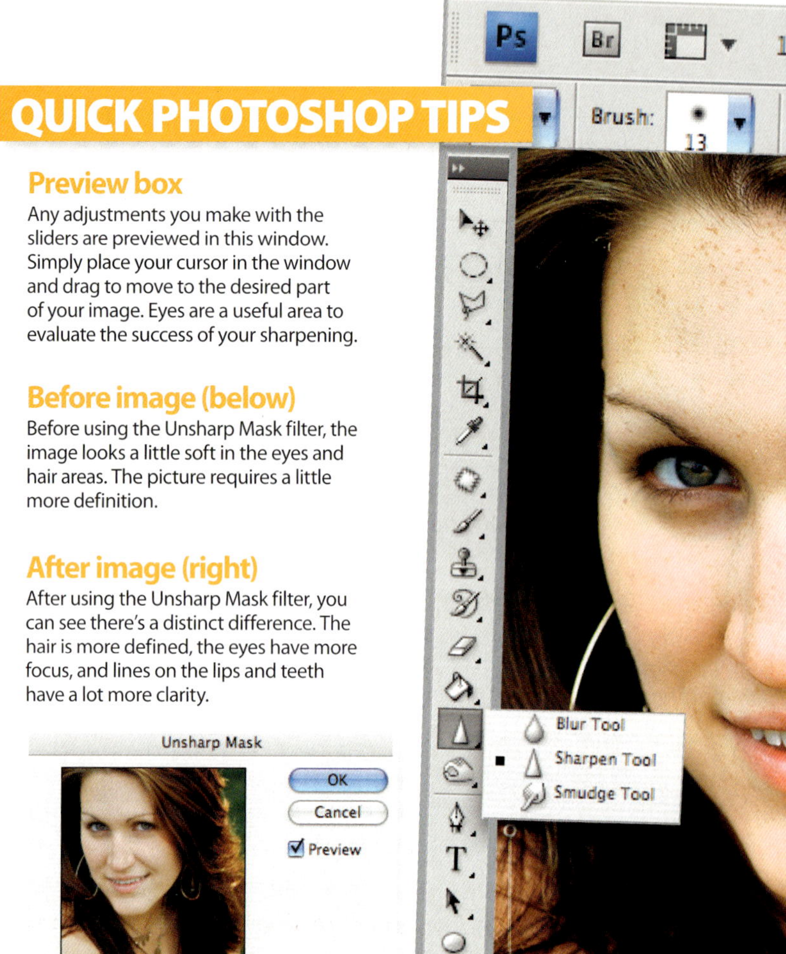

QUICK PHOTOSHOP TIPS

Preview box

Any adjustments you make with the sliders are previewed in this window. Simply place your cursor in the window and drag to move to the desired part of your image. Eyes are a useful area to evaluate the success of your sharpening.

Before image (below)

Before using the Unsharp Mask filter, the image looks a little soft in the eyes and hair areas. The picture requires a little more definition.

After image (right)

After using the Unsharp Mask filter, you can see there's a distinct difference. The hair is more defined, the eyes have more focus, and lines on the lips and teeth have a lot more clarity.

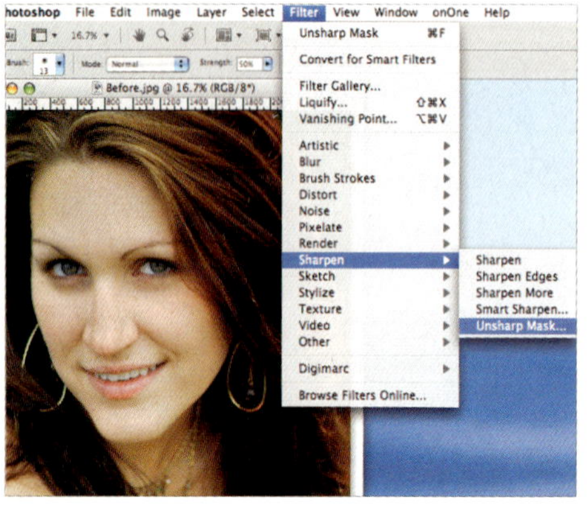

01 Select the filter

Make all the necessary colour adjustments and edits first. Sharpening should be the last thing you do. Go to Filter>Sharpen>Unsharp Mask.

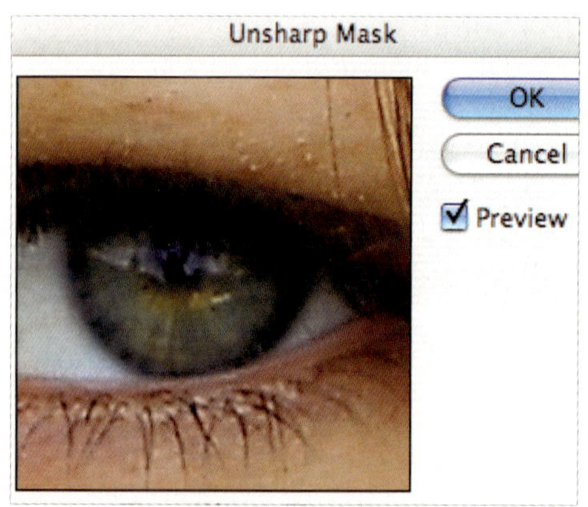

02 Set up the box

Make sure Preview is ticked. Move the cursor into the window in the dialog box. Hold the cursor and drag until you see a suitable part, such as the eye.

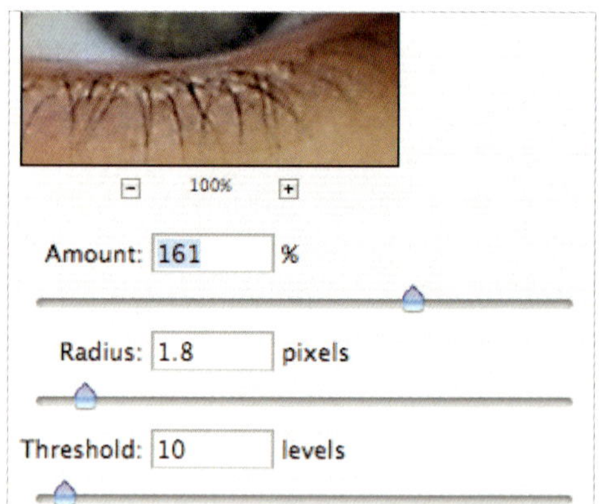

03 Make your changes

Start moving the Amount, Radius and Threshold sliders. Low-res images should be given low values for Amount and Radius to avoid harsh results.

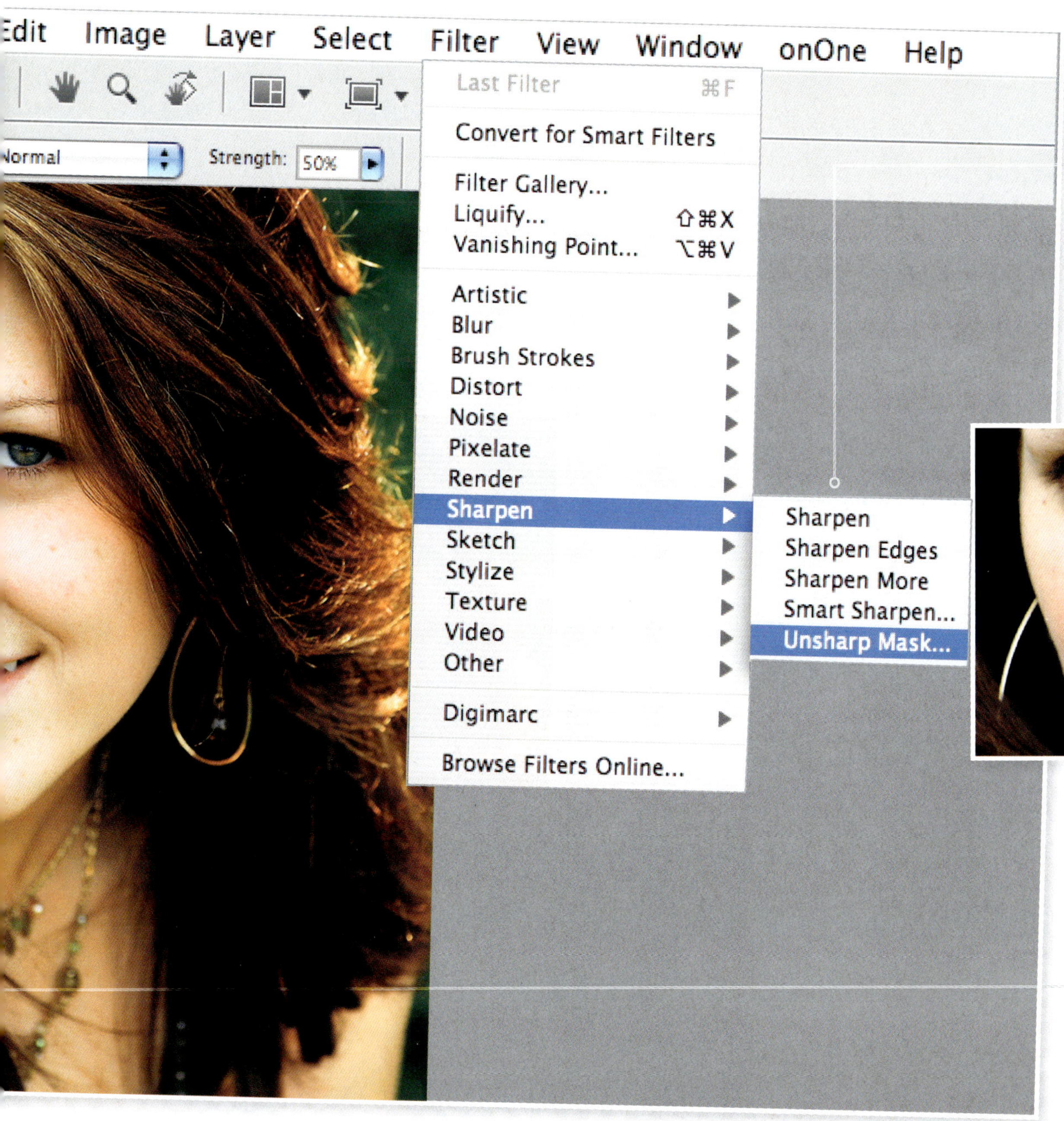

Filter menu

There are lots of sharpening options within the Filter menu. The Unsharp Mask filter and Smart filters offer the most accurate sharpening results. The Unsharp Mask filter relies on adjustment sliders to create the perfect amount of sharpening.

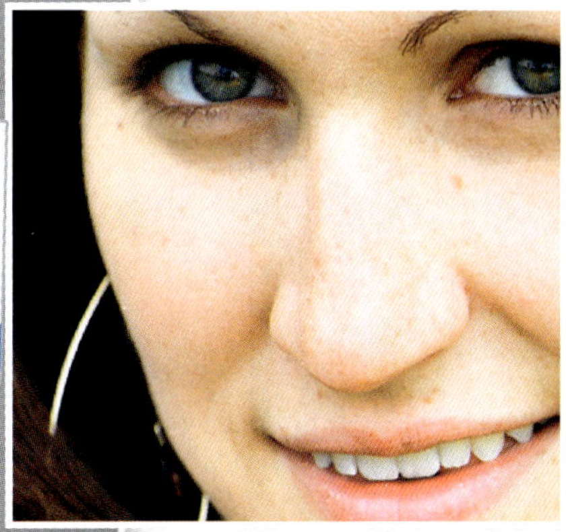

When to sharpen

All photos will benefit from subtle sharpening. You should always perform sharpening last, just before you print out your image.

The Sharpen tool

An alternative to the Unsharp Mask filter is the Sharpen tool. This works just like a brush and is good for very small, specific areas. The longer you hold down the cursor, the stronger the sharpening effect will be.

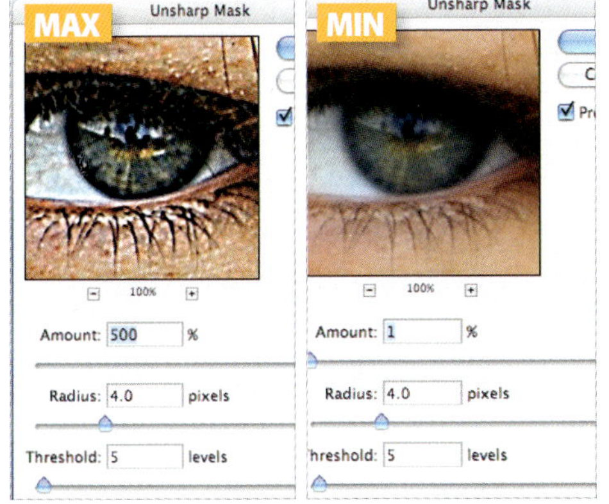

04 The Amount slider

This dictates how strong the sharpening effect will be. The higher you set the percentage, the more obvious the effect will be.

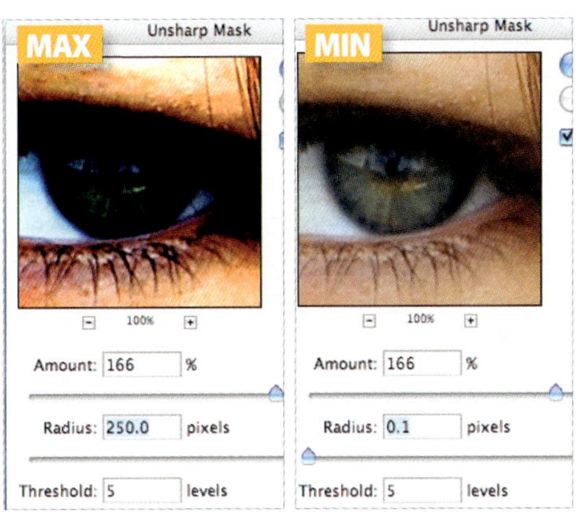

05 The Radius slider

The Radius slider is based on the edges, and you can choose how many pixels around the edge will be affected.

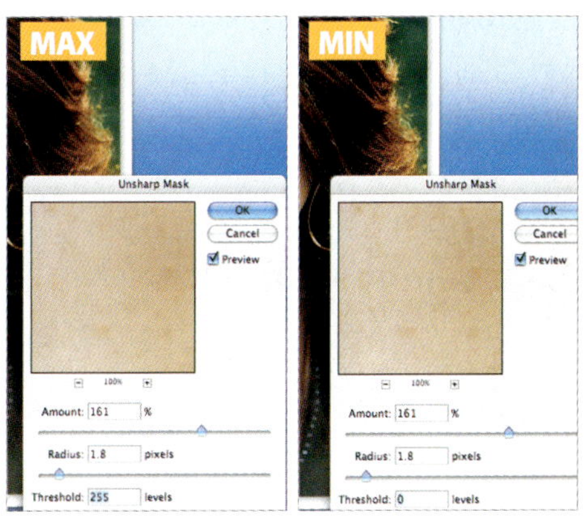

06 The Threshold slider

The Threshold slider enables you to choose how different each pixel must be from the rest in order to have sharpening applied to it.

Using the Sketch filters

Get a hand drawn look in minutes with this handy set of filters. Picking which one to use is the hard part…

The Sketch selection of filters are designed to simplify your photos into strokes and apply textures to them to give the appearance of various forms of natural media. The majority of the filters in the Sketch collection will limit the number of colours in your image, as well as softening detail. Hence, these filters work best on simple images that don't have too much going on.

Before you apply any filters, you need to check out your Foreground and Background Colors. You will find the current colours at the bottom of the toolbar on the left of the interface that holds all your tools. The square at the front is your Foreground Color and the one at the back is your Background Color. You can click on these squares to bring up the Color Picker and choose new colours for these. If you want the default black and white, just hit the keyboard shortcut 'D'. Many of the Sketch filters use these colours in some way, so you need to set them before you apply any filters.

You can pick any of the filters from the Filter>Artistic menu, which brings up the Filter Gallery. Then you are presented with all the thumbnails of effects that come under the Artistic category. Click on any to apply the effect. Click on another replaces the current effect with the new one. There are sliders on the right-hand side of the interface that can be played with to customise the effects to suit. Click OK when you're happy with the result to return to the main Photoshop interface.

> "The majority of the filters will limit the number of colours, as well as soften detail"

QUICK PHOTOSHOP TIPS

Finding the filters

To access the Artistic filters, take a visit to the Filter menu and scroll down. Here you will find a list of all 14 filters available in this category.

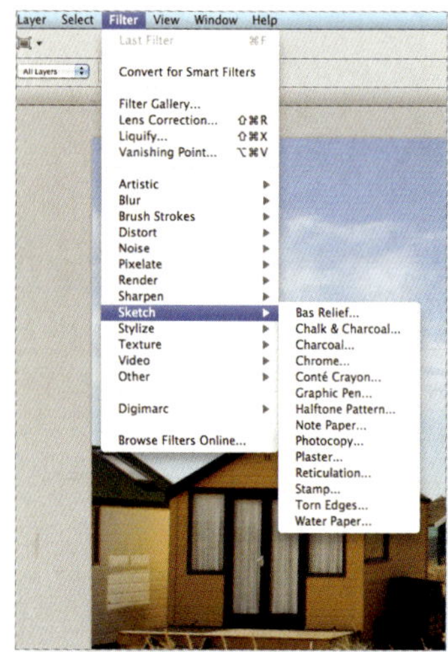

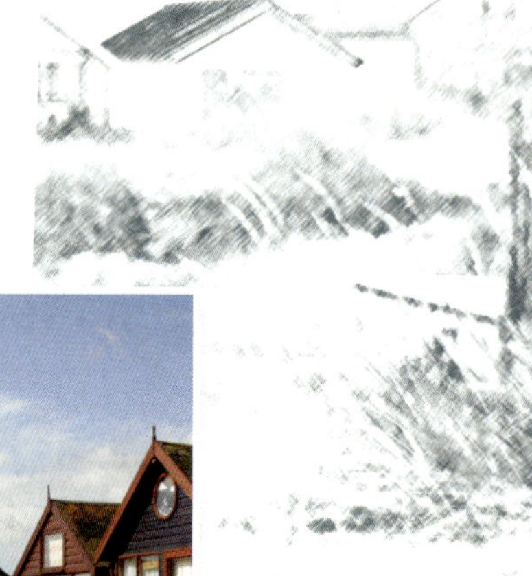

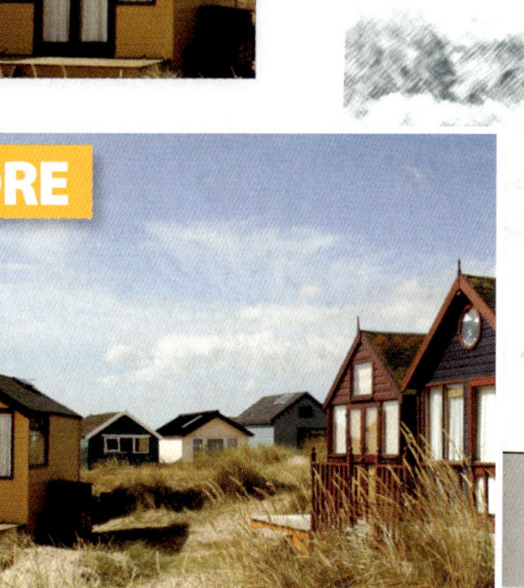

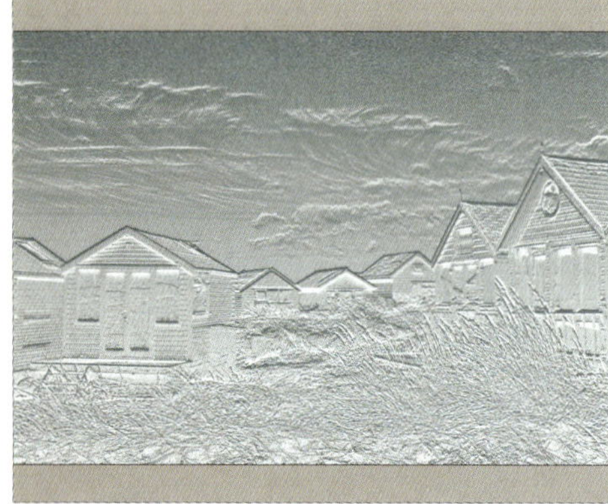

01 Bas Relief

This filter emulates the effect of a low relief carving made up of your chosen Foreground and Background colours.

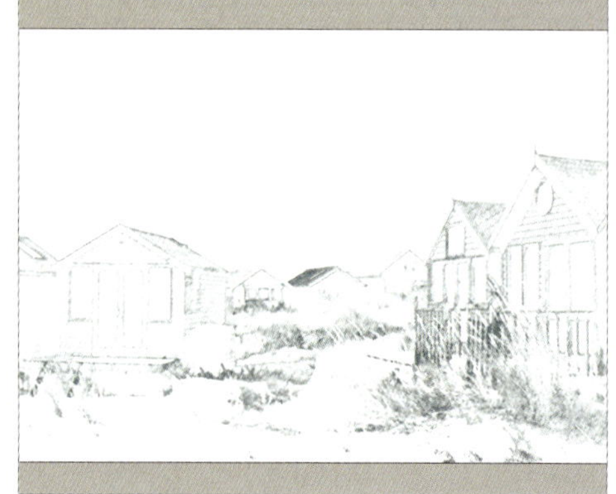

02 Charcoal

This creates a rough image that looks like charcoal. Your Foreground Color is the charcoal marks, and your Background Color is the paper.

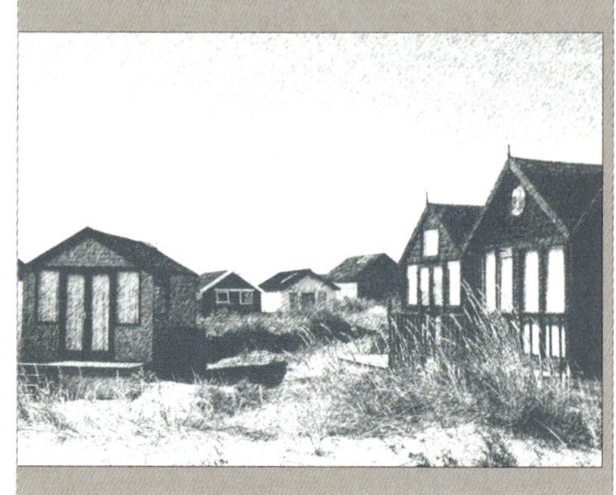

03 Graphic Pen

This re-creates your image in two colours. The Foreground Color is used for the pen strokes and your Background Color is used for the paper.

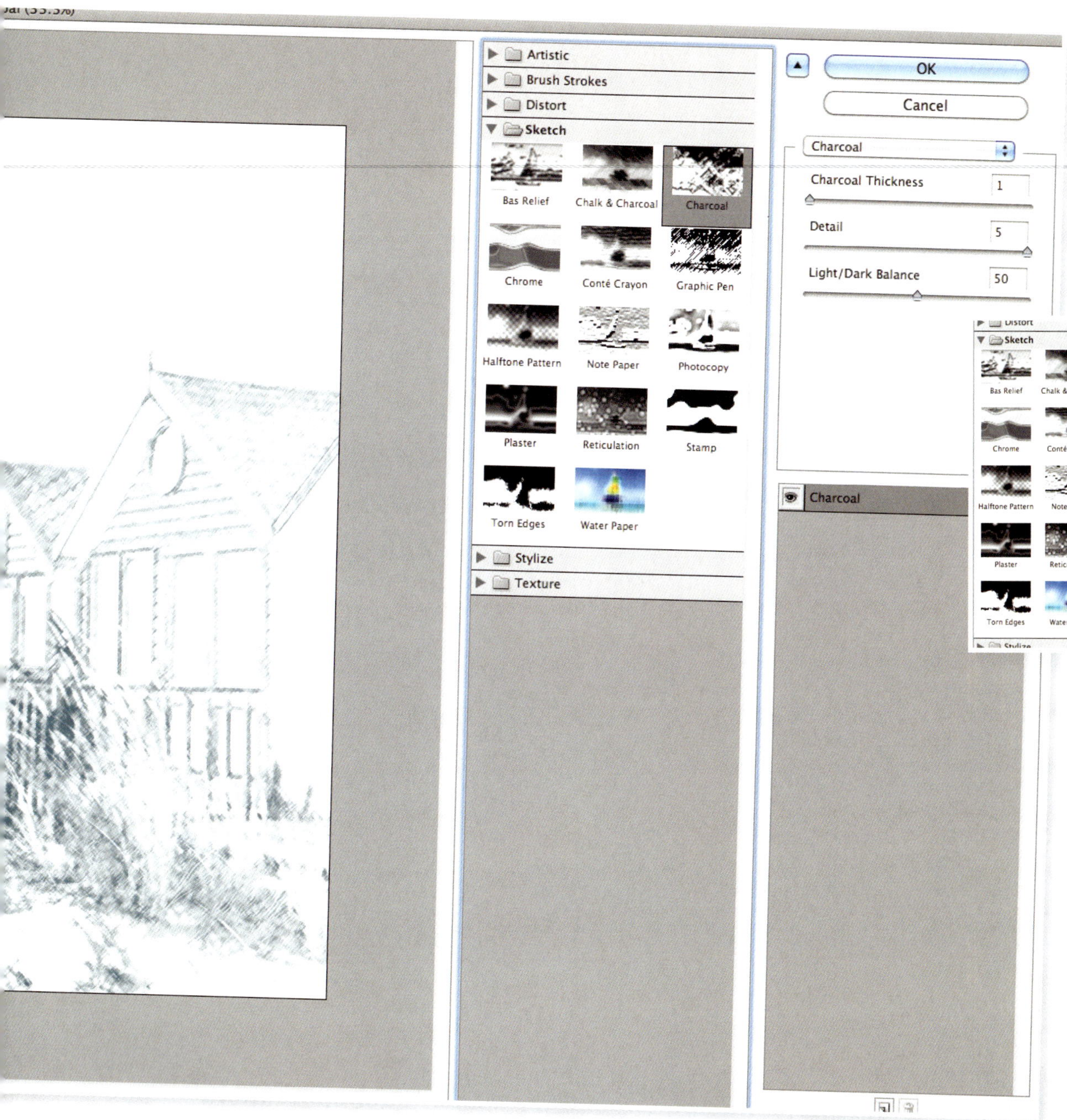

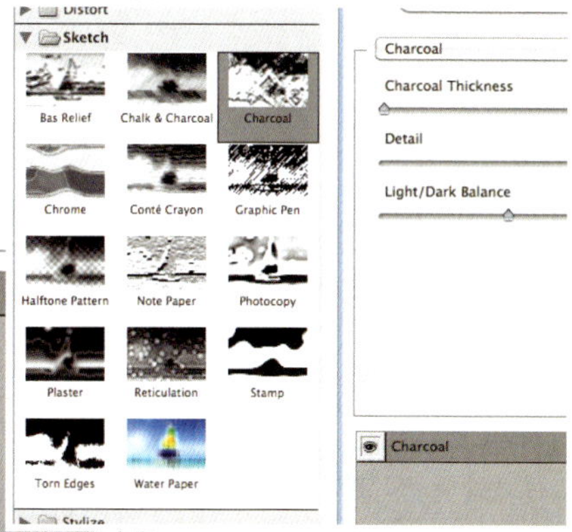

Preview window

The preview window enables you to see the changes that you are making live. You can zoom in or out of the image using the controls at the bottom of the window.

Filter options

Each filter has its own thumbnail and you just have to click once to apply it. Then, you can use the sliders in the right-hand panel to tweak it to your liking.

Apply the filter

When you are happy with your settings, you simply need to hit the OK button to apply the changes and you will be taken back to the Photoshop interface.

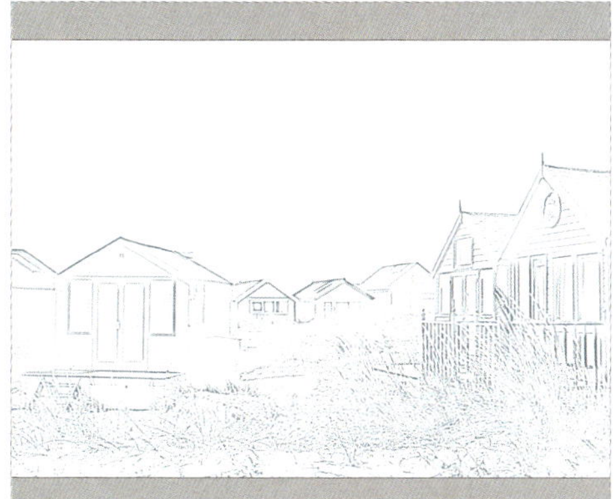

04 Photocopy

This filter uses your Foreground and Background Colors as paper and toner to create a rough photocopied version of your photo.

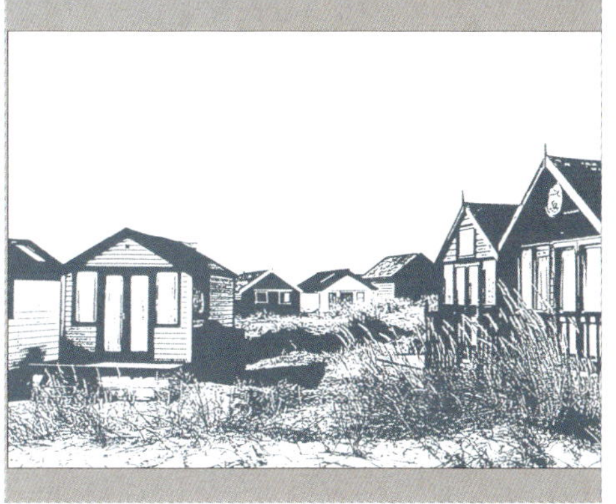

05 Stamp

This filter uses the Foreground Color as the background and the Background Color as the ink from the rubber stamp.

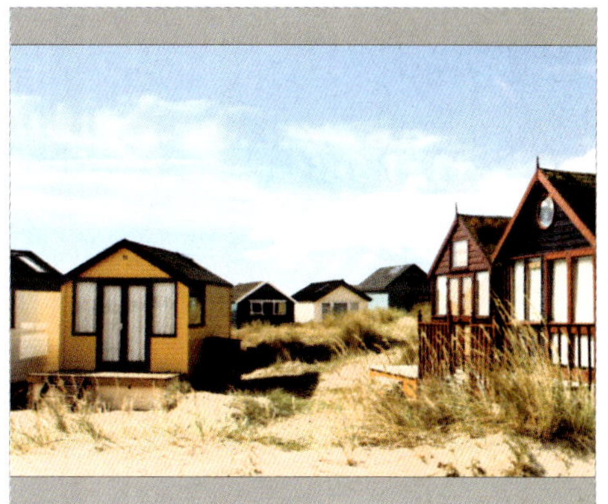

06 Water Paper

This filter essentially waters down the colours in your image, which gives it this soft, painterly style. Perfect for landscape images in particular.

Using the Liquify filter

This feature has a bad reputation, but it can be used for some very practical applications, as we show you here

The Liquify filter suffers from a bad reputation as many people tend to use it purely to add bulging eyes to photos. However, these pages will reveal how it has many practical applications and teach you how to use the options more effectively for your image-editing work.

Find the Liquify feature under the Filter menu in the top bar. Here you can push, pull, reflect, bloat and pucker pixels within an image, plus you have the safety net of being able to repair the damage by using the Reconstruct tool if needed.

Using this filter in a photography project can let you slim waistlines and faces with the Forward Warp feature or make lips fuller with the Bloat tool. Many professional photographers rely on this tool in post-production as you can make dramatic improvements to photos, especially portraits. Just remember to always duplicate your background layer before starting as the effects applied are permanent; once OK has been hit your layer will be altered.

Retouching is often the primary use for this filter but it can also add creativity to a project. Try adding a ripple effect to still water, create a wood look from scratch or add a reflection to a plain landscape. We will show you the possibilities of the underestimated Liquify filter.

"Using this filter in a photography project can let you slim waistlines and faces"

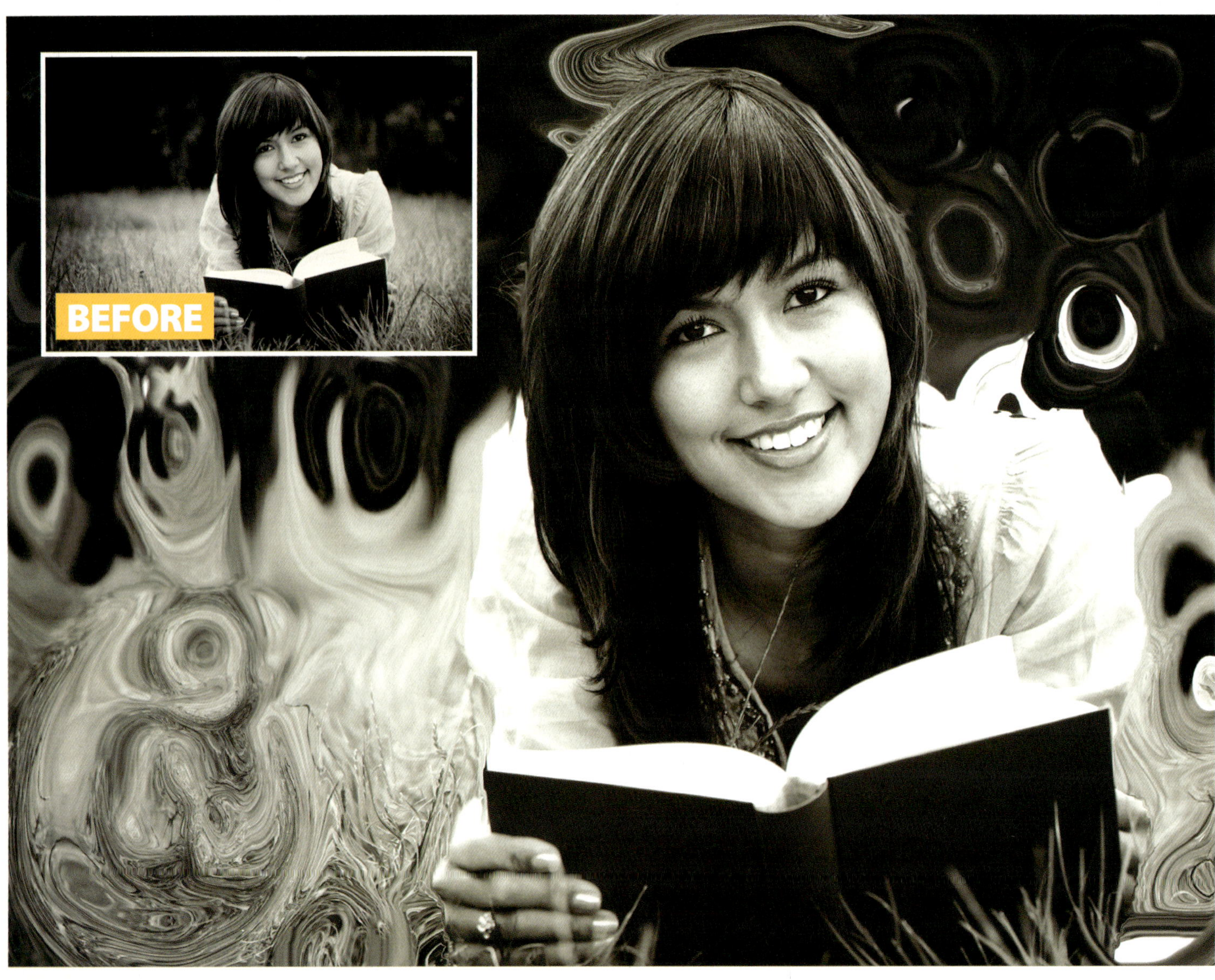

QUICK PHOTOSHOP TIPS

Twirl Clockwise

All aspects of this tool can be edited in the right hand menu depending on the level of effect you're after. The brush size can be altered and editing the Pressure setting affects the strength of the tool. Edge Hardness is the density setting and the speed of the pixel movement can be tweaked by increasing the brush rate. A twirl effect is created by clicking and holding down the mouse or by clicking and moving the mouse around. This can be used to create a wood effect. Fill two layers with brown colour, one dark one light, and add a Clouds effect (Filter>Render>Clouds). Open the Liquify filter, select the Twirl tool and move the mouse over the canvas to apply the effect.

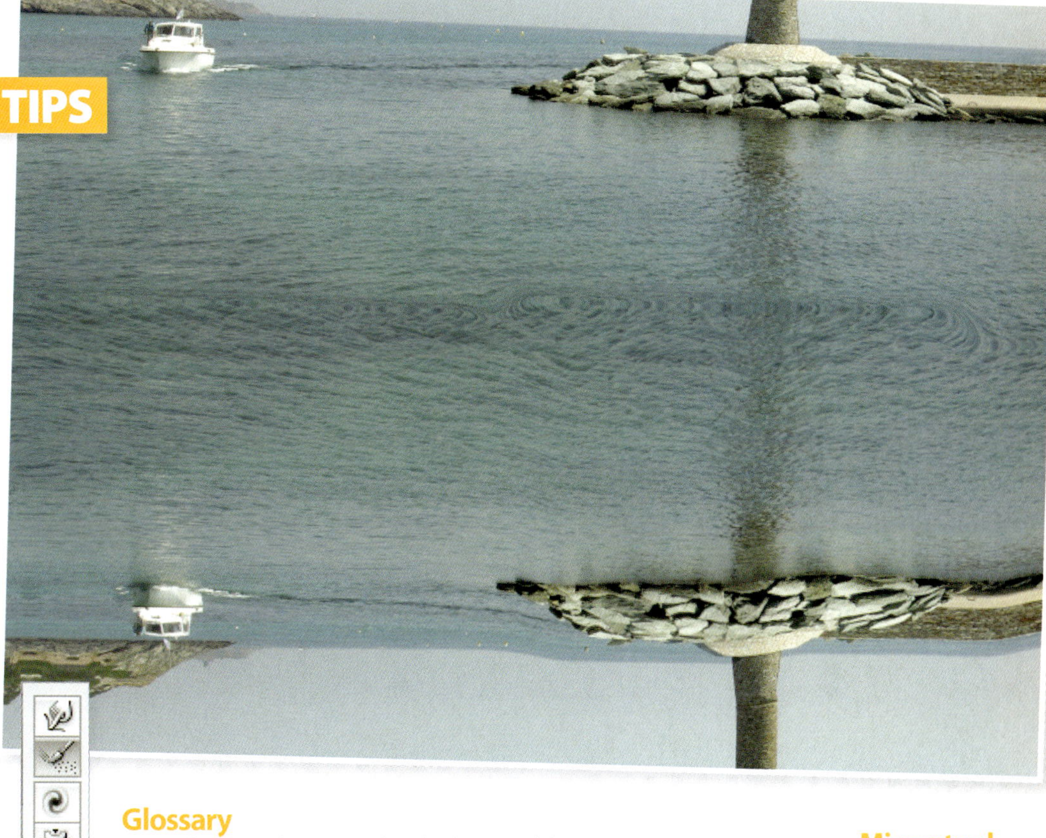

Glossary

Forward Warp tool: Moves pixels in the direction of the mouse.
Reconstruct tool: Reverts areas back to their original state.
Twirl Clockwise tool: Rotates pixels in a clockwise motion. Hold down Opt/Alt to change direction.
Pucker tool: Pinches pixels. Holding down Opt/Alt bloats them.
Bloat tool: Works like the Pinch tool with the opposite movement.
Push Left tool: Pushes pixels in the opposite direction than the way you move your mouse.
Mirror tool: Flips pixels to create a reflected image.
Turbulence tool: Causes pixels to create a ripple effect.
Freeze Mask tool: Adds a mask.
Thaw Mask tool: Edits or removes a mask.
Hand tool: Allows you to move around the image.
Zoom tool: Zooms in on your image. Holding Opt/Alt switches direction.

Mirror tool

This is a clever and quick tool that can add some spark and excitement to bland landscapes. To use it just draw a horizontal line in your image. You will see it has mirrored the pixels that sit above where you have drawn the line. To use this in projects creatively, increase the canvas size so there is blank space at the base (Image>Canvas Size). Open the image in Liquify, select the Mirror tool and paint under the image in the blank space. Moving your mouse to the left adds a reflection while moving it right takes it away again.

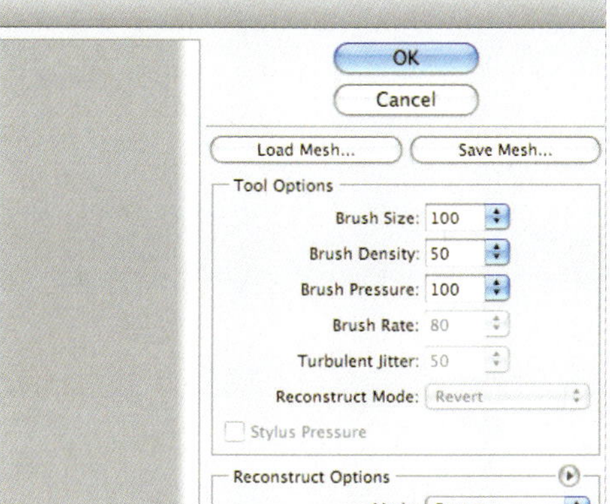

01 Forward Warp tool

To make an area smaller select the Forward Warp tool and set your brush up in the right hand menu. Keep the brush small.

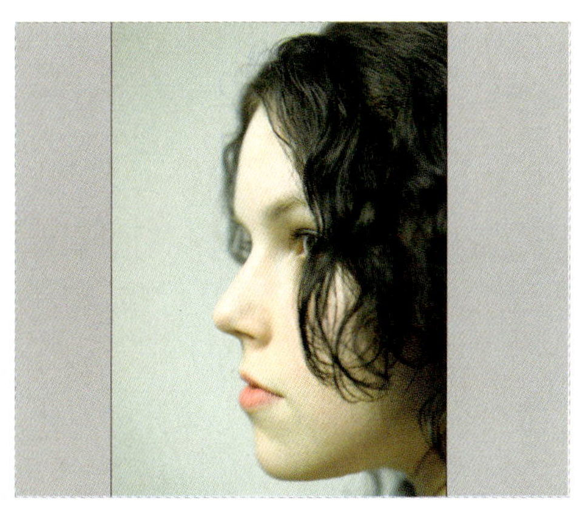

02 Move those pixels

Click on an area of the jaw line and then simply move the mouse upwards. Work in small movements. Zoom out and check its realism.

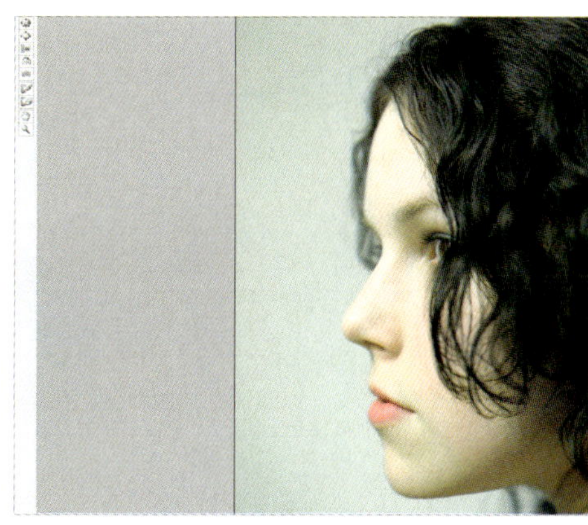

03 Keep it natural

If the chin needs shrinking more, repeat the process. The same technique works on anything that may need shrinking a little!

The wonder of Vanishing Point

Perspective can be a tricky thing at the best of times. We explore the miracle that is the Vanishing Point filter

It's not unusual for many of the tools in Photoshop to leave you really impressed at just how good they are, but there are a few – still surprisingly overlooked by many novices – that truly have the power to leave any digital imaging enthusiast quite breathless at the sheer brilliance and virtuosity contained within them. The Vanishing Point filter in Photoshop is just one of those examples – it's quite simply just brilliant!

Essentially, Vanishing Point is all about perspective, and within its magical realm you'll start off by actually creating planes of perspective, simply by plotting points and dragging out multiple planes from them. But that's only part of the story. Once these planes of perspective have been established, you'll be able to do a myriad of things with them. You can add type that conforms to the perspective in your images seamlessly. You can also clone, just as you can in Photoshop normally, but this isn't the usual kind of cloning. Because it's based on the planes of perspective you've created, the Cloning tool will actually clone while conforming to the perspective in your image, making cloning over imperfections with brickwork, for instance, an absolute breeze!

And it doesn't end there. You also have a magical Marquee tool, which again conforms to perspective and with which you can copy and paste existing objects and paste them in another part of the scene, marvelling as they diminish realistically.

"Leaves any digital imaging enthusiast quite breathless at the filter's sheer brilliance"

QUICK PHOTOSHOP TIPS

Magical cloning

The Clone Stamp tool within Vanishing Point allows you to clone over objects with any sampled texture of your choice, and even have that texture conform precisely to the original perspective in your image.

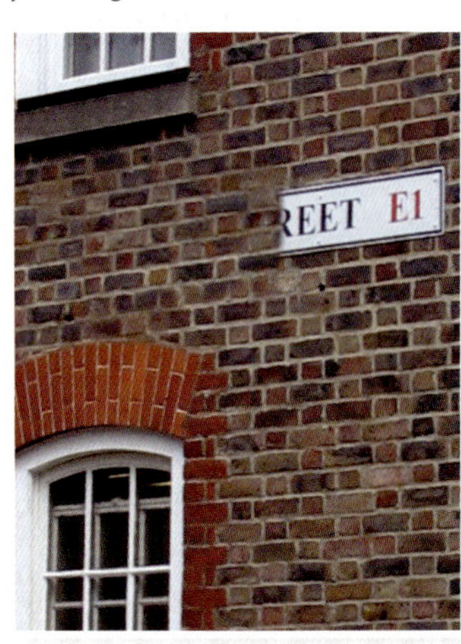

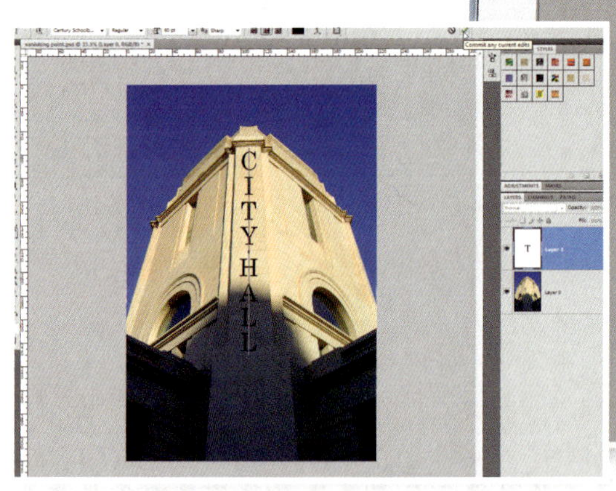

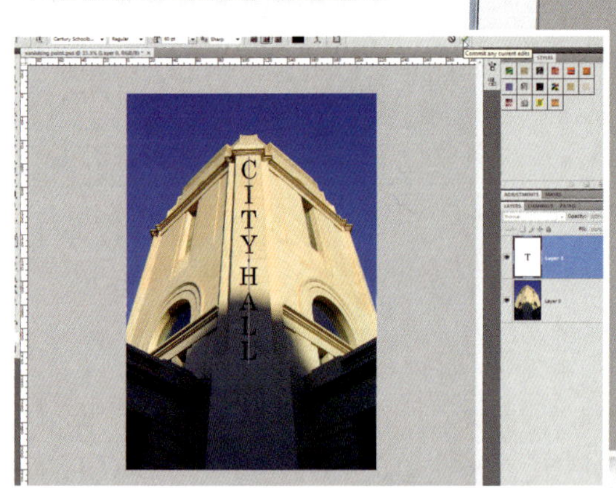

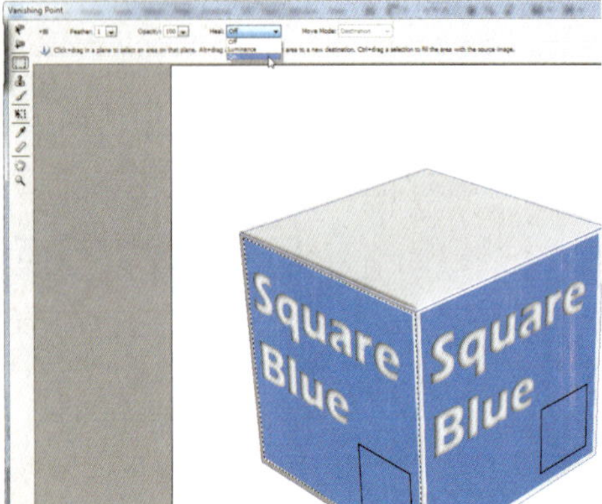

01 Magic healing

Clone an object to another surface. By Opt/Alt-dragging an active selection, the selected area can be dragged to a new location.

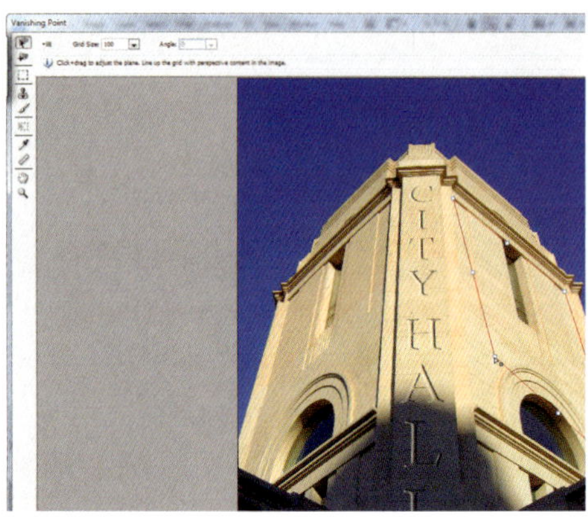

02 Grid accuracy

Blue grids are accurate. Yellow indicates that the plane could be made more accurate. Red indicates a plane that is unusable.

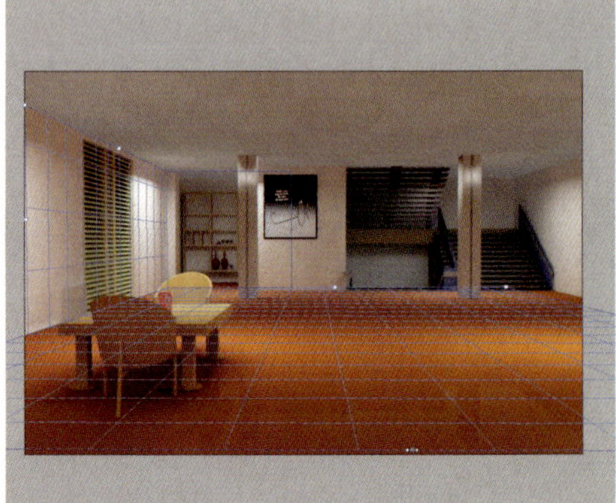

03 Adding multiple planes

Hold Cmd/Ctrl and click and drag out from a central handle on one of the perpendicular edges of the plane to create more planes.

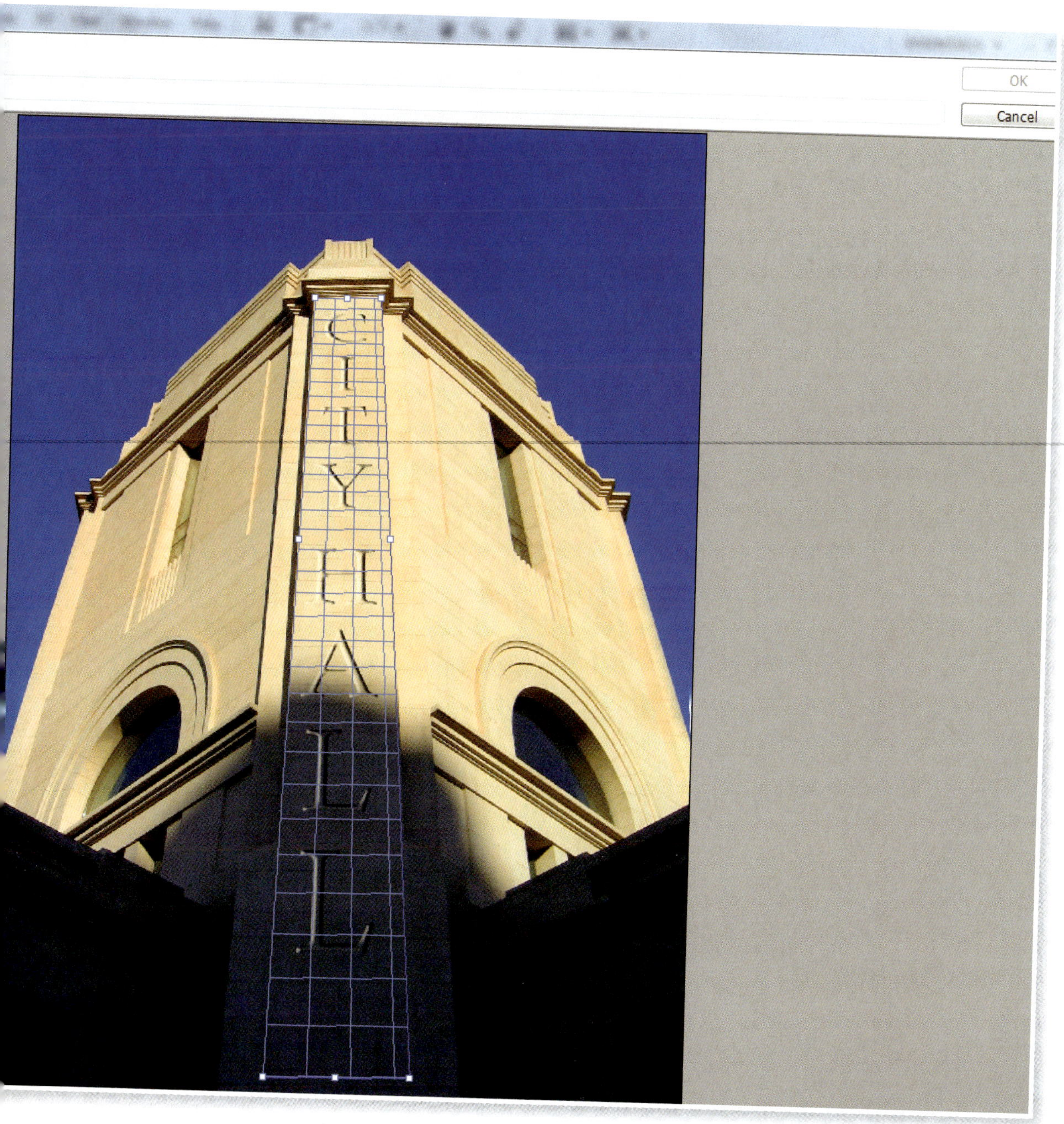

Magic transformations

As you can see here, Vanishing Point has the power to conform any element to the perspective within your images. Here we've used it on the carved type to make it look completely convincing.

Toolbox

The Vanishing Point filter has its own exclusive toolbar. You'll find it at the top left of the dialog, and it's where you will go to select the tools that you use for Vanishing Point.

Perspective plane points

These points around the edges of the perspective planes are what you use to adjust the shapes of your planes and create additional planes from existing ones.

Perspective planes

These planes, or perspective grids, are key to using the Vanishing Point filter correctly and using it accurately. These grids establish major planes of perspective within your image.

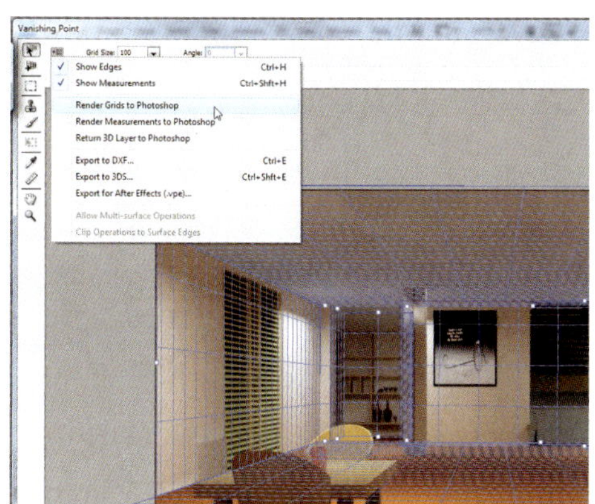

04 Planes as pixels

Try rendering the gridlines to a layer as pixels. Click on the small arrow in the Vanishing Point dialog. Choose Render Grids to Photoshop. Click OK.

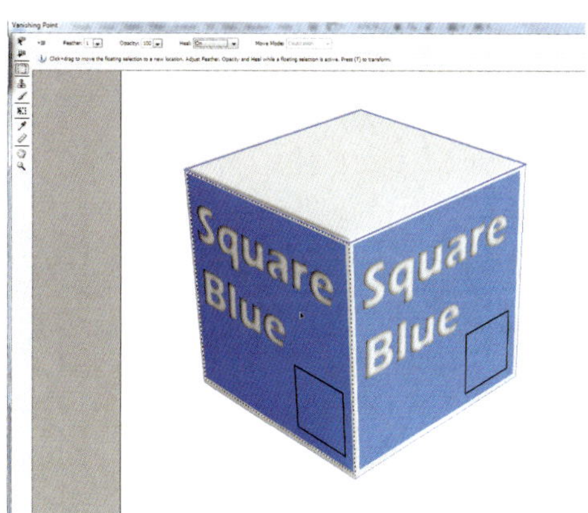

05 Magical marquee

Choose the Marquee tool to select an object. As you drag around, the selection conforms to the perspective of the underling perspective plane.

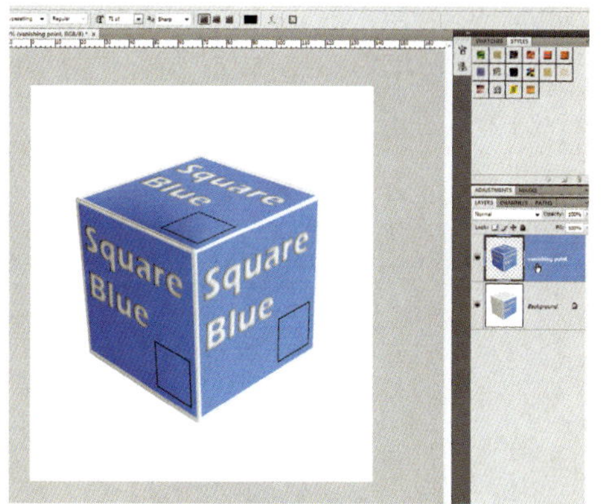

06 Lovely layers

By adding a new layer before you begin to clone within Vanishing Point, you give yourself much more flexibility.

Using the Lens Correction filter

Reshape those awkward angles in your photos for improving perspective and removing distortion

Lens correction techniques sort out issues that can occur when taking an image at an angle. It is one of the most common problems in photography. You snap a tall building for example, and when you look at it later, it looks as though the vertical edges of the building are bending inwards. Luckily, because it is such a common problem, Photoshop has the answer within its Filter menu. You can employ some of the following techniques to straighten things out like wonky horizons, or you can increase the perspective for more creative results.

If you're taking a picture straight on, such as a square object requiring perfect right angles, there are a range of tools you can call upon to make these subtle adjustments. The Transform commands, for instance, can be used to reshape subjects on separate layers. But it's the Lens Correction filter in Photoshop that holds the ultimate array of image adjustments. You can correct and apply colour shifts, better known as fringing, which is visible around the edges of brighter subjects in your image and introduce vertical perspective.

We take you through the features of this filter so you can straighten up horizons and add vignette effects to your images. When corrections have been applied we also show you some of our favourite image adjustments to improve colour, brightness and sharpness post-filter. The final results can be a dramatic improvement on what was originally a flat and out-of-shape photo.

We have supplied our beach chairs shot for you to practise all these techniques on, so you can give the tutorial ago. Or, you can pick up nay image with similar problems and see for yourself how easy it is to sort out your image collection's flaws.

"Straighten out wonky horizons or increase the perspective for more creative results"

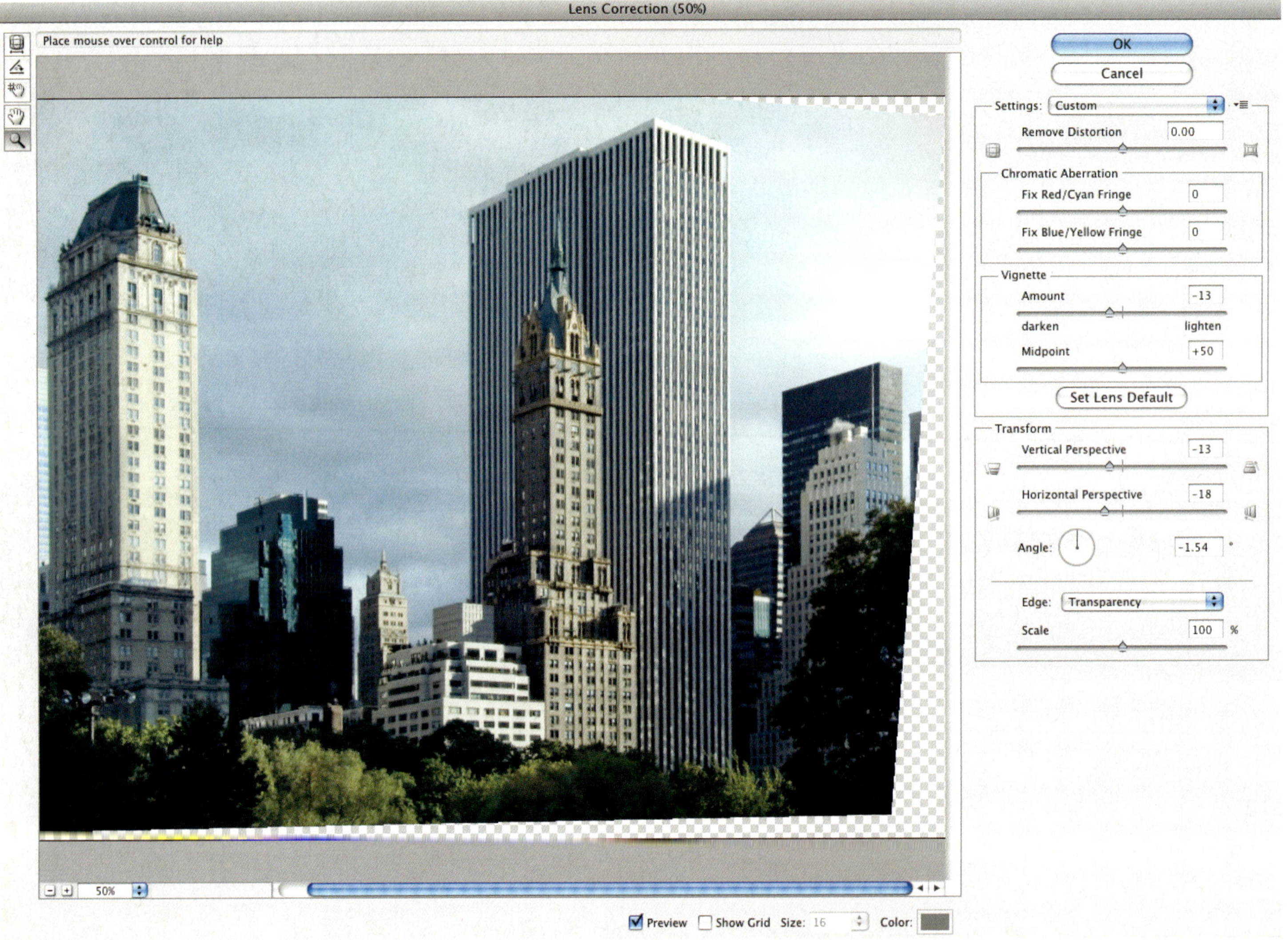

Basic problems solved! We look at the Lens Correction filter

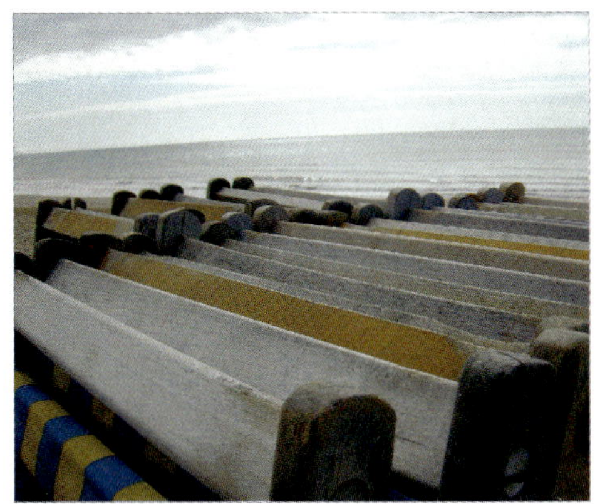

01 Assess the damage

Open the provided image. The horizon is not straight and due to the earth's curvature, it's also bowed in the centre.

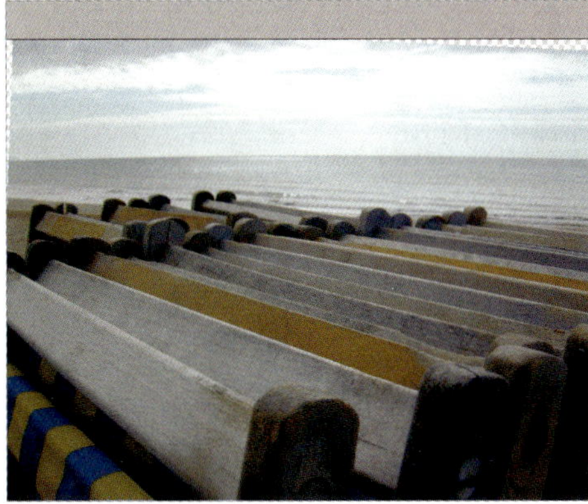

02 Level horizon

Go to Filter>Distort>Lens Correction. Uncheck the Grids option and select the Straighten tool. Click and drag along the horizon line to level it out.

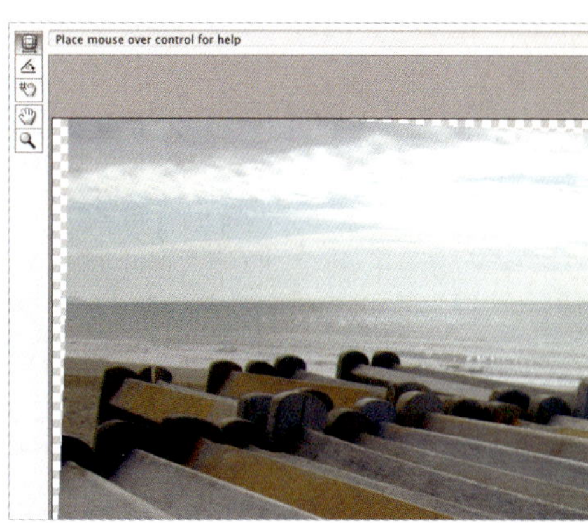

03 Reshape curvature

Select the Remove Distortion tool and drag the image from the top edge inwards to bend the horizon until it's flat.

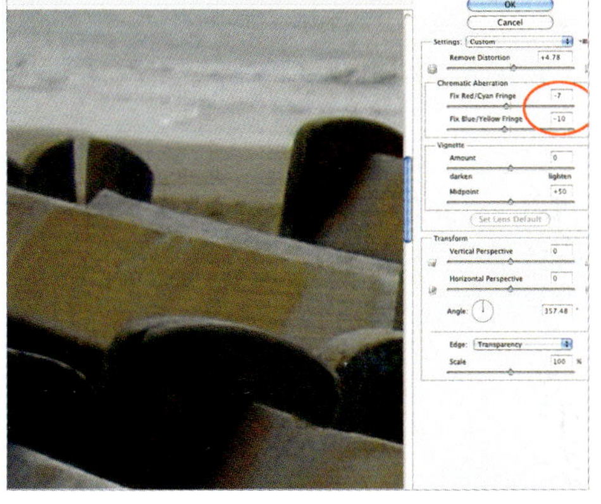

04 Remove fringing

Zoom in to the top of the deckchairs. There's a hint of yellow and blue fringing. Under Chromatic Aberration, move the Fix Blue/Yellow slider to -10.

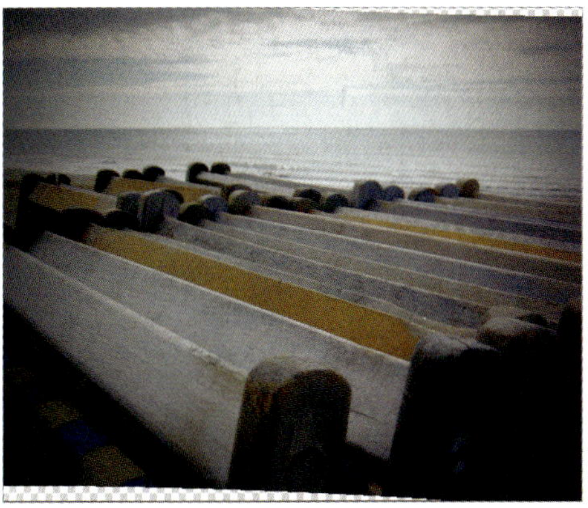

05 More dramatic

The Vignette controls are used to adjust overly light or dark corners of the image. Change the Amount to -100 and set Midpoint to +30 for a cool effect.

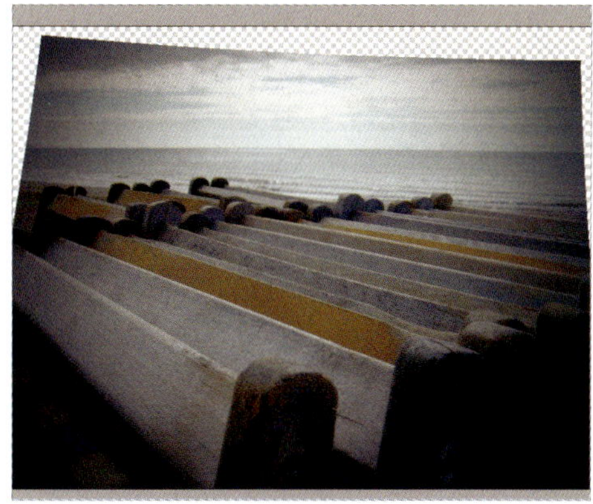

06 Tilt the perspective

The Transform controls in the filter change the vertical and horizontal perspectives of an image. Change the Vertical option to +30 here.

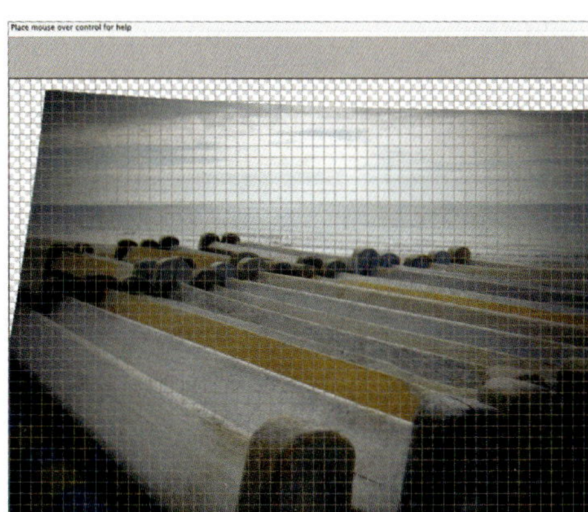

07 Re-assess angles

Click on the Show Grid option to make sure the image's horizon is level. If not, use the Straighten tool to tweak it once more and make it level.

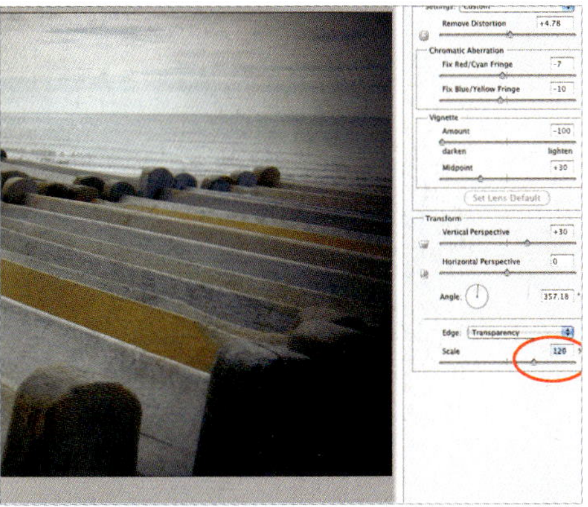

08 Scaling up

Some of Photoshop's chequerboard background is visible. Adjust the Scale slider at the bottom of the Transform controls to 120%. Hit OK to apply.

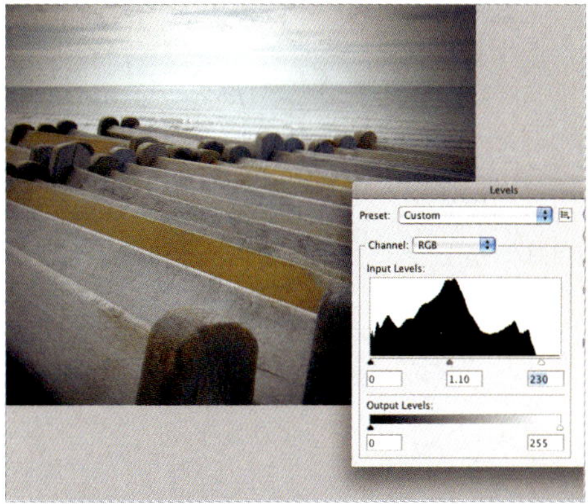

09 Post-filter adjustments

The image's exposure and sharpness can still do with improving, so go to Image>Adjustments>Levels and tweak to suit.

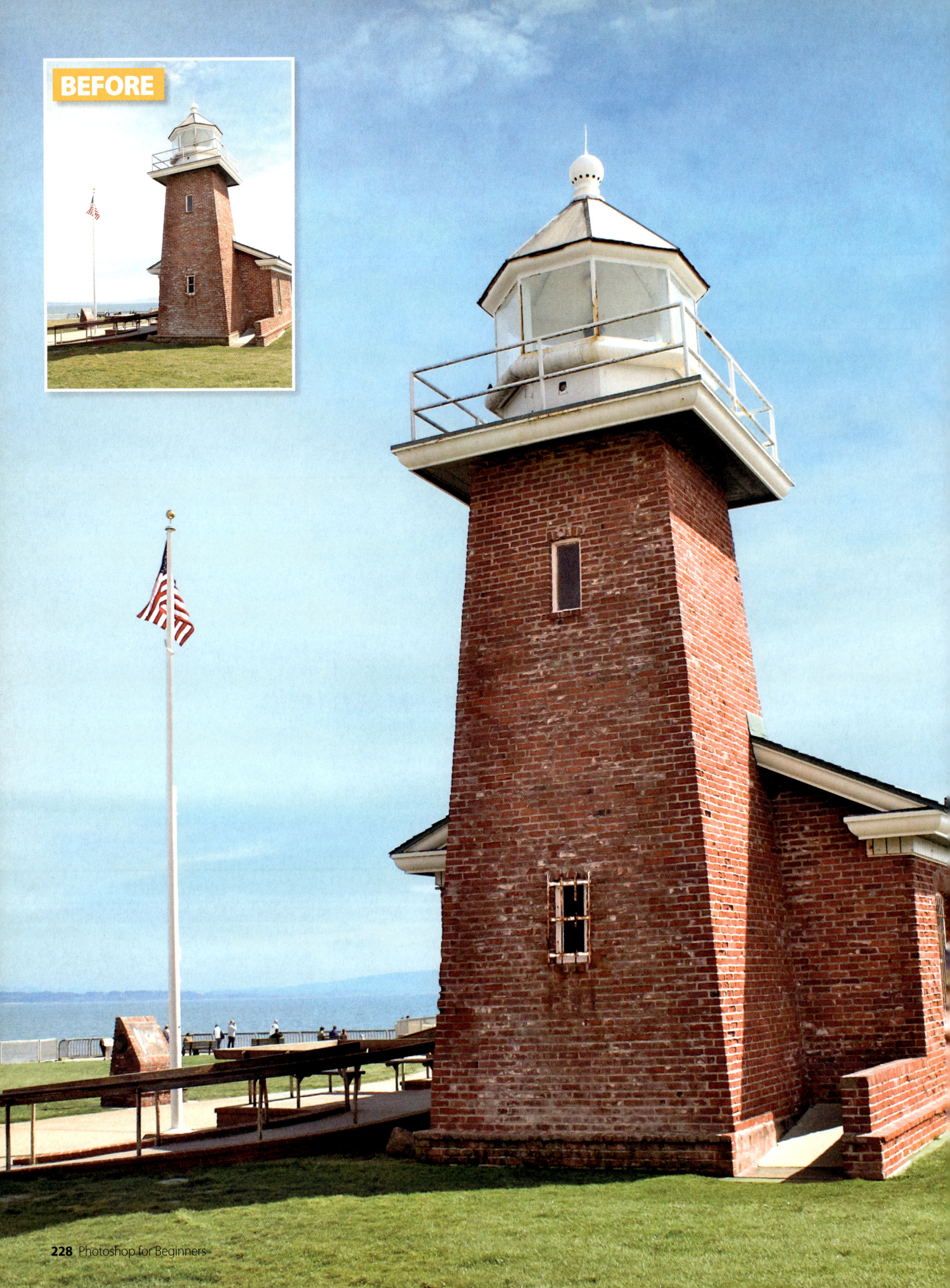
BEFORE

Edit colours with Photo Filter

Take a leaf out of traditional photographers' books and use coloured filters

Colour is a vital part of most people's photography and there have been all sorts of inventions to add zing to an image's tones. Traditional photographers have long used coloured filters in front of the camera lens to improve the colour balance and temperature of a photo. This is applied over the entire image or is graduated to concentrate on one area (such as the sky).

The Photoshop equivalent of this is the Photo Filter tool. Found lurking in the Adjustments menu (or Filter>Adjustments if you are using Elements), it enables you to gently coax extra colour out of your image or push things further for more dramatic effects. The easiest application of this tool is to make light work of dodgy white balance by reaching for the Warming Filter (80) or Cooling Filter (80) settings. These fix the two most common balance problems (too blue or too yellow, respectively), but if you have suffered a more unusual blight, just pick a complementary colour to tame things down.

However, we are going to be concentrating on a different aspect of the tool, namely that of editing colours. The beauty of using the Photo Filter over something like Hue/Saturation is that you are provided with a batch of ready-made improvements. This makes it less likely for you to create something that looks fake. The start image for this tutorial is supplied to practise on, or use one of your own snaps.

"It enables you to gently coax extra colour out of your image"

USING PHOTO FILTER

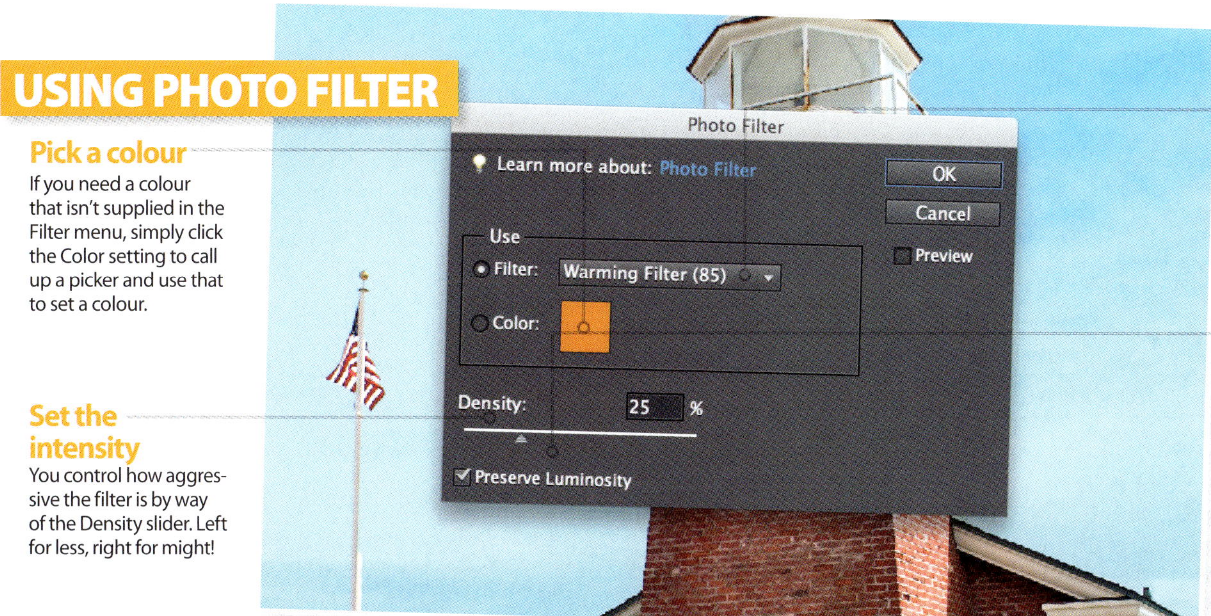

Pick a colour
If you need a colour that isn't supplied in the Filter menu, simply click the Color setting to call up a picker and use that to set a colour.

Set the intensity
You control how aggressive the filter is by way of the Density slider. Left for less, right for might!

Pick the filter
Use this dropdown menu to select one of the supplied filter colours. Most of these will do what you need.

Light show
In most cases, the Preserve Luminosity option should be left checked, as this keeps the highlight detail in the image. However, if you have areas where you want to kill the highlight, simply uncheck the box.

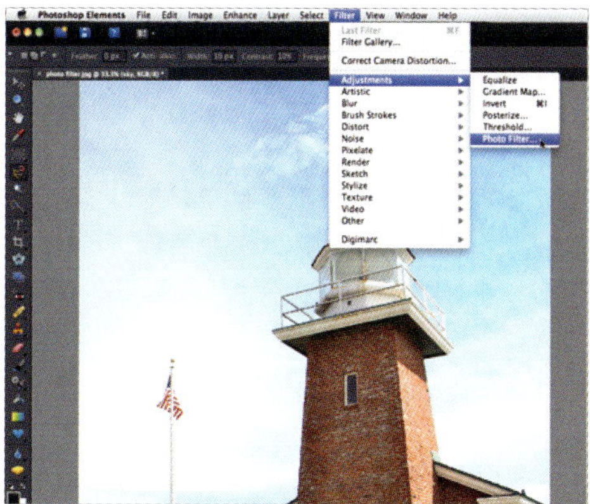

01 Make the adjustment
Go to Image>Adjustments>Photo Filter (Photoshop) or Filter>Adjustments>Photo Filter (Photoshop Elements).

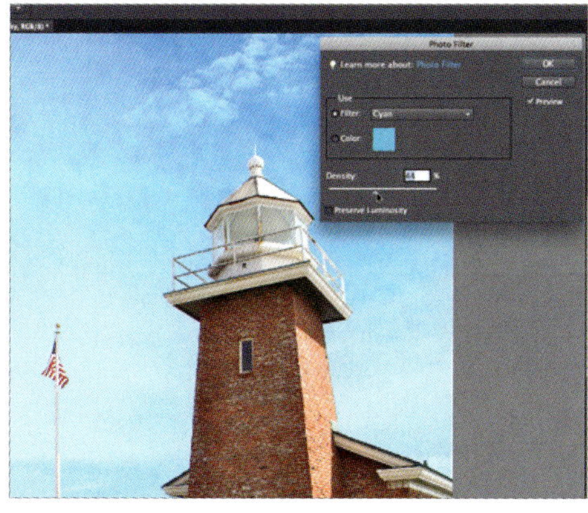

02 Choose a filter
Now you can choose a filter from the dropdown menu. Try a few to see which one looks the best, using Density to control its strength.

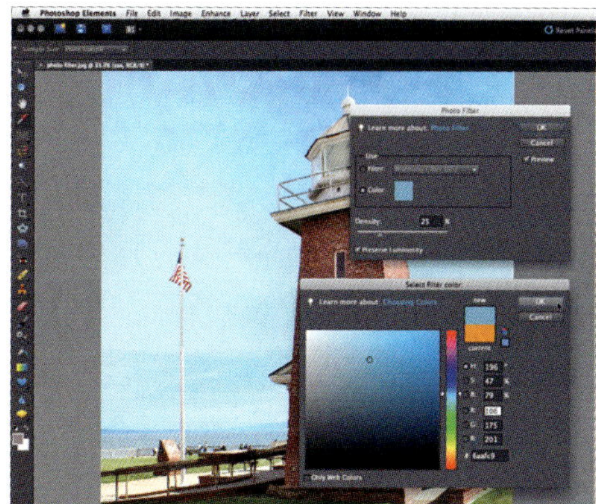

03 Color Picker
If none of the filter presets are exactly what you need, then select the coloured square by clicking on it twice and you can choose your own colour.

Resizing with plug-ins explained

Push pixel dimensions to their limits with dedicated plug-ins for that resizing job

Imagine this nightmarish situation: you've created your Photoshop masterpiece, and it's time to print at large format. However, the image's pixel dimensions are too small… What's the next step?

Well, there are a couple of routes to take to rectify this dilemma. The first is to use Photoshop's own resizing controls found under the Image Size menu. This option can be highly effective, producing excellent results quickly (see right for our comparison of this to a plug-in). But there is an alternative option for enlarging your image – using a dedicated plug-in for this precise purpose.

In this guide we've gone for a professional plug-in, Genuine Fractals 6 by onOne. Such industry standard plug-ins offer additional options alongside simply editing pixel dimensions. One example in Genuine Fractals is having control over the level of texturing in an image once enlarged. The secret lies in the plug-in's own technology that it uses for the enlargement. There are different methods, and where Photoshop uses a Bicubic method, plug-ins such as BenVista's PhotoZoom Pro 3 use a patented S-Spline technology to smooth out pixelation synonymous with image enlargements.

There are many plug-ins available for professional standard enlargements, especially if poster prints are your thing. Many companies offer their plug-ins as free 30-day trials – a great way to get a taste for what's on offer. Read on to find out how to use Genuine Fractals for resizing.

"There are many plug-ins for pro standard enlargements"

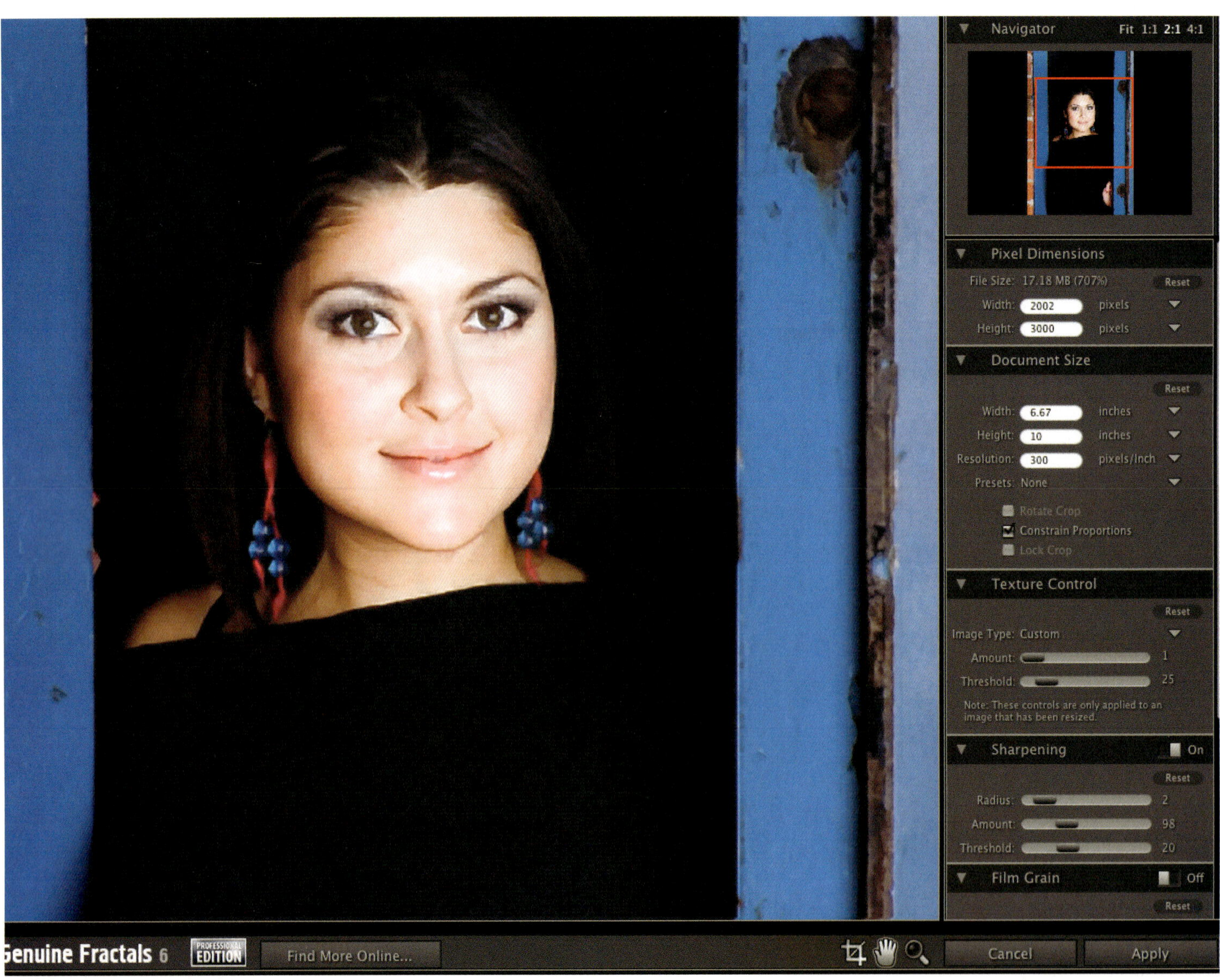

QUICK PHOTOSHOP TIPS

Photoshop vs plug-ins

Photoshop has multiple methods for undergoing enlargements to an image. These include Bicubic, Bilinear and Nearest Neighbor (preserves hard edges), all producing different results and found in the Image Size menu. We tested and compared the results of these options to those of Genuine Fractals 6, and the differences were amazingly subtle. Using Genuine Fractals 6, however, we achieved a more defined and smoother enlargement – best if you're going to huge proportions. Effects were noticeable when applying an enlargement to a low resolution image to start with.

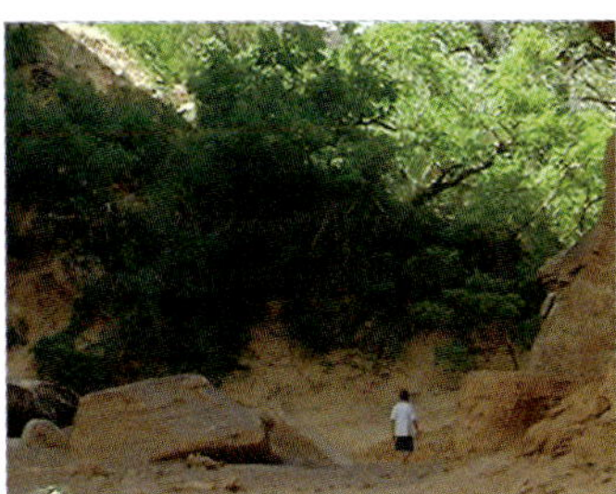

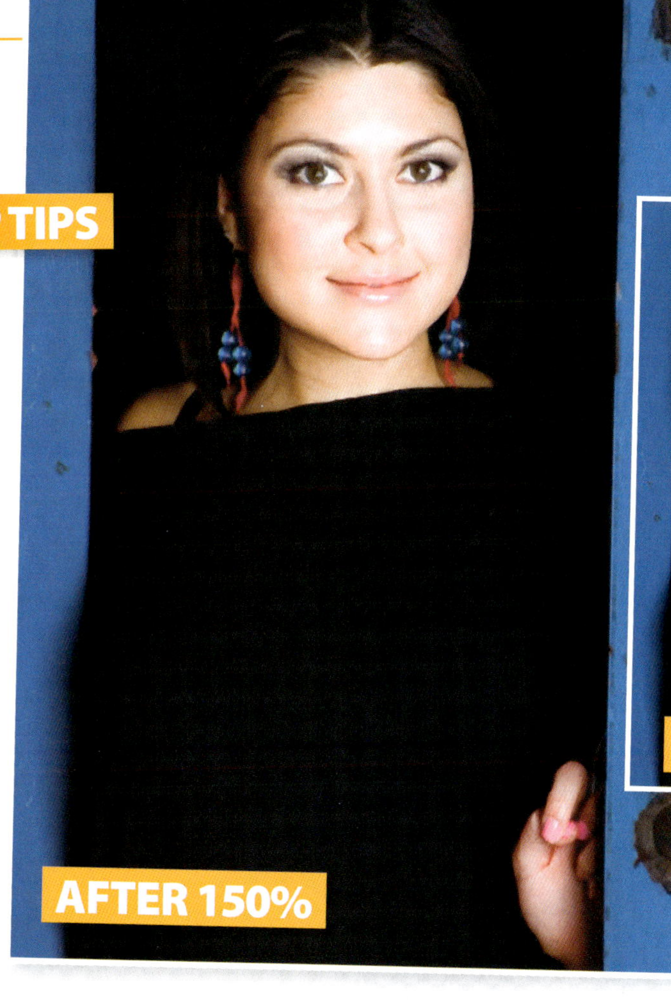

AFTER 150%

BEFORE 150%

Alternative plug-ins

Look out for what the competition offers. BenVista (**www.benvista.com**) offers PhotoZoom Pro 3, using the unique S-Spline technology for blowing up artwork to massive sizes. Alien Skin (**www.alienskin.com**) produces an exceptional plug-in for this specific task, called Blow Up 2 and boasts easy-to-use features with great improvements to definition. Magnifier by AKVIS (**http://akvis.com**) also resizes images with minimal distortion. Take advantage of the free trials that can be downloaded from the manufacturers' sites.

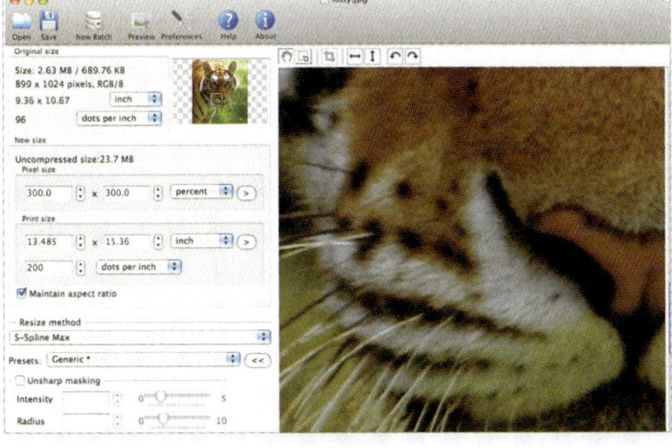

Features of Genuine Fractals

Genuine Fractals 6 has much more under its belt to justify its high price tag (for the Professional Edition). The plug-in is capable of batch processing for group enlargements, as well as offering controls for adding texture to an image to bring back detail in the surfaces. Also available is an authentic film grain effect to help remove pixelation, and the Tiling feature divides the enlargement into segments, easier for printing on individual sheets of paper. The plug-in also offers sharpening controls to make enlargements look their best.

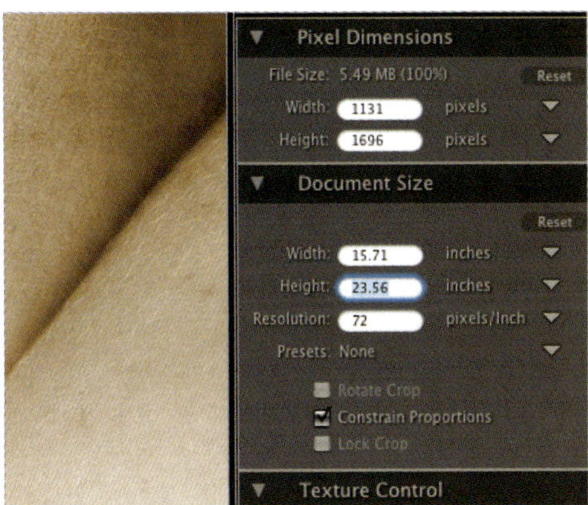

01 Pixel dimensions

Using the Document Size fields, set the new width and height. The percentage is indicated, and check out your new pixel dimensions.

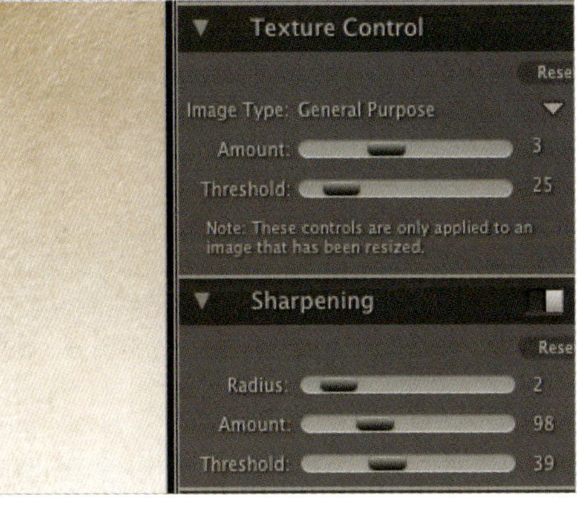

02 Texture and sharpening

Texture is similar to detail, and it takes effect after an enlargement is applied. Add some sharpening, and your enlargement looks more natural.

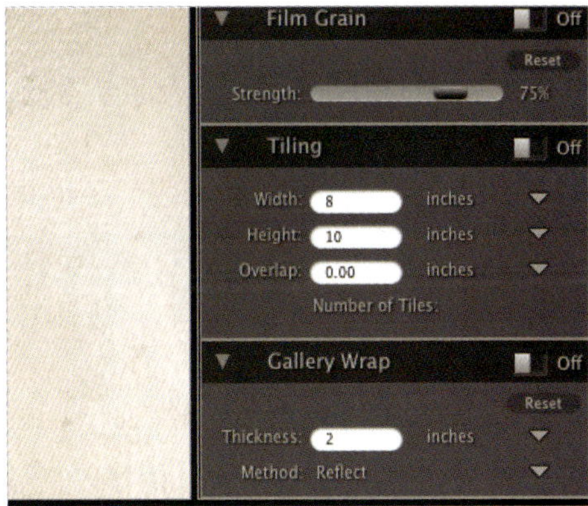

03 Finishing touches

Add a hint of realistic film grain, apply Tiling, which allows you to print segments of your image, or use Gallery Wrap to extend the edges of your image.

Output

Photoshop File Edit Image Layer Select Filter View Window Help
CREATIVE IDEAS
We have lots of photo projects to help you do much more with your images
Print
Copies: 1
Print Settings...
Cancel
Done
Print

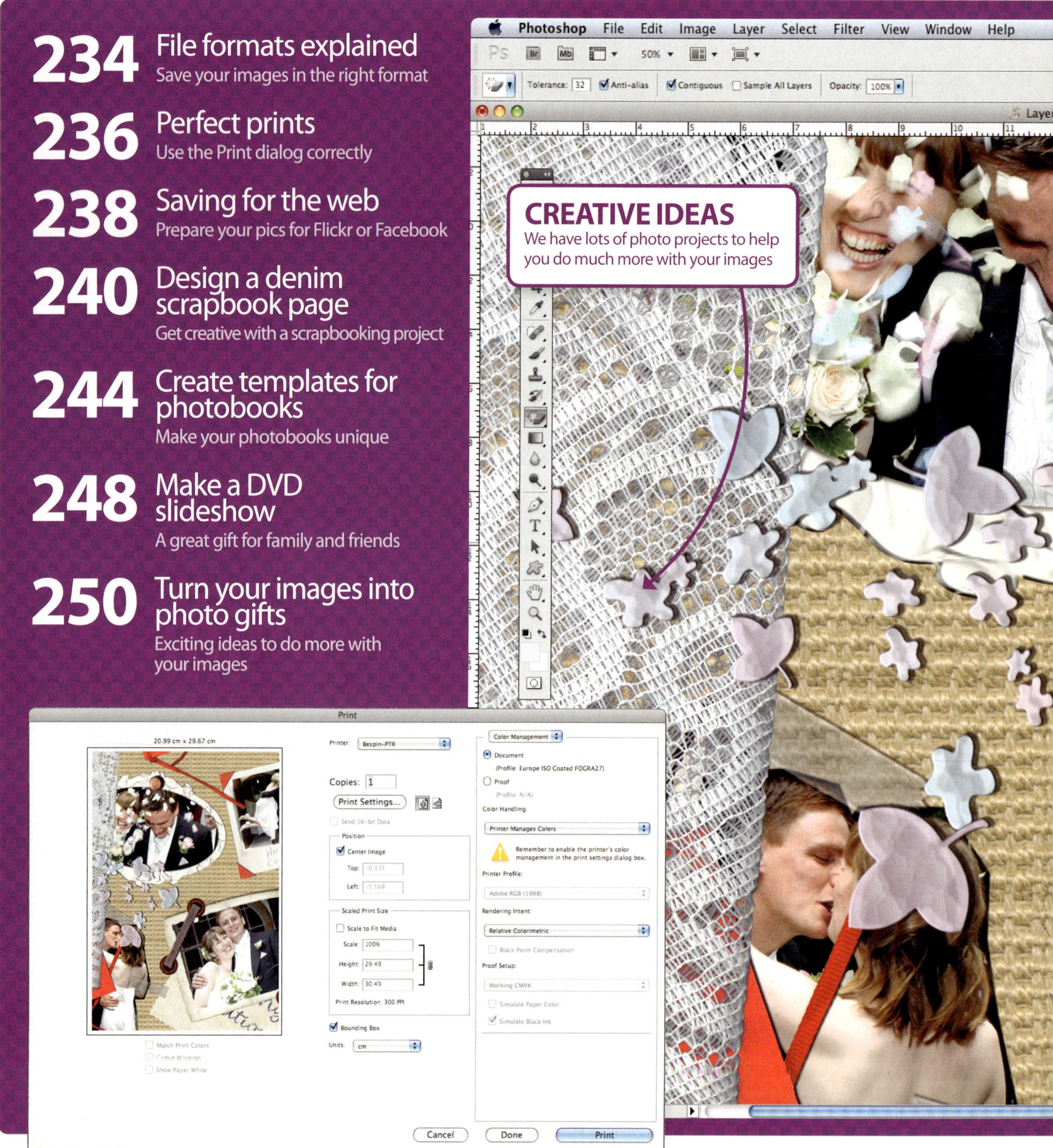

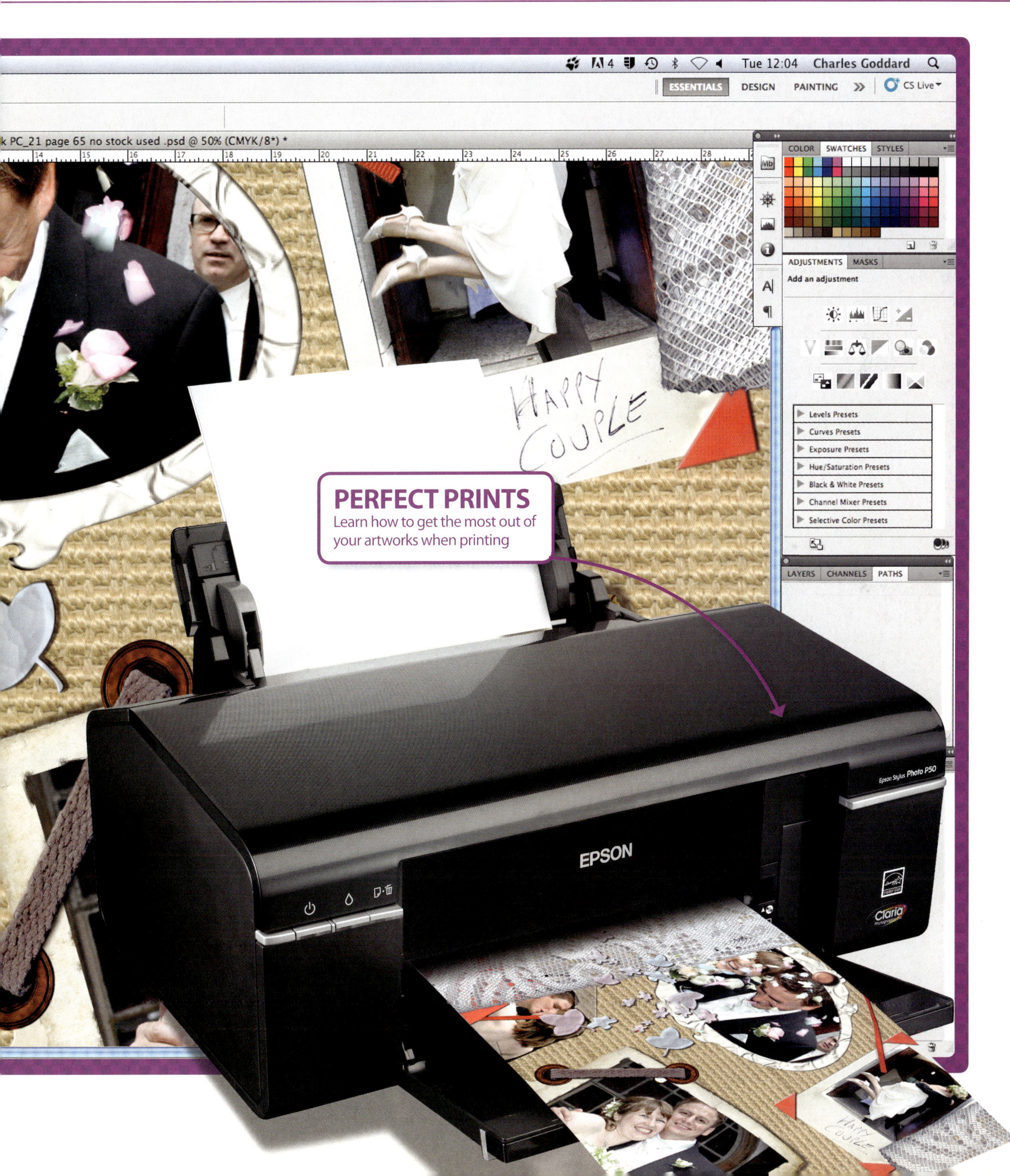
PERFECT PRINTS
Learn how to get the most out of your artworks when printing
Tue 12:04 Charles Goddard
ESSENTIALS
DESIGN
PAINTING
CS Live
k PC_21 page 65 no stock used .psd @ 50% (CMYK/8*) *
COLOR
SWATCHES
STYLES
ADJUSTMENTS
MASKS
Add an adjustment
Levels Presets
Curves Presets
Exposure Presets
Hue/Saturation Presets
Black & White Presets
Channel Mixer Presets
Selective Color Presets
LAYERS
CHANNELS
PATHS
HAPPY COUPLE
EPSON
Epson Stylus Photo P50
Claria

File formats explained

Saving your work in the correct format can be confusing. We help you choose the best way to store your precious projects

Everything is designed and built for a specific purpose, to achieve different results and provide different services. In the building trade a hammer is designed to knock in a nail, while a screwdriver helps to secure screws. In the computing world, it's file formats that are designed for specific purposes and programs, and in this quick-fire guide we'll help you understand the differences.

You can generally tell the type of format that a file has been allocated by the extension added on to the end of the file name, for example '.pdf'. Within Photoshop alone there's a massive range of formats, each designed with a specific purpose in mind.

When working with a file, you always have a target output in mind, either print or digital. When working for print, the file size isn't really a priority, whereas image quality should certainly be high up on the list. When designing for the internet, it's important that a balance of image quality and file size is found. Optimising download speed and yet ensuring that the image isn't too pixelated will provide those browsing through your images with the best experience possible.

Choosing the best file format for your desired output source is important, and will make or break the success of your image. Here's our handy guide to just a selection of the most useful file formats that you'll discover when working with Photoshop.

"When working with a file, you always have a target output in mind, either print or digital"

QUICK PHOTOSHOP TIPS

BMP

BMP files, otherwise known as bitmap, are another widely used file format across all platforms. However, it's most commonly associated with Windows.

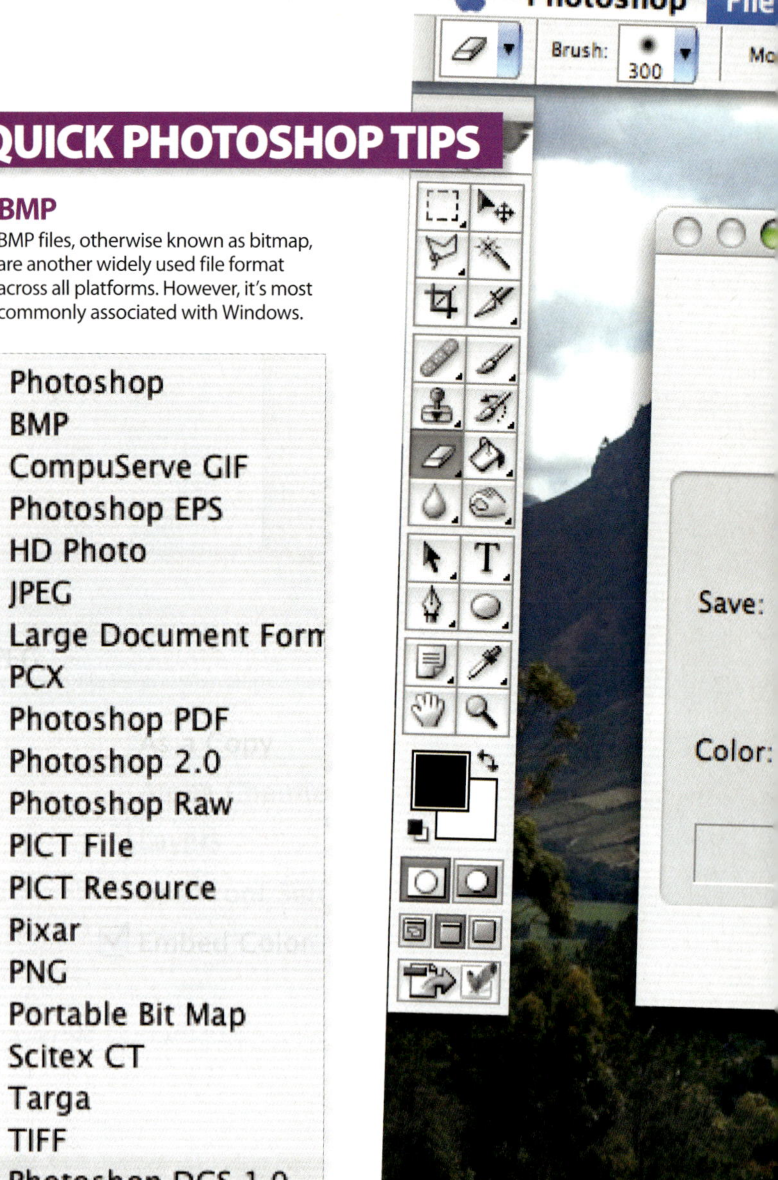

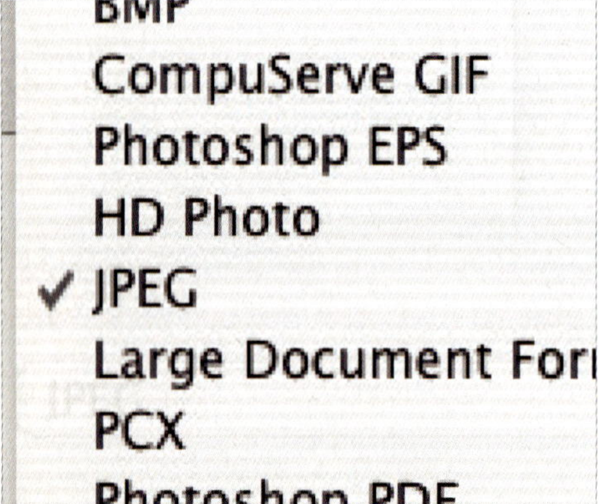

01 JPEG
Widely accepted as the standard format used to save images, JPEGs are used in a variety of media output sources, such as publications and websites.

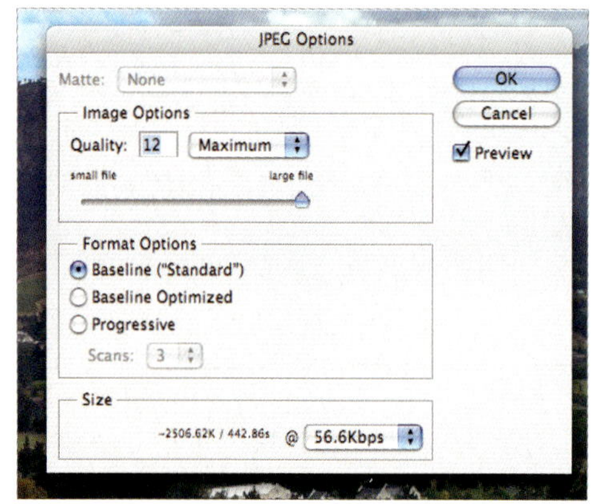

02 Compression and quality
A JPEG file keeps image size down by using 'lossy compression', compressing and flattening all layers that may have been used to construct the image.

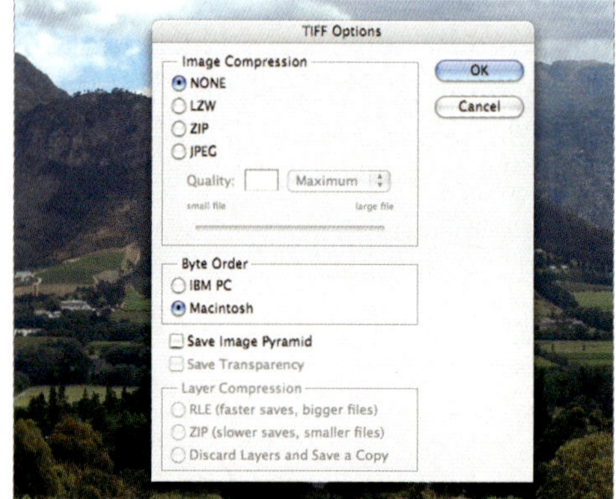

03 TIFF
When working in the desktop publishing industry the TIFF file is used. By using 'lossless' compression a TIFF file keeps all image data.

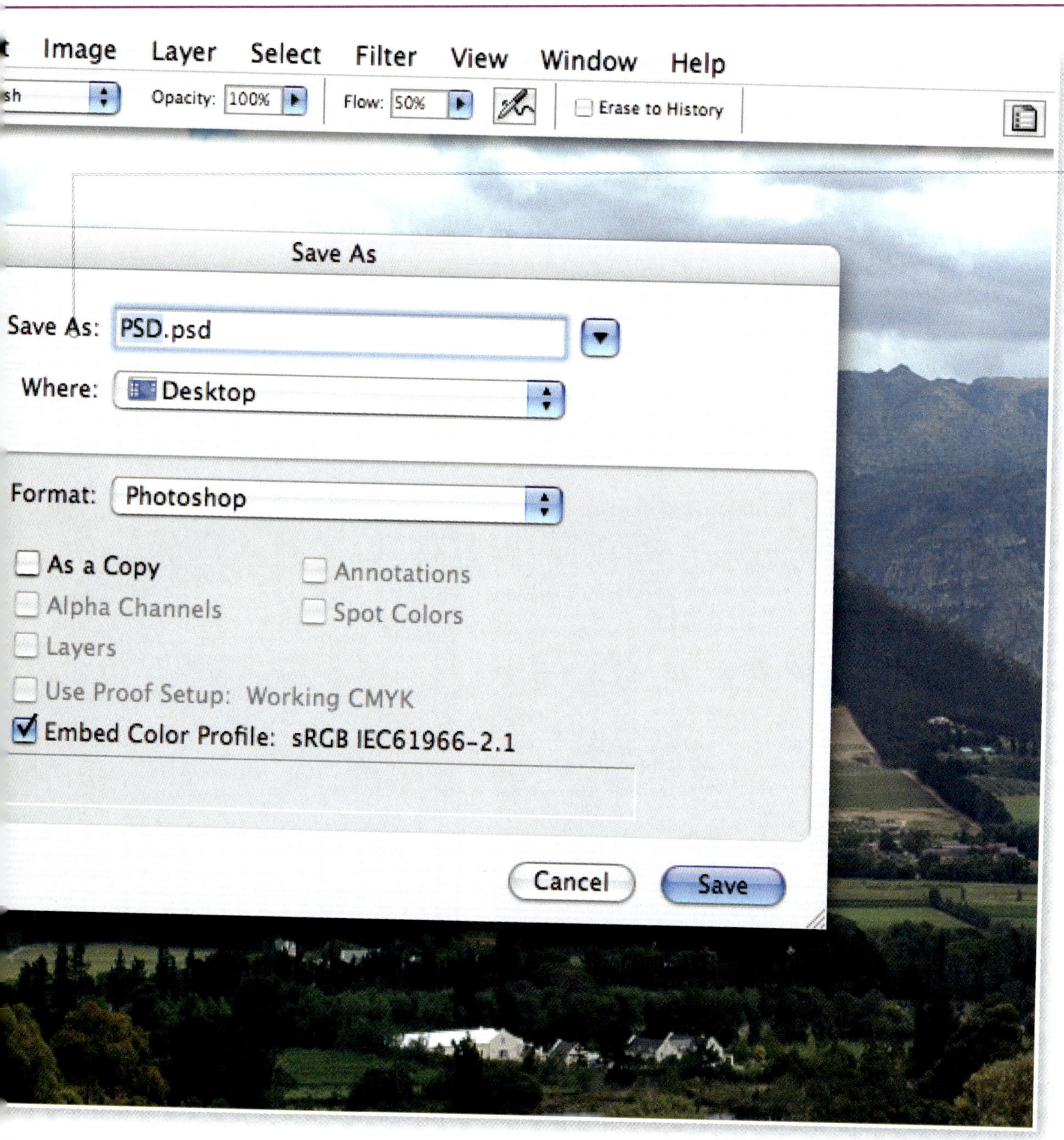

Save As

This is the standard window for saving your documents – you've no doubt noticed it by now! Here you can choose your format, file name and Save destination.

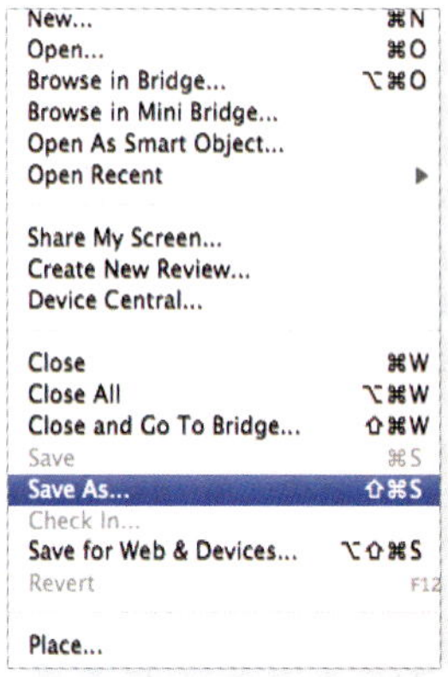

RAW

RAW files are created from digital cameras, storing the raw camera processing data such as white balance, saturation and tones. This data can then be adjusted later on, using Adobe's Camera Raw editor.

PDF

Most commonly created from another Adobe product, Acrobat, this type of file can be viewed on every computer platform using the freely available Adobe Reader program. This format is often used to preview and share desktop publishing documents.

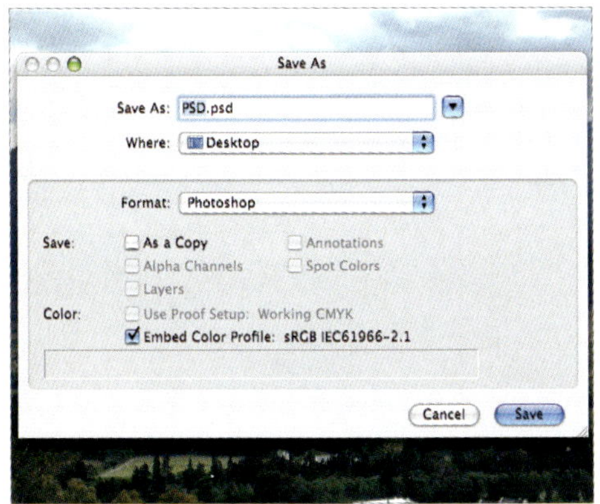

04 PSD

Used throughout Adobe programs, PSD is at the heart of Photoshop. No compression is used when saving a PSD file, so sizes can get fairly large.

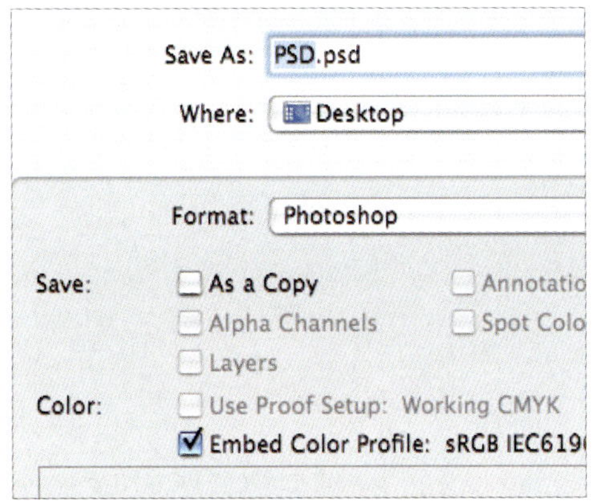

05 Saving with layers

Images composed with layers can be saved as a PSD file to allow further editing. The Layers button will be ticked if the image has multiple layers.

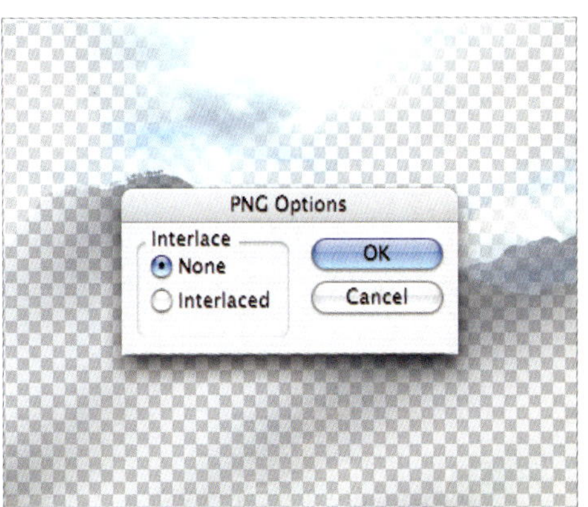

06 PNG

PNG allows any files with transparent sections to hold their properties. Image quality and size are important, so finding a compromise is important.

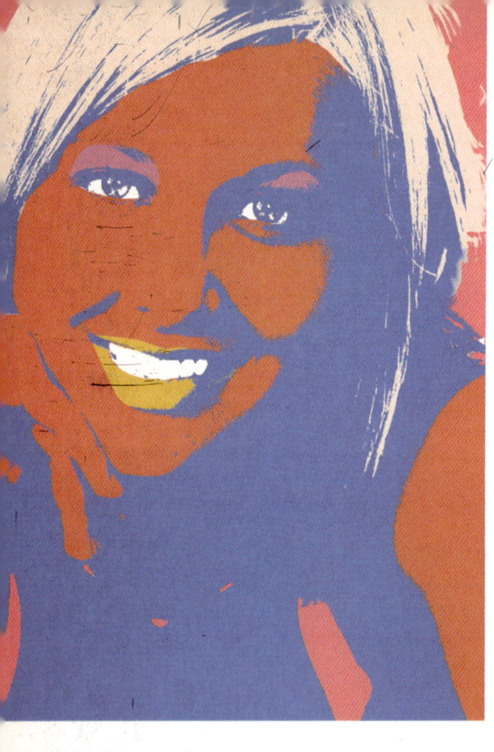
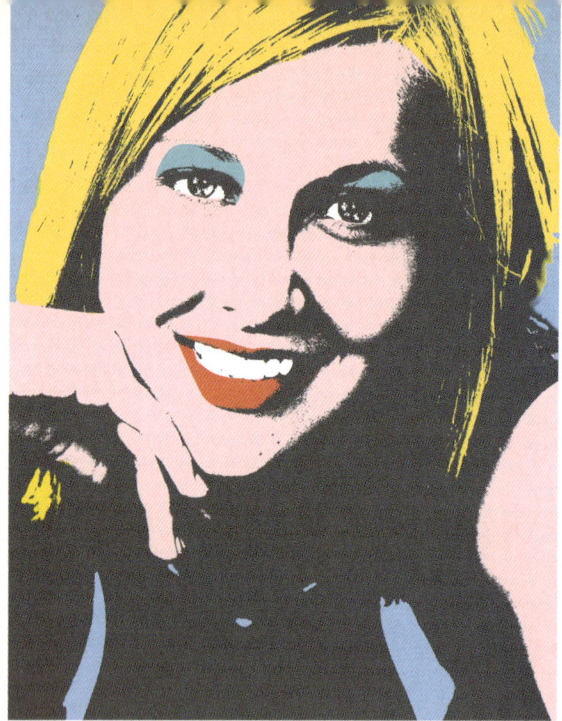
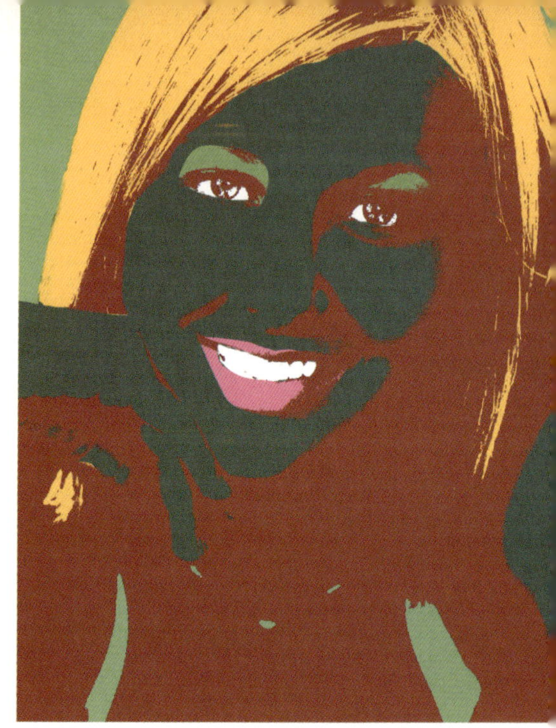
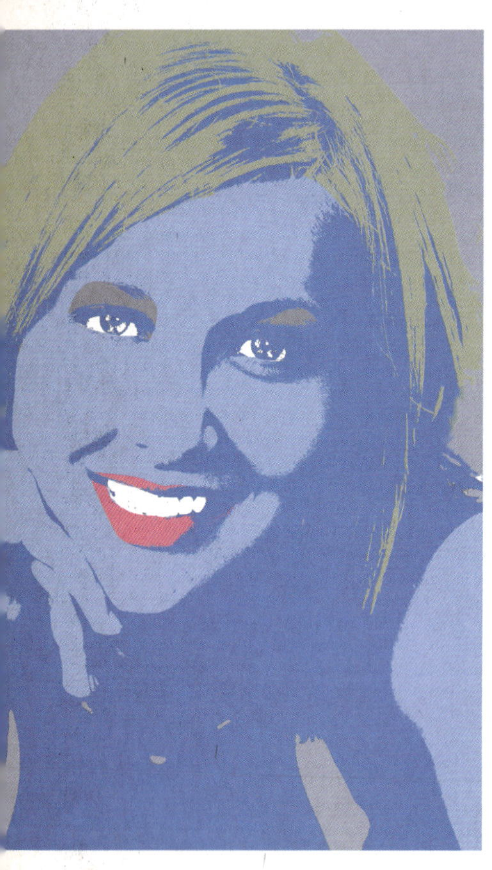
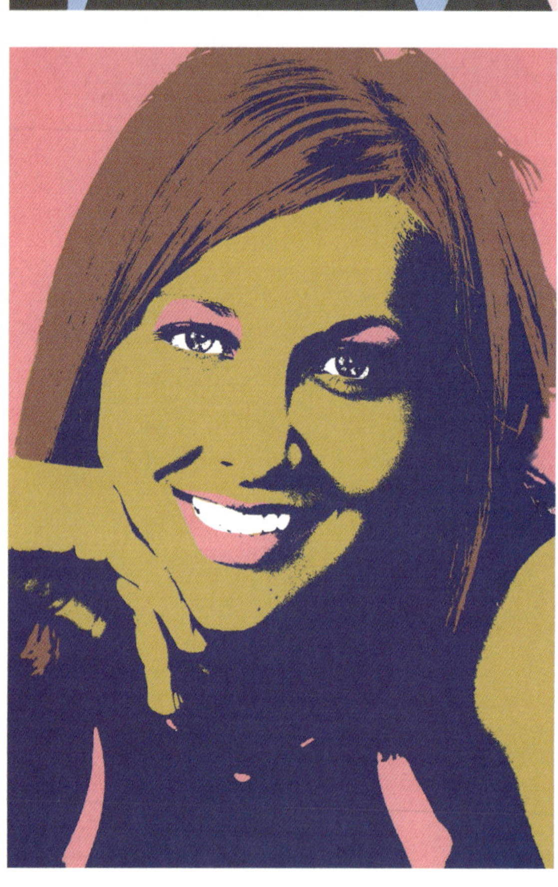
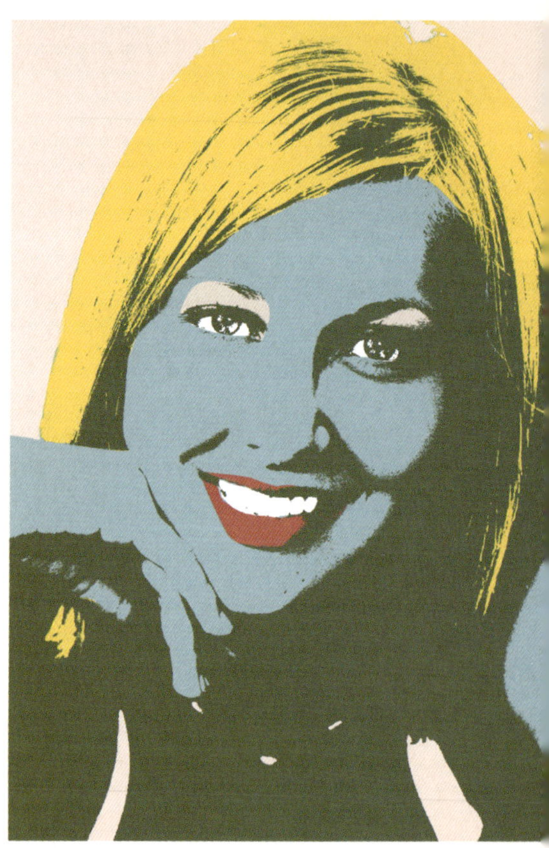
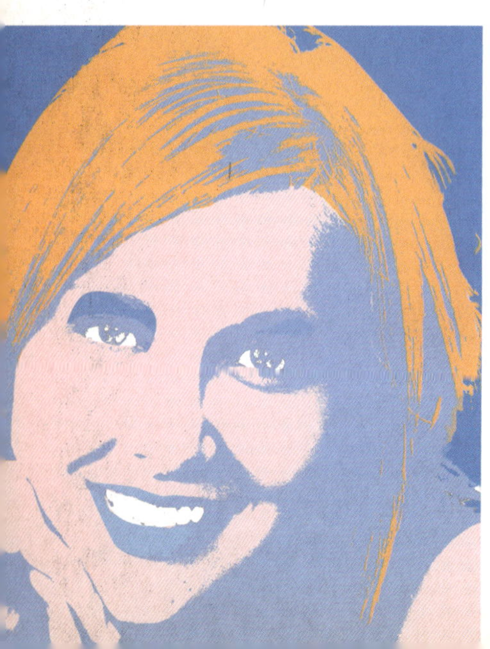
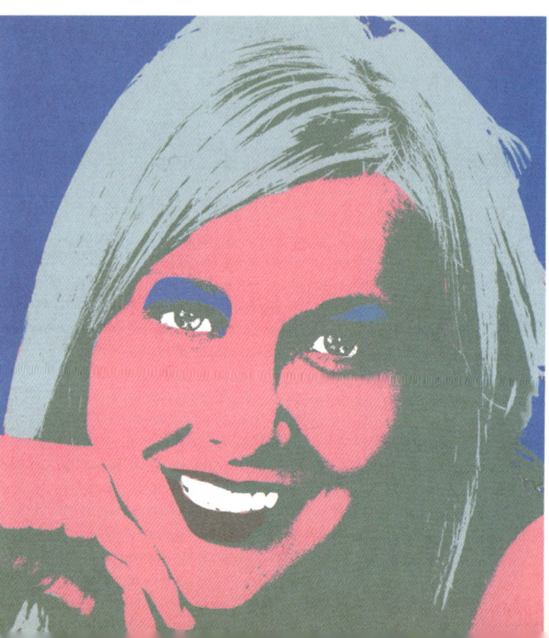
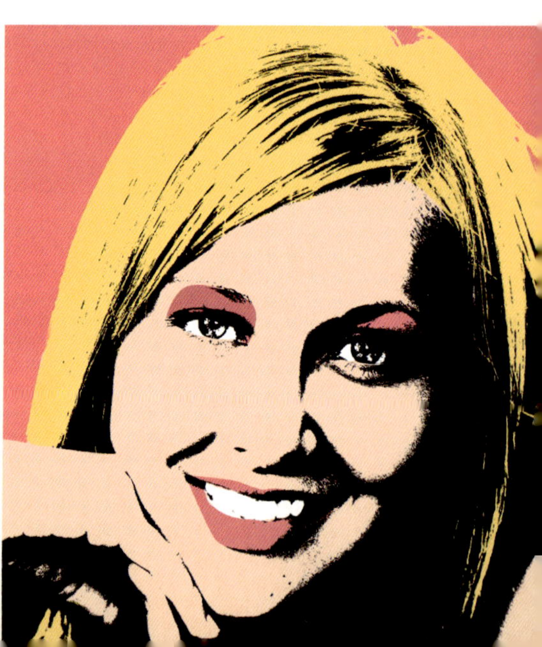

Perfect prints

When it comes to printing images, you need to get to grips with Photoshop's Print dialog

Printing images is a straightforward enough job in Photoshop. You can just hit the handy shortcut, Cmd/Ctrl+P and up pops the Print dialog box. Hit OK and you're done, right? Well, not always. You need to make sure that your artwork is set up correctly to your printer, otherwise the result might not be quite what you expected.

First of all – and this may sound really obvious – you need to make sure that you have selected the right printer. If you have more than one in the house, you don't want it to be flying off to the wrong printer. Next, check the number of copies that you want. As soon as that is sorted, you can work on how you want the image to be positioned on the page, whether it should be scaled and at what size it should print. Once you have these setting right, you should get a good print.

Occasionally you may find that the colours don't match up. In the Print dialog you can choose whether Photoshop or your printer controls the colours, so try both until you get the best result. Also, make sure that your image is in the right mode for your printer. Your printer will usually be in CMYK, so if you print an RGB image, it may look a bit funny. You can easily change the Mode of your image using the Image>Mode menu.

> "Your printer will usually be in CMYK, so if you print an RGB image, it may look a bit funny"

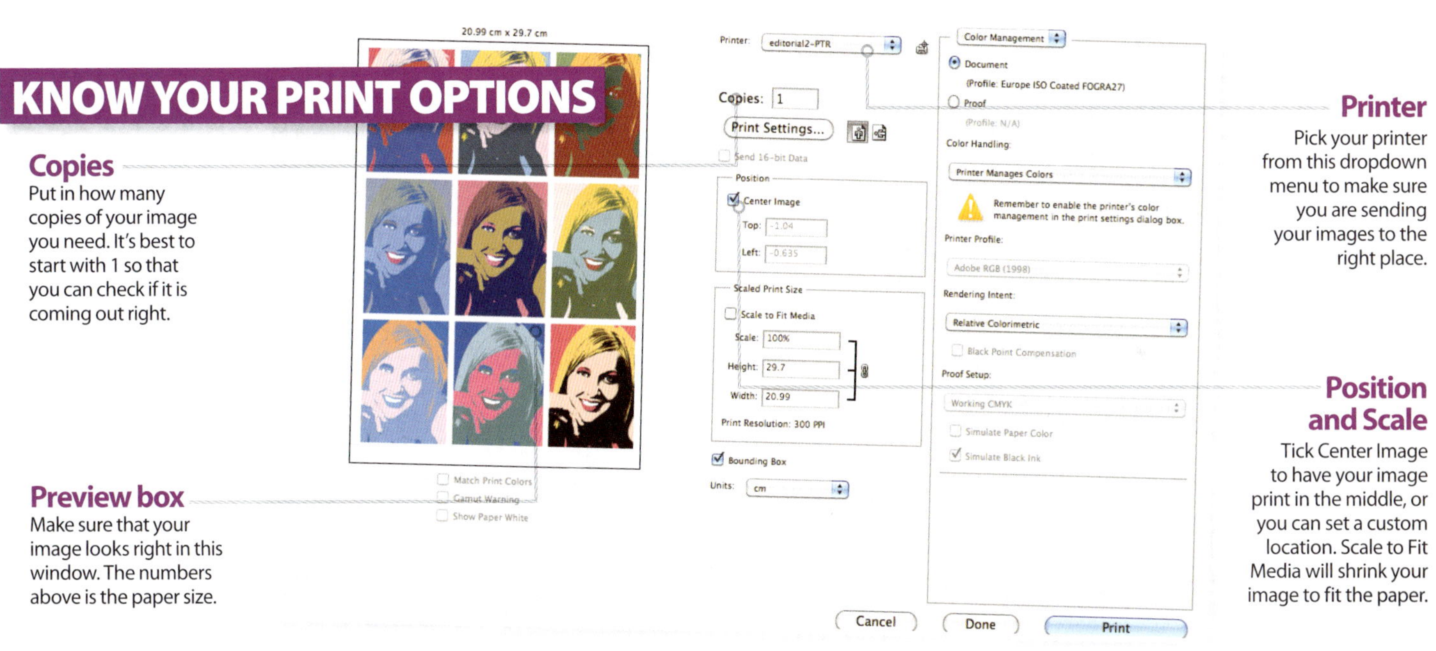

KNOW YOUR PRINT OPTIONS

Copies
Put in how many copies of your image you need. It's best to start with 1 so that you can check if it is coming out right.

Preview box
Make sure that your image looks right in this window. The numbers above is the paper size.

Printer
Pick your printer from this dropdown menu to make sure you are sending your images to the right place.

Position and Scale
Tick Center Image to have your image print in the middle, or you can set a custom location. Scale to Fit Media will shrink your image to fit the paper.

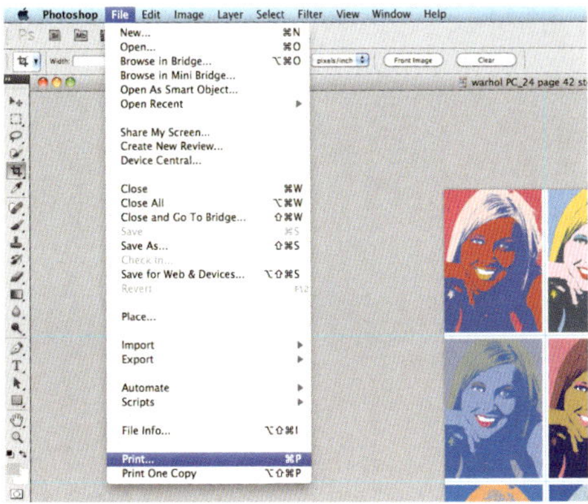

01 Open the Print dialog

In CS5, you need to go to the File menu to get the Print dialog up. There is also a Print One Copy button for quick prints.

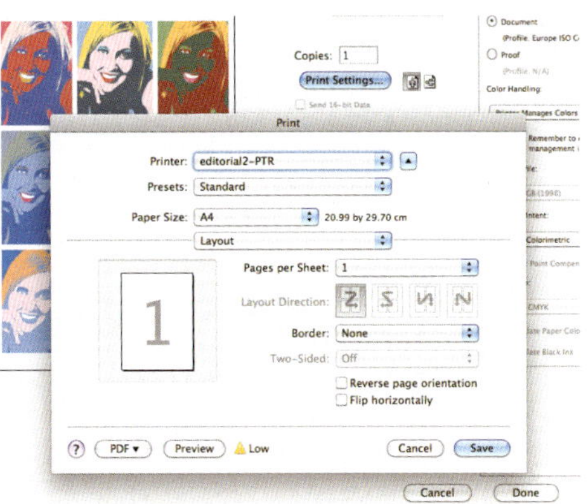

02 Print Settings

Here you will see a button marked Print Settings, which enables you to change the way that your artwork is presented when printed.

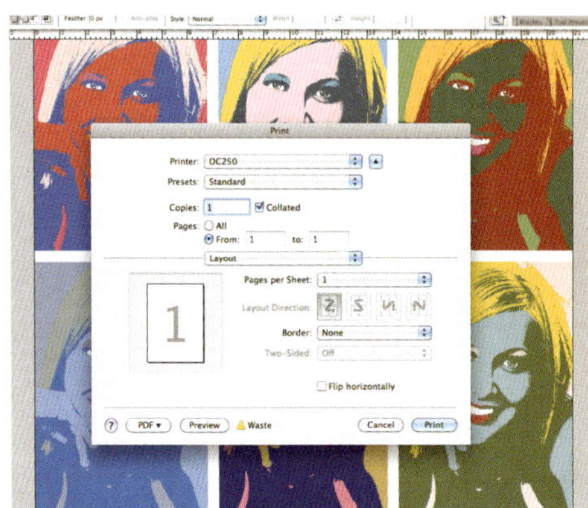

03 Earlier than CS5?

If you don't have CS5, you still need to go to the File menu. Pick Print, ensure the settings are correct in the window and click the Print button.

Output

Save images for the web

Produce optimised images that are web-ready with a little help from the Save for Web feature

Saving photographs or graphics to be used on the web is a bit of a balancing act between the image's file size and quality. Although you don't want blurry images to appear on a web page, saving a file at an unnecessarily high quality will increase its size and can mean it loads up extremely slowly. An image needs three things to be web-ready; it needs to be 72dpi (dots per inch), in RGB colour mode and reduced in file size to make sure the web page loads quickly. And this is where Photoshop's Save for Web tool comes in handy. With this straightforward tool you can ensure your images are optimised and prepared for the web. As well as allowing you to save photos or graphics as small as possible without reducing the quality too much, the Save for Web feature makes sure web-safe colours are used so the images will display correctly on a site. Within the control window you can choose between different types of file (depending on how complex the image is) and there are many other controls to play about with too.

Although the command was created to help people get images web-ready, it's also a great way to resize images for any use, especially if you aren't confident with using the Image Size route. So let's start having a look around the features of this powerful tool to ensure your images look their absolute best for the global audience of the web.

> "Saving photographs or graphics to be used on the web is a bit of a balancing act between the image's file size and quality"

QUICK PHOTOSHOP TIPS

Sizing up

Within the Save for Web dialog box there is an area for Image Size. As well as displaying information about the image's height and width, its proportions can be constrained using a checkbox. The size of the overall image can be changed by entering a new amount in the Percent box too.

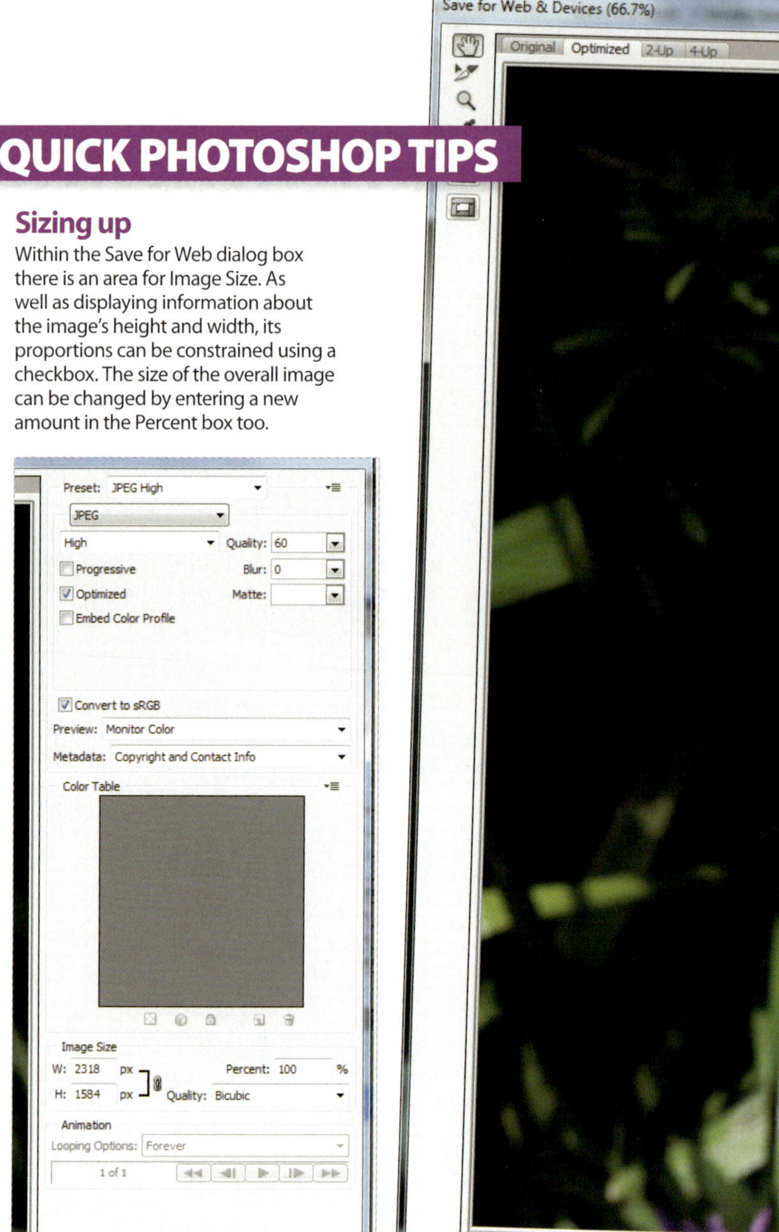

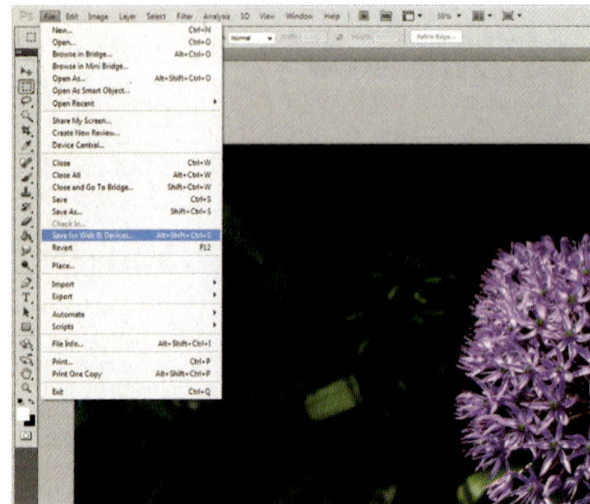

01 Select the file format

Go to File>Save for Web & Devices. In this case we're saving a photograph, so will select the JPEG format using the Optimized drop-down menu.

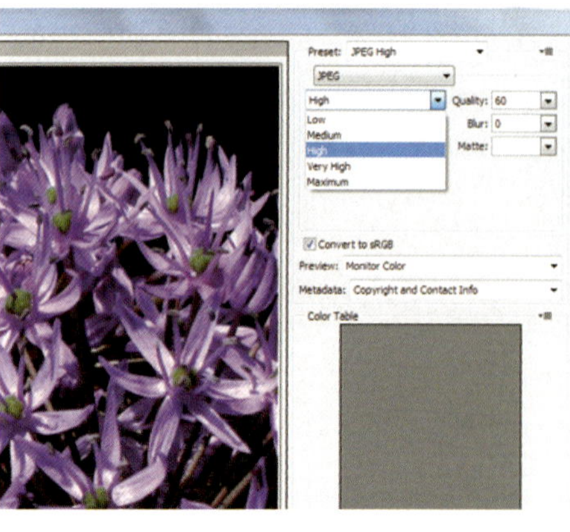

02 File quality

For most photos, you will use JPEGs. Use the Quality slider or Compression quality drop-down menu to change an image's compression.

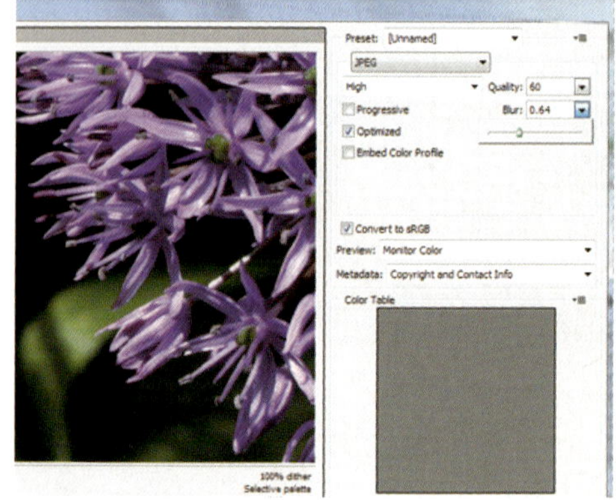

03 File size tricks

The Blur slider is good for shaving file size. The Progressive box creates images that load gradually but increases size. Get a size you like and click Save.

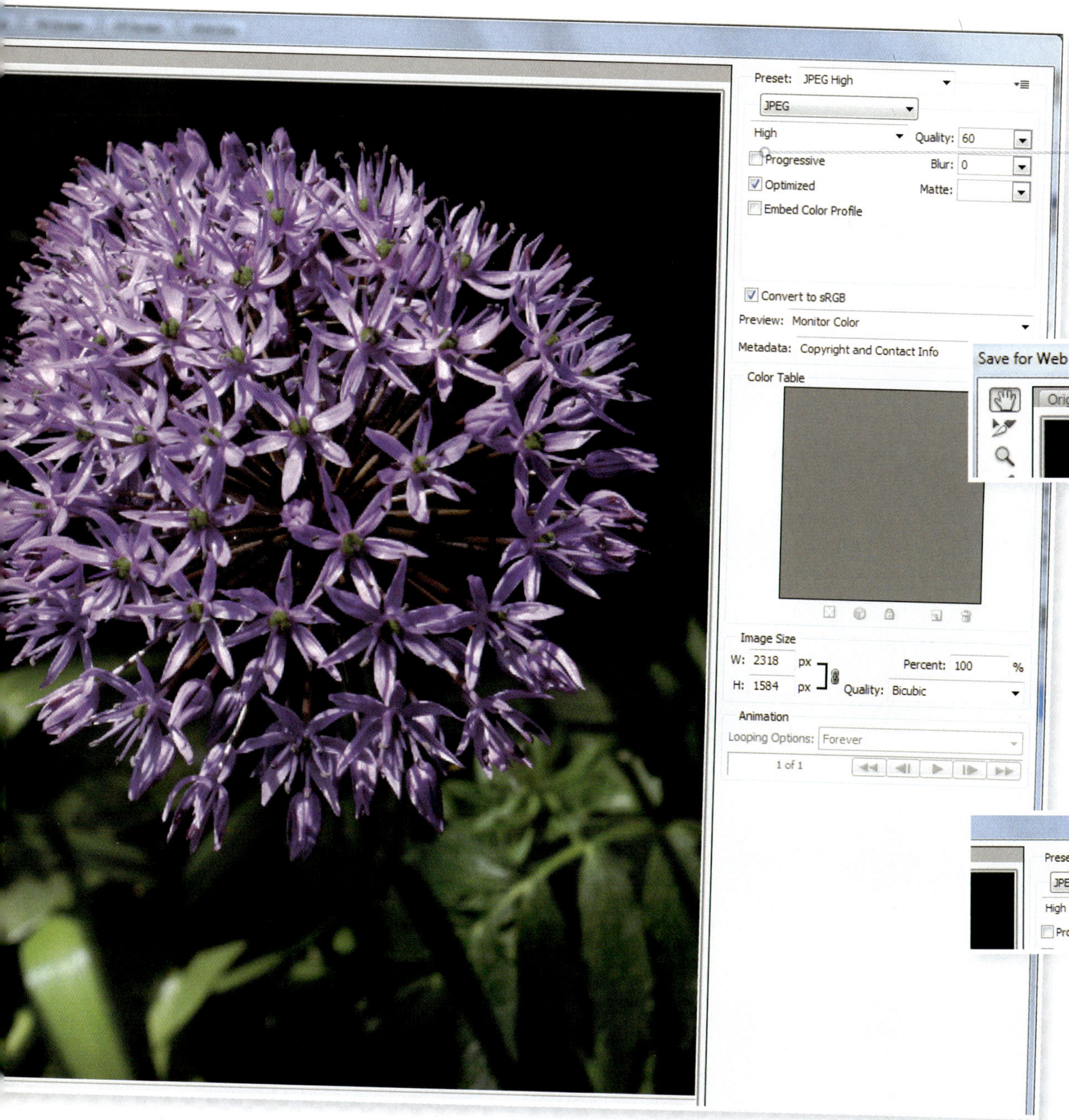

Making progress

Ticking the Progressive checkbox means your image can be displayed quickly and in high quality.

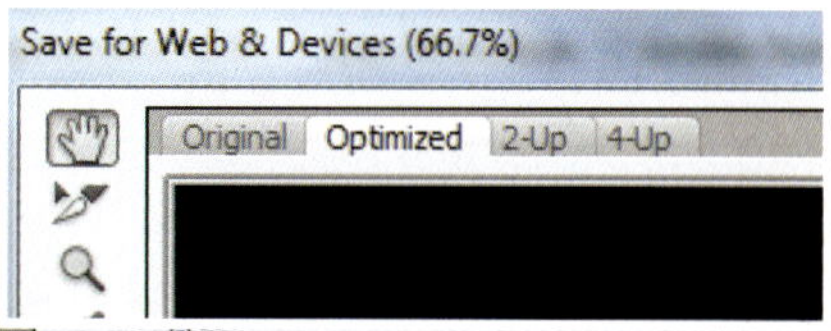

Pick a view

The tabs in the top left corner allow you to switch between views. Original displays the unchanged image and Optimized shows it with the Save for Web settings applied. To compare images, use 2-Up or 4-Up for a view of two or four images of different qualities.

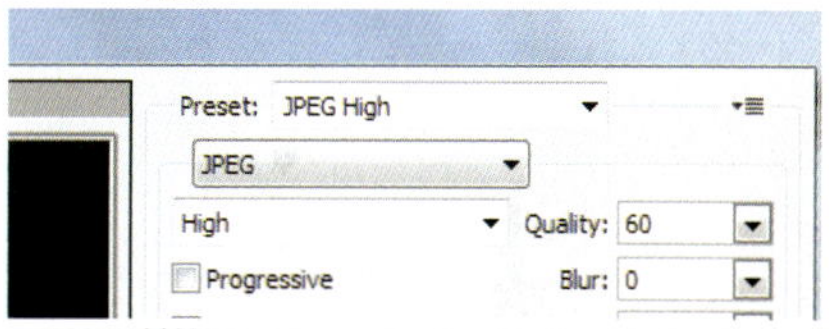

Presets

Many settings can be altered within the Save for Web tool. However, to make it easier to optimise images there is a Preset drop-down menu for each of the file formats.

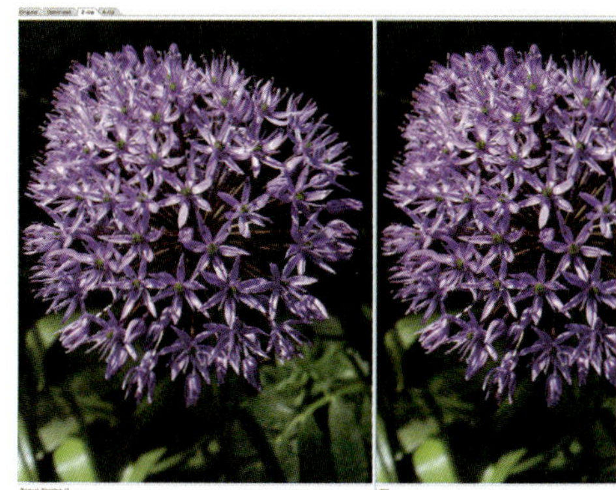

04 View before and after

If you are unsure as to the effect your edit has on your image, click the 2-Up tab at the top of the window. You will see a before and after shot.

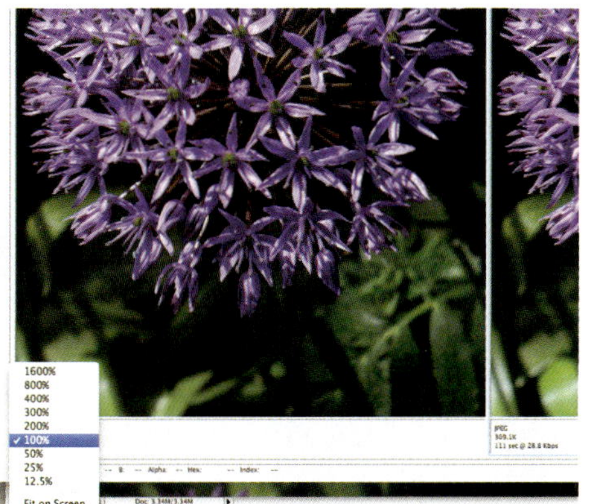

05 Change the view

You can also zoom in and out of the image. Click the down arrow next to the percentage value in the bottom left. Choose the option you want.

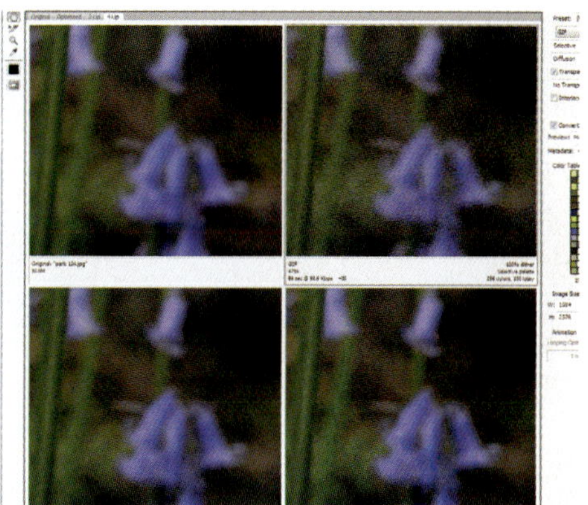

06 Lossy

If you are saving as a GIF file, lossy is a useful control that removes some of the detail from your image to further reduce the file size.

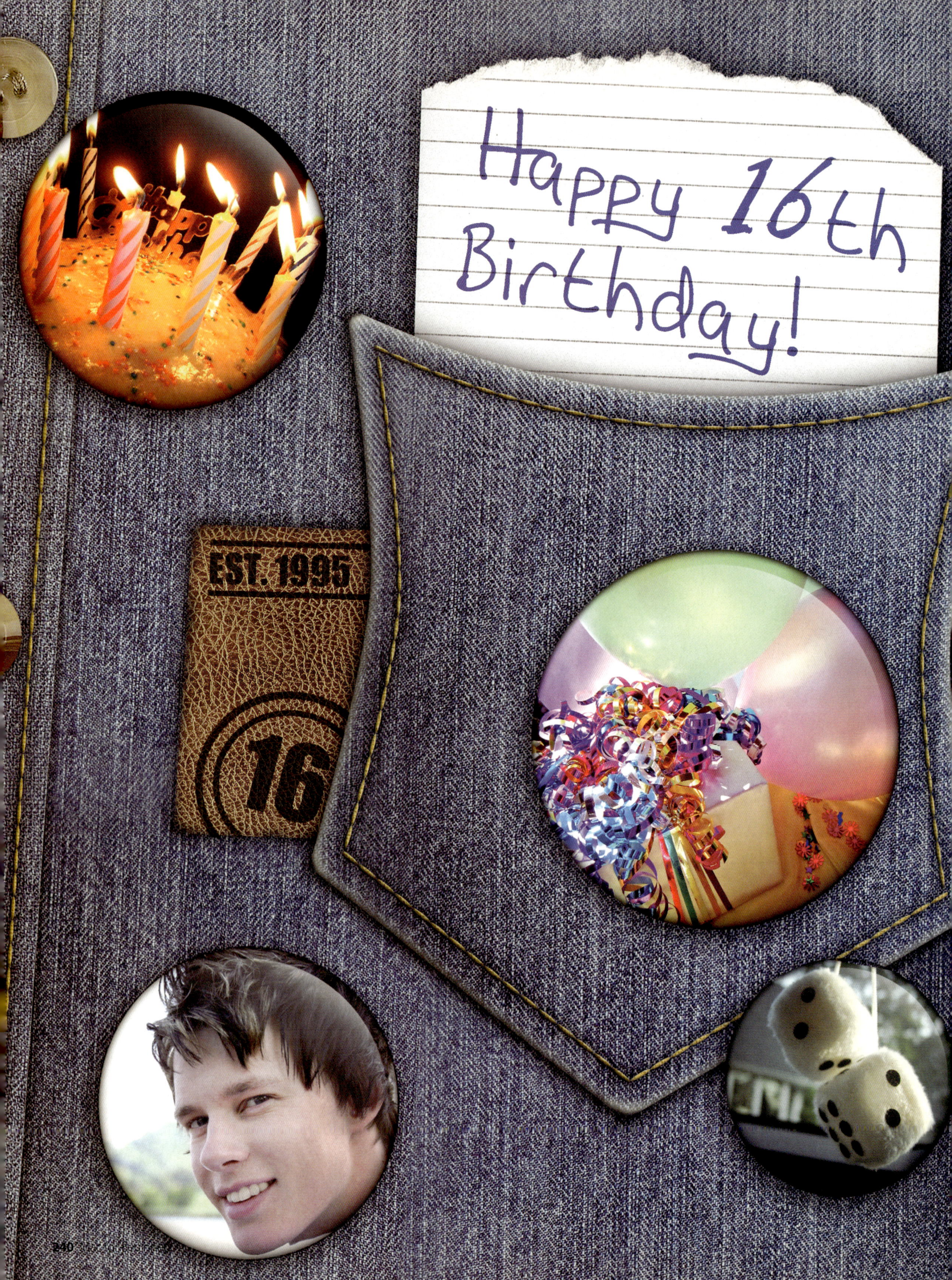
Happy 16th Birthday!
EST. 1995
16

Design a denim scrapbook page

Discover how to turn your photos into button badges and then present them on a denim-style scrapbook page

In this tutorial, we'll take you through the process of creating a scrapbook page in the style of a denim shirt. You'll be creating the pocket, adding buttons and notepaper and presenting your photos in the style of button badges.

To create a realistic appearance, we'll use layer styles, including Drop Shadows, Inner Glows, Outer Glows, Pattern Overlays and more. You'll be amazed at just how much can be achieved using only layer styles.

You may have a theme in mind for your scrapbook page and want to use your own photographs. Here we've chosen a 16th birthday theme, and if you'd like to follow the tutorial using the same images they are all available to download from Stock.XCHNG (**www.sxc.hu**). The image ID numbers are as follows: 680169 (the birthday cake), 1214995 (the fluffy dice), 337654 (the teenage boy) and 519222 (the balloons and present).

To complete this tutorial, you'll also need the leather texture for the logo patch which, again, is on Stock.XCHNG, image ID 1154337. Everything else is included for you with this book

One of the files provided for you is the denim texture which will be the base for your artwork. If you'd like, you can scan in your own denim texture. We've also included a nifty custom brush that has been designed specifically to create a stitching effect when used in conjunction with Paths and the Pen tool. So, once you have all your files ready, let's get cracking.

"You'll be amazed at what can be achieved using only layer styles"

CREATE STITCHES

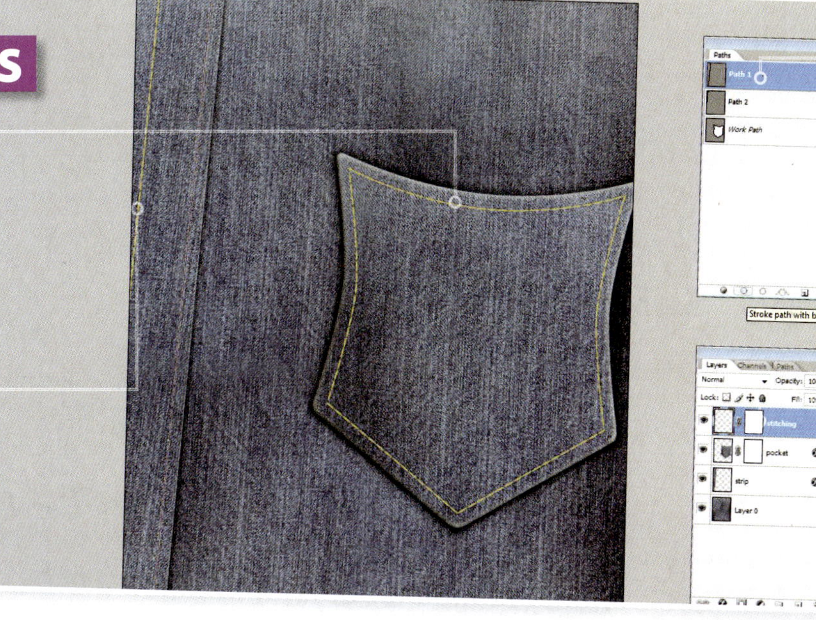

Pocket paths
Make the path for the pocket's stitching by going to the Paths palette, click to select the path of the pocket, right-click and choose Free Transform Path and then shrink and reposition appropriately.

Seam path
To create the path for the straight line of stitching here, select the Pen tool, click to place a point at the top and then click to place a second point at the bottom.

Stroke the path
To apply the stroke, go to the Paths palette and, with your path active, press 'B' to select the Brush tool and then click the Stroke Path With Brush icon.

Custom brush
Create a new layer (press Shift+Cmd/Ctrl+N) and add the stitching by applying a stroke to a path using the brush on the CD with a colour of R:226 G:177 B:58.

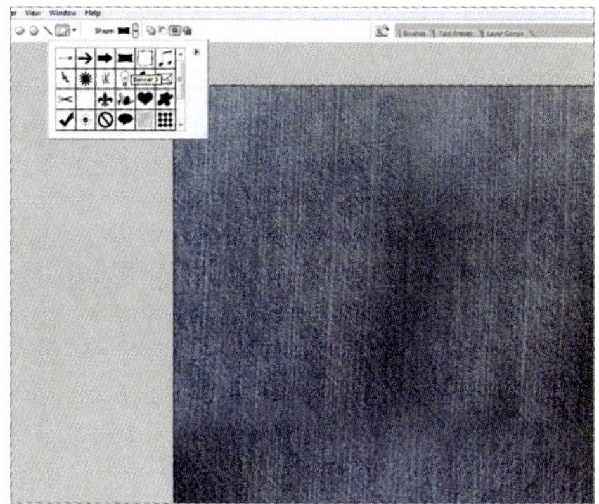

01 Create a banner
Open 'denim background.psd', select Custom Shape tool. Set the tool to Paths. Choose Banner 3 from the Shape menu. Now create the shape.

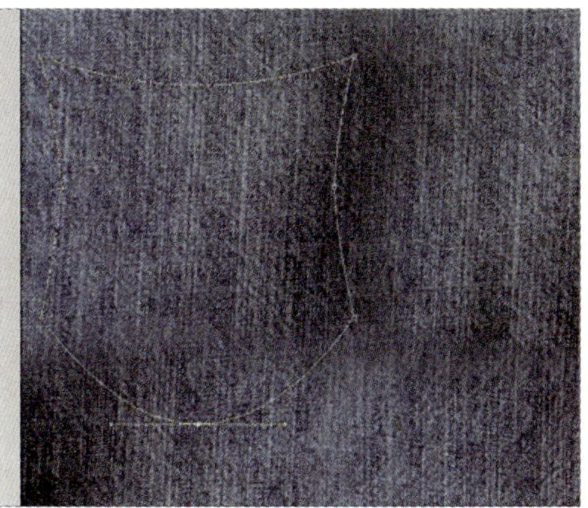

02 Make your point
Select Pen. Click in the middle at the bottom of the shape. Drag this point downwards. Hold Opt/Alt and click the point to turn it into a pointed angle.

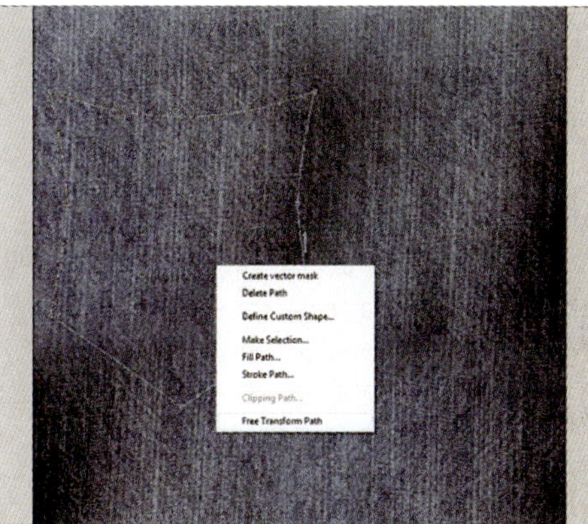

03 Get in position
Hold Cmd/Ctrl and select the path. Ctrl/right-click and choose Free Transform Path. Holding Shift change the size of the path to suit your image.

Finish the pocket

Apply some layer styles to complete the effect

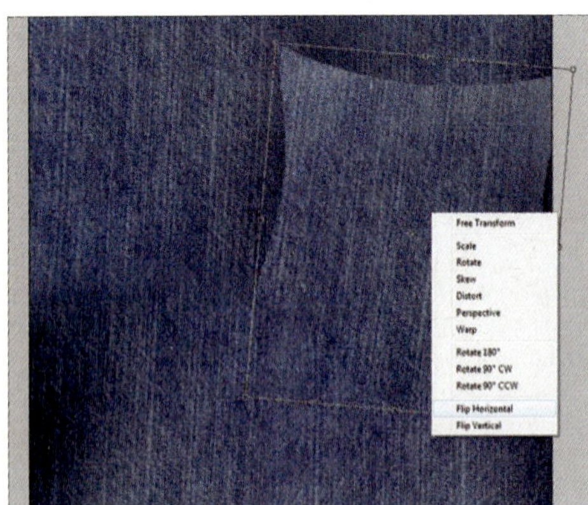

04 Duplicate it

Press Cmd/Ctrl+J to duplicate the selected area of denim. Press Cmd/Ctrl+T and right-click the pocket, and then click Flip Horizontal.

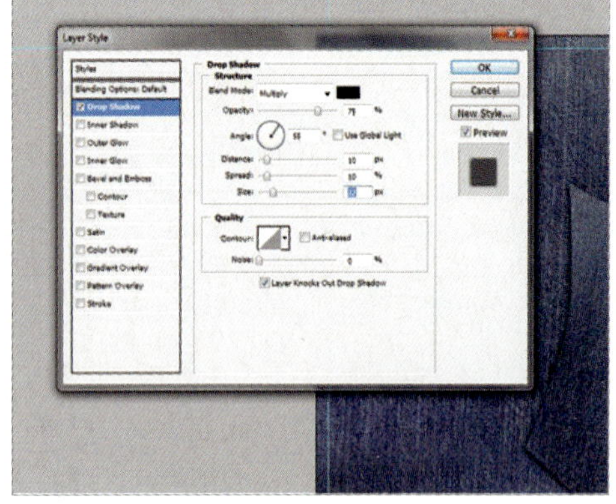

05 Spatter and spray

Make sure the photo is the active layer and hit Add Layer Mask. Use the Spatter, Sprayed Strokes and Displacement filters to give the fabric more texture.

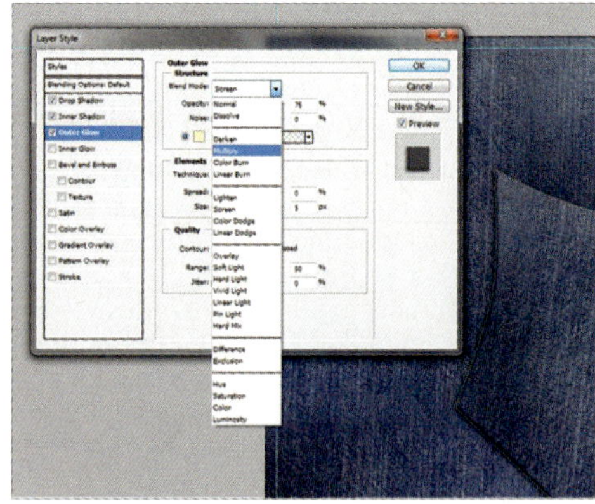

06 Give it a glow

Tick Outer Glow, set mode to Multiply, colour: black, Opacity: 30%, Spread: 24%, Size: 84px, Range: 70%. Tick Inner Glow, Choke: 10%, Size: 40px, Range: 85%.

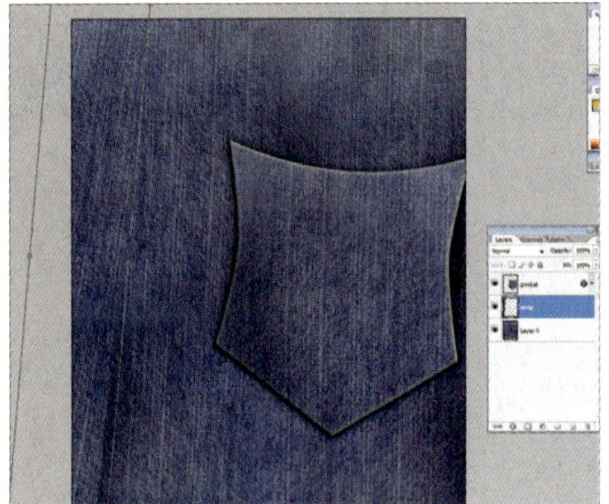

07 Add a hem

Select a strip of denim, press Cmd/Ctrl+J. Move to the left. Add a Drop Shadow, untick Use Global Light, Angle 115, Distance 14px, Spread 8%, Size 43px.

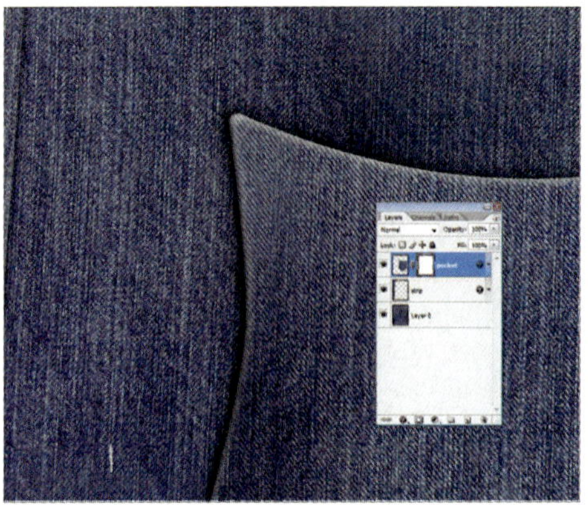

08 Soften the corners

Add a layer mask to the pocket layer. Use a small black airbrush on the mask to soften the edges and corners of the pocket slightly.

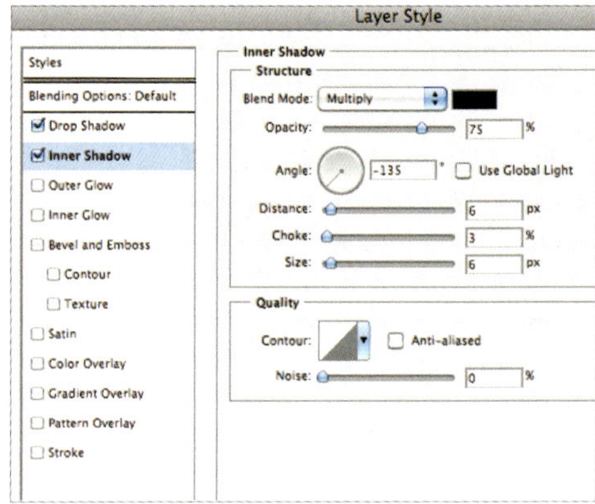

09 Add the shadows

Add a Drop Shadow to Stitching layer. Untick Use Global Light, Angle: 49, Distance: 3px, Spread: 0%, Size: 3px. Tick Inner Shadow, use the settings above.

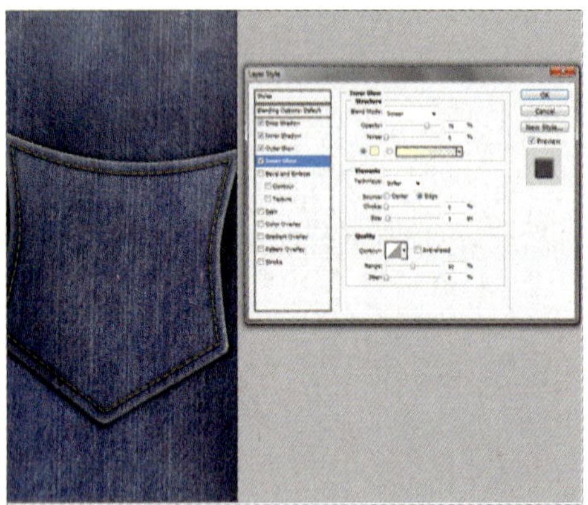

10 More layer styles

Tick Outer Glow. Set mode: Multiply, Opacity: 40%, colour: black, Spread: 15%, Size: 40px, Range: 55%. Tick Inner Glow, Choke 0%, Size 3px, Range 50%.

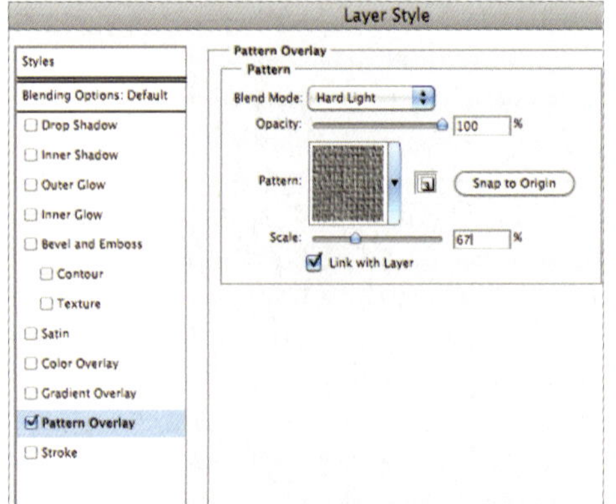

11 Create some texture

Tick Pattern Overlay. Click Pattern menu, load Artist Surfaces. Choose Dark Coarse Weave and enter the settings above. Make a new layer called Badge.

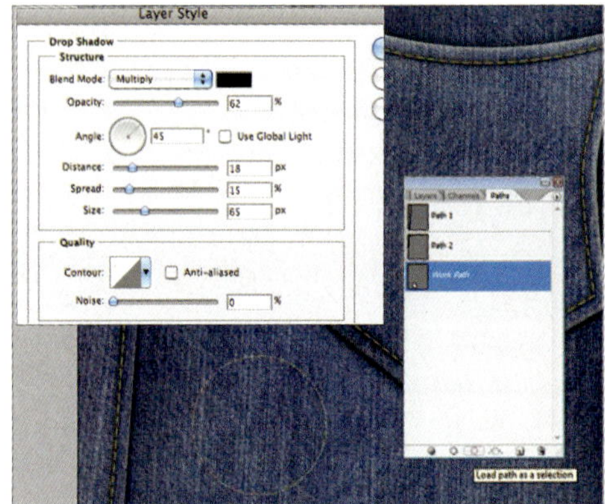

12 Draw your circle

Pick Ellipse tool, hold Shift and drag. In the Paths palette, click Create Selection from Path. Fill with any colour. Add a Drop Shadow, settings as above.

Make the badges

Finish the stitching and build your photo badges

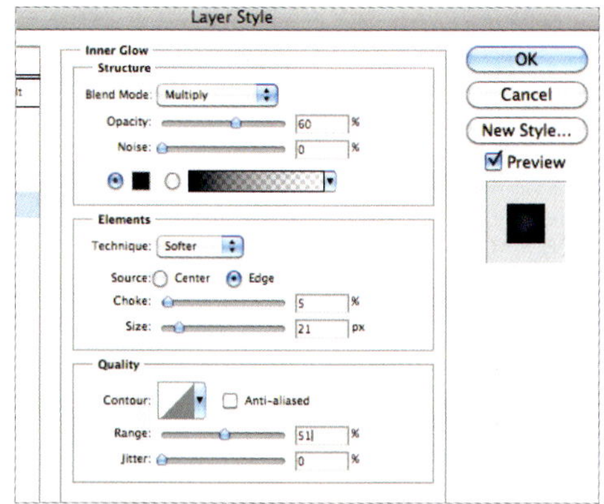

13 Even more layer styles

Add an Inner Shadow, deselect Use Global Light, Angle -66, Opacity 60%, Distance 13px, Choke 11% and Size 46px. Add an Inner Glow, settings as above.

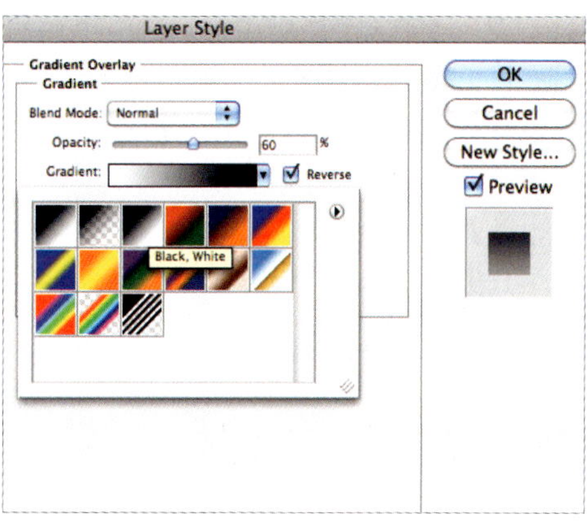

14 Gradient sheen

Add gradient overlay, Opacity 60%, tick Reverse, choose Black, White gradient and Radial style. Reduce the layer's Fill to 0% in the Layers palette.

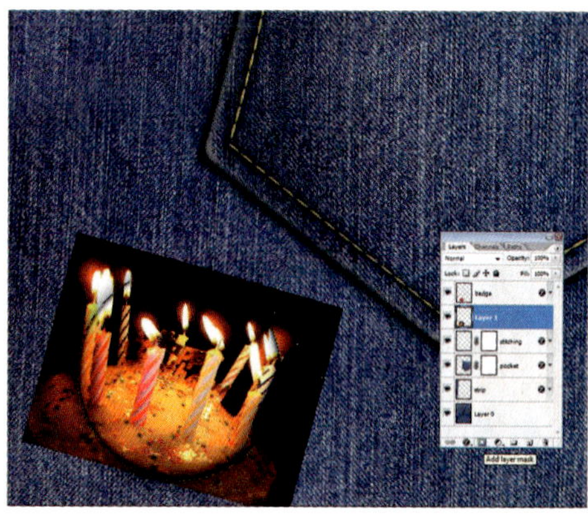

15 Drop in your photo

Paste in your chosen photograph underneath this layer. Right-click the circle layer's thumbnail and then add a mask to the photograph layer.

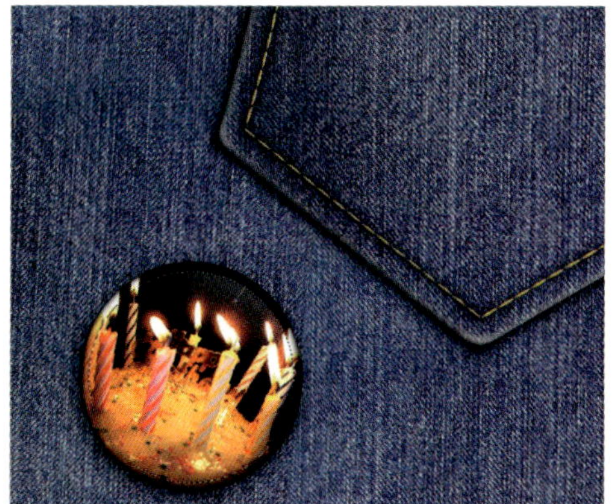

16 Give it some shine

Add a layer above the circle layer. Create a smaller circle, select the Gradient tool, Linear Gradient, Opacity 33% and colour white. Drag down and left.

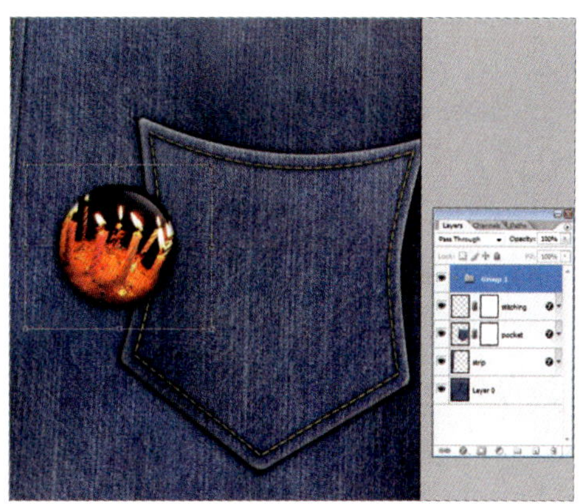

17 Group the badge layers

Hold Shift, click badge layers, press Cmd/Ctrl+G. Press Cmd/Ctrl+T to transform and move. Duplicate the circle and sheen layers and bring in photos.

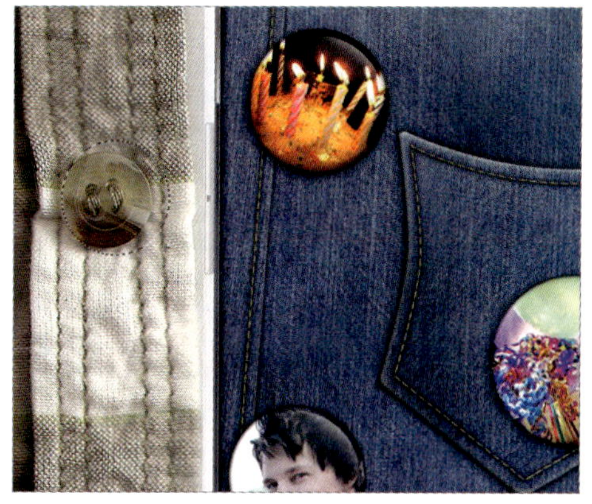

18 Bring in some buttons

Open 'shirt.jpg'. Select a button, copy and paste into your work. Press Cmd/Ctrl+J twice. Press Cmd/Ctrl+T to move to the left-hand hem.

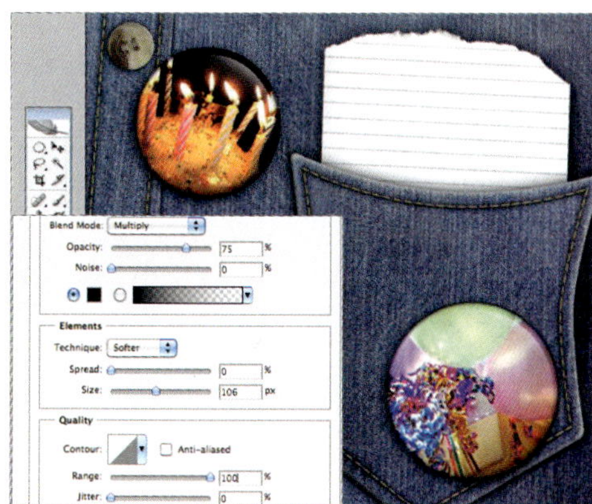

19 Make a note

Copy and paste the notepaper from 'paper.psd', below the pocket layer. Use Cmd/Ctrl+T to position. Add an Outer Glow, settings as above.

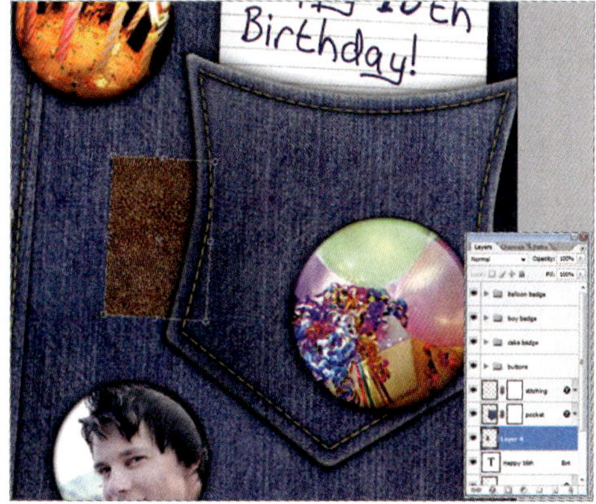

20 Paste in the leather

Add your text to the paper. Set the layer to Multiply, 70% Opacity. Copy and paste the leather under the pocket. Cmd/Ctrl+T to shrink and angle.

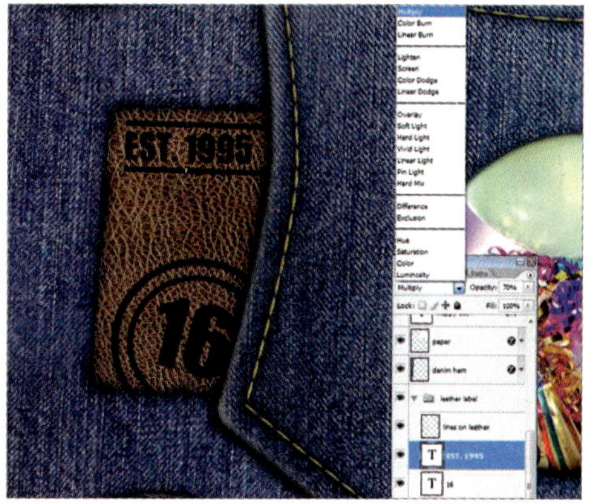

21 Finish with layer styles

Add an Outer Glow, mode to Multiply, black, Spread 14%, Size 59px, Range 88%. Add text above the leather layer, mode to Multiply and 70% Opacity.

Create a template for a wedding

Get a individual look for your photobook

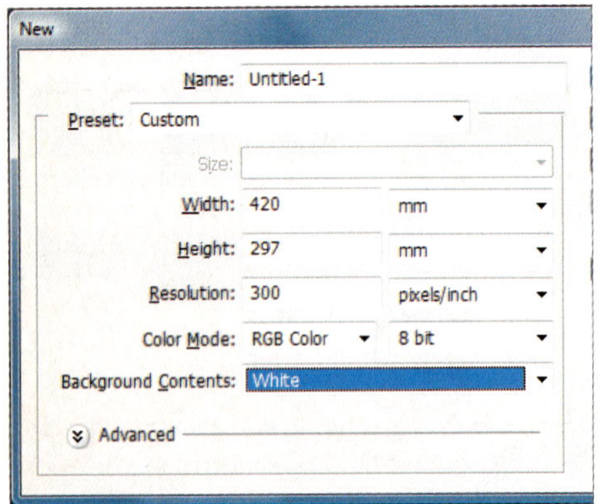

01 Create the pages

Go to File>New and enter 420mm x 297mm in Width and Height. Enter the Resolution as 300 pixels/inch and Background Contents to White.

02 Set the areas

Go to View and tick Rulers. Go to View>New Guide, select Vertical. Set position to 21cm. Add guides at 1 and 41cm and horizontal ones at 1 and 28.7cm.

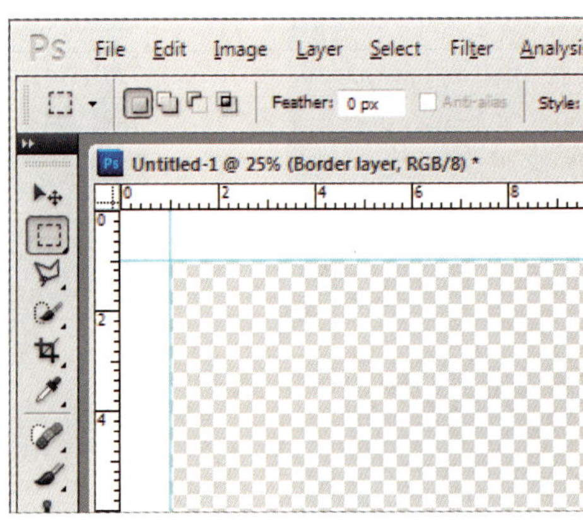

03 Mark it out

Pick the Rectangular Marquee and set Style to Fixed Size. Enter Width as 40cm, Height as 27.7cm and click where the guides intersect in the top left.

04 New layer

Go to Select>Inverse, Edit>Copy and Edit>Paste. You now have a new layer for the border. Click the eye icon for your Background layer.

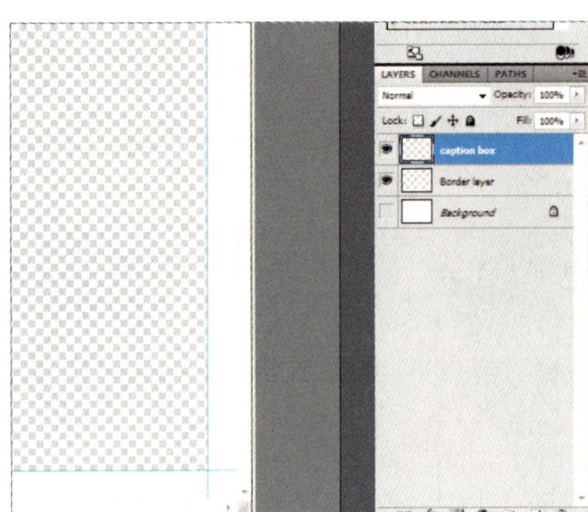

05 Caption box

On a new layer, select Rectangular Marquee and Set Style as Fixed Ratio. Set Width to 15cm and Height to 2cm.

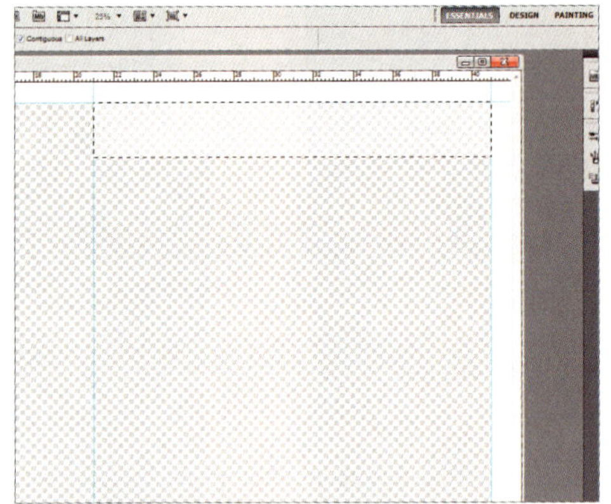

06 Add colour

Drag from the top mid-point to the other guide. Pick the Paint Bucket, set the foreground colour to white and choose an Opacity of 50%. Click to fill.

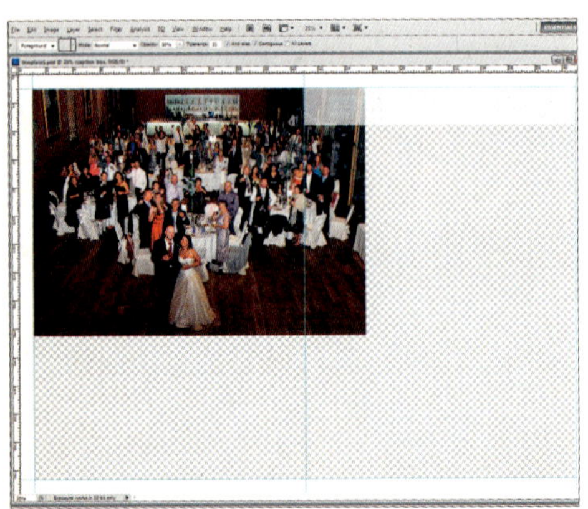

07 Save and use

Drop a photo between the border layer and the background. You may need to use Edit>Transform to scale the image up or down.

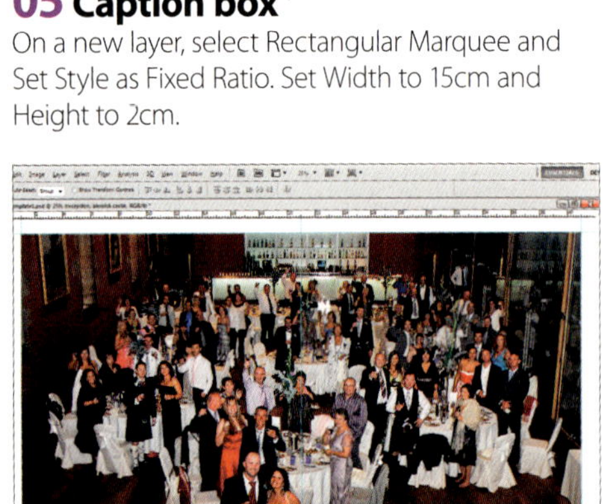

08 Add text

The caption has its own layer, so move it to the best position. Click on the Text tool, choose your font then click on the image and enter the text.

09 Add more picture slots

Create a new layer and pick the Rectangular Marquee. Set Style to Fixed Size, Width to 2cm and Height to 29.7cm. Click the 20cm mark at the top.

Multi-image layout Add in extra images and shapes

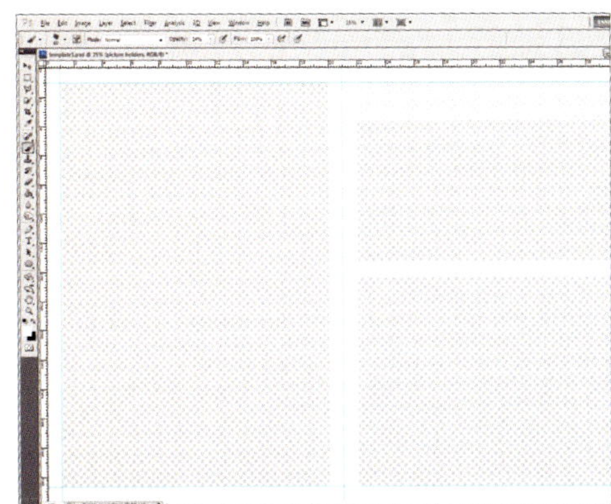

10 Expand the layout

Use the Paint Bucket to fill the column. On a new layer, use the Rectangular Marquee to click at 21cm wide and 1cm high. Click 13.3cm down and fill.

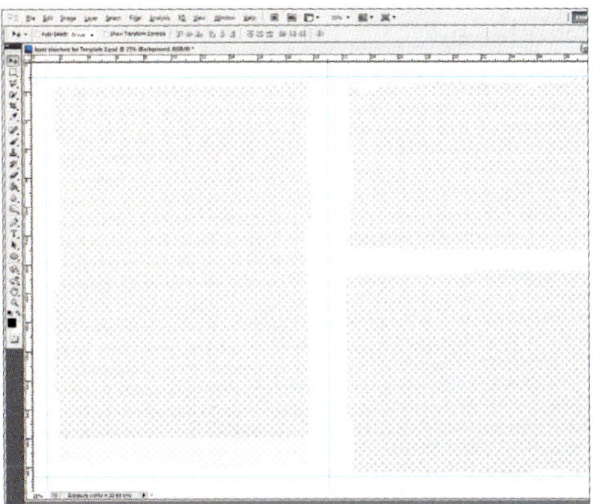

11 Rough edges

Select the Chalk brush (size and Opacity of 70). Brush white around the square edge of the picture areas. Move the caption box to the bottom left.

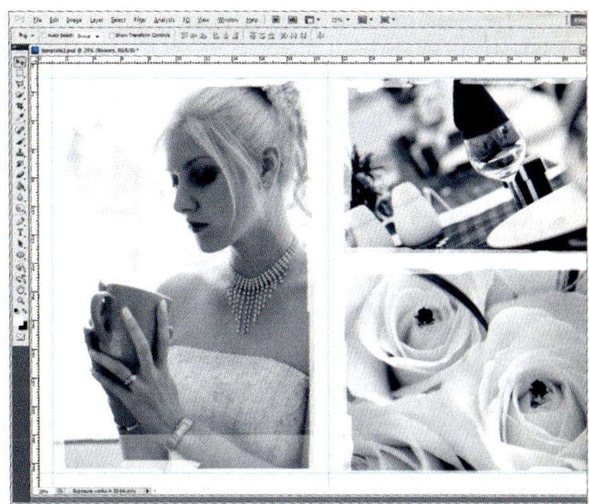

12 Drop pictures in

Save this template for future use. Now drop in pictures underneath all of the border layers. Rescale any if they are too big.

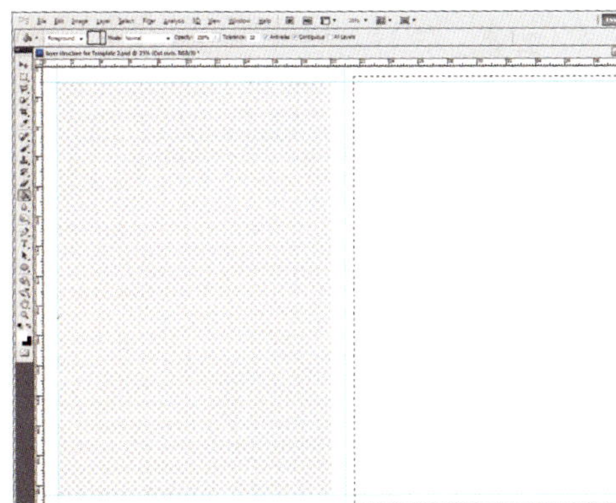

13 Once more template

Open an existing template, delete layers except the centre and border. Add a new layer. Select the right with the Rectangular Marquee and fill with white.

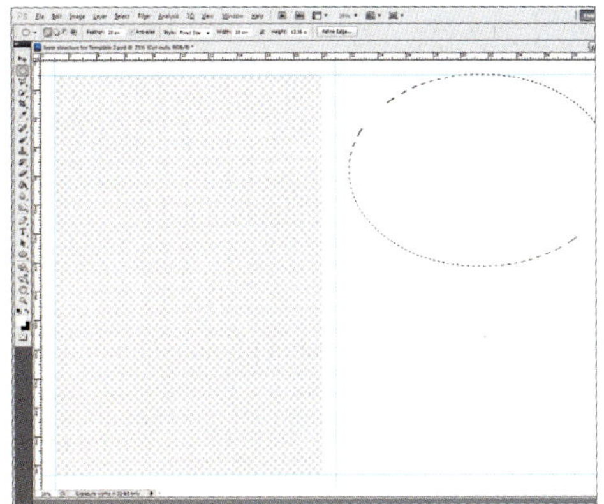

14 Create an ellipse

Pick the Elliptical Marquee, set Feather to 20px, Style to Fixed Size, Width to 19cm and Height to 13.35cm. Click and hold the right side of the page.

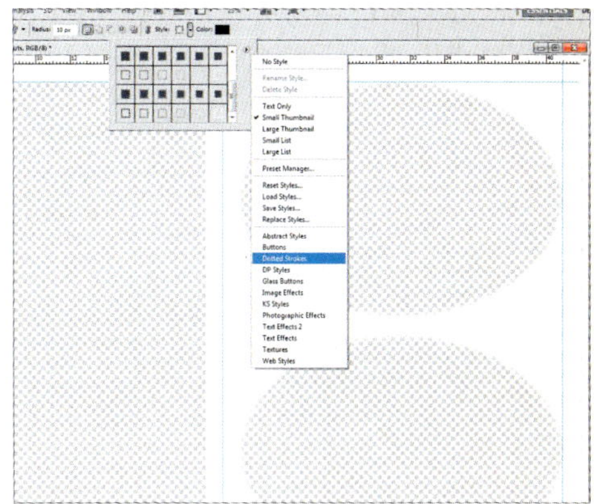

15 Cut it out

Go to Edit>Cut. Add another ellipse below it. Pick the Rounded Rectangle. Load Dotted Strokes from Style selection and use Black 3pt No Fill.

16 Add effect borders

In the Rounded Rectangle options, fix Width to 19cm, Height to 27.7cm and click on the top left corner where the guides intersect to drop it on.

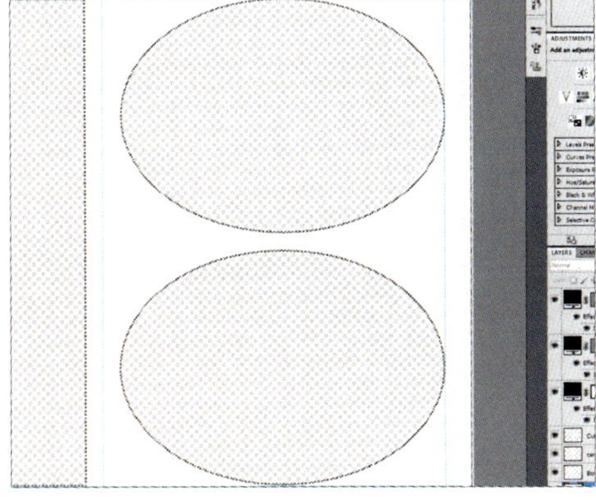

17 Now the ellipse

Select an Ellipse with Width 19cm, Height to 13.35cm and position it against the top and right guides. Add a third for the last hole.

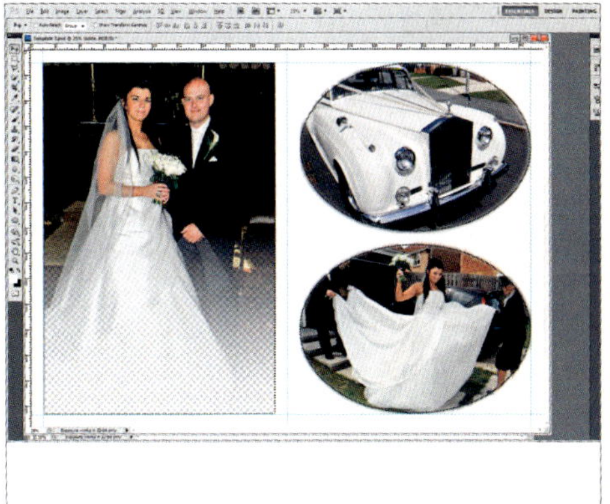

18 Add in the photos

Open up your photos as before, making sure that they are place underneath the border layers, resizing or moving to fit.

Make a DVD slideshow

Sometimes you need an easy way of showing off your photos and a slideshow is perfect

Photoshop can be used to create or modify photographs in many different ways and formats, but did you know that you can also use Photoshop and Bridge to create a PDF slideshow? This is very useful if you want to send examples of work to potential clients or even if you just want to share some of your holiday snaps with friends and family. In this tutorial we will be looking into how we can use Photoshop to make a template for your holiday photos as well as using Bridge to make a fun slide show.

We start by making our template, which is going to be an A4-sized picture so printing will be easy. We will also set a background image. We chose one from morgueFile (**www.morguefile.com/archive/display/162896**), but feel free to use any picture you want. We set up guidelines, which are used to position the title, comment and photo boxes later on. Guides are very useful when designing templates as you can set exactly where elements go in your design. Next we add two Rectangular Marquees that we fill with white. These will be our title and comment box. Finally we make a portrait and landscape version of the photo holder that we will use to position the photo within our template. Finally we use Adobe Bridge to automatically build the slideshow, which can then be customised by choosing from its options to suit your individual wants and needs to enjoy your images. You can follow the tutorial through from the beginning, or use the templates provided.

"Did you know that you can also use Photoshop and Bridge to create a PDF slideshow?"

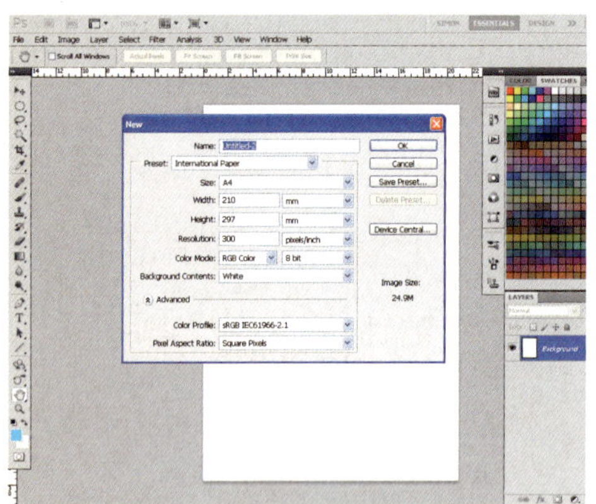

01 New document

Make an A4 document (File>New>International Paper>A4). Set the Background Contents to White and then save it as 'Template.psd'.

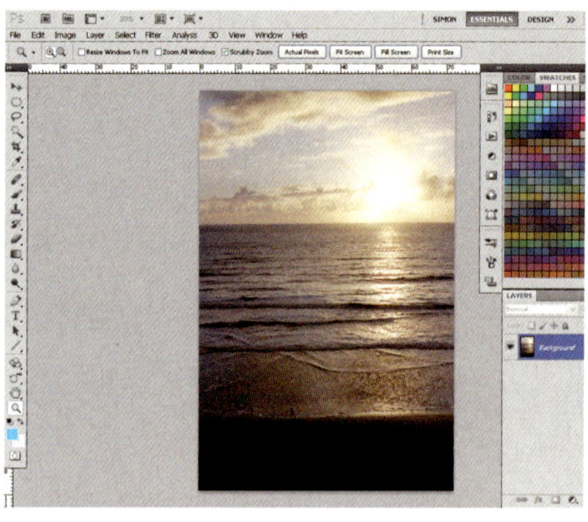

02 Build a backing

Open the image you want to use. Go to the Layers palette, hold Opt/Alt on your keyboard and drag the Background layer to Create a New Layer icon.

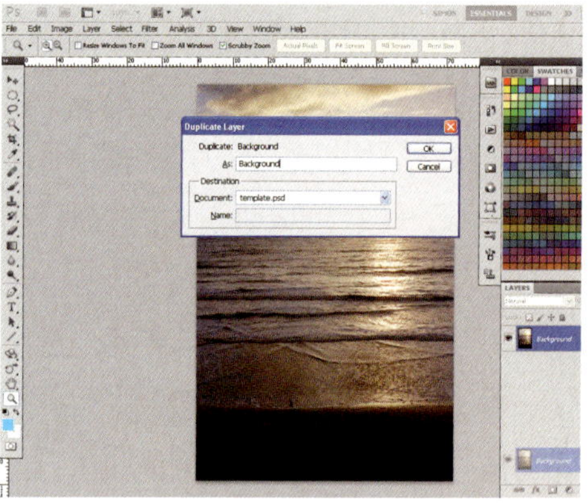

03 Apply to template

This will open a dialog box. From this, select the Template file and click OK to copy the Background layer onto the template file we created in Step 1.

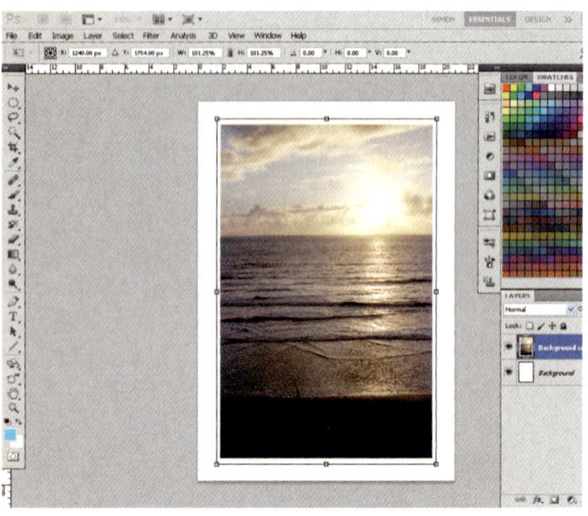

04 Resize

Go to Edit>Transform>Scale, hold the Shift key and drag the corners to the edges. Rename as 'Photo background' and reduce the Opacity to 50%.

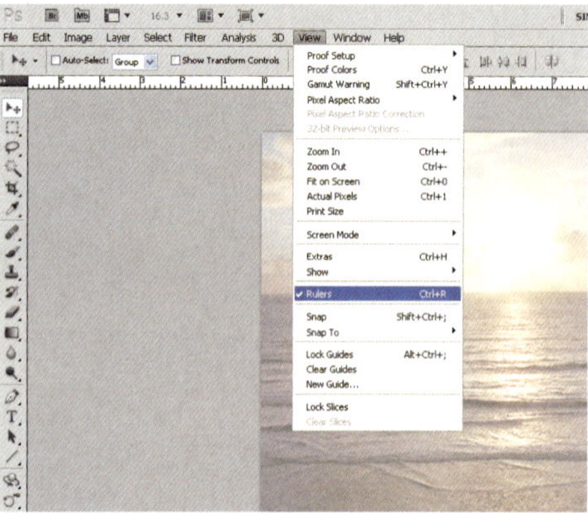

05 Set your rulers to stun

Go to View>Show>Guides and View>Rulers. Right-click a rule line and pick Inches. Grab the Move tool, click-drag from the top Rule to pull out a guide.

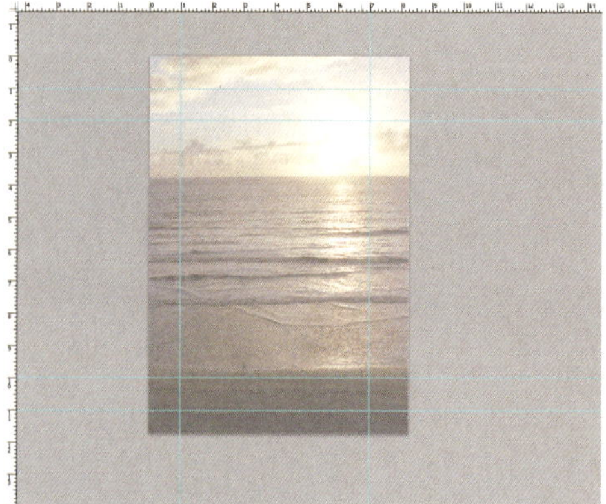

06 Making guides

Move one guide to the 1" marker on the top rule, one to 7" and drag two horizontal guides to 1" and 2". Pull a guide to 10" and 11" for a comment box.

Add more elements Build up the areas of your template

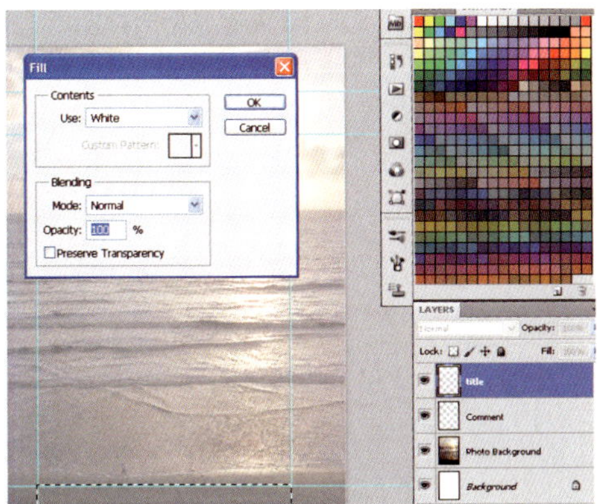

07 Rectangles rule

Make a layer called Title. With the Rectangular Marquee tool, draw a shape using the top guides. Go to Edit>Fill>White. Repeat for the comments.

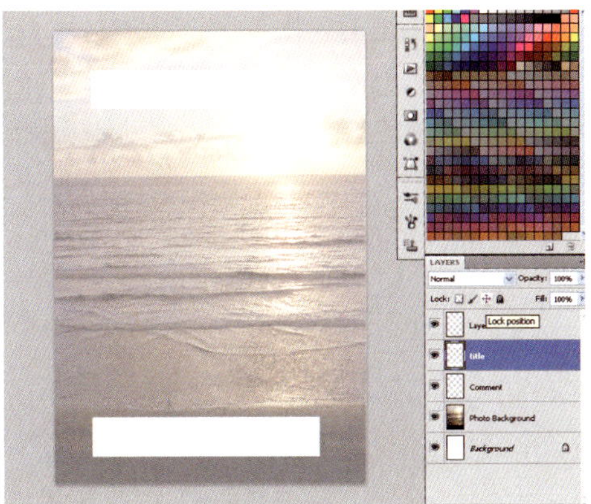

08 Lock and load

The Layers palette has four icons preceded by the word Lock. Click the Title layer, then the third icon. Repeat for the Comment layer.

09 Photo placement

Remove the old horizontal guide lines by dragging them back to the rulers. Position new horizontal ones at 3" and 9" and vertical lines at 2" and 6".

10 Portrait placeholder

Make a new layer called Portrait. Place a rectangle between the guides. Lock the shape in position and tick the eye in the Layers palette to hide it.

11 Landscape choice

Make a layer called Landscape. Set vertical guides at 1" and 7", and horizontal ones at 4" and 8". make a white rectangle and lock in place. Save as a PSD.

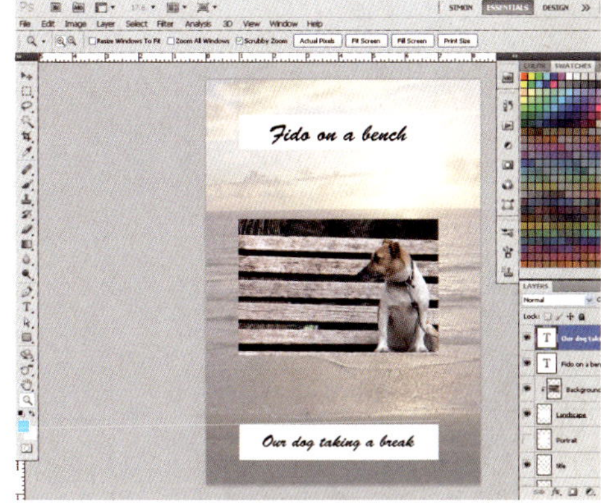

12 Add some details

Copy a photo you want to use and place it over the template. Clip it in place. Using the Text tool, add a title and comment in the boxes. Save as a JPEG.

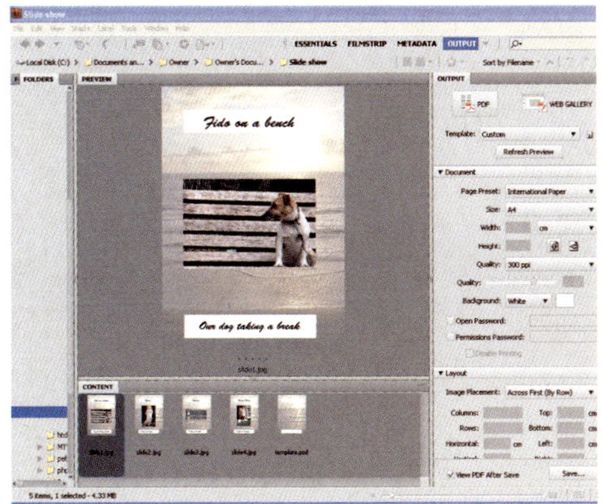

13 Slideshow

Repeat for your photos, then go to File>Browse in Bridge. Locate your folder and go to Window> Workspace>Output. Pick PDF in Output options.

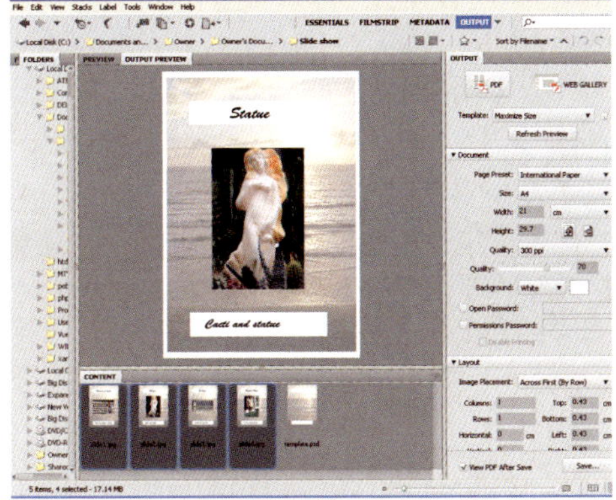

14 Add the slides

In Contents, highlight the slides to use. Choose Maximum Size from the template list, International from the page presets and A4 from the Size list.

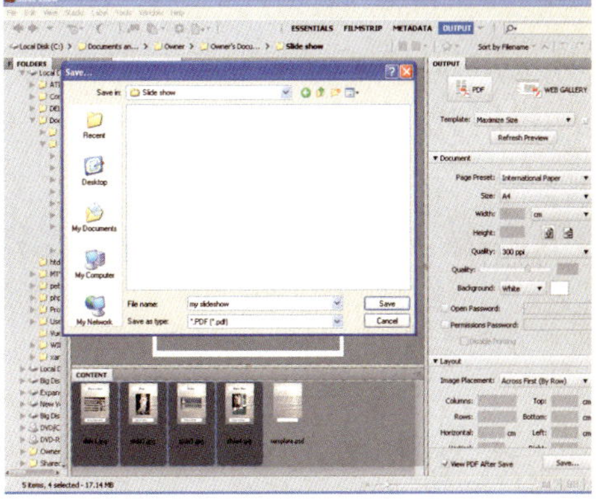

15 Save and preview

Set Column and Rows to 1 in Layout, untick 'File name' in Overlay. In Playback, tick 'Open in full screen' and 'Automatically advance to next page'.

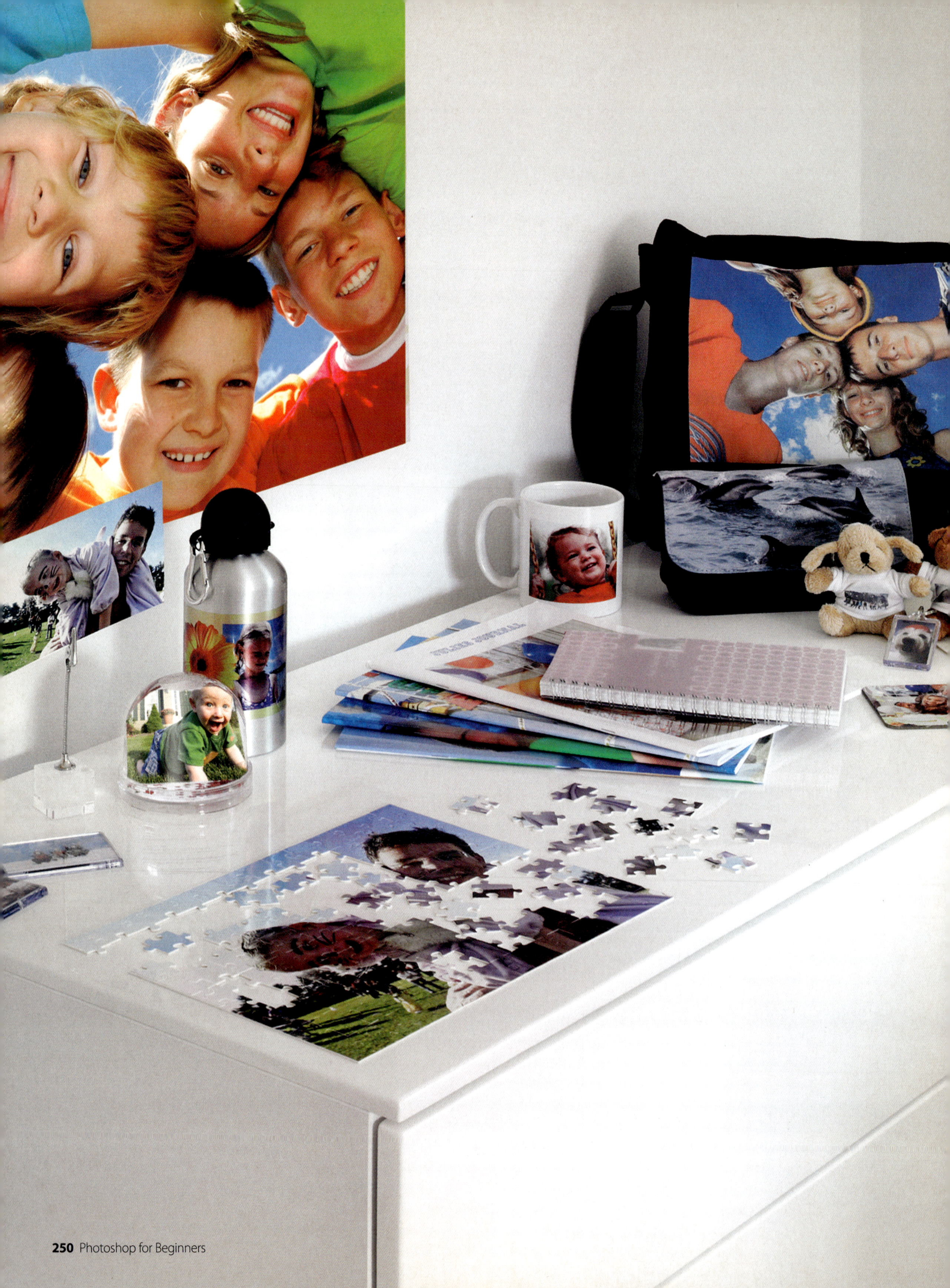

Turn your images into photo gifts

Don't keep your images imprisoned on your desktop, discover the endless possibilities of printing and transform your work into pieces of art

In this digital era, it's easy to leave images in desktop folders or hidden away on a hard drive. . It's an unfortunate fate for the results of all your hard work and memories, especially when there are so many printing options available. Beyond the realms of regular 6"x"4 glossy or matte prints lies a whole treasure trove of photo gifts. Household items such as calendars, mugs and cushions can become as individual as you are by embellishing them with your photographs. There is something to suit every one and every kind of budget, from as little as £2.

Simply typing 'photo gifts' into an internet search engine calls up thousands of online retailers promising to offer high quality, customisable commodities so it can be overwhelming to decide which one to opt for. That is why we have done the hard work for you and put together some of the best companies and the kinds of goods they offer over the next few pages. It is always worth shopping around once you know the gift you wish to purchase, as some retailers will have discounts to take advantage of.

These photo products vary from the novelty to the professional and make a thoughtful present. Most items offer different designs and templates to choose from, making the purchasing process even easier. However, always bear in mind that products will take a few days to be delivered and some retailers will charge extra for post and packaging.

"There is something to suit every one and every kind of budget"

TOP PHOTO GIFT SITES

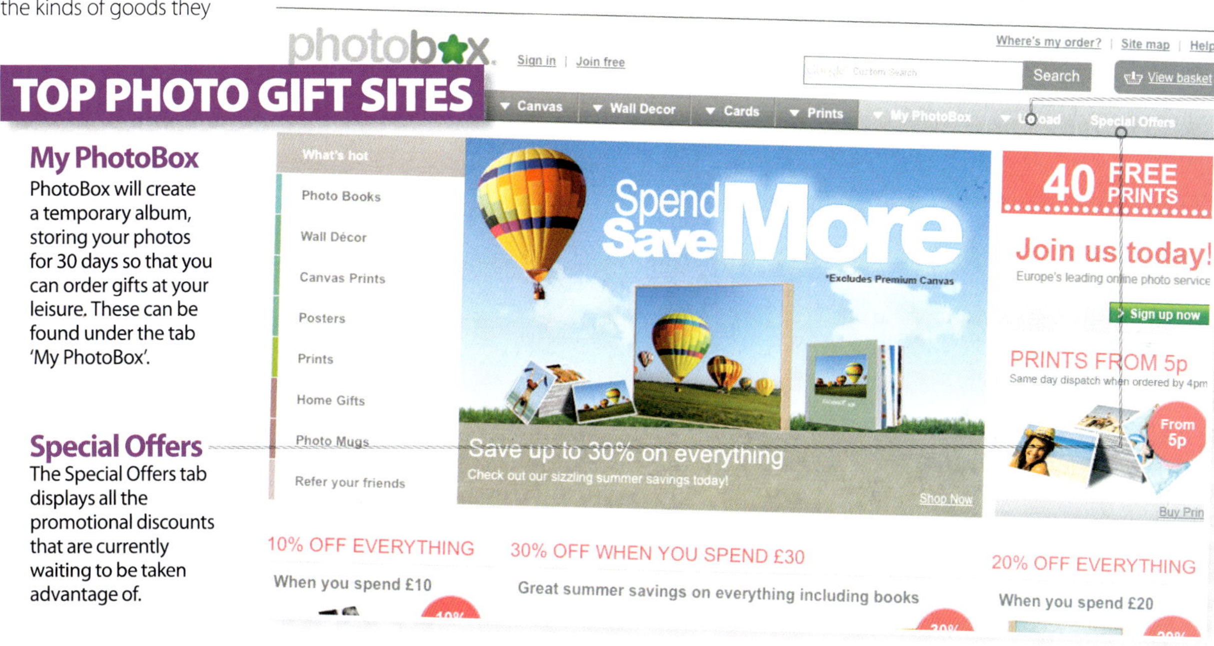

My PhotoBox
PhotoBox will create a temporary album, storing your photos for 30 days so that you can order gifts at your leisure. These can be found under the tab 'My PhotoBox'.

Special Offers
The Special Offers tab displays all the promotional discounts that are currently waiting to be taken advantage of.

Image Upload
Click on the 'Upload' tab to quickly select the photos you want to transform into fun photo gifts. There is also a step-by-step to make it even simpler.

Shop Around
The 'Shop' option calls up the whole range of photo gifts that PhotoBox has to offer, organised into eight categories.

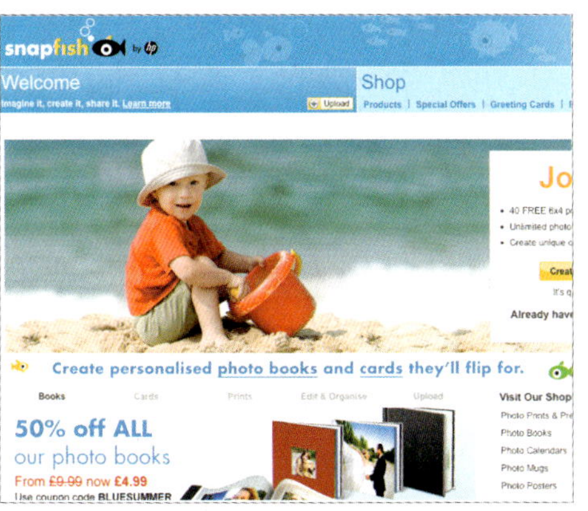

01 Snapfish

A leading retailer with over 90 million members and a wide variety of products. Print, share and store images online, with unlimited free storage.

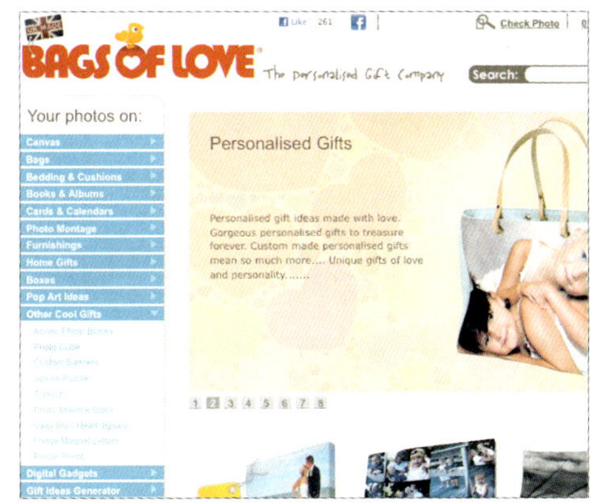

02 Bags Of Love

Don't be misled by the name, Bags Of Love offers a vast amount of unusual personalised gifts for Him, Her, newborn babies and even your pet.

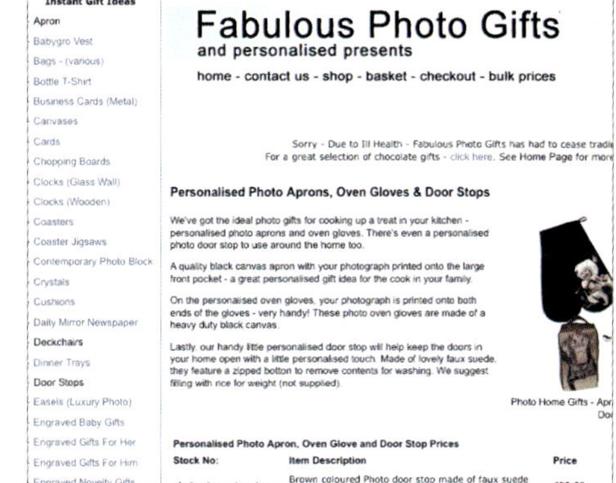

03 Fabulous Photo Gifts

Aprons, deckchairs, clocks and chopping boards – you name it, Fabulous Photo Gifts will print your photograph on it. A very fun, creative company.

Creative options

We take a look at the most popular photo creations

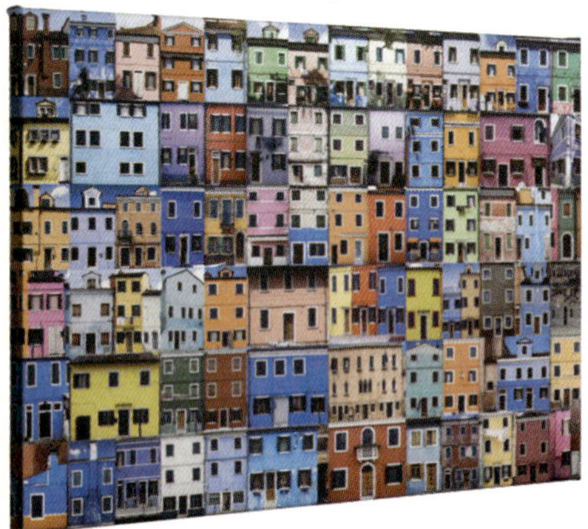

01 Canvas

Transform your photo into a true work of art. They come in a variety of sizes and orientations, but ensure it is UV protected.

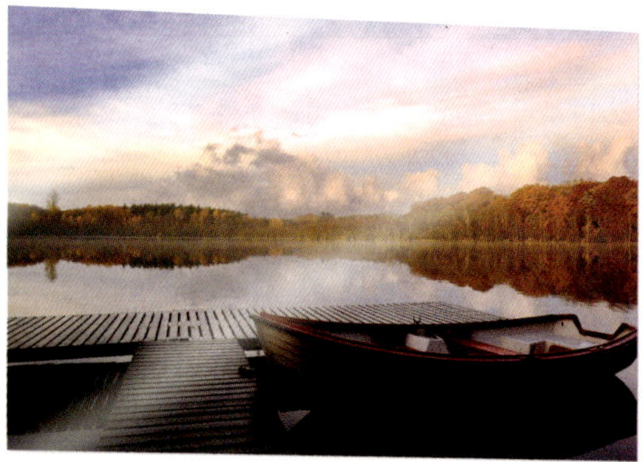

02 Poster

Go super-sized and decorate your home by turning your picture into a vibrant poster that you can't buy in the shops.

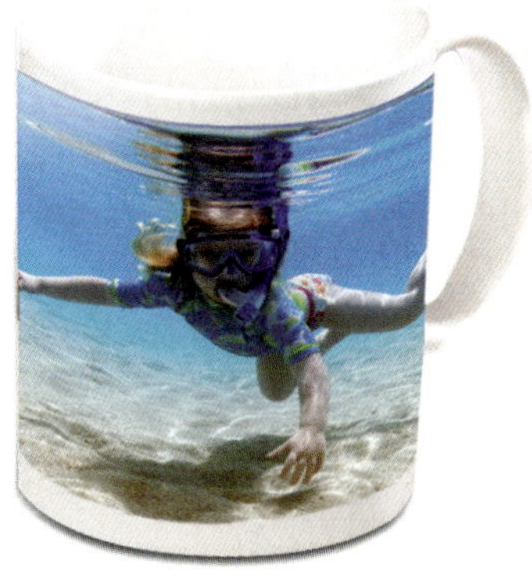

03 Mug

Make a hot beverage extra special by using a collage of photos or one panorama that stretches around the whole cup.

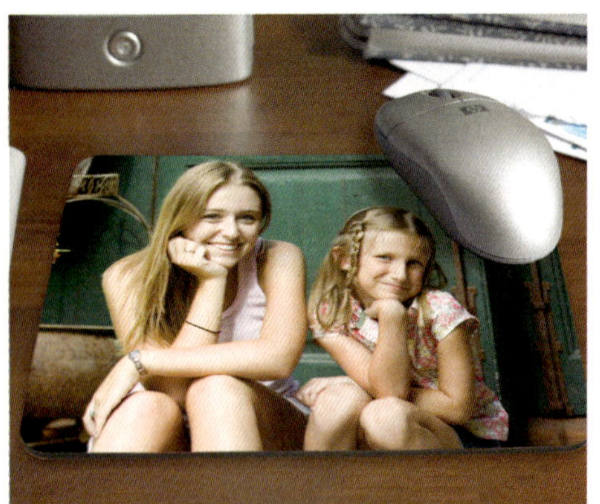

04 Mousemat

This is an item that office workers will clap eyes on everyday, so make it a more pleasurable experience by placing a picture of family onto the surface.

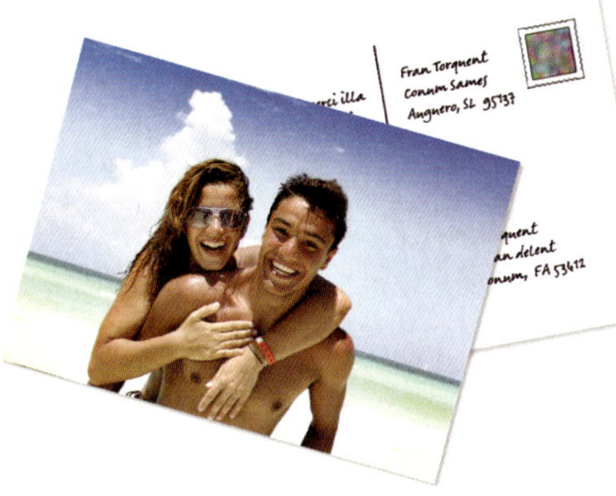

05 Postcard

Create your own postcards with your favourite holiday snaps. Some retailers have a variety of templates to design a professional-looking card.

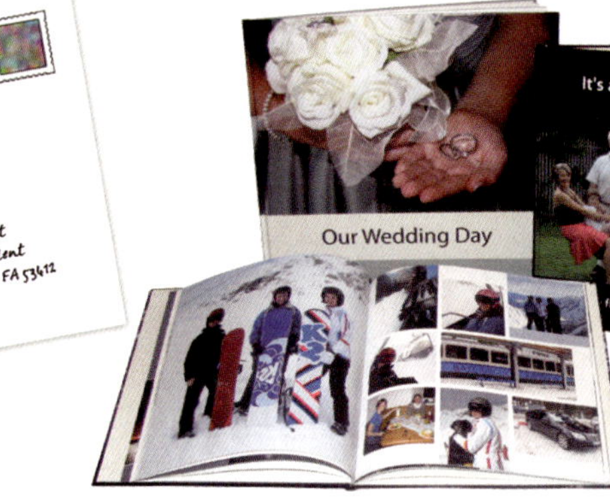

06 Photo book (hardback)

Publishing your photographs in a hardback photo book is a professional way to present your images. They make fantastic coffee table talking points.

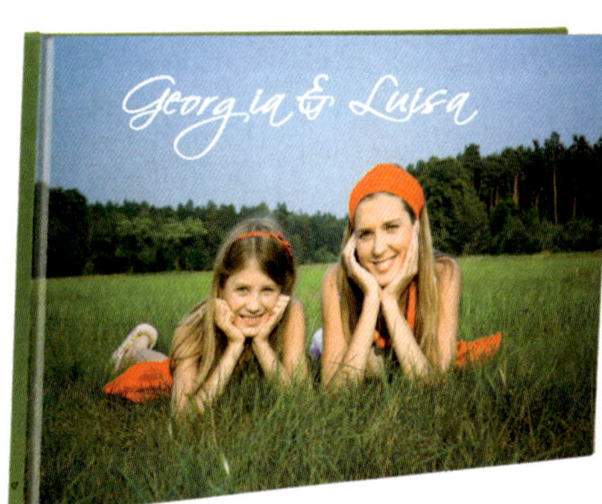
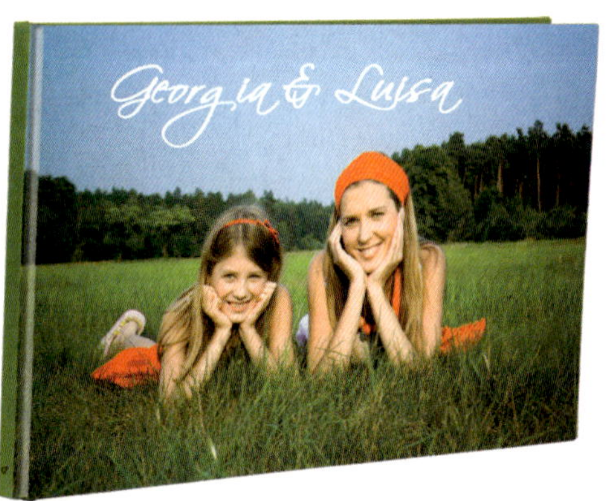

07 Photo book (pocket sized)

The smaller the book, the smaller the price. These pocket-sized books are great for showing off occasions to your friends and family.

08 Occasion books (themed)

A theme can enhance your images. These can range from clip-art adorned pages, through to themed layouts such as gallery or portfolio.

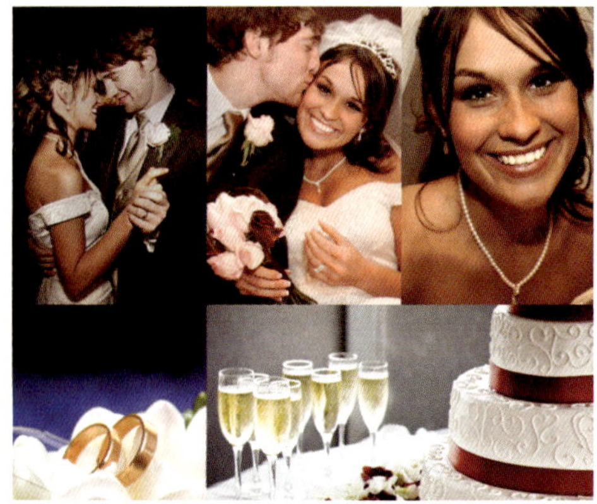

09 Collage prints

Can't decide which image to display in your home? Opt for a collage and group all of the best pictures together in one, high quality print.

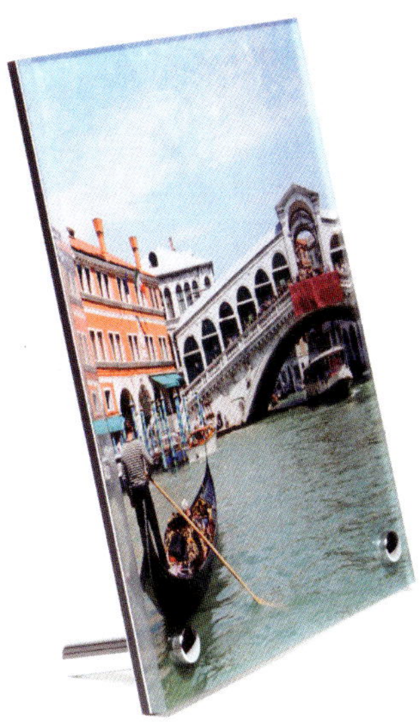

10 Acrylic prints

A modern way to display your images; acrylic lends a luminous effect to prints and gives UV protection, as well as being less breakable than glass.

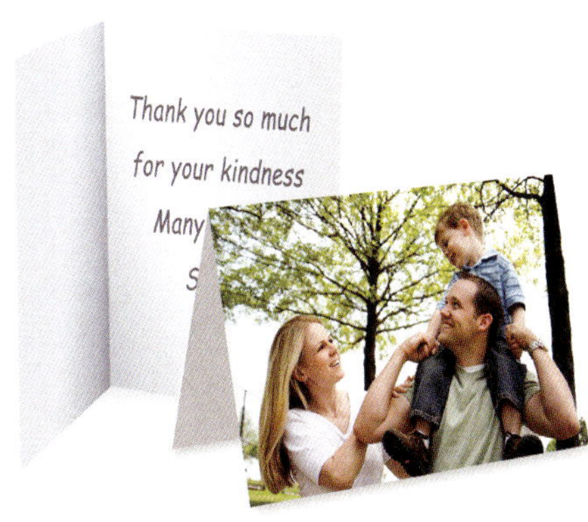

11 Cards

Birthdays, announcements, weddings and any other occasion, you can create greeting cards for all of them.

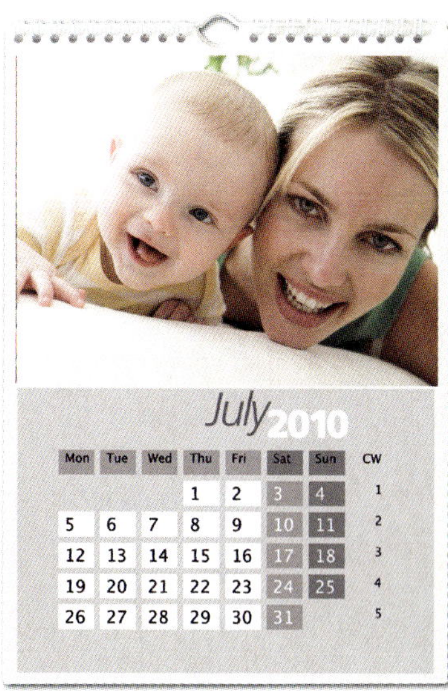

12 Calendar

Brighten up each month with your own image. Choose different orientations, sizes and whether to emphasise the dates or the photographs.

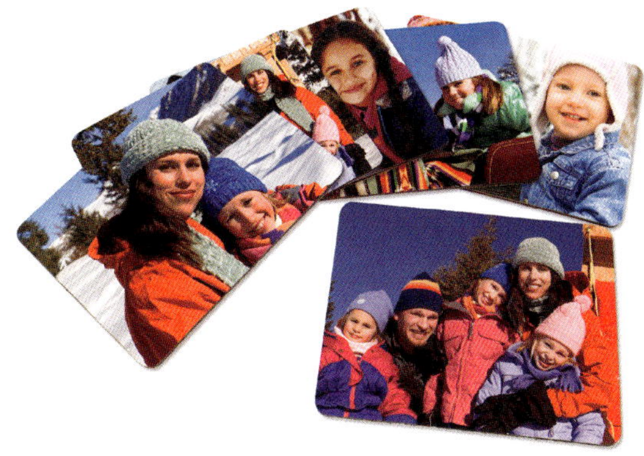

13 Placemats

Perfect for family meal times or fun dinners where you could plant a portrait of each guest on their individual placemat.

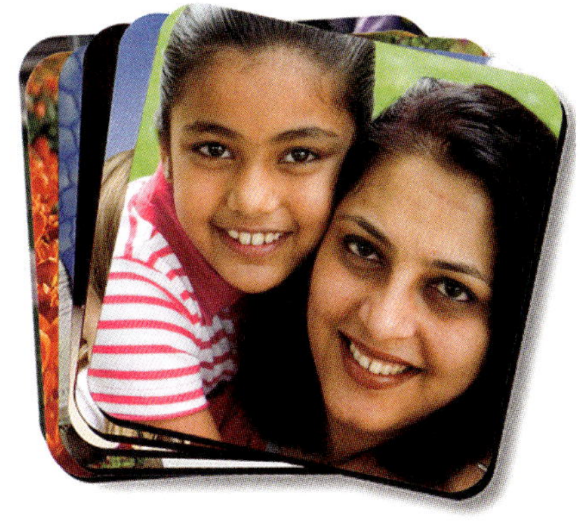

14 Coasters

Take care of the little touches around your home by creating a coaster set. Check they are heat resistant and choose between glass or hardboard.

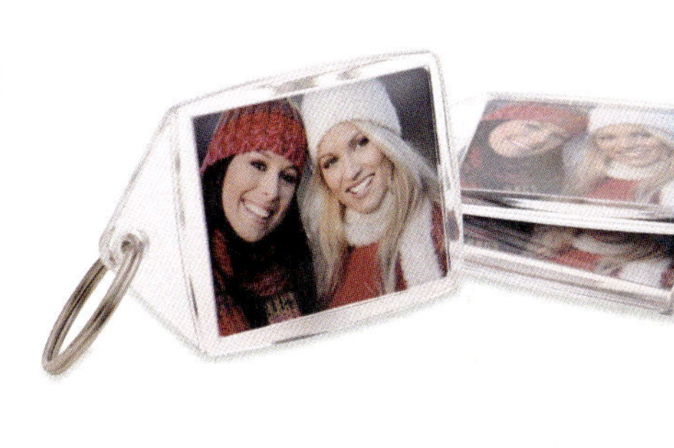

15 Keyrings

Small items such as keyrings are inexpensive and are a high quality alternative to having a photo in your wallet.

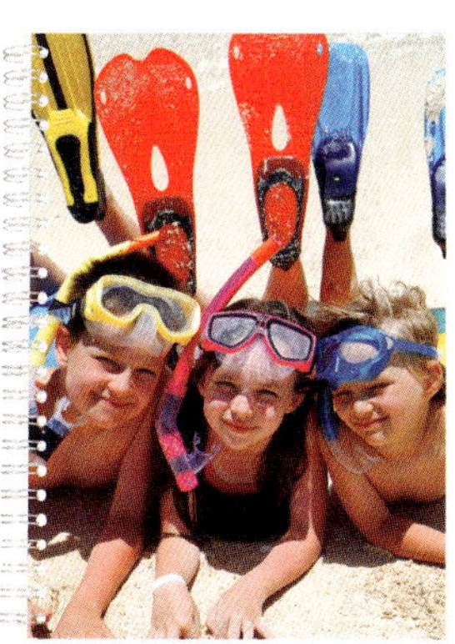

16 Notepad

A functional photo gift that is great for taking to work or school, bringing a personal touch to functional stationery.

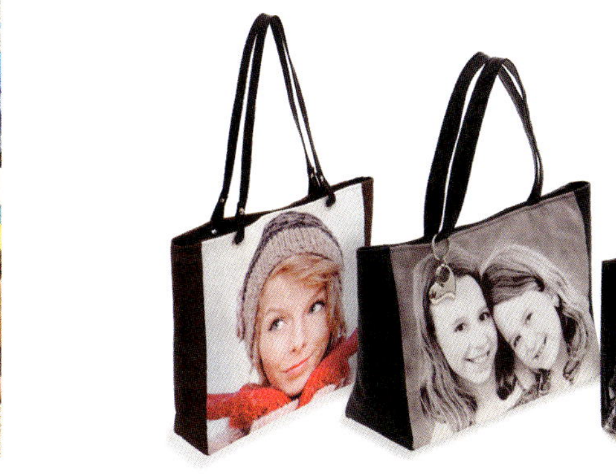

17 Bags

A practical gift that come in a wide variety of shapes, sizes and materials to suit every taste. Washbags and shopper bags are also available.

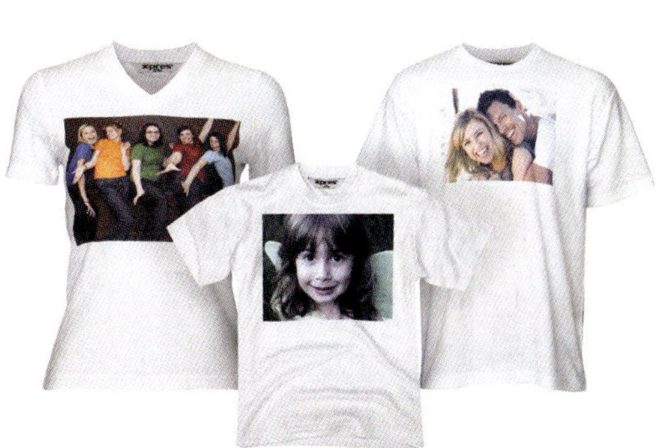

18 T-Shirt

Personalise your wardrobe by turning your digital image into a t-shirt. Great for themed socials and parties or even sports events.

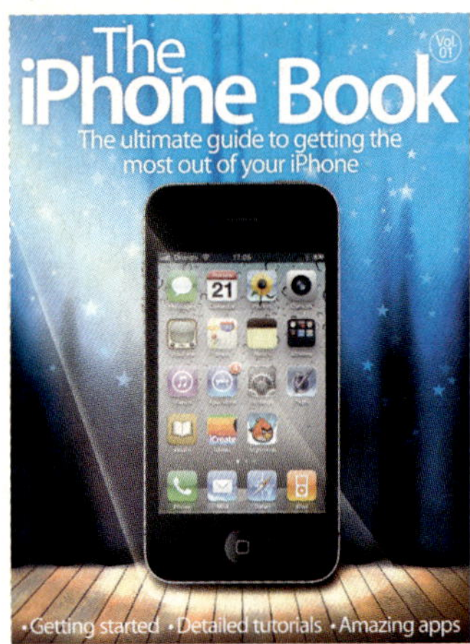

The iPhone Book vol 1
Whether you are new to the iPhone or have had one for a while, **The iPhone Book** is the ultimate resource for getting the very best from your Apple device.
SRP: £9.99

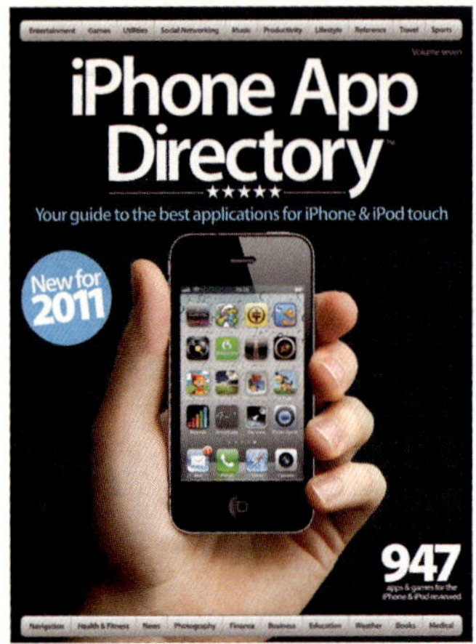

iPhone App Directory vol 7
The latest collection of iPhone apps are reviewed right here, including the very best available for iPhone 4.0, with every single App Store category featured inside.
SRP: £9.99

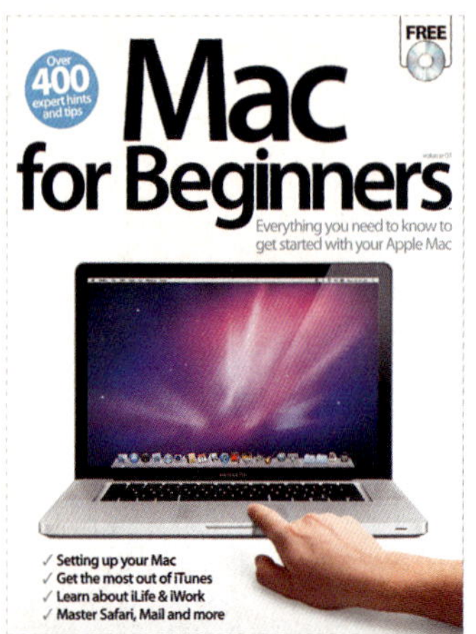

Mac for Beginners 2011
Starting with the basics, this essential guide will teach you how to master all aspects of switching to Mac including OS X, Snow Leopard, Mail and Safari.
SRP: £12.99

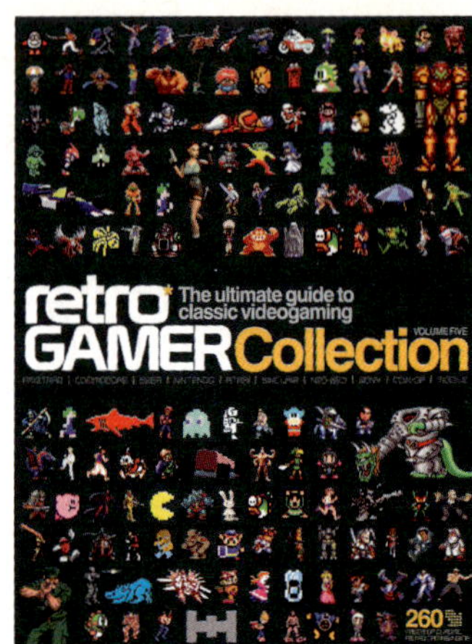

Retro Gamer Collection vol 5
An unmissable selection of in-depth articles featuring timeless games and hardware. From Zelda to Asteroids, this book covers all the classic games from days gone by.
SRP: £9.99

The world's best cre
to collect and keep

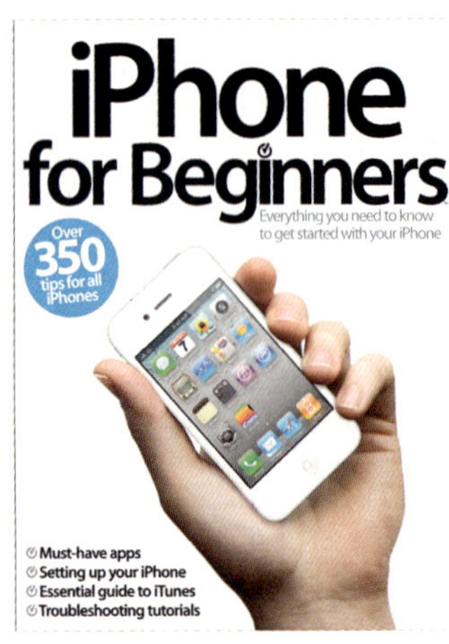

iPhone for Beginners
Everything you need to get started on your iPhone. With step-by-step tutorials, the 100 essential apps and a troubleshooting guide, this is a must-have for iPhone owners .
SRP: £9.99

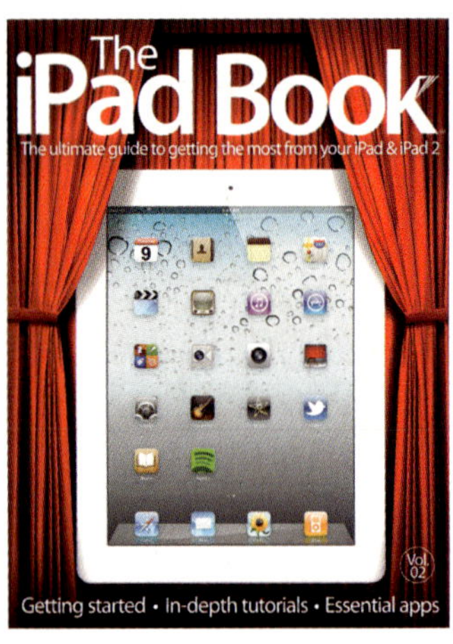

The iPad Book
The ultimate guide to iPad and iPad 2, this comprehensive book brings you a wealth of productivity, entertainment and lifestyle tips, along with all the top apps to download.
SRP: £9.99

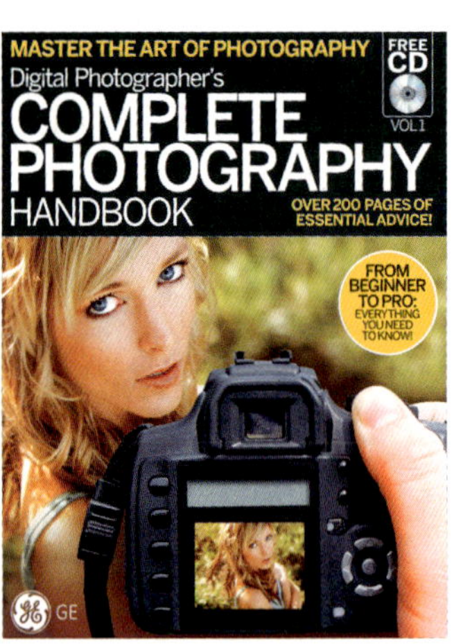

Complete Photography Handbook vol 1
With fantastic shooting ideas and a wide variety of practical tips, this tome is the only resource for digital photographers.
SRP: £12.99

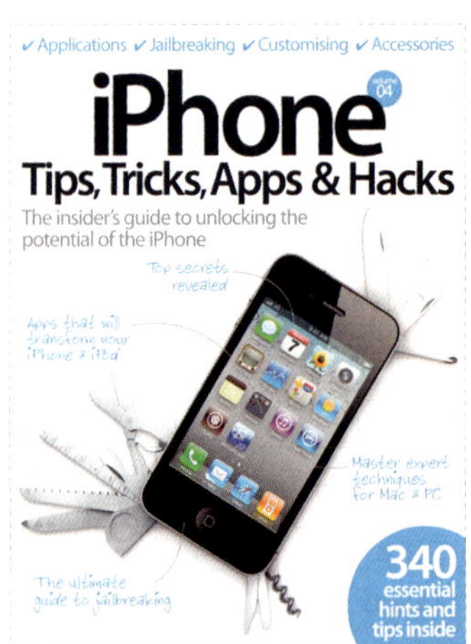

iPhone Tips, Tricks, Apps & Hacks vol 4
Step-by-step tutorials and in-depth features covering the secrets of the iPhone and the ultimate jailbreaking guide make this a must-own book.
SRP: £9.99

Prices may vary, stocks are limited and shipping prices vary

Order online www.im

On your free disc

Essential creative resources for Photoshop projects

There's much more to this bookazine than the pages within, as it also comes with a fantastic free CD packed full of features. We have the essential tutorial files that you need to get cracking with many of the tutorials that we have featured. If you want to try out the techniques on other images, then we have a set of 30 photos. There is also a resource pack full of brushes, textures and vectors, so you can really get creative. As if that's not enough, we have ten more tutorials in video form, which will really help you get to grips with the basic tools and techniques in both Photoshop and Photoshop Elements.

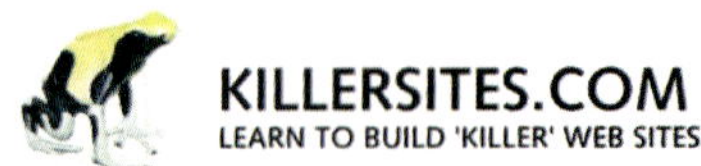

PHOTOSHOP CS5 BASICS

Layerstyles Window Part 2

by Santo Romano

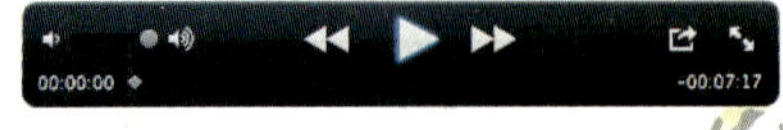

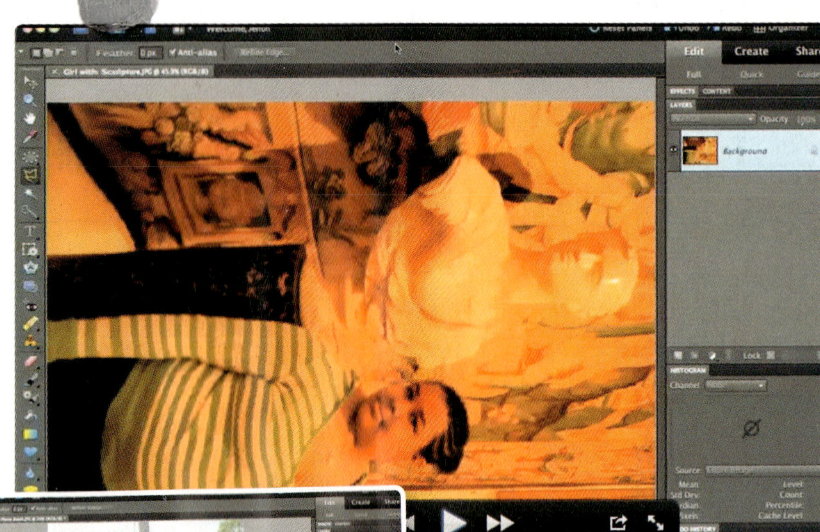

Video tutorials

We have got ten bonus tutorials on the disc as video guides. These show you how to make basic edits, such as colour and tone, selecting areas and changing colours, as well as some tutorials breaking down the new features that can be found in Photoshop CS5.

30 stock images

Free with this book are 30 high-resolution stock images that you can use in your personal projects and to try out the tutorials on the disc. We have everything from animals and people, to macros and landscapes. You can access these by going to the Stock Images option on the main disc interface.

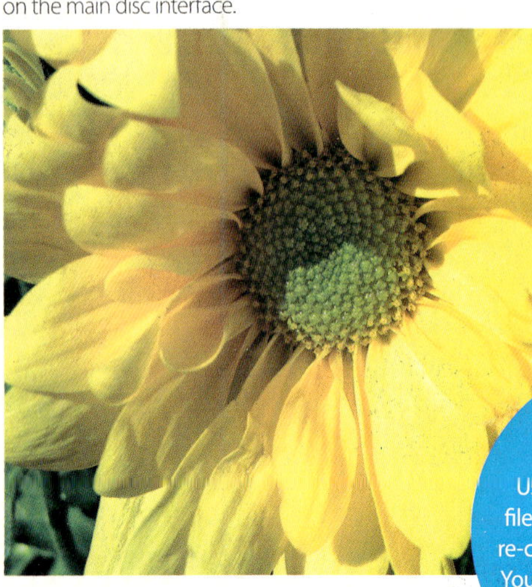

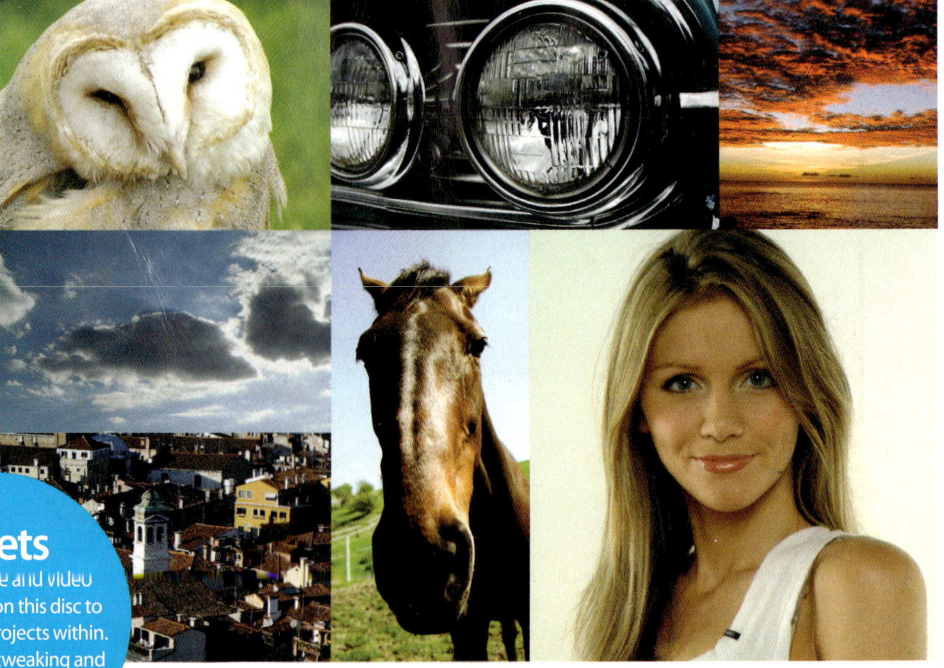

Assets

Use the image and video files supplied on this disc to re-create the projects within. You'll soon be tweaking and editing like the pros!